An Existentialist Aesthetic

The Theories
of Sartre
and
Merleau-Ponty

An Existentialist Aesthetic

The Theories of Sartre
and Merleau-Ponty

Eugene F. Kaelin

THE UNIVERSITY OF WISCONSIN PRESS
Madison, Milwaukee, and London, 1966

Published by the University of Wisconsin Press
Madison, Milwaukee, and London

U.S.A.: Box 1379, Madison, Wisconsin 53701
U.K.: 26-28 Hallam Street, London, W.1

Second Printing, 1966

Printed in the United States of America
Library of Congress Catalog Card Number 62-14413

To D. W. G.

who may not approve of the direction it has taken
but who nonetheless lighted the way

Foreword

Aesthetics today is like a savage child who wanders gaily through the corridors of the House of Man's Knowledge, without ever managing to settle down in a home of his own. On some occasions he refuses to let a willing person adopt him; on others, he is thrown out after a while because of his strange and independent nature. The University of Paris has even offered a chair to this forlorn child, but it is located in the Home of the Philosophers, where absolute anarchy reigns in regard to his ultimate destiny. How far we are from Socrates conversing with Phaedrus on the banks of the Ilissus, and building up the first structures of the science of Beauty!

Ever since the *Critique of Judgment,* philosophers have periodically been tempted to give aesthetics an epistemological status. I recall the well known article by André Lalande, in which this famous logician tried to prove the parallel structures of the normative sciences—logic, ethics, and aesthetics—which are dominated by specific values and which thus establish rules for the true, the good, and the beautiful. This call for a unification of axiologies went unheeded, and despite the efforts of the philosophers of values, such as Louis Lavelle or René Le Senne in France, aesthetics still encounters the same uncertainties concerning its origins and future. From time to time it appears as a philosophy or it is annexed by educational theorists or leaders; but whatever its avatars, aesthetics remains on the outskirts of intellectual activities at the very moment when its metaphysical and historical importance is recognized and magnified. Is this not the case when Gaston Berger, seeking to give his con-

temporaries a dynamic ethics by recommending a "prospective" attitude, declares, "Imagination must become the fundamental virtue of
our time"?

Thus, even when we are conscious of aesthetics directly influencing the details of our daily life and our spiritual efforts to control
our destiny, we find it difficult to grasp, to organize, to situate. Let us
consider the vague question: What are we when we study aesthetics?
This inquiry has as a background the intricate discussions about the
status of the sciences of Man without mentioning the uncertainties
of aesthetics about its own nature.

But why do we not continue to accept these doubts as justifiable,
as the characteristic trait of aesthetics? This could be a decision. But
such an attitude does not satisfy the modern mind; furthermore the
problem of aesthetical values and behavior has suddenly become
vitally significant to the evolution and the future of mankind. This
is our first debt of gratitude to Professor Kaelin. The work for which
he asked me to write a foreword is a vigorous and honest attempt to
determine the nature of aesthetics itself, that is to say, of a branch of
knowledge which is not simply a subdivision of psychology or social
psychology, nor a normative science, but which is rather the theory
of aesthetic creation—aesthetics proper, as he justly says.

In addition, this step towards an "aesthetics proper" is in itself
meaningful. It is proposed as a critical study of existentialist aesthetics, that is, aesthetics as seen in the works of Jean-Paul Sartre and
Maurice Merleau-Ponty. Those proponents of French existentialist
phenomenology in reality only indirectly discuss questions concerning aesthetics. But Professor Kaelin is right in believing that this
philosophical attitude, as understood by the two French thinkers, in its
basic assumptions raises the central problem of aesthetics: the problem of human creation.

Another merit of Professor Kaelin's book is that it apprehends
French non-Christian existentialism from an especially revealing
point of view. This historical analysis is of real interest to everyone
who wishes to make a careful study of the intellectual history of our
times and who is not contented with the usual general studies made
without precise reference to the sources and internal development
of philosophy. Sartre and Merleau-Ponty are true technicians of
philosophy, and Mr. Kaelin has undertaken to show the development of their techniques in its most subtle forms and details.

But let us leave to the reader the joy of further discovery along this rich and varied road. Now, I do want to stress one important idea presented by the author—an idea that is essential to an understanding of European philosophical ideas and that permits the clarification of certain theoretical difficulties encountered by aesthetics. Mr. Kaelin observes with acuteness and penetration that, in spite of his open recognition and use of Husserl's language, Sartre merely appears to be a phenomenologist; he is in reality a "critical philosopher" in the Kantian sense of the word. He seeks to write a new *Critique* of Man and recently has clearly shown his intentions in the first volume of his book, *Critique of Dialectical Reason*. On the other hand, Merleau-Ponty was a more faithful disciple of Husserl, or at least he considered phenomenological method as a means to reawakening the problem of the consciousness in its relations with the external world and other consciousnesses.

Thus, the difference between these two philosophers is significant evidence of a fundamental contradiction in the problems of contemporary aesthetics—that of perception and imagination. And one might ask if it is only by chance that André Breton, the "theologian" of surrealism, presents this duality of perception and imagination as the cardinal antimony which must be overcome in order to attain that level of spontaneous aesthetic creation at which opposites are either reconciled or absorbed.

Existentialism has not experienced the surrealist search for an earthly transcendence, which is the synthesis of the imaginary and the real; nor has it been concerned with surrealism's conception of the poetic act as a means of access to a miraculous universe. Existentialism is not prophetic; it is radically critical and concerned with the empirical world to which reflection applies. Sartre and Merleau-Ponty are in agreement over the philosophical role and mission of reflection. They are by vocation committed witnesses of their time, and not mere passive bystanders. Thus we find a sort of desire for synthesis different from that of surrealism: a desire to reconcile reflective consciousness and practical consciousness, to reconcile the spectator and the man of action.

The orientation of their thoughts is strictly moral. Like his predecessors in France, the existentialist philosopher is above all concerned with the influence on the individual of the historical destiny of men. Does that mean that aesthetics must await the solution of the moral and social problem, as if it were a superfluous or secondary matter to be considered once serious affairs have been settled and there is at last time to think of lighter concerns? Such an attitude is not completely foreign to Sartre and Merleau-Ponty, or else they would not be French philosophers! In spite of themselves, they moralize in all circumstances, especially when discussing the role of aesthetics in modern societies. We must, however, realize that they have understood the originality of the problem of aesthetics and its central place in all philosophical speculation better than have most philosophers during the past century. For this reason I feel that Professor Kaelin has chosen an especially good focal point for this analysis.

It is curious to note that according to Mr. Kaelin the two philosophers, as a result of their initial choices—one in favor of the problem of the imagination being identified with that of consciousness, and the other in favor of the problem of perception being likewise assimilated with that of consciousness—have been going down two complementary blind alleys. Sartre, who tends to make human consciousness (the *pour soi*) a creative function in constant danger of escaping into an unreal world, is incapable of differentiating between image and sensation, while Merleau-Ponty painstakingly explains the relation between perception and reflection or judgment.

Yet these divergent difficulties are derived from a common source which has been inspiring post-war French existentialism: the desire to discover in the very heart of consciousness the free act by which man establishes himself as a human being in the society of men. That act of freedom is also the source of aesthetic creation, the promoter of new meanings and therefore of new communication of thoughts between men. Professor Kaelin's analysis of Merleau-Ponty's proposed distinction between "primary and secondary expressions" is therefore extremely important. Here again one has the impression of having probed to the depths of the problem and of having thus reached the limits of what can be positively known or suggested in the realm of aesthetic creation. Merleau-Ponty's sudden death robbed us of the hope of learning his answers to the unavoidable questions which arise when expression is considered to be an immediate response of man to the universe, and especially deprived us of his solution to the crucial problem of the relation between expression and meaning and communication.

Depending on one's point of view, Sartre's approach might be preferred to that of Merleau-Ponty, or vice versa. In any case, both lead to the field of "aesthetics proper" as Mr. Kaelin calls it; each has oriented his analysis to avoid both traditional metaphysics and the objective method of the behavioral sciences. Their method is the autoanalysis of the consciousness defined by its immediate relationship with the world—forming it, forming itself with it and by it, making the world human and making itself human at the same time. . . .

Belonging myself to the French philosophical tradition, I am eager to express to Mr. Kaelin the gratitude of our philosophers for his having so admirably understood the current aims and problems of French philosophy through two of its most important representatives. His study of this problem is truly revealing. The essence of French culture is philosophical, which for a Frenchman means "reflective." Reflection is always a secondary moment. There can be felt the importance of the problem of perception and of the distinction between sensation and image, as posed by Descartes' *Cogito*. Phenomenology has clarified certain fundamental points of the problem, by attracting attention to the question of meaning and expression, thus relating the problems of reflection and language.

A desire to prophesy is a dangerous thing, especially if, as Merleau-Ponty believes, philosophy is the critical conscience of cultural institutions. However, today it is easy to predict a rebirth of aesthetics, and even a new impetus for aesthetical researches, linked to the evolution of modern society, an impetus of which this book is an indicative and revealing sign. Perhaps the savage child which is now wandering through the House of Man's Sciences will eventually play the role of the Prodigal Son.

EDOUARD MOROT-SIR
*Representative of French Universities
in the United States of America*

*New York
9 May 1962*

Preface

For the completion of this work I am indebted to too many individuals to mention each of them in this place. I wish, however, to express my gratitude to the following organizations for the financial support which allowed me to undertake the study here presented: the Research Committee, Graduate School, University of Illinois; the Research Committee, Graduate School, University of Wisconsin; and the American Council of Learned Societies. To the first, for its grant of a post-doctoral fellowship, which permitted me to return to France for an intensive year of research into my subject matter; to the second, for two grants of summer salary support, which made it possible for me to draw up the initial draught of the treatise; and to the third, for a post-doctoral fellowship spent at the Institute for Research in the Humanities, University of Wisconsin, where the final manuscript was prepared.

A special debt of thanks is due Professor William H. Hay, of the Department of Philosophy, University of Wisconsin, and Professor Germaine Brée, of the Institute for Research in the Humanities, for having read the entire typescript of the study. The errors it still contains are not to be attributed to them, nor to my assistant, Mr. John Atwell, nor to my wife, Pierrette, who as usual suffered most from my prolonged concern with scholarly affairs.

After completing the manuscript, I learned of the death of Merleau-Ponty, who at the age of fifty-three succumbed to a coronary attack in Paris on the fourth of May, 1961. Besides serving as an introduction to his works for English-speaking readers, it is hoped that this study may constitute, in some limited degree, a memorial to the life of this gifted son of France. For him, to philosophize was to criticize the conditions of life.

E. F. K.

Institute for Research in the Humanities
University of Wisconsin, Madison
June, 1961

Contents

ILLUSTRATIONS

An Existentialist Aesthetic

The Theories
of Sartre
and
Merleau-Ponty

. . . if books on aesthetics do not quite take the prize for dreariness, at least they stand very high on the list.

J. A. Passmore
"The Dreariness of Aesthetics," Mind (NS), LX(1951)

I

The Philosopher's Interest in Art

Traditionally defined as the love of wisdom with the whole of human experience as its purview, philosophy has suffered many of the same pressures as its sister disciplines, science and technology, to restrict its area of interest to a specialized frame of reference, rather vaguely denoted as the universe of "meaningful discourse." And, since the sciences one by one have left philosophy in the pursuit of their own areas of this universe, presumably there will, in the extension of this process, be no uncovered corner of the world left for a strictly philosophical investigation of the traditional sort. The development of science has in this respect produced the same effect on philosophy as on mythology and religion. When the complete scientific account of human experience has been written, the assumption is that there will be no field of inquiry left for philosophers, seers, or prophets. And Plato would have shown no little consternation at seeing the lovers of wisdom classified with men bereft of their reason, whose opinions are only slightly more trustworthy than those of poets or outright fools. The great wit of the tradition has become today's madness. The supposition goes, in consequence, that the former holy trinity of human values expressed in the true, the good, and the beautiful will have been exhausted, in our own or a slightly distant time, into a single general law from which more particular laws may be deduced; and the total system of scientific laws will constitute the rational explanation of the world which may be experienced by any form of human agency.

In the face of this restriction in subject matter, philosophers have

3

been forced to a reformulation of both the aims and the procedures
of their own activity. The "first philosophy," or attempt to investigate the first causes and principles of all knowledge, has given way
in our time to a new conception of the philosopher's job of work.
No longer primarily concerned with the nature of reality, the philosopher has become concerned with the problems inherent in man's
attempt to symbolize the events of human experience. It is no longer
the fashion to be interested in metaphysics; it is, on the contrary,
strictly *à la page* to investigate the language of physics and other sciences in a concern which has come to be called "meta-linguistics."
And, obviously, there are various ways in which this discipline may
be practiced.

Where, before, a simple criticism of a philosopher's opinion was
like that of the scientist's, that he was wrong, today it is heard more
frequently that a philosopher is wrong-headed—leaving open the
very interesting possibility that he may yet be right. As in British
politics, right thinking and thinking right are not necessarily the
same. Where the logical complement of being wrong was quite apparently being right, it is not yet clear where one stands if one is
other than wrong-headed; depending upon the philosophical stance
of the person making the judgment, the person so judged could be a
pragmatist, a metaphysician, an existentialist, or a Wittgensteinian
of either school, whether positivist or analyst. Quite clearly there is
implied in the judgment an appraisal of the very conception of an
opposing philosophical approach; where the conception of the nature of the philosophical discipline is at stake, the fortunes of aesthetics have been observed to be bartered away in the trade.

Metaphysically, idealism has produced the aesthetic theories of
Croce[1] and Bosanquet[2] and Collingwood[3] and by reaction, the realistic aesthetics of Alexander.[4] Positivism, in its avoidance of the metaphysical question, has produced the principles of literary criticism
made famous by I. A. Richards;[5] and the so-called school of logical
analysis has produced a book of essays in aesthetics and language.[6]
Following this latter trend, Professor Monroe Beardsley has published his *Aesthetics,* in which the area of philosophical inquiry into
art is limited to the language used by critics to describe their experience of works of art.

America in general, and Harvard University in particular, has
been extremely fortunate to have witnessed a series of aestheticians

interested primarily in establishing aesthetics as an autonomous discipline: George Santayana, D. W. Prall, and John Dewey, who was invited to Harvard to give a series of lectures in honor of William James, and who chose the subject of the philosophy of art. Although each of these men has had his students and disciples as well as his vigorous dissenters, I have chosen them as illustrative of the forerunners of contemporary American aesthetics.

George Santayana gave his course in aesthetics at Harvard from 1892 to 1895. The notes he had assembled for it and the discussions which ensued within it were later organized into his *Sense of Beauty,* which he called an outline of aesthetic theory. One of the first organized treatises on the subject of aesthetic experience to appear in America, the book gives ample evidence for understanding the low status of aesthetics in the academic world. The methods used by prior aestheticians were, according to Santayana, either didactic or historical, that is, either the exercise of one's taste in giving an actual critical judgment, or merely relating aesthetic experiences of one time and place with those of other times and places. Neither of these, he claimed, could have fruitful consequences, and so proposed a scientifically psychological method of investigating the facts of aesthetic experience as "phenomena of mind and products of mental evolution."[7]

Although he was astute enough to have perceived that traditional writers on aesthetics were "audacious metaphysicians and somewhat incompetent critics,"[8] and his own aim was to found aesthetics on the firm basis of his own competent criticism and naturalistic psychology, Santayana's break with the past was not complete. His book is a long single criticism of Plato's notions of an ideal truth and beauty; but he himself retains the notion of beauty, and deduces, as it were, the various forms beauty may take, given his naturalistic conception of man and the world. His work is significant, not for its definition of beauty, nor for its development of the categories of material, formal, and expressive beauties, but for Santayana's constant insistence that aesthetic theory be judged by its accuracy or inaccuracy in treating the facts of everyday experiences of beautiful things.

In sum, Santayana's aesthetics looks forward and backward in history; it tried to make a break with tradition and did so, but only to a certain extent. The very title of his principal book, *The Sense of Beauty,* indicates its Janus-like physiognomy. His retention of the

word "beauty" links him with the tradition; and "the sense of" indicates his desire to place aesthetic experiences in their naturalistic
context: the sensuous experience of ordinary individuals.

The work of David Wight Prall is concerned principally with the
sensuous character of aesthetic experiences. Following Santayana in
still a second way, by considering the area of the fine arts as a privileged locus of aesthetic feeling, he introduced the concept of an "aesthetic surface"[9] which, in his estimation, was useful to rejoin what
Santayana's three categories appear to leave asunder. Realizing that
materials, form, and expression may be separated only for the purposes of analysis, he chose to indicate that aesthetic expression is always a function of organized sensuous materials. His *Aesthetic Judgment* appeared in 1929, and was followed by *Aesthetic Analysis* in
1936. The first book was in preparation and came out during his stay
at California; the second, while he was lecturing at Harvard from
1930 to 1940.

Dewey's lectures on the philosophy of art, given in commemora-
tion of William James, were delivered in 1931; they grew during
three years of reworking into his monumental *Art as Experience.*[10]
Whereas Prall's doctrine of sensuous surface was criticized for having led to "purism," for extolling the surface qualities of a work of
art to such an extent that its depth qualities were lost sight of, and
for limiting aesthetic analysis too narrowly to the domain of the fine
arts, Dewey's work was a direct attack on purism, the "thin" doctrine
of aesthetics, and the separation of the finer arts from the common
aesthetic experiences of everyday life. For Dewey, the experience of
the fine arts was no differently conceived than the rather routine matter of having an experience of any kind at all.

Thus, in the movement from Santayana to Prall to Dewey, American aesthetics began with the attempt at a scientific description of
human sensibility, with special reference to the embodiment of feelings in works of fine arts; proceeded to a specialized treatment of
the surface qualities of works of fine arts; and finally culminated in
the placement of aesthetic experiences in the greater context of human experience in general. All three men were working, moreover,
with the legacy of Immanuel Kant, whose *Critique of Judgment*
(1790) may be said to mark the beginnings of modernism in aesthetics, considered as the philosophy of art.[11]

In more recent times there is less debate on what makes an aesthetic enjoyment a good, and still less on what makes a particular work of art good or bad. To a large extent Kant's antinomy of taste is solved dogmatically by espousing the thesis and ignoring the antithesis (or vice versa), just as in the general area of criticism critics continue to practice "legalistic" or "classical" aesthetic judgments in terms of some kind of normative standard; and their opponents, to ignore the classical criteria in favor of their own impressions. And currently, more often than not, discussions of the good and bad of aesthetic experience have been reduced to arguments as to what is meant by the words being used in the expression of judgment. Aesthetic theory, as a consistent body of knowledge purporting to explain aesthetic experience of one sort or another, is not now the fashion.

Noting that each era of philosophy, defined by a particular way of approaching philosophical problems, demands a corresponding change in the philosophy of art, Susanne K. Langer has developed a semantic explanation of the expressiveness of works of art.[12] Taking her cue from the words of Peirce, that philosophy's business is to make our ideas clear,[13] she has erected a semantic model by which to explain the manner in which the artist may be said to communicate with an audience. That model is, however, the one first suggested to positivists by Ludwig Wittgenstein in the *Tractatus:* isomorphism of symbol and referent, the symbol being, in Mrs. Langer's case, the structured work of art, and the "referent" (she more recently has called it "import"), a feeling.

This same model of symbolization, it could be noted, was already used by Santayana in his discussion of literary form:

Speech would be an absolute and unrelated art, like music, were it not controlled by utility. The sounds have indeed no resemblance to the objects they symbolize; but before the system of sounds can represent the system of objects, there has to be a correspondence in the groupings of both. The structure of language, unlike that of music, thus becomes a mirror of the structure of the world as presented to the intelligence.[14]

Nor can this idea be considered Santayana's property, since map makers have been using it almost since the dawn of cartography.

The significance of Mrs. Langer's position is that it calls attention to the expressive language of artists working as artists, and not solely to the language of critics at least one degree removed from the heat of creation. Hers is a philosophy of art, and not of criticism.

Still, the philosophical job of justifying the preference of "the studio point of view" over that of "the gallery"[15] needs further qualification by reference to a theory of aesthetic experience in general. And the semantic approach to art was not an original invention of Mrs. Langer; she was anticipated in this respect by C. J. Ducasse[16] and, in spite of her disclaimers, has been engaged in no little polemics with the students and followers of C. W. Morris,[17] whose own semantic philosophy of art was inspired by the aesthetics of Dewey[18] and the semiotics of G. H. Mead.[19]

Finally, to round out this sketchy view of the development of American aesthetics, our own times have witnessed the rather curious repudiation of his earlier work by Morris Weitz,[20] who, having traveled to England after the great awakening and discovered the later Wittgenstein, became convinced that "art" could not be defined. He concludes from this that aesthetic theory is impossible, and so dismisses his earlier work, *Philosophy of the Arts,* as misguided.[21]

For those thinkers who consider the philosophy of art as a theoretical impossibility, there is an alternative way of conceiving the job of aesthetics. We may call this move "philosophy in art." Considering aesthetics as a special branch of philosophy, aestheticians of this stripe endeavor to examine aesthetic experiences with an eye to showing how it involves certain more strictly philosophical problems, such as perception, theory of knowledge, or metaphysics.

Due to the etymology of the term, aesthetics is most often conceived, in the first place, as a special case of perception. One of the most influential aestheticians having pursued this course is Stephen C. Pepper, whose *Aesthetic Quality* is based upon the distinction between practical drive and enhanced quality perception, and one of the most vigorous writers on aesthetic perception today is Rudolph Arnheim,[22] whose work is inspired principally by the discoveries of the Gestalt school of psychology. Writing about the same time as Pepper in his psychological mood, Charles Hartshorne produced his *Philosophy and Psychology of Sensation,* which still has its devotees.

Croce is most famous, to consider the second case, for his attempt to integrate aesthetic perception into a general theory of knowledge; his work has had considerable influence on both philosophers holding to an idealistic metaphysics and critics looking for a *modus operandi* in the analysis of artworks. Spingarn's *Creative Criticism* is dedicated to Croce, and since the former is responsible for the term "the new criticism," it is not empty speculation to state that Croce has had a good deal to do with the motives and results of the school of criticism working under that rubric. Currently, John Hospers has been carrying aesthetics in the direction of epistemology, as is apparent in the title of his principal work, *Meaning and Truth in the Arts;* much of the contemporary work on iconography in art fits this same category of philosophical aesthetics.

Finally, in spite of the change in philosophical fashion, metaphysics is still not alien to aesthetic analysis. There come to mind as illustrations the work of Milton C. Nahm, whose *The Artist as Creator* is subtitled "An Essay of Human Freedom," and some of the discussions now going on concerning "the work of art." Here once again Pepper may be cited for his later work,[23] which has been criticized in articles by Donald Henze[24] and Paul Ziff.[25] Much of the criticism of Sartre's aesthetics by British and American writers has been leveled at his metaphysical orientation, and the very interesting problem of the relations between metaphysics and the novel has begun to attract some attention from literary critics.[26]

Aesthetics conceived as the pursuit of philosophy in art is a rich source of philosophical investigation, but its value seems limited to an intellectual understanding, and then only for those capable of grasping either the sweeping generalizations or the specialized jargon of professional philosophers. Those who object to aesthetics undertaken in this manner are precisely those who need it most, the common run of artists, art educators and students, and the "plain" man who may feel it profitable to spend a Sunday afternoon in an art gallery away from his television set. This disparity between the philosopher's attitude toward art and that of the practicing artist is nowhere more clearly pointed up than in Gilson's *Painting and Reality,* in which the author goes to some pains, in the preface, to make clear that he is looking at art as a philosopher, and not as a creator or appreciator.[27] It is difficult to conceive how philosophers can do more to avoid considering the problems of men engaged in ordinary human activity than to insist upon the separation of philosophers from the common run of individuals. No respectable scientist can afford to make a hard and fast distinction between his theory and its application.

If it is a safe assumption that aesthetic experiences of natural objects are proper areas of scientific interest, and as such the domain of psychology and social psychology, the field of aesthetics obviously overlaps to some extent with these sciences. Likewise, insofar as aesthetics is definable by reference to the creative and appreciative acts in human experience, the field of aesthetic inquiry includes these rather vague areas of value experiences from which scientists characteristically shy. And, since philosophy proper is thought to provide a method for reflecting on all human experience, aesthetics is correctly conceived as an area of philosophy.

Aesthetics is the philosophy of art, and more; it is in its broadest aspects a philosophy of human values. Whether, in Prall's sense, the field of aesthetics is defined as "the whole panorama presented to us through our senses, the surface of our experienced world . . ."[28] or, in Dewey's, as an investigation of art considered as the expression of all the "meanings," both surface and depth, of human experience, those technical philosophers who have treated aesthetics as a means of finding philosophical problems in the areas of art and aesthetic experience have unnecessarily specialized their interest. As aesthetics overlaps with psychology and the sciences at one extreme, it necessarily overlaps, as both Santayana and DeWitt Parker contended,[29] with criticism at the other. Thus, if philosophy is correctly conceived as the rationalization of, or reflection on, aesthetic experiences, then to be successful even in the limited attempt to illustrate the manner in which the subject matter of traditional philosophy is implicit in the experiences of works of art, philosophers must be prepared to show how this subject matter aids in the control of creative communication mediated by existing artifacts. In short, philosophers must become more perceptive in their criticism and less theoretical in their perceptions.

Moreover, this critical job of aestheticians must be performed without doing violence to the facts of an artist's or of his audience's experience. That the "separatists"—psychologists, logicians, and metaphysicians—have failed to comply with this injunction is eloquently attested by the numerous complaints against aesthetics coming from practicing artists and their students. If we continue to separate our philosophical specialty from an honest attempt to raise our ordinary experiences of beautiful things, whether natural or artificial, to the level of intellectual comprehension, we are most certainly open to the charge of inhabiting an ivory tower.

If, however, the philosopher could be persuaded to take a step outside his tower, to consider as his domain the field of aesthetic experiences and to consider it whole, he will find an almost unlimited area for aesthetic investigation. Most human individuals and societies show some kind of taste, and artists thrive on finding new means of expression. Each new means they find poses a new problem in aesthetic communication. The journals of literary and art criticism add to the common sense approach to appreciation, and considerably swell the legitimate field of aesthetic investigation. In fact, the only limit that could be placed on this field is that whatever is said concerning the experience of a work of art be judged in terms of an actual experience, and not on the authority of the speaker or the prestige of his philosophical approach.

As the title of its review, *The Journal of Aesthetics and Art Criticism*,[30] indicates, the American Society of Aesthetics is not limited in its meetings or in its publications to a discussion of the relations between philosophy and art in either of the senses explained above. And following the tart comment of Stuart Hampshire, that when aestheticians argue from the particular to the general they are moving in the wrong direction,[31] the editors of the many journals of literary and art criticism are devoted almost exclusively to analyses of particular works of art. The philosophical role to assume here is the criticism of criticism; the method used in its pursuit is then no different, and need be no more or less technical, than the method of philosophy as it is applied to any other field of primary human activity.

In sum, aesthetics has been conceived of by some as an autonomous discipline similar to other sciences in that it develops a method for treating an area of human activity divided into the experience of natural beauty and the arts, and by others as a special field of philosophy devoted to the discussion of philosophical problems as they arise in the same or related areas of human experience. The former stresses philosophy as a method; the latter, as a special kind of subject matter. We have called the one "philosophy of art," and the other "philosophy in art."

Since the pursuit of philosophy in art has produced few results of value to those who should benefit most by a philosophical discussion of art, and the philosophy of art tends to be abandoned through a growing skepticism in our own time concerning the validity of aesthetic theory, it has been proposed that the role of aesthetics be re-thought in such a way as to avoid the critical weaknesses of the one and the theoretical shortcomings of the other. To this yet unfound theory, whose existence has been stipulated, I have given the name "aesthetics proper." The field of aesthetics will be properly conceived only when aesthetic experiences are understood in the full range of their implications concerning the conduct of human individuals living in a changing social and cultural environment. Like any other intellectual discipline, it must establish a method which allows for continual discovery of additional facts. Its methodical pursuit, then, is both descriptive of these facts and, as they include the evaluations of men, critical of their use and abuse in the total organization of the human economy.

The foregoing historical notice is not offered as definitive or complete. I have indicated the broad range of historical disagreement concerning the nature of aesthetic inquiry only to show the degree of confusion existing among philosophers themselves on the central problem of laying out the domain of aesthetics proper. And in light of this considerable confusion, there should be little wonder that aesthetics finds itself in the position of the unwanted stepdaughter in departments of philosophy in the American university system.

What, then, is the purpose of introducing American readers to the context of existentialist aesthetics? The presumption may be that one more aesthetic theory will only add to the already considerable confusion, but to a skeptical mind there is always the hint of a doubt: how does one know unless one tries? And will not the demonstration that one's attempt is confused actually help to relieve the confusion now generally associated with aesthetics?[32]

This book has been written for such a skeptical mind. All the previous failures to theorize about aesthetic experience may, after all, be a mere prelude to a success in the future. If the human animal does learn by its past mistakes, there is always that possibility. Nor does the hope of success necessitate complete fulfillment. In considering a foreign manner of philosophizing, one may be led to discover a fruitful conception of aesthetic investigation which would not only allow a rational explanation of aesthetic experience, but also permit one to rationalize the very institutional structure of American education, which latter investigation may in turn show a dividend in better education for students of the liberal arts.

Moreover, certain conceptions of philosophical and aesthetic inquiry are more apt than others to show the place of aesthetic activities in the general social life of society, corporately conceived. When the brunt of aesthetic analysis is brought to bear upon the language of critics or the logic of value judgments, attention is drawn away from the experiential problems undergone by men who live face to face with conflicting value claims: on the one hand, that of the artist, that his expression be limited only by the resources of his materials and the strength of his own imagination, and, on the other, those of the various institutions of society which tend to add further conditions—economic, political, religious, and so on—to the artist's freedom of expression. Immediately there is brought to mind the socialist's contention that art is a people's activity, a language working for the cohesion of society and promoting the ideals of its dominant class. Except for the recent book of Professor D. W. Gotshalk, *Art and the Social Order,* there is little interest in American aesthetics for a continuation of the work begun in England by William Morris and others on art as a social function.[33]

It may be concluded, therefore, that what is being sought is a conception of aesthetic inquiry within the more general scheme of philosophic activity which has as its aim the criticism of social institutions. Technical competence there must be, but philosophers must be brought to realize that their special area of technical competence can be applied to the solution of the problems arising in the lives of men. It is not suggested, a priori, that existentialism with or without its phenomenological basis will provide that conception of philosophy and aesthetics; it is suggested, however, that art activity is of sufficient social import to be brought to the attention of philosophers in that light. And one of the critical criteria to be used in evaluation of the existentialist aesthetic is the degree to which its philosophical orientation allows practical decisions to be made in the lives of individuals both aesthetically and socially considered. A philosophy of art which solves more philosophical problems than those involved in actual aesthetic communication is, from this point of view, of less value to both philosophers and their audiences than one which stems from an examination of the facts of aesthetic experience, and, no matter how involved its theoretical involutions may become, returns its practitioners and their readers to a richer, more enlightened aesthetic life; not, as some of our artist friends insist, in spite of our theoretical involutions, but because of them. Such is the philosopher's interest in art, and I have given an exposition of the existentialists' aesthetic doctrines in order to measure their efficiency against this test.

The method used in the sequel of this study is first of all to expound what I have called "the existentialists' aesthetic doctrine." As a cursory glance at any secondary source on existentialism will confirm, there is no general agreement on what constitutes existentialist philosophy; and it is more than slightly ironic to be asked for an essential description of any mode of thought which denies, in essence, the validity of essential descriptions of a growing institution. Either, then, we are reduced to silence, or we must adopt an arbitrary method of procedure.

My method is arbitrary in a double sense. In the first place, the investigation is limited to French writers, rather than extended to include the Germans and Russians, primarily because of my limited linguistic competence: the primary sources are French; the secondary, English and German. Secondly, of those French writers associated with the existentialist movement, attention is centered upon the writings of Jean-Paul Sartre and Maurice Merleau-Ponty. Since Sartre is already widely known as a leader in the movement and is one of the few philosophers of note in contemporary thought who has willingly accepted the title, his inclusion is axiomatic. Merleau-Ponty, on the other hand, is almost completely unknown to American readers. None of his works has been translated; moreover, due to their considerable difficulty, none is likely to be translated in the near future. Once a working companion of Sartre,[34] a life-long member of French academic circles, and holder of the Chair of Philosophy at the Collège de France, Merleau-Ponty erected a philosophy which offers an unparalleled example of comparison and contrast with the controversial doctrines of his erstwhile associate.

Part I of this book is dedicated to an exposition, interpretation, and critical evaluation of Sartre's aesthetics; Part II, of Merleau-Ponty's. In each case the exposition is not a matter of translating an already existing aesthetic treatise; Merleau-Ponty never undertook, nor has Sartre yet undertaken such a project. I have accordingly been forced to scan various of their books in order to cull an aesthetic doctrine. In an effort to be faithful to the intentions of the original authors, I have adopted a style which allows the subject author to speak as much as is possible for himself; consequently, quotations are many and long. In the body of the text the citations are rendered into English, and the original French has been relegated to a section of notes.

The meaning of the word "context" may be made clear by reference to my second task, the interpretation of the doctrines. In order to give added significance to the bare exposition, I have traced the historical line of development in the thought of both men. Both have been generous in the statement of their sources; both owe an allegiance to the phenomenology of Husserl; and both have been influenced by the substantial body of philosophical and aesthetic writing, of primarily European sources, which has preceded their own thought. Principal among these are the various authors of manifestoes for artistic movements, essayists, critics, and aestheticians of the French intellectual tradition. For readers who may be unfamiliar with that tradition, I have included comparisons and contrasts with current British and American writers and issues. Finally, I have submitted the doctrines, as interpreted, to both philosophical and aesthetic criticism.

In the conclusion I have critically compared the two authors, given an evaluation of each in terms of the purpose of aesthetics as stated above, and indicated some lines of development which a future existentialist aesthetic investigation might pursue. The two appendices are included as inessential to the argument of the thesis, but as casting an oblique light on the conclusion. In order to limit the historical scope of the study, I have arbitrarily adopted as a basis for my discussion the period of nineteen years from the appearance of Sartre's *L'Imagination* in 1936 to the publication of Merleau-Ponty's *Les Aventures de la dialectique* in 1955.

Part I JEAN-PAUL SARTRE

Phenomenology in Sartre's Theory of Images

The evaluation of the work of a contemporary figure is never easy, and when the figure is as controversial as Jean-Paul Sartre,[1] the task becomes doubly difficult. Besides the obvious fact that at any moment the living philosopher may add to, and thus change, the body of his work, we already have at our disposal a voluminous literature of great variety: Sartre has written philosophy, novels, plays, screen scenarios, and literary and social criticism; during his maturer years only poetry seems to have escaped his attention.[2] He is, and rightfully enjoys the reputation of being a man of letters.

In a culture where there is no disparagement connected with this designation, he is a man of parts; in our own culture, where a littérateur is not a philosopher and the philosopher is anything but a littérateur, "respectable" practitioners of the trade tend to look down upon their colleagues who take the pains to write well, as well as informatively, as popularizers. Putting aside the question of how the social evaluation of these academic philosophers is justified, we must face the more profound criticism of those non-academic philosophers for whom Sartre is the spirit if not the incarnation of the intellectual bogey. Even in France undoubtedly the greater part of the secondary literature on Sartrean existentialism stems from such non-academic sources. Marxists and neo-scholastics in particular have seen in him a potent rival, all three schools of thought being predominantly humanistic in character, but each making contrary dogmatic claims within the field of values.

If there is nothing to be gained by opposing one's own prejudices

19

to those of another school, it is equally true that no one is the wiser
for blindly accepting the tenets of a rising school of thought. We
might cite on this side of the balance the attitudes toward Sartre's
views expressed by Simone de Beauvoir[3] and Robert Campbell,[4] as
well as the social idiocy of the existentialist "rats," habitués of cafés
of dubious repute. Maurice Merleau-Ponty, who succeeded Bergson,
LeRoy, and Lavelle at the Collège de France following his tenure as
professor of philosophy at the Sorbonne, was a collaborating member of Sartre's existentialist review, *Les Temps Modernes,* before dis-
senting and elaborating a phenomenological philosophy of his own.[5]
And, for those who care to read novels that way, Simone de Beauvoir
has given a rather faithful fictional account of the inner workings of
the existentialist movement in her *Les Mandarins.*

In order to interpret this massive body of primary and secondary
literature, can we now construct a body of principles which will enable us to evaluate Sartre's contribution, if any, to philosophy? I
think we can. And the number of such principles need not be excessively large. First, although the social message communicated by
existentialism was adopted in extreme form by the younger generation seeking liberation partly from the arbitrary decisions of parents
and partly from the political strictures imposed by the occupying
Germans, we should admit that the head of a movement is not necessarily responsible for the conduct of his would-be followers. Moreover, to a great extent these pseudo-existentialists have been transformed through time and circumstance into parents themselves; the
Germans no longer occupy France; and the "rats" have become assimilated into the new social order. In the second place, we can avoid
the extremes of unthoughtful acceptance or rejection of the philosophy in favor of an impartial analysis of its claims, if only we can
isolate the distinguishing marks of that philosophy. For this task,
the third, it is not unreasonable to separate the literary efforts of
Sartre from his already dense body of purely philosophic work. Our
ground here is not that literature cannot be philosophy, but that
historically considered, the literary interpretations of his philosophy
are secondary; they were intended, in the main, merely to reach that
larger section of his audience which is composed of readers for
whom philosophy is too forbidding a fare. *Les Mouches* illustrates,
but does not defend, the thesis of personal freedom; *La Putain
respectueuse* illustrates, but does not defend, the bad faith of society;

Le Diable et le Bon Dieu shows the consequences in a fictional context of personal choices of good or evil, as the unfinished tetralogy, *Les Chemins de la liberté,* shows the plight of the existentialist individual "condemned to be free."[6]

Only one novel has a truly ambiguous character. It has been said that *La Nausée* holds a peculiar status among the works of the author. Is it an essay or a novel? Is its purpose to illustrate without defending a thesis, or to develop an idea which will later be defended at greater length? It certainly can be read as either, and if we are inclined to consider it here as an essay rather than as a novel —as it should be, according to its publisher[7]—our reasons are historical and textual. Textually, the theme of *La Nausée* is the subjective reaction to the discovery of one's personal existence as a free individual. If it presents a philosophy, it is philosophy considered as a philosophy of life. But as a matter of historical fact, the notion of freedom as the defining property of consciousness was already exposited in the first of Sartre's works: *L'Imagination,* which appeared in 1936. And the psychological case history suggesting the connection between the freedom of consciousness and the experience of metaphysical anguish is described in an article of the *Recherches Philosophiques* of 1936–37. *La Nausée* appeared in 1938. To this extent, *La Nausée* represents illustration of a thesis. But freedom is not an easy thesis to uphold in an age of territorial occupation or of philosophical positivism. A thoughtful reader of the book could recognize the thesis, but would feel unsatisfied at the lack of evidence for it. How is freedom possible? This is the question Sartre spent so much effort to answer, first in *L'Imaginaire* (1940) and at still greater length in *L'Etre et le néant* (1943). When the historical relations of these texts are thus established, the ambivalent nature of *La Nausée* becomes more apparent: it fits into the general sequence of Sartre's work, marking a clear-cut stage in the development of his thought; but, at the same time, the style of the work is predominantly literary rather than analytic.

Besides his books, Sartre has written several articles of a purely philosophical nature, the consideration of which sheds light upon the development of his early philosophy: in addition to "La transcendance de l'Ego," mentioned above, he has presented "La structure intentionnelle de l'image," (in *Revue de Métaphysique et de Morale,* 1938). Both of these indicate the extreme dependence of

Sartre's beginnings on the work of Edmund Husserl, a subject to which I shall return. The second of these articles appeared as the first section of *L'Imaginaire*. A third article, "Une idée fondamentale de la 'phénoménologie' de Husserl, intentionnalité," (*Nouvelle Revue Française*, 1939) was written in the concise, almost poetic, style identified with the person of Alain,[8] and appeared in the same journal as the essays of the latter. The article heralds a new theory of the passions, which Sartre took the trouble to outline in a book published by Hermann in the same year, *Esquisse d'une théorie des émotions*.

Finally, there appeared two books of a more special interest. The first of these is *L'Existentialisme est un humanisme*. Since this work is nothing but a series of offhand answers by Sartre to unconnected questions concerning his theories, we would incautiously extend the meaning of "primary source" should we include it in that capacity. It appeared in 1946, well after the theoretical justification of Sartre's philosophy had been attempted. And I may cite for those interested in aesthetic theory *Qu'est-ce que la littérature?*, which appeared in serial form in *Les Temps Modernes* from February through July in 1947. Although this too appeared after the greater philosophic effort of Sartre had been expended, it is not a mere capsulized version of his thesis; it represents, rather, an extensive inquiry into the problem of the freedom of the creative literary artist, and is best read in connection with the general aesthetic theory outlined in the *Esquisse* and the *Imaginaire*.

In sum, the following list gives a selective bibliography for the primary sources of the early Sartre. The arrangement is by date of appearance, no respect being paid the distinction between books and articles:

1. *L'Imagination*, 1936.
2. "La transcendance de l'Ego," *Recherches Philosophiques*, 1937.
3. *La Nausée*, 1938.
4. "La structure intentionnelle de l'image," *Revue de Métaphysique et de Morale*, 1938.
5. "Une idée fondamentale de la 'phénoménologie' de Husserl, l'intentionnalité," *Nouvelle Revue Française*, 1939.
6. *Esquisse d'une théorie des émotions*, 1939.
7. *L'Imaginaire*, 1940.
8. *L'Etre et le néant*, 1943.
9. *Qu'est-ce que la littérature?*, 1947.

Keeping in mind always that at any day there may appear further contributions to his work (he has, for example, promised a book on the positive aspects of ethics, foreshadowed by Simone de Beauvoir's *Pour une morale de l'ambiguïté,* which would counterbalance the criticisms of pessimism, despair, or misanthropy that have been hurled at his *magnum opus, L'Etre et le néant*), we might consider this list as definitive. Within his earlier period, it contains the bulk of Sartre's philosophical output.

The question that remains is, What can be done with such a list? The research which heretofore has been primarily bibliographical yields a corpus of literature too vast to be fairly exposited, much less meaningfully interpreted and justly criticized. I propose, therefore, to isolate the peculiar problem posed by this whole list of works, to point out the distinctive marks of the method adopted by Sartre to solve this problem, and finally to evaluate Sartre's claims to having solved the problem by the methods he has adopted.

The keynote of Sartre's whole philosophy was struck in the first of his truly philosophic works, *L'Imagination.* And since this work is little read, it is not difficult to understand the lack of knowledge exhibited by British and American readers concerning the development and internal consistency—or lack of it—in Sartre's theme. In brief, it is concerned with a very traditional problem of philosophy: the theory of knowledge, in particular, the problem of perception and its derivatives. In an act of perceptive awareness, according to this early work, the perceiver becomes aware of himself intuitively as a spontaneous agent while "intending" external objects by means of images.[9] Consider the object I know as a blank sheet of white paper. In looking at it, I can truly say that I see the paper; and when I do so, I am reporting on my immediate impression of a white expanse, which in some sense is situated out-there in my perceptual field. When I turn my gaze from the paper, its image may rest in my consciousness for a time before disappearing. When this after-image disappears, I can say that the paper no longer exists for me; but there is no reason to suppose that the paper ceases to exist in-itself.[10] The defining characteristic of a being in itself is, for Sartre, merely the fact that it is, that it may become the object of someone's perceptive experience. Later, in *L'Etre et le néant,* the "in-itself" will be characterized by two other marks: we may say, by force of logic, only that it is, that it is what it is, and that it is not other than what it is; but in the work under consideration being-in-itself is described as nothing more or less than whatever can become the object of perception. It exists *in* itself, but *for* some perceiving subject.

The perceiving consciousness, on the other hand, can never be the object of someone else's perception; nor, for that matter, of its own perception. It does not exist for something else, since it can be known only directly, without the mediacy of images, and even then only by itself. It is characterized as existence for itself. In terms of Hegelian logic, consciousness becomes, in Sartre's theory, the negation of what is. To say, as Sartre does in *L'Etre,* that consciousness is what it is not and is not what it is, is perhaps to play needlessly with paradox, and may have as its consequence the cessation rather than the stimulation of further thought. Moreover, at this stage of the development in his thought, Sartre has as yet no ontological basis for the resolution of such a paradox. Consciousness, that which exists, but not for someone else's perceptive awareness, must be said to exist only for itself.

We have therefore two kinds of existences, each with a different defining property. Call them subjects and objects, mind and body, or the ideal and the real, whenever such a situation arises there is a problem: what is the nature of the relationship between the two in an event implicating both? What is the nature of man, that being who is a consciousness in and of the world? Alphonse de Waelhens has written that Sartre never succeeded in harmonizing this dualistic ontology with the phenomenological method and that Sartre's insistence upon ontology has gravely prejudiced phenomenology.[11] This charge is evidently dual, and only one of its elements concerns us here. For the moment it is immaterial whether Sartre has been faithful to or dissident from the methodological principles laid down by Husserl; as a matter of fact, Sartre thinks that Husserl was wrong concerning the function of the image in an act of perception, so it is not surprising that he would be considered a dissident by the more orthodox phenomenologists. One can still learn by the mistakes of others. It remains, of course, to see why Sartre thinks that Husserl did make a mistake.[12]

The first charge made by de Waelhens formulates quite clearly our overall task, which is to show that Sartre is concerned with one of the most traditional of philosophic issues, the mind-body problem, and that a modified form of phenomenology lays some claim to solving the problem. In comparing Sartre's position to that of Descartes, however, de Waelhens' interpretation is as misleading as it is instructive: instructive insofar as the general statement of the problem given above fits both Descartes' and Sartre's descriptions of it, but misleading should one pursue the analogy to the extent of attributing any statements about substances to Sartre. None such has ever been made.[13]

What has been done may be more readily explained by outlining the number of possible positions on the problem.[14] At one extreme, for example, one might deny the predicate "real" (however it may be defined) to consciousness (however defined); this is the metaphysical position of the materialist. And in this respect one might recall Huxley's attempt to find a mechanical equivalent for consciousness similar to that found for heat. But none such has yet been found, and it is even doubtful whether it is possible to maintain the position of an ultramaterialist. Hugh Elliot, who denied any form of existence other than that studied by physics and chemistry, was himself forced to envisage at least a psychical accompaniment to certain material configurations and to call this phenomenon "consciousness." Given the admission of some form of consciousness, the logic of absolute materialism is patently deficient; for in speaking of consciousness as "unreal" it uses words in a very odd way. To be consistent in the application of an established semantic rule, true materialists would be forced to say that "consciousness" is meaningless, in that there are no instances in which it is proper to use the word; but by applying it to certain accompaniments of physicochemical processes they admit that the word does have meaning. It is for this reason that metaphysicians who would be consistent materialists are constrained to adopt the compromise position of epiphenomenalism, as Samuel Alexander seems to have done in his *Space, Time and Deity*. Idealists, at the other extreme, deny the predicate "real" to any form of matter. Here Berkeley's three dialogues are a case in point; for him the concept "matter" is explicitly qualified as either self-contradictory or meaningless: meaningless in that there is nothing perceived to which the word might be applied, and absurd as a cause, an instrument, occasion, or the permanent possibility of perceptions. It might be noted in passing that Berkeley's arguments are consistently developed, and need none of the apology one must devise for the supposed materialists. Between these two extremes we find a number of mean positions. I have mentioned epiphenomenalism and must add, in order to complete the account, the parallelism of Spinoza, and the various forms of interactionism, such as the dual substance theory of Descartes and the occasionalism of Geulincx and Malebranche. The two extremes of this series are monistic— with respect to metaphysical categories—while the mean positions are dualistic.

Sartre's major philosophical attempt is to arrive at a metaphysical system which would avoid the untenable extremes of idealism and materialism[15] without embracing either epiphenomenalism or the dual substance theories of reality. Such is the aim of *L'Etre et le néant,* and the ground of this work was being laid in the prior works on the imagination. Sartre became a metaphysician through his early attempts at criticizing accepted theories of the imagination and at constructing his own allegedly more adequate phenomenological theory. In his first philosophical work, he has examined the views of various classical thinkers concerning the existence and function of images, showing that most of them rest upon a naive error in ontological assumptions. What light he could find on these matters came from the more recent theories of Alain and Husserl.

Consider in the first place Sartre's evaluation of that period of philosophy usually called "modern." Whether the theory of knowledge involved is predominantly rationalistic, as in Descartes or Leibnitz, or predominantly empiricistic, as in Hume, there is according to Sartre a similar elementary error in the formulation of the theory of images. Although images play different roles in their respective theories of knowledge, Descartes, Leibnitz, and Hume are all said to be guilty of conceiving the image as if it were a thing, an object of the same nature as any perceived object.[16] What is for Descartes an obscure idea, an affection of the body (see *Regulae,* XII), is for Leibnitz an inner state of the perceiving monad; it is a sign, or expression, of an extended body in the mind of the perceiver (see *Discourse on Metaphysics,* XXVII; Correspondence with Arnauld). And, as for Descartes, the difference between an image and an idea is, according to Leibnitz, only that of clearness. For Hume, on the contrary, the impressions (images) are "opaque" entities possessing, in Sartre's interpretation, "a mysteriously phosphorescent quality"[17] enabling them to be associated, as if by magic,[18] according to the relations of contiguity, resemblance, and the like. The rationalists explain the obscure by the clear: because we possess clear ideas of the objects we perceive, the objects are recognized; for example, we accept the three seen edges of an object as an integral part of a cube. If in this example Sartre has overlooked the detail of Descartes' distinctions, such as that between simple natures having no existence without the mind and perceived figures distinguishable only in thought from the material bodies of perception which are external to the mind, his purpose was merely to show in what sense conception illumines perception. The perception we might have of a material body is both indistinct and unclear. It is indistinct in that I cannot perceive a figure without perceiving the extension of a body; it is unclear because what I actually see is only three sides, the others being obscured by what I do perceive. Yet by the laws of perspective I know that the three obscured sides of the cube must be present. The knowledge I have of the simple nature of cubicity suffices to render the perception clear. It must be remembered that clearness is, for Descartes, a function of being present before an attentive mind. For Hume, however, there is no such power of deductive explanation; in his scheme, our general ideas are abstracted from particular copies of our impressions.

It is clear, then, that the image plays a different role in a rationalistic theory of knowledge than in an empiricistic one. Sartre's claim is that the rationalists are mistaken in supposing that the appearance of images needs any rational justification; images appear, and this is reason enough. Sartre is aware that the empiricist might be willing to accept such an explanation; but in doing so Hume, in particular, leaves us with another problem: that of the unconscious.[19] Since ideas exist only in our perceptions, as objects internal to thought, and since they are not always consciously entertained, being called into play by the gentle force of association, they preserve their peculiar mode of existence, as material objects do, without our being conscious of them. The question of whether Hume actually held this view is of some consequence here. Indeed if Sartre were asked to put his finger on the text, he would be forced to back down. His reading of Hume is based upon the *Treatise* in full, and he means that Hume's position *implies,* in some sense of this term, the existence of the problem he describes. Psychologically speaking, he seems to be right. On purely associationistic grounds this subtle interplay between the conscious and the unconscious is sheer magic. We must be able to escape both the rationalist's need for an explanation of images and the empiricist's avoidance of the problem, which poses other problems equally unsolvable on his own terms; and we can do so, says Sartre, if only we avoid the initial error, which is to consider an image as a thing. An image is a consciousness, or intentional act.

"Consciousness" used in this sense is a neologism which Sartre has carried over from the German *Bewusstsein* to indicate a particular structure within a global consciousness. The sense intended in the second instance of the term is what is usually meant when we misleadingly say that consciousness is composed of acts or states.[20] We think by images, but not on the occasion of images; that is, a perceptual image is the crudest type of knowledge (by acquaintance), but when we have such images our thought is unmixed with an object. It is all thought, a "translucent" apperception and not an opaque entity.[21] If it were the latter, our mind would be completely passive before the object, which in no sense of the term can be conceived as possessing the power to act upon a subject. In a word, the image is a spontaneous structure of consciousness existing for and by itself. It should be noted that this sense of causation—power or efficiency—is exactly the sense denied by Hume, and we shall see later that Sartre's denial of it, on different grounds to be sure, poses other problems.

What does it mean to say that a consciousness exists for and by itself? Sartre offers a concise definition of these terms when he says,

That existence is called spontaneous which determines itself, which brings itself to exist. In other words, whatever exists spontaneously exists for and by itself. Only one reality therefore merits the epithet "spontaneous," and that is consciousness. For it, in fact, to exist and to have consciousness of its existence are one and the same thing.[22]

Whatever exists by the fact of being aware of its existence is, by this explanation, freely self-determined. Consciousness is *of* an object; it posits the existence of its object. But in the same event it is aware of itself "non-positionally." It is known as a lived experience is known, and can become the object of another consciousness only in an act of reflection. Hence, wherever there is consciousness of an object there is self-consciousness. In denying that the image is a content of a global consciousness, that is, in denying the status of an object to the image, Sartre was led to accept the thesis of a self-determining subject within a conscious event (*Erlebnis*).[23]

Sartre contends further that any successful theory of the image must be capable of two explanations: first, how images function in an act of knowing, and second, how images properly so-called differ from percepts. At this stage in his thought, he accepts no distinction between the act of conceiving and that of perceiving which can be only quantitatively differentiated, as the distinction between the clearness and distinctness in the theories of Descartes and Leibnitz, or between the force and vivacity of impressions and ideas in the epistemology of Hume. To think by conception is one way which consciousness has of referring to the world, to think by perception is another; both are structures of consciousness. As will be shown later, both acts are intentional; but both acts intend the world in a different manner. There would thus be a difference in kind and not only in degree between imagining and conceiving, between an image and an idea. The second criterion—that of explaining the difference between image and percept, imagining and perceiving—has been thoroughly discussed by two more recent theorists of note, Alain and Husserl; Sartre examines the claims of each to having satisfied this criterion.

Alain was a Cartesian rationalist; to perceive was, in his theory, to judge that the object perceived was such or such. The difference between a veridical perception of an object and the image of the same object is that in the first case there is no error in judgment while in the second there is. When I imagine that I see an object and mistakenly take it to be what it is not, I have no reason to doubt that my receptor organs have been stimulated, but my interpretation of that stimulation can always be in error, especially when I see things under the influence of my emotions. Othello's treatment of Desdemona is understandable in these terms, and Iago knew it. But for Iago's complicity Othello's perception was a clear case of self-delusion. And so are dream experiences: asleep before an open window when it happens to rain, I can feel the moisture as it comes into contact with my skin senses, and it is not a mystery why I interpret this stimulation as the engulfing waves of the sea in which, in my dream, I have been shipwrecked. If imaginary experiences are of this nature, there is no need for images at all. Alain's position is therefore similar to that of earlier behaviorists who likewise denied, as a heuristic maxim, the existence of images. This denial of images constitutes a metaphysical postulate whose purpose is to allow the development of a purely scientific description of physical experience. Thus Alain's rationalism and the empiricism of behaviorists constitute another instance of congruence in supposedly antithetical methods.

Moreover, Alain's theory has an advantage in Sartre's estimation: it avoids the naïveté of mistaking an image for an object; but this advantage is greatly overbalanced. Following the line of reasoning explained above, Alain was led "to construct a theory of the imagination without images." And this would not be too serious a charge, but for two disconfirming consequences of the hypothesis. The first of these pointed out by Sartre is a matter of consistency: if imagining is sufficiently explained by the uncritical acceptance of belief in the existence of an object which is not as judged, then fictions of the imagination, such as illusions and hallucinations, are likewise based upon judgments. And this attributes too much activity to the imagination, which will later be seen as "motivated" by external objects in such cases. The second disadvantage is more directly empirical: any theory which denies the existence of images, says Sartre, is blindly denying an experiential fact, such as the image anyone might entertain of an absent friend. In concluding his refutation, he states that an image is a real psychic fact, and hence the proper subject of scientific investigation.[24]

In Sartre's opinion, the most scientific of recent investigations into the facts of the imagination has been that of Edmund Husserl in *Logische Untersuchungen*. The theory of knowledge contained in this work is allegedly unique; it expressly denies what Sartre has called the "alimentary" and "digestive" character of the idealism of contemporary academic French philosophy. In this denunciation occurs the oft-quoted spider image: "We have all read Brunschvicg, Lalande and Meyerson: we have all been led to believe that the mind, like a giant spider, attracted things into its web, covered them over with its white spittle and slowly swallowed them, thereby reducing them to its own substance."[25] In a word, that idealism is misguided which reduces objects to images or collections of images, considered as states of consciousness. In logic, this error had been denounced by Husserl as one phase of psychologism.

If logic is equivalent to a method of inquiry, then one must, in a logical analysis, start with whatever is empirically given. And, according to Husserl, in any act of knowledge, there are two irreducible given factors: an object which is intended and the consciousness which intends. It follows therefore that all objects of knowledge, whether physical or ideational, a thing or an essence, transcend consciousness. Note that "transcend" here means nothing more or less than "are other than." In an act of *reflective* self-awareness, the object is a prior consciousness and in this sense transcendence is predicated of consciousness itself; the object is immanent to consciousness only when the consciousness becomes aware of itself "nonpositionally." This use of "transcendent" and "immanent" is quite different from, although related to, the notion of movement of the self within its environment, of the self's development, or of the difference between the body as "facticity" and the consciousness as transcendence. These later acceptations of the terms are explained by Sartre in their metaphysical and moral contexts in *L'Etre et le néant*. The confusion of these terms within Sartre's total philosophy is unfortunate, and has given rise to much controversy.[26]

How does the notion of intentionality enlighten us on the nature of the image? It is clear that if an image is no longer a content of consciousness, but a structure of the consciousness itself, then to describe the image we must take into account the structure of the consciousness in the act of imaging. In other words, we must perform the reduction, put the world in brackets, so to speak, and consider consciousness without reference to the world of objects it intends in its empirico-naturalistic attitude. This putting the world into brackets is a metaphorical expression of the effect of doubt; as a methodological procedure, it allows a suspension of belief in the existence of objects and puts into evidence the structures of the consciousness itself. Sartre accepts the phenomenological reduction, as this bracketing of the world is called, and even follows Husserl in the second of his reductions. Thus if psychology is to be a pure science, the psychologist must consider only the essence of the structure involved. The method of knowing in this *époché* is intuition, and the reduction is called "eidetic." The consciousness in this reduction no longer intends the world, but meanings or significations, directly, without benefit of mediating signs.

Sartre's reason for refusing to follow Husserl into the third and final of his reductions, that which places the transcendental subject into relation with its own subjectivity, is explained in an article: "La transcendance de l'Ego" (*Recherches Philosophiques*, VI: 85–

123, 1936–37), in which he traces the sense in which the ego might be said to be transcendent, becoming an object of awareness to some consciousness. The gist of the article is that the "I" is never the object of direct experience, appearing as it does only at the horizon of experience as reflected by another, succeeding act of consciousness. In contradiction to Husserl, Sartre maintains that the field of transcendental subjectivity not only is, but must be impersonal. What appears later in *L'Etre* as the pre-reflective cogito appears here as a criticism of Descartes' *Meditations* as well as Husserl's *Cartesianische Meditationen.*[27]

Although Sartre applies Husserl's method, he accepts only the first two reductions as valid. In the first, the image is considered as image, a constitutive act of the consciousness referring to an object by virtue of a psychic matter. Husserl called this matter a "hyle," which is informed by the intention. The image is therefore not an object, nor even a content of consciousness; it is a process or event in which a certain mental configuration is related to a transcendent object. It must be noted here that "intention" and "hyle" are correlative terms, neither definable without reference to the other. The intention is always a formal characteristic; it is sometimes called a manner or way of referring. The hyle is what is referred.

This distinction of matter and form within the image has, in Sartre's opinion, a clear advantage over the classical formulation of the image as a simulacrum of an object, as well as over the pseudo-distinction between image and idea explained above as an important part of both rationalism and empiricism. An example may show why. Husserl had examined, in the *Ideen zu einer reinen Phaenomenologie und phaenomenologischen Philosophie,*[28] an act of attending to Albrecht Dürer's etching, *A Knight, Death, and the Devil.* What we actually perceive is (a) the presented physical character of the lines in the etching, but what we become aware of is (b) the representations of a knight on a horse, the personification of death, and the devil incarnate. The imaged objects (c), a knight in flesh and blood, the emaciated and snake-ridden figure of death, and the diabolical incarnation, are the objects to which the representations refer. (a) and (b) have the same hyle, the same psychic configuration; only their intentions, their manner of referral, differ. The presentation does not further refer to an object, but the representation does. Hence, the intention of the presentation (a), which is self-referring,

DÜRER, *Knight, Death, and the Devil*

differs from the intention of the representation (b) of a transcendent object (c). In the description of these acts, we might add, there is ample theoretical grounds for distinguishing an act of immediate from an act of referential expression in aesthetics: for example, when we attend to the physical properties of a painting without taking into consideration the reference such physical properties might make to objects outside the painting as a thematic expression, we are attending to and appreciating the purely formal characteristics of the painting; when, on the other hand, we attend to the representations qua representations, our appreciation is of the subject matter or content of the painting. Sartre, of course, was not blind to the implications Husserl's theory carries for aesthetics.[29] In fact, the conclusion of *L'Imaginaire* contains a sketch of an aesthetic theory, which will be discussed in the following chapter; he does not press the matter here, because he thinks the distinction Husserl has drawn between hyle and intention is itself a tenuous one.[30]

How can it be explained that a consciousness is directed differently to an object in the two cases above? What is the distinction in the acts informing the matter-in-image of the representation and the matter-as-perceived of the perception? Husserl appealed to the motivation of the consciousness involved. If one is motivated to see the pictorial value of paintings, then one will not, in the same act, perceive the purely formal values, and vice versa. Sartre points out that this is an inconsistency. Our investigation was to be eidetic, and not empirical; but motivation is an empirical fact. Motivation is as extrinsic a character of the imagining consciousness as was the correspondence, for Leibnitz, between the inner states of the monad and its outer environment. And if, on the other hand, the hyle is the same in the two acts of awareness, how could one explain the difference between a percept and a true image, for which there is no perceived object at all? If we remain within the eidetic reduction, says Sartre, the appeal to motivation is patently inconsistent. He concludes therefore that both matter and form differ in nature in the acts of perceiving a real object and perceiving the representation of a real object.[31]

In sum, Sartre contends that if one's aim is to add to the body of scientific knowledge concerning the relation of consciousness and its environment, one must still investigate the nature of the image; and if one were to consider what he calls the "errors" of Husserl, one need only avoid them in order to arrive at a fuller comprehension of the world of the imagination. Such, at any rate, was the program called for by Sartre, who sought to formulate a phenomenological psychology of the image; the work appeared in 1940 bearing the title, *L'Imaginaire*.

Having learned what he could from his predecessors, Sartre tried in this first original work to develop an internally consistent and empirically adequate theory of the imagination. This work will be discussed under the following four headings: the method of phenomenological inquiry, the description of the image, the classification of images, and his conclusions.

In the first place, the method of any inquiry is to some extent determined by the object or class of objects one is inquiring into. Sartre wants to limit his attention to those images which refer to objects not in the presence of the observer. These are images properly so-called, and Malebranche had already used the word "image" in this precise manner (*Recherche de la vérité*, II, I, 1.). This usage implies that when I have the image of a friend, for example, that friend need not be in my presence. My image refers to an object, my friend, who happens not to be directly perceivable. It must be noted that what I observe in a case of veridical perception is that the image by which I become conscious of an object is, in itself, not perceived. I perceive another object by means of it. The image itself is unobservable. Should I deny this, I would be guilty of the same naive ontology as that criticized by Sartre in traditional rationalism and empiricism. The image can be known only by an act of reflection. This reflection might very well be considered a kind of second level observation; it is an act which permits the statement, "I had an image." Sartre seems to be mistaken when he says "I have an image,"[32] since it would appear that a consciousness given over to the image could not, without changing its intention, be aware that the object of its awareness is non-existent. Only an act of reflection could establish this fact. What was perceived in the first instance is then established as an object of a past awareness. My reflective act is intuitive and admits of no error —barring bad faith in my pronouncement. The object of this intuition is an essence. By having one, I know what an image is; and by reflecting upon its kind, and only thus, can I intuit the essence of the imagining consciousness. It is not a question here of the essence of a transcendent spatio-temporal object.

To understand this process, however, one must keep in mind the unique position of examples in general phenomenology.[33] Not being a matter of observation and empirical generalization, the procedure involves no multiplication of examples. There is no induction and, properly speaking, no deduction. One example suffices to establish the fact, and intuition grasps the essence of the example as a pure possibility. The job of the phenomenologist is to describe these intuitions, and it is in this sense that Husserl maintained that his method was purely descriptive. The method of the phenomenologist consists therefore in a three-fold technique: contemplation of an example, reflection on the essence of the example, and description of that essence. Moreover, since Sartre's phenomenological analysis is of images, his procedure is to produce an image, to reflect upon it, and to describe the essence reflected upon. Anyone with the proper apparatus is capable of verifying the first two of these steps, so Sartre jumps immediately to a description of the essence he has intuited from his example.

We have therefore, in the second place, an inventory of the necessary or essential properties of images, those without which the existence of an image would be impossible. The formulation of the phenomenological reduction as Sartre uses it here is clearly not unrelated to another procedure formulated by Kant and called the "transcendental deduction"; I merely note this fact in passing, the validity of neither process having been demonstrated. The necessary characteristics which compose the inventory are four in number.

According to Sartre, in order to be a possible experience of some subject, the image must first be considered *a conscious event*. The force of this assertion is really a denial. Sartre means that the image cannot be conceived as a content, immanent to the imagining consciousness (global sense). Hume, it is said, was deceived by this "illusion of immanence," when he explained objects (*Treatise,* I, IV, 2) as unknown correlates of a constant and coherent set of impressions. Strictly speaking, an object is never perceived, according to Hume, since we are aware only of our impressions and ideas. The distinction between a perceived object and its image is therefore a matter of greater or less coherence and constancy of their appearance, of which we are aware. But what does it mean to say that we are aware of our impressions qua impressions? Sartre insists that if a content of consciousness is to be observed, it must be of the nature of an object. And if this is so, to be able to observe that object-content one must have another content, and so on indefinitely. But this is absurd, since no one would in the end ever have perceived an object in the first place. Obviously, this *reductio* argument is valid only if one holds that objects themselves are perceived. Hume does not hold this. In an effort to validate his claim Sartre takes issue with the external relation Hume supposes to exist between our ideas and their objects (*Treatise of Human Nature:* I, I, 7). If to form an idea and to form an idea of an object are one and the same process, says Sartre, the chair one perceives is not an object of wood and cane, for example, upon which one might sit, and which might serve as criterion for judging the difference between it and other objects such as tables and inkwells. Yet our ideas are supposed to be *of something.* Sartre concludes that Hume meant no distinction at all between the idea of a chair and a chair as it is perceived; or in other words, that for Hume the idea of a chair is an observable content of consciousness. And the proof of this interpretation is taken to be Hume's contention that whatever is valid for our ideas is valid for their objects.[34]

If it cannot be contended that an image is an object of consciousness, it must be supposed that images are consciousnesses, acts by which one becomes aware of transcendent objects. Although we are not directly aware of images, we become aware of objects by means of images. This doctrine is not new; we find it in St. Thomas (*Summa Theologica,* I, Question 85, article 2), who found the theory already at least adumbrated in Aristotle (doctrine of sensible forms). If Sartre has not garnered it from its more original sources, it has been obtained from his Neo-Scholastic contemporaries; or barring this possibility, more indirectly through Husserl from Brentano. Whatever its historical source, Sartre's view maintains that an image is a synthetic organization within experience of psychical elements referring directly to its object. The essence of the image is precisely to refer to its object in the peculiar way that it does. As a conscious event, the image is the way in which the consciousness "gives itself an object."[35] In other words, the image is a conscious event whose intention is an object.

In relation to the second property of images, Hume's so-called error becomes still more apparent. *The attitude of the imagining consciousness* is said by Sartre to be *that of quasi-observation,* and the object of the image a quasi-observable. To explain this predicate, we shall have to consider an act of veridical perception. When I perceive an object, I judge it to be such or such. The object is merely a "series of projections"[36] (Husserl's *Abschattungen,* profiles). In order to perceive these *Abschattungen* as a unified object one must understand the concept which unifies them. In a word, to perceive an object one must have formed the concept of that object. Moreover, these perceived objects are seen in relation to other objects, and as transcendent to the perceiving consciousness. In an act of the imagination, on the other hand, not only is the concept which illumines the perception not formed, but given in the act; but the objects referred to by images lack relations to other objects, since they are not a part of the environing world, and are, properly speaking, constituted by the act itself. The difference between an observed object and an imagined object is therefore dual: there is a difference in the role played by concepts, as well as in the intention of the consciousness. In an act of perception the consciousness intends a real object, which transcends the consciousness and is related to other objects of like kind; while in an act of the imagination the consciousness intends an unreal object, which does not transcend consciousness, being constituted by it, and which therefore has no relation to other objects.[37]

Sartre expands this notion of an unreal object as a third characteristic of the imagining consciousness. Images are said to *posit their objects as non-existent.* As in the phenomenon of quasi-observation, comparison with veridical perception is helpful. A truly perceptual image refers to a transcendent object; the perceptive consciousness poses the existence of a real object. The imaginative consciousness, on the other hand, may posit the existence of its object in one of four ways: as non-existent (so-called fictions of the imagination), as absent (for example, the image I am now having of my friend, who is not in my presence), as existing elsewhere (such as the image I may have of my friend who is not only not here, but situated in some other, imaginally defined, context), finally, as making no claim to any kind of existence at all. The thesis of the act of positing in this last way is completely neutral (for example, my present image of a beautiful dancer whose existence is not in question although she might exist). Each of these positional acts bears an element of negation, and this negative element constitutes the essence of the imagining consciousness. The imagined object is given, but given in a peculiar way; it is given as absent. Foreshadowing some of his later metaphysics, Sartre claims that the image envelopes a certain nothingness.[38] Is it nonsense to say that an image refers to something which isn't there? If not, Sartre's concept of nothingness has authentic operational credentials.

It may be of some help at this point to examine the authenticity of these credentials. When we say that the image is a consciousness which posits the non-existence of its object, what are we committed to? It is clear that we do not mean the belief or disbelief in the existence of unreal objects. Belief or disbelief is a matter of subsequent intention, a judgment of the truth or falsity of the object of the primary intention. Nor can it mean that we are aware of our images but not of their correlative objects; this would be to commit the error of immanentism: we are not aware of our images directly, only of their objects. But the object of an image is non-existent. Either we are talking nonsense or a distinction must be drawn.

The distinction Sartre has in mind is that between an object actually before the perceiving consciousness and one which is defined by its conception alone. The unreal object is a "quasi-observable"; it is created by the intention, or concept. One could therefore say the object of the image is a mere possibility. The beautiful dancer which appears to me in image could be explained by my *intending* her to appear. This would be the point of telling someone to imagine such an object. I entertain the concept of a beautiful dancer and the sensuous elements necessary for the apparition occur: a tall slender form in gracious movement, as it were, before my very eyes. The object of my image is the dancer, who, for all I know, may exist nowhere outside of my own consciousness. If so, the object of images may be said to be "unreal" in this sense. If I were to try to observe the dancer in person I could not; if the image, I could not. In creating images my consciousness is in the state of quasi-observation. I can not move around the object, feel it, enter into its dance; for its only existence is defined by the concepts I must use to conjure it up. Imaginary objects are thus creations of the imagining consciousness. And should we insist that the word "real" adds nothing to the concept "object," and hence that the word "unreal" added to the same concept is absurd, Sartre asks us to consider the following conditions which allow for the appearance of "absent" objects:

The condition necessary for a consciousness to be able to imagine is . . . dual: one must be able to posit the world in its synthetic totality, and at the same time posit the imagined object as out of touch with this synthetic whole, that is, at the same time to posit the world as nothing with respect to the image.[39]

Because the world, or situation in which we live, is real, the image we project upon that situation is readily perceived to be nothing. But should we attend to the image, the world recedes into nothingness for that act of consciousness. Like figure and ground, image and the world are complementary notions: one exists at the expense of the other, and between them there is tension. When I walk into a café looking for my friend who happens not to be there, I could say one of two things: either I see the interior of the café but not my friend; or, since my image was unconsummated, I perceive the absence of my friend. In sum, "The intentional object of the imagining consciousness has this particularity: either it isn't there and is posited as such, or it doesn't exist, and is posited as inexistent or not posited at all."[40] The image is a consciousness which intends its object in one of the aforementioned ways.

The object intended, however, is a very peculiar one; it is given, so to speak, *in absentia*. Not being before the subject, it is neither the cause nor the effect of the subject's cognition. It is inert, inactive. Lest some unwary reader assume that this condition of unreality in the imagined object negates the very existence of the image, Sartre warns that no evidence could be found for the denial of the representation in essence of an object or idea, of the defining intention, or of the motor-affective analogue (the psychic hyle) which represents the object. To repeat, an object is unreal when it is referred to by some consciousness in such a way that its existence or presence is expressly denied, or that its existence is a mere possibility. And in this way the imagining consciousness posits the absence of the object it represents.

Any qualities that such objects might have must therefore be absolute, in the sense of "non-relative." All relations such objects may have are purely internal and intrinsic; the imagined object is a concrete totality. There is, however, a sense in which space, time, and movement are dimensions of unreal objects, and we must make clear what that sense is. It is manifestly impossible, for example, to locate an unreal object topographically. If I have an image of a friend to my right, I do not necessarily have an image of that friend to the left of an object which is directly before me. This is true because all localization of the unreal object is within the image. The localization of the object, like its being, is determined by my consciousness. I may have an image of my friend as he is seated in his room before a desk, but if I do, my friend-in-image is then related to his room-in-image. The room in this image is the object of a secondary intention. Like the object of the primary intention, it is given in absence.

Similar considerations establish the intrinsic character of the time involved in an imaged object. In a dream, the actual time passed by the dreamer is infinitely shorter than the time of the dream sequence. The intention of the dream image determines the sequence of events in the dream, and the acceptance of the dream events as real, or life-like, is explained by a supplementary intention defined by the belief itself. And like time, so duration: each is absolute within the image. Moreover, within a dream sequence, fatality correctly describes the relation between the events: the future determines the present. And this too is possible only because there are no causally related parts to the image. In a dream, I intend the full development of an act, or sequence of events; the unity of the intention defines the unity or sequence between events. In a word, within the image there is "a shadow of time which is suited to that shadow of an object, with its shadow of a space."[41] All these shadows constitute the unreal world; whence, the ambiguity, the evasive and apparently contradictory qualities of creative intelligence. Within this world movement is possible; but this movement, like the time it entails and the space and duration it consumes, is a purely intentional phenomenon. One could imagine a turning wheel, but one could not within the same image, by one intention, imagine a turning wheel which reverses its direction.[42]

The final characteristic of the image, according to Sartre, is its *spontaneity*. Consciousness, whose existence is its self-awareness, comes into being whenever there is consciousness of something. The image, which is a consciousness, reveals itself to reflection as creative. The object does not determine the consciousness because the object of the imagining consciousness is non-existent. Whereas in perception the consciousness is to some extent passive before the object it perceives, in the act of imagining the consciousness is completely self-determining. This means, among other things, that I can conjure images at will. If one should offer an objection to this explanation, by an appeal to memory, concluding that in the first instance my image was a perceptive, and therefore passive, experience, I should counter, with Sartre, that even so I can at any given moment will to recall that image in the absence of its attendant object. We have insight here into what he will later distinguish as *motif* and *mobile,* as objective and subjective motivations without which the discussion of freedom in Sartre's thought is profitless.[43] My situation determines what I see and in this sense my situation motivates my perception; but even in the most compelling of situations I sometimes see what I want to see, and in this sense too my conduct is motivated. But neither of these motivations takes away the spontaneity of my actions, in Sartre's opinion, since either my situation or any of my prior decisions may be changed by a free and subsequent decision. This thesis need not be defended here; suffice it to say that the image owes nothing to its object since the object is produced and preserved—as non-existent—in the very act of imagining. It is because of this spontaneity that artists, imaginative creatures par excellence, are correctly said to be creative.

The foregoing examples, taken from empirical cases, have quite purposely been varied. Reference to pure fictions, to hallucinations, to dreams, and to aesthetic objects, is not intended to predispose the reader to particular conclusions in the realm of aesthetics proper, nor to emphasize a criticism often laid upon Sartrean existentialism, its concern with the bizarre or the morbid. Rather, the image in each of its forms is of some value to the phenomenologist; if one were incautious, however, one could easily be misled to the conclusion that Sartre wants to attempt an inductive and empirical investigation of the field of images in order to arrive at a proper description of the imagining consciousness. This is not the case; he has chosen a variety of examples to indicate that any one of them suffices to give an intuition of the essence of the imagination. His intuition is described in the following definition: in its generic sense, the term "image" means "an act which, in its corporeity, aims at an absent or non-existent object by means of a physical or psychical continuant which is not given in itself, but [which is given] in the guise of an 'analogical representative' of the object aimed at."[44] Besides showing a heavy dependence upon the conclusions of Husserl, hyle and intention still defining the image, this definition affords a means of classifying images according to the greater or lesser extent of the creativity of the consciousness in the imaging act. Likewise, it is evident from the possibility of a physical continuant within the image that Sartre does not limit himself to purely mental images. He is trying to get at the essence of these by a process of abstraction from cases which are at least partially non-mental. The more matter is abstracted from the analogue, the more spontaneous is the creative act. We may therefore consider our third heading, the classification of images according to the increasing order of spontaneity within the mental act.

Thirdly, in the loosest sense of the term, portraits and caricatures are images. In cases such as these, the matter of the analogue is a perceptual object; it is physical and has little relevance for the world of physiology or consciousness. The movements and feelings of the perceiving subject are alien to the physical portrait. But they are put into play by the portrait,[45] and in this sense the portrait constitutes a way of visualizing its subject. The conceptual activity of the intentional consciousness is limited to the recognition of a resemblance.

Still physical in its matter is a sign, such as a plaque reading "Office of the Under-Secretary." The reference no longer takes place by means of resemblance, and Sartre could find no processes better than convention or habit to explain how one could take the printed words to stand for their object, the office itself. He is saying, however, that marks on plaques, like those on paper, have meaning through stipulation and inference. The meaning of words is assumed to be conventional and their understanding a matter of habitual use. Unlike the portrait, moreover, the sign does not posit the existence of its object; the sign, as image, has an empty intention, and convention is responsible for its reference.

In a third level of abstraction from matter, we have pantomime. The mimic gesture is taken to be the sign of a real act. Consciousness must therefore become aware first of the miming motions and subsequently of their reference to a completer, more real act.

Similarly, an abstract design, such as a line drawing, is merely a two-dimensional representation of a three-dimensional reality. Such is the fourth level of abstraction. The abstraction of the line drawing, moreover, shows clearly the extent to which conception determines the image. In responding to such drawings, we interpret by means of a hypothetical concept which is *savoir,* or knowledge. We might very well say to ourselves, This could be a bird; our hypothesis produces eye-movements which actually yield the object anticipated.

Something similar occurs, according to Sartre, when we are led to see faces in a flame, spots on walls, or rocks in a human shape, examples of the fifth level. The matter of such images is even more abstract than that of a two-dimensional line drawing, being sheer appearance: not what is there, but what is taken to be there. Again a hypothetical concept and the eye-movements of anticipation are assumed to explain the appearance of the unreal object.

On the sixth level, we are on the fringe of self-delusion. Hypnagogical illusions, those arising from a relaxed state of attention and which are usually accompanied by phosphenes if the eyes of the subject are closed, have no material analogue whatsoever. The object which appears has no transcendent correlative. The abstractive process has therefore been completed. The role of the self-deluding consciousness has gained in spontaneity, but it has not yet become completely determinant of the experience. The consciousness has become fascinated by itself in a sort of auto-suggestion. Knowledge, the concept (*savoir*) which defines the possibility of the experienced event, always precedes the illusion. There could be no auto-suggestion without this kind of knowledge, and the physiology of sensation is such that anticipation produces the intention. But this intention is empty and the experience is illusory because it is taken for a fulfilled intention, one which has a real object. Under hypnagogical illusion, my consciousness intends an object as if there were true representation; "I really see something, but what I see is nothing."[46]

One final step remains in Sartre's abstractive scheme. In the mental image properly so-called, there is a voluntary creation of the analogue, now purely psychic in matter. There can be only a logical distinction between the matter of the image, its hyle, and its form, or intention. To repeat, in the mental image, the intention creates the object. At the moment we reach this upper limit of abstraction from physical matter within the image we reach the limit of the possibility of observation. In order to reflect upon a given image to investigate the relation of matter and form in its constitution, our consciousness, which is investigating and which at the same time is the investigated subject, must change its intention. In giving way to reflection, it loses the image it seeks to investigate. One is therefore led to a final choice point in the maze: we can have the image as a whole, with no distinction of matter and form, hyle or intention, or we can try to reflect upon the psychic matter of the image without its informing intention; but in this case the consciousness grasps no image at all, and therefore no matter. The psychic matter of the purely mental image is consequently postulated as necessary in essence. Although it is not given in isolation, it must be given; and should we try to say more about it, we must appeal to conjecture, if only to the improved method of conjecture which constitutes the essence of experimental psychology.[47] We are forced to leave the realm of the certain, that of essence, and to enter that of the probable, the realm of individual psychic events investigated by the empirical scientist. It is not our purpose to follow Sartre there.

In the fourth place, the results of Sartre's phenomenological investigation of the consciousness may be summarized in the following way. The phenomenological method, which is described as the intuition of the essence of a consciousness considered without reference to the object it intends (the bracketing of the world), leads to an impasse when the consciousness investigated is an image. We cannot intuit the psychic matter of the image even within the stream of our own global consciousness because in the attempt to do so the image disappears with the change in intention from image to reflection on the image. Sartre is led, therefore, to accept the existence of a "transcendental" psychical continuant, which he misleadingly calls a content.[48]

The word "transcendental" in this context is suspect. But the distinction between a transcendent and a transcendental object is not new. He had been using "transcendent" as equivalent to "other than the intending consciousness"; and in this sense the epithet is proper only to the object before the reflected consciousness in the context described above. The psychic continuant is, of course, immanent to the imaging consciousness, being the matter of the image itself. It is transcendental in the sense of being unknowable or unobservable. The word does not mean "external" in the sense which would make the image transcendent to the consciousness. This apparent exteriority of the image is the basis for what has been described above as the "illusion of immanence." One question we may ask of Sartre, however, is the sense in which this continuant (*continu*) can be called a content (*contenu*), warning that if "content" is meant he comes as close to being the dupe of the illusion of immanence as he found Hume to be. How has he avoided taking the image for an object if the psychic matter of the image is a content of consciousness, transcendental if not transcendent? Only by distinguishing, one might repeat, between consciousnesses. A global consciousness is a stream of constituent consciousnesses. But so was it for Hume, who called these consciousnesses "perceptions." The difference is that in Hume's case the sense data are capable of being related to others in such a way that ideas and distinctions between ideas are, as it were, observable, hence knowable. For Sartre there are no "sense data," and the matter of a mental image must remain transcendental.

In short, Sartre's analysis of the phenomenology of the imagination contains descriptions of at least three different knowing processes. In an act of perception, consciousness intends an object. I perceive a chair as a spatio-temporal continuant capable of supporting my weight. The role of conception in my act, which is my knowledge of the essence of the object, is clear since all objects are perceived as such or such. In the intuitive act, consciousness intends meanings, the essences of objects or universal mathematical truths. The essence of an object is defined, in *L'Etre,* as the *ratio* (reason) of the appearances of that object.[49] In an imaginative act, on the other hand, consciousness tends toward, or intends its object by means of the image. Intuition is a direct awareness; perception and imagination, to some extent indirect or mediate. Moreover, perception and imagination are clearly different mental processes, since the object of the first is given as present; of the second, as absent. To understand the essence of the perceptive act another analysis must be undertaken; there must be another bracketing of the world and another intuition. And the way is open for such an analysis, in Sartre's opinion, once we have renounced the hypothesis that objects are amalgamated wholes of qualities[50] and that there are such things as pure sensations, or pure sense data.[51]

Maurice Merleau-Ponty has attempted such an analysis in his *Phénoménologie de la perception,*[52] and his case will be considered in the second part of this treatise.

If the foregoing is a faithful account of Sartre's early philosophy, a further analysis of the method he has used, this time from a critical viewpoint, will be helpful to show to what extent his theory solves the problems he claims any successful theory of the imagination should solve; to evaluate his criticism of Husserl's use of the phenomenological method; and to point out how the weaknesses in his theory were created in his difference from Husserl, weaknesses which necessitated further elaboration in *L'Etre et le néant.* As these last two points are related, they will be treated as a unit.

Consider, first, Sartre's claims to theoretical success. From his point

of view, both classical rationalism and empiricism failed to solve the
problem of perception because of a naive ontology of the image,
which he calls "the illusion of immanence." The "obscure" idea in
rationalistic theory is no closer to a solution of the problem than the
impressions of sense in empiricistic theory. To have succeeded, says
Sartre, either would have had to show in what way images of a purely
mental kind differ from percepts, and how images function in an act
of knowledge. True, these requirements for any theory to qualify as
successful were written into his first work, *L'Imagination,* and his
own attempt at successful fulfillment of them appeared in the subsequent *L'Imaginaire.* But if we take his work as a unified whole, we
may express serious doubt as to whether he fulfilled his own requirements.

The first seems to be satisfied almost by definition, and this would
not be surprising to a scholastic for whom an essence is what a definition signifies. One must keep in mind, however, that Sartre claims
to have intuited the essence of an image. As a result of this intuition,
images are said to differ from percepts as a structure of the consciousness differs from an object which it intends. In an act of the imagination, consciousness creates its own object; in an act of perception,
consciousness is placed before an object. Here is the first difficulty.
For Sartre, consciousness is pure spontaneity. In what sense therefore
can an object affect a consciousness in perception? Sartre claims that
it does not. But if this is so, what is the relation between consciousness and object in an act of perception? The statement which constitutes the phenomenological axiom, "Every consciousness is consciousness of something," solves the issue by fiat and the question is
begged. We still face the issue of discriminating between percept
and image. To call the one an object and the other an intention is
perfectly valid, if only one can describe the nature of the relation
between object and intentions in an act of purely perceptive awareness. It is for this reason that Merleau-Ponty saw the need of ground-
ing phenomenology in perception.[53] And de Waelhens seems to have
touched upon the difficulty implicit in Sartre's position; since Sartre
chose to bind himself between two disparate explanatory categories,
the *pour-soi* and the *en-soi,* spontaneity and determined essence, he
has failed to solve the problem of perception,[54] as others have failed
for similar reasons. The question of the interaction of the two orders
of existents has clearly been begged. At best he has shown that the

discussions of perception and imagination should be separate issues. Sartre can easily suggest, therefore, that his main interest was to separate the two problems; and this might be considered legitimate if he had not appealed to acts of perception as already successfully described or as sufficiently known to be taken for granted. And the extent to which Sartre follows Husserl on this matter is not clear in these early works.

As for his second claim, that his theory solves the question of the function of images in an act of knowledge, here too there arise serious doubts. In an act of perception and in an act of the imagination there is a concept. But the concept is formed in the one, given in the other. I form a concept, according to Sartre, by unifying the various perspectives of a physical object into a single idea. I do not see a cube; I take what I see as three converging planes to be a solid of six intersecting planes. To this extent perception does imply judgment; and of course, judgment implies the existence of concepts. Now Sartre is aware of this, but takes for granted the question of how we know concepts. Without such knowledge his later discussion of the degradation of pure *savoir* to *savoir imageant* to images per se seems unfounded.[55] His weakness on perception theory has already been indicated. The imagination, on the other hand, intends its object with reference to a concept which has already been formed. When I look, for example, at a shimmering flame and "see" a face of a diabolical personality exhorting me to evil, I must already possess the idea of the devil and his ways. Thus both perception and imagination entail conception. But what is the source of our concepts, if not our past experience? This past experience, moreover, was a matter of perception, which necessitates, *ex hypothesi,* prior acts of conception. Let us suppose that this indefinite regress of perceptions necessitating acts of conception were truncated, that our circle were not vicious. How are we to explain the fact that in a given act of the imagination I decide to see what I actually do? Surely there is no explanation, and Sartre admits it; my act is purely gratuitous, absurd. One consciousness does not cause another; between any two consciousnesses within one global consciousness there is nothing at all, no connection, no reason. It is in this sense that Sartre has claimed that nothingness eats at our hearts like a worm. In spite of his dislike of gustatory images for characterizing knowledge, Sartre has come up with a beauty in his ontology; being-in-itself becomes an apple gnawed at by a living consciousness. And the consciousness we take of this fact creates metaphysical anguish, which Sartre and some of his early and close followers, at least, have claimed to experience.[56]

Moreover, it is difficult to see in what way an image which is purely mental can be considered cognitive at all. The image refers to an object, but its object is nothing. Can we have knowledge about unreal objects? Surely in a limited sense only. I can be acquainted with my image and with its reference to an unreal object, and I can describe that unreal object in essence. This happens in every dream I remember; but a dream is empirically motivated, as Alain has shown,[57] and the hypnagogical images described by Sartre afford another example of this kind of motivation. The problem of interaction thus re-inserts itself into the query. If, in order to avoid it, we consider the purely mental image, where there is no interaction, we find the following data: I am acquainted with it, and I can describe its unreal referent, but only in terms of concepts, and what I describe is by nature related to no other objects. What good is this knowledge, if I cannot communicate it to someone else—the possibility of inter-subjectivity of conceptual understanding not being shown—or if this knowledge relates to no other knowledge? The notion of the unreal object may be useful for describing the so-called detachment, or aesthetic distance, of art objects, but the utility of such knowledge reduces, it would seem, to a state of enjoyment. And this can be considered knowledge in a very thin and modified sense, certainly not in the sense of a full-blown epistemology. Only a complete statement of the phenomenology of knowledge would allow us to admit Sartre's claim to have described the role of images in its acquisition and communication. We may conclude therefore that at this stage of his development Sartre failed to fulfill his own claims.

In the second place is the task of evaluting Sartre's adaptation of Husserl's phenomenological method. The example considered by Husserl was the difference in the perception of the physical qualities of an engraved etching from the imagination of the object represented by means of those qualities. He claimed that this difference is one of intention, and that differences of intention are a matter of motivation. But motivation is an empirical fact; in introducing it, he has violated the reduction. Sartre's claim is that Husserl was inconsistent in his appeal to empirical data, and that this inconsistency is between methodological principle and applied method. This charge is at least plausible since Husserl's investigation was to be eidetic, and not empirical. But how has Sartre remained consistent? Only by denying the relevance of an act of perception in his own analysis. Stopping with what he could "know" as certain, he denies all relevance of perception theory to a purely phenomenological analysis. One wonders then about that section of his book entitled "the probable." Hasn't Sartre merely removed the inconsistency one degree? His own analysis appeals to conception as defining the intention of the imagining consciousness.[58] If we assume that conception is impossible without perception, as we have done above, the inconsistency becomes apparent; but if this assumption is not necessary, the theory is incomplete until a further explanation of the conceiving consciousness is given which does not appeal to perception. We could find ourselves back at the stage of innate ideas, but this is not clear.[59]

There is, however, a hint of the solution to this problem in L'Etre, where the essence of an object is said to be the *ratio* of its appearances.[60] If we may analogize with geometric progressions, we may say that in order to perceive the ratio of that series we must be given a starting point and two other points of the progression. I may perceive the ratio of 2 only after I have performed the division of the second member of the series, 6, by the first member 3, and verified it by dividing the third, 12, by the second. That is, given a segment of the progressive series I can calculate its ratio. If this is an intuition, it certainly is an intuition which follows the performance of the operation involved. Sartre is correct in stipulating that the *ratio* is inherent in the series, but it would seem that the series, or a segment of it, must be perceived before one can intuit its *ratio*. To revert to objects and their essences, if the analogy suggested by the terms "series" and "ratio" is valid, then one should have to have various appearances of the object before being able to judge that the object is a such or such. In what sense therefore can the essence of an object be said to precede its existence? One sense is that the object is created to be what it is by its maker, as when I intend to make a chair and do so.[61] This sense of the existentialist slogan is adaptable for all cultural objects, such as chairs and gateposts, but in what sense is the slogan adequate for natural objects, the sum of which is investigated by the natural sciences? To appeal to the exemplars in God's mind, to divine intentions, if you like, is clearly as impossible as the concept of God itself (as *en-soi-pour-soi*) in Sartre's system. There is no escaping the conclusion: in an effort to save consistency, Sartre has neglected empirical adequacy.

Moreover, Sartre, no less than Husserl, appeals to motivation in his classification of the kinds of images. But it must be noted in his favor that this classification represents a means to his intuition and not its rational, eidetic, explanation. In showing the increase of the spontaneity of the consciousness from the perception of a physical portrait to the purely mental image, he has claimed only the latter as his true subject of investigation. Yet there is a clearly perceptible sense in which his theory lacks consistency. He has claimed that no object external to the consciousness, nor any prior consciousness, has the power to determine another consciousness. Within the scope of his ontology, and not in his methodological principles, he must show how a consciousness can be spontaneous and yet motivated. Whence the tortuous passages of *L'Etre* containing the distinction between *mobile, motif,* and *fin.*[62] This concept of the end exposes what one most probably would suspect from the outset: that the very notion of intention is an ambiguous concept in phenomenological theory, referring at some times to the way in which a consciousness aims at (*vise*) its object, and at others, to the object aimed at.

The third and final criticism. It is current knowledge that Husserl disclaimed the use of critical techniques (transcendental deduction)[63] as a substitute for phenomenology. Since Sartre used them in both of his treatises subtitled "phenomenological,"[64] one might very well pose the question which motivated this study, In what sense is Sartre's method phenomenology? In order to answer the question, we need only consider the first of the characteristics of purely mental images. As it was formulated, Sartre maintained that images *must* be conscious events, and not contents of consciousness. Failure to see this necessity was the alleged cause of Hume's naive ontology of the image. How does one intuit this necessity? By trying to conceive of the possibility of contradicting the statement that every image is a conscious event, and failing? Certainly not, this would be an empirical fact and Hume, for one, did actually conceive such a contradiction in positing images as contents of consciousness. The necessity must therefore be of a logical nature. Should we be inclined, with most of the empiricists, to contradict the statement that every image is a conscious event, we would be led, says Sartre, to some contradiction within the theoretical structure. This is the nature of his argument as outlined above,[65] and as it has occurred throughout the history of philosophy. But it is not a direct intuition of an essence; it is a discursive argument, rationalistic in character, which assumes that any statement is true whose contradiction is unthinkable, that is, entails a self-contradiction. It is the basis of the *reductio ad absurdum* argument; but the validity of the *reductio* argument is strictly dependent upon the mutual exclusion and exhaustion of the universe of possibilities by the two assumptions made. This may be true by definition of Sartre's two orders of existents; but, if so, an old problem arises to plague us. How do the two orders interact, as we know they do, in perception? Sartre thinks he has found the answer in his phenomenological analysis of the imagination; but again this only shifts the question. How do I know that the only alternative to conceiving the image as a content of consciousness is to conceive it as a conscious event? Rationalists prefer one explanation and empiricists another, but these two methods are not essentially exclusive of each other; nor are they exhaustive of the possibilities. Kant himself had tried their synthesis, and in so doing invented the method of determining what must be the case for our experiences to be possible. In following Kant rather than Husserl, Sartre is led to talk of the presuppositions of experience. But presuppositions are still suppositions, and we look in vain to find the source of the necessity by which they are claimed to be valid. The argument, if it is an argument, would have the form of *tollendo tollens* since the conditions involved are necessary rather than sufficient; but the connection between the antecedent and the consequent of the conditional statement itself remains a mystery. In sum, it can be said that Kant's rationalism is taken as a substitute for phenomenological analysis in Sartre's theories, and the impartial student of the history of philosophy may wonder if this substitution is acceptable, especially since the "hyletic" content of the mental image remains a transcendental object (hypothetical construct) in Sartre's account of the imagination. Sartre and Hume could both be wrong; and we should still rest assured that we not only can, but do have knowledge. But the question remains how knowledge is possible, and what part perception plays in it. Thus we are in need of a theory of perception which does not beg the question.

To conclude, Sartre's distinction between perceptive and imaginative consciousnesses depends upon his acceptance of Husserl's account of perception,[66] but the force of this acceptance has been obscured by Sartre's use of Kant's method of transcendental deduction. Moreover, his claim that images may give knowledge of a certain sort is unsupported, pending a fuller account of the function of the imagination in acquiring knowledge. Since the imagination is said to function at its highest (most spontaneous) degree when it creates its own object, and this is assumed to be the case in aesthetic experiences, if we are to evaluate more fully the extent to which his theory has achieved this specific aim, we must proceed to consider Sartre's theory of the aesthetic image.

III

Aesthetic Theory in Sartre's Phenomenology

A complete analysis of Sartre's specifically defined aesthetic ideas entails a good bit of scholarly spadework. Several texts must be collated before any attempt at a just criticism can be made. It is far too easy, on the contrary, to bracket those aesthetic theories which draw a distinction between the artifact or physical object constructed by the artist and the so-called artwork which emerges, results from, or otherwise appears by means of the artifact; to label them "idealist," and to declare, for some unknown reason, that they are unworthy of our attention. This is the procedure of at least one contemporary English aesthetician.[1]

But is it fair to cite, as does Margaret MacDonald,[2] the theories of Croce, Collingwood, Alexander, and Sartre as being of a kind with respect to the property cited, and then to criticize the kind, thinking thereby to settle the difficulties in the claims of all four thinkers who, though admittedly alike in some respects, may be quite unlike in another, perhaps significantly different, respect? If this difference between the members of the kind—one hesitates to write "family"—is a possibility, then each of the theories must be considered on its own grounds, and in terms of the claims it makes toward explaining the facts of our aesthetic life. This is precisely what I should like to do for the theory of Jean-Paul Sartre. The easier alternative to this kind of critical scholarship is rightly called the setting up of a straw man. Whatever one thinks of Sartre, one cannot with sincerity refer to him as a straw man: straw men do not write theories of any sort, nor even the sketch of a theory, and it is for this reason that the ideas of straw men are so easily refuted.

But how can one come to grips with a theory which exists only as a sketch? The answer is simple: by considering the context in which the necessity or the usefulness of that sketch was thought to arise. Sartre's notes on the aesthetic object occur as the second part of his conclusion to *L'Imaginaire*. In that conclusion he is trying to show how his phenomenological psychology of the imagination might serve to settle some of the outstanding aesthetic questions, of which he mentions three: the ontological *situs* of the work of art, the nature of aesthetic pleasure, and the "paradox" of the actor. Moreover, since Sartre alludes to a difference between aesthetic pleasure and the emotion of the work of art, the scholar must seek what information he can concerning Sartre's ideas on the emotions from another of his works, *Esquisse d'une théorie des émotions*. Finally, although he is talking in his psychology of the imagination about the status of art works in general, he speaks at greater length in another of his works, *Qu'est-ce que la littérature?*, about the status of literary works of art in particular. These then are the texts to be collated, and my analysis of the problem will include two major sections. The first of these will be a general discussion of the function of the imagination in the production and the appreciation of works of art; and the second, a consideration of the aesthetic problems Sartre thought to be definitively resolved within the context of his psychological theories.

THE CREATIVE IMAGINATION

In the art process there are at least three points of specific interest: the creator (1), makes something (2), which means something to an audience (3). Note that it is not assumed that what the artifact means is necessarily the content of a value judgment, although what is meant by the artifact may be the object of a value judgment. Sartre is concerned primarily with the descriptive phase of aesthetics, not with its normative or critical phase, and this is in general keeping with the way the subject of aesthetics is taught in the French educational system, where aesthetics is a subdivision of psychology, and not of axiology. Moreover, any aesthetic theory which limits itself to a description of one or the other of the three dimensions within the art process would seem to lack completeness.

In a complete act of artistic expression the aesthetic object mediates two different subjective states, that of the creator and that of the appreciator, who, of course, may be the creator in a different moment from the first. To consider the process from the point of view of the creator—and no theory which does not is likely to be taken seriously by artists themselves—is to consider an act of creation, or to use Sartre's terms, to describe the function of the imagination in the production of an art object.

The prime requisite for such a description would be an adequate account of the artist's freedom, and according to Sartre no purely deterministic psychology can do justice to the artist's ability to rearrange the elements of his perceptual experience. After all, even Hume granted to the imagination this property of freedom, and defined it in similar terms.[3] In *L'Imaginaire* Sartre was attempting to describe the conditions which would permit the appearance of images to consciousness; an image, in his view, is a spontaneous conscious event in which the attitude of the subject is a quasi-observation of a non-existent or absent object.[4] But the subject is in the world, and can attend to an object which is not so situated only by negating the relevance of the objects of the world for the given experience: "To entertain an image is to constitute an object on the margins of the totality of the real world; thus to hold the real world at a distance, to free oneself from it, in a word to negate it."[5] Nothing mysterious is being claimed here. I can have an image only when I am but marginally aware of the world. The world is the background upon which my image appears. If I were not in the world, there would be no background and hence no configuration could appear within it; and if I did not back off, so to speak, from the world to attend to the object I imagine to inhabit its nether places, the object would not appear in image. In sum, the existence of an image precludes to the structure of the world the presence of the object which appears to me in imagination. When I say that I am having the image of a centaur, I could equally well say that there is no such thing as a centaur in the world.[6] To repeat, the conditions necessary for the appearance of such an image are the ability one has to posit the existence of the total structure of a universe made up of objects which appear in an act of perception, and in a succeeding act of consciousness to posit the inexistence of the imaged object within that total structure.[7]

Although few serious psychologists or philosophers may wish to deny the existence of images, not a few of them may well wish to deny the fruitfulness of Sartre's language to describe them. But the person who insists upon the fruitlessness of Sartre's categories to describe the phenomenon in question assumes the burden of giving an alternative set of categories which will be more adequate to the description of the conditions under which statements of the follow-ing kind can be said to be true: "Hamlet saw the ghost of his father." Nor will it do to follow Richards too closely and claim that such sentences serve merely to organize our impulses and attitudes.[8] Richards' theory of aesthetic expression will be refuted from Sartre's point of view in the second part of this chapter.[9]

The Model of Idealism.—If, on the other hand, we are willing to grant an author the privilege of speaking in the way he sees fit, we may proceed to the clarification of some common misunderstand-ings which have plagued aesthetics for some time. It has too often been assumed, for example, that the referring property of images enables the appreciator and the creator to have the same mental content when each contemplates the artifact in the same or at least a similar fashion. Should we linger a while on the two modes of contemplation, we shall see that they are different. The artist's con-templation is active; the movement of the arms necessary to sculp-ture, to paint, or in some way to produce a work of art, brings about a physical change in the world. But the appreciator's contemplation is to an extent passive; under optimal conditions he remains un-moved, his consciousness guided by the work of the artist.[10] The creator, then, exemplifies the ideals of an active, creative synthesis of diverse elements, while the appreciator must first perceive the artifact, and then entertain the image to be associated with it.

A second misconception in traditional aesthetics concerns more particularly the nature and the functioning of the creative imagina-tion in art. It is the thesis made famous by Croce, and infamous by his followers, that the artist's creative act is the intuition of a novel form which is independent of the manipulation of the materials which embody the intuition. Expression is intuition and intuition is expression; the whole process is strictly a mental affair, and the making of an artifact is extraneous, mere technique. One need only consult Croce's *Aesthetic,* Chapters I and XV,[11] to see that this was intended seriously.

According to this theory, every "externalization" (the word is

Croce's) is only a more or less successful expression of its ideal correlate, the orginal vision of the artist; putting the theory to practice, some critics have maintained that the artist enjoys a privileged position for judging the success of this external expression since only he possesses the original intuition. It must be said in Croce's favor that some artists do claim that their work is guided by intuition, or a vision of some sort; he quotes Michelangelo to this effect. But the psychological grounds for such a claim are conspicuously absent. More artists seem to agree that their intuitions arise from the manipulation of the materials of their craft. The painter must think as a painter with his brush, and the primary data of any aesthetic which would be scientific are constituted by the efforts of artists to express themselves. Sartre's aesthetics, like Susanne Langer's,[12] is one which emphasizes the activity of the creator, thereby adopting what Langer has called the "studio point of view."

At this point there has been established one important difference between two aesthetic theories of an idealistic kind, a difference which has been obscured by Miss MacDonald's cryptic statement of Sartre's position; she says: "For Sartre, too, the work of art is 'something unreal' for which the artist constructs a material analogue in the external world."[13] Her error is to have thought in kinds, rather than in terms of complete individual theories. Nor was Sartre, at the time he wrote *L'Imaginaire,* unaware of the kind of theory we might call "naively realistic." Again, to show this one need only refer to the historical context in which his work was written.

The Model of Realism.—As early as 1920, Emile Chartier, who wrote under the pseudonym, Alain, had presented his *Système des beaux-arts* in which there is developed a complete aesthetics, not merely a collection of notes on critical appreciation, based upon the assumption of the non-existence of mental images. Alain, too, adopted the studio point of view, and Sartre was aware of this. The whole gist of the debate is contingent upon the question whether naive realism does justice to the facts of our psychic experience[14] and not upon the propriety of talking about "mental states" or "ghosts" as exclusive alternatives to talking about physical objects.[15] To make clear what the alternatives are, as Alain and as Sartre saw them, I shall first sketch the realistic theory of Alain, and then show the reasons for the exception Sartre takes to it.

Like Sartre, Alain appeals to the imagination to explain creation.

But here all psychological resemblance ceases. For Alain, the imagination is not a mysterious faculty for joining together what nature has put asunder, nor is it a manner of referring to unreal objects, however these might be defined. I can imagine, says Alain, only what I falsely perceive. I perceive what is there, and can only imagine what is not. And when I perceive an object I take it to be an object of a certain kind. In every case of perception, therefore, there is first sense stimulation, which, when clear and distinct, is infallibly interpreted or judged as what it is.[16] Thus in every perception there is a judgment of the existence of an object.

Imagination differs from perception, in Alain's view, as a false judgment differs from a true one; one of the principal causes of the error of my judgment is the condition of my body at the time of perception. Especially if I am under the influence of my emotions when the "tumult in the body" is taken as sufficient grounds for the existence of an object am I subject to such errors in judgment. The artist, in the frenzy of inspiration, searches for an object which is supplied by further movements of the body as it operates upon itself, its social situation, or the external world. According to this theory, the art object is not distinct from the artifact; it is the artifact in so far as the latter answers to the emotional state which has produced it. Alain called this creative process, proper only to art, "the fixing of our imaginary experience."[17] As creator, the artist is not a visionary; should he give way to his impulses to imagine things which do not exist, it is highly improbable that he could create a thing which does. The artist's vision results from a manipulation of his own body in contact with the external world. His idea is his expression, but his expression is a physical fact.

Since the artifact, in Alain's aesthetics, is a compound of formed matter, since, in other words, matter and form are correlative aesthetic terms, and the materials of art are relatively limited, it becomes imperative to consider his treatment of form. In order to do so, we shall have to examine more fully the place of technique in the arts.

The artist's activity is forming activity. To deny the relevance of discussing this notion of form is to invite the departure of our artist friends who are indissolubly wed to their techniques. Technique is what the arts and the crafts have in common; he who would be an artist must first be an artisan. We have here the basic ambiguity in the word "form." Both artist and artisan are making an object: the latter with reference to some prefigured form; the former discovering some new form by applying the rules of his craft. Making an object with reference to some prefigured form Alain, following Kant, calls "industry"; and industry is not completely alien to art. A poet who would write a sonnet must use the prefigured, conventional form; to this extent the poet is an artisan, or maker. The same is true of any other artist who follows some general compositional "form." What makes one sonnet more interesting than another, one symphony more expressive than another, however, is the style of the individual artist using that form. The style of the author is his personal contribution. If style is not the man, it is certainly, as Buffon has said,[18] of the man.

"Style," Alain assures us, comes from "stylus," the word used to designate the instrument which gives its form to what is written.[19] "Style" and "form" are related concepts, yet refer to significantly different aesthetic notions. Both refer to techniques which are capable of being formulated and taught; both describe how an art object is made, hence, its form. The notion of style, however, has the added connotation of personal identification with a given artist. It is in this sense of the term that we can properly speak of the style of Rembrandt, of Leonardo, of El Greco. The style of the artist is his hallmark on the object; although it may be imitated, copied, and even taught as the technique definitive of a given school, the value for the discovery of the style is always attributable to the personality of the discoverer. To ask why a given artist creates in the way he does may pose an interesting psychological query; but in posing it, we tend to draw our attention away from the object of aesthetic inquiry, the artifact as it has been formed. Leonardo, it has been noted, was left-handed, whence the quality of his drawings, the lines slanting downward from left to right; Rembrandt lived in Holland's northern bleakness, whence the sombre tone of his palette; El Greco was astigmatic, whence the elongation of his figures: so many instances of interesting psychological facts, pertinent cultural data, but for Alain, the aesthetician, so much non-aesthetic speculation. What is important for the aesthetician is the expressive quality of the object, formed as it is. The artwork is the object given, and an adequate explanation of the artwork's significance must go beyond the mere tracing of a supposed cause and effect relation. Alain knew

Taine's positivistic literary criticism well; he called it a crime against humanity.[20]

Crime or not, Taine's brand of positivism has failed to explain the significance of artworks. So Alain had recourse to the writings of another positivist, Auguste Comte, for a more adequate explanation of meaning in the arts. Comte's theory of signs was developed into a theory of immanent expression of art objects in Alain's aesthetic writings.[21]

It is perhaps necessary here to distinguish between the notions of immanent and referential expression[22] in order to make more fully comprehensible the extent to which Alain's theory is naively realistic. An artwork is expressive in the referential sense when the object as a whole refers to some meaning external to itself. Michelangelo's *Leda and the Swan* refers in this sense to the mythological seduction of Leda by Zeus. Literature and drama are of necessity referentially expressive; they tell a story. All symbols used in such arts are discursive. Their meanings are fixed by convention, and if they refer as a whole to a subject outside the work, the reference is founded upon resemblance or is dictated by convention. Whence the iconographical approach to art interpretation. But there is another dimension to the "meaning" of artworks. Even the discursive symbols of literature and drama when interpreted as a whole can be considered non-discursively.[23] Alain calls this non-discursive content of art the "absolute character" of an art language: ". . . the absolute language is found in all the arts, which in this sense, are similar to enigmas, signifying imperiously, and very much, without one's being able to say what."[24] Taken as a whole, artworks are not conventional signs or symbols; in Alain's terms, they are primitive signs. While the meaning of symbols is fixed conventionally, that of primitive signs grows out of the interpretative process. The artwork is a gesture, however complex; its meaning is the response one makes to it.

If this speculation on the meaning of artworks is correct, there is no one true meaning to the work of art. Each individual appreciator must contribute to the communication process, and classics become what they are by the growth of the meaning called out by the work. Not referring to anything outside itself, the artwork can be considered only as referring to itself. This reference is the immanent quality of the work of art.

It has been thought that any work of art which is bound to symbols as its medium cannot be immanently expressive. A good deal of Susanne Langer's efforts, as of Alain's, has been spent to dispel this error. The literary work of art can be judged by the same formalistic criterion as the most abstract kind of expressionistic painting. It suffices to consider each art medium and the kind of object it allows, and within that medium to consider the idea expressed, ignoring the intention of the author, which for any number of reasons may be other than the idea expressed. If we commit the intentional fallacy, we are judging the author as an artisan, and not as an artist. In Alain's words,

Always, insofar as the work is that of the artisan the model for the work is outside the work; but insofar as the work is of an artist, the work constitutes its own model. In a word, what refers to another object is flat; to the wisdom of the author, pedantic; but when the work corresponds with itself and instructs its author as well [as its audience], then it has style. And it is not an accident that this beautiful word ["style"] also designates the pointed tool which formerly molded writing.[25]

So convinced was Alain that the work of art was a physical object that he accepted Mallarmé's "white page" theory, according to which a poem is engraved on a blank sheet (cf. *Un coup de dés*), and even went so far as to suggest that students recopy Stendhal's *Chartreuse de Parme* word for word, comma for comma, if they wanted to learn how to write.[26] He had, of course, exaggerated an obvious truth: if the artist wishes to communicate with an audience, he must give a permanent physical object to the appreciation of that audience. Only extreme idealists would disagree with the statement that a painting hangs on a wall and that a poem is written or spoken; without these outward physical marks no one would claim that an artwork existed. But few aestheticians will agree that the poem itself exists on a page: if so, in whose book is *the* poem? Sartre and Alain agree that works of literature exist as imaginary constructs, but their theories of the imagination lead them far apart.

For Alain there were no images; an imaginary construct was an erroneously perceived object. Since emotions were thought the primary source of error in human perception, and they were defined as movements of the human body, the artist's emotion and his creative activity were one and the same thing. The object, which results from that activity, fixes the imaginary experience; the emotion is given an object, and is transmuted thereby into feeling. It is in this sense that the work of art gives insight into the human situation, and that the arts called "liberal" are liberating.

Although Alain has made this attempt to account for the value of art, it is not clear whether he was aware of an apparent and implicit contradiction in his thought. If the work of art refers to nothing, if not to itself, the reference of the work to the author's affective life would seem to suffer the same fate as the reference to any other object outside the work. He affirms this exclusion in denying the validity of the historical approach to criticism,[27] claiming that appeals to the author's private life are unjust.

Alain's purpose was to deny moralism and to affirm his own formalistic aesthetics. Remember that form is style and style is of the person. What we perceive of the author *in the work* is his style. If the work of art refers in this sense to its author, however, the reference is not a meaning reference, neither semantic nor pragmatic (in Morris' sense). One must distinguish between significance and signification. According to Alain, the arts "refer to" humanity in the same sense that the wear of a bench or other human tool refers to the human act of sitting or working; they are natural signs of man's estate. Since they are interested primarily in this *signification,* anthropologists usually study artworks from that approach; but from the appreciator's point of view, the *significance* of a created form is felt as a harmony of diverse psychological elements:

As in music, one recognizes here [in poetry] an agreement between intellectual processes and corporeal nature, which led Kant to say that the beautiful contains a purposiveness without an exterior purpose. In other words, the beautiful makes us feel within ourselves the agreement between the higher and lower [faculties] so vainly looked for by the wise.[28]

It is said that the value of the arts is the settled feeling they provoke. The meaning of artworks could therefore be called emotive in Richards' and Ducasse's sense.[29] Natural signs of humanity, the arts liberate their audiences from an exclusive preoccupation with petty passions. In this sense humanity itself becomes the object of every successful work of art. Such was the very influential, realistic theory Sartre was led to combat.

The Phenomenological Model.—What are the shortcomings of the realistic aesthetics? Sartre found several in Alain's theory. First, as explained in the general theory of the imagination, Alain's denial of images as such rather crudely emasculates, from Sartre's vantage point, the phenomenal experience of imaginary objects.[30] A theory of the imagination without images was considered, in Sartre's *L'Imagination*,[31] as an absurd contradiction in terms, and psychologically speaking, a most unabashed kind of physiologism, not to say "behaviorism." Sartre maintains that anyone has the means of producing the primary data of the experiment: when I go looking for a friend, I carry with me the image of that friend whether or not he happens to be where I am looking. There is no need to repeat here the conditions under which such an experience is possible; the fact speaks for itself.

Besides the violence Alain's theory allegedly perpetrates upon the facts concerning the existence of images, there remains a consideration more strictly pertinent to aesthetics: the referral property of images. If we look more closely at this property from Sartre's point of view, we may be led to see a shortcoming in Alain's explanation of the meaning of the arts. To this we now turn.

The plurality of meanings of a single artwork seems repulsive to a reasoned explanation. When Alain claims that the meaning of artworks varies from spectator to spectator even though the work is described as a unique form fabricated by the artist out of the materials of his craft, he is trying to be as faithful to the facts of artistic appreciation as to those of creation. And it does seem a fact that different people listening to the same symphony hear entirely different things, or take what they hear as entirely different things. Moreover, if the "meaning" of the symphony is the direct reaction of the audience to the sounds of which it is composed, a mere glance at an audience during a performance of the music will suffice to show the difference in reactions. Aldous Huxley's *Point Counter Point* contains a lucid interpretation of this difference.[32] Can the same music "mean" so many different things? Alain's answer is a flat yes; the music means whatever one finds there. For him, this is not a paradox, but a fact. The work of art is an enigma, to be resolved by whoever will, and by whatever means. After all, since meaning is a relative term, why shy from the relativity of the experience? Sartre could answer that Alain has been misled from the facts about the artwork itself in trying to be too exact in his explanation of the experiences of creation and appreciation. Perhaps the question of the meaning of artworks could be better answered if we look more closely at the nature of the works themselves.

For example, if the works are images, and not merely objects corresponding to the physiological processes by which they are created and appreciated, a distinction is necessary between the artifact (the image) and what the artifact means, whatever is referred to by the image. Communication would then take place in the usual manner: the image intends an object which is understood in its unique sense by the person having the image. There is no relativism here. Nor would one have to commit oneself to the claim that the artist has the image before the object is made, since the object made is the means of entertaining the image. Even in Sartre's terms the artist could discover his own idea. In other words, if one distinguishes between the artifact and the artwork, the image and its referent, one does not relegate the activity of the artist to "industry," in Alain's sense of this term. The artist's creation can still be considered a personal discovery. The object emerges once the image is formed, and it is a truism to state that in an act of communication the artist and his appreciator understand the work in the same manner. Note that if this is a proper description of Sartre's aesthetic theory in outline, there is at least this significant difference between Sartre and Croce on the aesthetic object.[33] The artist is not in a privileged position to understand his own intuitions. Nor is he forced to create, being "big" with his work and at term of gestation.[34]

PROBLEMS IN AESTHETICS

Ontological Status of Artwork.—Sartre has developed his notion of the aesthetic object as the referent which the artifact intends in the *Psychology of the Imagination.* In doing so, he is attempting to answer that old teaser, Where is the art object? C. I. Lewis, whom few have accused of being an idealist, has written a lucid chapter on the same subject in his *Analysis of Knowledge and Valuation.* According to Lewis, all art objects are "abstract," which is to say that they are "separable and separated from their physical presentation." But "The kind of abstractions which, like poems and musical compositions, have aesthetic value, *can* be presented through the medium of physical things: they are sensuous or imaginal though repeatable in different exemplifications."[35] In short, for Lewis the work of art is an essence, not to be confused with a particular rendition of itself or with the intention of the author, which we may never know.

Between Sartre and Lewis there is little difference. And in general, where the only differences are metaphysical, a common sense description of the phenomena of the experience described will bring out the underlying unity of explanation. Lewis begins his analysis of the aesthetic object with the question of what kind of entity Beethoven's *Fifth Symphony* is. For him, as explained above, the symphony is an essence, an ideal, a non-actual event; it is very complex, but not impossible to analyze. The reason for its being considered essential, ideal, and non-actual is the obvious absurdity of identifying it with any one particular interpretation. One might say, in comparison with literary objects, that the symphony exists only as intended by the series of notes which is the recipe for its performance. It would therefore enjoy only a kind of intentional being. The performance of the symphony merely concretizes the abstract essence. The clue to the phenomenal identity of the interpretations of Lewis and Sartre is, first, this notion of the intentional being of the object; and second, a common desire to avoid the absurdity of identifying the symphony with one of its performances. But in the hands of Sartre (to lapse into Alain's terminology), the aesthetic object loses its essential character. Non-actual and ideal it remains: ideal, in that the aesthetic object is the referent of an image; and non-actual, in that it is non-existent. Therefore, the real *Fifth Symphony* is never heard—not in heaven or on earth, or in any other conceivable place. (cf. Shaw's hell in *Man and Superman*.) Sartre's laconic, "The work of art is an unreal object,"[36] expresses this truth well; at least as well as Lewis's statement that what is enjoyed when one hears the symphony is the physical thing as interpreted, and that what is contemplated is the aesthetic essence.[37] Realism or idealism, the difference here is a word.

It has often been suggested that the only basis for choice between the two words is a metaphysical bias. But this suggestion covers a truth with not a little dogmatism; in matters aesthetic, not all metaphysical positions need be biases. Sartre has chosen his "idealistic" position precisely because of his assumption that phenomenology, as it had been developed by Husserl, was a more faithful account of aesthetic communication than realism. And in the phenomenological description of communication the primary notion is that of the intentional act. When an artist creates an object, according to Sartre, his consciousness intends an "absent" object via the physical object he creates. But the complete act of communication necessitates a second consciousness, that of the appreciator, who by assuming the aesthetic attitude intends the same unreal or absent object. It would follow, therefore, that in an act of artistic creation there is a physical object (a presentation or image or analogue) which serves as an instrument for uniting two consciousnesses in one act of communication. Both consciousnesses intend the same object, the unreal, that is, ideal or non-actual, object which is the work of art. Students of American criticism will recall the "objective correlative" theory of T. S. Eliot, according to which a poem is an object serving to correlate two subjective states, those of the creator and the appreciator.[38] Creation described as a process of communication is well served by assuming the phenomenologist's hypothesis.

The Aesthetic Object.—Nor is the plausible description of the process of communication the only benefit of Sartre's aesthetics. Assuming the same hypothesis, he lays claim to having definitively answered Lewis's question, What is a symphony? If the symphony is an unreal object, it exists nowhere. It could be said to form a world to itself, and that it does. Each note contributes to the creation of the work of art; the sounds in relation produce the unique quality we call the symphony. And there is nothing strange about the notion of a universe of one individual. Again, there is only a difference in words used to describe the experience of that universe. The contemporary American aesthetician, Susanne K. Langer, prefers to call the artistic universe an illusion—to be distinguished from a delusion in that the former does not disappear in an act of analysis.[39] And an illusion is an ideal, not a physical entity. To say that it is ideal or illusory is to say that the work of art is given only in the act of perception. Thus for Langer, it is sheer appearance, but an appearance which is perceived. Sartre would classify her psychological position as being based covertly on the "illusion of immanence";[40] he maintains that we do not see our images (mental images as such), but only their objects. Consequently, the notion of "sheer appearance" is ambiguous: it may be the presented object considered in itself (the physical thing, which Langer calls the materials of the "semblance" as opposed to the elements of the creation); or it may be the presented object as presented, the quality of the physical thing in the act of perception (the "semblance" properly so-called); or, finally, it may be conceived of as the object referred to by the physical thing (the so-called aesthetic object). Such would be the three possible positions with respect to the aesthetic object. Whether a particular aesthetician would elect one or the other of these substitutions for "sheer appearance" would depend upon his metaphysics, or if this word is still too obscure to mean anything concrete, the theory of perception and imagination used to reinforce the aesthetic theory.

It will be recalled that, for Sartre, perception and imagination are two different acts of consciousness. One is primarily passive, and the other more readily contemplative and active. By assuming the contemplative attitude of aesthetic activity, the audience is said to enter the world uniquely defined as a "provoked dream"; in passing from this world to the real world, in leaving the theater for example, the play-goer is said to experience an authentic awakening.[41] "Aesthetic distance" is the accepted term for this aesthetic attitude. And the work of art can truly be said to take place, or "come off" only within its bounds.

But what exactly constitutes its bounds? How does this illusion function in aesthetic communication? Sartre's reason for rejecting any such notion as Langer's "virtuality" has already been explained: virtual time, space, and experience, which are the primary or secondary illusions of artworks in Langer's theory, exist only for perception, even if within a uniquely determined *Gestalt*. If the sheer appearance is interpreted as the object referred to by the physical thing made by artists, if it is a perceived illusion as Langer insists, then the artwork is conceived of as a content of the perceiver's consciousness. And Sartre considered this a basic metaphysical error, the illusion of immanence. A more complete answer to our questions will be derived from an analysis of the emotion in the act of artistic communication.

Aesthetic Pleasure.—A second reason for rejecting Langer's aethetics would be precisely its relative inability to render justice to the so-called aesthetic pleasure, the third question Sartre considered answered within the context of his "idealistic" aesthetics. Continued comparison with Mrs. Langer's views will establish the importance of the issue in contemporary American aesthetic theory, an issue

which may have been foisted upon aestheticians by the artist's insistence that his work is made of feeling or feelings. But if the artist
is right in his contention, a serious paradox results for anyone who
would construct a consistent categorial explanation of the phenomena
of art.

This paradox has been expressed in various ways throughout the
history of aesthetics. As early as 1896 George Santayana had formulated his definition of beauty as objectified pleasure;[42] but the paradox, which unites a tertiary quality, pleasure, with the primary and
secondary qualities of the object, could be solved only within the context of an idealistic theory of objects as a unity of a manifold of
sensory data. The German aesthetician, Otto Baensch, dissatisfied
with the idealistic description of objects, sought another explanation,
but gave another paradox. In his article, "Kunst und Gefuehl," published in the volume of *Logos* for 1924, he distinguished between
"subjective" and "objective" feelings. Subjective feelings are those
expressed by living things; as such, they are feelings which are felt.
Objective feelings, on the other hand, are those given to a perceiver
as an intellectual content, the quality of an object; these are possessed by the object itself. Ordinary language expresses this concept
when it labels the weather "moody," or a landscape "serene."

According to Baensch, we do not sense this feeling quality; the
feeling of the weather or of a landscape is said to be a non-sensuous
quality of the object. Whence the paradox. The feeling content of
objects is said to be "intellectual," in that the quality is understood
as a function of the organization of the parts of the object in question. When the subject has assimilated the other sensuous qualities
of the object, the non-sensuous feeling quality is understood as an
emergent property of the form, that is, the relationships among the
sensuous qualities of the object. In the closing portion of the article,
the emergence of this property is related to what Baensch calls "the
principle of form," under which he discusses the aesthetic values of
rhythm, structure, rules, regulation, and the aesthetic audience's attitude in experiencing form. The difference between Santayana's "objectified pleasure" and Baensch's "unfelt feelings" thus hangs upon
a distinction which insensitive perceivers persist in labeling "verbal."
And not a few of these insensitve perceivers have been artists themselves. Langer takes over the paradox from here.[43] She is intent upon
doing justice to the activity of artists without repudiating the

theorist's abhorrence of paradox. Indeed, she thinks the job of the philosopher is to reduce paradox by making consistent the apparently inconsistent statements of untrained reasoners.[44] In her opinion, Baensch's article contains two truths: that the feelings of the art object are unfelt (cf. aesthetic distance), and that the understanding of artistic feeling is associated with the form of artworks.

In Langer's aesthetics a careful distinction is made between feelings which are expressed "symptomatically," and those "embodied" in the work of art. When a person screams "ouch," he is symptomatically expressing his pain. And most expressionistic theories of aesthetics make their initial error in assuming that the artist expresses his feeling in this way.[45] Alain was combatting this error when he maintained that the emotion of the artist is purged of its intensity and transmuted into feeling for contemplation in an object. Where Alain himself erred was in making the expression a case of evoking feelings in the audience; this is the upshot of his "immanent theory of expression," according to which the artwork means whatever it calls out. Langer is quick to point out that a theory such as Alain's would readily give way to sentimentalism: the work does not express the audience's feeling any more than it does that of the artist. Both the feeling of the artist and that of the audience are "irrelevant" to the work of art. She is saying, of course, that the exhilaration of creation and that of understanding the created work are not essential properties of the objective work. The audience little cares for the agonies of the artist; and the self-respecting artist seems to have little regard for the feelings of the audience. Only in ignoring each other can these two parties communicate through the objective work. Yet feelings are said to be expressed. They are expressed as the meaning of sentences is expressed; one might say that the artwork intends its feeling as the words intend their meaning. Whence Langer's semantic approach to art.

Based on Wittgenstein's "A proposition is a picture of the universe,"[46] her claim is that the form of a work of art is analogous to the form of a feeling; the one "pictures" the other. The form of a work of art is describable in terms of the balance of its tensions, the rhythm of its development, the harmony of its resolution; and so might the duration and intensity of a feeling be described. She has, in a word, given a fuller statement to Schopenhauer's idea that music is a universal language of feeling. That she has difficulty in generalizing his insight is evident from the strained logical quality of her descriptions: poetry has as its primary illusion "virtual experience"; the novel, "virtual past"; drama, "virtual future"; the movie, "virtual present." In each of these discussions she is more concerned with the nature of the artistic illusion than with the manner in which the illusion symbolizes human sentience. In fact, in calling poetry virtual experience, she seems to have mishandled her own categories. The work of art is said to be an illusion and to symbolize a pattern of human sentience. If virtual experience symbolizes a pattern of human sentience, it does so because the one is similar to or the same as the other. If the illusion is only similar to its referent, then the artwork refers to something beyond itself, and the feeling is grafted onto the form of the work by the person enjoying the work; if the same, then the artwork (symbol) and referent relation no longer holds, and we are back to pure Baensch. Still another attempt must be made to find a place for feelings embodied *in* works of art.

Sartre's ideas on the subject must be synthesized from two sources: *L'Imaginaire*[47] and *Esquisse d'une théorie des émotions*. As early as 1939 he had promised a "new treatise on the passions";[48] and, as Alain had incorporated Descartes' original treatise in his own aesthetic theory, so Sartre adapted the Husserlian notion of intentionality to his own ends: first, to explain the phenomenon of emotivity, and second, to describe by its means the emotion of aesthetic experience.

In this adaptation, the emotions, like knowledge, are considered facts of consciousness; generically, they are a set of ways a subject may be related to the objects of the world. This relation is that of intentionality. A psychological subject does not feel his emotions in a vacuum, in spite of what one might be led to believe by the density of Proust's novels and the subtlety of his analyses;[49] in every intentional phenomenon, according to Husserl, the world and consciousness are both given. To hate, love, fear, suspect are merely so many ways to be related to certain objects; and an object of love appears to the subject as lovable; of hate, as hateable; and so forth. In sum, this theory treats the emotions as properties of objects. Applying this Husserlian principle to the objects of art, Sartre seems to have foreseen some such study as the present:

To be terrible is a *property* of this Japanese mask, an inexhaustible, irreducible property which constitutes its very nature, and not the sum of our subjective reactions to a piece of carved wood. Husserl has reinstated horror and charm to things. He has given back to us the world of the artists and prophets; frightening, hostile or dangerous, with havens of grace and love.[50]

We have, in this insight, one of the more essential differences between Sartre and Alain on the subject of aesthetic experience; one, it might be added, that Sartre himself has never pointed out. As for Langer, her semantical analyses seem to leave us with the paradox she was attempting to solve: how feelings could be objective. The feelings described in her theory are merely symbolized and understood, not felt; those described in Alain's theory are not bogusly "objective," since they are as a matter of fact felt by the audience. Sartre would tend to agree with Langer and Baensch that feelings can be objective, but would disagree with their intellectualized emotions; at the same time, he would agree with Alain that the emotions are important for the creation and appreciation of art objects. The mechanism used to explain the objectivity of feelings in the art communication process remains to be explained.

Sartre reviews, in his treatise on the emotions, the general methods of psychological investigation he calls "positivistic," with an eye to showing their shortcomings. He puts special emphasis on the theories of James, Janet, the gestaltists, and the psychoanalysts. It is not to the point here to consider each of these; it suffices to indicate that any method which is properly called "positivistic" consists in observing facts in an effort to reach an ordered explanation of them. And the various schools cited have chosen different ways to observe psychic phenomena. The difficulties of these methods are patent: facts are by nature accidental and contingent, and make their appearance in disarray; whereas scientific explanation demands knowledge of the essential, the necessary, the ordered. But according to Sartre, any attempt to reach an essence by adding similar events is destined to failure: "Psychologists do not take into account, in fact, that it is quite as impossible to attain an essence by piling up accidental properties as to arrive at unity by indefinitely adding figures to the right of 0.99."[51] Moreover, the "observation" itself must at best be indirect. Positivistic psychologists are limited to the tracing of correlations between bodily reactions and presumed states of consciousness. And on these correlations only two points of view are possible: the intellectualist theory, which states that the inner state is the cause of bodily reactions; and the peripheral, which claims that

the causal order is reversed. In either case, says Sartre, there is a refusal to consult the "general and essential structures of human
reality."[52]

The most pertinent question to pose at this point is, How does the
phenomenological method avoid these pitfalls? Simple to ask, but
not quite so simple to answer. Phenomenological analysis starts with
phenomena, whatever appears to some subject. The phenomenon itself is had, experienced, enjoyed; a brute interaction between the
world and a self. In his efforts to get at and interpret the dumb impression of phenomena, Husserl invented the eidetic science of
phenomenology. Its results are considered intuitively certain: in the
eidetic reduction, the investigator arrives at the essence, or meaning,
of phenomena by an unerring intuition. The whole of the experience
is grasped as a simple configuration. Unfortunately, however, in the
Esquisse, as in L'Imaginaire and in L'Etre, Sartre substitutes Kant's
method of transcendental deduction for eidetic intuition; that is, he
tries to investigate the conditions of possibility, those presumed facts
of the human situation without which the experience of an emotion
would be impossible. In general, his approach is to reflect upon a
given instance of an emotional reaction to the world.

In this reflection, the emotion is seen as a structure of consciousness, having a meaning for the subject's psychic life. This meaning is
not unlike the phenomenon of belief in magic. The person believing
in the efficacy of magic has built his own world in which the laws
of nature no longer hold. The will of the person produces changes
possible only to his befuddled state of mind. Likewise, the world,
which is nothing but a brute fact, becomes the object of hate only
because the subject is angry.[53] But what, precisely, does it mean to be
angry? The emotion of anger itself is nothing more or less than a
bodily disturbance, the behavior of a human organism in a certain
state, as Alain had insisted. And, as in the positivistic theories considered by Sartre, there are then two elements in correlation: the behavior and a mental state. But the causal inferences usually supposed
to relate the two elements are almost dogmatically denied by Sartre.
The state of mind alone would not call out the bodily reaction; in
an extreme state of emotion the mind of the subject is destroyed: one
can be rendered immobile by the joy of ecstasy as by the stupidity of
fear. Moreover, the behavior usually associated with the state dissi-

pates into sheer play-acting if it is not reinforced by the emotional state. A particular emotion is considered as a unique function of the two; it appears in a body overwhelmed by an objective situation and displaying a characteristic pattern of behavior. The bodily disturbance might very well outlast the expression of this behavior pattern, but the pattern of behavior "constitutes the form and the significance of the disturbance."[54] Consider, finally, the behavioral pattern characteristic of a given emotion without its relationship to the bodily disturbance associated with it; such a pattern would be a "pure," that is, an "empty" meaning, an abstract affective schema.[55] The emotion is therefore a synthetic form of the consciousness, as that consciousness is embodied; ". . . in order to believe in magical patterns of behavior, one must be bodily disturbed."[56]

If this interpretation of the facts of our emotional life is accurate, then it is not improper to abridge Sartre's description of the structure of the emotional consciousness as follows: the emotion appears, or takes hold of the person, in the spontaneous, lived, degradation of the consciousness in its relation to the objective world. Frustrated in its attempts to perceive the world in the customary rational manner, the consciousness breaks down, goes to sleep, and in a dream-state creates for itself an unreal universe. Under emotional strain, the organism approaches hysteria; and the bodily disturbance reflects its belief in the reality of the unreal world it has created for itself. This notion of belief is of prime importance, for in the emotional state, the consciousness is not thetically aware of itself as consciousness; rather it is said to be aware of an object corresponding to the particular emotion. But reflectively, through the bodily disturbance, the consciousness becomes aware of itself as object in the world, as it would, so to speak, be seen from an external point of view. One will recall Alain's contention that a work of art is created under the influence of emotion, and reflects the human personality undergoing the "tumult of the flesh." Sartre says as much in practically so many words:

Consciousness is not limited to projecting affective meanings into the world surrounding itself; it lives the new world it has just constituted. It *lives* this world directly; takes an interest in it; suffers those [feeling] qualities its behavioral patterns have outlined. This means that, when all other routes are barred, consciousness throws itself into the magical world of emotion, throws itself there by degrading itself; it becomes a new consciousness before a new world. constituting the new world with what is most intimate to itself, leaving no distance [between itself and what it has created] from its own point of view.[57]

The feelings reflected in the magical world of art are not unfelt; they are indeed, as Alain had pointed out, a pre-condition for the creation of that world. But it remains to be shown in greater detail how the structures of the imagining and the emotive consciousness may be communicated from the artist to his audience. The complete act of communication necessitates two distinct conscious states; or more properly, two distinct phenomenological consciousnesses.

Bodily disturbance, or tumult of the flesh; belief in the reality of an unreal world, or erroneous perception: the "idealist" Sartre and the "realist" Alain use shockingly similar language. The similarity will become even more apparent when we further neutralize the metaphysical differences between the two thinkers. For the idealist, consciousness creates, to some extent, the world in which it lives; for the realist, on the contrary, the world is given. Sartre's and Alain's accounts of artistic creation reflect this difference. According to the latter, the artist is moved by a fit of passion to see what does not exist: the dancer first feels her emotion throughout her body; and in executing her movements, in reacting kinesthetically to her environment, she gives objectivity to her feeling. Thus for Alain, the dance is the series of overt reactions, movements of the body; for Sartre, these movements are only the physical analogue of the aesthetic object we call "the dance." We may observe here, however, that once a dance is choreographed, Lewis' type-token distinction must be taken into account. "The dance" does not exist in the same fashion as its various interpretations; it is non-actual. Sartre calls it unreal, an absent object merely referred to by its token representation, the given performance. But if an object is unreal, then it cannot be perceived, and any "perception" of the dance must perforce be erroneous. At this point the idealist and the realist meet on a common ground.

A second similarity between Sartre and his predecessor is the attitude of belief attributed to the consciousness of the creator. Without this ability to give oneself away to the unreality of the erroneous perception, no artist would be led to create an object which corresponds to it. The artist must always live in the world of the "as-if"; he can create only with his imagination. The real world must be projected, so to speak, into the ideal, which is made real by the physical movements of the body, whether these be the graceful movements of the body itself, which forms the material of the art form, or whether the body be merely the instrument of creation, as when the hand flourishes a painter's brush or pounds a typewriter key. This is Alain's physicalistic account of creation. For Sartre, the consciousness must "degrade" itself into acceptance of the world it creates, out of matter to be sure, but which is constituted according to the laws of magic rather than those of cause and effect. It no longer is self-conscious, no longer the subject of knowing, but refuses the real world as an object of knowledge, pushing it into nothingness, and accepts for legal tender what is from the realist's point of view base, imitative coin. The aesthetic object is the object of this "erroneous" belief; and it appears on the fringes of the real world. As in every case of the imagining consciousness, when the unreal object is accepted as real, the real world disappears from consideration. The result is the active, productive attitude of the artist, who lives as in a dream creating objects, like a hysteric, merely by assuming a peculiar point of view on the world.

The appreciator's consciousness differs from the creator's in the passivity of its attitude. Where the creator's must degrade itself, must deceive itself in its reversal of the image (artwork) and its background (real world), the appreciator's consciousness is guided by the artist's work. The appreciator is willingly deceived by the other; his attitude, if he would understand the artistic creation, is the willing suspension of disbelief: Picasso's curious lines must be accepted as a human head seen from multiple points of view at the same time.

Aesthetic pleasure arises in this context. It is defined as "a manner of apprehending the unreal object, and, far from directing itself toward the real painting, it serves to constitute the imaginary object by means of the real canvas."[58] In other words, aesthetic pleasure is as necessary to the apparition of the aesthetic object as the second, receptive consciousness is to the completion of an act of communication; and an emotion is the manner in which an aesthetic object is apprehended. The emotion is real and felt, but its object is imaginary. Langer's description of aesthetic pleasure as a psychic by-product, the exhilaration concomitant to creation or appreciation, is as erroneous, from this point of view, as her semantic analysis of artworks in general. If an aesthetic pleasure is a by-product of creation or appreciation, it is a feeling symptomatically expressed and would be known by introspection. Sartre does not wish to distinguish feelings which are only symptomatically expressed from those which are embodied in works of art. And in neither case is our knowledge of the feeling a matter of "introspection."

We are thus led to a final point of comparison between Sartre and Alain, the realist: the nature of the social interaction between artist and audience. A physiological psychologist, believing neither in minds as such nor in ideas and feelings which are not expressed, Alain could not conceive of artistic communication on the model of speech or conventional language. For him, there was no idea in the head of the artist which was later sketched on canvas and understood by an audience; no transference of idea from head to head through a work of art. In short, in a purely behavioristic scheme, an artwork does not mean an idea. To explain communication, therefore, he was led to suppose the generation of meaning via gestures which, before being made, were understood neither by the artist nor by any one else. The proper model for this type of communication is: gesture, reaction-1, reaction-2. The two reactions need not be similar, but when they are, the gesture has been "understood."

Note that this scheme of the communicative process is especially fitting for modern art, in which the artist may be "playing around with colors and tones" until he finds a pleasing arrangement. When he stops playing around, his work is finished. The meaning of the work is private for the artist, as it is for each individual in his audience. In an art of understatement, the reactions of the audience are necessary to complete the work. Frequently in Japanese art, the artist merely suggests, and the reactions of the audience complete the artistic statement. As contrasted to western art, oriental art in general is an art of understatement. (Alain was fond of Japanese art, and wrote a letter of condolence to a Japanese friend following "the crime of Hiroshima" against culture.) One of the grave weaknesses of the idealistic model of communication is that it disparages much of the oriental and too much of our contemporary art as meaningless. Oriental and modern artists as well as the realistic aesthetician will merely comment that it is always fallacious to look for a meaning which was not intended, merely because artworks do not intend anything at all. All the meaning and all the feeling is inherent in the work itself. This problem will be considered further in the evaluation of Sartre's intentional theory of the physical art object.

Let us assume for the present that the intentional theory is workable, as it is for the representational arts. Using the phenomenological model to explain communication, Sartre again is not far from Alain's realism. There is a society which emerges from the attitudes of artist and audience, and this becomes clear when one insists upon the art process as communication and not merely as expression. Someone must respond to the physical object in such a way that the ideal, aesthetic object appears. True, the second, more passive, consciousness may be that of the creator in a later moment, but without someone assuming the attitude of aesthetic contemplation the artwork will not appear. The carpenter may look at the painting only as something to be boxed for shipment, but even he may for a furtive moment glance at the painting in another attitude[59] and see something he has never seen before, something he could never put in a box precisely because it does not exist independently of the glance he has stolen, let us say, of a nude's inviting stance. The pleasure he feels in this glance is proof that he has helped create the artist's work. For literary objects, again, it is quite clear that one must read the words, supplying their associated meanings, before the novel may take complete shape. It is for this reason that one critic insists that a novel and a poem, like a musical composition, must be performed:[60] an interesting and enlightening ambiguity. The audience in some sense cooperates with the artist in the creation of the work of art. This was true for Alain, as for Sartre; the only difference between the two is that the "sense" in "in some sense" has two different meanings.

To illustrate further how a feeling may become a phenomenally objective property of aesthetic objects, I turn to a special case of emotive expression, the experience of acting.

Paradox of the Actor.—One of the most interesting claims of Sartre's aesthetic theory is that the appearance of an aesthetic object depends upon the attitude taken by an audience of appreciators. In two words this means that there is no non-communicated art and that the active participation of the audience is necessary to the achievement of art. Thus it would seem to follow that all the arts are in need of some kind of "performance," in the double sense described above. The orchestra interprets a musical composition, but even this sort of performance is incomplete until the composition is heard by some audience. In other arts, as in poetry and the novel, the interpreter and the performer are the same person. For those arts in which there is an interpreter who comes between the source of the aesthetic "idea" and its logical consumer, Plato had already attempted to render justice to the art process. In the *Ion,* he calls attention to the transference of inspiration from the muse through the poet and his rhapsode to an appreciative audience. Although it has gone out of fashion for poets to appeal to the muses as sources of their inspiration, Plato's inclusion of the muses serves well to indicate that the selection of a starting and an ending point in the process of artistic communication is, after all, a logical necessity. The reader of a novel or a poem is both interpreter and consumer, and as such his activity is a necessary part of the appearance of the work depicted in the object he contemplates.

Some new light may be thrown on Sartre's view of the aesthetic object if we consider here, and in more detail, the activity of an interpreting artist per se: the actor, whose job is evidently to cooperate with the dramatist in producing the "physical analogue" of the aesthetic object, the play. The classical formulation of this problem in French letters is due to Denis Diderot (1713–1784), encyclopedist, essayist, philosopher dedicated to the introduction of English thought on the continent, dramatist, critic, literary correspondent, and aesthetician. Although his dialogue, entitled *Paradoxe sur le comédien,*[61] was written in controversy with the author of *Garrick ou les acteurs anglais,*[62] which was translated into French by an Italian actor, Antonio Fabio Sticoti, in 1769, the work was first published in France in 1830. The lapse in time between the date of its conception and its official publication has led some bibliographers to doubt the authenticity of its authorship.[63] Diderot was incensed by the poor style of the offensive treatise, whether of the original English or of the translator's French, as well as by the acceptance in France of certain commonplace ideas which were patently false. A truism, indeed, must first be true.

The most current of these commonplaces was the notion that a good actor must "live" the role he is playing—a thesis taken up by the recent Russian actor, Constantin Stanislavski. The problem has some interesting theoretical implications, as well as a great deal of practical application in the actual playing of theatrical roles. I mention Stanislavski, rather than Garrick, to indicate the contemporaneous importance of the issue. Stanislavskian "realism" is the accepted method of acting in American movies and on the legitimate stage of many so-called national theaters; it has been erected into "the Method," and as such has become the accepted theory in schools of acting and departments of speech in American universities.

The question is, Just how much feeling must an actor put into his role in order to create the illusion of his craft? Contemporary Stanislavskians insist the actor must feel his role, but Diderot had already formulated the rebuttal to this insistence in 1769: if the actor gives himself away completely to the life of his character, it would be psychologically impossible for him to control his body sufficiently to give a convincing picture of the character. Whence, the "paradox": to make it appear that the actor is experiencing the events in the life of his character, he must "feel" as little as possible. His job is to act, not to live. The feeling of the role is felt, not by the actor, but by the audience. The more the audience is convinced of the feelings expressed by the actor, the less the actor actually feels the feeling expressed.

The reasons given by Diderot to support his thesis are, on the surface at least, psychologically sound. The actor studies his role, his gestures; he practices before a mirror, and rehearses until he has achieved the proper attitude. Even after rehearsing the role a hundred times, the least change in pitch of voice, manual gesture, or bodily posture may make the actor miss the role. In short, the actor must study life to learn the external signs of the emotions he intends to portray; in portraying them, he must study his own performance to control the continued communication of his part. This, said Diderot, is too much study, too much control demanded of someone who, if he were actually feeling the emotions depicted, would be incapable of fulfilling the demand. If the feeling is not felt by the actor, to be felt, it must be felt by the audience which completes the illusion:

It's you who take in all these impressions. The actor is tired, and you full of sorrow; and the reason for this is that he has worn himself out without feeling a thing and that you have felt everything without wearing yourself out. If the case were otherwise, the life of the actor would be the worst of all possible; but he is not the character, he plays it. He plays it so that you take him to be the character: the illusion is for you alone; he, the actor, knows well that he is not the character.[64]

Compare this statement with that of Stanislavski, one actor who evidently forgot that he was not the character:

Once on the boards and all that seemed to be so easy while you were in the auditorium becomes devilishly hard. The hardest thing of all is to stand on the boards and to believe and take seriously all that takes place on the stage. But without faith and seriousness it is impossible to play satire and comedy. . . . One can play at that seriousness, but then the comedy revenges itself. *To live over or to play at living over*—there is a difference between natural, organic comism, and the outer antics of a talentless court fool.[65] [Emphasis added.]

The issue to which Sartre is addressing himself is therefore a living one, if I am allowed the pun, felt by actors who claim to know their business.

The task of the aesthetician in a case of this kind is to clarify the terms of the issue so that those more intimately connected with the problem may have for their opinions a more solid basis in fact. This clarification may be begun with the statement that actors themselves are not in a privileged position for a greater insight into their work. Acquaintance and description are still two different processes, and paradoxically enough the one most intimately acquainted with the job of acting may by reason of his extreme intimacy be incapacitated for a reasoned description of it. This seems to have been the case with Stanislavski. Secondly, as was made abundantly clear in the dialogue of Diderot, the actual test of the theory is in practice, if practice is not too narrowly conceived. We must not become dupes of the paradox. A more complete notion of the actor's practice will take into account the reception of the actor's performance by the audience. Here again, the actor is not in a privileged position for knowing. In making an appeal to the total act of communication, Sartre assumes the only role proper to the aesthetician.

The actor's paradox, according to Sartre's phenomenological aesthetics, is not an irreducible conjunction of contradictory claims. Those who claim that the actor must not accept the existence of the character are not in the least contradicting those who claim that the actor does in fact become victim of the character's life. And the supposed contradiction is not resolved by clarifying the possible confusion of the "must not" with the "does in fact"; there has been no confusion of an imperative, or rule of the actor's trade, with a statement of psychological fact; but confusion there has been. Two kinds of worlds have been confused: the ideal with the real. It would be sheer idiocy to assume that the actor "believes in" the existence of Hamlet as this character is portrayed in Shakespeare's play, even if it were true that the character Hamlet had an actual historical counterpart. Whence the aberration of certain critics who search for the real events corresponding to some others which resemble them in a novel's context, and of certain art historians who claim to enlighten the public on an art object by delivering up the facts on the lives of models used by a painter. The pictured model has an ideal existence, and so does Hamlet. His existence must be believed in as such for there to be such a thing as a play. The "thesis" of the actor's belief is therefore conditioned by his knowledge that Hamlet does not exist. In Sartre's terms, the consciousness of the actor at the time he assumes his role posits the non-existence of the character. And it is for this reason that, in accepting the "unreality" of Hamlet, we maintain the reality of the world of ordinary objects. The reality of the world and the unreality of an imaged object are mutual implications. The one appears on the background of the other, and we become aware of the one or the other as our attention shifts from the real to the unreal world. But according to Sartre this does not mean that the actor must completely control the presentation of his character as Diderot had insisted. At least a part of his portrayal is not consciously motivated. He must use all his own feelings, his own gestures, to produce the physical analogue for the creation of the unreal character. His complete performance is lived, but lived "sur un mode irréel."[66]

The tears shed by an actor are real, but the actor becomes aware of his own tears, as does his audience, as mere physical analogues of the tears shed only ideally by Hamlet. In a word, it is not true that the character becomes real through the feelings and gestures of the actor; if we look at the psychology behind acting, says Sartre, we shall be led to admit that the actor assumes the unreality of his character.[67] The actor's own consciousness does become lost, so to speak, in its own creation, just as the consciousness of the sleeper first creates its dream and then loses itself within it. And whenever a real object becomes part of the unreal world, as, according to Alain, sense stimulation which does not cease in the state of sleep becomes a "misinterpreted" part of a dream, that object must become "unrealized"; the real tears shed by an actor must be projected into a purely imaginary realm. In painting of a realistic kind this projection is actually performed by the painter and guided by the rules of perspective; and any actress who is experiencing stage fright may actually be aided in portraying the timidity of Ophelia:[68] all she would have to do would be to project this real emotion into the realm of the unreal world defined by Shakespeare's play.

If the philosopher keeps in mind the distinction between kinds of theses, whether the knowing consciousness posits the existence of an actual or of an ideal (unreal) object, the conflicting claims of schools of acting may be solved: the actor does feel his role and this feeling may help create and communicate the play, but the actor feels his role in such a way that this feeling has no consequences in the real world. And the distance between the real and the unreal worlds is properly described as "aesthetic" distance. Thus, natural organic comism is not unalterably opposed to the outer antics of a talentless court fool. To understand this we need only ignore the question begging character of Stanislavski's epithets and keep our theses straight, as moralist critics never seem to do. As conscious agents we can become aware of objects that are real or unreal, but not of both at the same time. If we become aware of the outer antics of the actor as such, either his acting is hopelessly inept or he is a "ham." When we become aware of his outer antics only instrumentally as analogues of another life which is lived in another world, he has succeeded in creating a character, in helping its author put on a play.

The moralist critic, who fails to distinguish the real from the unreal worlds, goes one step further in his confusion and takes the unreal object depicted in the acting as a real object of moral appraisal. The admittedly close connection between the real feelings of an actor which become the vibrant core of the imaginary character in a play and the feelings of a reader which likewise form the emotional cast of the world of a novel or poem will be touched upon in the next chapter of this study, where we shall consider the phenomenological theory as applied to literature, the art in which the interpreter and the consumer are the same individual. In the same chapter the problem of aesthetic judgment, and its correlate problem, the censorship of the arts, will be considered.

What has been accomplished in this chapter is a "contextual" analysis of Sartre's phenomenological theory of the aesthetic imagination. I have striven to compare and contrast it with other aesthetic theories, of both American and foreign aestheticians, who have been trying to solve a select group of queries concerning the aesthetic experience of individuals engaged in the pursuit of art.

The first and most scathing criticism of Sartre's method is perhaps what Miss MacDonald really had in mind when she reproached him for distinguishing between the physical artifact and "the aesthetic object."[69] However, what is at issue here is not the distinction, which certainly can be drawn for some kinds of art objects, but just what sense can be made of the expression, "the aesthetic object." Moreover, since the basis for the distinction between artifact and aesthetic object is clear for certain arts, it is not the expression "aesthetic object" which is the offender, but the definite article "the." One can perhaps with more justice reproach Sartre for the generality implicit in his use of the definite article, than for his idealism, which is, as it must be for an analytic philosopher, beside the point. To repeat: before the pursuit of aesthetics can become "respectable," it must be separated from metaphysics. This is not because the pursuit of metaphysics is essentially nonsense, as some contemporary philosophers maintain; but because any discipline which would be scientific must develop its own categories for the interpretation of the experiences it attempts to describe or explain. To consider a case in point, a novel can certainly be described as existing only in intention—not the author's prevised purpose, but the context of meaning referred to by the words used to depict the events in the novel—phenomenology here makes sense. The error committed by Sartre, the aesthetician, is in having generalized a theory adequate for one art, to cover other art forms for which the theory is inadequate.

Let us consider the facts: there are representational and non-representational arts; the drama, literature, some forms of painting and sculpture, and even music may give us a picture of the universe. The works of all such arts intend objects other than themselves. But what of those arts called "pure": the majority of music, some kinds of poetry, sculpture, and painting, architecture, landscaping, civic design. No one whose aesthetics would be complete would exclude these arts unless he were to adopt the dogmatism and question begging, of those who exclude from analysis what does not fit a pre-designed theory. The question is simply this: if an aesthetic object is an ideal entity, what can be said of those art objects which do not refer to anything beyond themselves?

Sartre was indeed aware of this question. He considered the ontological status of works of music, often considered the most "pure" of the arts, and came up with some conclusions rather ominously similar to those of a realistic aesthetician, C. I. Lewis.[70] And the similarity of these conclusions may astonish all save a non-metaphysical aesthetician. Any art form which depends upon a performer for the completion of the communicative process must distinguish between the object and a mere rendition of it. The issue is, therefore, whether a metaphysically neutral vocabulary can be invented to cover this distinction. We may attempt to discover such a vocabulary by paying closer attention, not to music which is usually "pure," nor to opera or literature which is always "mixed" in its form of communication, containing elements only of immanent or of both immanent and referential expression respectively, but by considering an art form which is easily either of these, depending upon the tastes of the artist. Any work of abstract expressionism will suffice to illustrate painting containing only immanent values of expression; any portrait will illustrate that containing both. A usual difference noted by the museum habitué is that the totally abstract work bears no name, only an opus or composition number; the portrait usually bears the name of the person it resembles. The abstraction means nothing; the portrait "means" its subject. What is the ideal entity defining the abstract expressionist painting, which exists only in one copy and which refers to nothing beyond itself? Only a theoretician deluded by his own theory will find one. What is important in the appreciation of a non-representational painting, as a composition by Jackson Pollock, is it phenomenal appearance, determined by the physical properties of the object. "Texture" is a suitable term for the ensemble of such properties. One of the important innovations of Frank L. Wright and Corbusier is their use of "architectural" concrete. The concrete used as wall or ceiling in buildings by these masters is important for itself; it imparts a texture to the edifice impossible to achieve in other materials. Likewise, much of the architectural effect gained in the construction of prairie houses is in the use of mixed textures: wood, metal, brick, and stone may be used in varying ways to produce the art object. Metaphysical idealism simply cannot do justice to the aesthetic quality of textural materials.

The naive realism of Alain, on the other hand, does render justice to the textural qualities of art objects, but as Sartre pointed out, realism tends to under-emphasize the intentional, or referential, aspect of those art forms which do intend meanings. Following the insight of Susanne K. Langer in her extension of the notion of "logical form" to cover that of an aesthetic expression,[71] I should propose the term "structure" for the formal qualities of these intentional objects. A structural analysis of a painting will entail the description of the similarity between the physical artifact and the scene depicted; of the novel, of the development and resolution of the forces influencing the lives of the imaginary characters. Texture and structure are thus two different properties of art objects; but not of all art objects, since in some there is no referential meaning. And if these two terms can be applied to art objects in any degree of completeness, there is further elucidation for the ambiguity of the aesthetic term "form." In speaking of the formal properties of the "pure" arts, of those whose main concern is with the creation of a physical object, or with the manipulation of a physical medium, we are obviously speaking of the texture of the art object. If, however, we use the term "form" in the two senses explained in Alain's theory to refer to both style and compositional rules or guides, a still further ambiguity is noted. "Style" itself may refer to textural or to structural qualities of artworks. For example, Marcel Proust has a very distinctive textural style; he was fond of the flowing epithet conducive to long sentences with "punch" endings; in fact, someone has said that his style (textural) is like the movements of a cat: no matter how many involutions it makes when jumping into the air, it always lands on its feet. At the same time, there is a very distinctive quality of Proust's structural style, defined ultimately by the theory of the past incorporated in the novel, as well as by his method of analyzing the minutiae turned up in his labyrinthine psychological introspection. To explain these features of a given work of art, one must, of course, consult the work in question. I refer to them merely to illustrate a point.

The utility of any aesthetic categories lies in their ability to settle outstanding disputes concerning the nature of art objects. To what extent does the dispute between realistic and idealistic metaphysicians, whose aesthetic theories are colored by their metaphysical presuppositions, prevent the development of a useful set of aesthetic categories? Since even in Sartre's estimation the aesthetic object is the referent of an image, or the physical analogue of an imaginary entity, it would follow that all the arts have some kind of physical basis. The appealing feature of Alain's realism is that it allows for this universal quality of texture, even if it minimizes or ignores structure. Sartre's alleged idealism, on the other hand, minimizes or ignores texture. Still it might be unfair to make the statement: Sartre's metaphysics was developed after he had already clearly formulated his psychology of the imagination.

Since there are some arts having texture, but no referential structure, the question normally arises as to whether a work of art is an image. Certainly not, if we mean by "a work of art," all works of art. The compositions of Pollock or the abstractions of O'Keefe and Mondrian are cases in point. If a painting refers to nothing, if it resembles nothing, how can it be considered an image? Are there such things as "abstract" images? One contemporary English philosopher maintains that there are.[72] Anthony Flew, in criticizing an article by J. M. Shorter, claims that some images are abstract because they resemble nothing, refer to nothing. In effect, it is not true that every image is *of* something; obviously, claims Flew, since abstract paintings are of nothing and yet are images. The very meaning of the word "abstract" as it modifies "painting" is that the object is not intended to be *of* or *like* anything, and is thus not pictorial. Flew's analysis seems to be valid; if it is, the reason is that it begs the question, namely that all paintings are images. Analysis will show why.

Shorter had maintained that there is a fundamental difference between the uses of "seeing" and "seeing in the mind's eye." An obvious truth, if by "seeing" is meant perceiving a real object; and by "seeing in the mind's eye," imaging the existence of a real object, which in Sartre's eyes would be positing its non-existence. Shorter, in a word, agrees with Husserl and Sartre that every image is of something; his statement follows the postulate of phenomenology that every consciousness is of something. Flew states two reasons for denying the validity of the postulate as it applies to images.

It simply is not true, he thinks, that all "picturing" or "visualizing" must be representational because, first, there are some visual images which are not produced by visualizing, and not even all of those which are so produced are representational (cf. non-representational painting); and secondly, since any subject's imagery is private, it cannot be discussed without a preliminary description of it. Mr. Shorter seems to Flew to have confused the uses of "to visualize," "to picture," and "to see in the mind's eye" with that of "to have mental imagery." Sartre would not argue with the expression, "to have mental imagery"; he would, however, take issue with its use which entails our seeing the mental image, as Mr. Flew seems to imply in his second reason. Just what is being described when he describes *the image?* Is it the object visualized, the referring image itself, or some element common to both? Sartre's phenomenology seems to have the edge over the common Englishman's language here: the word "imagery" hides a multitude of referents. Moreover, if it be remembered that an image intends its object as a concept intends its meaning, the connection between having an image and being able to describe its referent is immediately apparent: any description of the image would have to be given in terms of the concept which "motivates" its appearance. As for Flew's first reason, it is statement and not proof. Aestheticians are still looking for a convincing reason for calling a painter's abstraction an image. Merely calling it such is not sufficient to make it so. There must be a legitimate sense of "visualizing" which has escaped Mr. Flew.

A clue to the settlement of this issue is to be taken from the realistic aesthetics of Alain. An abstract painting is not an image at all; it is, rather, a percept. And this is the reason for including both the physical aspects of the work of art and its referential qualities in a listing of aesthetic categories. Some artworks are perceived, that is, seen as physical objects having physical characteristics. We perceive the work of Mondrian, for example, as a certain geometrical shape. We can describe this shape as it really is, and when we do so, we describe its texture. The shape is achieved by the manipulation of a surface. The reason for the frequent lack of critical perception concerning Mondrian's work is that people continue to look for something to be "seen by the mind's eye" instead of what is there to be seen by the body's eye. I am saying, of course, that a total abstraction has no imaginative content; it *is,* it doesn't mean anything. Such a description does not mean that all paintings are mere percepts. When a painting represents an object of nature, it obviously refers to that object; and in so doing, it has imaginative content. Thus, we are led to the conclusion that it is a mistake to found one's aesthetic theory solely on the facts of perception or of the imagination. *All* aesthetic objects have some kind of texture, something which we see or hear or otherwise perceive; and *some of them* have some kind of structured imaginary content, which we can see only "in the mind's eye."

Finally, if we consult the volume of reviews Sartre published as
Situations I, we will find that he was as much occupied with stylistics
and texture as with the structure of the plots of novels.[73] And a
comparison of those reviews with his treatment of the sculptor's medium will show that Sartre was aware of the distinction between texture and structure as general aesthetic categories. In *Situations III* he
has evaluated the imaginary space creations of Giacometti and the
real movements of Calder's mobiles; it is there that we find his description of the imaginary qualities of a realistic sculpture:

> Here, at this time, is matter: a rock, a simple segment of space. With space
> Giacometti must fashion a man; he must put mobility into total immobility,
> unity into infinite multiplicity, the absolute into pure relativity, the future
> into the eternal present, the chatter of signs into the obstinate silence of
> things.[74]

Besides having a familiar ring for anyone conversant with the aesthetic theory of Alain, this passage indicates a necessity, in any aesthetic theory, for the distinction between the seen and the imagined.
More apparently consistent with his own general phenomenological
theory is Sartre's distinction between the perceived artifact and the
imagined aesthetic object.

> Ganymede on his pedestal. If you ask me how far he is from me, I will
> answer that I don't know what you are talking about. Do you mean by
> "Ganymede" the youth carried off by the eagle of Jupiter? In that case, I
> will say there is no *real* distance relation between him and myself, for the
> simple reason that he doesn't exist. Are you alluding, contrariwise, to the
> block of marble the sculptor has fashioned in the image of the loved one?
> In this case, you are asking about a real thing, an existent mineral, and we
> can measure.[75]

An ideal object existing only in an imaginary space, the statue is
viewed absolutely, outside of time and space; that is to say, only in
image. But some statues do not come off unless viewed at a certain
distance, or from a given perspective. Contradiction? Not all all; the
perspective from which the imaged object will appear depends strictly
upon our standing in the proper spot. The next time a painting seems
to be too small or too large for its image to appear, step back or forward, and it may.

Still other works never come off as representations at all. When
Sartre viewed Calder's mobiles he saw them as all texture, with no
imaginary structure:

> Calder suggests nothing: he catches real living movements and fashions

them. His mobiles signify nothing, refer to nothing but themselves: they exist, and that's the end of it; they are absolute. In them, the "part of the devil" is stronger, perhaps, than in any other creation of man. They have too many springs, and [are] too complicated for a single human brain to foresee all their combinations, even the brain of their creator.[76]

In this description, Sartre has returned to Alain's theory of aesthetics pure and simple. Calder is said to create physically, rather like the devil than like God, by the fortuitous combination of elements; he discovers his idea *after* having expressed it.

To conclude: in practice, if not in theory, Sartre is a better aesthetician than contemporary philosophers of other persuasions will give him credit for being. And the reason for this is that in practice he always observes the work of art before pronouncing upon it. In general aesthetics as in any other scientific enterprise, when theory comes before observation the theorist can only explain away, and when it proceeds as a natural development from the observation of facts, then and only then can the theory fulfill its explanatory claims. Realism or idealism? Metaphysical terms, which can only be out of place in a scientific aesthetics.[77]

IV

Literature of Commitment

The title of this chapter, in conjunction with the phenomenological description of art objects which has preceded, may serve to indicate the main puzzle concerning us here. If a work of art has only an ideal existence separable in each instance from any physical representation of it, if words are merely intentional devices indicating meanings, if the reader of a work of literary art is provoked into a dreamlike state, is not the Philistine's attitude toward art advisable for any one of a realistic turn of mind? I think not. Besides the considerable vagueness in aesthetic theory, already exposed, of the terms "idealism" and "realism," it is quite evident to any self-conscious reader that the distinction between a word and its meaning is not only permissible, but necessary if one is to understand the structure of a novel, and even, to some extent, the appeal of a poem. Thus, if the Philistine's attitude results from a stiff-necked dislike of the "otherworldliness" of the literary object, he has been misled by the meaning of a word; if literary objects are as Sartre has described them, it is likewise true that they function in the manner he has described: to permit communication between members of a society, and even more importantly, to create a society where before the writing and its appreciation there was none. Art is communication, and not empty expression.

When we stress the process of art as communication, rather than self-expression, we are emphasizing the sociality as opposed to the individuality of artists whose vanity is to believe perhaps too strongly that theirs is the dominant personality engaged in the artistic communication. Even so, the process must be visualized from both its end-points, as well as from the central and mediating object which unites them. The general characteristics of an art object as a mediating link between two consciousnesses, have been discussed at length in the preceding chapter. All arts must be per-formed; and thus the consumer is as important to the total process as the producer. The purpose of this chapter, then, is to discuss the activity of the author[1] as well as that of the reader of the literary product. The sources for the present study are to a large extent still in the making: Sartre is writing philosophy, literature, and criticism, social and political as well as artistic. Fortunately for the student of the contemporary movement called "French existentialism," the manifesto for existentialist writers has already been composed. With the breakdown of the Third Republic in 1939 and the rebirth of French society in the Fourth in 1945, the time was ripe for an evaluation of the writer's conscience. Old patterns were outworn; the new could be left to happen (as a "historical" critic will insist that they do anyway), or they could be established in conformity with a plan. The writers who grouped themselves together to form *Les Temps Modernes* chose the latter alternative.

Both Sartre and Beauvoir as self-conscious artists have written on the function of literature as it relates to philosophy and to social life;[2] Merleau-Ponty, the academician of the group, was especially interested in the relationship of philosophy and literature.[3] Moreover, since the founder and director of the journal is Sartre, it is not surprising that the greater part of the organizing load was his. Three of his articles in the earlier issues were dedicated to establishing literature as a profession rather than as a waste of time or a mechanism of escape; they form the second volume of *Situations* and the nucleus of my commentary. As important as these three articles are for understanding the literature of French intellectual life today, it would be a mistake to limit our attention to them alone. If the centrality of Sartre within the group known by some of its critics today as the "mandarins of the left,"[4] is important, then so are Sartre's growing sympathy with the French Communist Party, and the recent political polemics within and without *Les Temps Modernes,* though they are not, as such, works of fine literature. Finally, in keeping with the plan of attack already used in this study, the analysis will be contextual: I shall endeavor to indicate the historical context of the theory exposited and evaluated, as well as some doctrinal affinities with literary and political movements within our own culture. The ultimate significance of the existentialist movement is to be gauged by the context in which it occurred and is still evolving, as well as by reference to a similar set of conditions which produced a comparable movement in our own country. And the aim, in comparing the foreign movement with the literature and life of our own culture, is to indicate some of the universal conditions under which literature is created and enjoyed.

One of the paradoxes of comparing the literatures of two cultures as different as the French and American, is that in general Americans have looked to the older, more firmly settled patterns of individual expression characteristic of Europeans, whereas in this case the Europeans are going through a phase through which, on the whole, Americans have already passed. European students have begun to come to America to study our literature, and the same interest is reflected in some of Sartre's criticism. He has labeled Dos Passos the "greatest writer of our times,"[5] has praised the techniques of Faulkner in at least two articles,[6] and has had translated for publication in Les Temps Modernes such disparate American authors as Richard Wright and Nelson Algren.[7] If one were to speculate on the reasons for this reverse influence of cultures, one might indicate the greater freedom of the American writer for experimentation: American authors have been engaged in establishing a national literature and hence have not been bound to the reproduction of the classical models definitive of an older, more well defined tradition. This is to some extent true, but more scientific explanations would light upon the similarity of conditions in present day, or recent, French society and those through which American writers have already passed. For example, the breakdown of the moral and social values of the twenties, followed by the economic depression of the thirties was not unlike the breakdown of the moral and social values of French society following defeat in World War II, and the prolonged period of German occupation.[8] And it is perhaps a truism to remark that the literature in the United States which reflects this struggle of values for survival is not unlike that in France which mirrors a similar struggle. Besides this similarity, there is a single factor which may be found in both literary scenes: the role played by Marxist economic, social and political theory in the functioning of the social and literary institutions of both countries.

In speaking of the relation between a society and its literature, it is all too easy, as I have done, to use such verbs as "reflect," and "mirror." They are verbal covers for considerable vagueness and ambiguity which need uncovering. Is the real world in which the author lives merely projected into an ideal, non-real context? If so, why? Does the artist have to express one set of values rather than another? If so, why? And why is the literature which does reflect the values of society, or any of its sub-groupings, better or worse than any other kind of literature? Is there a distinction between fine literature, usually called "pure," and propaganda? Or are these terms, too, merely different ways of categorizing the same objects? However the aesthetician would answer questions such as these, an analysis of the process of art communication must be found in the background. Consider three cases in which American authors and critics have given some kind of answer.

Granville Hicks, a Marxist writing in the thirties, has examined the literature of America from the close of the Civil War to his own day.[9] One need not read far into Hicks's criticism before coming into contact with the "mirroring" metaphor. Great social and political changes were going on, and they had found their way into books of fine art. This is an obvious fact; no one who has read both history and literature will deny it. But as Hicks proceeds, his attention shifts from the books produced by authors living in certain conditions, to the lives and moral worth of the individuals themselves. There are, in his method of criticism, decent authors, renegades and—even worse, from Hicks' point of view—"escapists." Here we have the mirroring process: "The confusion in Lowell's political thinking gives some clue to his failure as a literary force."[10]; and here the moral judgment: "So Lowell passes from the scene, never wholly traitor to the bright impulses that had roused him in his youth, but to the end bewildered."[11] But we are not so interested here in the reasons for an author's conduct, as we are in those of his critic, for this is eminently the job of an aesthetician. And as a more extensive study of Hicks's work will show, each of his critical judgments is based on the assumption that any literature and consequently any author that ignore the conditions of class struggle, which for a Marxist effectively describe the evolution of any society, are *eo ipso* bad literature and an immoral author. The judgment on the literature is allegedly aesthetic; and on the author, moral. But on what grounds are these judgments made? On nothing more secure than the individual political preferences of the critic? Perhaps this would be unjust, even to a critic of the stamp of Hicks. Behind his judgments, as behind any critical judgment worth considering, is an aesthetic assumption. Hick's assumption is that the goodness or badness of literature is to be judged on a functional basis; the more a literature functions to produce the new society, regardless of its merits as "pure" art, the better that literature. And there were more than one Hicks writing both art and criticism in the thirties. American communist sympathizers of that time were appealing to the service to which a professional writer not only could, but must, devote himself if his conduct were to be considered "ethical." This is not a sense of the word with which we should be unfamiliar.

This narrow, functional, point of view was refuted by James T. Farrell, whose criticism furnishes the second case to be considered. Armed with the more complete aesthetic theories of Mead and Dewey, and the insights into aesthetic experience gained from Prall's *Aesthetic Judgment*,[12] Farrell sought a finer balance between the aesthetic and the technical, or functional, aspects of the total experience of a work of art. In fact, Mead's suggestion that in the experience of a work of art each functional unit becomes suffused with the character of an end, vitiates the distinction between the functional and the final *aspects* of the total experience. However, this is not to say that the distinction can never be made; critical dogmatism is always an error. The integrity of the work will decide which of the aspects is determinant of the total experience. Thus, Farrell cautions:

I must say parenthetically that I have used the phrase *aspects of experience* because I do not seek to establish my categories as absolutes. One or the other, the functional or the aesthetic, is given more emphasis because of particular purposes, situations, and necessities; moreover, when experience is harmonious and coordinated, there is no split between the functional or objective. Any complete divorcement of categories here leads to the vice of oversimplification; and unfortunately, both in the practice and in the theory of aesthetics and literary criticism, there have been glaring instances of such a divorcement.[13]

Spingarn's "New Criticism," although correct in proclaiming the integrity of the art object, degenerated into the empty aestheticism of of impressionistic criticism, according to which the critic merely writes the impressions called out in the experience of the work.[14] Here was obviously an oversimplification on the side of the aesthetically "pure."

Oversimplifications on the side of the aesthetically functional were found in the critical writings of humanists, Catholics, and Marxists; according to the codes of each of these, the duty of the critic is to evaluate the ethical significance of the work. The humanist had his touchstones of purifying literature illustrating the ethical conscious-ness, and so did the Catholics and Marxists, but in each case the ethical consciousness was different. The error in this kind of criticism is, of course, to bring a critical canon to the work of art instead of examining works of art to find the critical canon. If our demand upon the literary artist is such that he must express such or such an idea, then we are asking for propaganda, and the institution of art which has its own way of functioning in a free society is poorly served.

Farrell has given an enlightening chapter on the relations between the functions served by literature; it bears the title: "Literature and Propaganda."[15] If we cease to insist that literature must serve this or that function, we should allow ourselves the time to discover what functions it can and does serve. Even the so-called reactionary themes of a Marcel Proust serve a social function when they are taken in context. If we exclude the work of Proust, dedicated as it is to bourgeois values (even if in decadence), on the ground that the theme is forbidden, we are not only violating the freedom of the artist to function as he can, we are at the same time doing a double injustice to literature. First of all, condemnation of a work on the basis of only one of its elements, subject matter, as opposed to its form or technical achievement is aesthetically indefensible;[16] sec-ondly, should our prohibition of such literature take effect, the very test of literature's effectiveness is rendered impossible. As Alain always pointed out,[17] it takes time to make a classic; and literature often generates a controversy whose assimilation in criticism takes much longer than the actual, historical resolution of the conflict of values depicted in the controversial novel.[18] Such is, after all, the risk of writing a literary piece whose subject matter is of topical, moral interest.

The conflict between two "liberal" critics of the thirties illus-trates a very important point. Both Hicks and Farrell were artists of sorts; both were evaluating the professional consciousness of writers; both used some kind of aesthetic judgment in proclaiming their theories. Thus the judgment between them can be made only on the grounds of relative merit in their aesthetic theories. Sartre is proposing a similar examination of the writer's conscience, and like his American predecessors he bases his examination on an aesthetic theory. It is of further interest to note that none of these men claims the exalted position in society due the "genius" of writers; this romantic notion has been buried for the better. In a later article, Farrell does a masterful job of analyzing the institutional background of the writing profession: a theme expressed in an earlier article by R. P. Blackmur, "A Feather-Bed for Critics—Notes on the Profession of Writing."[19] Such critical self-examination is the mark of a responsible critic, and the antithesis of oversimplification.

It would be a mistake, however, to charge all social minded critics with inept oversimplification. Kenneth Burke, writing in the *Nation* during those depression years of the thirties,[20] had recourse to the "psychology of art" in an attempt to settle the issue of the moral functions of literature in society. Unfortunately, however, this psychology was nothing newer than Aristotle's catharsis theory applied to the so-called "pure" arts. Recognizing the intimate connection between work and ethics, the struggle of society to achieve the fine balance between competitive means to cooperative ends which is so often upset in a capitalistic economy, and the stratification of the social group according to class interests in conflict, he also claims that the only virtue of pure art is its power to produce acceptance of the values of the dominant group. The audience of such art, in Burke's view, is delivered from the struggle. Naturally, therefore, if "pure" art is not to be condemned, but allowed to thrive, the underlying moral system must be sound. Thus, in his attempt to avoid one kind of oversimplification, Burke was led to another. Art for art's sake is good (allowable) only when the audience is already living in a stable, sound society. Since the necessary conditions for the appreciation of such pure art is the possession of a sound social system, if we would have our arts pure, we should first produce that sound state of society. Otherwise the literature of agitation, functional literature in Farrell's sense, is a necessary corrective of the abortive society in which the author and his audience must live.

The subtlety of Burke's thesis is remarkable: there is no conflict between literature and propaganda. At one end of the social cycle, we have pure literature which functions as a cathartic producing acquiescence in the values of the society; at the other, functional literature, or literature of reaction, which produces dissatisfaction

with the values of the ruling class of society. Nor is his oversimplification the statement that society must be changed before pure literature becomes possible; this would be to place the whole burden of social change on the social and political forces, on institutions of society
other than art. In claiming that writing is a profession in which the
author expresses himself within the total institutional framework of
the society, changing at times the conditions under which he lives,
Burke reaffirms the democratic structure of the total society and the
place of the artist within it. He seems to err only in ignoring the fact
that whatever an author writes is a result of the author's choice.
Even granted the institutional setup of society and the institutional
nature of art, there is no reason to suppose that a given writer will
choose to write for himself, and thus "purely," rather than for others,
and thus "functionally." Hicks at least recognized the relevance of
the artist's choice, and condemned the bourgeois artist for precisely
that reason. But where Hicks had been victim of the pure-functional
distinction in aesthetics, Burke fell victim to the individual-social
distinction in social theory.[21] In the remainder of this chapter we
shall consider Sartre's attempt to erect a theory which commits neither
of these oversimplifications.

CREATIVE COMMUNICATION

The term "creative communication" is used here to indicate the
kind of synthesis of aesthetic ideals made possible by Sartre's phenomenological analysis of literary activity. The aim of the theory is
to give to each its just part: the individual, the social, the purely aesthetic, and the broadly functional aspects of literature. The epithet
"creative" is used here to indicate the part of invention due to the individual author's vision and to the aesthetic quality of the work by
which that vision is shared; the term "communication" lays stress
here, as always, upon the society of author and audience, which,
ideally, is ever-expanding, as well as upon the functional value of
the author's work in contributing to the grounds of solidarity in this
ever-expanding society of appreciators.

Since the subject matter of literature in general is life in general,
it is perhaps a truism to assert that the subject matter of the novel
is some aspect of man's achieving a personality. In order to achieve
complete selfhood, man enters into relations with his environment
both natural and social, struggling oftentimes with each of these

environments, as with himself, to become something other than what he is.[22] The general theme of literature is therefore somewhat fixed. One novel will differ from another according to the treatment given by the individual novelist to this theme: according as novelists' metaphysical assumptions (implicit or explicit) differ, their description of the environment and their protagonists' relations to that environment differ (cf. the metaphysical structure of Sartre's own *La Nausée* with that of an American naturalistic novel, such as Farrell's *Studs Lonigan* trilogy). And, since some novels are predominantly moral, rather than metaphysical in tone, their structures are consequently predominantly moral, and differ according to the moral assumptions made by the author (cf. the differences in structure of Malraux's *La Condition humaine* with that of Huxley's *Point Counter Point*).

Besides illustrating the manner in which philosophy serves the practicing man of letters, if not his critics, this insight into a novel's structure throws some light upon the inventive task of the writer: he must find the technical device for portraying his metaphysical or moral idea in a concrete situation (although intentional, or ideal). The diary device used by Sartre in *La Nausée* is more apt than the same device used by Dostoevski in *Memoirs from the House of the Dead* because the device is more formally functional; it is, in fact, an aesthetic necessity following from the nature of the metaphysical situation depicted. The diary is the work of a reflective man, and only a reflective man such as Roquentin could have been led to the discovery of the meaning of his own existence. Likewise, the cause and effect relation of the deterministic metaphysics of the naturalists necessitates a technical device for starting the story; since no novel's beginning can be traced back to a first cause (out of consideration for the reader's boredom, if not for the logical difficulties in proving God's existence with the causal argument), the novelist must find a way for beginning his causal sequence of events. Farrell's flashbacks in *Young Lonigan* constitute the technical device needed. Metaphysically each of these novels hangs together as a formal unit. Sartre gives a hint at the critical device explained here in his treatment of Faulkner's exploitation of time in *The Sound and the Fury*.[23] The form of the novel and the author's techniques are mutually determinant.[24]

It would be a mistake to assume, however, that every novel will lend itself to either a metaphysical or moral analysis. Some, and a prime example is Proust's *A la recherche du temps perdu,* have a more restricted foundation in the psychology of the individual protagonist: psychology may then yield the structure of the work. In Proust's case it is at least in part the psychology of Bergson with the importance it gives to the instantaneous recall of complete blocks of lived experience. Sartre scrutinizes the technique of Proust as typical of the "bourgeois" novelist.

The question which naturally arises here is, What makes a novelist bourgeois? The easiest answer is not the most enlightening: a bourgeois novelist might be considered a member of a certain class (the ruling class of a capitalistic economic society, the owners of the means of production who have succeeded in overthrowing the older ruling aristocracy), who is writing either for other members of that class (enjoyment) or for members of the working class to produce acquiescence in the values of the bourgeoisie (function); the theme of novels produced by such writers will usually be some facet of the bourgeois world. This interpretation would be consistent with Kenneth Burke's theory of art in a capitalist society. Proust was a bourgeois living on the fortune of his mother and writing for his own and his readers' pure aesthetic enjoyment, and his theme was partially the struggle of the rising bourgeoisie against the older, now decadent, aristocracy: a bourgeois novelist writing on a bourgeois theme to produce acquiescence in bourgeois values. However, like most apparent analyses, this one is too simple: Proust is much more an aesthete than a propagandist;[25] and if bourgeois, he was not determined as such by his mother's wealth, but by his own choice.[26] We must therefore find another sense of the term having more meaning for our purposes.

Sartre found it in the political assumptions of the bourgeoisie: the equality of man whose so-called natural rights flow from the very essence of humanity. In such a state of affairs a man was to be respected simply because of the universal essence of humanity inherent in his own personality; and when the individual finds himself exploited by growing capitalistic concerns (which are legally endowed with a personality), the bourgeois society institutionalizes charity in the name of the same universal essence of man.[27] But something is wrong with the society which institutionalizes the effects of its own malfunctioning, and Sartre sought to find the cause. In explaining this cause, we shall find a suitable meaning for the term being explicated.

Sartre has given a two-point definition of the bourgeois class: complexes within it are necessarily reducible to a collection of simple elements; and these ultimate simples are the referents of the term "social reality."[28] Characteristic of the bourgeois society is thus its atomistic structure. The individual person belongs to or joins certain groups which are considered neither more nor less than a simple summation of its members, and since equality is the catchword, even the offices held by certain of these members cannot be used as a means of functional differentiation within the total structure. When the novelist sets for himself the task of examining the individual element of the social group, he is led to use the same atomistic assumptions in treating the individual's psychological make-up: each act of an individual may be analyzed into motive, decision, and action proper; this last is seen as in turn influencing the environmental situation which reshapes the motive and produces further decisions and actions. In a word, the bourgeois novelist is wed to the method of analysis.

Sartre considers Proust's work the fullest achievement of this analytical technique; it is intellectualistic, relating feeling with motive, atomistic, separating motive from motive, and mechanistic, relating motive with decision and action. The difficulty with the work of Proust is that its author was not a typical man:

A pederast, Proust thought he was able to take advantage of his homosexual experience when he wanted to depict the love of Swann for Odette; a bourgeois, he presents this feeling of love by a rich leisurely living bourgeois for a kept woman as the prototype of love. The reason is that he believes in the existence of universal passions whose mechanisms do not differ sensibly when one modifies the sexual character, the social condition, the country, or the epoch of the individuals who feel them. After having "isolated" these immutable affections, he will be able to reduce them further to their more elementary particles. Faithful to the postulates of the spirit of analysis, he did not even imagine that there might be a dialectic of feeling, but only a mechanism.[29]

There follows upon this description of Proust's technique, a fourfold reason for rejecting it: first, the love passion is not on a priori grounds a constitutive element of the human mind since a feeling is always an expression, in Sartre's eyes, of a certain kind of life and a certain outlook on the world which are common to a whole class or to a certain epoch, and since feelings are not triggered by a given internal mechanism as much as by historical and social factors;[30] secondly, human affections do not enter into complexes without modifying each other since a man is an organism, and not a machine; what is called for then is dialectical synthesis and not analysis; thirdly, the love of homosexuals is not of the same character as love between heterosexuals; in the latter's evolution there are not the qualities of Black Mass necromancy, spirit of international freemasonry, and implied damnation of its participants, since love between heterosexuals is not forbidden in society;[31] finally, the origin, the class, the milieu, the nation of the individual are not simple concomitants of his affective life; rather each human affection manifests the social life of the individual having it.[32]

In denying the validity of Proust's analytical method, Sartre was forced to another, more synthetic view of the nature of man, "whose principle is that a whole, whatever it may be, is different in nature from the sum of its parts."[33] Whence the picture of the total man, as opposed to a group of passions; a man essentially situated in an environment, having to be born and to die. In order for the novelist to "achieve" such a character, he must depict an individual as existing in the world, in a certain milieu along with other men. In short, the total man is he whose metaphysical structures are described in *L'Etre et le néant*. It is not to our purpose to comment fully upon Sartre's major metaphysical opus at this time; others have assumed this task with greater or less sympathy.[34] The sources for Sartre's concept of the total man are mentioned here only to indicate the complexity of his aesthetic thought, and to reaffirm the principles of a scholarly cross comparison of an author's works before pronouncing thereon. This dual influence—of phenomenological psychology of the imagination and the ontology of existentialism—is the distinctive mark of Sartre's aesthetics of the novel, but in theory there are contradictions which are yet to be worked out.[35] Psychology or ontology? The difference may be explained thus: Sartre's discussions about the kind of object a novel is, are based on the theory of the imagination, and those about the kind of object a novel represents, on his own existential ontology. But more of this later.

In sum, if the bourgeois author is known for his analytic treatment of man, the existentialist author will be known for his dialectically synthetic treatment of the same subject. A function of technique, rather than of subject matter, the difference is formal rather than contentual. Nothing would prevent an existentialist author from treating a "bourgeois" theme; in fact, this is one way of producing those novels of reaction of which Burke had spoken: to depict the underside of bourgeois society, its pathetic shortcomings and abortive justice. In the literature published in *Les Temps Modernes* we thus find the themes of prostitution, homosexuality, antisemitism, colonialism, racial discrimination; in short, those called by Farrell " 'bottom-dog' literature."[36] In Sartre's terms, the best way for literature to become a social force in addition to being an aesthetic object of worth in itself is for the author to adopt the point of view of the least favored, or what is more poignant, of the most disfavored individuals in contemporary society.[37] This is the way existentialist authors were encouraged to produce certain changes in their own society, and not merely in the souls of their readers (the job of authors with a restricted clientele).[38] Existentialist literature was to be social action. It intended to produce social change by offering its audience a conception of the human individual consistent with (ironically enough) its true nature: man in face of his co-efficient of adversity, a given individual working out his dentiny within an unfriendly environment. Thus "tragedy" is the accepted term for the existentialist predicament.

With those who define tragedy according to the principle that formal excellence of aesthetic expression overbalances the negative value of a real pathetic experience, Sartre exhorts his associates not to forget the aesthetic quality of their works:

In effect, I should like to recall that in "committed literature" the *commitment* must not, in any case, make one forget the *literature,* and that our preoccupation must be to serve literature in giving it new blood, just as much as to serve society in trying to give it the literature fitting its circumstances.[39]

The difference Sartre hoped to establish between bourgeois literature and that of the existentialist movement is a greater social consciousness on the part of the existentialist author who must retain his truly aesthetic purpose. Such a difference will explain in what sense authors other than those closely associated with the movement can be truly labeled "existentialist."[40] The bourgeois writer was exercising his *human* right to express himself as he saw fit. In service of the bourgeois class, using its presuppositions, its method of analysis and, in general, producing acquiescence in its values, he was repaid the emolument of royalties for services rendered to a class, rather than to men. The result, according to Sartre, was professional irresponsibility: in France the bourgeois writers became "a nest of singing birds" devoted to the production of more song rather than to the resolution of problems of pressing social need. The new writers, on the other hand, could congratulate themselves on "having found a good professional conscience and for having made of literature what it should never have ceased to be: a social function."[41] It was with this analysis, and this hope, that Sartre and his co-founders, in 1945, presented *Les Temps Modernes*. But a statement of aim is not a fully conceived manifesto. *Qu'est-ce que la littérature?*, the existentialist manifesto, appeared in 1947.

As mentioned earlier, the question posed in the title of Sartre's literary manifesto has a historical setting: social, political, and literary currents were flowing together in such a way as to demand an examination of conscience. And the conscience being examined was both professional and aesthetic. Too often there has been an arbitrary split between an author's consciousness as artist on one hand and as a member of the literary profession on the other; but if the writer's personality is necessarily schizoid, Sartre would say that it is so following the premises of the analytic method of bourgeois thought. For the existentialist, a writer is a professional and an artist at the same time; he, too, is a total man facing a simultaneous duty to himself and to the society in which he must live. Having stated the writer's social reponsibility in the presentation of *Les Temps Modernes,* Sartre considers the writer as professional artist having a place in a functional society, in the longer work now under consideration.

The artist works with a medium, and the medium of the literary artist is words. When asked why, in its earlier stages, *Les Temps Modernes* published little or no poetry, another art whose medium is words, Sartre made a reply which can hardly be understood without some reference to the French literary scene. Having suffered a series of poetic movements such as symbolism, dadaism, and surrealism, a French critic, in this case Sartre himself, could make the statement that poetry is not literature. And he had good aesthetic authority for the statement on the part of Alain,[42] according to whom poetry is an art of incantation more like music than literature, whose essence is the telling of a story.

In terms of the aesthetic doctrine propounded by Alain and of the poetry written by Paul Valéry, the poet uses his medium in a way completely alien to the literary artist; in Sartre's terms, he uses words inside out:[43] the poet considers language as a structure of the external world rather than as the living extension of the poet's own body.[44] A word, as a sign, is after all an ambiguous thing: a sign-vehicle which intends a meaning; in reading words one may become aware of the physical qualities of the signs themselves, or be led to an intellectual comprehension of their intentions. This is precisely what had happened in symbolist, dadaist, and some surrealist poetry; there was an exploitation of the physical appearance of language, not without some loss to intellectual comprehension. Sartre accepts this trend as definitive of the poetic medium:

". . . the poet has withdrawn from [the] language-instrument in a single movement. Once and for all he has chosen the poetic attitude which considers words as things and not as signs. For the ambiguity of the sign implies that one can penetrate it at will like a pane of glass and pursue the thing signified, or turn his gaze toward its *reality* and consider it as an object.[45]

Whatever one thinks of this acceptance, no one will be led to deny too vigorously the grounds upon which it is based. Logically, of course, there has been an error; species (lyric poetry) and genus (poetry) have been equivocably converted. There were, after all, poets trying to justfy the ways of God to man, so the complete value of all poetry is certainly not purely medial. Alain and Valéry excluded didactic poetry from "pure" poetry precisely because it tells too much of a story.

When we look through the medium of literary works—other than poetry, to grant Sartre his point—we find exactly the same function claimed by the didactic poets: the novelist, essayist, or even journalist, is using words to disclose some truth about the world; if he fails to communicate, he does not thereby become a poet or philosopher, but merely a bad writer, talking but saying nothing. In a word, "The writer is a *speaker;* he designates, demonstrates, orders, refuses, interpolates, begs, insults, persuades, insinuates."[46] All of these actions call forth a reader, if only to be insulted. The writer thus finds himself in a social situation:

The speaker is *in situation* in language; he is invested with words. They are prolongations of his meanings, his pincers, his antennae, his eyeglasses. He maneuvers them from within; he feels them as if they were his body; he is surrounded by a verbal body which he is hardly aware of and which extends his action upon the world.[47]

Behind the mystery of these words one will find an implicit assumption concerning the nature of the ultimate human reality, the onto-

logical transcendence or *pour-soi* (consciousness) in relation to the
en-soi (thing in itself) in which it seeks to become other than itself.
This dialectical relation between consciousness and its "facticity" is
the subject of *L'Etre et le néant*. Sartre does not distinguish mind and
body; the body is merely one way the consciousness lives out its
freedom, using whatever means it has to achieve its ends. Words are
such means. Although Merleau-Ponty's concept of metaphysics differs from that of Sartre, he uses a similar notion of the extension of
the physical person beyond its spatio-temporal limitations when he
speaks of a corporeal schema. This metaphysical difference will be
examined in more detail in a later chapter, when we consider
Merleau-Ponty's phenomenology of perception.[48] The importance of
the distinction is capital for an understanding of the different aesthetic theories. Both men owe a good deal to Alain and Valéry,[49] two
able French aestheticians much concerned with artistic media, and
with a theory of bodily aesthetic creation.

The act of putting words on paper, as conscious or unconscious as
it may be, is only the beginning of the literary creation which is completed in the act of reading. Thus the total creative process involves
three moments: the author's expression, the reader's contemplation,
and the aesthetic object which emerges in the reader's comprehension. Following the phenomenological model of communication, we
have the union of two consciousnesses via a significant, public object,
language. Again, it must be repeated that language is an ambiguous
vehicle: "the literary object, though realized *through* language, is
never given *in* language."[50] The literary object is thus an emergent,
intentional object, arising out of the social process of communication.
But more of this later. Meanwhile, Sartre continues his discussion of
the writer's situation under the threefold division noted above.

Author.—The logical starting point in a commentary on the social
act of literature is with the activity of the author; hence, Sartre begins by asking the question, Why does one write? Two obvious answers are rejected as trivial: some writers seek to escape from the
undesirable conditions of working for a living; others to exercise a
vain will to power.[51] But whatever his motive, the writer's decision
is one of choice. Following the principles of "existential psychoanalysis" Sartre could say that Proust chose to be bourgeois, and the existentialist, to reveal the world. Thus Nietzsche's "man, the creator"
was changed to read "man, the revealer." Here, once again the casual

reader of *Qu'est-ce que la littérature?* faces nothing but bafflement if he refuses to collate texts. The reference is to another section of *L'Etre,* in which Sartre explains the sense in which man is responsible for the world in which he lives.[52] Although motivated by the external situation surrounding him, man must choose to change it, or to go along with the consequences of accepting his situation as it is. In either case choice there must be: one either chooses to change, or chooses not to change the world. Besides showing the close connection between the metaphysical and the ethical aspects of Sartre's thought, the task of personal choice placed upon the writer illustrates quite lucidly in what respect Sartre's system can be correctly called "idealistic"[53]: since most of the objects in the world are cultural, created by man for his own purposes in conformity with preconceived notions, ideas, or essences, only man's existence precedes his essence.[54]

Sartre's stipulation of auto-determination on the part of a writer affords an illustration of the multiple influences on his aesthetic theory. When explaining the nature of communication, and of the aesthetic object, Sartre speaks as a phenomenologist; when talking of the writer's moral responsibility, he slips into his ontological and quasi-ethical language. This is the same confusion of categories noted in the distinction between the aesthetic object qua intentional object and the life of the individual depicted therein. But at least one can say that Sartre is consistent in the confusion: the kind of life depicted in literature is assumed to be of the same kind as lived by authors, the only kind of life possible as a result of the so-called metaphysical structures of man's being.

An author, like his characters, must choose to reveal the world as it is; this is his commitment as professional artist. He expresses his freedom in addressing himself to the freedom of another: ". . . the writer has chosen to reveal the world and particularly to reveal man to other men so that they may assume full responsibility before the object which has been laid bare."[55] Thus, in sharing the writer's situation, the reader is called into a society of communicating "freedoms," which Sartre likens to Kant's concept of the kingdom of ends, the principle of autonomy by which the moral law binds all free agents. And this reference to Kant is not an oblique play on words: the existentialist ethic of never treating another trancendence (person) as if it were a thing is an acceptance of Kant's second formulation of the moral law, according to which a person is always to be treated as an end and never as a means.[56] Within the kingdom of ends, where only free personalities communicate, the aesthetic object called a novel appears. In no sense can the novel be identified with a book (a mere solicitation on the part of the author to produce the work, an invitation to its performance), or with an idea in the author's mind (a purely subjective myth). The condition necessary and sufficient for the appearance of the literary object is therefore the "free cooperation of the reader" in the author's attempt to reveal the nature of the real world.

A new paradox enters the discussion when it is recalled that the aesthetic object is an imaginary construct. But the solution of this paradox has already been outlined in the preceding chapter. In the treatise now under consideration, Sartre merely repeats the observations of the *Psychology of the Imagination* with specific reference to the literary work. In particular, he repeats his denial of I. A. Richards' positivistic "expression" theory that the work is an attempt by an author to evoke feelings for the purpose of organizing, controlling, or merely enjoying them. The last aim above all, associated as it is with an emotive theory of value and romanticism in art (art for art's sake, or for the sake of producing valued feelings), ignores the true character of aesthetic distance: the reversal of the real and ideal characters of the world in aesthetic contemplation. It is to be remembered that an image involves the denial of the relevance of the real world. Thus Raskolnikov's crime is not an act to be purged from Dostoevski's novel because of a blatant violation of a moral law; such moral objection to the novel's content is misguided: ". . . it is not his behavior which excites my indignation or esteem, but my indignation and esteem which give consistency to his behavior."[57] The reader is truly moved; but he is not moved to act. His emotive consciousness is one which posits the non-existence of the novel's situation. And what gives the illusion of reality to the events in the novel is precisely this awakening of the reader's emotive consciousness. Feelings, per se, having nothing to do with the art process; all feelings which are evoked by the author are evoked for the purpose of concretizing the novel's illusion. Thus instead of evoking feelings which are enjoyed for their own sakes, art is said to use the feelings of a reader in making vivid the situation of the author's ideal characterizations. The aesthetic emotion, properly so-called, is the joy accompanying the comprehension of the world itself, proposed in the imagination as "a value, that is, a task proposed to human freedom."[58] It is in this communication of freedoms that both reader and author find commitment to a specific mode of action through the aesthetic object. And it is at this point that critics of Sartre object: what distinguishes the commitment of literature from ordinary propaganda? To answer this query, Sartre refers to the aesthetic properties of the literary work.

The Literary Work.—Time honored, albeit inadequate, is the analysis of the work into its subject matter and form.[59] If we accept the analysis, and at the same time accept the equivalence of technique and form, the description *in abstracto* of the literary work is not difficult. The subject matter of the novel is the life of some individual: "*Praxis* as action in history and on history; that is, as a synthesis of historical relativity and of the moral and metaphysical absolute, with this hostile and friendly, terrible and derisive world which it reveals to us. There is our subject."[60] The protagonist is placed in a specific time and a specific place, and the novel becomes a cultural phenomenon necessitating historical criticism. For example, Americans may find it hard to accept some of the conditions portrayed in a novel of the German occupation, such as Vercor's *Le Silence de la mer;* or the same novel's effectiveness may change with a change in the real world's situation. Thus, Sartre explains, following Pétain's conference with Hitler at Montoire (24 October 1940) in which the German dictator sought the active collaboration of the Vichy government in a proposed war against England, the attitudes of the French readers to Vercor's book would change. The old man of the story, resigned to the political state of affairs and his approaching death, would be the central character of the book before collaboration became the principal aim of the German forces; but when collaboration was dictated, rather than freely chosen, the young girl who resists the appeal of the gallant German occupying officer would become the center of the tragic *récit.* Although the psychological principle he uses seems sound, Sartre forgot that Vercor's book was not written until 1941, one year following the meetings of Laval and Pétain with Hitler. And to indicate that even the attitudes of the French resistants did not significantly change the quality of the novelette, one need only point to its inclusion in the *Editions de Minuit,* the unified collection of the resistance writings published clandestinely in 1944. In his analysis, Sartre was merely repeating the principle that the attitudes of the readers contribute some of their vibrant reality to the subject matter of the book.

The form of a novel must be suited to the subject depicted. "Poetic prose," a hybrid medium in which part of the artistic effect depends upon the "obscure harmonies" of words which may be in contradiction with their clear meanings, is proscribed. We recall the exclusion of poetry itself on much the same basis.[61] As we shall see later, the style of the author is to be regulated by his aim of reader comprehension, and will therefore depend upon his audience, rather than on his own personal taste. Here, a difference from Alain. If we inquire about the concrete form of the novel, about the subject matter of the novel in the manner it is stated—as opposed to the more abstract considerations of style—we shall have a greater insight into the formal properties of the existentialist novel. What follows from the novelist's situation? A point of view: "Since we were *situated,* the only novels we could dream of were novels of *situation,* without internal narrators or all-knowing witnesses."[62] Proscribed therefore were the techniques of the omniscient narrator, all those intrusions of an author which tend to destroy the aesthetic distance of his work; proscribed likewise is the third person, or internal narrator through whose eyes a gullible public is asked to view the work. The first of these techniques is idealistic; the second, dogmatically realistic in metaphysical presupposition.

Having banished the method of analysis used in Newtonian mechanics[63] for the more synthetic notion of "Einsteinian relativity," Sartre asked that the points of view depicted in the novel reflect half-lucid, half-overcast minds; the characters are to interact with others only half understanding each other; and the novel should not have a definite end (so much for Aristotle's beginning and middle): as in life, the completion of an action in a novel should be hazardous; there ought to be a suggestion of a given ending, but no possibility of other developments should be excluded.[64] In this description of the events of a novel, there appears a much clearer picture of the metaphysical structures of the so-called ontological absolute than in *L'Etre et le néant.* But so far, no one has sufficiently collated the two works: the job of a philosophical critic, or of a philosopher not averse to literary criticism.

Sartre himself calls the metaphysical position of existentialist writers "historical relativism"; the books of these men are to exist

by themselves, held together by the network of relations between
characters and their environments:

We hope that our books remain in the air all by themselves and that their
words, instead of pointing backwards toward the one who has designed them
[as Alain assumed to be the case], will be toboggans, forgotten, unnoticed,
and solitary, which will hurl the reader into the midst of a universe where
there are no witnesses; in short that our books may exist in the manner of
things, of plants, of events, and not at first like products of man. We want
to drive providence from our works as we have driven it from our world.
We should, I believe, no longer define beauty by the form nor even by the
matter, but by the density of being.[65]

This dense, living object was to be the existentialist novel. Merleau-
Ponty concurred with this pronouncement in his "Le roman et la métaphysique," where the philosophical novelist's task is explained not as
an abstract dissertation, as some critics read Sartre's La Nausée; but
as an idea put in the form of an "immediate presentation": in an experience of the novel, a philosophical idea comes to exist in the manner of things.[66]

Any critic interested in tracing the relations between philosophical
ideas and the novels in which they are expressed will find valuable
material here. A philosophical idea is not the content of a novel, but
it may dictate a novel's concrete organic form. Any other solution
of the problem of the relation between philosophy and literature will
tend to aggrandize the one at the expense of the other. The work of
literary art, in its integrity, is a concrete form.

Audience.—There remains a final step to trace in the writer's situation, his relationship with a cooperative audience. Anyone is a
member of that audience who is capable of reading the words of the
author in such a way that their meanings fall together into a self-
consistent and whole imaginary construct. The task Sartre proposed
to his followers was to change this "anyone" to include everyone.
We may be brought to understand the logical subtleties of this
change if we divide the literary audience of existentialist literature
into three categories: the actual, the virtual, and the ideal reading
publics. Consider the actual reading public of a novelist in the situation of Richard Wright.

According to Sartre, Wright is thoroughly committed; he writes
not for the universal man who really doesn't exist, being only an
essence; nor for the poor "black peasants" of the South, who can't,

on the whole, read. Rather the actual reading public of Wright's novels is composed of the cultivated Negroes of the North—a judgment borne out by a quick glance around the audience of a Chicago showing of the film version of *Black Boy*—as well as for those white Americans possessing enough good will to allow themselves to be led to an understanding of the Negro's problem of adjusting to a predominantly white society. These whites were thought to be found among intellectuals, "Democrats of the left," radicals, and CIO workers.[67] The mention of the CIO, rather than the AF of L, is significant. The CIO, a union of unskilled workers embracing a whole industry instead of the narrower trade affiliation of skilled workers in the AF of L, would contain members less likely to be prejudiced by the status due the "skilled" qualification, and hence more likely to understand the problem of discrimination. The recent merger of the two American federations of unions, however, takes away much of the point. There is a similar problem of discrimination in the French labor movement.[68]

As the psychological make-up of the literary audience changes, the style of the author's works must be changed if he is to gain an ever wider society of appreciators. In a word, style follows audience sought after. If Richard Wright were writing solely for those educated Negroes of the North, his novels could have been elliptical. Writing as a confederate to his readers, his tone could be elegiac, but since he sought to communicate also with the sympathetic white audience, his novels had to be prolix; and at times, his tone is abusive and his aim didactic. Thus, an author interested in producing understanding must couch his work in terms capable of being understood, since those who do actually understand form the actual reading public of the author concerned.

The virtual reading public of any author, on the other hand, would be the class of all men. Here once again, social and political conditions enter into the aesthetician's considerations, for not all readers are so situated as to be able to understand readily the import of a novel. It is for this reason that style cannot be the end and aim of the man of letters: even when the author refuses to accept the responsibility to commit himself to a given situation, the reader cannot allow himself the same irresponsibility if the appreciation of literature is to have a function in his life. If the style does not follow the audience, it is not unlikely that the audience will not follow the style.

Moreover, since all men do not enjoy the same social and political situation, the conditions necessary for obtaining the virtual public of all men may never be realizable in the life span of any given society. There must therefore be the acceptance of some workable idealization of the class of virtual appreciators. Sartre finds in the Marxist ideal of a classless society the fitting solution to his problem: if the virtual public is hopelessly divided into varying social and political classifications, then an author, to be understood by the greatest number of individuals, must address himself to the whole of man as unclassed. Moreover in so doing, he may help to bring about the communist ideal of the classless society. Note that there is no talk of propaganda here; the process is a strictly literary affair. But when the literary process is described in such a way as to include the cooperative audience, and the desire is to extend this audience to include as many men as possible, the only practical solution to the problem of committing literature to a social function is to "unclass" literature, and hence society.

This unclassed literature Sartre has called *littérature totale:* "The fact is that only in a socialist collectivity would literature, having finally understood its essence and having made the synthesis of *praxis* and *exis,* of negativity and construction, of doing, having and being, deserve the name of *total literature.*"[69] Total literature, thus described in Sartre's metaphysical terms, serves to integrate the artist with his audience and the audience with the total society; it becomes authentic in that the writer has become aware that there is no distinction between his subject and his public: man-in-the-world. Gone are the days of the bourgeois writer with his genius for analysis and the consequent separation of his genius from the audience with which it would communicate:

. . . as long as the virtual public remained like a dark sea around the sunny little beach of the real public, the writer risked confusing the interests and cares of man with those of a small and favored group. But, if the public were identified with the concrete universal the writer would really have to write about the human totality.[70]

Thus, instead of defining bourgeois literature as that which has for subject matter some aspect of bourgeois life and values, Sartre defined it as an aberration of artistic communication producing a false separation of author and audience by virtue of a series of false assumptions: that a group is only a sum of its members; and that literature, to be committed to a social function, must be propaganda, or aesthetically inadequate. That much committed literature has been aesthetically "impure," giving something less than a concrete significant form, is incontestable; but that it must be so is nothing more than an aesthetic, or a political *parti pris.*

Having tried in this way to clear the theoretical ground for an aesthetically sound and committed literature, Sartre considers some practical problems facing the author committed to a given metaphysics as well as to his social situation. And a great deal of light may be thrown upon Sartre's rejection by his bourgeois contemporaries, if we take into account the unifying thread of this double commitment. In fact, the existentialist author is only apparently faced with a double responsibility. A man-in-the-world addressing himself to others similarly situated, the author has a social commitment and his metaphysics is an attempt to explain the conditions of that commitment. It is for this reason that Sartre is not easily understood by his contemporary scholastic and communist critics: phenomenology can be traced to scholastic thought,[71] so there is at least that common ground between Sartre and his Catholic critics; and existentialism has in common with the Marxist's ideology its interest in a classless society. Only on metaphysical grounds can there be a difference of opinion: an atheist and an existentialist, Sartre seems to his theistic and essentialist adversaries a hopelessly confused aesthetician;[72] claiming to be neither idealist nor materialist, he has been called "unrealistic" by the materialistic Marxists.[73]

If a set of metaphysical presuppositions is all that separates the three outstanding non-academic philosophies of France today, Sartre would claim that the simpler set of assumptions made by existentialist thinkers to explain the commitment of the literary artist is a mark of its superiority over the scholastic and Marxistic theories, according to which the commitment of an artist is dual: if a Catholic or a Marxist takes seriously his metaphysics, and tries to embody it in his artistic work, he can only produce a work of propaganda. We have all read literature giving us nothing more than a sermon of one sort or another. To avoid sermonizing, to avoid producing a *roman à thèse,* the existentialist author adopts the following purpose: ". . . to create a literature which unites and reconciles the metaphysical absolute and the relativity of the historical fact, and which I shall call for want of a better name, the literature of great circumstances."[74]

A final consideration of the writer's audience concerns the manner in which the existentialist author would expand his actual audience to include more and more of his ideal audience in his attempt to attain the virtual audience. In 1947, when the work under consideration was written, the actual audience of existentialists were the intellectuals; it is still a moot question whether existentialism has become academically respectable in France, not to mention elsewhere. Those groups from the virtual audience most amenable to inclusion in the actual were thought to be teachers, the petty bourgeoisie (small business operators, shop owners, government functionaries), and the nearly indifferent non-communist factions of French political life. If works of fine literature are lost to these groups, the existentialist must adopt other means of communication for his social purpose: the radio, the cinema, and newspaper and periodicals publishing editorials and political reportage afford other avenues of development. If the writer's profession is not limited to the aesthetically pure, neither is it to be restricted to hack journalism: a novel can have all the merits of purity and function, and not all journalism need be hack. At this stage, Sartre is arguing for a complete social consciousness on the part of the individual who lives by his pen. And when the conditions of society have become such as to provide the leisure of reflective activity to the entire classless society, in part through the efforts of writers themselves, more people will have more time for consumption of the aesthetically pure. This is the hope and the task of the existentialist, committed, man of letters.

The final portion of *Qu'est-ce que la littérature?* is dedicated to an analysis of French letters from the point of view of their consumption by some kind of public. In short, his analysis is as follows: from the twelfth to the sixteenth century the profession of writing was limited to clerics writing for other clerics (a tradition maintained in contemporary academies); in the sixteenth and the seventeenth centuries, it was pre-empted by the aristocratic intelligentsia, and situated primarily around the salon. But with the rise of the bourgeois class in the eighteenth century, various philosophical points of view, all committed to the technique of analysis, were expressed in literature; Sartre mentions in this respect idealism, psychologism, determinism, utilitarianism, and seriousness, that is, the assumption that one's existence is necessary. In the nineteenth century there was a brief reaction in the form of romanticism, based upon an "independent" ideology which extrolled the virtues of the individual as a center of feeling; Sartre felt that the romantics' appeal to human feeling had at least the virtue of universal reference. The situation of the writer in 1947 was thought to have grown out of these evolving points of view, according to each of which the writer took some kind of stand in relation to his public.

Sartre's evaluation of French literature immediately preceding World War II is reserved for later consideration. That is a problem of criticism, and not, essentially, of the creative process.

V

Existentialist Criticism

In order to participate in the literary process the critic has a clearly definable role: his is the task of producing understanding; obviously if he is to produce the understanding, he must first himself have understood. The critic is therefore one member of the author's audience who may function to widen the literary artist's actual audience to include as many as possible of the virtual audience. Thus it follows that the critic's is a double role of cooperation: first, to have per-formed the work; and second, to help others do the same. If everyone were an existentialist, convinced that literature is a process of communication, and not an empty expression, the whole would have been said for the art of criticism. Unfortunately, however, these two conditions do not obtain. Sartre's judgment is that while many French critics are convinced that they should be concerned with aesthetic values, they know little about aesthetic theory; others dedicate themselves to the consecration of literature as part of the French national and public domain; still others think they have explained everything in classifying the works of various authors according to historical influence, philosophical presupposition, or literary school. The result is what Sartre has termed a "crisis in the art of criticism."

This crisis forms the subject matter of Sartre's introduction to the second issue of *Les Temps Modernes:* "La nationalisation da la littérature," later published as the second part of *Situations II.* In that article Sartre deplores the French critics' search for great men, behind which he sees two rather misguided assumptions: that the great man is the literary genius, who by virtue of his gift for language lives off the top of society rather than serving it in the way proper to his profession; and that the works of genius become a tribute to the national culture, a public benefit which may vie with French wine and perfumes on the international commercial market. Both of these assumptions have produced aesthetic aberrations in the past: the cult of genius has served the ends of the bourgeoisie, and the consecration of the national literary product has led to the battle of culture which brought "cultivated" Frenchmen to accept the exclusion of art works deriving from other national cultures. The stand taken by Romain Rolland during the first world war against French provincialism indicates that other writers have been aware of the problem Sartre is attacking in the second of these points;[1] his own analysis of Proust's work has served to focus attention upon the first.[2]

To be fairer than Sartre to the journeymen French critics, one might indicate the aesthetic basis of their search for great men, and let others judge its value. It is not inappropriate to point out that critics have always sought out the great man because style is of the man, and style gives form to expression. The identification of style with form and form with aesthetic value is not without some recommendation, as Alain's aesthetic theory testifies. Thus when Vendôme puts a series of questions to Sartre's literary manifesto,[3] thinking thereby to criticize it, he seems merely to repeat the list of great men: Montaigne, Balzac, Stendhal, Flaubert, Proust; actually, he is making the implicit assumption that genius can be known only through its works, and that the works of this list of great authors speak for themselves, if their readers are capable of listening to the "voices of silence." Some time may be spent on Vendôme's position since it throws considerable light on Sartre's critical theory.

Applying Sartre's ideal of committed literature to the history of French letters, he could find only four writers of a national literary stature who had deigned to commit themselves to a social function; Sartre had mentioned each: Pascal in the Jansenist controversy (*Les Lettres provinçiales* went a long way toward fixing the classical style of French prose.); Voltaire in the trial of the Huguenot, Jean Calas, executed on the charge of complicity in the death of his son who had been converted to Catholicism (see *Traité sur la tolérance*, 1763); Emile Zola in the Dreyfus Affair (*J'accuse!*); and André Gide in his declarations against French colonialism in the Congo (*Voyage au Congo*).

Vendôme asks whether a critical canon such as Sartre's commitment, which produces a favorable judgment on so few authors of known and venerated genius, can be an acceptable critical tool. The answer to this question is simple: commitment is not a critical canon, and the value of the literature qua literature is not to be judged in reference to the degree of commitment of the author. The judgment of an author according to his commitment is a moral judgment on the profession of writing. Whence, in a free or democratic society the profession of writing as an institution of the society in which it is practiced is properly made only by the writers themselves. Sartre's approval of Pascal, Voltaire, Zola, and Gide is therefore an approval of their moral stand, and not of their literary value. The question of literary value will concern us later. Here it suffices to state that Vendôme forgot to take into account the import of the sequence of articles in *Situations II:* the statement of a need for an examination of the writer's conscience in the "Présentation," the appeal for comprehension on the part of critics in "Nationalisation de la littérature," and the existentialist literary manifesto in *Qu'est-ce que la littérature?*

A second serious misinterpretation of Sartre's critical views occurs in Vendôme's statement that commitment, as a literary canon, would exclude all literature of the past from approval as "great literature." Here again, the basic misunderstanding is of commitment as an aesthetic, rather than a moral canon of judgment. But there is more: the misunderstanding of the function of history in the literary process. The literature of the past is, precisely, of the past: the critic cannot commit the author who no longer writes, whether because of death, emigration, or "political suicide" (on the part of those authors who continued to write during the occupation and thus became collaborationist). The last of these categories of non-functioning authors committed themselves, but to the wrong social order; in some circumstances the right thinking consciousness must not write at all.[4] In each case the writer's commitment is a matter of personal choice. If no one can change the objective character of the past, no one can foresee with certainty the color of the political future.

The past and future, modes of escape for the writer, are intellectual props for the critic:

We will try in vain to become our own historians: the historian himself is an historical creature. We must be content to *make* our history blindly, from day to day, by choosing from all the possible moves the one which seems the best in the present; but we shall never be able to take on that history those cavalier views which made the fortunes of Taine and Michelet: we are within [the process].[5]

As with the writer, so with the critic:

To read, for a contemporary of the author, rolled up within the same historical subjectivity, is to participate in the risks of the enterprise. The book is new, unknown, without importance: one must enter into the situation without a guide. Perhaps we shall thus let pass the rarest of qualities without seeing them; or, on the other hand, a superficial brilliance may lead us into error.[6]

To judge the value of a contemporary work, therefore, the critic must guess, take a chance, bet—unless he claims the ability to disengage himself from his historical situation. But an angelic viewpoint is possible only to the angels; the critic, such as Vendôme, can disengage himself only in retrospect, and then only upon the proviso that his vision be armed with the proper method. For how do we know that our judgments of the value of literary works of the past are sound? By intuition? So much Bergsonian mystification,[7] an affectation of the guardians of the portals.[8] Although his attitude here is clear, Sartre himself comes close to the same mystification in his study of Genet: "a technical invention and a work of art have a positive content which remains irreducible [in historical analysis]; when you will have explained Racine by his epoch, his milieu, his childhood, there will remain the *inexplicable Phèdre*."[9] [Emphasis added.] Whether a given work is explicable or not, the least assertion being made here is that Taine's positivistic method, modern historicism, fails to explain the unique quality of an author's expression.

Yet the question of "aesthetic" versus "historical" criticism is not clarified by maintaining the dichotomy of the two points of view. If a writer is situated in a certain time and place, under given social and political conditions, a certain historical knowledge is necessary to understand the structure of the work reflecting that situation. And if the job of the critic is to produce understanding, it is hardly possible for him to be ignorant of the social background which enters into a novel's imaginary structure. Here is precisely the point: only those historical data are relevant to the explanation of a work of art that enter into the structure of the imaginary object; the rest is historical pedantry. Aesthetic analysis begins where the historical research leaves off; it traces the internal development of the work of art. The judgment of aesthetic value follows upon the understanding of the concrete form of the structured aesthetic object. Vendôme would replace this conscious judgment by a feeling of the work's import, and we are thus led back to the discussion of "the aesthetic emotion."

As is usual when a critic of opposing ideology goes to work on the efforts of his adversary (Vendôme, who writes in the Jesuit-founded *Etudes,* berates Sartre for his "ill-conceived atheism"), the rebuttal of the criticism may be found in the work being criticized, if it is read with a bit more sympathy. If the aesthetician would seek to avoid Vendôme's mysticism, he must look into the grounds for aesthetic value judgments. The study of existentialist literature thus brings us to a consideration of means and ends, and the relation of the literary work as an end in itself to the experience of aesthetic enjoyment. Our source: *Qu'est-ce que la littérature?*

The difference between the propagandist and the man of letters is perhaps only in attitude toward the completed literary work, in the value they attribute to their literary efforts. Is the work nothing but a means to some further end? the propagation of an idea, philosophical, economic, social, or political? If so, the author never escapes his propagandist guise, even if his work shows all the stylistic excellence of a literary masterpiece. How philosophical ideas enter into the formal structure of the work of art has already been shown, and the structures of the imagination which allow an author to project real social and political conditions into an imaginary framework have been described. In a word, I have attempted to show how ideas *are* the work, and not intended by the work, when the work achieves its "density of being." Those who read the plays and novels of the existentialists and find nothing but propaganda, a philosophical proof, or sermon, merely give evidence of not yet having learned to read. Vendôme cites *La Nausée* as if it were a bare philosophical treatise.

But Catholics are not the only ones who hold a fixed position and see the evil hand of the propagandist in works of art structured from a different point of view; Marxists, too, find propaganda when they read because they make propaganda when they write:

. . . the CP today has entered the infernal circle of means. It must take and keep key positions, that is, means of acquiring means. When ends withdraw, when means are swarming like gnats as far as the eye can see, the work of art in turn becomes a means. It enters the chain. *It is governed from the outside.* It takes man by the belly or the short hairs. The writer maintains the appearance of talent, that is, the art of finding words which gleam, but something is dead within. Literature has changed into propaganda.[10]

And in answer to the Communists' charge of being a "gravedigger," Sartre could very honestly reply that he would rather be a gravedigger than a lackey. When literature is forced to serve an ideological end it loses its autonomy.

Two points are being made here: Sartre's early disagreement with the French Communist Party is cited to foreshadow the later developments in his idea of commitment, as well as to indicate the supreme value in the existentialist hierarchy of values: freedom. And on this point Sartre will continue to be misunderstood until his critics take the time to read *L'Etre et le néant.* Each personality is a transcendence whose fundamental structures include the power of imagining the universe other than as it is, and although each is necessarily defined by reference to a human situation which it is capable of transcending, the human person is therein described as absolutely free, even when the body is cast into chains.[11] Being in the world is a condition of this absolute freedom: there is no transcendence without a situation, its facticity, to transcend. Nor should it be supposed that Sartre is talking of a relative absolute, which is a blatant contradiction in terms. The person is free because he is situated, and not in spite of his situation. In terms of a specific action, a man is free only to achieve his real possibilities, and not merely to imagine abstract or logical possibilities.[12] Thus the freedom which has all the appearances of relativity can be called absolute because it is a property of the concrete human reality in its totality, and not of an abstracted mental faculty, or will. The work of art, mediating two human consciousnesses, is not a tool; it is an end in itself because the communion of consciousnesses is a good in itself. Hence Sartre could say, in agreement with Kant, that the work of art does not have an end; "But the reason is that it is an end."[13]

Continued comparison with Kant's aesthetics may aid comprehension. In the *Critique of Judgment,* Kant explains the relational judgment of taste, based upon the purposes called into play within the act of judgment, as the contemplation of an object having a purposiveness (*Zweckmässigkeit*) but no external purpose (*Zweck*): the object has no end, either as an object of knowledge or an act of the will, although it has the form of an end, which may be cognized by the feeling of harmony which the contemplation of this object may produce in our cognitive faculties. In our own words, we could say, with many of the didactic critics, that the aesthetic object might be considered an object of knowledge; or, with many of the moral critics, that it might be considered the object of a moral judgment. That the aesthetic object may be so easily misinterpreted as a theoretical or moral object merely points out the need for caution in our purely aesthetic judgments. As with history, the only relevant bits of conceptual knowledge or moral evaluations are those which enter into an artwork's structure. And it is the perception of this structure which occasions "aesthetic pleasure." Yet Sartre seems unwilling to admit the validity of Kant's concept of purpose, or rather, purposiveness without purpose (*Zweckmässigkeit ohne Zweck,* which is translated into French as *finalité sans fin*). His question arises from the fact that the finality of the aesthetic object is in actuality only the appearance of finality in Kant's scheme of things: the beautiful object solicits the free and ordered play of the imagination, which is both regulative and constitutive of the aesthetic experience, but is judged as beautiful only by virtue of the pleasure felt when the imagination and the understanding are harmonized.

The difference between Sartre and Kant on the aesthetic object is precisely the manner in which each treats "the free and ordered play of the imagination," within which the object is said to appear. For Kant, the object does not refer beyond itself; it is self-contained. Whence his formalism, not unakin to that of Alain. Its principal value is thought to be the "disinterested" pleasure taken in contemplation of the object (judgment of quality), although Kant does maintain that the beautiful may be "symbolic" of morality (see *Kritik der Urteilskraft,* Sec. 59). For Sartre, on the other hand, who is quite willing to grant that the imagination is regulative and constitutive of the aesthetic object if the imagination is interpreted phenomenologically,[14] the value of the object is not to be associated with the pleasure evoked by its contemplation. In fact, when imagination is conceived as the "absentification of the present or the presentification of the absent,"[15] as Sartre does conceive it, the value of the imagined object becomes the revelation of the world as it is:

Each painting, each book, is a recovery of the totality of being. Each of them presents this totality to the freedom of the spectator. For this is quite the final goal of art: to recover this world by giving it to be seen as it is, but as if it had its source in human freedom.[16]

For all attentive readers of both *L'Imaginaire* and the *Kritik der Urteilskraft,* the semantic equivalence of "having its source in human freedom" and "the imagination's being regulative and constitutive of the aesthetic object" will be apparent.

The pleasure which Kant assumes to be constitutive of aesthetic value—and he is followed by Vendôme—is, in Sartre's eyes, a formal characteristic of the aesthetic experience. We may recall here his treatment of aesthetic joy (the so-called aesthetic pleasure). Far from denying its existence, as Vendôme charges, Sartre treats it as one of the necessary conditions of a work's achievement. The aesthetic emotion (as distinguished from feelings which may be embodied within an artwork's structure) is an intentional act; as such it is a manner of apprehending the work of art, be it literary or otherwise, as a "transcendent absolute end which, for a moment, suspends the utilitarian round of ends-means and means-ends."[17] The work itself is an appeal from consciousness to consciousness; and the aesthetic experience, as a total process, is a communion of disparate consciousnesses. The work is a value, or in Sartre's terms, the fulfillment of an experienced lack.

Only the phenomenology of this aspect of aesthetic experience remains to be explained. Repeating the principle he had proclaimed in an earlier work, Sartre distinguishes between kinds of awareness. When I am occupied with the perception of the work itself as completed in my own act of the imagination, I am aware positionally of the value of the object (the world as disclosed), and non-positionally of my own freedom.[18] "Positionally" and "non-positionally" here refer to the act of positing the existence of the object in question. As in each act of the consciousness, I am positionally aware of a transcendent object; and by the pre-reflective *cogito,* I am aware non-positionally of my own act of awareness. Here once again, the ontology of *L'Etre* reinforces the phenomenology of *L'Imaginaire.*

But in spite of the contentions of "romantic" artists and critics, the value of the object is not necessarily the emotion that object may call out. As pointed out above, my feelings may go toward constructing the imaginary object, but these feelings are not to be confused with "the aesthetic emotion." Nevertheless, the emotion we call aesthetic enjoyment likewise has its phenomenological explanation.

If, in contemplation of the literary work, I become aware of my own enjoyment (and many are those who read for their personal titillation), I am positionally aware of my own enjoyment, and only non-positionally aware of the object as a value.[19] Figure and ground are easily reversible, and it is this reversibility in perception of the form of an object and the tone of our perceiving faculties themselves, which allowed Kant to speak of a felt purposiveness as opposed to a purpose of an object which is perceived either subjectively as a personal interest or objectively as a telic construct. This is what is meant by those authors who describe an aesthetic object as autotelic. If a work of art embodies its own purpose, it cannot be said, essentially, to contain an external purpose.

In sum, the critic's job is to participate in the literary process, which is basically a communication between consciousnesses. Efforts on the part of critics to assume the task of intuiting value are either aesthetically or psychologically or methodologically unsound. The value of the literary work is to disclose being in some aspect of its totality; and the critic has fulfilled his function when he has analyzed the texture and the structure of the work under consideration in such a way as to disclose the manner in which it reveals the inner structure of the world, society or consciousness. All efforts to classify a literary work according to one or another of its properties will miss the essence of the work itself, the imaginary object with its own "density of being." Whatever its subject matter, within or without some party's line, the concrete work of art can be judged on aesthetic grounds, just as the author's act of writing may be judged on grounds primarily moral. If these considerations are kept in mind, no one need continue to interpret committed literature as propaganda.

The most natural corollary to a discussion of literary criticism is the problem of censorship. Public censorship is the result of a moral evaluation of works of art, which has as its end the control of the behavior of members of the society in whose name the work is judged unfit for publication: Plato banished the poets from his ideal Republic because of the unruly passions they were thought to foment amongst the citizens. But Plato was a philosopher, and his judgment of the poets was not without some reference to the metaphysics of aesthetic experience. "Poet" means maker, but poets could at best make only a second degree copy of "real" things since real objects in Plato's sense are conceived, and never made at all. Thus besides fomenting passions which could only be detrimental to the well-being of the Platonic state, poets were inveterate liars at worst, and at best slavish contemplators of shadows flickering by on the walls of a cave. Plato's interpretation of the whole non-philosophic world is comparable to a modern phenomenon, that of a gullible American movie-going public who take the events of their films as an escape from the problems of day-to-day living. Whatever its merits, Plato's case against the freedom of expression of the artist is instructive: the aesthetics of imitation demands realism of its artists who, when too realistic or imitative of non-desirable persons, things, or events, are condemned in the name of a metaphysical or moral commitment.

Sartre, on the contrary, has been trying to form a philosophy in which aesthetic, metaphysical, and moral judgments are not necessarily contradictory. In fact, when Sartre's phenomenological ontology replaces Plato's transcendental idealism, poets become liberated from the latter's moral condemnation on the very same metaphysical considerations which brought about the proposed censorship. If the artist is dealing only with an analogue of the aesthetic object, which is unreal, there is no longer any ground for the charge of fomenting the passions of the peasants. The attitude of aesthetic contemplation precludes the activity which is thought detrimental to social well-being. Lost in the contemplation of a beautiful woman, no one can put into action the fulfillment of his desire: the beautiful woman qua beautiful is untouchable; the person in flesh and blood, who can become the object of desire, is merely the physical analogue of the ideal contemplated. Thus Sartre's distinction between artifact and aesthetic object clears the air of much of the absurdity in the discussions of obscenity in the art of painting. A nude in a painting, no matter how much she may be "non-idealized," or may resemble a real prostitute, is not a nude in the flesh and, for those who realize this, cannot become the object of sexual desire: "It is in effect impossible for us to place ourselves simultaneously in the aesthetic attitude in which there appears that unreal person-itself which we admire and in the realistic attitude of physical possession."[20] In the above quotation, Sartre was referring to a real woman contemplated as beautiful; how much more so, then, for the painted nude, the copy of the copy of the ideal of beauty. Aesthetic contemplation, all action, has nothing in common with the physical passions of an un-

informed audience. So much, in general, for Sartre's attitude toward
the moral evaluation of art objects. In his eyes, informed aesthetic
judgment clarifies the problem of censorship. And it is true that in
most discussions of the problem of censorship of arts the case for the
artist has been poorly argued.

Much subtlety has been expended, for example, on the discussion
of obscenity. A contemporary American aesthetician, Abraham Kaplan of the University of California at Los Angeles, has tried a classification of the forms obscenity may take in art, in an attempt to describe the obscene as as aesthetic category.[21] We choose not to follow
Kaplan on the grounds that aesthetics is not a classificatory science
and that his description of the alleged aesthetic category gives little
basis for a judgment of the morality of "obscene" art. The problem
is to balance the claim of the artist for freedom of expression against
the claim of society that his expression must not produce undesirable social effects. Both of these claims are moral; but, for the case of
the artist to be understood, some knowledge of the facts of aesthetic
experience is requisite.

The artist, arguing for his freedom as a member of a political
body, demands to be judged as artist; society all too often judges
him by the contingent side-effects of his artistic work, as if he were
never anything but a crude propagandist. The artist would be judged
as a member of a profession playing in the total social structure a
role which may become institutionalized without losing its integrity,
whereas society tends to condemn the individual artist for the shortcomings of his audience. Moreover, if the judgment of "obscenity" is
detrimental to the freedom of the artist on the grounds stipulated, the
problem becomes a relatively simple matter to adjudicate. Audiences
change; what is unfit for a child may be fitting for an adult. To limit
the expression in any given society to what is fitting only for children
or mental deficients is to bring the level of the whole society down to
adolescence or imbecility. And there are institutions of society, besides the legal, which may better serve the role of censoring "undesirable" materials, institutions such as the family or the school. Thus,
on the basis of audience judgment, the case seems clearly in favor
of the artist's freedom. On the other hand, what about the expression
of the artist whose work, in itself, is as perverted as the artist's own
personality? What about the literary works of a Marquis de Sade?

of a Jean Genet? Existentialist authors have already assumed their
defense: Simone de Beauvoir for Sade, in "Faut-il bruler Sade?",[22]
and Sartre for Genet, in his *Saint Genet comédien et martyr*.

For society to judge a work of art obscene, there must be in evidence a conflict of values between those of the society whose existence is threatened and another, divergent, system of values espoused
by the author of the obscenity. Perversion is obscene to a society of
"normal" heterosexuals; extreme cruelty is obscene to a society of
"charitable" Christians. Any value may be perverted, and hence any
deviation from the accepted standards of value may produce a different variety of obscenity. The obscenity of Sade and Genet is
principally sexual, but our discussion is not limited in relevance to
sexual morality. Sade and Genet are selected as illustrative of the
moral judgment on literary creations within a society which is
nominally "free," whence the title of Mme de Beauvoir's essay,
"Must we burn Sade?" Must we burn the literary work of a perverted
author whose name has become the symbol of cruelty, a new word in
the vocabulary of the society which has always condemned his way
of life? A question very easy to answer in a fascist community; not so
easy in one dedicated to the free development of its member's po-
tentialities. The answer to Beauvoir's question quite naturally depends upon the nature of the society which stands to gain or lose by
the suppression of the individual's freedom, as upon the very nature
of the individual himself.

The first consideration is the point of view of the individual. From
the existentialist position, the individual is not once and for all a
this or a that, be it a pervert or a prostitute. Each individual is a
transcendence who chooses to become this or that from moment to
moment in the course of a life full of contingent circumstances. A
pervert may become an author, and an author may become a pervert;
the case at hand would certainly not be solved by considering the
individual as one or the other independently of the second. Beauvoir's purpose was therefore to delineate the possible effects certain
choices of a given individual may have for certain other choices of
the same individual; whence her evaluation of Sade's writings as of
an author-pervert.[23]

As she recounts them, Sade's erotic eccentricities became his way
of life, and his way of life became his ethics which was given imaginary expression in his literary creations. Thus, however perverted his

personal life, ". . . he helps us define the human drama in its generality."[24] Even the perverted author discloses being. Moreover, if one consider the imagined excesses of this prince of excess, one will not find many vices which are completely original: treatises of psychiatry are full of cases at least as strange as his.[25] On the other hand, if we compare the moral tone and the philosophical "content" of Sade's work with that of other authors, we find his ideas consistent with those of later thinkers and deducible from a general philosophical climate, that of his own time. Ethically, Sade's works foreshadow the appearance of those of Nietzsche, Stirner, and Freud; literarily, those based upon Freudian psychoanalytic theory, surrealism being a case in point. As for his own time, he did nothing more than to adapt the atheism of the Baron d'Holbach, according to whom moral problems are social problems and do not affect the individual in his individuality. When the individual is left to his own devices, he quite often takes up hedonism, and in Sade's case hedonism became excessive.

Sade, the sensualist, became too limited by the confines of the real world. One sexual partner did not suffice, nor did one mode of sexual intercourse; he multiplied the former as much as the latter, and was jailed for his Dionysiac excesses. From the confines of his prison cell he could express astonishment that he should have been condemned for having reached sexual climax by whipping a "miserable prostitute." After all, a prostitute is already a social outcast, and in Sade's estimation deprived of her rights as a member of the society which was condemning his activity. He had an intimation of the bad faith of society described by Sartre in *L'Etre et le néant*.[26] But he failed to realize that he, too, was immoral in denying the transcendence of the girl he whipped; he had treated her as an object. Cut off from the real expression of his tastes, he turned to their imaginary experience; he became an author. As Beauvoir puts it,

In choosing eroticism, Sade chose the imaginary. He could succeed in inserting himself with certainty only in an imaginary realm without risking deception. He repeated it throughout his work: "The rapture of the senses is always regulated by the imagination." "Man can pretend to happiness only by giving in to all the caprices of his imagination."[27]

So much for the intimate connection of Sade the pervert, with Sade the author. But the question remains as to the value of the imaginary expression of the perverted author's experiences.

Beauvoir concludes her appreciation of Sade's literary efforts by proclaiming him a true moralist in the great tradition. Enemy of the bourgeois virtues of chastity and moderation, Sade illustrates the value of free choice, even when that choice is of evil: "Sade's merit lies not only in having proclaimed aloud what everyone admits with shame to himself, but in the fact that he did not simply resign himself. He chose cruelty rather than indifference."[28] For us, the readers of Sade's works, there is the value described above: the disclosure of being. Reading Sade's work is an invitation to thought, not to action: "The supreme value of his testimony is that it disturbs us. It forces us to re-examine thoroughly the basic problem which haunts our age in different forms: the true relation between man and man."[29] The bourgeois society, confirmed in the efficacy of its own value system, will always condemn the deviate, even when the deviate might conceivably improve that society. This has been the case against Sade, as it had been against many another reformer of social values: Socrates, Jesus of Nazareth, and even Karl Marx. Social deviation, as such, is never condemnable in principle. If it were, the possibility of social change would likewise be condemned in principle.

The close interplay between the social body and the individual member is thoroughly handled, and with as much good taste as is possible for the subject, in Sartre's study of Jean Genet, the foundling living on public charity, ignorant of his parentage, who became in turn thief, vagabond, pervert, informer, jailbird, poet, dramatist, and finally "respected" bourgeois man of letters. Where Beauvoir's interest was primarily in the individual, Sartre's is placed more explicitly in the interaction of the individual with his society; we are thus led to the second point of view to be taken on censorship.

Genet's case is so many-splendored, so full of the existentialist struggle with a wayward destiny, that it challenges all the dialectical skill of a thinker such as Sartre. Let us make no mistake here: Genet lived the experiences which gained his unsavory reputation, and he wrote about them with complete candor. Some of them were so repulsive that Sartre refuses to mention or comment upon them.[30] And Sartre himself is no prude. While Genet's work as a whole is given the value of liberating its audience through horror, parts of it evidently defy comment. They are written in gutter French, or if you prefer, with all the expressiveness of the vulgar, slang idiom possible only to the person who has lived in the most vulgar of societies, or even outside of them. Sartre analyzes the linguistic texture of the works which Genet claimed to have excreted, the structure of their situations, and the concrete whole as an act of an author who was banished from polite society by his habits, who sought salvation in evil, and who, ironically enough, actually achieved the redemption of readmission to French society through his literary efforts. An outline of Sartre's treatment of this antisocial author is included here because it is one of the most thorough attempts ever made at literary criticism.

If Sartre's conclusion sounds more like psychoanalysis than literary criticism, we need only keep in mind his assumption that literature is action producing social consequences, and that literary communication begins with a complex gesture on the part of the author inviting an audience to consider the nature of the universe. He had already presented a study of the poetry of Baudelaire (*Les Fleurs du mal*) based upon the principles of "existential psychoanalysis";[31] in *Genet* he gives his aim retrospectively in a complex statement which will be analyzed here into its constituent parts.

Sartre states that the study was composed ". . . to show the limits of psychoanalytic [Freudian] interpretation and of Marxist explanation, and to show that only [an analysis of] freedom can give an account of a person in his totality. . . ." Both Freud and Marx, being determinists of one sort or another, could give only a partial account of Genet's early life; Sartre relates the events of Genet's experience to encounters with being and nothingness. In the long introduction (578 pages, not 800 as Luethy claims[32]) to Genet's "dungheap," we are presented with a consciousness, its relations with things, and its hostile social environment.

". . . to show that freedom struggling with its destiny, at first crushed by fatalities, then turning back upon them in order to digest them little by little. . . ." Genet became a poet at the taunts of fellow prisoners, became a prose writer with the realization of his poetic deficiencies.

". . . to prove that genius is not a gift, but the way out one invents in cases of desperation. . . ." We have seen the bourgeois use of the concept "genius," which may take from the author the responsibility for his work, as Plato's Ion found, by Socrates' questioning, that he was inspired by Homer, who in turn was inspired by the muse.

". . . to find the choice a writer makes of himself, and of his life, and of the meaning he attributes to the universe by referring to the formal character of his style and composition, the structure of his images, and the particularities of his tastes. . . ." Form and content, the concrete aesthetic object, offer a clue to the writer's personality, expressed for all to see in the way in which only imaginary objects are given to be seen. Through the imagination, the author liberates himself from the control of his passions; the reader may do likewise.

". . . To retrace in detail the history of a liberation: that's what I wanted to do; the reader will judge whether I have succeeded."[33] With such a complex purpose, there can be no wonder at the study's length. Mr. Luethy, who could find no copy of *L'Etre*, found *Genet* boring, so multiplied the number of pages in his report on it. If he had been able to find a copy of Sartre's metaphysical treatise, the ideas he found unintelligible in *Genet* might have been understood, and his report more accurate. No further comment upon each of the aims is necessary, as our discussion of the study is limited to parts of it relevant to the present topic: censorship.

The very title of the study, *Saint Genet comédien et martyr,* indicates society's complicity in Genet's case: the homosexual-vagabond-poet attains his sanctity, martyred by the community of "normal" people who have assigned him his role. Excluded from the approval of the just (self-)righteous, pillars of society, Genet chose evil, as had Sade, and to be sure that all society, even the unjust, would exclude him, he committed the only crime possible in the society of outlaws—he betrayed an accomplice. At all times he chose to be an incarnation of the Other. The irony of Sartre's title epitomizes the paradox of Genet's final acceptance by the society he repudiated, himself having been repudiated by it. We shall try to follow this paradox in an attempt to understand the irony.

Like Sade, so Genet: once imprisoned, the only way the individual had to express his will to evil was the channel of the imagination. What he wrote is called by Sartre "les belles lettres considérées comme un assassinat."[34] The connecting link between the aesthetic attitude and the outlaw's malevolence is precisely in the will to destroy reality:

Since the synthesis of the Non-being of Being and the Being of Non-being is appearance, and since appearance is a manifestation to the wicked person of his terrifying freedom, what would happen if Genet, by an extraordinary effort, transformed his acts into gestures, his being into imaginary experience, the world into phantasmagoria, even himself into a mere appearance? What if he substituted for the impossible destruction of the universe the destruction of its reality? What if this young man would transform himself—like Divine [one of his characters]—into an imaginary woman? And what if, by this play-acting, he would bring everything—trees, plants, tools, animals, women and men into a reality-destroying maelstrom? We shall learn later on that this mad attempt to replace the entire world by an appearance of a world is called "aesthetic" and that the aesthete is a wicked person. Genet was an aesthete for ten years of his life, and beauty was, at first, nothing more to him than a hateful dream of universal conflagration.[35]

Note that Sartre here is not identifying the aesthetic life with the evil life, but merely pointing out that the two modes of living have a common basic metaphysical structure. The wicked are like aesthetes; they show a common dislike of reality, which as existent may be good, but not necessarily beautiful. The wicked flee the good as the aesthete flees the existent in pursuit of his dream reality.

Society, in condemning the contents of Genet's "directed daydream,"[36] becomes an accomplice to his literary crimes as it had been to his real crimes: "What rather well attests that these imaginary confessions are attenuated crimes is that society regards them as felonious. The poem of a bad action is itself a bad action."[37] Thus the books are condemned as obscene, unfit for public consumption. If this were the whole story, Genet's life and letters would be of little interest in the present study. That it is not all is illustrated by Genet's final acceptance: at first by critics, and finally by the entire French bourgeoisie.

As pointed out above, since critics serve in the process of literary communication, in a real sense they are the guardians of the portals: theirs is the task of separating the truly from the apparently valuable, or so it seemed to Sartre in his consideration of the ambiguous nature of literary value. On the one hand, paintings, sculpture, and other works of art are endowed with a certain economic value on the market of "culture"; in wars they are evacuated, protected, and if not, stolen. They may figure with special mention in treaties of peace. This is one kind of value attached to the artifact itself. Society is not without responsibility for this source of value, since its economic institutions determine to an extent the kind of art it enjoys.[38] But a second and more important kind of value is that which is attributed to the aesthetic object qua aesthetic. Sartre characterizes this ambivalence of the value of artworks in the following passage of *Genet:*

. . . the *reality* of society implies the socialization of certain *unrealities.* Imaginary insofar as they relate to events which have never happened or to characters which have never existed, at times even to laws which are not those of our universe, "accepted" works are *real* in that they provoke real actions, real feelings, and determine the historical development of a society. To tell the truth, social collectivities defend themselves as long as possible against the images: "critics" are charged, as specialists, to retard their admission. Genet knows it; but he knows also that, if he wins, he will re-enter with the honors of war into the community of the Just which has exiled him.[39]

How, then, could one win the bourgeois critics? The answer to this was easy for Genet: by flattering their prejudices with style, with significant form. And here we have the source of Genet's ironic return to righteousness. The critics who condemn the vocabulary and the content of his work, have praised its style, its form. We recognize the old abstraction of the formalist aesthetics. But if the work of literary art is correctly described as a concrete form, as an expressed content, the abstraction of a significant form from an unacceptable content is nothing more than an expression of the bad faith of the bourgeois critic:

They stop at the vocabulary of Genet in order to prevent themselves from entering into its delirium; they admire the form in order to keep themselves from realizing its content. But form and content are one and the same thing: *this* content demands *this* form; as long as you play at staying amoral, you will remain on the threshold of the work.[40]

The organicity of content and form has been explained above in the metaphysical analysis of the imaginary object. The aesthetic mechanism is not new: Sartre had pointed it out in his article on Faulkner.[41] But besides simply reiterating the aesthetic canon of literary judgment, Sartre argues here for the organicity of morals and metaphysics. If we insist on the amorality of our aesthetic judgment, we shall miss the concrete character of the work, since the structure of the work is moral as well as aesthetic and metaphysical. The reader must enter into the subject, and live vicariously the experiences even of the author-pervert. The ultimate value is an understanding of the nature of the world, and censorship of the work will preclude the possibility of such an understanding. So the existentialists have asked, why burn Sade and continue to martyrize Genet?

That Sartre is not merely grinding a special metaphysical and moral axe is evident from his rather closely reasoned analysis of poetic form in its distinction from prose,[42] of the two predominant modes of structuring images in contemporary poetry,[43] and his critical comparison of the poetic styles of Genet and Breton.[44] If we include the time spent by Sartre on his earlier treatises on the imagination, twenty years or more of work went into the preparation of *Genet.* Read the purely aesthetic criticism of *Situations I,* the case for committed literature in *Situations II,* the existential psychoanalysis of *Baudelaire,* the application of the principle of commitment to recent French literature in connection with Sartre's phenomenological psychology of the imagination and his ontology of being and nothingness, and *Genet* will seem to be something other than the work of a fool.[45] It shows, rather, the culmination of a lifetime spent by one artist in the pursuit of the understanding of his craft.

To conclude, in this chapter I have tried to establish the philosophical and aesthetic bases of Sartre's criticism. When Bosanquet classified the judgments of Greek art by the Greeks themselves into aesthetic, moral, and metaphysical, he was no doubt referring to the aesthetic works of Plato and Aristotle;[46] what his own idealistic metaphysics prevented him from seeing was that aesthetic, moral, and metaphysical categories are not necessarily contradictory if' one espouses an aesthetics in which ethics and metaphysics have their rightful plate. Sartre claims to have found the unifying thread of philosophical activity in contemporary phenomenology, and the greatness of his aesthetic writings is precisely that he has found that thread.

VI

Committed Literature, Second Phase

Because he had read *Genet* and understood little of it and because Sartre seemed to him to be becoming more and more professorial, pursuing his interest in sociology, social psychology, and economics to the point of re-reading Marx and Engels, Luethy, the Swiss journalist, historian, and economist living in Paris, could criticize the work of Sartre as that of a "simple, guileless fool, whose scandals and indecencies were only those of any other of our pure fools."[1] It was another matter when one of the original co-workers of *Les Temps Modernes* composed a more subtle analysis of Sartre's "flirtation with communism," which for all its subtlety may be reduced to the same *ad hominem* argument used by the Swiss.[2] A pure fool without guile or malice in Luethy's estimation, Sartre became in Merleau-Ponty's analysis the personification of the mandarin, deluded by a set of metaphysical categories stretched to the point of cracking in his attempt to justify Marxian theory and communist practice. To understand these charges we must refer to the events and the works they occasioned. In so doing, we shall be led to an exposition of a new development in the theory of committed literature, and a new evaluation of Sartre's aesthetics, in particular of its synthesis of phenomenology and existentialist ontology.

The events which brought about the new development occurred on the twenty-eighth of May and the fourth of June, 1952. On the first of these dates a communist demonstration in Paris was interpreted as a riot and immediately put down by force of police arms. When, in retaliation, a general strike was called for the second of these dates, the proletariat refused to respond. A political farce? dissolution of the Party? or merely general discontent with Party policy by the rank and file of the working classes? Sartre endeavored to find out which, and published his findings in a series of articles entitled "Les communistes et la paix," which was almost two years in the making. The first two of the series appeared in July and November of 1952, and the third in April of 1954. In the interim between publication of the second and third of the series, Sartre felt obliged to compose an answer to one of the critics of the first two, Claude Lefort, who wrote "Le marxisme et Sartre," published in *Les Temps Modernes* in April, 1953. Sartre's "Réponse à Lefort" appears in the same issue. The question to be investigated here is not a squabble between Marxists and Marxist sympathizers, but a supposed change in the direction of committed literature. Never a materialist or a determinist in the strict sense of these metaphysical terms, Sartre was always opposed in principle to the French Communist Party, of Marxist persuasion. His "I'd rather be a gravedigger than a lackey" was sincere, and many were the readers of *Les Mains sales*—Vendôme, for example —who identified Hugo, the non-recuperable bourgeois whose intellect was placed at the service of the Party, with Sartre himself. Marxists read the play as anti-communist propaganda, but Sartre has denied this characterization, referring to it as an example rather of committed literature. A brief summary of Sartre's critical writings, taken from *Qu'est-ce que la littérature?*, may serve to indicate the context of the issue.

According to Sartre's literary manifesto, the French literature of the Third Republic could be divided into three historical divisions. Before 1914, and the war to end wars, there was a reign of the "geniuses": Gide, Mauriac, Proust, Maurois, Duhamel, Romains, Claudel, Giraudoux. Sartre's association of the cult of genius with the methods of the bourgeois republic has been explained in the preceding chapter. After 1918, the theoretical end of all wars, the literary scene was a bit more diversified: the cult of genius survived in the works of Cocteau and Arland; surrealism flourished in Breton, Peret, and Desnos; letters likewise took on, in Sartre's terms for the surrealist movement, the character of literary chapel or spiritual college, church, or secret society, in the works of Drieu-la-Rochelle (later suspected of treason) and Morand; finally, the disciples of Alain, who were radicals and sons of the petit bourgeoisie, such men as Bost, Prévost, and Chamson, continued writing for no better reason than to earn a living. Starting in the thirties, with a growing awareness of the impending social disorders of fascism, bolshevism, and nazism, and the historical examples of the Chinese and Spanish civil wars (for example, the Marxist-inspired works of Malraux), French letters became committed in fact.[3] *Qu'est-ce que la littérature?* served merely to indicate the direction just outlined and to justify that move with aesthetic theory.

Literature in its commitment, following the second World War, was interpreted as "the conscience of the revolution." Merleau-Ponty, who was in a position to know, stated the original policy of *Les Temps Modernes* in the following way:

Commitment was first of all the resolution to show oneself externally as one felt internally; to confront behavioral patterns with their principles and with each other; to speak out on everything, therefore, and to re-weigh everything; to invent a total behavior pattern in response to the whole of the world's events.[4]

Excluded therefore from the journal's policies was any allegiance with church, party, or social club, since such allegiance would prevent the unbiased measurement of the world's course of events. As Merleau-Ponty points out,[5] this policy is nothing more or less than a literary statement of Sartre's metaphysical notion of liberty and precludes any close relationship between Sartre and the Communist Party. Thus when Sartre proclaimed, in the second of his articles on "Les communistes et la paix," "It is true, the purpose of this article is to declare my agreement with the communists on certain precise and limited subjects, reasoning from *my* principles and not from *theirs;* we shall see why,"[6] the rumor started that Sartre was about to give up his status as gravedigger for that of lackey, and literary critics could rightly pose the question of the new status about to be assigned in practice to committed literature. The answer to this question, quite naturally, is to be found in the reasons why Sartre prefers his own to the principles of the Marxists; I shall attempt an explanation of those reasons.

First of all, it must be noted that we are no longer in the realm of fine literature. Sartre in this period is at best playing the role of director of an intellectual's review, of a neutral and dispassionate journalist trying to discover the meaning of contemporary events for the world's history; at worst, of a propagandizing sympathizer with the Communist Party. One word of caution, in French, and in France situated as it is between two powerful states of opposed ideologies, the word *sympathisant* carries with it none of the derogation implied by the American-English "sympathizer," and Sartre's basic sympathy with the Communist ideal of the classless society has already been given its literary interpretation. Such sympathy would seem to indicate that Sartre has always accepted the theory of class-structured society, as well as the theoretical class struggle described by Marx. In his meditation on the events of May and June of 1952, he was led to compare the theories of Marx with contemporary sociological theories of class stratification. He found the work of Sorokin, Gurvitch, and Halbwachs "mechanistic," full of "ersatz concepts" created *ad hoc,* and having as its effect "mystification" rather than explanation.[7]

In answer to a formulation of the class structure of society according to the grouping of individuals enjoying the same status, one could reply that status in its real sense refers to a privilege resulting from classification; that stratification, like the unity of any class, "can be neither passively received nor spontaneously produced."[8] Passivity in the individuals, mechanism in the group—such was the sociological theory of his contemporaries, in Sartre's view already refuted by the activist theory of Marx:

The class, the *real* unity of historical crowds and masses, is manifested by an operation having a certain date and relating to a specific intention; it is never separable from the concrete will which animates it, nor from the ends which it pursues. The proletariat realizes itself by its daily action; it exists only in act, is act; if it ceases to act, it dissolves.[9]

The proletariat, or working class, is as distinct from a passive mass as action is distinct from passion itself.[10]

Ideally, when the reason for social struggle no longer exists, the unity of the proletariat will be expressed as pure relation: "The ideal would be that the proletariat be pure relation, that which arises wherever two workers are together."[11] But in order to achieve the ideal, action is called for, and the Communist Party is the vehicle of proletarian action: "In a word, the Party is the movement itself which unites the workers by leading them on to the assumption of power. How do you expect, then, that the working class disavow the Communist Party?"[12] No more glaring example of a speculative argument (the logical fallacy) was ever penned: the facts of the matter indicated, on the fourth of June, 1952, that the working classes of France did disavow the dictates of the Party; Sartre shouted that it should not have been the case. It was at this stage that Lefort compared, unfavorably, the articles of Sartre with the theories of Marx, and that Sartre continued to search for the reasons why facts and theory did not coincide.

The third article in the series shows a remarkable change in tone. Sartre exchanges his interest in general sociological and economic theory for a more scientific examination of the facts of contemporary French economics; he seeks the causes of the obvious growing discontent amongst the workers with the policy of the Communist Party. Although it may not be described properly as "eating crow," the following citation illustrates the change in attitude:

For my part, I hold that the development of capital, taken generally, explains the common aspects of all workers' movements. But these considerations of principle will never explain, by themselves, the particular traits of the struggle of the classes in France or in England between a given date and another. A concrete fact is, in its fashion, the singular expression of universal relations; but it can be explained in its singularity only by singular relations: to wish to deduce it from an absolute but empty concept or from a formal developmental principle is to waste one's time and trouble. Indeed, there are dialectics and they are in the facts; it is up to us to discover them, and not to put them there.[13]

Sartre then applies this scientific principle in his search for the causes, which now have supplanted the more general "reasons" he outlined in articles one and two. Accordingly, there follows a description of the French economic scene: too little production and too high prices; economic dispersion; the rampant Malthusianism of the French bourgeoisie refusing change, even after the disasters of 1848 and 1871; the collective avarice and hoarding of the average French household; the division of labor between skilled technicians and unskilled flunkeys, which is reflected in the division of laborers' unions and produces dispersion in collective bargaining practices.[14] Here at last are some facts, and in general, the statement about them seems true. But a group of facts, even collated and interpreted, mean nothing if their explanation cannot be acted upon or put to use. Two reactions to Sartre's efforts are of note, that of the Communist Party and that of a fellow phenomenologist, Maurice Merleau-Ponty.

Writing in *L'Humanité*, official organ of the French Communist Party, on February 22, 1954, two months before Sartre's last article,

Jean Kanapa condemned the efforts of certain of France's intellectuals to revise the official Marx-Leninist line of the Party. Sartre objected, in an open letter to the editor of *L'Humanité,* to having his own journal associated with certain others of rightist complexion, as well as to a few epithets which seemed directed to himself: "intellectual flatfoot" (*intellectuel-flic*) and "philosopher of St. Germain-des-Prés." Sartre quite rightly pointed out that the inclusion of such an article in the official newspaper was tantamount to Party acceptance, and that such acceptance would tend to disunify the left and dissuade those intellectuals who sincerely try to hold on to their principles while allying themselves with the Party. But oddly enough, Sartre's open letter was published alongside the offending article itself in *Les Temps Modernes,* and not in *L'Humanité.* Kanapa wanted a party of workers, of a real proletariat, and not of renegade bourgeois intellectuals; presumably, the Party agreed with him.[15]

More serious, and perhaps more important for our study, is the reaction of Merleau-Ponty, who has given, in *Les Aventures de la dialectique,* the most complete analysis of Sartre's theory of literature in practice. According to this onetime collaborator of Sartre, there are two phases in the theory of committed literature: the first is evident in Sartre's description of literature as social action in *Qu'est-ce que la littérature?* and the second, in "Les communistes et la paix," where literature was conceived as a "pure" political action.[16] The difference in the two moments, then, is in the conception of the action of the man of letters. As described above, during the first phase, the littérateur never loses his eminently cultural function: his action is to reveal the nature of the world and of man's place therein; writing always in search of a wider portion of the virtual audience containing all men, he is committed to his own time and situation and communicates with his fellows, inviting them to consider the universe from his point of view. In committing literature to this socal function, Sartre has, in Merleau-Ponty's eyes, at the same time "uncommitted" (or separated) politics from the dilemmas it faces in day-to-day practical decisions.[17] This charge is an important issue in Merleau-Ponty's analysis: it affords the clue t6 the change in Sartre's attitude; but its meaning is anything but clear.

How does one "uncommit" politics by committing literature? Two answers suggest themselves, both of which are supportable from a reading of Merleau-Ponty's text. First of all, the writer is an individual; committed as he may be to a particular time and place, his point of view is restricted, in Sartre's theory, to a single transcendence working out its life's project. The political situation of the writer is in consequence a part of the situation being surpassed by the freedom of that transcendence. For this reason no existentialist writer was to be tied to a particular political point of view; all was to be weighed in the balance of justice and truth. In this, the first phase, Sartre is the gravedigger, and not the communist lackey. Secondly, politics may be "uncommitted" or disengaged from the problems of a given time precisely because the writer searches the universal, the meaningful, the true and the just. Politics, on the other hand, works itself out in particular situations where truth, meaning, and justice are easily compromised on behalf of a particular goal. Thus, in describing the universe from his own point of view, the only point of view anyone can express, the author is forced to generalize his standpoint; in consequence, the historical events of the world take on the color of the writer's particular situation. And this is so following the premises of Sartre's metaphysics, which admit only two sorts of entities: men and things; meaning, in this metaphysical world view, can only be the reaction of a given man to the world of things. Public, universal history is never attainable.

From Merleau-Ponty's vantage point, this is precisely the fallacious conclusion of Sartre's ontology; their metaphysical differences will be discussed at greater length in another chapter. It suffices here to state the import of those differences for the issue at hand, the writer's commitment. Merleau-Ponty would agree with the separation of the writer's literary from his political activity:

There is a center of history which is political action, and a periphery which is culture. There are infrastructures and superstructures. Things are not the same in the one as in the other. A writer fulfills his role when he depicts typical situations and patterns of conduct, even if their political commentary remains to be done; even if, in the words of Engels, the work is still in progress.[18]

With the Sartre of *Qu'est-ce que la littérature?*, therefore, Merleau-Ponty has only a metaphysical squabble; he accepts the description of the writer's social function, and has contributed to the theory by describing, in one of his earlier essays,[19] the relation between metaphysics and the novel.

On matters literary the difference between Merleau-Ponty and

Sartre began when Sartre abandoned his original separation of politics and culture. In this second phase, literary activity becomes purely political; the concept of literature as the conscience of the revolution no longer suffices; the writer's act is said to be a political event:

For Sartre . . . since there is no single history behind us to which our literature and our politics both belong, since their unity is our own affair, since he considers both as having a unique source in consciousness if either is to come into contact with things, literature must treat of politics; and action, like a novel, must stick to the event with no separating distance.[20]

Thus, the political action called "Les communistes et la paix" changes the free and proud gravedigger into a political lackey. In Merleau-Ponty's eyes Sartre became an "ultra-bolshevik."

Having distinguished two phases in Sartre's conception of the writer possessed of a social consciousness, Merleau-Ponty then proceeds to show that there is a single unifying thread binding the two together. As if to cement their differences and to change a firm friendship into an open literary feud, if not personal hatred, Merleau-Ponty become sardonic in his description of the aberration in Sartre's application of the concept "freedom": it was in the name of freedom that Sartre first denied allegiance to the Communist Party; it is in the name of freedom that he becomes *sympathisant*. Thus, from Merleau-Ponty's point of view, Sartre, having imprisoned himself within the limits of two metaphysical concepts, having excluded the validity of a universal public history, enjoys freedom of consciousness, but has excluded himself from the company of others. Conscious of this separation, he repents and, Merleau-Ponty comments, "There is folly in the *cogito* which has sworn to rejoin its image in others."[21] Besides referring to Sartre's Cartesian foundations, Merleau-Ponty points out the pessimistic conclusion of *L'Etre:* "L'homme est une passion inutile."[22] Love, masochism, sadism—any conceivable relation between transcendences will fail to unite them. The gravedigger has truly repented.

But the repentance is form without substance. Sartre still refuses to become a Communist. He sympathizes, but his action is to be pure and not contaminated by the daily changes in the party line. By analyzing the structures of the act of sympathy, Merleau-Ponty tries to show that Sartre's new approach to the problem is likewise destined to failure. If sympathy is a pure political action, it is really no action at all. The Party claims absolute allegiance to a changeable

line; it wants nothing to do with the purity of an intellectual's motives or of his principles. If Sartre persists in being communist in
spite of the Party, his action is taken from a point outside the Party.
He may preach co-existence, but he too serves the bourgeois world
if only by taking the point of view of the most disfavored subjects of
bourgeois exploitation: "At the same moment he affirms a sympathy,
in principle only, for communism, he is placing himself in the non-
communist world, and he is still not speaking about communism."[23]
Any opposition from without can only be rivalry or menace to the
Party which has excluded those who demand to see, and not to act.
Sartre's pure action is nothing more than that of seeing, understanding, and can have nothing in common with a militant doing. For all
his inanity, Kanapa was probably right. To insist on interpreting the
action of seeing as a pure doing is possible only for those deluded
by the myth of the mandarins:

> The action of revealing has its facilities and its torments which are those of
> contemplation. They are problems and solutions of mandarins. The myth
> of the mandarin reunites the fantasy of a total knowledge and pure action.
> By virtue of his knowledge, the mandarin is supposedly present everywhere
> a problem presents itself, and capable of acting immediately, no matter
> where, without distance and by pure efficacy, as if *what he did* fell into an
> inert milieu and as if it were not, at the same time, only theater, manifesta-
> tion, object of scandal or enthusiasm. The spectator-consciousness is too oc-
> cupied with seeing to be able to see itself as a "special" consciousness, and
> it dreams of an action which would be another sort of ubiquity. Such is the
> naïveté and the ruse of narcissism.[24]

If we accept this description, nothing has been changed from phase
one of committed literature to phase two: Sartre is still Sartre; he
still clings to the metaphysical principles which were the initial
source of his undoing. Merleau-Ponty maintains further that pure
political action is a farce: "The conclusion of Sartre is no longer
pure action, but pure action contemplated at a distance, in other
words, sympathy. On the grounds of concrete politics, Sartre will
re-appear tomorrow as he really is, pacified, conciliating, and uni-
versalist."[25] In a word, Sartre has succeeded in deceiving himself; he
too is a victim of bad faith.

The corrective for such self-deception is, of course, to renounce
the myth which makes it possible: to admit the difference between
thought and action and the existence of a history in which both come
together and part, thereby allowing room for the true action of the

writer, which is to think, and that of the politician, which is to act. Thus,

To recognize literature and politics as two distinct activities is perhaps the only way to remain faithful to action as to literature; and, on the contrary, when one is a writer, to propose unity of action with a political party is perhaps to attest that one remains in the universe of the writer . . .[26]

After all, two political parties may meet, if only in disagreement; they both manipulate the same object, the human masses of a single government in a single purpose, the direction of that government. The writer manipulates only words if he rest true to his profession, and has nothing with which to deal on equal terms with a political party. Either he becomes a propagandist and manipulates masses with the party, or he remains true to his profession. Should he wish to compromise his profession, he can do so either by accepting the delegation of the party's function to himself, as in the case of Kanapa; or as Sartre has done, by deluding himself that writing is a pure political action:

To judge otherwise one must live in a universe where everything is meaning, politics as well as literature; in a word, one must be a writer. Literature and politics are really united to each other and with particular events [of history], but in another way: as two divergent viewpoints on a single symbolic life, or history.[27]

History is the common medium of cultural (literary) and political activity; within its total symbolic structure both culture and politics may meet and mutually influence each other without the one becoming a part or the whole of the other.[28] And to admit their separation is the prime condition for the efficacy of each. Such is the case of Merleau-Ponty against the later development of Sartre's concept of commitment.

But this was not the end of the matter. Simone de Beauvoir, piqued by Merleau-Ponty's reference to the mandarin myth,[29] immediately composed a refutation of the latter's interpretation of Sartre's case. Her title indicates the basis of her counter-criticism: "Merleau-Ponty et le pseudo-Sartrisme." Against his appeal to the mandarin's total knowledge, she quotes at some length the factual references of the third communist article cited above. Although she admits the phenomonological basis of Sartre's ontology has some weaknesses (precisely those which Merleau-Ponty had pointed out: the impossibility of communion between the self and the other, the

isolation of the individual transcendence from public history, etc.),
she states with confidence that Sartre is working on them, and that
Merleau-Ponty knew this quite well.[30] But when she appeals to
Merleau-Ponty's own use of the phenomenological method, and to his
teaching at the Collège de France, she does nothing for us but indicate our next major task: to outline Merleau-Ponty's theory of perception, and how he uses it to found a rival theory of aesthetics. But
this is a later project.

However, her *tu quoque* does not solve the weaknesses in Sartre's
theory; on the contrary, it as much as admits them. After all,
Merleau-Ponty's assumption that an author's work is the author's
responsibility is sound, until the author takes the trouble to repudiate
it in whole or in part. And this Sartre has not yet done. Moreover,
even if Merleau-Ponty had failed to refer to *L'Etre et le néant,* instead of deducing Sartre's new attitude from the categories described
therein, Beauvoir could have made the same charge as she did under
the existing circumstances, that Merleau-Ponty set up a straw man in
the interest of blowing it over. The service he has rendered us in
the pursuit of the commitment of literature, is to have pointed out
that the "newer" approach to the relations of a writer and his political situation is really not new at all, since both phases of Sartre's
position are readily deducible from his metaphysics. In itself, this is
no negative criticism; it becomes such only when the metaphysical
principles are compromised in their application to an alien ideology:
"To feel oneself responsible for everything before everyone, and
present in all situations—if that leads one to approve an action,
which like all actions forces these principles, then one must admit
that he has enclosed himself within words."[31] And when an individual insists upon creating his own history, at the expense of a universal public history made symbolically by the concurrence of all
actions, that individual, be he Sartre or Beauvoir, has "deliberately
taken up a position in the realm of the imaginary."[32]

Once a writer, always a writer; but any writer—and here we must
agree with Merleau-Ponty—has his own peculiar way of serving the
social body of which he forms a part.

When scholars consider literature as a fine art, they are not in the
least committed to the exclusion of function. Some of the functions
of fine art, in fact, are to generate a culture where one does not exist;

to propagate one that does exist, either by aggrandizing it in ascendence or rejuvenating it in decadence; or to re-structure one in which the growth of an individual has become thwarted or impossible. Literature is a cultural institution; to function as it can and ought, it must be allowed to function freely. To what extent does Sartre's theory of committed literature coincide with an ideal of a free literature, and to what extent does it deviate from that ideal? In the first place are its merits.

The existentialist defense of writers espousing non-bourgeois values, such as Sade and Genet, is a sign of cultural health, for no one set of values, even if they be of the dominant class of the culture, can be considered determinant of the whole of culture; even if they were, censorship of an opposing point of view would preclude the possibility of cross-fertilization within that culture. Even if literature be committed to a particular political point of view, and become the conscience of the revolution, it will not fail to serve the total culture which includes the bourgeois as well as the proletarian class in revolution. Nor should it fail to serve the bourgeois class itself: it is never without some value to see ourselves as others see us, be we proletarian or bourgeois. In short, the censorship of literature is deleterious to the whole culture as it is to each of its member factions.

The basis for Sartre's argument in behalf of the freedom of literature is the freedom of the individual, and the immorality of treating the human transcendence as if it were an inanimate object. The strength of his argument, therefore, would seem to depend upon the validity of the metaphysical underpinnings of his aesthetic arguments. And even here we can find some support for his theory in the methods of science. A word of explanation: the so-called law of universal determinism, which Sartre denies, is nothing more or less than an assumption of the scientific method; without appealing to the indeterminacy principle which governs the location of particles, a would-be defender of Sartre's idea of spontaneity may appeal to the operation of *Verstehen*[33] as it is sometimes used in the social sciences to compensate for the proverbially unpredictable character of human behavior. There is a difference, of course: Sartre's theory concerns a metaphysical absolute, and the operation of *Verstehen* is a relative procedure which may be, and in fact is, disregarded by many scientists, when the laws of social science approach the range of predictability known as scientifically certain. But in general, social sciences have not reached this range when dealing with human subjects; Sartre can very well say that the reason for this is not to be found in inept techniques of the social scientists, but in the nature of the subjects under investigation. Call it "spontaneity" or what you will, the behavior of human individuals alone or in groups is to some extent unpredictable. Perhaps it is for this reason that society is composed of institutions for social control. If we continue to object to the Sartrean metaphysics on grounds of scientific principle, we are not doing so because the two are mutually contradictory. But the moral principle involved does seem more obviously in accord with general moral feeling than Sartre's metaphysical principles are with the scientific principles discussed above. And it has been said that existentialism has had such a vogue with French intellectuals precisely because it arose at a time when the members of the French population were being treated like things rather than human personalities. Sympathy for the underdog—or bottom-dog—is a fundamental human trait.

Sartre meant to bring his aesthetic theory into harmony with his metaphysics and morals. And to a certain extent he did: by stating the imaginary character of the object of art, he allowed for the aesthetic description of the literary object as an isolated universe constructed according to principles of the same metaphysics and morals he had outlined elsewhere. The critic, when he is giving an aesthetic criticism, limits himself to pointing out the texture and the structure of the so-called unreal object. And since the structure of the unreal object is a function of metaphysical or moral principles, it is readily apparent in what sense the aesthetic critic must understand these principles in order to understand the content of a novel. Furthermore, when Sartre indicates that form follows content, he is stating that structure and texture are mutually dependent, and accepts the description of a novel as a concrete form. His argument against the cult of genius is precisely against the separation of matter and form, the latter considered as style. All of this is to Sartre's credit, and his aesthetic knowledgeability is attested in his critical writings.

Yet from the point of view of literature as a cultural enterprise, two very definite shortcomings are masked in that knowledgeability. The first is his insistence on a particular metaphysics. There is no apparent reason why an aesthetician should adopt his view of "total literature" merely because the kind of life depicted in a novel is the same as that lived by its author. In literary terms this would be tantamount to admitting the superiority of realistic novels. Some realistic novels are aesthetically excellent and some are not: literary excellence still depends upon the author's ability to find the technique which best suits his subject. And not all realistic novels are existentialist: those of the American school of the thirties and forties are based on quite another metaphysical presupposition, universal scientific determinism, and they are quite as good as any of the existentialists'. Like the bourgeois class, the existentialist philosophy is only one element of a general culture. The criticism of Sartre here is only for narrowing his aesthetic viewpoint to a particular ideology. If his virtue was to have sought the unity of aesthetics, metaphysics, and morals, his vice is in having found too much. Even Claudel's *L'Annonce faite à Marie,* for all its resemblance to a medieval miracle play, is a beautiful aesthetic structure based upon the Christian morality in which the chief virtues are faith, hope, and charity. And to fail to see and understand this when one reads the play is to miss a part of one's cultural heritage. But Sartre was a very decent critic before he established himself as one of France's leading metaphysicians: when he invited readers of a novel to correlate the techniques of an author like Faulkner with a set of metaphysical views on time, his aesthetic knowledgeability was evident; he could call for a "total literature" only after having written *L'Etre et le néant,* when in general the narrowing in his aesthetic viewpoint began to take place. In the same vein, *Baudelaire* and *Genet* could not have been written prior to the exposition of the principles of existential psychoanalysis in *L'Etre,* which, it will be remembered, appeared in 1943.

A final cultural point. The psychoanalytic criticism Sartre has adopted in both *Baudelaire* and *Genet* may be thought to have contributed more to the science of psychology, as it no doubt did, than to culture, as it ought to have; but that criticism will also seem to contradict an explicitly existentialist aesthetic aim. Recall its first statement:

We hope that our books remain in the air all by themselves and that their words, instead of pointing backwards toward the one who has designed them, will be toboggans, forgotten, unnoticed, and solitary, which will hurl the reader into the midst of a universe where there are no witnesses . . .[34]

The question is why an existentialist like Sartre could not grant Baudelaire and Genet the same favor he has asked for himself: to be forgotten personally, and to have their works speak for themselves in the way it is proper for aesthetic works to speak. Literature is a process of communication through gestures, and to be able to understand its import for culture we must be able to read rather complex signs.[35] A defender of Sartre on this topic, however, may very well point out that not all criticism need be aesthetic, and the point may be granted. But if it is, the counter-critic need only retaliate that if this is the case we are no longer considering literature as a uniquely cultural institution.

Merleau-Ponty's analysis of the second phase in Sartre's idea of commitment seems sound. The separation of the cultural and the political functions of literature is the only means of maintaining a free culture and a free politics, but we need not accept the theory of history espoused by Merleau-Ponty in order to make his point. For it is not Sartre's idea of history, as much as his idea of society, which is at fault. The two ideas are not unrelated, of course, but should we consider the structure Sartre imputes to society in his second phase, rather than the isolation of the individual's history from the universal, public history, which is characteristic of his first phase, we shall find that he assumes its arrangement into classes united along divergent lines of unified action, two classes being more or less unified into single groupings: the bourgeoisie and the proletariat. At best, this is nineteenth century sociology, worthy of Marx who lived in that century, but completely disreputable for a social scientist of contemporary society. But even granted the nineteenth century sociology at its base, there seems little reason to prefer one of these classes to the other if we, as writers, should like to keep our actions pure, and if our action is to be a true reflection of our own deliberate choice. Proust chose to be a bourgeois, and Sartre chose to be a communist sympathizer. Wherein lies the difference? Like Genet, who went all out for evil, Proust went the whole way for the bourgeoisie. But as Merleau-Ponty has pointed out, Sartre went for nothing; he chose to remain Sartre. There is no aesthetic ground for choosing one or the other of society's classes, if only as an object of sympathy. Moral grounds, perhaps; but to insist upon these would be to advocate an external criterion by which to judge the literary institution, and thus limit its freedom. This is, after all, the manner in which Vendôme had interpreted the idea of commitment. But if he was right, Sartre is wrong, and Sartre's criticism would be reduced to the level of its American counterparts in, for example, Granville Hicks[36] or Howard Fast,[37] both of whom put the same extraneous moral demand upon the freedom of the writer.

The argument here is for literature as an institution which can function properly only under conditions of freedom. Sartre could certainly not have been unaware of the treatment of certain of Russia's musicians, subjected to a similar extraneous demand. Pasternak's recent case furnishes a literary example of this. Regardless of its source, such a demand prevents the institution we call art from serving as a free institution should. Our hand is played: contemporary society is structured, not by a set of conflicting classes (France seems to be composed of as many peasant farmers as of the two classes named), but by a system of overlapping institutions or formalized patterns of individual behavior. The art institution is perhaps the only institution in a democratic society in which the function served is to channel and liberate the individual impulse to excellence; its product is cultural, and although it may be taken as a sign of the malfunctioning of society in its present state that this product is preserved for future generations in such minor or sub-institutions as the museum or library, its purpose is to induce this same value, the function it serves, in those who are led to appreciate it. To destroy it as such, as unification with any extraneous institution may destroy it (Witness the death of art in academies of art!), is to destroy one of the reasons man has found for continuing to live.

A second benefit which derives from considering the arts as a functional institution in the system of overlapping institutions we call "society" is the opening up of a neutral ground upon which the discussion of the morality of the arts may be dispassionately discussed. Thus Sartre could claim allegiance to the proletarian class only on the grounds that there are more members in it than in its opponent class, since under conditions of strife each tends to exploit the other, thereby denying someone's transcendence. But whether it is a question of happiness or of the development of transcendences,[38] the issue of numbers is utilitarian in essence, and affords no compelling proof of the rights of the greater number. If art is truly an institution it possesses the twofold nature of all institutions: first, it restricts human behavior in that it channels conduct into a formal pattern; second, it liberates the human impulses which find means of expression there. A discussion of this twofold nature will afford the grounds for judging the morality of a given aesthetic expression. An argument can be made for censorship and for freedom of expression precisely because the individual's freedom is relative to the institutions of the society in which he must live—not absolute, on the basis of a given metaphysical system, which at best is only one way to organize one's world view. The case of the freedom of the artist versus dictation by a group of vested interests is still to be written. But that is another work.

Finally, should we consider art as an institution of society, which is a system of overlapping institutions, the question of the artist's livelihood is easily solved on less emotive grounds. When Sartre condemned the Alainians as petit-bourgeois writing for a living, he condemned himself for the same reason. The point is that he need not condemn an artist who is a financial success. The economic institution is not alien to the artistic; if it should ever become so, we should very soon have no more art for having killed off the species of artists. Economics, as an institution, becomes fatal to art only when it dictates to the artistic: such appears to be the case in the American cinema, where business or financial success, rather than artistic expression, is the goal of the enterprise. The ideal society keeps its institutions in balance. Art can do nothing but suffer from dictation, whether from economics or from politics. And Sartre should know it. Total literature must, in a meaningful sense, remain "free."

Having examined Sartre's conception of images as a phenomenological experience, of works of art as images, and of literature as works of art, we are now in a position to consider his claim that images may give knowledge of one sort or another—the task postponed since the second chapter. There, it will be remembered, the imagination was found to be motivated by concepts (*savoir imageant*), which enabled consciousness spontaneously to render present what is absent from, or absent what is present in, an immediately perceived environment. But from a strictly empirical point of view, since concepts are presumably formed from previous bits of knowledge gained from prior experiences, and these prior experiences depend to some extent upon our past perceptions, Sartre's distinction between perceptions and imaginary experiences would seem to have been considerably blurred. Moreover, this blending of our perceptual and imaginary experiences has been shown to be corroborated by Sartre's account of works of art, which always exist physically as perceptual objects, which in turn "motivate" the appearance of the image, or aesthetic object. For Sartre, the physical artifact is an analogue of the aesthetic object whether this object be representational or non-representational in character. Given this interplay between the perceptual and the imaginary in our aesthetic experiences, what sense can be made of Sartre's claim that images may give us (new) knowledge? We may facilitate the discussion by considering a literary work of art as the most complex form of imaginary experience.

Put on this ground, the puzzle is not a new one. Plato averred in the *Laws* (Book II) that, on second thought, "imitative" poetry and music need not be banished from the ideal state if they be judged from considerations of truth rather than from those of any vulgar pleasure they may excite. And the truth of art was to be measured in terms of the exactness of representation of the quality and quantity of the thing represented. Thus, good poetry was good in so far as it represented a truth which was symbolic of the Good, or ultimate ideal of harmony according to law.

Like Plato, Aristotle was bound to a mimetic theory of art, but his discussion of the truth of artistic imitations (*Poetics*, 9) allowed for a distinction in the kinds of truth which may be represented. Both history and poetry, for example, were said to represent actions; but history is tied to a particular action, whereas poetry may represent a universal one. History must report what has happened, and gives limited knowledge; poetry may represent what might happen, and so gives knowledge tied to no particular place or time. Finally, since poetry does exceed the stricter limits of historical reportage, its representation is of something either probable or necessary: its statements are acceptable if they might be true or if they must be true— given the poet's artistic insight, or, as Sartre would say, given the writer's situation.

For all their difference in metaphysics, Sartre's account of the literary object agrees rather well with Aristotle's description of the knowledge gained through literary art. Both seem correct in their agreement that ". . . poetry is something more philosophic and of graver import than history."[39] But Sartre's theory of the literary image may throw some new light on this distinction between history and the more universal knowledge of art.

If a literary art object is a complex image and images are motivated by a perception of the world, in constructing such an object the author is exercising his ability to render absent the present or present the absent. The psychological mechanism which allows this reversal is the separation of an image from the background on which it must appear. In our account, the image is the literary work and the real world is its background. Since the author is situated in the real world and takes his inspiration from that situation, it will come as no surprise that an author's personal life, and his physical and cultural environment will be mirrored in his work. But to read the work as if there were no more content to it than an autobiographical statement, or a realistic description of a given milieu, is to look at the piece only for its historical, or literal, content. That this has been the practice of many so-called historical critics can not be denied, but neither can it be denied that such historical criticism misses the essential artistic import of the work being criticized.[40] The author puts the real world out of contact with the image; that is, whatever he accepts from his environing situation as valid for his expression is put into a new, imaginary context which stands out from the world. No matter how realistic his work, the author makes an abstraction and so "renders absent the present." In the context of the artwork's abstraction he must project "situations" which are probable—or necessary—given his over-all point of view. The question as to how the literary image gives us knowledge, and of what kind, must be answered in terms of this general scheme.

Following the description of the knowledge of images in the second chapter of this study, we should maintain that the knowledge is one of direct acquaintance; it is had or not by the person who enjoys the image. And since the image is a unique object to which no concept is applicable its knowledge can be had in no other way. The critic's task in the communicative process is to analyze the texture and structure of the image in such a way as to allow a third person to enjoy the work. Can this knowledge be further characterized?

The answer to this question may be forthcoming from an analysis of the second power of the author: the "presentification of the absent." The author's "vision" is of a probable or necessary state of affairs, of one which *might* exist under favorable circumstances; in a word, of a given value. It is in this sense that Sartre describes the work as an appeal from consciousness to consciousness made under the conditions of freedom for the mutual enjoyment of a given desideratum.[41] And once the vision is shared, the value communicated, the social consequences of the communication may very well take the course Sartre has predicted for all valid works of literary art: they may become effective political actions. The artist indicates a new direction, a new meaning, a new value for all who share the common interest; he enriches culture by his proposal of a new value and may actually produce a work having political repercussion. Thus, if it is obvious that "culture" conditions the appearance of literature, it is also apparent how literature may effect profound changes in the culture of both the author and his audience. When literary criticism is at its best, it functions to show how a value is communicated in the work of art. And this it can do only by showing the manner in which the work's literal "historical" statement is conditioned by the author's "gesture" to elaborate a single concrete, significant form which embodies the new value. In its most essentially artistic aspects, then, the image gives us knowledge of projected human values. It is for this reason that literary art objects are prized, and that an author may become an effective political agent.

The second part of this treatise is dedicated to the examination of the aesthetic theory of Maurice Merleau-Ponty, whose primary philosophical concern has been with a criticism of human institutions, one of which he considers art, the specifically human activity of finding new directions for the development of history. I shall begin that examination with Merleau-Ponty's account of the manner in which forms may be said to become significant, that is, embodiments of a specifically human value.

Part II MAURICE MERLEAU-PONTY

VII

A New Direction in
Phenomenological Philosophy

Maurice Merleau-Ponty was graduated by the Ecole Normale Supérieure in 1931, and like most of his classmates who began immediately to instruct the subjects taught them at the Normale in various lycées about the country, he spent a considerable period in secondary education before being named to a university post at Lyons in 1945. He remained there until 1949, when his nomination to the Sorbonne brought him to the ultimate goal of most aspiring French academics. Finally, at the death of Louis Lavelle[1] in 1951, he was tendered and accepted the still rarer distinction of the Chair of Philosophy at the Collège de France, which he held until his death in 1961. In keeping with convention, his inaugural lecture, delivered at the Collège on Thursday, January 15, 1953, was limited to a eulogy and an outline. Eulogized were his predecessors, Lavelle, LeRoy, and Bergson; sketched in very thin outline were his own latest speculations upon philosophy as "expression," a linguistic architectonic developing from the contingent events of the universal history of mankind and flowing back thereto, in its happiest moments, to redirect the original historical movement.[2]

In this last phase of Merleau-Ponty's thought, philosophy was conceived as "the algebra of history," one institution in the total historical context of institutions which was always the object of his philosophical inquiry. Albeit little known to the British or American reader, his studies in Marxist theory and practice, *Humanisme et terreur*[3] and *Aventures de la dialectique*,[4] are among the best on the continent. The second treatise, which attempted to place the Marxist

159

movement in its proper historical context, alienated him from earlier connections with both orthodox Marxists and the group known as the "Mandarins of the Left," centered around the persons and writings of Jean-Paul Sartre and Simone de Beauvoir.

While Merleau-Ponty was writing his observations on the recent developments in dialectics and branding Sartre's position (stated in the series of articles in *Les Temps Modernes* on the communists and peace[5]) as "ultra-bolchévisme,"[6] Sartre himself was busy with an apologetic study of the relationship between existentialism and communism, rationalizing the difference between the two as a mere "question of methods."[7] It therefore fell to Simone de Beauvoir to counter Merleau-Ponty's criticism, and she rose to the occasion with her biting article "Merleau-Ponty et le pseudo-Sartrisme," in which he is charged with recently having intentionally misread Sartre, with always having been too academic, and with at long last having betrayed his original phenomenological inspiration in Husserl. The orthodox Marxists were angry for other reasons. Henri Lefebvre found the public airing of the falling out between Merleau-Ponty and the mandarins ridiculous; more serious in his opinion was Merleau-Ponty's falling away from the scientific method of Pavlov. In an attempt to expose the pseudo-scientific character of the concepts used by Merleau-Ponty in *La Structure du comportement* to evaluate the scientific claims of psychologists, Lefebvre began to publish a series of articles purporting to re-investigate Merleau-Ponty's thought from its very beginnings.[8]

It is the purpose of the present chapter to follow the lead of Beauvoir and Lefebvre, not grinding any particular axe, but in order to discover the extent to which Merleau-Ponty's theory of perception can be truly considered an improvement upon that of Sartre.[9] The latter has been criticized mainly upon the grounds that it begs the question of perceptual knowledge.[10] Following Merleau-Ponty's own desire, we shall investigate both *La Structure du comportement* and *La Phénoménologie de la perception* in an effort to understand his essential philosophical position. As he himself always maintained, a reading of the second presupposes a reading of the first. Each is phenomenological in that it posits the phenomenon, an appearance to a consciousness, as the starting point of philosophical inquiry, the task of which is to describe the human being as a man-in-the-world. The Belgian historian of contemporary philosophy, Alphonse de

Waelhens, has already attempted to show the analytical superiority of Merleau-Ponty's method over that employed by Sartre in *L'Etre et le néant*. A brief sketch of de Waelhens' criticism may afford a suitable introduction to our inquiry into Merleau-Ponty's theory of perception.

In *L'Etre,* consciousness is defined by Sartre as an emptiness of being (*néant d'être*) describable only as an act of negating what is. What is, is in-itself, the *en-soi;* consciousness, the negation of what is, exists for-itself.[11] Thus, when I perceive a white sheet of paper, the paper exists in itself, but for me. In the act of perception I am precisely that aspect of the experience which is not the paper. Were I to turn my gaze from the white expanse, my consciousness would for a moment still be of the paper, but it would intend the absent sheet of paper via the image which endures. Since there is no consciousness without an object, each act of conscious intention implies both the aforementioned "ontological structures," the *en-soi* and the *pour-soi.*

At a later stage of Sartre's ontological treatise, knowledge is defined as a recognition of the plenitude of the *en-soi,* and the emptiness of the *pour-soi.*[12] Ontologically, then, consciousness and knowledge are practically identical. The difficulty with this conclusion is that it controverts the common-sense distinction usually made between the two: one kind of knowledge is direct and consummatory, while another is indirect and merely descriptive. We experience the lived, and usually distinguish it from the kind of knowledge purveyed, for example, by our scientific descriptions. Thus the distinction drawn in French between *le vécu* and *le connu* corresponds roughly to that referred to in English philosophy, since Bertrand Russell's famous distinction of the types of knowledge, as knowledge by acquaintance and knowledge by description.[13] Moreover, Sartre is well aware of the importance of the distinction; his proof of the existence of the "prereflective *cogito*" depends upon a "non-positional" awareness of consciousness—by direct acquaintance—at the same time consciousness intends "positionally" a given transcendent object. Russell's argument, as stated in his *Problems of Philosophy,* differs only in language. Further, Sartre is aware of the practical difference between consciousness and knowledge when, in *L'Esquisse d'une théorie des émotions,* he shows that feelings and conations of an experiencing subject are likewise consciousnesses—in the sense of

Bewusstsein introduced by Husserl—but neither feelings nor conations can be properly called "knowledge." De Waelhens concludes
that Sartre has prejudiced the perspectival character of perception
upon which phenomenological description rests by retreating to the
level of ontology, and charges further that in so doing Sartre has
come dangerously close to a radical distinction between mind and
body, which it is the virtue of phenomenology to avoid. This is
precisely the point on which Beauvoir has critized Merleau-Ponty's
reading of Sartre. It is true, for example, that Sartre intends to avoid
the mind-body dualism; but in the absence of the philosophical
treatise Beauvoir claims Sartre was preparing (1955) to overcome
the difficulties of uniting ontology with phenomenology—knowledge of which Merleau-Ponty is alleged to have possessed at the
time of his criticism[14]—this issue can be settled only by considering
Sartre's analysis of a specific act of perception in order to determine
whether in one part of his treatise he does in fact what in another
he has disclaimed doing in intention. And this is exactly the task
de Waelhens has performed.

Consider our knowledge of a particular quality. In a given act of
perception a subject is faced with the presence of a thing. This presence is at once immediate and at a distance. I perceive the color red,
for example, as the red of a given notebook. The quality is grasped
as belonging to the notebook. The book is this color, and I myself
am not the color. My own consciousness is grasped as an emptiness,
determined in this instance by the quality red. The red is there before
me, but at some distance; the perceptive act yields a colored expanse
spread out in my visual field.[15] If this analysis is correct, our knowledge of the quality is an intuition; it is had or not, and for our
knowledge of the visual object no multiplication of points of view
is possible or necessary. The problem here arises only from the
ontological point of view; given the two structures related by "internal negation," the *pour-soi* and the *en-soi,* it becomes incomprehensible, on the level of a phenomenological analysis, why an empirical consciousness must go through the process of multiplying its
points of view in order to grasp an object. De Waelhens goes
further: ontologically speaking, consciousness is not in-the-world,
since by definition it is not engaged in the thing it perceives; therefore, consciousness could not, in principle, interact with the environment in such a way as to perceive. Sartre's ontological concepts

produce a radical separation of consciousness and its object, and applied to an act of perception produce a classically rationalistic explanation of perceptual knowledge. But Descartes and Spinoza at least had the escape route of natural confusion (unclearness, indistinctness) to explain perceptual error. Sartre's *pour-soi,* a complete translucency, lacks this saving grace.[16]

Phenomenology, on the other hand, holds that the consciousness must be engaged in the world, and must collaborate—by interacting with the environment, to use Dewey's terms—with the world in order for there to arise sense knowledge, which is patently perspectival in character. As a phenomenologist, Sartre is aware of this. We do multiply points of view taken on an object. Although we may start with a sensory intuition, the indubitable knowledge of quality, we must, because of our situation in the world, continue to explore the object from many points of view in order to complete the significance of the object to our perception. Thus in de Waelhens' view Sartre errs by gratuitously assuming that consciousness is forced to multiply points of view as a matter of ontological principle: if consciousness which yields sense knowledge were not a detailed viewing of an object, it would become identified with its object and hence destroy itself as a pure existent *pour-soi.* But this is a presupposition, the result of Sartre's use of the transcendental deduction, and not a descriptive feature of an act of perception. In other words, de Waelhens claims, as we have shown above,[17] that Sartre begs the question of perceptual knowledge. A thorough-going reconstruction of perceptual theory is required in order to save the phenomenological foundations from ontological falsification. Such was the task adopted by Maurice Merleau-Ponty.

The remainder of de Waelhens' trenchant analysis is devoted to showing the parallel problems attending Sartre's phenomenological and ontological descriptions of bodily existence.[18] As we shall see, Merleau-Ponty settles both of these issues by considering the problems of perception and of body, not as parallel or analogous, but as one and the same issue.

In sum, it is claimed by de Waelhens that Sartre's ontology gravely prejudices the truth of phenomenology: the postulation of two radically different structures or principles of ontology compromises the reality of the only object of phenomenological inquiry, man as a being-in-the-world. Merleau-Ponty was to attempt to save this insight, and to produce an existentialist metaphysics without appealing to a set of presuppositions. In order to achieve this *voraufsetzungslöse* inquiry, he begins by critically analyzing the methods of those whose only office is to describe human consciousness: practicing psychologists. Methodology is still within the philosopher's purview. The role Merleau-Ponty assumes here is that of existentialist philosopher of the science of psychology, much the same as that played by Sartre in his now famous critique of Freudianism.[19] It is not without point, at this stage of our exposition, to state general agreement with those critics of Sartre who claim that as a dramatist he has shown great insight into human motivation, and that as a phenomenologist he has shown equally great comprehension of the general principles of psychology by finding the example which adds poignancy to his treatise (such as the caress, the look, dread, or shame); but the inferences he draws from the examples, governed by the method of transcendental deduction, have failed in the long run to convince. In search of a more convincing interpretation of the phenomena of our experience we may now turn to Merleau-Ponty's critique of the methods of psychology.

What if the psychologists are right, after all, to assume that human behavior may be explained by purely objective or physiological data? Sartre's assumption that every consciousness is of something, that each intends an object present or absent in a spontaneous act, may have given his metaphysics an unduly idealistic appearance, in spite of all his verbal disclaimers. The nature of intentionality may be adequately described as "minding," a particular physiological function of the human organism.

Merleau-Ponty considers two basic theoretical concepts current at the writing of his first treatise (1938). They are the reflex arc and the conditioned reflex. The arguments of other psychological schools are considered as modifications of these two basic modes of explanation. A bibliography of the psychological and philosophical texts used by Merleau-Ponty is given on pages 243–44 of *La Structure du comportement,* and may justify the following procedure, which is to consider the theoretical constructs in a critical fashion without giving credit to the particular psychologists who performed the experiments involved.

The simplest, perhaps the most naïve, of the physiological explanations of mental behavior is by way of the reflex arc.[20] Basically, this explanation attempts to avoid the mentalism and anthropomorphism rife in earlier treatises on the psychology of man and lower animals respectively. In the quest for a thoroughgoing objectivity, theorists of the reflex arc ignore the notion of intentionality, seeking to explain the more complex physiological processes by the simple stimulus-organism-response configuration, in which the organism serves as locus of connection between simple "longitudinally" defined incoming and outgoing pulsations. Each of these concepts is analyzed in its turn.

In the first place, the notion of stimulus. Attempts have been made to describe stimuli in terms of their nature, their spatial location, and their physical intensity; but in laboratory experiment it has been found that none of these is as significant as the total form of stimulating elements in the production of a reflex response. In one such experiment a cat was submitted to the stimulation of water alone, alcohol alone, and a mixture of the two. The reaction to the mixture, the feline highball, was found to be entirely different from the reactions to either water or alcohol alone, even though there is no known chemical combination of the two liquids which could produce a different kind of stimulus. Merleau-Ponty concludes that the cat in some sense responds to the stimuli of water and alcohol in summation, and suggests that, instead of first looking for the simplest stimulus and then 'composing' a more complex stimulus of it with other simple stimuli, psychologists seek the reason for the difference between the responses to the simple and the complex stimuli within the organism itself. A stimulus is not a purely physical event; it is a biological phenomenon. Each species selects and determines its *own kinds* of stimuli.

The models used to envisage the organism's physiological structures, in the second place, have been for the most part mechanical. Picture the organism as a keyboard played upon by the encroaching stimuli, or as a telephone dialing system which produces a specific result by the process of composing the letters and numbers into a single telephone number to be dialed. The keyboard model is obviously circular. Any melody which results from the contact of felt-covered hammers on taut strings is not produced by the instrument itself, but by the movement patterns of the hands which strike the keys controlling the hammers. The form of the response is thus determined by the form of the stimuli, supplied in this model by the organism playing the piano and following the form supplied by the musical notations of the score. The automatic telephone seems a better model, but it too has deficiencies. Depending upon the sequence in the letters chosen, the same letter will become a part of a distinctive response composed to a certain extent by the effective organization of the stimuli; but this organization, precisely, is not effectuated by a mere summation of "longitudinal" connections, as the necessity of the "transversal" connections of the central switchboard amply demonstrates in any case of successful telephonic communication. Consigning these transversal connections to the dark confines of the central nervous system merely illustrates the necessity of supposing the activity of the organism as a whole in the definition of a meaningful behavioral reaction. By its selectivity, by its attention, the organism has as much causal efficacy upon the environment as the environment has upon it. Conceptions of the organism as a mere locus of connection between incoming (afferent) and outgoing (efferent) waves of impulse fail to explain either the specificity of the stimulus or the specificity of a response. All theories of internal combination of stimuli seem doomed to failure. Since there are roughly five times more afferent paths than efferent, one must assume that there is a common segment in which a same nervous path can produce qualitatively different reactions. The simple reflex-arc theory must therefore be patched. Moreover, the same response may be called out by different stimuli; to explain this phenomenon the simple connection theory necessitates more patching by appeals to such concepts as inhibition, internal accommodation, and habituation.

Finally, even if it were supposed that stimuli, receptors, and nervous paths were to function specifically, it would not suffice to explain the adaptation of a particular response as the reflex called out by the given stimulus: in some cases the reaction differs according to the position of the stimulated organ. In the knee-jerk reflex, there are different reactions depending upon the position of the leg when the knee is tapped. Merleau-Ponty concludes that the situation, the total environing set of circumstances, conditions each response taking place within it. And if this is true, psychologists can no longer suppose that sensory receptors and motor responses are related in certain specific ways before being brought into contact by the direct play and interplay of an organism on and within its environment. The effect of the situation is to give "meaning" to a stimulus. Consider the example of the man walking through a woods: if he catches his foot on a tree root, his foot muscles relax and the body reacts in such a way as to continue the general relaxation which will allow the man to disentangle his foot; but in a different situation the bodily reaction may be quite the opposite, as when a man is walking down hill, thumping his heel on the ground before the rest of his foot. Here likewise the foot muscles relax, but the body reacts by contraction in order to allow the continuation of the descent.

In sum, says Merleau-Ponty, the concept of the reflex arc as the basic atomic structure is not suited to the task of explaining all more complex behavior. Simple reflexes do exist; they are not empty hypothetical concepts. But reflex acts are pathological; they occur in extraordinary circumstances, where the organism is isolated from a total environment which determines the normal life situation. Thus the conditions under which they appear are, if not unreal, at least unrealistic.

According to Merleau-Ponty, when the conditions of behavior are studied in their realistic context, the structures of the central nervous system must be supposed to vary concomitantly with external stimuli; whence the possibility of adaptation of the organism to its environment. The afferent paths of the nervous system are thus conceived as an organized field of force harboring at one and the same time a disposition of intraorganic tendencies and the influence of a given external stimulus. The forces within this field tend to equilibrium via certain "privileged" connections, and thus produce the response appropriate to the stimulus. Once these responses are called out, there results a corresponding change in the organized nexuses of the afferent system, which, in collaboration with new stimuli, work toward the production of still another, modified response.[21]

But if such a supposition is an adequate description of the intimate connection between the organism and its environment, there remains the question of describing in purely physical terms the mechanism by which the adaptation of internal and external structures takes place. Some psychologists have suggested the notion of "gestalt" as sufficient to the task, and it is in this connection that Merleau-Ponty considers the gestalt hypothesis.

The attempts of Wertheimer, Koehler, and Koffka to account for the "transversal" phenomenon in nervous connections are worthy of special mention. They were based upon the then new concepts of "form." A form, whether physical and inorganic or strictly organic, as would be the structures of the nervous system, is defined as a system whose properties are different from those of a mere summation of its parts. It is characteristic of such forms that a change in any one of their constituent parts results in a radical change of the whole, but a corresponding change in each and every one of the parts results in no change whatever in the whole. Forms, then, may be transposed totally, without loss of identity, like a musical melody which remains recognizable though written in a different key.

The physiological conditions which fulfill the requirements of the definition of a form have already been made apparent: the complex response of an organism cannot be reduced to a mere summation of simple physical stimuli; all the relations between the elements of the afferent portion of the nervous system, as between those of its motor reactors and between the two systems together in a single interaction between the organism and the environment, are internal. Merleau-Ponty accepts the bases of the melodic analogy as sound, but at this point brings to bear a brace of criticisms.

First of all, he questions the possibility of describing the essentially physical character of certain "forms." In attempting to avoid physiological atomism—the anatomical approach to physiology—the gestaltists are said to have left themselves open to perhaps more serious charges: anthropomorphism, and, ultimately, circularity of explanation. When we make appeal to certain "oriented" or "ordered" processes perceivable within the physical environment, we are evidently projecting the forms of our own mental behavior into the environment, much as Kant insisted we do in any act of knowing. The very notion of "adaptation" of response to a given stimulus, or of a "coherent" sequence of motions, betrays the projection of human norms into a supposedly purely inorganic situation. This confusion of essentially human characteristics with those of a physical situation is nowhere so evident as in the ambiguity of the French word *sens* to indicate both the direction and the "meaning" of a stimulus and response, as well as the organ of reception itself. The relations between the meanings which define any order are the results of our own internal constitutions; in using these terms as investigators, we do not find the order in any objective physiological process unless we have first projected whatever order is there to be observed. Even explanation of privileged behavioral patterns by computation of the statistical frequency with which the pattern results under conditions of known stimulation can be said to be anthropomorphic in this sense, since the notion of "frequency" is an ideal concept and in the strictly physical interactions of physiological structures and environment there occur only singular events which are to be explained by particular causes.[22] The charge of circularity of explanation follows immediately from the gestaltists' basic anthropomorphism: since any order which exists in the stimulus is a function of the order of responses, the attempt to explain the order in a given response by appealing to a supposed order within the stimuli is manifestly circular.

The second criticism by Merleau-Ponty of the gestalt school is to question the necessity of the new category of "form" for understanding the phenomena of nervous connection. Could one not avoid "anatomizing" in physiology by adopting a more functional approach according to which nervous routings are viewed as determined by connections established from moment to moment, like resonating bodies, by a synchronization of neurons? This is the solution of Lapicque, French physiologist, who invented the term *chronaxie* to refer to the time value required in stimulating a given nervous organ to an intensity of twice its normal threshold. This time value is found to vary from nerve fiber to nerve fiber, but to be constant along any given fiber under certain conditions. And it is supposed that nervous paths of similar chronaxy may be stimulated occasionally as in sympathetic frequential resonance of sounds. Consider the phenomenon of irradiation: when a certain stimulation travels beyond its given path without producing the expected motor response to produce a reaction associated with a neighboring path, the connection is assured by a momentary synchronization of the two afferent paths. There is no choice, but simple resonance between fibers of like frequency. The problem is then to explain how the proper synchronization takes place within the organism. Lapicque's answer is to suggest a total functional relationship between periphery and center, between receptors and cortex.

We may illustrate this mechanism as it could be used to explain the difference in effective response in the patellar reflex. The knee jerks, it has been noted, in different movements depending upon the position of the leg when it is tapped with the examiner's hammer.

It is supposed that the time values (chronaxies) of the various fibers implicated in the stimulation are altered by a modification of the relative positions of the body's members. Hence, as in the phenomenon of irradiation, a different response is called out due to a synchronization of the stimulated fiber with another connected with the given response. The same principle might be used to explain the difference of bodily reaction to having one's foot caught during a walk. And if the periphery is unified by the center, the time values of the various central neurons are not absolute, but varying according to conditions of cold, heat, or electric shock; in other words, according to peripheral stimulation. But here again, we quite obviously lapse into circular explanation: the initial variations in time values of the peripheral nervous fibers are thought to be controlled by the center, whereas it is empirically observable that the organization of the center is in its turn a function of stimuli arriving from the periphery. The cybernetic function of the central nervous system is not a secret or hidden response of a particular part of the whole system as much as it is a functional relationship obtaining between all its members. Moreover, what the concept of variable time value is calculated to accomplish is the explanation of the integration of multiple stimulus with simple response. It remains to be shown that the resultant simple response usually has, in the concrete environmental situation, a specifically biological value, which is the result of adaptation. Lapicque has succeeded in pointing up the role of the central nervous system as the organizing principle of the given response, and the moment by moment, or temporally differential, character of the organization of each response. In so doing he has made clear what the problem actually involves even though he too failed to solve that problem.

In general, Merleau-Ponty claims that Lapicque was in error in supposing the existence of a mechanism "hidden behind" the cerebral processes to explain their organizing function in behavioral responses. When the necessary conditions for a given response obtain, the response is evoked; in the absence of any one of such conditions the response does not result. Why continue to search for a "cause" which would transcend the conditions? Moreover, since each neuron's chronaxial characteristic is dependent upon that of the others, no simple part by part analysis will ever yield the possibility of a real synthesis of the parts analyzed. Thus we return to the meta-

phor of the melody and the notion of the gestalt, as internally determined; and it would not be playing with words to indicate that when
an organism adapts itself to an environment the former must be "in
tune" with the latter. The nervous system contains only global phenomena.[23]

The work of Lapicque is thus seen by Merleau-Ponty as a corrective to an inadequate description of physical *Gestalten*. Lapicque has
merely replaced emphasis on the organism in the stimulus-organism-
response configuration, but where he uses a language of "mechanistic realism," the gestaltists have used one which tends to "finalistic realism."[24] Thus the notion of "form" merely expresses the
descriptive properties of certain natural groupings. It is true that it
makes possible the use of a finalistic vocabulary. But that very possibility is founded, according to Merleau-Ponty, in the nature of
nervous phenomena; it expresses the kind of unity realized in them.[25]
The only way to avoid mechanism and finalism in psychology is to
avoid as scrupulously as possible all appeals to causal explanation: a
difficult injunction, but one which Merleau-Ponty heeds in his explanation of order, to be explained later in this chapter.

Having considered the simplest explanation of behavior, consisting of the description of conduct in terms of a reflex-arc mechanism,
as amended by the concepts of. *Gestalt* and *chronaxie,* and found it
wanting, Merleau-Ponty proceeds to an examination of Pavlov's
doctrine of the conditioned reflex. The normal responses to stimulation by food are salivation and mastication. If, by presenting secondary stimuli along with the food, an experimenter succeeds in producing these responses to the secondary stimuli—usually visual or
auditory—when presented alone, he has conditioned the reflexes of
the experimental animal. And such laboratory experimentation has
led Pavlov and his followers to suppose that non-directed conditioning may take place in more realistic non-laboratory situations.

Situated in an environment more realistic than a laboratory, the
animal is assumed to be under constant influence of an almost unlimited series of stimulations. If any stimulus may be substituted for
another in the function of calling out the response appropriate to
only one given stimulus, the effect of this indiscriminate conditioning
may be the transference of response to any stimulus whatsoever.
Such is the result of the law of irradiation. In order to limit the
scope of the irradiation, it was necessary to conceive the operation

of a second law, the law of inhibition, according to which the transference of response from one stimulus to another may be reduced
in effect or prevented altogether by the effect of a third, inhibiting
stimulus. Thus, in order to explain the specificity of response to the
normal stimulus isolated from the total situation, one was forced to
envisage the response of the animal as being produced by a series of
stimuli each affecting the other; those stimuli which have become
reflexogenic by virtue of association with an already secondary stimulus, if they are not also associated with the primary stimulus, lose
their power to provoke the response, and eventually become conditioned inhibitions.

Merleau-Ponty describes one of the control experiments in which
this general theory was put to the test. One stimulus, a light, associated with food produced a strong salivary reaction, and was
itself associated with a sound, which became only slightly reflexogenic, and never being associated with the primary stimulus, finally
became a conditioned inhibitory stimulus. When the sound was
presented along with the original associated stimulus, the light, no
reaction occurred. Then a third stimulus, the rhythmic beating of
a metronome, was added to the first two associated stimuli and the
whole series again presented with food; the series of three stimuli—
light, sound, metronome—became reflexogenic, but to a lesser extent than the original light. The supposition is that the quantitative
difference in the response is due to the presence of the inhibitor, but
that the third stimulus acts in such a way as to prevent full inhibition. The following set of figures are given as results in the control
experiment: the light alone yields ten drops of saliva; the light and
metronome, ten; light and sound and metronome, ten; light and
sound, none; sound and metronome, four; the metronome alone,
four; the sound alone, none. The critical cases occur in the combination of sound (the inhibitor) with the light and of sound with the
metronome. In the first there is no response; in the second, the response proper to the metronome alone. The presence of the sound
inhibits the response to the light, but does not inhibit the response
to the metronome.

Merleau-Ponty views the interpretation of these data as revealing
the "premise of realism" upon which the experiment is based. The
effect of the sound is to inhibit that of the light; the effect of the
metronome, that of the sound. The effect of each successive inhibi-

tion is calculated on the basis of a "real synthesis" of the properties of each stimulus considered alone. If the light will always contain the potentiality of producing a given response (here, ten drops of saliva), the sound which inhibits that response must likewise possess its positive power of inhibition; but this is exactly what does not occur when the combination of sound and metronome is presented. The effect of the multiple stimulus cannot therefore be calculated as if each stimulus puts into play a given section of the physiological structures capable of combination by the simple arithmetic or algebraic processes of addition and subtraction.[26] If such were the case, the addition of the metronome to the combination of the light and the sound ought to yield four and not ten drops of saliva. To explain this differential functioning of the counter-inhibitory stimulus, Pavlov supposed a kind of nervous equilibrium, which, taking place in the higher centers, was not further specifiable. In so doing, he has supposed a third law to be superimposed upon the first two, and again proved the need for an explanation of the transversal connections within the central nervous system. And such is no doubt the case. The reason, according to Merleau-Ponty, was already apparent in the studies of the French physiologist, Piéron: the effect of a combination of stimuli is not a mathematical or quantitative procedure. In one experiment, conditioning was produced by a combination of elements each one of which was inhibitory; this is possible because each new combination of elements is interpreted by the subject as qualitatively different. In a word, the true excitant of conditioned responses is neither a sound nor an object considered as an individual thing nor a grouping of sounds or objects considered as ensembles at once individual and indistinct; it is rather the distribution of sounds in time, their melodic suite, and the relations between the sizes of objects; or, in general, the precise structure of the situation.[27] Pavlov's theory remains a theory, and as such it is imposed upon the facts. Having its source in physiological atomism, it supposes in psychology entities proper only to the universe of things—physics—and wholly unobservable in the universe of organic reactions—biology.[28]

Merleau-Ponty's final evaluation of the method used by Pavlov is perhaps the most convincing. The latter's supposition of a complex physiological process of stimulation, inhibition and counter-inhibition has the apparent effect of removing any possible discrepancy between theory and fact. Two forces working in opposite directions are posited as determining any given reaction: if the reaction takes place, the experimenter appeals to the positive force; if not, to the negative. Thus the theory cannot be invalidated by experiment; but neither can it be validated. A footnote reminds the reader of a similar "scientific" procedure in physics: Michelson, who wished to prove the existence of ether, tried to explain a negative result by a special property of the ether itself, or by another substance constituting a counter-effect to that of the supposed ether.[29]

Moreover, Pavlov's very insistence on the strictly physiological character of his psychological theories is suspect, resting, as it does, on a semantic confusion. Those facts are usually labeled "physiological" which are directly observable in the nervous system of the organism examined, and those which are mere constructs or intervening variables, to use more modern terminology, we are led to suppose on the basis of observable characters of external behavior. Pavlov's analyses are made in accordance with the second of these meanings of the word, and his science is therefore a science of supposition. Like the musciologist who would reduce the experience of music to that of the physical properties of sound, Pavlov, in reducing psychology to physiology, has used methods proper only to the studies of chemistry and physics and has accordingly missed the purely psychological event. What is needed, according to Merleau-Ponty, is not a physiological and explanatory method, but a psychological and descriptive one.

Nowhere is this need so apparent as in Pavlov's attempted explanation of the cybernetic function of the central nervous system. In effect, the supposition that complex behavior is describable in terms of simple addition and subtraction of stimuli precludes any further notion of motor or even receptor coordination. Tracing the afferent nervous paths to a point in the brain where a connection either positive or negative is made and the appropriate response put into action, Pavlov considered the case of complex stimulation as one in which the various stimuli reinforce or inhibit each other at the points of connection on the mosaic-like, punctiform structure of the brain; the only effect of the addition of the stimuli is to permit or prevent the reaction controlled by the point of reception. The qualitative nature of the reaction cannot be modified by the conjunction or disjunction of the individual stimuli. This alleged lack of a possibility to change qualitatively the nature of a response leads Merleau-Ponty to doubt whether Pavlov's model will ever be adaptable to human speech, in which there is obviously a remarkable adaptation of part to part in the complex reactions, in the rhythmical organization of grammatical periods. Furthermore, reflexes have been conditioned in species having no cortex (fish) and even in invertebrates, a fact which would seem to suggest that the conditioning of reflexes is either a general nervous or biological phenomenon requiring no particular anatomical mechanism having its seat in the cortex.

Having thus cast doubt upon the generality of Pavlov's physiological concept, Merleau-Ponty suggests the solution of the problem of localization within the nervous centers by considering their global functioning rather than their supposed atomistic structure. The authors whose work he scans for some kind of agreement are worthy of mention. They are principally Buytendijk and Plessner, from whom he has borrowed the critique of Pavlov's method, Fischel, Piéron, Gelb, and Goldstein. He abstracts three conclusions:

First, even if a lesion has been localized in a particular sector of the nervous system, it is capable of producing structural difficulties affecting the organism's entire behavior; and similar difficulties may be produced by lesions localized in different sectors of the cortex. This first result casts doubt upon the specificity of function of a given sector of the nervous system, even if the empirical difficulty of localizing the lesion is overcome; but it suggests a third empirical difficulty, that of describing the biological nature of the pathological response in terms of the normal functioning of the organism with all its centers intact. In certain cases of aphasia, for example, it is not strictly true that the subject, following lesion, has lost the power to pronounce certain words; he can be trained to repeat them by rote. What he has lost is the power to *use* them, to associate a given stimulus with the name of a class of stimuli, that is, to perform a certain *kind* of act and not a series of movements. Quoting Goldstein, Merleau-Ponty states, "Each time the patient is forced to depart from a concrete and real situation in order to enter the level of abstraction known as the 'possible' or the 'conceived' his conduct is blocked."[30] And the same results obtain whether the response be acting, perceiving, willing, feeling, or using language. How then is one to characterize this pathological condition? Obviously not by merely observing the content of the behavior, but by understanding the total context of its manifestation:

The conduct of the sick person is not deducible from that of the well by a simple subtraction of parts; it represents a *qualitative* alteration [of normal behavior], and precisely to the extent that certain actions demand an attitude of which the patient is no longer capable are they electively pathological. The need appears, then, of a new kind of analysis which no longer consists in the isolation of elements, but in understanding the shape of a manifold and its immanent law.[31]

We have here the first glimpses into Merleau-Ponty's understanding of phenomenological description. The pathological phenomenon cannot be understood as a thing, power, or cause; rather, it is a process uniting a variety of symptoms according to a logical relation of ground and consequent; or of sign to meaning.[32] The center of nervous connections, consequently, is ill-conceived as a mosaic of points or an apparatus of specific mechanisms dedicated to particular movements; it is better envisaged as a regulating system capable of giving a functional direction to various general modes of conduct, which are either adapted or not to the requirements of a specific situation.

Secondly, Merleau-Ponty concludes that it is, nevertheless, possible to treat the functioning of the nervous system as a global process in which all the elements have an equal importance. A specific nervous function is not independent of the physiological substrate supporting its action. This conclusion Merleau-Ponty has derived from a consideration of certain physiological commonplaces: that given cortical centers have privileged status for the functioning of certain sense organs; a lesion of the occipital lobe, for example, seriously impairs visual perception, and a lesion of the temporal lobe impairs audition. But one patient of Gelb and Goldstein, whose occipital lobe had been destroyed by a piece of shrapnel, experienced more than a serious impairment of visual perception. He was found deficient in any intuition of a manifold of impressions; in a word he was incapable of conceiving. The temptation here is to explain the general conceptual difficulty by appealing to the obvious perceptual malfunction. But the explanation could be reversed: the wounded soldier's perceptual difficulties could very well be explained by his obvious disability to grasp as a whole the units of the sensory manifold. Thus, to function properly the specialized occipital region would need the cooperation of the central regions of the cerebral cortex, and vice versa. The higher nervous centers are functionally related, and the specificity of a function which has been localized in certain centers of the brain is not proof that the centers are the seat of the corresponding function, but that these centers are merely the privileged means of realizing the given function. Finally, quoting Piéron, Merleau-Ponty writes: "Modes of thought and associative processes can be innervated about a predominant sensorial nucleus with significant differences for different individuals, and even for the same individual under different circumstances."[33]

His final conclusion is that the notion of location within the nervous substance has as a consequence an equivocal interpretation. One must accept a concept of plural localization, and of functional parallelism. This third result follows from the examination of the concept of space as applied to the brain. To consider the brain as so many cells or neurons related *pars extra partes* is to miss the point of the functional relationship between nervous centers collaborating to produce the behavior in question. Behavior is not *contained* in such a space. The effect of cerebral lesion is measured by the inability to perform a certain *type* of function or to attain a certain *level* of conduct, and this localization of function is usually labeled "vertical." Of another stripe is the horizontal localization. On the level of correspondence between the nervous substance in its punctiform structure and two sets of attendant phenomena likewise punctiform in structure—the sensuous receptor and the muscles in their relations to the external stimuli and movement of the body respectively—the effect of lesion is merely to remove from the access of the organism certain stimuli or movements. The task is to explain how these two types of behavioral "localizations" are functionally related in both normal and pathological cases. Certain subjects with elementary visual difficulties—deficient horizontal functioning—which are not due to cortical lesion have experienced malfunctioning of color perceptivity, which progresses to complete insensitivity to light. It is almost impossible to specify this qualitative difference in perception merely by appealing to isolated centers of control. Instead, Merleau-Ponty supposes the following process:

Local excitation distributed across the surface receptors undergoes, on entering the specialized centers of the cortex, a series of structural differentiations which dissociate the stimuli from the context of spatio-temporal events whence they emerge and re-orders them according to the original dimensions of organic and human activity.[34]

In summary, some physiological events may be localized on the horizontal level, and others on the vertical; the psycho-physical parallelism about which one could speak is not the one-to-one correlation of certain physiological processes with a given content of awareness, but a loose correlation of the two sets of physiological processes which work together functionally, in a more or less well integrated fashion, and which constitute the substratum of organized human behavior, likewise more or less adapted to the human situation.[35]

Though space and color perceptivity are considered, the most complex test situation given for these three conclusions is that of human speech. We shall treat this case at some length because of the importance of the concept of expression in Merleau-Ponty's later philosophy.

Whatever the model by which one is led to conceive the action of the central nervous system—be it transmitter, switchboard, dialing system, or transformer—the facts to be explained in current speech seem to surpass the possibilities of sheer mechanics in which verbal images act as counters. Such a mechanism must be capable first, of receiving an indefinite number of counters, many of which from a purely acoustic point of view are identical; secondly, of combining the same counters according to different patterns never before received; and finally, of making this combination, not merely by a process of addition or spatial juxtaposition, but by interpreting the meaning of each counter, which may, however, vary for the same counter in a different spatial position. The very notion of such a mechanism seems to Merleau-Ponty a self-contradiction: first of all, a machine is constructed for a limited set of operations; secondly, the automatic functioning of any machine can never be put into operation without first being set for certain specified conditions. Since a machine could not set its own conditions as the human animal does in speech, the physiology of speech needs a non-mechanistic interpretation. In speech,

the coordinated elements are not merely placed side by side. They constitute together, in their very order, a whole which has its own law and manifests that law even from the moment the first elements of excitation are given, just as the first notes of a melody assign to the whole structure a certain kind of resolution.[36]

Each element entering into the whole has its own meaning re-interpreted for its position in the whole. The same note in two different melodies are absolutely unrecognizable, whereas the same melody in two different keys remain identifiable throughout a complete change in the elements. Thus "meaning" and "structure" are correlative notions, and the nervous centers must be capable of creating a unity of meaning which is expressed through the juxtaposed elements of the structure, through the relations of the terms, without taking into account the physical reality of the terms themselves—the case of homonyms, in language. Whatever ambiguity there may be in the individual terms, the context in which they occur must be such as to remove the ambiguity. To linger too long in the search for the right word is to prejudice seriously any meaning of the sentence in which it is to occur. If the subject is forced to revert to each individual counter in the development of his sentence, more likely than not there will be no statement. Contemplation of verbal counters, or verbal "images" is perhaps possible, but only in the pathological conditions of the physiologist's laboratory.

In the very act of pronouncing the words of a sentence, a subject must accentuate the first words and give them a rhythm proper to the total structure which is not yet pronounced, even if its ultimate pronunciation is prefigured by the initial sounds. As in music, the key to meaning is the context, the global unit, the form, the whole whose immanent law gives significance to each of its constitutive parts. And it is for this reason that Merleau-Ponty looks toward a revised gestaltism for a corrective to Pavlov's physiological psychology. The physiological processes implicit in the understanding of the meaning of a word must be improvised and actively constituted at the very moment of perception.[37] What is understood is the meaning of the whole sentence; if by chance one must inquire about the meaning of a word, the process of analysis must be applied to the whole unit of awareness. It is impossible to conceive how the meaning of a sentence is constructed out of individual parts, each containing a prior absolute signification. In short, perception cannot be explained by substantive physiological processes, but must be given a descriptive analysis in the manner prescribed by Husserl: the experi-

ence must be had and described according to its essential characteristics. How could one trace the physiology of word comprehension,
when the phonemes, as vibrations in the air, either spoken or heard,
depend for their meaning upon the meaning of the entire sentence?
An inquiry is to be made into the global functioning of the organism,
and not into the physiological substratum, if psychological events are
to be understood. Again Merleau-Ponty insists that psychology is
richer than physiology; its laws are more complex:

As one approaches the center of the cerebral cortex, the conditions of behavior, instead of being found in the nervous substance itself, as is the case
on the periphery of the nervous system, are found more and more in the
qualitatively variable modes of its global functioning.[38]

What is needed, then, is a theory of complex orders of conduct varying with the kinds of forms or structures of perceived objects. But
this is the subject of a later section of this chapter.

Before outlining the elements of Merleau-Ponty's philosophical
anthropology, it would be profitable to consider the criticisms he has
leveled at other latter-day practitioners of physiological psychology,
the behaviorists who have tried to use the conditioning process to
explain all learning. By "learning" is meant the acquisition of a new
behavioral pattern which allows the animal to adapt itself to varying
situations. Here again, Merleau-Ponty comments upon the experiments made by others: principally, Watson, Thorndike, Miller; and
borrows his criticisms from psychologists whose work is more congenial to his own interests: Buytendijk, Koehler, Koffka, Guillaume,
Tolman. He proceeds by distinguishing the laboratory situation from
the more realistic and concrete situations of the natural life processes
as they take place in nature.

In situations of the first type, an experimental animal (a rat) is
conditioned to run a maze to seek an incentive; and, following a
series of "trials and error," supposedly succeeds in fulfilling his
drive. Under the pressure of hunger or sexual deprivation, the animal is led to perform a series of unrelated gestures one of which is
rewarded, and the others of which are either merely unrewarded or
"punished" by an experience of pain. As the theory has it, the reward
tends to fix the successful response, and the punishment to inhibit
the unsuccessful. Without the reward and punishment—intrusion of
the experimenter on the rat's experience—it would be difficult to
conceive why the rat continues to try running the maze after its first

errors, which should inhibit any future response; or even why the one effective response is adopted. In answer to the latter question Watson had supposed a law of "repetition." But this repetition is not always performed in the same manner as the first successful trial. For example, a test animal will often repeat unsuccessful trials—which responses should have been inhibited—while at other times only one successful trial suffices to fix the response. It is difficult, therefore, to conceive how the learning process can be explained by the chance innervation of previously existing connections. What appears to happen, especially in the case of a single trial which fixes the successful response, is that the organism in some manner evaluates the situation in which it finds itself; it is precisely this evaluation, the assignment of means to end, which the strictly behavioral interpretation of the situation is not theoretically capable of explaining.

To amplify this charge, Merleau-Ponty criticizes more thoroughly the theoretical suppositions of behavioral explanation. According to the theory in question, the series of stimuli and responses in which successful auto-conditioning takes place are thought to be related externally, with only the connecting link of immediate temporal contiguity: each leg of the maze must be run after the other without actual sight of either their interconnections or of the goal object. But since the successful responses are only some of the total set of possible responses, by what process do they become fixed for a second run of the maze? For those responses to become fixed, the actual attainment of the goal object must in some manner recall the whole series of preparatory gestures which led to the first success. If this is so, the temporal contiguity of the process of learning has been reversed: what was last becomes stimulus to what was first; but this is contrary to the original hypothesis. Moreover, according to the same theory, conditioning is capable of fixing the successful response only according to the pattern of preparatory responses traversed in the process of learning. But this theoretical principle is flatly invalidated by the facts: if the correct response is a slight pull of a string, a cat has been observed to do this first with its teeth, and next with its paws. Merleau-Ponty concludes that "learning is thus never restricted to rendering oneself capable of repeating the same gesture, but of bringing to a situation an adaptive response by different means."[39]

The animal is led to "understand" the situation; it reverses the temporal direction of end and means. At the time of Merleau-Ponty's treatise, behavioral theory had not yet explained the animal's sense of "direction," the intentional relation between preparatory acts and attained goal; in a word, how the goal gives a single meaning to a series of diverse acts. Here again, a phenomenological analysis is the suggested alternative.

The real life processes of the animal considerably complicate the discussion. Learning a maze in the laboratory under the tutelage of a rat psychologist is not learning per se. Not only must the animal be capable of bringing the same or similar solutions to different problems, but the "sameness" and "difference" here must be measured by the total situation in which the problem occurs. Koehler's monkey experiments have shown that the test animals actually succeeded in solving problems by establishing known connections in entirely different situations.[40] Merleau-Ponty interprets this phenomenon as follows:

> The conditional stimulus acts only as a stand-in for a whole category of stimuli which have become reflexogenic at the same time as the first; the movement of the primitive response is fixed only as a particular case of a general aptitude capable of variations about a single fundamental theme.[41]

True learning is general and takes place in fact on the level of chimpanzees. But however such learning takes place, "there must be in the organism a principle which assures a universal significance to the learning experience."[42]

In retrospect, the trial and error method of learning may be characterized by the following dilemma: either the trials contain no internal law, and hence no significance for the problem solving animal—in which case there is no learning—or there is learning, and the organism must be capable of establishing between different possible solutions to the same problem, or the same solution to different problems, and between the problems and the various solutions, a kind of relation by which the solutions to the problems appear as means to that end, that is, as possibilities. In solving their problems, even the lower animals must be capable of *evaluating* the problematic situation. And for Merleau-Ponty this is another way of saying that a stimulus must be understood as more than a *stimulus in itself* (physically or chemically determinable), and ultimately as a *stimulus for the organism* involved in the problem. In other words, no stimulus as such is given to the organism, but instead is elaborated into such by the life processes of the animal itself.

Behaviorists have objected at this stage of the discussion to the anthropomorphic character of Merleau-Ponty's language: the "evaluation" of the total situation, the "general import" of learned responses, the very notion of "problem" smacks too much of the experimenter's own experience to be a fitting characterization for the behavior of the lower animals. And Merleau-Ponty is sensitive to the charge. He admits that a strictly objective interpretation of animal behavior would be limited to the description of particular movements effectuated by particular stimuli; but insists that his own anthropomorphic description of problematic situations seems to fit some experimental learning processes and not others, and that this difference must be accounted for by an adequate theory. After all, it has been shown that some animals respond only to particular stimuli, and that others succeed in adapting their responses to varying situations. To exclude the facts is not to exclude the anthropomorphic language used to describe them so much as it is to exclude science itself. What is being defended in the objection is not scientific objectivity, but physiological realism and, ultimately, epistemological nominalism. Any scientific law which is not given as a fact is given, but which does find its expression in the facts themselves, would be subject to the same criticism; should the objection be pushed to its extreme, the very terms of "colors," "lights," and "pressures" would be excluded from scientific psychological terminology.[43]

Since man is the experimenter, any terms used to describe the conditions of the animal experiments must ultimately derive from the context of human experience; they are valid when the terms used faithfully describe the objects named; invalid, if they do not. Thus, according to Merleau-Ponty, pure objectivity in psychological experiments is an impossibility. The only problem is to decide which of the data are original and which derivative. Experiment has shown that responses to the structure of certain situations cannot be considered derived from the basic elementary, physically described, nervous responses. If the scientist continues his endeavor to discover the ultimate simples of biological response, he will continue to be subject to the charge of incoherence: he must continually revise his general theory to fit the facts of experience, or frankly abandon the theory itself. The latter alternative may provide a fresh start, by merely abandoning the elementary-complex distinction between behavioral responses and by adopting what Merleau-Ponty calls a "holistic view," according to which the structure of the experience is given in the content considered to constitute the experience, or results within the experience as a developing theme.[44] In either case, the structure of behavior seems clearly to dominate any given simple stimulus or response.

The rest of this chapter will deal with Merleau-Ponty's holistic, or structurally centered, view of animal behavior.

PHILOSOPHICAL ANTHROPOLOGY

The critique of psychological methodology has furnished Merleau-Ponty a set of concepts he will ultimately use to constitute his own "philosophy of ambiguity."[45] I have given it the name "philosophical anthropology" since it is an attempted description of human behavior based upon an analysis of various structures or formed responses evident in part on the lower levels of evolutionary development, and completely only in man. Its method is not metaphysical in the sense of appealing to "transphenomenal" realties, but reflective in the sense often intended to include scientific inductive procedures and their critical evaluation. This interpretation of the philosophical method is similar to Heidegger's[46] supposition that metaphysical inquiry (direct personal encounter) is a broader concept than the method of science, and the ultimate court of appeal by which the claims of science to validity are judged. Merleau-Ponty calls the method, simply, "reflection." And for this term to have any meaning, in Merleau-Ponty's view, the reflection must be on the non-reflective responses of lower orders of behavior.

For the purposes of this commentary, the substantive portion of his analysis is divided into three parts: the orders of form, the dialectic of orders, and *les aventures de la conscience,*[47] an historical résumé of the mind-body problem which exposes what Merleau-Ponty considers the erroneous bases of the distinction between mind and body, and which serves the added purpose of making clear his own historical sources.

The Orders of Form.—The first level of formed response is composed of what Merleau-Ponty calls "syncretic forms." These are behavioral patterns linked with certain abstract characters of a situation, or certain complexes of stimuli found within the animal's environment, and limited to the natural conditions of response set up by the physiological structures of the animal in question. For example, it has been shown that the reaction of a spider to a fly caught in its web is not directly called out by the stimulus of food incentive: when a dead fly is placed in his web, the spider fails to respond to the situation; but when a vibrating tuning fork is placed there, the same spider immediately responds to the food a fly's presence would imply. Evidently then, the spider's reaction is to the vibration of his web, and not to the presence of food. In this example there is apparently a correspondence between the abstract character of the situation—the vibrating web—and the "rhythm of the insect's life" which includes disturbance, motion toward vibrating object, and contact with its prey. This correspondence between the external and the biological factors of the total situation always implies a series of relations which are nonetheless concretized within a specific kind of situation; because of this limitation to the specific situation, little learning of the sort which implies generality is possible.

Earlier writers have referred to this kind of response as "instinctive." Merleau-Ponty cites Buytendijk's discovery that conditioning of toads is impossible except in situations which strongly resemble those in which the so-called instinctive responses—to a fixed complex of special stimuli—are called out. The experiments run as follows: presented with an earthworm behind a glass screen, the toad continues to nip at the moving morsel in spite of the inhibition which should have been effectuated by the presence of the screen. The "instinctive" response dictates continuous pursuit of the moving prey. But while only one contact with a "bad tasting" ant is enough to inhibit further trials at contact with ants of the same hill, the inhibition brought on by the toad's having nipped a piece of black paper dangling on a thin thread is overcome, and further trials are made to capture the moving prey in spite of the prior unsavory experience. Any stimulus is reflexogenic to the toad only insofar as it resembles the natural stimulus for the reacting organism. It is not the essential nature of the stimulus, in this case the food, or a prior experience of the taste, so much as a constellation of occurrences to which the organism is attuned by its very nature.

The second level of forms apparent in the experiments made upon the behavior of the lower animals is said to be composed of "mutable forms." A formed response is mutable when conditioning to a given stimulus is transferable from one situation to another, the transference taking place by the presence of signals, or sign-gestalten. Conditioning, it had been supposed, takes place only by the relation of spatial or temporal contiguity of conditioned and unconditioned stimuli. But consider the following experiment: a hen was conditioned to peck at a pile of grains of corn colored a light shade of grey, and given an inhibitory response to another pile similar to the first in every respect save its darker shade of grey. Given the alternative between the lighter shade of grey and a still lighter one, the hen pecked not at the first positively conditioned stimulus, but at the "neutral" color. Again, when it was given the alternative between the first negatively conditioned stimulus, the darker pile, and a still darker pile, the hen's reaction was to peck at the original inhibitory stimulus. In every case of choice, the hen pecked at the lighter of the two shades. Gestaltists have concluded that the hen had been conditioned to react to a directly perceived relation, "lighter than." The sign, the grey of the edible grain, is a configuration, and not an absolute physical stimulus, determinable solely by spatio-temporal coordinates or qualitative sameness. And, if so, the relation between the conditioned stimulus and the conditioned response is a relation between relations: between the configuration of the stimulus and the organized motor responses of the animal.

In his objections to a similar conclusion by Tolman in his "Sign-gestalt or Conditioned Reflex," Neal E. Miller has claimed that simple conditioning of reflexes may explain sign behavior without an appeal to internal or external structures within the experimental situation.[48] Tolman had performed the following experiment: a rat was conditioned by the presence of a white door to take the proper turn of the maze to secure food. The question is whether the temporal sequence—white door, food—has effectuated the conditioning, or whether the white door is merely an element in the total configuration of stimuli. The latter would be the case if the animal, when presented directly at the end of the maze, without having first passed through the door, and given a shock along with the food, would lose its positive conditioning to the white door on subsequent runs through the maze. If such a result were found to obtain, the temporal sequence would not be the only basis of the conditioned effect, but rather the configuration, white door—"value of goal."

Miller's reply has become classic. First of all, Tolman failed to produce the anticipated result; but even if he had, a more strictly behavioristic interpretation of the results would have been possible. Appealing to a law of anticipation, Miller pointed out that acquired responses tend to be anticipated in the stimuli which precede the conditioned stimulus itself. Thus a rat begins to go through his learned responses immediately upon being placed in the maze; if the conditioning is negative, it suffices to explain the rat's refusal to run the maze to consider the prior negative experience with the goal object as "residual" or trace phenomena. Should one change the goal object, for example, to water when the shock is given, the anticipation is less strong; the rat runs the maze, but more slowly than before the negative experience. The white door has not lost its positive value, and the anticipated goal response would still be the determining factor in the experiment.

The gestaltists have answered this objection by pointing out that the refusal by the rat to run the maze is qualitatively different from his reaction at the time of the shock—the same physiological processes are not innervated—and the movements the rat must make to follow the right side of the maze are different from its reaction at the point of turning itself. Its reactions are not anticipated, but prefigured, or pre-formed. Thus, the same movements have not been transferred from the later to an earlier stimulus, or vice versa, but the earlier stimulus tends to call out those movements of the animal which have a significant relation with the change of the sign (value) of the final stimulus. An error or a shock ultimately acts to change the value of the sign, a structural relation within the total situation.[49]

If animals react to the structure of signs more than to the physical matter, or content, of the stimulus, it is likewise evident that there is a natural limitation on the animal's adaptability to external structures. Children have proven superior to monkeys on their responses to serial order, reacting successfully from the second try on to "plus one" in situations where the goal object is placed successively in second, third, and fourth, containers; the same advantage is enjoyed by the human animal in its response to a means-end relationship. In Koehler's experiments with monkeys it was shown that the instrumental value of an object decreases for the subjects in direct relation with the distance of the object used as instrument from its correlative end. Monkeys are apparently cabable of relating means and ends, but only within their direct field of spatial vision. The reason for this superiority is alleged by Merleau-Ponty to be man's ability to use symbols, and to construct objects embodying symbolized relations. A monkey builds scaffolding, and succeeds in using it to attain a goal object, while a child would succeed only in breaking its neck in an attempt to use the monkey's "scaffolding." Here again, the reason is that "the thing" exists only as a possible response within the monkey's organism, which is more agile than the human's in maintaining its equilibrium. On the level of sign behavior, structures of stimuli are correlative to structures of response, and the "meaning" of any sign is the response it may call out.[50]

But as intimated above, not all signs are signals to a fixed response. The third and highest level of formed activity is called "symbolic." The signs learned by the lower animals appear to remain on the level of signals, that is, pointers to a specific response within a well-defined situation. Signs become symbols when a response can be made in the absence of a specific stimulus, and when the sign itself becomes a thematic development of an activity which is its "expression." An animal could conceivably be conditioned to type a given word or sentence; the presence of the keyboard and the order of the experimenter would suffice to produce the reaction. But this activity would still be a reaction to signals. Symbolic activity admits of variations; the typist, the organist produce certain adjustments in their behavioral responses not in reaction to a note or to a group of notes, but to certain grammatical or musical phrases. In order to play the organ, the organist must understand the correspondence between the configuration of the graphic text, the structure of the heard melody, and the prescribed digital patterns of his own motor responses, as they are linked in a common bond of signification: the developing theme. Without this internal bond, musical notation would not be a language, nor the organ an instrument, nor the musician an organist. This intertranslatability of structure constitutes the essence of symbolic behavior. A true sign, a symbol represents what is signified not by virtue of a simple empirical association, but by its relations to other signs when the object for which it stands is related to the objects for which they stand in correlative patterns of structure. For this reason, the "key" to lost languages has been found in certain cases by an internal analysis of the text which has indicated the external dimensions of the represented universe. Finally, in symbolic behavior human conduct expresses a stimulus for its own sake: behavior no longer merely has a meaning; it is a meaning.[51]

This is the root of Merleau-Ponty's later doctrine of expression, which is merely sketched at this stage of its evolution in order to complete the enumeration of the hierarchy of formal behavioral structures. He is sensitive, for example, to a possible charge that the illustrations he has chosen to elucidate symbolic behavior may presuppose knowledge of symbols.[52] The aptitude necessary to create meanings by composing them on a typewriter or piano keyboard may possess the structures claimed, but both sets of physical responses can be set in motion only by the prior symbols, either words or musical notations, which are to be re-formed into another set of structures: the typed sentences or the melody as heard. But his answer seems somewhat weak. He claims that every acquired aptitude for the utilization of a given object is an adaptation on the part of the human subject to that object consisting of a synchronization of organized motor responses with a complex of stimuli organized by these same responses into an "object." In fact, objects appear only by virtue of this close correlation with human responses.[53]

This last sentence would indicate that a stronger answer could be made to his would-be objectors. It is quite true that a typist who is merely copying an already composed text is doing much the same thing as a musician who is presenting the music composed for him by another, and that both of these aptitudes seem to be describable as mere signalizing behavior. But the typist who is composing a poem for the first time, and the composer who runs his hands over the keys of the piano in search of a melody, are constituting by their acts a new "meaning," objects which did not exist before the act of typing or playing. In each case the new cultural object acts as a stimulus for any other person who would reproduce it by any other means. The "meaning" of the new piece is then the structure common to all the structures by which the piece is to be presented. What Merleau-Ponty must do, then, is to explain how new symbols come into being through the interplay of bodily responses. Since the precedent for such an explanation already existed in the aesthetic theories of Alain and Valéry,[54] it is no mystery that Merleau-Ponty's aesthetics is based upon that of Valéry, and that the aesthetic creation of symbols is envisaged in Merleau-Ponty's epistemology as a necessary first step in acquiring knowledge. But of this, more in a subsequent chapter.

In terms of human behavior, the significance of aptitudes is a relation between the structures of stimuli and those of responses. Given a structured set of stimuli, the typist or the organist "understands" the situation when he is capable of making the ordered set of responses, a series of movements not merely spatio-temporally juxtaposed, but bearing an intrinsic connection designatable as the grammatical or the musical meaning of the piece. Thus "true *aptitudes* demand that the 'stimulus' become efficacious by the internal properties of a structure, by its immanent significance, and that the response be symbolic of it."[55] The possibility of mediation between the symbol and its meaning is thus clearly conceived as formal isomorphism, and abstraction can be made of the content of either stimulus or response, as of a specific situation. Cognition then becomes possible as a kind of abstract response which may be made to varying contexts, and man is liberated from the strict biological determination of his situation here and now. For example, a scientist in the laboratory may manipulate his own particular stimuli in search of a general statement of their relations, which would be valid in non-laboratory situations as well; or he may manipulate his own formalized responses which have already achieved symbolization in the language of mathematics or logic; or, if the general concepts are empirical in nature, the scientist may manipulate them in abstraction of their source in past experience—in terms of their relatedness *inter se*—and search for a future authentication in experience whether in a laboratory or not. "Truth" takes on a new meaning at this level of behavior as the relation between the symbol and the symbolized becomes specifiable in more general terms.

Merleau-Ponty deduces two sets of conclusions from this doctrine of formal responses. First is the re-evaluation of Pavlov's theory of the conditioned reflex. Either the conditioned reflex is a pathological phenomenon, or a second order reaction to a complex biological situation. At a certain stage in the training of one of his dogs, Pavlov had noticed a complete inhibition of any response whatsoever; he called it a "freedom reflex." But if one considers each stimulus an absolute physical process, this reflex of liberty, not being absolutely determinable, is a theoretical surd. It is more proper, says Merleau-Ponty, to interpret the liberty reflex as an expression of behavior determinable according to a higher order, the response of the animal to a situation having a total biological significance. That the conditioned reflex is abnormal is attested by the fact that it is more easily observed in children than in adults; among children, in the younger; and among children of the same age, in the more backward. Moreover, in adults who have mastered complicated aptitudinal responses, it has been found that in order to produce a simple movement in the total complex movements involved in the response, the adult must analyze the total gestalt of movements in order to be able to produce one of its elements in isolation. This act of analysis is a reaction to a reaction, and is possible only in a species which is capable of symbolizing to itself, without actually performing it, the complex reaction demanded by the stimulus. But in either case Pavlov's doctrine is seriously compromised: the conditioned reflex is a pathological dissociation of responses in a species whose activity is mainly syncretic; as a strictly physiological explanation of symbolic behavior, its shortcomings are made apparent by the necessary appeal to analysis.[56]

The second set of conclusions is relevant to the philosophical method one must employ to understand the significance of animal behavior. Pavlov's alleged errors have their source in his attempt to explain the "superior" by the "inferior," mental activity by physiological matter. Similar difficulties would be experienced should one attempt to explain the inferior by the superior, the existence of things by the laws of the minds which intend things as goal objects. In explanations of the first kind all the relations considered are external; of the second, all internal. According to the one we would have the world of things (realism) and to the other a world of minds (idealism). Obviously a new metaphysics is needed which avoids both these monistic extremes. We need a metaphysics of behavior in which behavior is considered as such, dependent upon neither its higher nor its lower manifestations, but expressing itself in both as a series of variations upon structural themes. When an objective world is viewed by a subject, the reaction of the subject is to regard the world as a means of accomplishing a possibility inherent in both the world and the subject. And if this happens in fact with every act of knowledge, it is plainly true that a knower is not a spectator of the objective events of the physical universe; nor is he a pure consciousness, as Sartre would have it, for whom there must be objects having an ontological substratum in pure being (*en-soi*). The gestures of an animal aim at (*vise*) being for the animal, at a certain environment in which the species is comfortable. Thus an unstable placement of boxes may be scaffolding for a monkey, but the occasion of an accident for a child. Nor do the gestures of the animal in question reveal a consciousness whose essence is to know, but merely a certain way of handling the world, a certain way of existing. Finally, the problem of other minds is clearly understood in the same terms, as occurring only in the symbolic order: when two animals use gestures in the same way to refer to the one physical world, they communicate. In essence, then, I have evidence for the existence of another mind when the symbols I use call out similar responses in its and my own experience.[57]

Before passing on to a more detailed examination Merleau-Ponty has given of the recent history of the mind-body problem, I shall attempt to elucidate further Merleau-Ponty's doctrine of forms by commenting on his theory concerning their functioning in the "dialectic" of orders.

The Dialectic of Orders.—Since the older physiological psychology had been predicated on the foundation of physical absolutes, each stimulus and each response uniquely determinable in terms of a linear causal series, and Merleau-Ponty has done his utmost to show that such a theoretical construction has no empirical authentication, he must face the task of showing how organized behavior is possible within the three orders he has presented. To him, the very notions of stimulus and response are ambiguous. The stimulus may be considered a physical event, or a biological one; its value may be quantitative, or a structured situation having a particular meaning for the organism in question. Likewise the response: it may be described geographically as affecting so much energy and displacement of objects within the organic situation, or as a series of movements related harmoniously and given a meaning by reference to the achievement of some goal object. And, in their highest order, the result of organic responses is the setting up of *aptitudes,* that is "the general ability to respond to situations of a certain kind by various reactions which have nothing in common but a meaning (direction, sense, intentionality)."[58] This preordained and non-reflective ordering of an organic species to its environment suggests a new principle of relationship. Where the linear causal sequence breaks down, in the performance of organized responses, and the mutual determination of organism and environment is evident—Pragmatists have referred to this connection as "interaction"—Merleau-Ponty suggests the existence of a dialectical ordering principle whereby the discontinuity between atomistic elements would be explained by successive restructuring of "forms."

Early gestaltists (Wertheimer, Koffka, Koehler) had already shown the way, and at least one writer in our own time, L. L. Whyte, has continued to put "the accent on form" in scientific explanation,[59] when the gestaltists themselves have failed to follow through with the logical conclusions to be drawn from their original inspiration. Koffka is cited for his reasoning that a cause can be effective only in a single universe. Since it is known that the stimulus of behavior comes from the environing physical universe and the response is redeployed in the same direction, it was concluded that the physiology through which the nervous impulses had passed must be equally "material" or physical, the only difference from classical materialist doctrine being that the whole process is supposedly mediated by the homogeneity of the physiological and physical structures involved, rather than that of isolated atomistic particles. But this is to suggest that all *Gestalten* are physical, that nothing essentially psychical takes place for the impulse's having passed through the central nervous system, and that in the long run there would be no difference between the observable kinds of orders. Merleau-Ponty therefore assumes the task of re-thinking the theory of *Gestalten* as they appear in the physical, vital, and human orders.

First of all, a physical system is composed of an aggregate of forces in a state of equilibrium or constant change. No law is possible for any isolated element or series of elements; the vector quality of each line of force is determinable only by all the forces working within the total system. Thus all qualitative changes taking place within the system are the expression of a single immanent law. No external force working on the system more or less continuously can do more than redistribute the forces within the system itself, which "develops by bounds or crises," redistributing itself into qualitatively different events and varying historical developments.[60] Even the law of universal gravitation, as corrected by the general law of relativity, may express no more than a certain state of equilibrium of forces which determine the history of the solar system; and other histories are conceivable. Within the total system we call the "physical universe" we are thus led to admit "partial totalities without which there would be no laws, and which are precisely what was meant above by 'form'."[61] According to Merleau-Ponty, causal laws uniting absolute particles in a linear series—explanatory principles he calls "positivistic"—simply do not exist; in every effort to validate such presumed physical principles appeal must be made to other laws which operate in conjunction with the one being tested. The effects of such conditions as temperature, pressure, and altitude are never in reality negligible. A given physical change takes place under the pressure of a mass of converging laws, and a state of the total system at any one time, before or after a given change, is describable in terms of the relation between the partial structures.

Each partial structure is itself a dynamic unity having a persisting character; being a system having its own internal law, the very existence of structure implies that of law. But conversely, the existence of laws implies that of structures. Hence structure and law are dialectical moments of a single continuing historical process. A 'form' can then be understood as a theoretical limit toward which our knowledge of physical events approaches; it is not a physical reality, "but an object of perception, without which, moreover, the science of physics would make no sense since it is constructed on the foundation of such objects and for the purpose of coordinating them."[62] Physical forms are in essence perceptual, and hence can not be appealed to, as gestaltists have done in an effort to reduce mental activity to the physical. As limits toward which perceptions tend, laws are instruments of knowledge, and the structures they relate are the objects of our perceptive awareness. Both have meaning only in the context of our conceiving the perceived world.[63]

Simple physical systems react on the conditions forming them in a way organic systems do not. Whereas the external forces working on the physical form act to produce the equilibrium of the form, the reaction of the system's re-alignment on the external forces is comparatively small, and is such as to re-establish a new state of inertia, to relax the tension between the two. The electrodes of a current-producing cell, for example, become polarized by the very current they produce. But in the second order of forms, the organic, structures react upon the influencing environment in such a way as to reconstitute the environment, while the organic structure itself undergoes growth. And this reconstitution of the environment is effectuated by "privileged" behavioral patterns, which are the means used by the organism to produce its optimal adaptation. That behavior which is not privileged—for a given species as for a given individual—is the difficult, or the pathological response. The very life of the individual organism necessitates that it select from its environment what is best suited for its own continuance, as the limits shown above on the process of conditioning readily demonstrate. Each stimulus has a vital significance, as well as physical determination. What are *laws* for physical forms become *norms* for organic structures, and the lower forms of life "evaluate" their environmental situation according to fixed "instinctive" patterns. The very differences of perceptual thresholds among various species indicate that the organism governs what of the external situation will affect it as a living thing, whereas a physical form "feels" indiscriminately the accumulated effect of all external stimuli. The action and interaction of organism and environment is thus a truly circular process in which each force constitutes a "dialectical" order irreducible to a purely mechanical model.

It remains to be understood in what way this dialectic operates. The so-called causes of organic behavior, physical stimuli, cannot be considered mechanical forces; when the stimuli impinging upon the organism vary quantitatively, the reaction is a global response varying in a qualitative manner. Hence a one-to-one correspondence of vector forces does not exist between stimulus and response. In effect, stimuli cannot be considered causes at all, but rather the occasions of response.[64] Instead of depending upon the material properties of the stimulus, its quantifiable spatial and temporal properties, the response depends upon the significance of the stimuli to the individual's organic needs. And this relation is intrinsic rather than extrinsic; that is, the "meaning" (*sens*) intrinsic to the structure, organism-environment, depends as much upon the aptitudes of the organism as upon the environment. Hence we find, in this second level of orders, another dialectical arrangement in which one total structure having an internal ordering principle functions via two correlative variables:

In recognizing that behavioral patterns have a meaning depending upon the vital significance of situations, biological science is prevented from conceiving them as things which would exist, *partes extra partes, in* the nervous system or *in* the body; it [should] see embodied within them dialectical relations which irradiate out onto the environment implicit in their structure.[65]

Without having recourse to the vitalism of the nineteenth century,

or to a more primitive kind of animism, biologists must recognize
that the conditions of life include the norms of the organism, "the
unities of significance that a consciousness finds there, that it sees
being deployed before it."[66]

At this point Merleau-Ponty has opened himself to a serious
objection. A consciousness is said to find the significance of vital
situations, and in some sense of the term, this seems appropriate. But
the question remains, exactly whose consciousness "sees" the significance? Certainly not an individual of a species not capable of con-
ceptualizing; such a seeing could be nothing more than a metaphor.
And if it is the biologist's own consciousness, then Merleau-Ponty
is guilty of the same kind of anthropomorphism he has charged so
many others with. But there is textual evidence that he intends the
first alternative: "In reality . . . we have already introduced consciousness, and what we have designated under the term 'life' is
already consciousness of life."[67] One could admit his conclusion that
the phenomenon of life appears when the dispositions of the movements contained within a "stretch of extension" takes place by the
mutual effect of each upon the others, reflecting upon itself as a
whole and thereby beginning to express something, to manifest outside the system an internal structure,[68] without in the least admitting
that such consciousness is fully self-conscious, as this still seems to
be the property of the human animal. And even for some of these,
full self-consciousness seems to be more of an ideal than a fact. A
third alternative which would allow Merleau-Ponty to escape the
criticism as an appeal to an "impersonal" consciousness, such as that
described by Sartre in his "La transcendance de l'Ego," but the
impersonality of this consciousness appearing at the "horizon" of
one's experiences indicates that the consciousness involved is not
that of the empirical perceiver.

The third order of forms is precisely the human level of experience. Where we have found two lower orders of dialectic, total
structures definable in terms of action and reaction of partial forms
—condition-effect for the physical order, and lived situation-instinc-
tive response for the vital—an explanation must be given for the
distinctively human reaction, perceived situation-work. Taking a
wide detour around the philosophy of Bergson, which he alleges
has not surpassed the description of the purely vital level of activity,
Merleau-Ponty claims that a fully self-conscious perception has its

beginnings at the human level, thereby laying himself open to the criticism we have made above. Presumably unaware of the possibility of the criticism, he continues with the description of the higher dialectic: "Perception is a moment of the living dialectic of a concrete subject; participates in its total structure; and, correlatively, has for its primitive object not the 'unorganized solid' [cf. Bergson, *Creative Evolution*], but the actions of other human subjects."[69]

At its beginning stages, the perceptual consciousness is said to possess a double characteristic: it intends a human, or cultural object, that is, one of a possible use value, and grasps it in direct experience rather than as a representation, which is a still higher conscious structure. The experiences of children who are just learning to perceive, and of artists, which often resemble those of a child, show that what is initially given in perception is a large, internally indeterminate, and externally vague outline, a physiognomy rather than a face. In nowise can it be thought to be composed of discrete sensorial elements which the mind fuses into a single object; a perceptual form is "a configuration either visual, sonorous, or one antedating any experienced distinction of the senses, in which the sensorial value of each element is determined by its function in the totality and varies with it."[70] And these forms appear in a general "phenomenal field." An example of such appearances may be had in the practical activity of an athlete, who is conscious of each of his movements insofar as they are directed to the purpose of the play. With each turn of his body the movement takes on a new sense (direction), for the total structure of the movement patterns is determined by the end of the activity. But each player lives the situation more than he is fully conscious of his own intentions.

Human work provides another example. Whereas workers in a capitalistic system usually consider as the meaning of their labors the money which is their reward, actually the use to which the object is to be put, by themselves or by others, should serve to give direction to their activity. This use is guided by a whole network of human institutions. Moreover, the comprehension of the use of an object would seem to imply that the person is capable of performing the responses which have gone into the making of the object, one of which is its prevised utility, without any elaborate "logical" understanding of the situation in which the object was actually made, by another, for his own use. The correspondence between a series of responses he is capable of making and that which he sees symbolized in the object made constitutes this "understanding." But the problem is precisely to describe the processes which enable this double awareness to take place. Can one appeal to introspection for the awareness of internal responses, and to the mental organization of a manifold of impressions for the external? Evidently not. If the unit of perception at this level is the vague general outline of a form in which the element finds determination by its relations with the other elements, the manifold could never be given to consciousness; moreover, could it be given, by appealing to it, we should be explaining the less evolved conduct by appealing to the more evolved, and this inversion of the process is unthinkable. Kant is of no help. The spoken word is heard before it is understood; a face seen before it becomes the essential part of another person. But the meaning of both these phenomena comes from another person, rather than from the "categories" of the child's own mind. Furthermore, the child can desire, will, fear, without knowing exactly what is being desired, willed, feared. A primitive consciousness is prior to the representational awareness of its objects.

Cultural objects are understood in terms of the practical intention which unites the various motor responses making up the act of use. At the primitive level, there is no conscious distinction between ends and means; only an outgoing movement, an action. Clothing serves to warm the body; buildings to house its activity; words to coordinate activities. But the human animal surpasses these basic needs: clothing becomes adornment; buildings, architecture; and words, poetry. The strictly human environment is forced upon man, but at the same time, man projects new values into that environment and changes it to fit other desires: "What defines man is not the capacity to create a second nature—economic, social or cultural—beyond his biological nature, but rather that of surpassing the structures it has created to create still others."[71] And this movement beyond the given biological and elementary human environments is already apparent in man's capacity to do work. Where a monkey can make a tool of sticks to secure food, a man can make tools to make other tools to do the same thing, and even turn the tool into a thing of beauty. Not limited by his physiological makeup to a given environment, but able to relate himself to a virtual, or merely possible situation, man is capable of solving problems in the abstract, and even of creating problems where there was none in his original environment. Man's condition is therefore definable in terms of "ambiguity": his higher behavior patterns enable him to surpass the more elemental demands made upon his existence at the same time that the former grow out of the latter.

The precise mechanism—or, more properly, "dialectic"—of this ambiguity is the subject of the next chapter. We may proceed now to the final topic of this preview of man's condition: a consideration of some of the more outstanding "erroneous" opinions concerning the consciousness of man.

Les Aventures de la Conscience.—The purpose of Merleau-Ponty's analysis of the "structures of behavior" was to provide a background of fact against which various metaphysical systems, in particular those concerned with perception and hence psycho-physical relations, could be evaluated. It may be profitable to begin the discussion of perception, as Merleau-Ponty does, from the point of view of common-sense dualism. According to that point of view objects which are physically describable as material particles impinge upon the organism via its sensory apparatus, likewise considered as material mechanisms. This impingement takes place by images, sense data, or simulacra which are registered in the nervous system, and from its internal vantage point, the mind is thought capable of contemplating the received impression. The percieved object acts upon the body and the body upon the mind, via the simulacrum. Instead of three orders of structures integrated into "higher" degrees of individuality, there is a "single linear series" of causal connections. So runs the causal theory of perception. But why does Merleau-Ponty mention a theory held long ago by the Greek atomists, and discredited by Aristotle and others who distinguished between the thing perceived and the sensible species, calling the latter the means of perceiving the former, themselves never perceived? Only because the theory differs very little from the physical orientation of modern physiologists. Both explanations, the one metaphysical and the other "scientific," suppose the reality of the object and its representamen (image), and both are causally mechanistic. In the case of physiological psychology, there is the supposition of a "transversal connection" capable of making a single "mental image" of the two retinal images of a single object. In this modern form, Merleau-Ponty calls the theory "pseudo-Cartesian." Instead of appealing to

the pineal gland—a mistaken localization—the physiologists have
sought the connection of mind and body in various "zones of association," but these zones too can be nothing but mistaken localizations following the description of the structures of behavior outlined above. Moreover, had the physiologists read their Descartes
more closely (*Dioptrique* and *Meditations* with the various Objections and Replies), they would have seen that the first modern
philosopher denied the transitivity of an action from perceived objects to sensible species which impress their image on the brain,
where the soul in its powers to interact with the body was to find
them.[72] Nor did Descartes suppose that there is a necessary resemblance between an image and its object, since light, the medium of
its transference, is nothing more than a movement.

But Descartes himself did not avoid all reference to causation in
explaining perception. Insofar as his position approached realism,
that is, assumed the existence of the external object, and the corporeal impression was considered the occasion of the soul's activity,[73]
some mediating physiological principle or structure was needed to
establish the link between body and mind. And in the light of what
Merleau-Ponty calls "the modern pseudo-Cartesianism" of a physiological psychology, the hypothesis of "animal spirits" and the pineal
gland is not as outlandish as modern science pictures it. Be that as
it may, Descartes' substantial contribution to contemporary phenomenology rests upon his descriptions of the mind's internal activity. Thus while Merleau-Ponty tends to reject Descartes' realism,
he seems to accept the idealism of the latter's *Meditations,* where
Descartes blandly announces that it is easier to know the mind than
it is the body. Although the piece of wax exists beyond its appearances, even should I mistake my impressions of seeing or touching
it, I cannot mistake that I thought I saw, or thought I touched something. And should I doubt the veracity of my impressions, I cannot
doubt that I doubt them. Thus the *cogito* yields the indubitable
knowledge of my thought—if not of myself—and a method, to be
called "reflexion," by which I might seek the "pure thought" that
defines each lucid experience. From this point on in the history of
(continental) thought,

. . . perception could no longer appear to be the effect in us of the action
of an external object, nor the body as the intermediary of this causal action;
the external object and the body, defined as "the thought of the object" and

the "thought of the body,"—as the signification, "object" and the signification, "body"—became indubitable such as they present themselves to us in
a lucid experience at the same time they lose the occult "powers" realistic
philosophy gives them.[74]

Nevertheless, the intellectual bases of Decartes' theory are seriously
compromised by the mixture of body and soul which is human
experience, and fail to exhaust the content of perceptions. In a letter
to Elizabeth he had claimed that the relation between the perceptual
experience and the thing experienced supposes a more primitive
notion, understandable only in relation to itself, of an order of life
sui generis where the distinctions of the understanding no longer
hold.[75] But if this is true, the knowledge of truth is distinct from the
experience of reality; intellection from sensation. And this, of
course, is the fatal weakness of rationalism, which the French call
intellectualisme. Descartes' supposition of a lower order of life explicable only in its own terms is consistent with Merleau-Ponty's
notion of a hierarchy of structural forms; what he lacked, according
to Merleau-Ponty, is the notion of their integration in a concrete,
lived situation. Before considering this integration, we may consider
Kant's attempt to avoid Descartes' failure.

Kant's monumental distinction between the matter and form of
our knowledge of objects has important ramifications for the mind-
body problem. If the matter of our experience derives from a manifold of impressions having its structure from the a priori aesthetic
forms of space and time, and is further organized by the a priori
categories of the understanding, then reflection, according to the
principles of Kant's critical philosophy, proves the knowledge of
an object, as such, to be impossible. And if objects are unknowable,
so is the body, until it has undergone the ordering of the subjective
forms of the human understanding. In this theoretical structure, the
general forms of the consciousness cannot therefore be derived from
corporeal structures. Matter, which is given to consciousness, is
never given "in flesh and blood," but is, rather, posited as a limiting
concept to the functioning of a consciousness. This destruction of
objects in themselves constitutes a movement toward phenomenology
similar to that found in Descartes' methodological scepticism, for
Kant's analysis of an act of knowledge leads to the idea of a constitutive or "naturalizing" thought which subtends by its very structure the structure of external objects.[76] Thus from the critical (Kant-

ian) point of view, the characteristic structures of objects and the structures of the thinking mind are analyzable without an appeal to the purely objective quality of objects:

In order to point up the double characteristic of objects as being "intimate" to a subject and at the same time possessing in themselves the solid structures which distinguish them from appearances, one has called them "phenomena"; and philosophy, in so far as it retains this theme, becomes phenomenology, i.e., an inventory of consciousness as a general environment for a universe.[77]

The distinction between the subjective and the objective elements of experience then loses its significance; "subject" and "object" no longer refer to two different kinds of things, but to two different sorts of "meanings" offered to the understanding. And when a person perceives he grasps the object itself, in one of its manifestations, since beyond a certain signification, "thing," there is nothing to be grasped. Consider our understanding of our own bodily existence. The body as a thing is comprehended in either of two ways: primitively as the vehicle of intention expressed in an attitude or gesture, or derivatively as a corporeal thing spread out in space. Although Kant's epistemology constitutes a step on the way to phenomenology, it is nevertheless an incomplete explanation of our lived experiences, of the manner in which a body lives its intentions. What is needed here is a fuller concept of the body-proper as distinct from the body (corpse) of the human individual. Merleau-Ponty's notion of the body-proper is explained more fully in the next chapter.

To continue with Merleau-Ponty's criticism of Kantian epistemology, if the perceiver is not capable of grasping the relationships between what is given to his perception and the thinking structures which organize the primitive impressions, because these latter in their unformed state, as matter, are never known, the problem of knowledge is described without account for the most primitive element: sensation. If for example, one must grasp a certain swath of experience as "a color" or even as "this unique red," the original impression is subsumed under a more general concept, and the very perception of the colored patch is an act of conception. Kant, like Descartes, ends with an unadulterated rationalism which explains the lower mental function by appealing to a knowledge of the higher, when the higher is known by experience to develop from the lower. The human being thinks, conceives, has ideas, because it lives its situation in a distinctively human way. In his own theory of perception, Merleau-Ponty delves as low as the body itself to found the phenomenological description of knowledge. But for Kant the body is an object extended in space and interacting with other objects, and the perception of objects is equated with an intellectual judgment: "Every form of consciousness presupposes the highest form—the dialetic of epistemological subject and scientific object."[78]

Whereas Merleau-Ponty's phenomenology tends to agree with Kant's description of the transcendental subject, "which treats all conceivable realities as an object of awareness,"[79] he is unhappy with the implications of Kant's theory for the psycho-physical problem. If the body is a phenomenal object like any other object of nature, it too has to be "thought," and such a conclusion jars with our common-sense awareness of objects through the very attitude of our body, its habitual or learned responses which enable it to cope with its situation without first conceiving that situation: "In a living thing, bodily displacements and the temporal sequence of behavioral patterns can only be described in a language made to order, according to the categories of an original experience."[80] And this is what Merleau-Ponty's theory of orders—physical, vital, and human—is intended to do. The three orders are describable only in their own terms; each possesses its own dialectic. Thus when we say that a certain behavioral pattern achieves a human significance, we do not mean that the physical has caused the biological, and the biological the human, but rather that behavior has reached its ultimate form of integration, and, in agreement with Kant, that this highest form of behavior is the condition of the possibility of understanding the two lower forms: a physical gestalt is, after all, a gestalt only to a perceiving consciousness, as shown above.

The critical problem is to describe a supposed action of the body on the mind, and of the mind on the body. Neither interactionism, nor parallelism, nor epiphenomenalism contains the answer. In order to express the action of the mind on the body, one should say that the organized behavior of the animal has surpassed the level of significance attained in the purely biological order; in other words, the body comports itself as a truly human body.[81] Conversely, when one wishes to express the action of the body on the mind, "it would be more exact to say that the behavior has become disorganized, leaving its place to lesser integrated structures."[82] And this is exactly what happens in each case of cortical lesion. Pathology reduces one order of behavior to a lower form. When a man has reached the highest degree of behavioral integration, there is no distinction between his body and his mind; in a very true sense the mind is a function of the body's behavior. This is what is shown, unwittingly to be sure, by those who have pointed out the supposed astigmatism of El Greco, whose elongated figures are an expression of his way of seeing objects. But if this is true, El Greco has been remarkably successful in integrating his bodily "deficiency" by using it to create the new "spiritual" universe depicted in his paintings. For to create an environment, and then to surpass it, is of the essence of the human condition.[83] The human body is never pure object, nor pure idea. It is a structure of elements functioning at times on one level, at times on a second, and at still other times on a third:

. . . there is the body as a mass of chemical components in interaction, the body as a dialetic between a living thing and its biological environment, the body as a dialectic between the social subject and his group. . . . Each of these degrees is a soul with respect to the preceding, and a body with respect to the successor.[84]

Further elucidation of these relationships must be garnered from a closer study of the phenomenon of perception in which each order has its proper place.

Before moving on to the phenomenology of perception in the next chapter, we shall consider here the Hegelian contribution to the development of the phenomenological method. As readers of the *Phänomenologie des Geistes* will recall, the relation between mind and body is like that between master and slave, without our being able to say exactly which is master and which slave; just as the master has need of his slaves to retain his identity as master and in this sense becomes the slave of his own servants, according to Merleau-Ponty, the mind and body of the individual human personality are linked in dialectical fashion. There is no mind without the "infrastructures" of a body, and there is no distinctively human body which does not manifest some form of mind.

It is clear that Merleau-Ponty sees each order of his hierarchy growing out of, negating, or surpassing the preceding order. Starting on the primitive, or physical, level of order, the gestalt, which is described in natural philosophy as a series of coordinate functions in external relationships, has meaning only for the mind capable of comprehending the law immanent to, and therefore uniting by internal relationships, the elements of its configuration. On the level of vitality this primitive level of order is maintained, but it functions differently, as the organism retains the physical gestalt in its anatomy and physiology while creating a new series of actions and reactions with its environment. Finally, when the organism is minded, that is, functions in such a way that the prior dialectic is surpassed in the creation of a still newer, more essentially human, environment, both of the previous orders are retained, built upon, re-interpreted; each successive surpassing takes place when the organism in question is capable of grasping the "significance" of a more integrated gestalt. It is for this reason that Merleau-Ponty claims that the mind and body may be considered related as concept and word, each expressing the other as the exterior expresses the interior. Only two restrictions are placed on this act of expression: first, the word must be the *living word,* a gesture which is becoming significant, or taking on a meaning for the first time; and second, this must be under the conditions of an historical contingency.[85] In this sense Kant was wrong: by ignoring the metaphysical dialectic of mind and body, he placed the problem of knowledge at the center of the highest intellectual function (conception, judgment) taken in its purity, and thereby missed the dialectical moment of import when nature and idea, the presentation and the concept (essence, meaning) are grasped simultaneously in a more primitive act of perception. And for this description, qua descriptive science, Merleau-Ponty turns to the phenomenology of Husserl.

The foregoing analysis has provided a running commentary on Merleau-Ponty's *La Structure du comportement,* in order to comply with the author's own desire that his principal treatises be read in the sequence adopted within this study as a whole,[86] as well as to indicate, as John Dewey has done in *Art as Experience,*[87] the anthropological base upon which a complete aesthetic theory must ultimately rest. The present summary will contain a double project: the attempt to appraise the philosophical import of Merleau-Ponty's critique of laboratory psychology, and to relate his conclusions to Sartre's psychology of the imagination.

First, the import of Merleau-Ponty's philosophy of the behavioral sciences. It is clear that Merleau-Ponty is not posing as a practicing psychologist. As far as can be determined on the basis of a critical examination of his texts, he has performed no psychological experiments on his own, and he makes no claim to having produced a more adequate science of psychology. His aim was to show that the laboratory study of the behavior of living organisms is based, either explicitly or implicitly, upon a set of "ontological" assumptions and that these assumptions cannot be reconciled with what he calls the "natural attitude" of the forms being studied. De Waelhens has put the matter, perhaps as succinctly as it can be put, when he states

La Structure du comportement is concerned with a level of experience which is not natural, but, rather, scientific; and it tries to prove that this latter level of experience—the group of facts which, once exposed by scientific investigation, are said to constitute behavior—is not comprehensible from the ontological point of view spontaneously adopted by scientists.[88]

Nor can the psychologist avoid Merleau-Ponty's charge by stating that a scientific method precludes the possibility of any ontological reference since it is limited, qua scientific, to a strictly empirical universe of discourse. As de Waelhens likewise points out, the desire to avoid ontology in science has made it possible for scientists in general to make implicit ontological references and has thereby permitted psychologists in particular the luxury of thinking uncritically; in short, according to de Waelhens, the uncritical assumptions of scientists have in the main produced bad science.[89] In this respect we may recall Merleau-Ponty's exposure of the "realistic" language of the reflex arc and of the conditioned response theories, and the "finalistic" language of Lapicque's theory of chronaxie.

Further, Merleau-Ponty never casts doubt upon the veracity of psychologists' findings, for whatever they are. He admits that some actions are reflex in character, and that responses may be conditioned. He merely states that such facts are abnormal (pathological) in that abstraction has been made in the experiments of the normal life situations of the animals being tested. In light of such "abstraction" it is significant that the more objective psychologies of our own time are concerned primarily with rats, or at best with monkeys, for before either of these species allow themselves to have their psyches tested, they must in some sense have been domesticated— already a kind of pre-training in the lives of each experimental animal as it is separated from its "real" world. Even more significant is the fact that very little of importance for human psychology has been found in a comparative study of lower animal forms, and in any direct study on human subjects, the conditions of control which are ideal for laboratory experiment have worked toward falsification in the account of the more normal life processes of the human being as he exists in a real life situation. Novelists, if they are possessed of the genius for observation and analysis that was Marcel Proust's, may from this point of view be in a better position than psychologists to represent the truth of "the human reality."

Thus the work of Merleau-Ponty is not scientific in any empirical sense, but is critical of the method of scientists whose results lead to claims of validity which surpass the conditions under which their experiments have been made; the justice of Merleau-Ponty's criticisms seem borne out by the frailness of the figure cut by psychologists in the scientific world: very few predictions of a purely psychological nature attain to, or have attained to, the level of "scientific certainty." Merleau-Ponty may have given us an account of the reason why. It is his interest in phenomenological criticism which has led him to be called "pseudo-scientific" by his Marxist critic, Henri Lefebvre.

Another obvious charge which could be brought against Merleau-Ponty by practicing psychologists is that the experiments he has considered are dated, that psychology has developed to a point where his criticisms are no longer applicable. But this answer is one which would give evidence that the criticisms were not understood. What is at stake is not a particular set of facts or predictions, but the presuppositions of a method which can only yield facts and predictions of limited utility. As long as the methods being used at the present time are the same as those described in the experiments Merleau-Ponty has criticized, his criticisms will be cogent. Finally, it is a grievous *scientific* failing to allow uncriticized assumptions to creep into an experimental design, since the design of an experiment may well control what "facts" will be found. And it is for this reason that laboratory psychologists are so sensitive to the doubts cast upon the validity of their (overly) controlled experiments. In a rat experiment there is always the question as to whose psychic behavioral patterns are being measured—the subject animal's or the experimenter's. Thus Merleau-Ponty's charge is clear: the analytical and

atomistic approach of science can only work toward an oversimplification of the synthetic and "dialectic" nature of the human and
even of the vital "order" of experience.

We move, in the second place, to a consideration of Merleau-
Ponty's relationship to the earlier works of Sartre. It will be recalled
that Sartre considered his *Psychology of the Imagination* a continuation of the psychological method of Husserl. Both Sartre and Husserl conceived of phenomenology as an eidetic science, whose object
was to give us knowledge of essences; it was to bear the same
relation to empirical psychology as the essential relationships studied
in mathematics bear to the empirical study of matter in motion, and
by "bracketing" the real or empirical world, phenomenologists were
allegedly in a position to intuit the essence of the psychic act being
studied. Husserl and Sartre have thus shared Merleau-Ponty's distrust of empirical psychology; but Merleau-Ponty's distrust did not
prevent his considering the validity of empirical claims to psychological knowledge on the same terms as the psychologists themselves consider the matter. Fearing that the knowledge of essences
may lead the inquirer away from a knowledge of the world as we
see it constituted before us in perception, Merleau-Ponty interprets
the Husserlian reduction in the following way: "The eidetic reduction is . . . the resolution to make the world appear [to us] as it is
before any reflection upon ourselves; it is the ambition to make our
reflections equal to the non-reflective life of consciousness."[90] Once
again we recognize Merleau-Ponty's appeal to the "natural attitude"
of a consciousness which knows before it knows that it knows. It
is on the basis of this natural attitude that scientific abstractions are
made, and it is on this basis that our criticisms of scientific results
must be evaluated. Any further study of the non-reflective consciousness must be founded upon a true description of the manner in
which a "meaning" occurs within an animal's natural habitat. Merleau-Ponty considers the case for man in his longer work, *Phénoménologie de la perception,* which is the subject of our next chapter.

Whereas Sartre was interested in continuing Husserl's work with
special reference to the area of the imagination, Merleau-Ponty took
on the task of re-thinking Husserl's account of perception; and
while Sartre merely accepted Husserl's conclusions concerning perceptive acts of awareness, Merleau-Ponty proposed a critical re-
appraisal of them. It would seem an extraordinarily difficult task,

then, to compare Sartre and Merleau-Ponty on this particular issue. But Sartre has made the task a bit easier for us in his criticsms of the psychological assumptions of the novelist, Proust. All we have to do is abstract from our interest in Proust, the artist, in order to consider the kind of psychology Sartre found inherent in Proust's novel, *A la recherche du temps perdu*. Once this abstraction has been made, the comparison becomes readily apparent.

On two occasions at least, Sartre has referred to the "psychology" of Proust. In an article published in 1939,[91] he opposes Husserl's notion of intentionality, according to which feelings are described as peculiar psychic acts in which the emotive character of an object or situation is grasped, to Proust's detailed analyses of the emotive states of his characters' consciousnesses. For Sartre, Proust as psychologist has made the assumption that emotions are enduring *states* of a person's psyche, and as novelist has tried to represent these states of consciousness by analyzing them into *causes* of a purely physical nature which lead a given character to conceive of a particular *motive*, which in turn may produce an *act*. The character's acts then may be taken as expressive of his inner state.

For an illustration of this in Proust, one need only recall the lengthy account of the jealousy felt by the character Swann when he realizes that the woman he is keeping is and has been loved by others, including other women. While he is paying for the privilege of visiting her at night, someone else takes his place during the day. The realization that Odette is cheating him causes a jealousy the pangs of which are cherished by Swann as proof—or substitute—for his feeling of love, and when Swann no longer loves the girl, he marries her. That the marriage should have taken place at all is explicable only in terms of the successive degradation of Swann's principles under the force of his infatuation and its succeeding drive to full possession of his beloved. Proust's rather labyrinthine analysis of Swann's inner torment comes to a climax in a scene of mounting pathos: one night, when Odette has momentarily withdrawn the privilege of his nightly visits, Swann cannot stay away since he cannot lead himself to believe that she is merely tired. His suspicions are fanned when he thinks he sees a light in her apartment; but after knocking at the window, he is brought face to face with his own base condition in the sudden realization that he has mistaken apartments. On another occasion, Swann is not immediately admitted because of

a visitor he thinks is de Forcheville, an aristocrat whom he suspects
to be Odette's second lover. Angry and jealous, he reads her letter
to de Forcheville explaining an interruption in one of the latter's
visits, and is mollified by the fact that Odette refers to the inter-
rupter as "her uncle." Thus, although his spying on her has become
still more serious, since it was actually Swann who interrupted the
two, at least she was lying to de Forcheville too! Later, when his
jealousy provokes conduct which leads to his exclusion from the
bourgeois salon where he had met Odette, the reader is led to a
comprehension of Swann's fall by a description of the aristocratic
kind of salon he was accustomed to attend before his infatuation.
The contrast is so striking that even Swann is brought to a final
realization that he has fallen in love with a witless tart. But he
marries her, and they produce the child who becomes the first love
of Marcel, the narrator. In a later incident, Odette marries de Forcheville, the principal cause of Swann's jealousy, as "the second lover"
of the incident described above.

Sartre admits the convincing character of Proust's analyses when
he proclaims that Husserl's doctrine has for its effect a "deliverance
from Proust."[92] That he should have felt the conviction of Proust's
portrayal and yet think it to be false is indicative of an important
distinction. Apparently Sartre is distinguishing between the expressive character of Proust's novel as a work of art and the validity of
the psychological method of analysis which has made the novel what
it is. At this stage in his development, Sartre was clearly rankled by
Proust's analytical genius, which could produce the work that it had
in spite of its pre-Husserlain psychology.

In the second case of interest to the present analysis, Sartre has
re-evaluated his first appraisal of Proust's technique.[93] By this time
Sartre was convinced that no distinction could be made between a
novelist's technique and the form of the novel it produced. He still
recognized the "genius" of Proust by referring to his work as the
quintessence of the "bourgeois" writer. But it will be recalled that a
writer is "bourgeois," not because of his subject matter or his manner of living, but because of the atomistic approach he adopts toward the reality depicted in the novel. In Sartre's view, Proust views
the social classes he depicts as a mere collection of representative
members: the aristocracy in the Baron de Charlus and in the Du-
chesse de Guermantes, and the bourgeoisie in Swann, in the Ver-
durins and in the members of the narrator's own family; each of

these characters is further analyzed into various attitudes and reactions which are characteristic of the personalties as individuals rather than as members of their particular class.

A Proustian scholar may, with some point, doubt the latter of these charges, since the Baron de Charlus is obviously portrayed as a decadent aristocrat, and Swann as a confused bourgeois. Sartre's principal case against the method of Proust is the universality of the feelings represented: Swann's love for Odette is pictured, in Sartre's reading of the novel, as valid for a homosexual relationship, and therefore false to the setting of this portion of the novel. In a later scene which reflects Swann's jealousy, the love of the narrator for Albertine does take on a homosexual implication, since Marcel's jealousy is felt over the attentions Albertine receives exclusively from another woman.[94] A feeling, for Sartre, never has the same character twice; every feeling is modified by the situation of the character who is experiencing the particular feeling felt, as well as by the nature of the personality who finds himself in the given situation. It is for this reason that, in presenting *Les Temps Modernes,* he called for a literature "of situations."

The comparison between Sartre and Merleau-Ponty may now be pointed out. Sartre has raised objections to Proust's methods which are identical to those raised by Merleau-Ponty against the laboratory psychologists; at bottom, Proust is alleged by Sartre to have made the same error as that exposed by Merleau-Ponty in the work of behaviorists: Proust, like the behaviorists, has limited his work to an observation of atomistic particles which are then assumed to be operative according to their peculiar psychological "mechanism" in any and every human context. Finally, both Sartre and Merleau-Ponty suggest as an alternative to psychological atomism a synthetic method according to which a human character may be defined by his specific relation to the world, that is, by his situation. In a word, both Sartre and Merleau-Ponty are arguing for a synthetic representation of character, whether it be in a novel or in literature of a more scientific sort, to replace psychological analysis, and for a "dialectic" of feeling to replace causal mechanism in the description of human behavior. In describing the kind of an object a novel is, both men have recourse to the notion of "form"—an object of perception that is always more than a summation of its parts. It will come as no surprise, then, that critics have begun to speak of recent French existentialism in terms of *the* theory of Sartre and Merleau-Ponty.[95]

VIII

Phenomenology as a Theory of Perception

Whereas the search into the sources of Merleau-Ponty's phenomenology led into the labyrinth of physiological and psychological explanation of human behavior and showed him primarily as a critic of science and scientists whose uncritical performance constructed the maze in the first place, the present chapter will deal more directly with the philosopher's manner of formulating a theoretical account of human experience. Up to now Merleau-Ponty has been shown as a philosopher of science analyzing and criticizing the method and results of the behavioral disciplines; he must at present be made to play a similar role for the philosophers themselves. The work constituting his *magnum opus* is dedicated to this purpose; *La Phénoménologie de la perception,* which appeared in 1945, two years following the publication of Sartre's *L'Etre et le néant,* is a detailed analysis of classical epistemology. Using the same method he had employed in the earlier work, he passes in review the "classical prejudices" of early modern philosophy in order to show the need of founding the theory of knowledge on phenomenal experience.

It was shown in chapter II that Sartre had failed in his first studies on the imagination to surpass the rationalism of Descartes, and de Waelhens has indicated that Sartre's later interest in ontology has seriously compromised whatever claim he may have had to basing his philosophy in a phenomenological theory of knowledge.[1] Even Simone de Beauvoir had acclaimed the appearance of Merleau-Ponty's theory of perception for the contribution it made to the then dominant philosophical interest of the mandarin group.[2] That it would lead to an ultimate break between Merleau-Ponty and his fellow existentialists was little suspected in 1945, but then few philosophers outside of Beauvoir and a limited number of foreign scholars have taken the trouble to read the entire philosophical output of either Sartre or Merleau-Ponty. Lefebvre's interest was aroused by the political debate of *Les Aventures de la dialectique*,[3] published in 1955, ten years after the appearance of *Phénoménologie de la perception* and seventeen years after that of *La Structure du comportement*.[4] The purpose of this chapter is to show how Merleau-Ponty has avoided the rather easy criticisms applicable to Sartre's theory of knowledge; and if he succeeds in surpassing the dualism of empiricism and rationalism, it is not without the cost of lapsing into what some critics have called "a philosophy of irrationalism."[5] As Merleau-Ponty himself has put it, the method of reflection demands the existence of a non-reflective experience out of which all knowledge grows, and which it is exactly the purpose of our reflection to enlighten.[6] Taking whatever risks may occur, I shall consider in turn his criticisms of both empiricism and rationalism, and the alternative he has found in phenomenology. As in the preceding chapter, we shall use his method of "critical reflection."

If the student of Merleau-Ponty's thought were tempted to start by developing the themes of phenomenology as Husserl laid them down or as Heidegger later adapted them to his own purposes, and continue by comparing the Germans' use of the discovery that every consciousness is engaged in the world with that of Merleau-Ponty, he would most certainly be led to demonstrate that a direct influence exists. Such is no doubt the case. But nothing would have been learned in the comparative study: in the first place, the very considerable influence of Sartre on Merleau-Ponty would have been ignored; in the second, the essential character of Merleau-Ponty's method of procedure would have been completely missed. Since his approach was critical and reflective, his first task was to consider the grounds for various claims to knowledge made in current theories, letting his own ideas develop out of the conflict of claims. Kant had done something similar when he tried to synthesize the claims of rationalism and empiricism in his "critical" philosophy, but his too is a theory which must be weighed in the more reflective balance. In general, philosophers have given too much credit to their theories, and too little to the experience being theorized; those who have considered the basic experience have been led too readily into the metaphysical problem of mind and body, which, as Descartes had clearly shown, grows out of a more basic epistemological problem. According to Merleau-Ponty, ". . . the philosopher believes he knows more about what he perceives in an act of reflection than is known in perception itself."[7] To see his counter-claim, that this belief is unfounded, we must consider the bases of the classical epistemological "prejudices," the ground-concepts and assumptions made by empiricists and rationalists in their varying explanations of the source of human knowledge. Only then can we be on the way to phenomenology as Merleau-Ponty traveled it.

The empirical ground of knowledge is taken to be sensation; Locke's "nihil in intellectu quod non prius fuerit in sensu" epitomizes this position. The difficulty comes in interpreting the dictum. Is it merely a heuristic maxim, unprovable in itself and useful only as a guiding tool for the discovery of the facts? If so, Leibnitz's response, "nisi intellectus ipse," indicates that other heuristic principles are possible, and any settlement of the issue might be taken as purely arbitrary: empiricists choose one, and rationalists, another guiding maxim. In order to get beyond the arbitrary, one must reconsider the elements of sensuous experience, and how they function in an act of perception. A definition of terms is therefore not out of order. What after all are our simple ideas, or impressions? To what do such words as "red," "blue," "hot," and "cold," refer? Unfortunately for empiricism, no simple answer has been forthcoming. Sensations have been variously defined as ways in which a consciousness is affected, and properties of objects themselves; each of these definitions offers its own kind of difficulty to reflective analysis.

If sensations proper are particular modes of a given consciousness, attested by a certain psychical state, it may be objected that these are not objects of our experience; we *have* sensations, we don't perceive, or even sense them. If it were supposed that we could sense our sensations, we would then be possessed of another sensation by which we sense the sensation of our first sensation, and so on indefinitely. The first sensations we have obviously suffice to put our consciousness in relation to some aspect of the world. Moreover, it has been shown by experimental psychologists that even the lower animals react to relations between sensorial stimuli, and not to an absolute

stimulus,[8] and this evidence seems to indicate that the organism reacts to a global situation, rather than to an isolated element within
it. Descartes has already shown in his first *Meditation,* and Hume
in his analysis of space, that color and extension are both necessary
for a visual impression. A series of colored points appear as a figure
on a background, and a "pure impression" is an abstraction which in
itself will always remain unknown. The celebrated search for sense
data which characterized a period of British and American philosophy had no better foundation than this.

If on the other hand we assume that our sensations are properties
of the objects we perceive, it becomes a mystery how these objects are
related to the perceiving consciousness. Such is the naïveté of naive
realism; errors, hallucinations, all purely subjective dependent experiences, are vested with the reality of objects.

Two definitions, and two sources of error. The error of the first
position, considering quality as an element of consciousness, had
already been called the "illusion of immanence" by Sartre;[9] in his
scheme, quality is not a content *of* consciousness, but exists *for* a
given consciousness. And qualities can not be considered brute impressions, in themselves meaningless; they are full of meaning to the
consciousness that has them, or to put it more exactly, for whom they
exist. Behind this error there looms a rather prodigious assumption,
the existence of the "real" and "external" world, the physical correlative of our psychical states.

The error of the second position hides the same assumption, according to which the impression and its meaning are fully and objectively determined. Thus, realists attempt to compensate for their
naïveté by explaining away illusions through an appeal to the laws
of optics and geometry. The laws of perspective and projection enable us to determine the exact location of the physical object whose
images affect us in the way described. But at the same time they have
merely amplified the problem of appearance and reality. Phenomenology attempts to avoid the dichotomy between appearance and
reality implicit in the two definitions given above by avoiding any
reference either implicit or explicit to the external world. Husserl
referred to this process as putting the world into brackets; Merleau-
Ponty prefers to talk of a "pre-objective" domain of the human consciousness. Once objects are constituted by a consciousness within an
indeterminate situation, one could with some reason talk of proper-

ties of objects or images of objects, but until they are so constituted the assumption that they exist can only be called a "prejudice."

Perhaps the most enlightening point of view one can take on this pre-objective domain is that of the optical illusion. In the illusion of Müller-Lyer, where two "equal" straight lines arranged one above the other, but having angles pointing in opposite directions at both ends, the one appears to be longer than the other. The 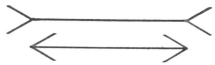 illusion depends upon our foreknowledge that the lines are equal in length, that is, upon an objective view of the universe. But if we limit ourselves to the pre-objective view of the perceiving consciousness, we shall find that the two visual experiences do not exist on the same plane in the same universe. The lines taken in themselves (*en-soi*) are fully determined by the laws of geometry, but for the consciousness they appear to be of different lengths. Within the experience of the observer, however, it is more exact to say that the lines are neither equal nor unequal, because in the world of indeterminate vision no comparison of their lengths is possible.

Like objects, which for Dewey are detached from an indeterminate situation which is "felt" or perceived globally as a quality,[10] the lines of the illusion stand out as an analysis of the visual field, and are not given in their full determination. With Dewey, Merleau-Ponty claims:

We must recognize the indeterminate as a positive phenomenon. It is in such an atmosphere that qualities present themselves. The meaning which they enclose is equivocal; it is an expressive value rather than a logical signification. The determinate quality by which empiricism wished to define sensation is an object, not an element of consciousness, and it comes on the scene late, the result of the scientific attitude.[11]

This conclusion seems to be supported by the results of Merleau-Ponty's earlier research, in which it was shown that an external stimulus does not affect an organism part for part, but only insofar as it offers a "meaning" to the organism's perceptive devices. Thus, if the structure of the organism's reaction depends in the long run on its biological functioning, and an organism structures its universe by reaching to or from stimuli which are favorable or unfavorable to adaptation,[12] the logical forms, or categories—which Kant took to be the necessary correlative of external impressions—are likewise seen to be derivative, rather than primary or biologically founded, constituents of experience.

Always immersed in an environing situation, the human being is constrained to construct its objects from a first, often confused, and always indefinite perception of a situational quality; and if this is a true picture of the matter, it can no longer be assumed that objects are the cause, even unknown, of our simple impressions. Having committed this first error in theory construction, empiricists are led to another in explaining how simple impressions are related, either as sets of "constant and coherent" affections of the human mind or as elements of objects themselves. The mechanism here is that suggested by Hume in his *Treatise*[13] and elaborated by psychologists into the dogma of associationism. The doctrine of the association of ideas claims that our ideas or impressions become associated by virtue of the relations of contiguity and resemblance between them. Once more Merleau-Ponty's answer resembles, if one may be forgiven the pun, that given by Dewey: for two impressions to be associated in any fashion whatever, they must first of all be dissociated from a prior total experience.[14] This much is already clear from the analysis of "pure impressions," but the question of the relation between the prior and the present experiences needs further elucidation.

When a figure detaches itself from a background and the subject sees an object, he is seeing more than a mere collection of parts. The colored impression is a representation; it intends an object which is figured on a ground. The figure itself may be interpreted as a contour, defined by empiricists as either a summation of local sensations or as contiguous blocks of space perceived in successive temporal durations. The question is to explain how *extrinsically* related elements (the colored points) become interpreted as a figure, for example a circle, in which the elements are formed according to a pattern of *intrinsically* related parts. No matter where my attention stops on the circular contour, and whether I take it in as a summation of points or of blocks, the perception of one unit calls out others not perceived, and what I eventually perceive is the circular pattern. One segment of the contour, an arc, may resemble another, and they both may recall a resembling contour perceived in the past as circular, the "meaning" of the present perception. But if this is the case, the question is how the prior experience has become "circular" when it was given as a series of points or blocks of space, related in fact by the same kind of arrangement (of summation) as the present case which is held in question. The very words "order" and "circle" are stripped of their meaning, which is the patterning character of the object perceived as a whole. In any given experience of pattern there are no indifferently given elements which form a figure of a thing because contiguity and resemblance are given; rather, these result from an analysis of a perceived totality. Given any series of impressions, the elements of which are thought to be associated, the unity of the object figured in them is a felt quality of the concrete situation in which they occur; it is by virtue of this felt quality of the immanent order within the situation that possible questions may be posed concerning the veridicality of any "perception" of objects it may include. An originally confused perception may become clearer. A grey form spread out indefinitely over a space may upon closer analysis become the black of a woman's dress. Thus the original impression is not fixed and absolute; nor is its object in any sense original, but a terminally verified content of the entire experience. Such "original" impressions have no power to associate themselves with others, any more than they can call up others without a prior *understanding* garnered from a past experience. Without this play of the understanding no two experiences can resemble each other to whatever degree purported.

Strict empiricists, however, wish to avoid any appeal to the understanding which may concede too much to the cause of rationalism. What we have called the "play of the understanding" has therefore been interpreted empirically as the projection of memory images on the present perception. And the effect of the memory on present perceptions has been treated to some extent by psychologists. First in relation to contiguity: a subject is instructed to commit to memory two series of syllables. The first is a masculine rime, *dak-tak;* the second, formed by a reversal of the letters, *ged-deg.* When the subject is asked to form a masculine rime for *ged,* his effort is much more prolonged than when he is asked merely to change the vowel. The set to reproduce what he has learned from the conditioning experience produces error in the first experiment, and its absence in the second allows for an immediate correct answer. Has association taken place? Hardly, if the force of association explains the error of the first experiment, it ought likewise to explain the success of the second. But the second response was not prepared in the conditioning exercises. Merleau-Ponty concludes that association does not act as an autonomous force: the given word does not call out another associated with it by the relation of contiguity. Rather, "It acts only to make probable or tempting the reproduction set; and only in virtue of the meaning it has acquired in the context of a past experience. . . ."[15]

Similar results have been found for association by resemblance. If a subject is conditioned to perceive a small geometric figure and then told to look for it in a larger geometric complex where it is camouflaged, he will find it with equal ease whether his conditioning was limited to five cases or was repeated hundreds of times. But a subject told to look at the larger figure without having gone through the conditioning almost as readily finds the smaller figure when told to look for one. In the case of the conditioned subject, the smaller figure can be recalled in the perception of the larger only when the larger is seen *as a possible representation* of the smaller; both perceptions must call up an identical meaning before remembrance is possible. When the past plays a part in a present experience, it does so not by association, but by an act of the present awareness intending a meaning. In general, appeals to memory to explain the organization of a present perception are doomed to fail precisely because they presuppose what they should explain: the formation of the given meaning and its imposition on the chaos of our impressions.

In summary, the weakness of empiricism is, like that of experimental psychology, its atomism. The reflective consciousness cannot understand the definition of its elements in separation or the description of the mechanism by which they are supposed to be united into perceived wholes. It is paradoxical that as long as one continues to think of the world in purely objective terms, no crucial evidence can be brought against the theory:

The atoms of the physicist will always appear more real than the historical and qualitative figure of this world; the physico-chemical processes, more real than organic forms; the psychical atoms of empiricism, more real than perceived phenomena; the intellectual atoms that are the "meanings" of the Vienna School, more real than consciousness; as long as one continues the attempt to construct the figure of this world, life, perception, and mind, instead of recognizing, as the most proximate source and final touchstone of our knowledge concerning them, the *experience* they afford.[16]

The atomism of the empirical approach to knowledge is particularly effective in covering over the effect of the human situation in perception, and in particular those cultural objects which are perceived on the ground of the natural world. How to explain the anger or pain one can perceive on a tortured face; the religious meaning in the attitude of hesitation or reticence; the laws of the city in the bearing of its police? Given the proper situation, one is seldom wrong in these perceptions. But how can one be right when even the natural world is explained as a mere summation of stimuli and qualities? In spite of the atomists, our reflection indicates that a background is continuous even under the figure we perceive—otherwise the phenomenon of space-tensions would be meaningless in painting —that a design is perceived as a whole and in its parts, and that the world continues to exist even when our back is turned to it.

Intellectualistic or rationalistic theories of perception start where the empiricistic leave off, with a concept of the organizing activity of the human mind. What was only a principle of activity in the theories starting with impressions becomes in rationalism a completely different heuristic principle: the mind's *attention* is thought capable of reducing the obscurity of an indefinite impression and changing what was indistinct into a clear and distinct image of an object. Both theories then attempt to account for the basic phenomenon of perception, which is the reorganization of the indefinite relation between a perceiving subject and its environing field. Both assume that an object is there to be perceived, if the screening effect of the body and its organs or emotions can be overcome and the clouds of the obscure vision removed. If one can control himself and pay attention, the obscurity will disappear and the world will appear completely formed in accordance with the ideas the mind already possesses. "Attention" is thus defined as the general power to give awareness to particular elements of consciousness.

For empiricism, however, this general power is never a datum of experience. If our impressions are associated, it is by force of the mysterious workings of some habit of the mind which can only be described, as it were, *ex post facto.* As shown above, the impressions themselves are powerless to operate any association on their own. But if the theory of "pure impressions" suffers from an overpassivity on the part of the individual *Bewusstsein,* rationalism suffers no less from the same defect. The act by which objects are constructed or reconstructed within a global visual field is itself lost to mental activity; it too is only posited, *ex post facto,* by an act of reflection on prior perceptions, and never grasped in a present perception.

If we have recourse to the experience of perception, we may describe the activity of becoming aware, of taking consciousness of an object, as a transformation of an already given, pre-objective, mental field. What happens when this field becomes reorganized into a clearer alignment of its constituent forces, so that the object now stands out clear and distinct while before it was confused and vague, is that the consciousness achieves a new manner of being present to its world. The child's experience in learning colors affords a clear example of this. Color recognition is not innate; it takes time for the child to arrange the perceived masses it receives in the way necessary to perceive new figures. If the indeterminate is to be made determinate, the object must appear as a change in the very structure of the consciousness itself. One of the first phenomena of which the child is aware is the "warm" or "cool" qualities of the colored patches, and the play of the warms on the cools and vice versa enables the child to perceive the "depth" of the color experience. On the ground of this depth, brilliance and dullness may appear; as the figure becomes more outstanding to the perceiving consciousness the blues and greens become differentiated from the yellows and the reds, and within the areas of warmth only, the yellows from the browns. What is experienced, or lived (*vécu*) comes to full knowledge by the act of reorganizing the pre-objective mental universe.

The philosophical interpretation of this experience has been given primarily by Descartes,[17] continued in Malebranche,[18] and more recently adumbrated in the rationalism of Lagneau[19] and his more illustrious pupil, Alain.[20] Descartes' second *Meditation,* containing the analysis of the piece of wax, is most probably the first modern occurrence of the problem. Always extended, a pliable and plastic substance, the wax is perceived either clearly or confusedly insofar as our attention enables us to grasp the simple ideas of which it is composed. If this is the case, all the attention can do is isolate the intuitable ideas which the understanding already possesses and is capable of grasping in this particular instance. The more attention paid, the clearer the idea becomes to a perfectly translucent mind; when I perceive badly or falsely, my understanding is prevented from working in its most precise or attentive manner. Alain uses the example of the moon which appears to be greatly larger on the horizon than at its zenith. If only one could manage the attention so as to cut off the disturbing elements of the entire indeterminate situation in which each perception takes place, he thought the moon (the real object) would be seen to be of the same size, regardless of its position.[21] A lens or even a cardboard tube permits experiment on the case in point. Once the attention has performed its task, the perceiving consciousness "sees" in every sense of this mystical expression.

A difficulty arises, however, in the analysis of the power of attention. According to Merleau-Ponty, the mind divisible into faculties of attention and understanding is incomprehensible. It is after all related in the same way to the objects of its perception, whether these objects be perceived clearly or not; the additional clearness brought to the experience by the act of attention produces no new relationship between the mind and its object. The "light" of attention has never been anything more than a metaphor; it is thought capable of illumining objects without itself ever being seen or even being absorbed by the objects in question. Thus if this light is brought to play, it is not conditioned by the objects. The connection between the first diffuse perception and the desire to sharpen it by paying added attention remains unexplained since the real object, the one perceived in complete clarity, is already understandable, if not understood, by the searching consciousness. Rationalists, like the empiricists, have confused the exact forms of the scientific, objective, view of the world with the perceiving consciousness insofar as the consciousness perceives correctly. The passage from indeterminacy to complete determination within the act of perception is impossible, since the indeterminate moment is foreign to the nature of the fully enlightened consciousness, which already possesses its object (a meaning).

Psychological experiments on the phenomenon of attention have cast further doubts on the very existence of the "general power to give awareness to elements of consciousness." Certain optical illusions cannot be reversed even though one knows beforehand that the reversal of figure and ground will produce a perception of two kinds of "objects." And the localization of a point at which one has been touched yields no sudden change in "local signs" enabling one

to perceive clearly what is given only vaguely, nor the sudden acquisition of a "secondary power of apprehension." There is however a
gradual transformation of the mental field which is in the first
instance created in an indeterminate fashion, and later dominated by
the subject in such a way as to isolate more precisely the elements
within it. The first perceptive awareness, which disengages a meaning from a total situation, is the act by which the consciousness
changes structure in apprehending its object:

Paying attention is not only the act of illumining to a greater degree pre-
existent data of consciousness; it is rather that of realizing within them a
new articulation by taking them for *figures*. They are pre-formed only as
horizons, and truly constitute new regions in the total world-situation. And
it is precisely the original structure they bring forward which produces the
identity of the object before and after the act of attention.[22]

Thus there follows a conclusion of supreme importance for aesthetics: an act of perception is already a primitive act of creation. It is
not caused by external impressions, nor given reason by an idea of
the mind. A reflective perception of the world is, however, motivated
by a prior non-reflective view on the same world.[23] This motivation
of one consciousness (*Bewusstsein*) by another is the central doctrine of Husserl's phenomenology, which will be discussed later.

The second rationalistic concept needed to complete the account of
perception is that of judgment. Like attention, judgment is an explanatory hypothesis rather than a constitutive element of the perceptive act. At first this thesis of rationalism was thought to be established by proving the absurdity of the passive, impressionistic view;
as a result of such a deduction—the rationalistic method used in a
secondary instance to establish its own validity in the primary—the
judgment itself came to be defined as what is lacking in the process
of sensation to produce an act of perception. Descartes moves in his
analysis of the piece of wax from the so-called secondary qualities to
a power of the wax to take on an infinite number of shapes and
forms, and beyond that to the substance formed. But obviously, in
the act of perception itself when there are no longer any qualities to
perceive, the "thing," which is after all a physicist's concept, no
longer exists. Science, by retaining this notion of a persistent substance, presupposes the existence of matter which is not given to perception. Alain, following the Cartesian tradition, argued that perception is a judgment, a pronouncement made on the basis of our re-

flective awareness of illusions. Given the impression of sense messages on the body, an illusion could have its illusory character only
if the judgment erred in its interpretations of the given stimuli. A
close student of the arts, he uses the example of a painter's creation
of an illusion of the third dimension to prove that for the eye to see
the mind must judge. Perception, in this process, is taken to be *an
interpretation* of received "sense messages."

In this form, the rationalistic theory of perception offers a host of
difficulties to the reflective consciousness. First of all, the judgment
is admittedly an hypothesis made for the purpose of explaining perception, and is not grasped in the experience of perceiving. Lagneau,
Alain's teacher in the subtle art of reasoning, admitted as much:
"Perception is an interpretation of a primitive intuition which appears to be immediate, but which is in reality acquired by habit and
corrected by reasoning. . . ."[24] Secondly, a series of paradoxical results
follow from the *ex post facto* hypothesis: the common sense notions
of "seeing," "hearing," "feeling" lose all primary significance, each
becoming a variant term for "judging," and this lack of distinction
between "seeing" and "judging" makes it impossible for us to distinguish a true from a false perception. What would be the criterion
for distinguishing between seeing and only believing that we see?
Merleau-Ponty cites two critical experiments to establish the necessity of such a distinction. Of two cardboard boxes constructed of the
same material but in different proportions, the larger seems to be
heavier even before any empirical trial of their relative weights.
Since the judgment and the sensation are identical by hypothesis, one
would be led to conclude that no sensation is necessary to perceive
the relative difference; but the example was first used by Alain to
show the sensory quality of certain illusions.[25] The second experiment concerns the varying aspect of a drawn cube, depending upon
whether it is looked at from one side viewed from above or from
the opposite side and viewed from below. Even if the person knows
that the cube will "change," he is incapable of forcing the change
by an act of judgment, and must wait until the perceptive intuition
changes structure within the visual field. In this example, it is clear
that the judgment must wait upon the realignment of the elements in
the perceptive experience.

In the face of the changing elements of our perceptual experience, sanity may be re-introduced, in Merleau-Ponty's view, by insisting on the totality of the experience. Differences of perceptions are not attributable merely to the form of the judgment; the sensuous materials are formed and the sense (the French *sens* may be rendered as "meaning" and "direction" as well) disengaged at the same moment. To perceive a unitary object the consciousness grasps the meaning which is given as immanent to the perceptual elements. The case of optical illusions, which depend upon the reversal of figure and ground of perception, shows that the data of the impression are not given in a moment anterior to the solution of the problem of reversal; the two perceptions follow each other, and each is an act creating the grouping of the data and interpreting its meaning in the same moment. That this process has tremendous consequences for the creation and appreciation of visual works of art will be made clear in the following chapter.

As a final note on the reflective criticism of empiricism and rationalism as theories of perception, we may consider the case of those who claim that each act of perception has an empiricistic and a rationalistic moment, that a full theory of knowledge must in some way unite the claims made by each. The Kantian theory of knowledge provides the example. If sense stimuli are the materials of perception and these are interpreted by the fixed categories of the mind, the total act of perception may be likened to a conclusion from given premises. But the isolable stimuli which form the substance of the premises are end-products of an act of perception. Whence, the premises have no foundation prior to the total act, and are impotent to ground any conclusion whatsoever. The same error can be seen in some of the more naïve kinds of psychology, in which disparate retinal images, the distances between objects deduced from apparent size, and the movements of the sensing organs are taken as *causes* of distinctions within our perceptions. The realism of these assumptions fails because it takes for granted the constancy of objects, the reality of the "thing" perceived. But idealism, which substitutes the notion of *reason* or *ground* for that of *cause* as intrinsic constituents of the phenomena perceived, likewise fails. If such empirical data as the retinal images noted above enter into the perception, they are not themselves perceived, but serve as *motivations* for the appearance of the object perceived within the phenomenal field. That they do so, and are the source of error in all erroneous perceptions is Merleau-Ponty's primary contention. But to make this clear we must attempt to clarify this Husserlian notion of motivation.

Consider the following psychological experiment. A certain subject afflicted with complete paralysis of the ocular motor muscles thinks that the objects he is perceiving move to the left when he is (falsely) under the impression that he is turning his eyes in that direction. The gestalt theory of perception instructs us that our perception of the position of objects does not depend upon an internal perception of the condition of our perceiving organs. The perceiver therefore does not know that the retinal images have remained stationary on his retinas; he merely "sees" the objects moving to the left. But an illusion does not result solely from external stimuli. There had to be the primary intention of moving the bodily organs to the left; the subject had to think that his eye moved. The illusion has no other source than the "signification" understood in the body complex, which "motivates" what is seen; this motivation is permitted by the fixed adaptation of the bodily complex, through its visual organs, with the environing situation. If a normal subject intends a movement to the left, without making it, the objects seen will remain stationary—after having "vibrated" for an instant—which result is not a learned response, but one of the constitutive structures of the human organism, an immanent meaning of the situation in which the vision is displaced to one side. When the vibratory effect is absent and we are conscious of the movement of our eyes to the left, the result is the perception of the movement of the objects to the left. The act of looking and the vista seen remain in close contact, and the illusory experience of the paralyzed subject is nothing other than the fixity of the objects within the vista, falsely motivated into "movement" by "a look" falsely taken to be in movement. Paralysis is neither an objective *cause* of the illusion as empiricists would have it, nor *reasons* or *premises* for a false conclusion as rationalists would have it. In Merleau-Ponty's terms, one meaning disengaged from the total psycho-physical situation motivates a second which is false to a more inclusive view of the same situation.[26]

The phenomenological notion of motivation is thus a corrective to what Merleau-Ponty calls "inadequate notions" of rationalism and empiricism. Both of these systems may be resumed in the following sequence of theoretical constructs, all based upon the same assumption of the objective character of the world; two ground concepts, mutually exclusive: *extension,* defined as co-existence of parts externally related, and *thought,* internally constituted and self-consistent activity, become arbitrarily united by means of a *vocal sign,* word or concept having a *meaning* apprehended by thought. The appearance of the sign *causes* the intellection of the meaning, given as the *reason* for the perceived phenomenon.[27] The work of Merleau-Ponty to this point has been dedicated to the destruction of the grounds for each of these notions, except perhaps the *concept* since he is dealing with a primordial or original type of knowledge which cannot suppose the existence of concepts or general ideas, which he takes to be derivative from the kind of experiences he is treating. In the place of these overworked notions of epistemological theory, he suggests the existence of a non-thetic consciousness (defined in Chapter II), one which does not possess full determination of its objects; that is, he makes an appeal to a logic of the lived experience possessing an immanent meaning which can become completely clear only in the face of further determinable evidence. Motivation takes place between the indeterminate consciousness and the later, more fully determinable consciousness. For this reason Husserl, in his later writings, referred to motivation as a "fluent" concept.[28] It relates two consciousnesses (*Bewusstsein*) not as two natural events are related in the sequence cause and effect, but by the meaning one suggests to the other: ". . . there is a *raison d'être* which orients the flux of phenomena without being explicitly posited in any of them, a kind of operative reasoning."[29] Such is the nature of the "lived logic," which never becomes explicit in an act of perception, true or false; non-thetic in character, it always remains implicit in the total perceptual situation. According to Merleau-Ponty, illusion and error are both explicable under the phenomenological treatment. The bare intention of moving the eyes to the left suffices to motivate the illusion that the objects seen likewise move to the left. Further elucidation of perception must be sought in the return to the description of the phenomena of our experience.

This last step on the way to a complete phenomenology of perception will concern itself with delimiting the phenomenal field of experience, from which all knowledge develops as a point of view taken by one constituent on the other constituents of this same field. Since both empiricism and rationalism, or more exactly the concepts of sensation and judgment, were found to be successful only on the basis of assuming the independent existence of the "real" world, before which the knowing consciousness is an ever so interested spectator,[30] the phenomenologist in his attempt to avoid all assumptions and whatever "errors" might derive from them, treats consciousness as being engaged in the world. Every consciousness, to repeat the slogan, is a consciousness of something, of some aspect of the world. The objects of the world—or as John Dewey maintained, of the situation—are detached from a background by each consciousness attending to some figure. Each organism, then, constructs the kind of environment proper to its species; there is no one unchanging mold which determines the behavior of the forms which must live in its environment. In its own way, each species and each individual has a characteristic manner of living, or in more strictly phenomenological terms, of being present to the world. The phenomenal field is created by the tension between the organism and its environment. And the difficulties attendant upon an adequate theory of knowledge are evident from the obvious impossibility of getting beyond the phenomenal field: the organism can never get beyond itself or its environment; any attempt to do so would only produce another self or another environment. Thus, the so-called ego-centric predicament tells only half the story; each organism is bound to its own situation as well as to its own point of view on that situation.

Attempts to study the phenomenal field have usually bifurcated nature into two disparate dimensions: the world of matter and the world of mind. The natural sciences specialize in the first; the biological and social sciences in the second. The claims of each of these sciences are open to critical reflection.

Consider first the physical sciences. Bending their attention primarily to physical objects qua objects, they have, according to Merleau-Ponty, presupposed the constancy principle without acknowledging it. According to the hypothesis of constancy, a physical object remains invariant throughout many experiences of it. Even in the more recent developments of physics, objects are calculated to exist in a certain geometrical location, if not by actual measurement then by statistical determination. In spite of our observations to the contrary or our inability to place exactly the position of a particle, in principle things are and remain what they are.

Psychologists, on the other hand, seeking to explain the knowledge gained by common sense concerning the meaning of bodily attitudes, gestures, and ways of accentuating words, have been all too eager to follow the physicists' model: the construction of a total experience by the cumulative effect of atomistic elements. Since it has already been shown that Merleau-Ponty evaluated the efforts of psychology to account for complex human behavior,[31] it will suffice here to state his evaluation of a behavioristic theory of knowledge given by Alain, who had claimed that perception is the beginning of science and science, a complete and methodical perception.[32] Faced with a difficulty of principle (explanation of the phenomenon of meaning) rather than of fact (complexity of the nervous system), classical behaviorists must be led to admit that the theory of perception has a pre-rational base, in short that perception can no longer be a beginning science, but that science is a perception which has lost sight of its origins and mistaken itself as complete.[33]

Within the phenomenal field, to which one must return if one is to keep track of the origins of perception, all the facts of consciousness take place. Gone is the world of introspection and any reason for the search after the "immediately given." As a matter of fact, nothing is ever immediately given. The phenomenon is neither a state of consciousness, nor a psychic entity. Consciousness merely happens to an organism in its environment, but only when the environment is ready to yield its significance. Examples of such consciousness are the sudden apparition of a figure which before its clear appearance was hidden in a confused background. Children's puzzles use this principle regularly: *Where is the rabbit in the forest?* Or again, we find ourselves suddenly "detecting" the movement of something in a background of haze. The meaning, the structure of the elements, almost spontaneously presents itself before our eyes. And any knowledge one may have of his own "psyche" can present itself in no other way. The best I can do to know myself is to look for the pattern of events in my life. This method of psychological analysis has been variously called "phenomenological" and "existential."[34]

According to the phenomenological method, what gives meaning to any event is the total pattern of its constituent elements. The pattern or gestalt is quite literally found, and not projected by the mind into nature. And if this is so, the problem of the "constitution of the world" cannot be given its usual idealistic solution, a transcendental Self which exists or subsists beyond the world of experience, giving form or reason to the changing course of nature. The transcendental field thus defined is meaningless idealistic jargon. For the phenomenologist, who would avoid the metaphysical extremes of both idealism and realism, the transcendental field is correctly conceived as a problem. The constitution of the world takes place moment by moment. Within the world the thinking self never has more than a single point of view; it is only partially determined and seeks to make itself more complete by reflection—which, in Merleau-Ponty's terms, means "philosophy." Whereas absolute idealists have had recourse to a completely determined self, to Reason self-contained, the critical phenomenologist is forced to adopt the reflective attitude and ask why 'reason' in any sense must be presupposed. In reflecting, the individual, situation-bound self can only think about itself in a prior state; when philosophy becomes thoroughly radical, the reflective being thinks about its non-reflective states, in a word, about its lived experiences as they are lived. Perception thus has its roots in pre-rational experience; and to account for this fact, Merleau-Ponty's theory of perception starts with an analysis of the body.

THE PHENOMENON OF BODY

Certain critics of Merleau-Ponty have employed the epithet "irrationalism" to describe his theory of knowledge.[35] And to an extent the epithet is exact, since he rejects both empiricism and rationalism, as well as the Kantian attempt to synthesize them. But traditional epistemologies have tried to explain our knowledge of a world already constituted for our perceptions, and in so doing have begged the serious philosophical question as to how there comes to be a world for perception in the first place. The question is metaphysical and demands a statement of the metaphysics implicit in a clearly thought out theory of perception. The irony of Merleau-Ponty's view on perception is that he avoids discussing the consciousness as such which traditionally has been taken to "constitute the world," the emphasis on which has given much of phenomenology an idealistic cast, in favor of a "pre-objective view of the universe" according to which an organism finds itself engulfed by an initially indeterminate situation. Since the "rationality" of both empiricism and rationalism hinges in the main upon the assumption of the permanence of the objects they describe, it is rather easy to understand the "irrationality" of Merleau-Ponty's position; he denies that this assumption may be made. But the epithet cannot be considered, as it usually is, a refutation of his view. The use of epithets may, after all, be nothing more than a special way of begging the question at issue.

The uniqueness of Merleau-Ponty's claim is that a correctly envisaged organism-environment situation allows the philosopher to approach the traditional mind-body problem, neither from the mind alone, nor from the body alone. When we speak of the body in any significantly human sense—Nothing is as empty or meaningless as a dead man's "smile"—we necessarily speak of a phenomenon, a lived event in which a rather unique object "appears" to a given consciousness under the guise of a quality or complex of qualities. In other words, his contention is that a metaphysically adequate description of the body already contains at least the sketch of a full theory of perception. In an attempt to make Merleau-Ponty's claim clear, we shall first of all examine the classical notions of the concept of the body as an object, proceeding in analysis from physics to psychology via physiology; then, noting his criticisms, investigate the bases of his existential analysis of the lived experience, which he summarizes in the concept of the "bodily schema"; and finally, follow his analysis of the body as a "primordial expression."

The Body as a Physical Object.—The physical analysis of a body starts out with a set of assumptions: that the living body, like. any other organized physical body, may be adequately described in terms of spatial and temporal coordinates; and that this description is objectively valid for any and all experiences of the body in question. That is, even where the physicist may be led to admit that perception establishes the "objects" within an organism's environment, it is further assumed that objects once constituted provide the rational basis of all further perceptions of them. A thing is, *ex hypothesi,* there to be seen; and since the human body is, qua physical object, also a thing, it is likewise there to be seen.

Merleau-Ponty counters this set of assumptions with another application of his "critical reflection." What, in fine, constitutes the experiential basis of the spatiality and the temporality of these privileged "objects"? As Santayana points out, objects are primarily the synthesis of the seen.[36] Any further analysis of this synthesis will eventually lead to the process of seeing, and from it to the act of looking (*le regard*). But the act of looking is nothing more than a familiar manner of acceding to objects which appear either at the focus of visual attention or on its margins. Thus there seem at least two ways of visually apprehending an object. A *figure* appears at the focus of attention, and a *background* recedes "behind" and "around" the figure so detached. The dialectical relationship between figure and ground in perception is patent, and constitutes the basis for the common "optical illusions." Whether we attend to a certain visual field in one way and perceive a pair of champagne glasses, or in another and see lovers embracing depends precisely upon the focus of our point of view, upon our manner of "inhabiting the object." Thus, as Sartre had already shown in *L'Etre,* the body is a privileged object;[37] it is the means by which a consciousness has a hold on the universe. Inhabiting a body, the consciousness takes in other objects from the body's point of view. Once the consciousness enters the universe in which things are seen, these objects become frames of reference to others. Changing its perspective from object to object, the consciousness experiences all objects save its body in a fluid background of other less determinate objects which, when central or focal to the consciousness' attention, become more determinate and constitute a perspective for the apprehension of other objects. Thus the perspectival perception of visual objects has meaning only in relation to one object, the body, which forms a point of view without a point of view.[38] The one fixed spatial co-ordinate is the body which the consciousness "lives"; and this lived object cannot be reduced to the system of relativity which constitutes the objects of the world. Hence, while it makes sense to describe objects other than the body abstractly as spatially determined, this sense may be understood only on the ground of one object's existence which is not so determined. The body is a living object, and its life modifies its physical character: there is nothing more expressive than a quick man's smile.

Considered from the vantage point of time, the body is likewise perspectival in character. The present is a point of view taken on the past and the future. As most conscientious historians are aware, the meaning of history is not objective; rather, it is the same meaning as an action taken in the present on the basis of a known series of past events and calculated to produce an estimated effect in the future. And if history has no absolute object, unchanging in character, since the objects of history change with the perspective of time, it is necessarily forced to a continual construction and reconstruction of the events in the "lived history." The life of a person, race, or nation thus constitutes the historian's primary source.

The relativity of space and time to a lived moment of history presents, from Merleau-Ponty's point of view, a difficulty of principle to a physical analysis of the objects of perception:

If it [an object] is to achieve a perfect density, if, in other words, there must be an absolute object, there must be an infinity of different perspectives contracted into a rigorous co-existence, and it must be given as through a single vision to a thousand different acts of looking.[39]

An absolute object is thus not one which could possibly be experienced. Because of this, both the method of science and the method of common sense assume that spatial location of the objects of experience is ideally determined, and described variously by different systems of geometry. This assumption, however, is the death of the transcendental consciousness, which is thought to constitute the objects of its environment. Moreover, the notion of a consciousness without its objects is sheer vanity.[40] The philosophical problem remains, then, to describe how there are objects (things *en-soi*) for us, perceiving consciousnesses.

Its Physiological Structure.—This philosophical problem has been given the uncritical attention of mechanistic physiologists. Their solution has been traditionally psycho-physical parallelism, according to which objects exist *pars extra partes,* as systems of co-extensive points. The organism is basically of the same nature, functioning by linear dependence upon the objects of an environment whose "influence"—in the strict, now archaic, sense of the word—of stimuli evoke the organism's response. In *La Structure du comportement,* Merleau-Ponty describes the forms of such behavior as syncretic, bound to the environment and its objective contents. That such forms of behavior are easily surpassed by living organisms is readily seen from the habit of even the lower animals to organize several stimuli into a significant form, or gestalt, conceiving, so to speak, its own peculiarly meaningful configuration of stimulants.[41]

Some rather common psychological facts militate further against the simple parallelism of the physiologist. Consider the effects of a paralyzed limb in comparison to the "experience" of an amputated one. The paralytic feels no sensation in a limb he still possesses; the amputee continues in rather peculiar circumstances to sense the member he no longer possesses. Where is the parallelism here? Does it arise between present psychic phenomena and cerebral traces, memory images, or whatever, brought together by association? Association has already been analyzed and found unsatisfactory.[42] Merleau-Ponty speculates that the experience of the amputee, as of the paralytic, may be given a more proper psychological interpretation as a kind of emotional shock following which the subject adopts the attitude of acceptance or rejection of the afflicted member. But, needed to explain the attitude is the subject's interaction with the parts of its body—no longer existing, but continuing to be felt; or existing in complete anaesthesis. And, in order to make sense, this interaction must be thought of as taking place on a level of experience he calls "pre-objective." The pre-objective view of the world is constituted by the fluid existence of the indeterminate objects of perception. If evidence can be adduced that the body is experienced at such a level, Merleau-Ponty will have found a workable alternative to psychophysical parallelism.

He finds such evidence in the area of comparative psychology. Consider the so-called instinctive reactions of insects and toads when a leg is injured. In such circumstances their behavioral patterns are broken. But if the injury is complete and the limb destroyed, a new and healthy limb takes its place. Nor can this replacement be considered a mere mechanical or teleological act; if it were, there would be a substitution when the leg is merely tied. In such a case there would be "conscious" effort—going out towards the world—felt by the organism. The substitution of a healthy limb for an injured one is one of the demands on the species for its continued life. Like nature's marvelous solution of the problem of minimal and maximal pressures in the spherical formation of an oil drop, the substitution of living members of the organism is an example of a higher kind of order determined by the movement of a living being toward the world. In this movement the global presence of the situation is felt and allows meaning to arise in perception. Thus psychic energy changes the world in which the psychologically organized beings exist: of two people who are becoming blind, one may accept his blindness before necessary and adapt himself to a world of darkness and inactivity, while another continues to live normally as long as possible.

Should we reconsider the case of the amputee and that of the paralytic in the light of this analysis, we may travel a royal road to

Merleau-Ponty's "irrationalist" metaphysics. Paralysis and amputation are no mere physical causes of the psychic events noted; there is no complete explanation available on the basis of the suppression or the persistence, as the case may be, of interoceptive stimulation. Considered existentially, the paralytic experiences *the absence* of a fragment of a more complete representation, whereas the amputee experiences the presence of a fragment of a more complete representation which in normal circumstances would not be given. The paralytic forgets; his judgment is negative. He does not perceive because psychologically he has willed to avoid the full awareness of his condition.[43] The amputee, on the other hand, remembers; his judgment is positive. He perceives his missing member in the same fashion as we continue to "perceive" a dead friend; we realize the friend is dead only because he or she can no longer respond to our attentions. In general, the ego continues to be engaged in the physical and cultural world in its accustomed manner; all present experiences carry with them the vestiges of our pre-objective view on the world. Playing with words, Merleau-Ponty concludes: "The patient therefore knows his condition exactly insofar as he is ignorant of it and is ignorant of it exactly insofar as he knows it."[44]

The solution of this paradox, reminiscent of both Sartre and Heidegger,[45] constitutes the "ambiguity" of the human situation. In the words of Sartre, the consciousness is what it is not and is not what it is. For Heidegger, an object which is at hand (*zuhanden*) is effective as a tool as long as it is instinctively (implicitly) used for its designed function; but should my writing be stopped by a broken pen-point, the object at hand (the pen) becomes an object of explicit awareness as an object on hand (*vorhanden*): an instrument for writing no longer functioning and needing to be repaired. The experience of the amputee is of much the same order. Conducting himself as he habitually did by trying to use the phantom leg to walk, he would fall, and thus become explicitly aware of his condition. Ignoring his malady, he knows it. But when he is acting as is proper for his actual state, taking full account of his amputation and compensating for it, his life may continue as if he were whole. Thus, knowing his condition, he may become unconscious of it.

Nor is it fair to limit the experience of human ambiguity to morbid cases. Remember that Sartre was called a "gravedigger" by the Communists because of his use of examples from the psychology of

morbidity. The conditions of human experience which make possible
a lived experience of an absent member likewise make it possible for
scientists to delude themselves into thinking that the human body is
nothing more than a system of spatio-temporal coordinates. Every
human being is both immanent and transcendent, bound up with a
certain environment and capable of surpassing it by changing it to
suit its own specific and individual needs. Thus, in my intentionality,
my particular relationship with the world, I can avoid what reflection
tells me is true—the incomplete and indeterminate grasp of my situation taken from the point of view of my own body—and accept
the common sense or scientific "prejudices" concerning the constitution of the universe. I may avoid my actual body and the things I
manipulate for my own purposes under present circumstances in
favor of the habitual body, the one I was accustomed to use in
manipulating things as they "must be" in any and all circumstances.
This psychological attitude Sartre calls "bad faith," or "insincerity"
(*mauvaise foi*). In such states the consciousness successfully lies
to itself, a situation which is possible since, phenomenologically considered, each consciousness is only implicitly aware of itself while
being explicitly aware of the objects in its environment.

In adopting the common sense or scientific point of view on the
objects of our environment, we abdicate from our power—and dig-
nity—of continually constructing or reconstructing the environment
to suit our purposes, thereby avoiding the anguish of individual
personal existence for the certainty and psychological reassurance to
be gained from espousing an impersonal, objective existence. In the
come and go of everyday existence, taking place on the background
of the subject's pre-objective view on the universe in temporal flux,
the consciousness moves continually from a state of facticity to that
of transcendence, neither of which is ever complete. That is man's
ambiguity. His consciousness must be committed to a certain situation for him to be able to see; but being so committed, his consciousness must lose a part of its absolute spontaneity.[46] The error of the
physiological view is to consider the human body and the consciousness inhabiting it as completely immanent, completely determined by
the physical properties of the environment-organism relationship.

Its Psychology.—When we turn to the classical psychological interpretations of the human body, we find various attempts to rationalize its privileged status. According to each, the body is an object

among other objects having some qualities like the others, but some other qualities which differentiate it from them. However, not many of these theorists have noticed that the presumed differentiating qualities of the human body are incompatible with its status, likewise presumed, as object.

Consider first, the body interpreted as a constantly perceived object, as opposed to the objects of the environment from which a subject may turn himself. Those who hold this view have not been aware of a host of difficulties connected with it. First of all, to be observed the object must be at some distance from the observing subject; and the consciousness inhabits the body, or more correctly, is the body in a peculiar function. Thus, secondly, for the body to be perceived at a distance the consciousness must possess a second body in order to perceive the first. Moreover, thirdly, as the body sees or touches the world—in the same fashion and with the same degree of certainty—the body can neither be seen nor touched. The hand touching and the hand touched have two different experiences. Thus the body cannot be considered as the object which is always present to consciousness. As a corrective to this point of view, Merleau-Ponty suggests that the presence or absence of objects is merely a variation within the primordial pre-objective field, and the body is merely our means of communicating with that field, the latent horizon of all our experience.

Second, the body may be considered the locus of a double sensation. The hand which is touched is felt by the touching hand and registers its own sensation as touched. This presumed quality of the human body is, obviously, no different from the first. It commits the same error. The same hand can never be experienced as touched and as touching. The exploring function of the hand is not perceived since it is the perceiving agent, although I may feel my left hand as an aggregate of bone, flesh and muscle by the right hand, which is moving, feeling, "determining" the other in its flesh and bone.

Third, the body may be considered an affective object, whereas all other objects are represented merely by stimuli. But if this is so, common experience belies the further assumption that the body is a spatially bounded object. Affectivity is diffuse, permeating the entire organism, and sometimes, as in the case of pain, exceeding its physical limits. Some toothaches are felt with such intensity that the pain seems to be felt in the surrounding environment.

Finally, the body has been considered as the locus of kinesthetic sensations, which are allegedly given globally and immediately, whereas the objects moved by the body are known by acts of mediate perception, accomplished perspective by perspective. According to Merleau-Ponty, what this experience shows is that movement has its origin in the body, not that the body feels its movement in a certain privileged fashion. Moreover, movement is a relation of succession in time through space, and as Bergson has shown, cannot be sensed directly in the same way it may be said to be understood by a correspondent "movement" in thought; consequently, our perception of the movements of the body are no more immediate than those of any other object. That is to say that the gestures of the body cannot be reduced to a mathematically calculable trajectory. As will be seen, they are lived through prior to the analytic process which decomposes, and "abstracts" them into a formula.

Faced with the failure of an objective point of view on the human body, psychologists have been led to interpret "psychic" events as those occurring in the interior of the organism and known by stimuli coming from the physiological center. The relation between the interior and the exterior is then assumed, and we have Cartesian interactionism and the metaphysical dualism of mind and body. But if we are to experience acts of consciousness, we must communicate with the world, our body, and others; each of these exists in the same phenomenal field composed of "objects" upon which we have nothing more than an indeterminate, pre-objective perspective.[47]

The Body as Lived: The Corporeal Schema.—The theoretical difficulties of the physicist, physiologist, and psychologist in explaining the experienced qualities of the human body have led to a search for a new point of departure. Since, as was concluded in the foregoing, the body cannot be considered an object like other objects—unless, of course, it is dead—the co-existence of external parts must be abandoned as the explanatory model. Already the notion of "organism" would seem to imply that the body is a biological object, different in kind from physical objects. Add in the human case the elements of social and cultural environment, and the physical model is still further removed from adequacy. In sum, when we have recourse to the everyday experiences of the human body, we recognize that the parts of the body are felt *inter se;* in some cases of physiological disturbance, it is not uncommon that a stimulus is "felt" in the right hand when it was applied to the left. Neither the hand nor the whole body is an externally related system of parts.

Certain German psychologists of the twenties and thirties had been tinkering with the notion of a "bodily schema" (*Körperschema*). According to Schilder, the bodily schema was defined as a kind of résumé of bodily experiences gained by the patient's awareness of interoceptive and proprioceptive sensations. Using the common sense approach to the problem, he appealed to the subject's immediate knowledge of any change in position, or its summary movements made in familiar gestures, and supposed that any normal subject could translate its kinesthetic impressions into visual patterns. The mechanism of this knowledge was supposed to be association, the constant readiness of the body to act taken to be evidence for the strength of the associational link.[48]

In revising this concept, Konrad appealed to the then current notion of gestalt, or form, to explain the subject's global consciousness of his own posture within an intersensorial world. But further evidence shows that the rudimentary notion of gestalt fails to fulfill the function supposed. The paralytic feels nothing of one of his members. His bodily schema, if he is possessed of one, is not a simple outline or sketch; nor is his consciousness taken globally of the truly existent parts. Thus the global integration, if such there is, must be an integration of dynamics; the body is definable in reference to its position in a field of objects, where "position" is understood as a certain posture in the total situation. When I am smoking my pipe, the act of grasping its bowl has nothing to do with my ability or inability to calculate the exact position of the pipe or my hand through the geometrical properties of these objects. I know the position of my hand with reference to the pipe it holds in a concrete situation.

Merleau-Ponty accepts Konrad's revision of Schilder, and adds his own brand of existentialistic metaphysics to the description. The notion of bodily schema not only surpasses that of a physical object, but expresses as exactly as possible the fact that my body is in the world. My body is always *here*, and *here* is the primary reference point of all spatial coordinates. All other spatial positions gain meaning from this first meaningful position. From here my body can grasp its objects. Whence the words "Come here," to the naughty child to be chastised, to the coquettish female to be loved.[49] The corporeal schema thus summarizes the situation of the body before its tasks. As

such, it is always the understood third term between the perception
of a figure on a ground; in effect every object of perception is
grasped as a figure on a double ground, that of external space which
creates a "spatial tension," which is in its turn registered by the perceiver on the ground of his own corporeal and schematic space. It is
for this reason that painters refer to the "rhythm" of their works of
art, and insist on its being "felt." Any skilled gesture is perceived *on*
the background of the global bodily schema. But the word "on" here
is not to be interpreted as objectively spatial. If it were, it would be
no more meaningful than others denoting abstract spatial relationships, such as "between," "beside," "under." The word "on" here
indicates the dynamic relationships of the body as a focal point of
interaction with its environment. In conclusion, it can be said that
my body is not a mere fragment of space; but it should be said that
there is space for me because I have a body. And if this is true, it is
unfortunate for Kant's intuitive forms of the sensibility, and the
transcendental aesthetic.

Having explained the nature of the bodily schema, Merleau-Ponty
takes on the task of amassing evidence to support his theoretical construct. He finds the evidence in the psychological case studies of
Gelb and Goldstein[50] on the relationship between vision and tactile
sensitivity, vision and movement, and on the difference between the
activities of pointing and grasping.

Consider the case history of Schneider, a soldier who, having suffered a lesion of the occipital nerve, subsequently lost his capacity to
make abstract movements—those not connected with an habitual,
real-life situation. The patient was further observed to have lost his
ability to execute a simple command to flex certain parts of his body,
to describe the position of his body, to tell where he was touched
when he was, and to infer the size of objects from his tactile sensations. He could act only when permitted to see the object implicit in
his action, and did so extremely well when aided in his preparatory
movements; he continued to ply his trade as a wallet weaver with
about 75 per cent efficiency. The problem to theory presented by this
case history is the explanation of the patient's superiority in performing "concrete" movements. The act of grasping a tool or a piece of
material according to fixed patterns of movement is considered more
concrete than that of pointing to a distinct object.

According to Merleau-Ponty, only the phenomenological psychologist has forged the concepts necessary to explain the privileged status of the more concrete actions. On this view, pointing and grasping are two different ways for a consciousness to apprehend space. Thus, while the classical psychologist limits himself to a single concept of space representation, the phenomenological psychologist makes an appeal to the corporeal schema, the phenomenal or concrete body as opposed to the abstract body described in strictly objective terms. Since these two bodies are "experienced" in different manners, it is quite possible for the same patient to react to the one with a higher degree of facility than to the other. The subject may be incapable of pointing to the spot on his body which has just been stung by a mosquito, for such action intends the body as an abstract object; but he has no difficulty at all in reaching for the spot in order to scratch the bite. In this latter instance, of course, the phenomenal and concrete body is the object of the subject's intention. The success of the concrete movement is thus explained by the non-thetic grasp of the body by the consciousness, whereas the failure of the more abstract movement is explained by faulty inferences by the consciousness which perceived the body externally. The afflicted consciousness therefore has in this example a better command of its lived situation than it has of abstract representations.

The phenomenological or "existential" analysis of Schneider's case yields a "meaning" or essence, and not a "cause" as empirical psychologists would maintain. Following the method of the objective sciences, the empiricists begin by observing the "facts" underlying present behavior, and then inducing the cause. For example, the patient's wound is noted as preceding his inability to fix objects in space, and this latter as preceding the patient's difficulty of movement. In repeated experiments, the constant conjunction of lack of fixation and inability to move is noted; so, by the method of agreement, the first is presumed the cause of the other. Likewise, when it is possible for the patient to look at the member he is expected to move on command, he does in fact succeed in moving the member. Thus, with the ability to see the object, there is conjoined the ability to move. By the method of difference, the initial presumption of causality is reinforced. Does this inductive analysis suffice?

Merleau-Ponty claims not. He points out, as Mill admitted in formulating the rules of inductive inference, that no "knowledge" results. What the empiricist has reached is a correlation between two events, without being able to tell which is the cause and which is the effect. And in the case of psychic disturbance it is not unreasonable to assume that the inability to move a member is actually the cause of not being able to see. In general, no psychic event can be established as "caused" since neither the event allegedly caused nor that causing is capable of objective observation. Certainly the visual representation of the leg, for example, is not the cause of moving the leg—although it would contribute to the cause, from the empiricist's point of view— for it too depends upon the ability to "project a spectacle" which is manifested in the abstract movement of the pointing gesture. If the power is lost in the one case, it should be lost in the other. The tactile experience and the visual experience considered apart from the corpo- real schema are abstract notions; to experience them abstractly is to undergo a pathological experience like that of the conditioned reflex outside the laboratory. The human individual in normal circumstances has one integral experience; the sensibility and motricity of its or- ganism are merely simultaneous and inseparable functions instan- taneously motivated in the same experience.

If empiricism fails to yield a psychological explanation of Schneider's case, can it be said that rationalism fares better? Can we substitute the concept of "reason" for that of "cause"?[51] The rational- ist notes that the empiricist supposes a "power" or lack of power on the part of the subject; but according to his own point of view, the consciousness does not have powers, it is power. The power that is consciousness is precisely its manner of grasping or apprehending the universe. In Schneider's pathological experiences, he is experienc- ing his body as facticity; it is seen, analyzed, manipulated as from without, and not lived. Thus the existentialistic concepts, metaphys- ical though they may be, are thought by Sartre and his followers to be sufficient reasons to explain morbidity.

Although Merleau-Ponty's explanation sounds similar to Sartre's metaphysical analysis, it must be said that he has no use for the en-soi and the pour-soi.[52] The two existentialists have the notion of "facticity" (the necessary connection of consciousness with a body and an environing situation) in common, but Merleau-Ponty is here objecting to Sartre's "rationalism." Consider his rebuttal of the meta- physical explanation. It is impossible to think a movement en-soi; when a patient moves his body to perform some habitual action thus acting in accord with the principles of the *pour-soi,* he must necessarily move the same segments of the arm as those required in the abstract movement, when the body is supposedly being acted upon according to the principles of the *en-soi.* It thus seems impossible to limit the physiological explanation on the metaphysical grounds contained in Sartre's system.

In sum, it is clear that both the physiological and the intellectual explanations, that is, both empiricism and rationalism, destroy the distinction between abstract and concrete movements. The distinction, which is lived and attested by Schneider's case history could be maintained only if there were several ways to be a body, which is the same as to say, "several ways to be a consciousness," or several ways for the same organism to be related to its environment. When Lefebvre accused Merleau-Ponty of using pseudo-scientific concepts, he referred specifically to those of "organism," "structure," and "environment."[53] But it is clear that Merleau-Ponty cannot be fairly called "pseudo-scientific," since he makes no pretensions to science, and consciously tries to give his explanations on a level of experience from which science abstracts its objects. More fairly, he should be called "non-scientific," or as he would have preferred, "existentialistic."

When we return to the existentialistic analysis of Schneider's case, we become aware of the epistemological problem to be solved. How are the linguistic, perceptive, and motor contents of an experience related to the form they received—their symbolic, conceptual function—which is neither a reduction of the content to the form, rationalism, nor that of the form to the content, empiricism? How, in other words, are we to understand Schneider's conduct, a motor, perceptual, and conceptual deficiency occasioned by his nervous lesion? He is capable of understanding "abstractly," since when presented with a pen he fails to recognize it as a pen but is capable of deducing the nature of both the instrument and its function by assimilating various individual properties of the object presented to him into a single pattern. How can the patient go beyond the particular contents he perceives when his illness is mental—faulty symbolic functioning *in concreto*—and produced by a known loss of visual acumen?

Merleau-Ponty formulates answers to these various questions by referring to the existential situation of the patient. In this world of "pure experience" as James called it, a normal subject perceives the harmony of content to the form of the object without the intermediary of hypothetical suggestion such as: "That could be a ———; it has a ——— ." The reason for this superiority of the normal over the pathological is that the normal consciousness is related to the objects of its environment by an "intentional arc." Even in the case of apprehending so-called intellectual relations the pathological consciousness is reduced to the construction of its objects by an analysis into its parts. When seeing the formulae, $5 + 4 - 4$ and $2 \times \frac{1}{2} \, 5$, that consciousness must perform each operation in the indicated order in order to arrive at the answer 5. Proceeding by abstraction, the mentally ill individual is incapable of feeling himself located within his human situation, and by the same token the human personality has lost a portion of its freedom. The sick consciousness is a victim of its old habits, and is unable to form new modes of reaction to the elements of its environment. When the intentional arc is broken, sickness sets in, whether the symptoms be manifest in the sensibility, the motor responses, or in intellection:

. . . the life of consciousness—knowing, desiring, perceiving—is supported by an "intentional arc" which projects around us our past, our future, our human situation, our physical situation, our ideological and moral situations; or, better, which is responsible for our being situated in all these respects. It's this intentional arc which gives a unity to the senses, as well as a unity of the senses to the intellect, and of our motor responses to our sensibility; and it's the intentional arc which gives way in illness.[54]

When the intentional arc "gives way" and the subject is forced to perceive its objects by having recourse to fixed concepts, the individual is no longer "in situation." He must rely on the "superstructures," the conceptual awareness gained from past experiences, without their being grounded in the stuff of pure experience. Finally, the connection between the physical accident and the psychical results may be explained in the same way. Consciousness is related to the world via the body. When the body is no longer capable of composing new variations on the older themes, the past, both natural and personal, becomes absolute, a set of objects without the vibrancy of relation to the living present[55] which is the intentional arc.

Following Grünbaum, Merleau-Ponty takes the motor responses to be the basic functions of the consciousness. The area through which the body can move is its situation, or environment. Nor is it

true that a movement can be made only following a subject's representation of objects in space. In certain cases of apraxia where the
subject sees and understands the function of a given object, he cannot use the object, making the appropriate motor responses. The
representation can therefore be made without the movements, and
all cases of habitual action suffice to show that the movements can
be made without representation.

Indeed, the most enlightening approach to the body's constitution
of its world is perhaps to be had in the analysis of habit and the
learning of habitual skills. In order for a given skill to become
"second nature," certain responses are to be "built into" the muscles
of the body. When beginning to learn, the subject naturally intends
its objects thetically, one by one in the prescribed order. The intentional arc has not yet become a part of the body. When it has, the
objects implicit in the action are never consciously intended. The
new driver intellectualizes his problem and drives poorly; the experienced driver reacts to each of the automobile's idiosyncrasies
without a thought. Whence the husband's distress at his wife's inability to feel the position of the front wheels following a turn;
until she learns this trick she will never be able to parallel-park. The
blind man "sees" with the end of his cane, but he never measures
the distance of his cane from the objects it touches. Expert typists
type by "touch," and may be incapable of indicating where each
letter is found on the keyboard; the hunt-and-peck artist composes
each word, following a more or less prolonged search, from his
thetic awareness of the position of each letter. If it seems absurd
to say that the world is understood by the body because to understand is to subsume a particular set of impressions under a general
concept, then in the face of the evidence we must either re-examine
our notion of "understand" or of "the body." And this is precisely
what Merleau-Ponty has done.

He starts with the body. Our body is the means by which we have
a world, and are present in a given situation. But situations and
worlds differ, and exist on different planes. The biological world
implicates only those gestures necessary for survival. The world of
free expression liberates the body from its devotion to survival; some
gestures, as the dance, are pursued for their form and others, as the
element of style in an athlete's motion, for their usefulness. Finally,
when the body has no natural means to relate with its intended

objects, it must construct instruments: the blind man's cane, a bridge, a boat, the wings of an airplane; all are cultural objects, all merely ways of extending the body's grasp of the universe. On each of these levels, from the biological to the cultural, it may be said that the body understands when the new habit is acquired. Motor habits are structures of bodily responses. "Meaning," "response," and "structure" are thus fundamental terms of the theory of knowledge, each capable of explication by a more thorough analysis of the corporeal schema. The primary meaning of the word "sense" is direction, an ambiguity retained in the French, *sens,* which also yields "sense," the organ, as well as "meaning." According to Merleau-Ponty's philosophy of ambiguity, it is the body which through its dynamic relations to a lived situation constitutes the first meanings an intellect may grasp, as if by proxy, in any later attempt to codify the experience in symbols.

The clearest expression of the relation between motor responses and the meanings of symbols in recent American philosophy is the work of G. H. Mead, for whom gestures take on significance through the interpretative responses of a society of individuals.[56] But Mead puts the emphasis on the adaptive responses of the interlocutor, while Merleau-Ponty stresses the initial gesture of a body in expression.

The Body as Expression.—Since the pathological as well as the normal consciousness may experience its body in two radically opposed manners, and does so either abstractly or concretely, the phenomenological psychologist must admit two different concepts of the body. What we refer to in the spirit of abstraction is the physical or objective body, and what we live—or as Sartre puts it, "we exist" —in full concrete relation to our environmental situation is the bodily schema. The objective body is not, moreover, the primary of the two experiences; it depends upon the schema, as the case of the injured frog noted above would seem to indicate. A stress felt within the schema produces a new leg for the one amputated. In the case of humans, paralysis shows that having a certain objective body is not sufficient for the formation of the schema, and persistent feeling of a "phantom member" following amputation proves that a whole objective body is not even necessary for a bodily schema to be determined. If it be argued that we see our body and construct from that vantage point the possibility of further tactile experiences, it may be answered that many subjects fail to recognize photographs of their own hands, or their own handwriting when a sample of it is placed with others. But we usually do not fail to recognize our own silhouette in a photograph; thus we recognize what we never see, and fail to recognize what we see a thousand times a day. In general, the felt unison of the elements within the corporeal schema cannot be translated into a summation of individual sense reports on the physical body. Here, as in art criticism, we must abandon the "spirit of geometry," for an exercise of the "spirit of finesse." Our knowledge of our body is given, in the language of Leibnitz, as "the law of successive changes" of the corporeal schema. The hand which touches and the sight of the touching hand are molded by a sense for style; we recognize the characteristic manner we have of moving the fingers and of holding the hands in relation to the rest of our physical economy.

Since the perception we have of our own body is of its stylized gestalt, the natural analogue suggested is our perception of a work of art, in which the aesthetic idea is "embodied" in a physical medium. Obviously enough, a musical composition is the pattern of sound heard; and a work of non-objective painting, a pattern of visual stimuli. But what about a work of literary art, which to some extent is composed of "ideas"? To Merleau-Ponty, it is likewise a pattern of gestures, in which the expression and what is expressed are one and the same:

The novelist's role is not to exposit ideas or even to analyze characters, but to present an interhuman event, to bring it to maturation and make it burst forth without ideological commentary, such that any change in the order of the events or in the choice of point of view would necessarily modify the *novelistic* meaning of the event.[57]

The aesthetic analogy Merleau-Ponty draws is taken from the position of formalism. As the subject of the next chapter is aesthetics, a statement of his point of view will suffice here. It is generalized in the following:

A novel, a poem, a picture, a piece of music are individuals, that is to say beings in which it is impossible to distinguish the expressive vehicle from its meaning, whose meanings are accessible only in direct contact, and which radiate their significance without leaving their temporal and spatial position.[58]

So much in this chapter for works of art.

In comparison, the body likewise radiates from a center of placement, and the means or vehicle of bodily extension is habit: our
habit of seeing, our habit of moving, our habit of "associating" what
we see and what we move. The blind man replaces a lost habit of
seeing with that of moving his cane over his immediate environment. The instrument gives him a new manner of extending the
influence of his body, and hence of acquiring a world in which to
live. Were we to stop and think about our habitual actions in search
of an intellectual analysis—one which would deduce its object from
the laws of perspective—very likely no action would take place. Such
an intellectual analysis would be fatal in the act of crossing a
crowded street. Separating the sign from what is signified can at
best produce a discursive alignment of superficial signs of action; in
situation the body grasps a meaning directly. The relative positions
of the body and oncoming obstacles are measured in the very act of
evasion. Moreover, seeing itself is a habit of the body, and in learning the difference between colors we learn a new way to use the
body. We acquire a certain style of vision, and undergo an enrich-
ment and reorganization of our bodily schema. Far from being an
object of representation to a perceiving subject, the body must be
re-interpreted as a structure of experienced meanings in process toward equilibrium.

Merleau-Ponty gives a useful summary of his position in speaking
of the sexual expression of the human body:

On this side of the conventional means of expression, which manifest my
thoughts to another only because within me as within him there is a meaning assigned to each symbol and which, in this sense, does not produce a
veritable communication, one must recognize a primordial operation of signifying in which the thing expressed does not exist outside of the expression
itself and in which the signs used themselves induce outwardly a meaning.[59]

The body in an act of love, as in a dance, is both vehicle of expression and locus of the feeling expressed, both instrument for the one
and object for the other partner; in the act of sexual communication,
as in a successful aesthetic "expression," there is no distinction to be
drawn between intention and deed. Perhaps no better example may
be found for the perfect union of body and soul. And if this union
of body and soul is anything more than a suggestive metaphor, it
would be false, in this most primitive form of human expression, to
claim that the body merely undergoes what a mind intends as if

it submitted to the action of signs communicated by a series of seductive gestures. For, as Sartre has pointed out, our human gestures of seduction intend the fascination of another consciousness, and put into play the eternal dialectic of the Self and the Other, each of which may become an object for the other but neither of which may ever dominate the other's subjectivity. The most delirious of our ecstasies give way to an awakening in which we realize that we have been abused by (masochism), or that we have abused (sadism), the other. In a successful act of sexual expression, the distinction between mind and body cannot be made, and what is enjoyed of the other is his consciousness as it lives its bodily experience.

In general, human existence may be characterized as an "expression" of the human body, not as an external accompaniment, which it may assume in life, but as an internal "embodiment," which it lives as a struggle to achieve equilibrium in an individually characteristic manner within its global environment. Thus Merleau-Ponty reiterates his case against "scientific" or "philosophical" abstraction: "The embodied meaning is the central phenomenon of which body and mind, sign and signification are only abstract moments."[60] And in all cases of human existence, we live first, and can reflect only on the matter of what we have lived, the ambiguity of the human condition. Further considerations of the act of expression as the embodiment of human intentions will be left for finer analysis when we turn to Merleau-Ponty's aesthetics.

SUMMARY AND CONCLUSION

In analysis and criticism of Sartre's theory of the imagination,[61] it was established that he had failed to found his phenomenological description of imaginary experiences since he contrasts the imaginary and perceptive elements of experience without making clear what, phenomenologically speaking, is involved in perception. Moreover, since the imaging consciousness was described as motivated by a prior consciousness fortified with the gains of prior knowledge in concepts, some question arises as to the phenomenological status of concepts. By posing the question, Whence concepts in the first place?, we have taken the empiricist's stand that all knowledge has its source in prior perceptive acts. But to this opposition Sartre would very likely object, since the question of the priority of concept or percept is, from his point of view, metaphysically unsound. Phenomenologically, the consciousness grasps a meaning when placed before an object; consequently the concept and percept are simultaneous moments in a single act of judgment. So far it would seem that Sartre and Merleau-Ponty are in agreement. Both admit, as phenomenologists, that the consciousness grasps the meaning, Sartre calling it the *"ratio* of a series of appearances," and Merleau-Ponty, "the immanent law" describing the unity of the object. Moreover, both contend that the cognitive act demands a base; Sartre finds it in the dialectical relationship of the *pour-soi* and the *en-soi,* and Merleau-Ponty in a prior epistemological situation, described likewise as a dialectical relationship between an organism and its environment. Thus the difference seems to be one of metaphysics. Sartre appeals to the "ontological structures" which establish the conditions of the possibility of knowledge,[62] whereas Merleau-Ponty stays within the realm of epistemology for his explanation and deduces his metaphysics of "ambiguity" from the primary organism-environment situation. In other words, both Sartre and Merleau-Ponty avoid the empiricism-rationalism controversy by claiming it is founded upon an experience derivative from a more basic one. Of the two explanations of knowledge, the preferable should be the one which stays within the realm of epistemology. If there is a superiority to be found in Merleau-Ponty's use of phenomenology, it would seem to be that.

But the question is not settled by this statement. It remains to be shown that the empirical and rational elements of knowledge, even if nothing more than simultaneous moments of an act of cognition, do in fact develop from a more primitive cognitive consciousness. The means used by Merleau-Ponty have already been made explicit. If it is true, for example, that both empiricism and rationalism are based upon an "abstract" view of mind and body—as Descartes clearly demonstrates[63]—and that the existence of the "real world" is assumed by each in its own way, Merleau-Ponty has rejected both epistemological theories for metaphysical reasons. With similar reasoning Sartre denies empiricism, which he considers founded on a "naive ontology" of the image, which he called the illusion of immanence. But in all fairness to Sartre it must be recalled that he treats the image as "a consciousness," an intention, or manner of being related to an "absent" object. Merleau-Ponty likewise uses the concept of intention, but re-interprets the notion in such a way as to make it, at the foundation of knowledge, a bodily act. Whence the intentional arc. In primitive acts of awareness the body "intends" the vague and indeterminate horizons of a "world", and "meaning" has its first meaning as "direction." Derived from this primary meaning of the word are the other translations of the French "sens," as a sense organ, with at least the possibility of a sensation, and a "meaning," a symbol having a constant referential function in varying contexts.

If this is the "direction" of Merleau-Ponty's epistemology, and it is clear from a reading of his two major works that it is, we have nothing more than a sketch of a theory of knowledge. What must still be shown is the manner in which a primitive awareness, or direction, of the body, or consciousness, develops into the more refined kinds of knowledge which even the most rigorous thinker would accept as "science." Moreover, since concepts are symbols functioning in discourse, it must be shown how the body's intentional arc develops from its vague pre-objective viewpoint into a consciousness capable of using symbols. Unfortunately no easy conclusion is possible here, as this explanation must be postponed until a further chapter. Like Benedetto Croce, whose aesthetic theory is couched in terms of a "general linguistic,"[64] Merleau-Ponty claims the conceptual knowledge is an outgrowth of "aesthetic knowledge," and that aesthetics is rightly conceived as a general theory of "expression." The hint of a connection between aesthetics and science is contained in Merleau-Ponty's theory of the body as expression, but its development must also wait upon the next chapter. Further remarks here are limited to an explanation of Merleau-Ponty's use of Husserlian phenomenology.

In the shortest and perhaps clearest expression of Husserl's principles,[65] Professor J. N. Findlay has described phenomenology as a theory of knowledge based upon a series of "reductions." In each, starting from the phenomenological axiom that every consciousness is a consciousness of something, a part of the dialectical relationship of consciousness-object is "put into brackets," that is, held in abeyance while analysis is made of the correlative term. The first such reduction is called the "phenomenological": it puts the world into brackets, and studies the appearance of something to a consciousness; whence, the world may be taken as reduced to a series of appearances. This is what Merleau-Ponty has done in denying the validity of the "objective" viewpoint in favor of a description of a consciousness (or body) as it intends the pre-objective domain. Thus Merleau-Ponty's originality is to have reduced the knowing act to a manner of the body's functioning in a given environment. And it is for this reason that his study began by "critical reflection" on the work of physiologists and psychologists of a physicalist persuasion.[66] The second reduction is called the "eidetic" and excludes the series of appearances from analysis while examining the "essence" of that series, again as grasped by a consciousness. It is at this level of analysis that the empiricist-rationalist controversy may be evaluated from the neutral ground of phenomenology.

If we ask ourselves the question, Which comes first, the cube or cubicity? it is readily seen that we are posing our question on the wrong level of abstraction. True, no one can ever perceive simultaneously the six sides of a cube; we are given a series of impressions, and from a judgment on the perspectives perceived, the mind establishes their unity in the object. Thus it is for the rationalist. The empiricist, if he is a radical one, may turn the cube over or walk around the object in order to perceive the "missing sides." But one cannot "walk around" the object without traveling through space. The empiricist position therefore presupposes the constitution of space. It assumes moreover that the cube is there and is capable of yielding further impressions of its shape. But the "space" enclosed by the "sides"—all of which are never seen together—is likewise invisible; it can only be thought. Even to be able to perceive of a cube what I do, I must put my body in relation to the same kind of space the cube is thought to be composed of; my body must make physical movements about a physical object. Since such movements are a property of the physical body, and an abstraction from the corporeal schema—and hence removed by abstraction from what is lived in the perceptual situation—even they must be thought. The absolute object, the cube in itself, can never be given; it is nothing more than the presupposition of the empiricist's method. The rationalist, on the other hand, presupposes the existence of the "meaning," cubicity. Take the notions "six," "side," "equal," "solid," and put them into a single formula, and the result is "cubicity." But just what in the lived experience controls the thought of cubicity on the presence of an object with six equal sides is left unexplained. In thought or imagination, I can think of the space inside, outside, on the surface, or whatever, but all I will have is a thought—of an absolute object. The very universality of the concept means that the object is considered from no particular point of view, but this can be known only in thought. The point of view I have on any object is established by the position of my body, the center of Merleau-Ponty's phenomenology:

If there is for me a cube with six equal sides and I can have an experience of the object, it is not that I constituted it from the interior; the reason is that I delve into the thickness of the world in the perspective experience. The cube with six equal sides is a limiting-concept by which I express the fleshly presence of the cube that is there, before my eyes, under my hands, in all its perceptual evidence.[67]

The thing is given with the experience of the body; its sides are not projections in space, but perspectives of the thing perceived.

Consider, as an example, Aristotle's illusion: when a subject crosses the index with the medial finger, and an object is placed between them, there is the distinct impression of two objects. Why? Because the mind is incapable of "thinking the distinct impressions into a single object"? Hardly. But the index and the medial fingers do not habitually work together under such conditions, and the illusion is the result of a temporary destruction of the bodily schema. The natural pattern of motor responses is surpassed, and the forced movement of the fingers can not grasp the object as a unity. The perception of the object and the perception of the bodily schema— called by Merleau-Ponty, "the body proper"—are two sides of the same act. To perceive a single object is to have two fingers working in their habitual way; to "perceive" two, in the case of the crossed fingers, is to perceive the break in the corporeal schema. In conclusion, "Every external perception is immediately synonymous with a certain perception of my body, just as every perception of my body is explainable in terms of external perception."[68] Whence, instead of leading the phenomenologist to a transcendental, world-constituting, consciousness, an act of perception leads Merleau-Ponty to a direct awareness of the body-proper. The third reduction of phenomenology puts the phenomenological epistemologist in contact with the distinctly human corporeal schema which, it will be remembered, is known by acquaintance and grasped globally, or totally, in one swoop of the intentional arc. I know my body proper by its potentiality of being moved through a pre-objective domain of experience.

In tracing the three "reductions" of Merleau-Ponty's phenomenology, we accede to his concept of the body proper, and paradoxically enough, return to Sartre. In *L'Etre et le néant* Sartre dedicates three chapters to a study of "corporeity." Comparison of Merleau-Ponty's conclusions with the first of these is quite revealing. We find the body described as the "facticity of a transcendence." Besides the figures of Husserl and Heidegger looming in the background, we can on closer analysis perceive some striking similarities with Merleau-Ponty's account. (*L'Etre* was copyrighted in 1943; *Phénoménologie de la perception,* in 1945.) We find in Sartre, for example, that the body is a point of view upon which it is impossible for the subject to take a point of view, a center of reference for the complex of instruments offered in the surrounding world, a situation lived rather than thought or perceived, a body "properly so-called" rather than a cadaver taking up so much space. These are most of the phenomenological descriptions used two years later in Merleau-Ponty's treatise. Missing from Merleau-Ponty's account, however, is the ontological description of the body as "the contingent form which the necessity of my contingency takes."[69] Again the reason for this absence is Merleau-Ponty's attempt to base his descriptions on categories other than "ontological." He preferred to criticize the methods and concepts of practicing psychologists, and in consequence drew the criticism of Lefebvre as being pseudo-scientific. That this charge is unfounded has already been explained. Like Sartre, Merleau-Ponty seeks to go beyond scientific descriptions, but in doing so appeals to our ever-present non-thetic awareness of the pre-rational elements of experience. Can this attempt be understood by English and American readers?

The answer to this last query is patent for American pragmatists. The "pre-objective domain" seems to this reader to be synonymous with William James' "world of pure experience."[70] But the more apparent similarity is to be found in Dewey's epistemology. Perhaps the best example to cite here is his essay on "Qualitative Thought," where Dewey deplores the traditional epistemological insistence on the fixed character of the properties of objects.[71] The result of this assumption has been an attributive logic and a classificatory science. "Objects" may be described and classified if we make the supposition, but the felt qualities of an experience have been relegated to a mystical limbo inhabited only by madmen and poets. But just what, on the other hand, has occurred in the realm of the scientific paradise? The experiences recounted have lost contact with the reality of the lived situation:

When it is said that I have a feeling, or impression, or "hunch," that things are thus and so, what is actually designated is primarily the presence of a dominating quality in a situation as a whole, not just the existence of a feeling as a psychical or psychological fact. *To say I have a feeling or impression that so and so is the case is to note that the quality in question is not yet resolved into determinate terms and relations;* it marks a conclusion without statement of the reasons for it, the grounds upon which it rests. *It is the first stage in the development of explicit distinctions. All thought in every subject begins with just such an unanalyzed whole.*[72]

The situation provides the background on which all objects are perceived; and insofar as they are perceived in some kind of relation, the situation provides the pervasive quality which is "felt" as a property of that relation. Dewey goes on to indicate that this aesthetic element may be conceived as the "art" of scientific observation, and contrasts it with the science or "logic of artistic constructions":

The logic of artistic construction and esthetic appreciation is peculiarly significant because they exemplify in accentuated and purified form the control of selection of detail and of mode of relation, or integration, by a qualitative whole.[73]

We may recall Merleau-Ponty's use of the analogy from aesthetics to throw light on our manner of being acquainted with the "body proper," the corporeal schema in situation.

I do not maintain here that there is an "influence" one way or the other across the Atlantic. As a matter of fact, a more inclusive reading of recent and contemporary philosophy will show that phenomenology and pragmatism are independent reactions to objective idealism and various forms of realistic metaphysics. But it is clear that both Dewey and Merleau-Ponty have maintained the primacy of aesthetic perception in a complete theory of knowledge. Merleau-Ponty's phenomenological language, however, does present some difficulties, and is, to say the least, strange to one untrained in the discipline. In appealing to the pre-rational, to the non-reflective aspects of experience upon which reflection must take hold if it is to have something to reflect upon—shades of the pervasive quality of the whole—his language is necessarily vague. Like Heidegger, he must categorically deny that "reason" is the ultimate court of appeal for matters logical.[74] But unlike Heidegger, he gives painstaking analyses of the methods of scientists, and in many instances reinterprets their experiments demonstrating that a more inclusive view is necessary to find a "meaning" in their work. Hence, where his language is vague he tries to supply examples, test cases, and case histories. There is little doubt that his examples throw light on his meaning, but phenomenologists are not agreed that examples are valid substitutes for "eidetic reduction."[75]

The second shortcoming of Merleau-Ponty's method of criticism is that where precision is intended, more often than not the explanation is mystifying. Consider the Husserlian notion of "motivation." In Sartre the reason for this middle ground between "cause" and "reason" is apparent: since a consciousness is defined as spontaneity, it can be determined by nothing, neither an external object nor a prior consciousness. But one consciousness can "motivate" another. I have criticized this notion earlier.[76] But in Merleau-Ponty, where consciousness is not conceived as absolute spontaneity and interactionism is the accepted relation between mind and body, the reasons for the appeal to motivation are harder to understand. Moreover, without the Husserlian distinction between a thetic and non-thetic awareness the concept doesn't make much sense; if, for example, it were not possible to be non-thetically aware of the horizons surrounding the objects perceived at the point of focus within our perceptual field at the same time that we are thetically aware of these objects, evidently no "perception" would take place. But no consciousness is capable of perceiving its own activity, and for this reason Descartes' *cogito* demands an act of reflection. Using the concept of a non-thetic awareness, Sartre appeals to a "pre-reflective cogito," by which each consciousness is aware of itself in the very act of being thetically aware of something else. Thus he finds himself in the same position as Merleau-Ponty with no more ground than the knowledge of the self as it is lived or "felt," in Dewey's sense, by the knowing agent. If the existentialistic doctrine of freedom is to be given a clear exposition, it will have to be made on the basis of a thoroughgoing analysis of the concept of motivation. But that analysis is a project which transcends the present purpose. As in the case where his language is vague, Merleau-Ponty's attempts at precision need the elucidation of example, and this at least he never fails to give.

But consider a final point. Phenomenology is supposed to be a method involving no presuppositions. Thus Merleau-Ponty criticizes both rationalism and empiricism for supposing too much: the objectivity of the world under two guises. But isn't any *motivation* which is only implicitly or non-thetically known likewise a supposition? The claim is that we experience it, but in such a way that no determinate description of the experience can be given. Is not this the same as to say that it is a "hypothetical construct" the existence of which is supposed, merely to give sense or meaning to an experience once it is had? If it is, and it happens that this is derived from a current school of philosophy, surely one would be excused for thinking that theory has preceded even the lived experience, and that the phenomenological descriptions of human behavior depend heavily upon the structure of phenomenological theory. The question then is not whether a supposition has been made, but which supposition resists further analysis. Although Merleau-Ponty shows that the "constancy principle" of empiricism and rationalism yields in analysis to his notion of a "fluid" determination within the intentional-arc, his own supposition cannot be further analyzed without a destruction of the nature of the event he supposes to exist. Or at least this seems to be the case in his critical reflections upon the human organism in its environment, which bring the reflecting consciousness face to face with a non-reflective experience of quality. Finally, if Sartre can escape this criticism of irrationality, it is only because he has taken refuge in his "ontological structures" to begin with; but as de Waelhens has made clear, Merleau-Ponty does not enjoy this refuge. It cannot be doubted, then, that Merleau-Ponty's philosophy rests upon at least a "non-rational" base. But that is what he intended it to do.

The quality of a lived experience or of an indeterminate situation no doubt exists and may be felt; our criticism begins when the theorist supposes, as Merleau-Ponty does not, that this quality may be precisely expressed in some terms other than its bare experience or its immediate bodily expression. Either the experience is had or it is missed. But this is the nature of an aesthetic experience and of our reflective relations to it in criticism; thus we may proceed in the next chapter to Merleau-Ponty's account of aesthetic experiences for further exemplification of his principle.

IX

Aesthetics as a
General Theory of Linguistics

It is clear from what has preceded in the exposition of Merleau-Ponty's philosophy, that further consideration of his aesthetic theory will involve a difficulty of principle. Recall that perception is a movement or direction of the organism from one position to another in which the surrounding field becomes organized and "interpreted" according to the creative intentions of the organism, and that the object perceived is the immanent law, or gestalt, of the appearances of the elements in the perceptual field meaningfully organized in the experience of the organism. If we recall further that knowledge of the formal properties of aesthetic objects was presupposed in his description of the manner in which an organism creates specific and determinate objects for itself from the basic non-reflective relationship with its environing situation, it seems obvious that simultaneous appeal to perception to explain aesthetic theory would constitute a case of circular explanation. Perception explains aesthetic objects, and aesthetic objects explain perception. The implication of such a criticism would be that neither explains the other, and that Merleau-Ponty's circle is vicious.

The only possible rebuttal to this criticism is to point out successfully that perception, in the basic sense of becoming aware of a new object in our environment, and the creation of an aesthetic object are indeed correlative notions, each needed to give a full explanation of the other, but that both activities depend upon a still more basic attitude of the human organism, the explanation of which is not exhausted by that of the one or the other, nor even by a com-

258

bination of the two. Such a concept is "expression." An organism may express itself without perceiving, as it does in every case of an unconscious or unskilled behavioral pattern; but if it perceives, the object of its perception is describable in terms of the laws of *Gestalten*.

Before proceeding to an elucidation of the concept of expression, a few preliminary observations would be helpful. First, it has already been shown that expression in its most basic interpretation is not a "mental" phenomenon in the sense that minds and their activities are conceived of as different in kind from bodies and their activities. Merleau-Ponty's notion of the corporeal schema allows us to bridge this distinction. Further, it remains to be shown that the activity of the organism in "reconstructing" its environment allows the same physical-mental field to express itself either on a higher or a lower plane in such a way as to appear merely physical or merely mental, and to demonstrate, using the same notion, in what way the organism capable of sheer physical reactions can transcend these in order to "create" for itself a mental, social, and cultural universe. In other words, expression takes place by degrees and knows no clear-cut distinction of kinds. If this is true, it would be false to say that the organism expresses itself physically for example in walking, and expresses itself differently in painting a picture. It will be recalled that Croce defined aesthetics as "a science of expression and general linguistic."[1] But expression for him was a mental act, that of organizing impressions into an intuition, so that the activity of painting was quite logically conceived as a bothersome afterthought for the painter's prior inner thought.[2]

For all of its idealistic metaphysics, the system of Croce is perhaps the most pregnant for comparison with Merleau-Ponty's aesthetics. For example, if it could be shown that even in its highest forms of intuition the organism's physical dimensions are intrinsic to the "mental" act, we might save a series of Croce's insights into aesthetic problems without at least the embarrassing consequence noted above. After all, the painter thinks by manipulating his paints; if he were not manipulating his paints he would have no symbols and hence no thought. The most pressing task, then, is to explain in what sense aesthetics is properly conceived as a general theory of linguistics. In so doing I shall attempt to demonstrate that the aesthetic moment is the first and most important in a complete theory of knowledge. On this point, again, Croce and Merleau-Ponty are in agreement.

In the second place, it seems apparent to anyone with a practical interest in aesthetic experience that no theory is valuable unless it gives a *modus operandi* for critical reflection on experiences of various art objects. The aesthetic theory must be such that it be corroborated in fact or in principle by the facts of our aesthetic appreciation, and should be designed to illuminate art at its highest potential. For example, if someone feels that he appreciates a work or the work of a given artist, but has failed to perceive the subtleties of that work, it might still be said that he "appreciates" the work, but such appreciation would not be at its highest potential; it would be low-grade. Furthermore, fully conscious and respectable criticism of art is self-critical as well as critical of aesthetic objects. This self-criticism of the critics can only be had in an application of the philosophical method—"reflection," to use Merleau-Ponty's term for it. It is for this reason that fully self-conscious critics seek the "armed vision,"[3] and ought to be able to find it in a combination of their own aesthetic experiences when these are illumined by creditable theory. This is the supposition which has motivated a whole school of critics working under the rubric of the "New Critics."[4] Thus the second task is to explain the philosopher's role as critic of the critics.[5]

Unfortunately for our project, however, Merleau-Ponty did not compose a complete and consistent theory of aesthetics. The scholar interested in elucidating his aesthetic ideas must begin by using the spade: several texts are to be dug up, sifted and collated. The general theory of linguistics has been exposited in Merleau-Ponty's magnum opus,[6] and applied in criticism of Saussure's linguistics[7] and Malraux's aesthetics[8] in his "Le langage indirect, et les voix du silence"; the criticism of criticism is contained in various articles and short works the principal of which are his inaugural lecture at the Collège de France, published as the *Eloge de la philosophie,* and the series of articles on aesthetics found in his *Sens et non-sens.* The following is a résumé of the primary sources for Merleau-Ponty's aesthetics:

1. *Phénoménologie de la perception.* Paris: Gallimard, 1945.
2. *Sens et non-sens.* Paris: Nagel, 1948.

3. "Le langage indirect et les voix du silence," *Temps Modernes,* VII (1952), 2113–44, and VIII (1952), 70–94.

4. *Eloge de la philosophie.* Paris: Gallimard, 1953.

There exist two blocks to the human imagination in its attempt to conceive an aesthetic theory in terms of the general epistemological problem of meaning. The first has been termed by G. H. Mead "the philologist's viewpoint" on the manner in which vocal gestures become meaningful; the second, a phenomenon I shall refer to as the "realist" or "traditionalist" view of art, assumes that artworks are significant because they resemble a part or parts of nature.

The philologist cannot work without a dictionary for a guide to the "meanings" of words or without the rules of grammar for constructing sentences. He may, in a real gush of genius, admit to ignorance of the fixed meaning of a given word, and try to deduce it from the position or the function of the word in a sentence. Well structured sentences, like well formed formulae, contribute to the "meaning" of the individual elements which enter into their structure, for in units of expression the whole governs the part. But the grammatical whole, the sentence, is as arbitrary a selection of a unit of linguistics as the word itself would be. Nothing but usage fixes grammatical rules, and usage changes even with the same user from time to time as it does with a society of users at any given time. A completely reliable linguistics must therefore be able to handle this dynamic element as well as the static one which has been the preference of philologists. We cannot continue to assume there is one idea for one sentence, one concept for one word. The most cursory glance at any dictionary will suffice to show the range of "meanings" for any given grapheme, but such a dictionary is an empirical one, and so would most naturally contradict the assumption of an "ideal" dictionary of the common man's philology. It will be shown later that Merleau-Ponty contradicts this assumption still further.

To deny the ideal relationship of a one-to-one correspondence between word and meaning is thought by some to entail the destruction of all meaningful discourse: no dictionary, no meaning; no thought, no sentence. In a sense there is ground for such a criticism: once a word has become established in a language it will tend to retain its meaning, and if anyone should insist uncompromisingly on his right to use words as he sees fit, he may tend not to communicate with his fellows who habitually use the word as its meaning has become conventionalized. But that is the extent of a language's fixity. If an under-imaginative analyst continues to insist upon the conventionality of word usage, in the name of a more adequate linguistics we must point out that both points made above were merely tendencies: words *tend* to retain their conventional meanings, and the non-conformist *tends* to non-communication. The expression "tendency" is used here to indicate that usage only approaches the ideal dictionary; we could go so far as to say that even if the ideal were actualized, our opponents would not have won their case. For we can always ask the question, How has the dictionary come about in the first place? Or in other words, How do our words gain a meaning in everyday usage? The answer to this question cannot be an appeal to another dictionary, for then we should have to dispose of another dictionary, and so on ad infinitum. In the beginning there is no word, but there is bodily expression. The linguist's primordial task is to explain how brute corporeal expression becomes refined into intellectual, cultural "meaning." And for this job there can be no dictionary.

The second difficulty for linguistic aestheticians has been the ordinary conception of artistic communication, and here again, theorists have been seduced by the obvious. Certain works of art, those which "imitate" nature, bear an obvious resemblance to natural objects. Because of this fortuitous "reference" beyond their own surface textures it is assumed by some theorists that a painting, a drama, a novel, have meaning. In rebuttal to the realists, others point out that works of music, architecture, the dance, and non-objective painting contain no such external reference. According to their point of view, therefore, the aesthetic language makes abstraction from any semantic reference and constructs its meanings as a system of internal cross references, each element of which is constituted by its relations to all the others in the same system. This is the position of the "pure formalist." But the formalists of this narrow school accept one obvious trait of expressive works while rejecting the other. If formalism and realism really do express what is obvious in aesthetic experience, it would seem that each is valid insofar as it goes. The difficulty standing in the way of a complete theory is that neither goes far enough. What is needed is a theory of expression, artistic and otherwise, which is capable of rendering the truth of each of the incomplete theories. To restrict our theory of aesthetic expression to an accidental resemblance between some works of art and natural objects is to miss the "message" of the artist who communicates, at least in part, via his style; but to look only for his style is to over-look perhaps the most obvious part of what he has had to say.

It will seem apparent on comparison that both of these theoretical difficulties—the linguistic and the aesthetic—are merely facets of the same problem: how a system of signs comes to acquire a signifi-cance to a society of sign-users. The philologist's conventional mean-ing and the realist's resemblance relation constitute a single point of view on two supposedly different contexts, and the grammarian's preference of the sentence over the word is strictly analogous to the formalist's preference of the artist's style. The remainder of this chapter will be a consideration of Merleau-Ponty's evaluation of Saussure's linguistics and of Malraux' aesthetics, and conclude with an exposition of his own concept of "primordial expression."

Saussure's General Linguistic.—Ferdinand de Saussure was Pro-fessor of Indo-European languages at the University of Geneva, having acceded to the chair of Joseph Wertheimer in 1906. His course in general linguistics, devoted in part to a comparative study of Indo-European languages, was given in the three following years: 1906–07, 1908–09 and 1910–11. He was one of those innovators whose major creative effort went into preparation of class lectures, so left no formal treatise on the subject; but his course has been passed on to the literate public by the effort of a handful of his students[9] whose notes have been restructured into the treatise Merleau-Ponty found congenial to his own reflection. The following abridgment of Saussure's system should make clear what Merleau-Ponty found there to his liking.

Saussure's starting point was a denial of the utility of dividing the field of linguistics into its three historical parts: grammar, philology, and comparative languages; better, he thought, was the attempt to cover "language" as a unitary phenomenon capable of a positive, that is descriptive or scientific, analysis. Grammar is by nature norma-tive; philology, linked too closely with commentary on written texts; comparative languages, in its beginnings at least, too closely tied with the classification of the different tongues. But Saussure credited the traditional tri-partite division with at least the virtue of handling as its object some aspect of "the living language."

The external points of view one might adopt, he lists and likewise rejects: physics (in the spoken language, the propagation of sound waves), physiology (the sensori-motor responses innervated in speaking or hearing), psychology (the association of the sound pattern with "concepts"), sociology and anthropology (the role of language in the formation of societies), and so forth. Each of these external points of view elucidates a facet of the linguistic experience without showing the integration of the facets into a general theory. In Saussure's view, a truly general theory of linguistics must be constructed on language itself: the phenomenon of communication by a codified language (*la langue*) is to be considered only a part of the more general science of semiotic (*sémiologie*) dealing with "the life of signs amidst [the more general] social life" and truly conceived as a subdivision of social psychology.[10] Saussure, of course, had no acquaintance with the theory of signs constructed by C. S. Peirce,[11] and a fortiori not of Peirce's successor, Charles Morris;[12] but his classificatory scheme seems prophetic of the social psychology of G. H. Mead,[13] centered around the notions of "participation" and "communication." He claims that what is true for the "heretofore unnamed science" (semiotic) will likewise be valid for any study of language.

The object of semiotic is taken to be the entire system of signs which have meaning because of a series of social responses; within it anything at all may be taken as a sign. "Communication" might be the broadest term of which language is only a limited part. And it seems obvious that "language" in this general sense must contain the codified language (*la langue*). The theoretical difficulty is to approach the one without the other. However, since the spoken language and its substitute, the written language, must be used to study the more general phenomenon, it seemed to him that a strictly internal point of view must be taken on the former; by a comparative study of the codified language with the other phenomena of general semiotic, the laws governing the general science could then be fruitfully induced.

But any science of the spoken and written language must treat two dimensions: its social aspect (*la langue proprement dit*), and its individual aspect (*la parole*). The first and social aspect contains the discussion of conventional meanings expressed in a living language, whether or not that language continues to be spoken. Latin,

Greek, and Sanskrit, thought "dead" languages, continue to exist for all those capable of uniting "vocal images" with "concepts" in the sign-signified object relation. The societies of Latinists, Hellenists, and Sanskritists continue to function in this way. However, where Saussure refers to a "collective consciousness,"[14] we would more properly say the phenomenon is intersubjective since communication takes place when two ideas are synchronized by the vehicle of the given sign. To this "synchronic" phase of the spoken language must be added the "diachronic" which has for its object the study of temporal differences of communication via the same signs. These temporal differences, both prospective and retrospective, constitute the historicity of the intersubjective experience of communication by the significant symbol.

The uniquely individual phase of language, on the other hand, can hardly be distinguished in English. Since we have rendered "la langue" as the "spoken and written language," the same English locution cannot be chosen to render "la parole." Strictly speaking, "la parole" refers only to the spoken word. The distinction between *la langue* and *la parole* is a matter of sociality-individuality: the former being the property of a speaking society and essential to an act of communication; the latter, of the speaking person who may quite contingently, even passively adopt the spoken language of his community in his own peculiar fashion. Of course, what has been the "parole" of a given individual may interact with "la langue" of his society in such a way as to enrich or impoverish it, and the element of individual will and intelligence implicit in *la parole* will be primarily responsible for whatever changes are noted in the "diachronic" changes of *la langue*.

Whereas signification is entirely "psychical" in communication via "la langue" (dual association of the concept with phoneme or grapheme), the act of expressing an original meaning, a function of the individual and hence belonging to a study of "la parole" is psycho-physical. In order to avoid the contingencies of the individual's manner of adopting the codified language of a given society, Saussure adopts the point of view he considers essential to linguistic communication, that of the codified language itself (*la langue*).

The unit of language is the sign, but one must be cautioned against interpreting the individual sign as a thing, or substance. Properly conceived, it is a functional relationship. Thus, Saussure:

The characteristic role of language with respect to thought is not to create
a material phonic means for the expression of ideas, but to serve as intermediary between thought and sound under conditions which are such that
their union necessarily produces reciprocally defined units. Thought, which
is chaotic in its very nature, must perforce be analyzed in order to achieve
precision. Hence, there is neither a materialization of thought nor a spiritual-
ization of sound, but rather a somewhat mysterious fact that a "thought-
sound" involves divisions and that language constructs its units by its constitutive relationship of elements themselves amorphous masses.[15]

In other words, a sign is a functional relation containing two factors:
the word or words (*signifiant*) and a meaning (*signifié*), but neither
of these factors has a positive determinate existence. Saussure conceives of them as two indeterminate waves of a fluid mass cross-cut
by the verbal unit, or sign, which unites them.[16] The sign is therefore
a form, and not a substance;[17] language is a system of values whose
units may be exchanged for another of its own kind or for a thought.

An analysis of the internal constitution of a complete sign involves
a knowledge of the total linguistic system. Again, to quote Saussure:

All the preceding amounts to saying that *in language there are nothing but
differences;* still more, that, since a difference would seem to imply in general that there are positive terms between which the relation obtains, language
is peculiar in that it contains differences *without positive elements.* If one
consider the sign or its meaning, language does not contain either ideas or
sounds which exist prior to the entire linguistic system, but only conceptual
and phonic differences which result from the system.[18]

With this paradox Merleau-Ponty's commentary begins. He approves
of Sausseure's holistic approach to language, appealing to the obvious nature of the sign. No particular sign has a fixed meaning out
of a given context, and all signs may have their meaning changed by
being employed in different contexts. This is to say that a knowledge
of both the grammar and the dictionary of a given language is necessary to adopt a new linguistic means of expression. But even this is
only a metaphorical statement since the eighteen year old presenting
himself for admission to a university already knows the meaning of
more words than he has had the time to search out in a dictionary,
and the reason for his knowledge is his living grasp of the forms and
structures of the total linguistic tool.

Furthermore, this native grasp of his language by each child who
has become thoroughly acculturated in a given society is strictly

analogous to Achilles' "solution" to the paradox of Zeno. Because any distance is infinitely divisible, the runner does not dispose of enough time to overtake a tortoise which has got off to a head start. When it is observed that Achilles' physical movement overcomes the incalculable differences stemming from the mathematical analysis of the problem, it is likewise observed that a native speaks his tongue without the ideal solutions of dictionary and grammatical rules. The use of the language suffices to fix the meanings occurring within it because language is composed of differential relationships,. or more exactly, because the terms of language are created by the differences which exist between them in the total linguistic complex.[19] If this is true, it can no longer be supposed that meaning is both "immanent" and "transcendent" to each word. Such has been the assumption of the philological point of view which considers each word as having its meaning fixed in a dictionary of the language, the immanence, at the same time it intends a thought which transcends its own structure, the transcendence. Philology must be surpassed or reconstructed.

Merleau-Ponty's attempts to surpass the philological point of view may be reduced to four points of analysis. First, we must give up the assumption that words are put together to express a given thought. As a matter of linguistic fact, a thought is never given without the words; no thought pre-exists its expression. When one thinks, and one is a human being, one uses words or other signs. But this denial is tantamount to a negation of the ideal of a complete expression. In fact Merleau-Ponty insists that a complete expression, an absolute truth, is unthinkable. Each thinker is reduced by his condition to struggling with his language *to discover what he thinks*. A mere repetition of the words which have allowed the discovery is no thought, and has no claim to the value of a thought.[20]

That this theory of linguistics has tremendous importance for a practical pedogogical situation is, or ought to be, apparent: the student who is allowed to recall or memorize the formulae of his particular interest without looking for his own discoveries is certainly not being taught how to think, nor allowed to contribute to the development of culture. Each individual who has any pretension to continuing culture must re-learn the lessons of the past, and re-learn them in such a way that a new development takes place for his command of the past knowledge. And this is at least the tacit hope of all educators, even of those who do nothing but stimulate the regurgitation of the past.

Secondly, the meaning of each word is lodged, not in itself as explained in the dictionary correspondance table, but in the entire language. Hence the dictionary is not an authority, but at best a guide to what has been thought. Words are limited only by other words, and the language as a whole becomes a tool with which to work.[21]

Thirdly, the meaning of each word is the "total movement of the language as it is spoken (*de la parole*)," and for this reason our thought is necessarily linked with the symbols of the spoken language. Language is thus an opaque entity, like a universe unto itself capable of containing the things of nature—on the condition that these things be reduced to their meanings, and that not all meanings be associated with individual verbal counters. Consider the case of obliquity: some meanings are merely allusions, implied indirectly more than stated explicity; Merleau-Ponty refers to this phenomenon as "the speech of silence": the indirect allusion contained in every formally polite discourse is a case in point. In comparing two languages, such as French and English, another example is readily available: the French woman says "l'homme que j'aime," and English speaking women render the same thought as "the man I love"; although the English speaker could supply the relative pronoun there is no need to do so since the apposition of the two expressions, "the man" and "I love," is sufficient to render the idea. Hence some expressions take place by the use of verbal counters, others by omission.[22]

Lastly, the expressive possibilities of a given language are exhausted by both kinds of expression: the direct statement of an idea which results from the discursive alignment of words in isomorphic relation to the elements of the thought expressed, together with whatever is expressed obliquely through the stylized phrasing of the discursive unity in that direct statement:

There exists for already acquired expressions a direct meaning, which corresponds point for point with the turn of a phrase, of forms and of words already instituted. Apparently, therefore, there are here no lacunae, no loquacious silences. But the meaning of expressions in the process of being achieved cannot be of this nature; it is a meaning which may be called "lateral" or "oblique," which is fused between the words—and that's another manner of shaking the linguistic apparatus in order to draw out of it a new sound.[23]

In order to understand the eloquence of silence Merleau-Ponty proposes a comparison with other "silent" languages, since "This meaning being born with the grasping of signs, this immanence of the whole in the parts, is found in the entire history of culture."[24]

If one were to elucidate this phenomenon, one could describe the effect of political and economic institutions on the behavior of the individual, as Merleau-Ponty has often tried to do.[25] This process of elucidation is, moreover, the job of philosophy; and Merleau-Ponty's performance of it was rewarded by the chair at the Collège de France. But since our interest is primarily aesthetic, the present discussion is limited to a consideration of the arts as "primordial expressions."

Malraux's Aesthetics.—Malraux, the aesthetician, is a rather latecomer on the French scene. Having established himself as a novelist of some importance in the thirties (*La Condition humaine,* 1933; *L'Espoir,* 1938), he continued his intermittent studies in art, which began in his youth and continued during his travels, in order to elaborate his central intuition (*le musée imaginaire*) into a two volume treatise entitled *La Psychologie de l'art.* In a later single volume edition of this work,[26] he notes the time of preparation as between 1935 and 1951. During those years France was invaded by Nazi Germany, lost a battle, and finally helped win the war. And in the war Malraux's career was as fabulous as those attributed to the heroes of his novels. Enlisted, he was captured and imprisoned. Having escaped, he joined the Resistance and was captured again only to be released forcefully by his own men. In the final stages of the war he commanded a brigade which was instrumental in the ultimate liberation of the Vosges. With the accession of DeGaulle at the fall of the Fourth Republic, Malraux became "cultural minister" of the Fifth Republic. He has rationalized the apparent switch from the earlier leftist novels to his present political position in a postface to *Les Conquérants,* the first of his novels dedicated to the Chinese Revolution of the twenties.[27]

The very title of Malraux's aesthetic theory, *Les Voix du silence,* explains Merleau-Ponty's interest in the work. If it is true that certain artifacts of culture are capable of "speaking," yet communicate what-

ever is said in the profoundest silence, this fact must be represented
in a general theory of linguistic. To repeat: the substantiation of the
alleged fact that artists communicate by using non-verbal symbols
is a logical requirement for the completeness of Merleau-Ponty's
aesthetics as a general theory of linguistics. To say that Merleau-
Ponty is "doing" aesthetics for the purpose of completing his general linguistics would be the same as to say that he is "doing" linguistics in such a way as to include an interpretation of the communication of novel meanings. In pursuing his task, he uses once
again the method of "critical reflection."

The central notion of Malraux's aesthetics is to institute an imaginary museum, or as it has been rendered, a "museum without
walls" in which would be represented characteristic works of all
periods and styles, reproducible by means of photography and photo-
electric engraving to any scale desirable. But to understand this concept is to refer to the function of real museums and the function they
play in aesthetic communication. When a work is acquired by a
museum, it loses all contact with any practical function it may have
been created to fulfill—such as tombs for burial, tapestry to combat
the ghastly draughts of age old castles, icons for religious meditation
—once isolated, the artifact takes on the acquired status of "art
work," a thing to be perceived and enjoyed as the genius of its creator. The one property each museum piece has in common with others
is considered its style. But "style" is an ambiguous word, even for the
science of aesthetics. It may refer to a general manner of making
certain kinds of artworks, such as a Renaissance style, a Byzantine
style, a Romanesque style, a Gothic style, or it may refer to the individual manner a particular artist has adopted or created for himself
to perform his works of art. In the latter sense we may refer to a
painting done in Gauguin's or Cézanne's style. What is contained
in both acceptations of the term, however, is a reference to the
manner in which a given artistic effect is achieved.

By using the method of photographic enlargement Malraux has
been able to point out that similarities in styles have existed between
works originating in times and places which themselves are separated by centuries and continents. He deduces a "spirit of painting"
which exists as a kind of collective consciousness guiding the individual choices of each individual artist; behind each painter, a
Master Painter whose effect is seen in each successful masterpiece,

man "expressing humanity." Malraux's anecdote concerning Stendhal illustrates this point. The critic, Sainte-Beuve, had met Stendhal, whose real name was Henri Bayle, and refused to believe that this personality could possibly have written literary masterpieces. Obviously, says Malraux, because the author and the social animal are not the same person: "M. Beyle is Stendhal, plus the foibles and minus the books."[28]

Even so, it is false to assume that an artist is born and not made. In a very important sense of the word the artist makes himself by copying and transcending those masters he has copied. Since an artist is an inventor of forms and an artisan is one who copies forms, it is very difficult for Malraux to make precise the moment when a given painter is an artist and no longer an artisan. His answer to the query is "When the painter or writer achieves style." Thus, style is the mark of the genius: ". . . the traditional plagiarist does not try to rival the genius; he tries to imitate his manner, or, if he is concerned with the periods of anonymity, the style of the epoch. This latter acts so forcefully on us that everything it marks becomes art."[29] In Malraux's scheme, style is the significance of the work: "Every style creates its own universe in 'conjugating' the elements of the world in order to allow the world to be oriented toward an essential part of man."[30] The imitation and the discovery of styles is then a historical process; as far back in the history of culture one may choose to go, it seems there is an antecedent to any given style. And there are parallel discoveries, and "metamorphoses" as well as "regressions."

The originality of Malraux's treatise is the ingenuity with which he has shown the historical development in artistic styles. A "metamorphosis" occurs when an established style is transformed into another living style; a regression is a change for the worse, into decadence. It is clear that in this historical process the individual painter may work in such a way as to change the "style" of his epoch.

Finally, in our own epoch, art has become "modern." In general, the mark of modern art is that abstraction is made of representative content. Since the entire attention of a viewer is brought to the sensuous surface of the painting, the painter is judged decadent in the moral sense. What happens in modern painting, according to Malraux, is that artists have returned to the subjective; instead of picturing some element of the objective world, each painter spreads out an intimate part of himself on the canvas for everyone to see. Moreover, since it is a fact that modern art has tended to become "non-objective" and the art of writing necessarily deals in words having a meaning, it would seem to follow that any comparison between the two arts is possible only by abstracting from the representative content of each. Styles can be compared, but pictures of something cannot profitably be compared with descriptions of the same thing. No matter what the materials of his creation, every artist is necessarily a creator of a universe, be it bound by a frame, a niche, or the covers of a book. A genius is a man who has created works of genius, and these are known by their style.

This brief account of Malraux's work is not offered to do justice to sixteen years' meditative effort. I have attempted to set up only the essential parts of the theory in order to give Merleau-Ponty's criticisms an understandable frame of reference.

The first point is to make clear the standard of comparison between "the indirect language" and the "voices of silence." In order to do this we need only collate the two lines of Merleau-Ponty's thought deriving from both Saussure and Malraux. The difference Saussure establishes between "la langue" and "la parole" is clearly evident in the two senses of "style" used by Malraux. The general codified language is that spoken at a given time by a community of persons; in aesthetics we speak of the style of an epoch or of a school. La parole, the individual spoken word, constitutes a variation on the community's language, and throughout a period of time the spoken word of a given individual may work to change the language of his community, to enrich or to impoverish it. In aesthetics, we may speak of the style of the individual, which, in Malraux's terms, may work toward a "metamorphosis" or a "regression." In both systems the units of expression are described as forms, units whose total significance transcends that of the sum of its parts. It is on this basis that the foundation of our comparison is laid.

But it would be misleading to stop at this point, for Merleau-Ponty has projected a set of rather serious disagreements with the method and results of Malraux's aesthetics. Consider the results. Malraux's position may be called "formalistic." If, in taking special note of the developments of modern painting one declares that art is necessarily abstract, it would seem at first blush that the praise one gives to the abstractionist artist works at the same time to dispraise works of more traditional art. Thus when Malraux denies the classical dictum of La Bruyère, that style is the discovery of *le mot juste calqué sur les choses,* his formalism becomes that of complete abstraction from the visible world; for all Malraux's insistence that the painter must plunge himself into time, the artist, in making the abstraction, detaches himself from his environment. In this detachment he can, of course, find only himself. This is the celebrated "return to the individual." But at what price?

The individualism of modern painting has paid a double price, if one accepts Malraux's explanation of the creative experience. First of all, completely detached from his situation, the painter loses all possibility of communication; secondly, it becomes impossible to pronounce an aesthetic judgment on either the traditional or the modern art. A word of explanation concerning both of these criticisms.

What is the problem of modern art? A celebration of the individual creative impulse? Or communication without the basis of a single objective view of the universe? For Malraux it is the first; for Merleau-Ponty, the second. "Communication of the subjective impulses of the individual" smacks too much of the outmoded concepts of "genius" and "taste"; it has produced in aesthetics a transfer of interest from the aesthetic object to the maker and appreciator. In the end, both of these concepts are mystical, or at least mysterious, being extrapolations from aesthetic experience itself. A genius is one who can create works of genius. How do I know? Because he has done it. Likewise for the "man of taste." But the proof is in the eating of this pudding: an artist's genius is the work he has done; and appreciator's taste, the works he enjoys. There need be no "subjective" reference for the two words. In deifying the genius, Malraux is said to have forgotten what he knows of writers in writing of painters: that they need constant contact with life, must live and breathe in situation. He himself had coined the phrase so dear to existentialists: the human condition. English readers know his novel as *Man's Fate.* When a work is placed in a museum, imaginary or otherwise, it loses its total significance; unfortunately, Malraux was right, once a work is placed there, only the style of the work remains. A book gathering dust on a liberary shelf likewise loses its power to communicate, however powerful may be its style.

The business of the artist, even the modern one, is not to display his immediate selfhood. Style he must have; but his style is only a means to the end of communication, via the indirect route, and not an end in itself. The problem of modern art then becomes the explanation of communication, through style, of a unique universe which may or may not be based upon "the objective or scientific view." In Merleau-Ponty's words,

Modern painting is concerned with quite a different problem from that of the return to the individual: the problem of knowing how one can communicate without the help of a pre-established Nature on which all of our senses are opened, how each of us is enmeshed in the universal by that which is most peculiar to ourselves.[31]

Where Malraux has been misled by his glorification of the individual in the face of a malign destiny—the theme common to his novels —into the falsely subjective concepts of genius and taste, as well as into breaking the continuum of means and ends by finalizing style, Merleau-Ponty will attempt to solve the problem he envisages in terms of a primitive perception of an environing situation. But of this, more later.

We may proceed here to a discussion of the second glaring weakness, as Merleau-Ponty sees it, in Malraux' aesthetic system. I have referred to it as the impossibility of judging traditional art on the basis of "modern" and vice versa. If we define traditional art as an appeal to the senses made by the picture of the objective world, art then becomes an imitation, but it does not for this reason become less an art. Even as Malraux has stated, painters themselves have not been outraged by the modernism of contemporary art. And the reason for this is that the very efforts of traditional artists to capture, for example, the velvety sparkle of a drape had already transferred interest from the drape to the sensuous characteristics which in modern art have become the entire painting:

Such is the reason that the works of classical painters have a different meaning, and more meaning perhaps than they believed themselves; that they often anticipate a style of painting freed from their canons, and remain the accepted means of every initiation to painting. At the very moment they believed to have demanded of the world, their eyes fixed squarely thereupon, the secret of sufficiently representing it, the artists produced without being aware of it that *metamorphosis* of which painting later became fully conscious.[32]

But note that if this is true, one can no longer define the traditional in art as a representation of objective nature and modernism as a return to the subjective side of the painter's personality.

This judgment may become clearer if we consider the principle of representation used in classical painting, that of linear perspective. Perspective is one artistic technique, developed primarily in the Renaissance, for representing a universe, or more properly stated, in creating the painter's universe. But as such it is not more "natural" than the technique of "flat" painting in non-perspective. After all, perspective in perception depends upon the balance of focal with marginal elements of the perceptive field. In order to see a new universe all anyone need do is to focus attention upon the empty spaces between objects rather than upon the objects themselves. The perspective of the traditionalist painters merely illustrates one rather than the other ways of ordering a perceptive field. According to Merleau-Ponty,

Perspective is much more than a secret technique for imitating a reality which would be given such as it appears to all men: it is the invention of a world dominated and possessed throughout by an instantaneous synthesis which the spontaneous "look" gives us, at least in a sketched form, when it tries vainly to hold together all the things [of the environment], each of which demands its entire attention.[33]

Thus, if traditional painting is creative through the use of one technique and modern art is defined by creativity as opposed to the imitation of the traditional, it seems that modern art cannot be understood as creative or as art in the same sense as the traditional. And it is true that what we have in modern art has always been present in traditional art: a canvas whose aesthetic surface constitutes a symbol by which communication takes place.

In Merleau-Ponty's view, modern painting is no different from modern thought (phenomenology): ". . . we are obliged to admit a truth which does not resemble things, which has no exterior model, no predestined instruments of expression, but which is nonetheless truth."[34] The history of art, like the history of thought, is composed of a series of partial expressions each demanding further interpretation in a changing context. Art and philosophy both demand continual reflective criticism. And this is precisely why art in a museum loses its significance; it needs constantly to be brought into contact with the living issues of contemporary cultural life. The "synchronic" stage of art, in becoming fixed, loses its life unless it continues to interact with the "diachronic":

One can no more take an inventory of a painting—say what is there and what is not there—than one can, according to the linguists, take stock of the elements in a vocabulary; and for the same reason: in the one case, as in the other, there is no question of a finite number of signs, but rather of an open field or a new organ of human culture.[35]

The discovery, and its elaboration, of the open perceptive field is the basis of Merleau-Ponty's claim to having corrected Malraux's aesthetics.

This correction has been effectuated by interpreting what is of value in Malraux in the light of three phenomenological concepts: perception, history, and expression. Perception, the act of the human being in organizing its environment into a single universe, in making the indistinct clear, in discerning things in a haze, is already the act of creation. The theme is stated here and explained at length in a succeeding section of this chapter:

Every perception, every action which presupposes it, in short every use of the human body, is already a *primordial expression*—not that derivative work which substitutes for the thing expressed a group of signs given as from elsewhere with their meanings and the directions for their use, but the first operation which initially constitutes the signs as signs; [i.e.] makes the thing expressed inhabit them by the sole means of the eloquence of their arrangement and their configuration; implants a meaning into what before had none; and which, therefore, far from being exhausted in the moment it takes place, inaugurates an order, and founds an institution or tradition. . . .[36]

Hence, according to Merleau-Ponty, every perception is a creative expression, and every expression must be worked out or interpreted in time.

History then judges the value of each expression. Malraux had foregone the "vertical transcendence" of God only to replace it with the "horizontal transcendence" of history, or a supposed Spirit of Culture. The truth of the matter, as Merleau-Ponty sees it, is that certain works have resembled others of different times because two artists have used the same instrument, the human body, in order to achieve their expressions. If this is the case, there is no reason to suppose any kind of transcendence to explain the direction and course of human events. History will judge the value of my expression because in my work my fellows are invited to join in my organization of the environment. No matter how abstract or modern my work, its creation is a social act: "Words, even in the art of prose, carry the one who speaks as well as him who hears over into a common universe by drawing them toward a new signification, by means of a power of designation which goes beyond any accepted definition. . . ."[37] In the creativity of art, men are brought together by the common presence of a new value, and a society is formed. It may be small at the start, as in the case of modernism whose first innovators were understood only by other painters; but when the critics caught on and were capable of explaining the new art to the masses of people, the institution of painting began to grow and continues to grow: "That spontaneity of language which unites us is not a command of authority; the history it establishes is not an external idol; it is ourselves with all our roots, our growth and, as it has been said, the fruit of our labor."[38] The history of art and of aesthetics is thus still in the making.

A final criticism of Malraux's aesthetics from Merleau-Ponty's point of view is an evaluation of its comparative method. Comparison, whether envisaged as an explanation of the regularities in cultural history, or a method of judging the aesthetic value of contemporary works on the basis of "the models" of tradition, is a limited tool. Noticing the similarities between styles found in prehistoric art and our own, Malraux infers therefrom a "spirit of art" hovering, so to speak, over the head of every artist. The effect observed is a certain demonstrable continuity of culture, and the cause inferred is a single "guiding spirit," as Malraux calls it, an anti-destiny constituted by the efforts of mankind to oppose what tends to crush it. And Malraux might well be understood if this inference were interpreted as a collective consciousness participated in by each artist in his search for the most expressive style.

Merleau-Ponty opposes to this apparently Jungian hypothesis his notion of bodily expression:

The whole marvel of a style already present in the invisible elements of a work amounts to nothing more than this, that the artist, working in the human world of perceived things, is found to have put his mark, without being aware of it, on the non-human world revealed by optical apparatus, just as the swimmer glides over a whole watery universe which frightens him when he sees it through an underwater telescope. . . .[39]

To use a phrase of Malraux against his own position, the similarity uniting diverse cultures is perhaps better explained by the human condition, the conditions of ambiguity which define man as a body-mind whose first expressions take the form of shaping an environment in which to live. Artistic creation is a spontaneous movement of the human body as it dominates its universe:

. . . like the functioning of the body, that of words and paintings remain mysterious to me: words, lines, colors which express my thoughts come from me like my gestures; they are forced upon me by what I want to say as my gestures are by what I want to do.[40]

And, in the long run, "The movement of the artist in tracing his arabesques in infinite matter serves to amplify, but also to continue, the simpler marvel of directed locomotion of [simple] grasping gestures."[41]

Thus it is clear that for Merleau-Ponty the mystery of painting, or of artistic creation in general, is not a matter of incomprehensible genius which can be grasped only by an equally incomprehensible taste: there is no spirit—of art, or otherwise—hanging over the human scene to direct it toward a predestined goal; at the base of creation is a much more fundamental mystery: how matter becomes organized into a living body, and a living body into a man. But this dialetic of the genesis of orders has already been explained in a previous chapter.[42]

The criticism of the comparative method of making value judgments in aesthetics is patent to everyone but those who make comparative judgments. Should I attempt to explain that a given work is "excellent" or "expressive" on the ground that it resembles my "classical" models, it seems incumbent upon me to explain why those models are, after all, models of excellence or expressiveness. True, the accuracy of objective imitation cannot be considered the standard for both contemporary and traditional art; they differ in this important respect. Thus, to judge a contemporary non-objective piece on the standards set up by traditional objective art is to work an injustice on both contemporary and traditional art: on the contemporary because it would be judged in comparison to something it is not, and on the traditional because it would be assumed to be excellent without a justification of the judgment. As Malraux himself had shown, it is the property of artistic styles to develop in time; choose any one and something comparable to it may be found in its temporal precedence. But if this is so, where is the model? Clearly, there is none.

For Merleau-Ponty the possibilities of the expressiveness of artworks are limitless, or at least bounded only by two factors: the advent (avènement) on the scene of a human being, and his entrance into the complex of social relationships we call "culture" or "society." The expressive gestures of one human being institute a new manner of existing:

> The central fact to which the dialectic of Hegel comes back time and again is that there is no choice between the *for-itself* and the *for-others,* between thinking for our own benefit and thinking with the category of the other; in the moment of expression, the other to whom I address myself and myself in the act of speaking are linked without reserve.[43]

Thus, in considering the basis of comparison between diverse arts, for example painting and writing, as Malraux has done, one need not seek an explanation by a mere analogy of the kind of abstraction possible in the one and the other; the explanation must be sought in a more primitive attitude of the expressive organism: the connections between the act of perceiving with that of expressing must be sought in the structures of human behavior. In a word, Saussure and Malraux are to be united in Merleau-Ponty's phenomenology of perception:

> . . . it is not a question here of a simple *analogy* between these two problems [painting and language]: we are interested in the expressive functioning of the human body which was already begun in the least act of perception, and which has since been amplified into painting and art. The field of pictorial meanings has been opened up since the time of man's first appearance in the world. And the first designs drawn on the walls of caves were able to establish a tradition only because they reaped the benefits of another: that of perception.[44]

Being a man has "motivated" a tradition of perceiving a universe and of constructing artifacts in a manly way, which is the same as to say, creating a culture in which behavioral patterns and reactions are ingrained in the human personality to such a degree that each person need no longer think about their "significance" in order to understand their import. The logic of cultural meanings is "lived," and not thought at all. Such is the basis of Merleau-Ponty's irrationalist aesthetic, and to conceive it more completely we need only turn to his own description of the mechanism of expression as a function of the corporeal schema.

Merleau-Ponty's Doctrine of Primordial Expression.—The tone of the article I have been expositing heretofore,[45] taken from a work which never did appear in the form then advertised, is light; its style breezier than the philosophical writing in Merleau-Ponty's *Phénom-*

énologie de la perception. Since the latter work was composed before the article had appeared, the comparative lightness of tone and swiftness of style may be due to the fact that the author had already mastered his thought in the philosophical tome, and was intent upon communicating it to an audience of quite another make-up. While the article exhibits a criticism of the linguistics of Saussure and the aesthetics of Malraux in the light of the results he had obtained in the *Phénoménologie,* the results themselves can be understood only by retracing the steps of the "critical reflection," the philosophical method as Merleau-Ponty applies it, on prior attempts to formulate the problem in which he is interested. That problem is to be understood here as the comprehension of verbal expression and its relation to the total human corporeal economy.

As a preliminary discussion, it would be well to consider the more "classical" treatments of the vocal gesture. In Hegelian fashion, Merleau-Ponty sets up an antithesis between empiricism and rationalism and effectuates in the end a synthesis by returning to an "existential analysis" of the situation.

Empiricists, whose emphasis has been placed upon the physiological substructures of linguistic expression, have understood the central phenomenon as verbal imagery. Physiologically, a verbal image can only be considered a trace left upon the psyche by a phoneme, the word as it is pronounced and heard. But in so viewing the subject of communication, the empiricist lets the speaking subject escape his attention: physiological traces are clearly bodily, and at best subconscious. Because communication does take place it is inferred that certain images are associated with certain nervous innervations; if this inference is correct, a man speaks "the way a lamp becomes incandescent," undergoing a flux of words without inserting an intention of his own. Since the meaning is given to the speaking individual with his words, the utterance of the word is not an act; the speaker evinces no directionality, no intentionality, at the heart of the experience.

The supreme difficulty with the physiological explanation, when it is taken as complete, is that a very common psychological phenomenon tends to contradict it. In a true case of aphasia, where the subject has lost the power to articulate words whether or not he has the express intention of articulating them, the pathology seems more "mental" than physiological. The word can be imagined and the innervation of the appropriate centers can be effectuated without the ability on the subject's part to pronounce the word in question. The trouble then is relegated to the darker regions of the psyche where associations are made. Since the principle of association has already undergone a pertinent criticism with the empiricist's theory of knowledge as laid down above, we may proceed to the rationalist's opposing viewpoint.

Gelb and Goldstein, in their work on the amnesia of color designations, have given a typical illustration of the rationalist position. Distinguishing between two kinds of aphasia—the inability to articulate words, as in the example above, and a true intellectual disability to understand the designation reference of names—the two German psychologists devised an experiment to test for the causes of amnesia of color names. The subjects afflicted with the condition were asked to classify a group of ribbons according to their color. After amassing a number of blue ribbons and coming to a particular pale shade of the color, some of the subjects blithely added a pink or a green about the same intensity as that of the last blue. It was as if the directions suddenly switched from color likeness to saturation likeness. Although it is difficult to ascertain the degree to which the design of the experiment controlled the results gained, the investigators concluded that the cause for the amnesia was the inability of the subjects to *comprehend* categorial classifications; told to put those ribbons together which went together, the subjects failed to subsume the particular samples under a single general idea, the name of a color.

Whereas critics of this series of experiments may easily point out that the subjects were already afflicted with amnesia of color designations and were hence incapable of understanding the concept of "blue," it was necessary to use the vaguer concept of "things going together." And since there are many ways in which a set of perceptual data available in the presence of a set of vari-colored ribbons may "go together," the error in the experiments could very well be charged to the vagueness of the instructions. In answer, the investigators need only point out the necessity of this vagueness, due to the condition of the subjects, and to the fact that once the "error" had been committed each subject ought to have been able to perceive that a double criterion of classification had been used merely by perceiving the difference of colors, even if the subjects under study could not name the colors seen. Thus it was concluded that to perceive an object is to be able to name it in some fashion or other.

But, says Merleau-Ponty, to name an object is to take away what is most individual and unique to it in any of its possible experiences, and to "see" it as the representation of an essence or category. In contradistinction to the physiological "explanation," according to which true aphasia is due either to the loss of verbal imagery or to faulty "connections" in the association process by which the image is linked with a given phoneme, the rationalistic solution is to claim, on the part of the subjects, a loss of the capacity to subsume a particular impression under a general category. In criticism of the rationalistic "explanation" Merleau-Ponty points out that it is really not so different from the empiricistic. "Association" and "subsumption" are evidently different names for the same psycho-physical process. And for both quasi-explanations it is apparent that a word has no meaning: according to the empiricists, the pronunciation of a word is not mediated by any concept; it is merely called up by a physiological process of innervation following strictly mechanical laws. The word then undergoes a continual devaluation from psychical, to physiological, to physical status, and as such loses its efficacy to name an object created in perception. But even for the rationalists it has no more efficacy: the interior recognition of the word as a sign of a certain class of impressions is thinkable without the real existence of the universal itself; after all, no one *perceives* a universal color.

Although Merleau-Ponty fails to indicate the fact, it is clear that we are at the heart of the old nominalist-realist controversy, which he must face and solve if his theory of perception is to succeed where Sartre's has been seen to fail.[46] At this point of the discussion he contents himself with pointing out that both empiricism and rationalism have failed to do the job. The empiricists have failed in their physiological explanation by not going far enough in showing how the meaning relation of a general name is successfully associated with the name; the rationalists have gone too far, one might say, into the subject's psyche in search of the explanation. The former have not been able to do justice to the subject who truly "speaks," while the latter have found a speaking subject but have sublimated him into nothing but a thinking subject.[47] To surpass these partial explanations of a complex phenomenon, it is necessary to start by asserting what seems obvious: that words have meaning for the persons who use them.

However, before continuing the exegesis of the existentialistic point of view, we must consider a further clarification. In speaking of the "word," Merleau-Ponty sometimes uses the more general "mot" rather than "parole," which is more proper to his thesis. It has already become customary in French philosophy to distinguish kinds of *paroles: la parole parlante* and *la parole parlée,* depending upon whether the spoken word is one which has already been instituted as a fixed vocable for an established meaning (*parole parlée*), or whether the word uttered is a creative act in which a new meaning becomes established in the language (*parole parlante*). Moreover, since the signs already instituted into spoken words are registered in the dictionaries of a given language, and there are no dictionaries for the neologisms to be included sometime in the future, any investigation into the field of *la parole parlante* might be reduced in essence to the apparently impossible quandary: how does one learn to speak a language having no fixed meanings? Merleau-Ponty's attempt at answering the quandary is contained in a series of reflections on the relation between "thought" and "expression," where his existential analysis of language begins.

The first of these reflections is that effective speech does not presuppose any thought. If our thought preceded all of our utterances, all speech would be a discursive alignment of already correlated sign-meanings. But this result is excluded by hypothesis; we are considering an "original utterance." The fact of the matter is that our thoughts tend toward physical expression for their completion. The thought and the words are co-terminous. On what grounds is this assertion made? Primarily on the basis of three observations from experience: that the most familiar objects of our awareness seem indeterminate if not named; that most subjects seem to be ignorant of their own thoughts if these are not given physical expression; and finally, that any "thought" which goes unexpressed is lost in unconsciousness. In sum, any thought we may rightfully claim as ours becomes such when we have given expression to it.

So far, Merleau-Ponty could be interpreted as writing an exegesis of Croce; but Croce uses the word "expression" to include only the "spiritual activity" of organizing impressions into intuitions. If our author is to surpass the idealistic metaphysics of the Italian, expression has to be interpreted in such a way as to involve the whole psycho-physical organism of the speaking subject. It may be useful for this analysis to consult the model Merleau-Ponty erects for a case of communication via the spoken word.

Considered from the angle of the speaker giving utterance to, "That is a brush.", the object coming into focus within the perceptual field is completed (*accomplit*) in the process of being named. Let there be no mistake here: it is not being claimed that the word "brush" has no preassigned designation; when it is said that this is a brush, what is being claimed is that a series of perceptual data comes to closure in the pronouncement. This is similar to the assumption of magical rites according to which operations in the physical realm of nature are thought to be produced by the pronouncement of the magical words. The primitive consciousness given to magic rites merely extends the naming process beyond its legitimate confines. As our color perceptions end in the naming of the hue and a child's ability to discriminate objects is immeasurably increased by a growing vocabulary, the physical act of expressng the thought does not *translate* a pre-existent ideal entity; the expression merely completes the thought process.

If we switch angles and view the process from the vantage point of the hearer, it is readily seen that the assumption of a thought pre-existing the expression is a patent absurdity. If the hearer already possesses the thought, if he has undergone the activity of subsuming the particular set of impressions under a general concept, there was in effect no communication between himself and the speaker. When there is communication, it is more proper to assume that a thought has been induced by the spoken words of the utterance. The job for the existentialist analyst here is to lay down the conditions according to which the communication has taken place. The task is especially difficult in all cases of novel communication. In general, it must be shown in what manner the speaker can be said to discover his thought—since he never just *has* a novel idea—in its utterance, and how this discovery may be said to become the property of a distinct personality, the interlocutor, in communication.

Non-existentialistic interpretations of communication have already made appeal to a kind of pre-rational social process wherein the gestures of one individual are interpreted as carrying a single "meaning." G. H. Mead, whose course in social psychology has been called

by one of his editors a "social behaviorism,"[48] has based his model
of communication upon the ability of the human organism to adopt
the attitude of the other, a second person whose reactions to the gestures of the first constitute the meaning of those gestures. When the
two individuals react to the same gestures in the same way, communication is said to have taken place. Although Merleau-Ponty would
most probably object to the behavioristic foundations of Mead's
thought, and to the extrinsic connection used to explain "meaning,"
he insists that the problem of understanding the thought of another
is solved in action by entering into the situation. Since the meaning
of a gesture, such as the movement of beckoning with the finger, is
immanent to the gesture which appears to an observer only within a
total situation, one will understand the gesture by a personal reaction to the situation as it is lived through.

Two examples are adduced to support this contention: the learning of a foreign language, and the understanding of the novel
thought of a philosopher. The two experiences have an important
factor in common. It is not enough to be able to associate an English
with a French word in order to understand French; to understand the
French language is to react to the words in the same way as the native
speakers. And this, in the long run, amounts to adopting the style of
living as defined in the culture of that language. The errors made by
beginning students in looking up meanings in a bilingual dictionary
are too common a phenomenon to linger upon here. The same point
is made by cross cultural influences. Many inventions of one culture
and affecting the institutions of the people speaking one language
have their names carried over without translation or transliteration;
the reason: there is no way of referring to the novelty on the basis
of the language of the borrowing culture. Likewise, where one institution exists in an area of a given spoken language but not in another
it is always false to use the same word in the two languages since the
connotations falsify the meanings for one or the other cultures: two
such words whose connotations are falsified between English and
French are *maitresse* (mistress) and *sympathisant* (sympathizer). In
"Les communistes et la paix" Sartre had declared himself *sympathisant,* and Merleau-Ponty wrote an article labeling him an "ultra-
bolshevik"; but to translate the word into "Communist sympathizer"
with all the connotations of "fellow traveler" and "dupe of a party
line" which this expression carries to the American is to falsify what

was intended in the expression used by Sartre. The difference, of
course, is in the attitude of the hearer to what has been said, and
these attitudes are indicated by the style of living to which Merleau-
Ponty refers.

In the second example, that of a new philosophy, the thought expressed is understood in much the same way. To read Spinoza correctly one must become a Spinozist, viewing the universe in the way
it was viewed by the master himself, and grasping his very style of
thought. Likewise, for Kant one must become critical, and for Husserl, phenomenological, in order to grasp the new way of thinking.
For a scholar, this means that a full exposition of an idea must precede its critical evaluation; there is no other proof that the scholar
has grasped the style of his author. Says Merleau-Ponty, ". . . I begin
to understand a philosophy by slipping into the manner of existing
indicated by that thought, by reproducing the tone and the accent of
the philosopher."[49]

The difficulty one may experience in the understanding of a new
thought, paradoxically enough, is presented by the conventional
meanings of the terms the philosopher must use to express himself.
For this reason certain philosophers have had recourse to a language
almost entirely their own; the most glaring example of this phenomenon in recent English philosophy is *Process and Reality* of
Whitehead. The thought is a system and can be understood only as
a system; each of the words in the system are definable only by the
consequences deduced from them in the total symbolic structure. But
it may be objected that the case is too easily made for the systematic
thought of a philosopher trained so highly in the rational techniques
of mathematics. And this may very well be justifiable. If so, consider
the case of the literary artist who likewise attempts to convey a novel
point of view on the totality of experience by using conventional
symbols or words. As formalist critics have always maintained, the
"meaning" of a poem or novel is not exhausted in an exact paraphrase of the sentences composing it. The meaning of the poem or
novel as an artistic expression is precisely what the ordering of the
conventional symbols adds over and above the assigned meanings of
the elements. R. P. Blackmur has called this surfeit of meaning "gesture,"[50] and Merleau-Ponty agrees to the propriety of this term. The
meaning of a poem is the gesture it contains: a primitive gesture, and
not a metaphorical or extended sense of this term.

For examples of literary criticism illustrating this concept, we may simply refer to Blackmur's brilliant essay, "Language as Gesture"; the purpose here is to consider the place of gesture in Merleau-Ponty's general linguistic. He claims that a reader of poetry does not understand the poem merely by thinking discursively the meanings of the words composing the poem's "sensuous surface." Nor does he merely represent to himself the synchronization of the words. Like the reader of a new philosophy, he must enter into the situation of the author and grasp the style of living implicit in the poem itself. When he does so, he finds that the successful author has managed to change the meanings of the conventional words he has used:

. . . the meaning of a literary work, properly speaking, is made up less of the common significations of the words than it contributes to modifying them. There is, then, in the person listening or reading as in the one speaking or writing, a *thought in the spoken word* which has not even been suspected by rationalists.[51]

And the thought can be said to be in the word in the same sense that the meaning of a gesture is immanent to the situation in which it has occurred. It need only be added that to understand a situation one must live through it, either actually or vicariously, as in the imagination.

The point here is not that conventional meanings are irrelevant to the structure of the poem; they enter into that structure and have their meanings modified by their immanence to that structure. The forms of which Merleau-Ponty speaks are "concrete" and not abstract containers to be filled by predescribed laws of replacement of variables. It thus becomes fair to ask to what extent the conventional meanings contribute to the meaning of the poem. How do discursive elements take a non-discursive or presentational form, to lapse into the aesthetic language of Susanne K. Langer?[52]

The answer to this question may be forthcoming if we consider the role of memory in the act of speech. The words of a given language always exist as the medium which is being worked by the artist; as such they constitute a background to all expressions in that medium. Thus the language I speak in expressing my own thoughts constitutes a field, a cultural world toward which I am tending in the act of expressing the thought. As my hand tends or may tend to a spot on my body which has been stung by an insect, my speech apparatus tends to the *mot juste* for my original thought. In the act, and in the use of the language, I use my body concretely; should I try to use it abstractly, by pointing to the bite or by quoting the word out of context, I shall as likely as not fail.

What Merleau-Ponty has done in this instance is to extend his concept of the body-proper to include a part of the cultural environment in the corporeal schema. It must be remembered that what unites the organism to the environment is an intentional-arc, the outgoing direction of the organism to the objects it constitutes in the immediate perceptual field. The process of choosing the right word to express my thought is not very different from the act of my consciousness in intending an absent object in image. Here Merleau-Ponty's debt to Sartre is patent.[53] Sartre refers to one of his acts of imagining the presence of a friend, Pierre. Pierre in image is nothing more than a "modality of my being in the world";[54] likewise any image I may maintain of an absent word is a modality of my phonetic gesture. I may recall the word, the person, or the spot in which I have been stung when the situation demands. In this process the life of the body, the living organism, functions to project the present situation into the past, as it can into the future; when the recall, or the projection, has been effectuated, I have successfully undergone my tendency outward in referring to the object in question. Finally, when the word is pronounced according to the phonetic rules of the language, the motor innervation has realized in a sonorous phenomenon the articulate style of my speech, and I have spoken.[55] It is in this way, claims Merleau-Ponty, that the individual *parole* produces its effect on the *langue* of a people. Saussure had isolated this phenomenon, and a cursory glance at any unabridged dictionary will show the same: in the special senses attributed to a word due to the novel uses of it by successful or "classical" authors.

To summarize Merleau-Ponty's position: in a creative act of discourse, a word is not a sign of a thought which may be given or entertained separately from itself; neither is given separately from the other. Nor, strictly speaking, should the word be considered the "final fixation" of the thought, as if the thought had a beginning without the word. To make sense of creative discourse, "The spoken and written word must, in one way or another, cease to be a manner of designating an object or a thought in order to become the presence of that thought in the world. . . ."[56]

When the novel thought has gained this worldly presence, the value of its expression becomes apparent. First of all it makes the meaning exist, almost in the manner of things, within the text in which it occurs. The novel thought comes alive in the organism of the words. And the principle of Plato and Aristotle so dear to classical aestheticians as "organic unity" is no mere metaphor. In the presence of this living thought, the hearer or reader comes to possess a new sense organ with which to view the world; the successful literary work opens a new field or dimension of experience. As an analogy, consider the formal structure of music. So-called absolute music has no meaning other than the sounds heard, the articulation of tonal elements. Or consider the way in which the character appears through the acts, words, and gestures of a player. Even to say that the meaning of the musical piece is internal to the articulated tones or that the character is internal to the player's gestures is a misrepresentation of the fact; music *is* the sounds, and the character, the gestures. Each is given in the other: in the articulation of the tones and in the articulation of the gestures. Meanings do not exist outside the world; they are made to inhabit the world by force of the novel structures given to the elements already found in the world. In the case of speech they are constituted by the relation of a bodily complex to its cultural environment.

The amount of confusion with regard to literary creation stemming from unenlightened criticism is easily understandable. Some critics read or hear only the words without the meanings; others lay some claim to having grasped the thought as if in spite of the words. Someday more critics will try to ascertain the manner in which a new thought has been expressed in the words. Three points of view, and three metaphysics. Ultra-realists take the poem to be the words irrespective of their meanings: symbolism and dadaism, or perhaps more clearly, "lettrism." The mistake here is an overemphasis on the sensuous surface of the artifact. Idealists, on the other hand, err by reason of illusion:

What produces our mistake on this question, what makes us believe in a thought which could exist by itself before being expressed, are the thoughts already constituted as such, already expressed, which we recall in a silent moment and which give us an illusion of an internal life. But in reality this pretense of silence bristles with words, and our internal life is an internal language.[57]

Only an idealist would imagine the existence of "mute, inglorious Miltons." The phenomenologist tries, on the contrary, to indicate the manner in which the novel thought is discovered. For Merleau-Ponty, it could be no other way, a new thought made to inhabit the world can be made to do so only by an operation on the already existing objects of this cultural world:

The novel significant intention can be recognized only by covering itself over with meanings already available as the results of prior acts of expression. The available meanings are suddenly intermingled according to an unknown law, and once and for all a new cultural being has begun to exist.[58]

And it exists as a gesture of one human inviting another to a sharing of values: "The spoken word is a true gesture, and contains its meaning as the gesture contains its significance. That is how communication is possible."[59] To understand the gesture, one need only participate in the situation it describes.[60] This is what it means to have an aesthetic experience.

From the foregoing summary, it is easy to understand the tag placed upon Merleau-Ponty's aesthetics by his earlier French critics; any theory which reduces verbal communication to an outgoing tension between the bodily organism of the speaker and his physical, social and cultural environment may fairly be called "anti-intellectual." But an epithet hardly affords a true and viable criticism. What must be done is to consider Merleau-Ponty's conclusion in the light of the evidence he has brought forward in its support. But this is a task much easier to accomplish following an account of the relation he sees between aesthetics and criticism.

X

Aesthetics as Criticism (of Criticism)

In deferring the evaluation of Merleau-Ponty's aesthetics, I have tried to allow for any further elucidations of his general theory which may derive from its application to particular expressions constitutive of general human culture. In his inaugural lecture at the Collège de France, Merleau-Ponty had examined the function of philosophy as the continual attempt to survey and criticize human institutions. In doing so he was opposing the Hegelian and Marxist idea of an objective history merely unfolding itself according to an immanent, if not predesigned, law or pattern. Human freedom, in such a scheme, reduces to a recognition of the inevitable. An existentialist recognizing only the contingency of human events as inevitable, Merleau-Ponty had to find a function for philosophy other than the recording of the historically inevitable pattern of events. Besides the fact that this view interprets history and philosophy as the same intellectual discipline, Merleau-Ponty saw in it the falsification of history itself. Thus the first step in his anti-Hegelian and anti-Marxian interpretation of philosophy is to separate the queen of the sciences from the crudeness of a purely historical analysis of human events. Philosophy becomes, in Merleau-Ponty's eyes, the criticism of human history in its broadest sense, including the establishment, development, and decadence of all human institutions.

One of these historical institutions may be called the aesthetic according to which the following codifiable behavioral patterns are exhibited: the creation of aesthetic objects as an expression of unique and individual "perceptions" of the artist, the functioning of these

objects in the lives of a society of appreciators, their "consecration"
as with museum pieces or religious objects. Further, the total aesthetic institution includes as one of its components the function of
criticism, which is to enlighten the less sensitive or perceptive of an
artwork's audience as to what is to be perceived in a work of art.
Since all perceptions are necessarily incomplete, since each movement
from an indeterminate and unclear awareness to a relatively more
determinate and clear organization of the environment never achieves
full determinacy or full clarity, the process of interpretation undergoes continual reconstruction. Philosophy, whose method is here still
interpreted as "critical reflection," can always be applied to more
primitive (in the sense of "primary") expressions; aesthetics is to be
considered the method of philosophy applied to the more primitive
expressions of artists and critics. Aesthetics, in this sense, is either
criticism proper or the criticism of criticism. In an effort to show the
derivation of this concept I shall trace the development of philosophy, as Merleau-Ponty saw it, in relation to the more primitive "expressions" of the human animal. We may start with the separation
of philosophy from history.

When an historian discusses the subject of his interest, he sometimes talks as if his point of view were taken from outside of history itself; but an "objective" historian in this strictest sense is a
manifest absurdity, or something other than a man. As the phenomenologist has pointed out, the world and our awareness of it are
given simultaneously; what we do to the world as a result of our
awareness of it acts to produce a different sort of world. To conceive
of the events of history as if they were all produced by a series of
antecedent causes leading to some unknown and unspecifiable future
is to deprive history of its meaning; in Merleau-Ponty's own words,
"History has no meaning if that meaning is understood as the direction [sens] of a river which flows under the action of all-powerful
causes toward an ocean, where it disappears."[1] To discover the meaning of history it is necessary to investigate the social and cultural
side of human events as they influence conduct and as they themselves are in turn influenced by individual acts.

To put the matter more concretely, each individual human event
has at least two poles of determination: its individual and its social
side. In acting, the individual must act upon something, presumably
upon what is already provided in his physical, cultural, and social

environment. The historical process, then, is not unlike that already explained as linguistic communication:

> The theory of signs, as it is elaborated in linguistics, implies, in a sense, a theory of the meaning of history which goes beyond the alternative of *things* and *consciousnesses*. The living language is that concrete union of a mind and a thing which is difficult to comprehend [in the alternative just mentioned]. In the act of speaking, by his tone and by his style, the individual attests to his own autonomy since nothing is more his own; but at the same time he is without contradiction oriented toward the general linguistic community and dependent upon the [rules of] spoken language. The will to speak is the same thing as the desire to be understood. The presence of the individual before the institution and of the institution before the individual is patent in the case of linguistic changes.[2]

In this statement Merleau-Ponty has achieved a number of effects: first, he announces that history is to be properly conceived as the locus of human expressions; second, that these expressions can be understood within the context of his general theory of linguistics, and not by compressing the events of history into a metaphysics of dualism which would embrace the world of objective events on one side and the historian's conscious awareness of them on the other.

The latter implies Merleau-Ponty's criticism of *L'Etre et le néant* as well as Sartre's later concern with the relations of existentialism and Marxism. It is significant to remember here that his article on Sartre as an ultra-bolshevik had not yet appeared and that his last article in *Les Temps Modernes* appeared in July of 1952. The statement was made as a part of his first lecture at the Collège de France, on the 15th of January 1953, a scant six months later. Whereas the article on the indirect language was dedicated to Sartre, the lecture is inscribed in honor of Merleau-Ponty's mother. Simone de Beauvoir has since pointed out that Merleau-Ponty had already become "academic,"[3] implying that he himself had thus become at least one step removed from the push and pull of historical human circumstance. The charge that an academic must by virtue of his profession ignore the events of contemporary history is, of course, absurd; moreover, in the existentialistic sense, it is unethical since it reduces Merleau-Ponty's transcendence to the functional role he assumed in university life.

The third effect of Merleau-Ponty's inaugural lecture is the reduction of history to process: a social process involving men and institutions. He proceeds to explain the manner in which this process is "understood." Like the implicit understanding of all social institutions, this one is not primarily conceptualized; it is lived through, but not understood in any primary sense at all:

Just as language is a system of signs without a meaning except as each sign is related to the other and has a certain manner of being used that is dictated by the totality of the language, each institution is a *symbolic system* which a subject incorporates within himself—as a functional style, a global configuration—without his needing to conceive it.[4] [Emphasis added.]

The words "symbolic system" have been emphasized here to point up the relation of institutional behavior in the scale and hierarchy of orders isolated by Merleau-Ponty in *La Structure du comportement*. According to this work symbolic behavior is definitive of purely human conduct and marks the manner by which mankind has been able to exceed the limits of its physical and biological environments. But such conduct has not as yet become "conceptual." Institutions are forms of behavior which are learned as an individual learns to walk; they govern our conduct as our habits govern our everyday life. We "live" them without ever becoming fully conscious of their effects on that life.

But to call human institutions "forms of behavior" is not to make them purely arbitrary, or metaphysical non-entities:

It is as such, as so many different logics of behavioral patterns, that there exist forms and historical processes, [social] classes and [historical] epochs whose locus of existence was our concern before. They exist in a social, cultural and symbolic space which is not less real than the physical, and which moreover is, ultimately, based upon the physical.[5]

History, in accordance with this, is the working out of social relations in a field of interaction between the institutions, or codified forms of social behavior, on the one hand, and individuals on the other. As such it is lived rather than conceptualized, and may take various directions according to the decisions of individuals to modify their patterns of conduct. Written history takes place much later and must be judged according to the accuracy with which the written account corresponds to the experienced events.

Philosophy enters the picture as reflection on the events of human history with the aim of understanding them in a fully conceptual fashion, and with the result that any light obtained by philosophical reflection may be used to change the flow of history to more intelligent ends. Thus its purpose is to change the tacit symbolism of the lived situation into a conscious symbolism; a hidden meaning into a manifest one. In this sense history is a lived process or primary human expression and philosophy is its criticism. Philosophy scrutinizes the primitive expressions of human individuals, institutional and otherwise, and evaluates their meanings. Wherever there is intelligent criticism of this type of first order expression, there is philosophy. The difference between the historian's activity and that of the philosopher is that the former merely describes, while the latter criticizes, evaluating and attempting to redirect the flow of historical events.

Moreover, in answer to the question, What is the place of the philosopher in the intellectual enterprise? Merleau-Ponty responds with a statement of the value of criticism:

Philosophy is directed toward the anonymous symbolic activity from which we emerge and toward the personal discourse which takes form within us, and which is our peculiar manner of existing; it scrutinizes this power of expression that the other forms of symbolism merely exercise without reflection. . . . it recuperates and thus pushes beyond any limitation the development of truth which presupposes at the same time it produces a single history and a single world.[6]

The philosopher is nothing more than a human being using his symbols of language in a peculiarly critical fashion; to be effective he must be in and of the world, and when effective he will change the world. Merleau-Ponty never completely lost this last trace of marxism. But neither had Dewey when he announced that philosophy will have become "recovered" when philosophers forget "philosophical" problems and start to deal with the problems of men.[7]

Dewey's maxim has often been misunderstood. Some interpreters have insisted that the interest of the philosopher is to be directed outward to the solving of problems posed by the position of men in society without regard to any of these so-called traditional problems of philosophy. If this interpretation of the doctrine were correct, it would be difficult to see why anyone should call on a philosopher, qua philosopher, to settle any issue. The presumption is that a philosopher is eminently qualified to deal with the living problems of men because of a special aptitude or characteristic which is the result of his long philosophical training, but apparently lacking on the part of those closely connected with the problem at hand. Examples of this are easy to find. Scientists who divorce the realm of

facts from that of values and then claim a unique interest in the
world of scientific fact are hardly in a position to understand how
human values enter into their considerations, almost in spite of themselves; especially is this the case in the science of economics where
the facts being studied are the values of goods and services. What
the philosopher can do in such cases is to bring his analytic powers
to bear upon the nature and functioning of value judgments as these
occur either explicitly or implicitly in the scientific enterprise.

Much the same kind of suggestion is made by Merleau-Ponty in
erecting philosophy into criticism of more primary human expressions
or institutions. A necessary condition to philosophic activity when
that activity is directed outward toward the problems of men is a
thorough-going understanding of the human processes involved in
the primary activity being reflected upon. Moreover, if the philosopher is to serve his role of enlightened critic, he must be assured
that his tools are in good working order. And as in the case above
these are primarily analytic in character. Insofar as we are interested
in the philosophy as criticism of the aesthetic institution of the general society, it seems clear that the traditional problem of philosophy
most pertinent to the present discussion is the theory of perception.
Since it it the critic's task to enlighten perception, it is not unreasonable to demand of him that he be informed on the process of perception in the first instance. To this end, Merleau-Ponty has developed his
phenomenology of perception, and following its development, has applied the theory to some of the problems in the criticism of the arts.

A cultivated Frenchman thoroughly imbued with the philosophy
and aesthetics of his own culture, Merleau-Ponty could hardly have
missed Alain's description of perception as the beginnings of a science.[8] According to Alain's *Système des beaux-arts,* the difference between an act of perception and that of imagination is an erroneous
judgment on the data of perception: to perceive rightly and to judge
truly are one and the same process; but under the influence of his
own passions, the creative artist is led to perceive falsely because he
has judged erroneously the objects placed before him: his own body,
his social situation, the external world. In the act of creation, then,
the artist constructs an object which "fixes the imaginary experience"
in such a way as to provide an object to correspond with the feeling
expressed.

The difficulty Merleau-Ponty finds in Alain's system is not so much the description of the qualities of the aesthetic object as that of the intellectual processes Alain claims are implicit in the creation of the object. First of all, to place perception on the level of an intellectual judgment is to start with too sophisticated a process: "Perception is not a kind of beginning science and a first exercise of the intelligence; we must find a relation with, a presence to, the world older than intelligence."[9] Aesthetic reactions are pre-rational; in Kantian terms the judgment of taste does not relate its objects to a pre-existent concept, and it is in this sense that they are labeled "aesthetic" as distinct from "logical." This is not to deny that concepts may form a part of an aesthetic object, but only that an object, if thus formed, is fully rational. If pre-rational, aesthetic reactions form the basis for all further rationality. On this point once again Croce and Merleau-Ponty are in agreement.

At least two distinct kinds of perception, the scientific and the aesthetic, would seem to result from Merleau-Ponty's observation. The scientific is derivative, and represents the analytical processes illustrated in the observations of scientists and philosophers using theoretical constructs; it is their job to interpret human experience through concepts and categories. However, this is the sense of the term in which perception is non-aesthetic. The "older relation of the organism with its environment," on the other hand, can only be the pre-rational experience of the human organism as it reacts to the world with all its feeling centers still intact and functioning to give a first significant form within what before was the "undifferentiated aesthetic continuum." Such perception is, in contradistinction to the above, first, primary, and synthetic. To adopt the analytical point of view, describing objects as if they were divisible into various sensations localized into a particular area of the perceptual field, is to misinterpret the primitive aesthetic response: "My perception is . . . not a summation of visual, tactile or auditory data. I perceive with my whole being without dividing the object; I grasp a unique structure of the thing, a manner of existing which speaks to all my senses at once."[10]

The psychological data put to use in Merleau-Ponty's theory of primitive perception is the work performed by the gestaltist school, in particular that of Gelb and Goldstein. In describing the manner in which a film conveys its meaning, Merleau-Ponty reasserts his gestaltism:

The permanence of colors and of objects is not constructed by the intelligence, but grasped by "the look" in so far as it conforms to, or adopts the organization of the visual field. . . . The objects and lighting form a system which tend toward a certain constancy and toward a certain stability, not by any operation of the intelligence, but by the very configuration of the field.[11]

In a word, it is an analytic falsification of experience to distinguish sensation from perception, and to assign the value of a sign to data of sense and that of a meaning to the concept interpreting those data. But this is what has been said before; aesthetic reactions are pre-rational, or non-symbolic. Alain's doctrine of the imagination as erroneous judgment blurs the distinction between analytic and synthetic perceptions.

A second objection to Alain's system which may be based upon the gestalt principle is the function attributed to the emotions in the aesthetic attitude. It is as if the creative personality were blinded by its own affective state into perceiving falsely, or imagining to exist what in reality does not, with the object created corresponding to the affective state. If this were correct, there would be a separation of the object perceived by an aesthetic viewer and its meaning, the affective state which gave rise to the object's existence. Once again there would be a separation of sign and meaning incompatible with our understanding of a gestalt. As Merleau-Ponty claims, since an object is organized by the needs and attitudes of the entire organism and not merely by a single sense modality, there is no reason to suppose that the "meaning" of a given aesthetic object is primarily an idea or concept; feelings may be engaged in the very act of perceiving the gestalt. Clearly this is what one does in "perceiving" the anger of an opponent as a configuration of given acts and gestures,[12] and the job of any actor is to express the personality and emotions of the character through his own acts and gestures. In fact the character has no other existence. In terms of perception, this idea is usually expressed by saying that the meaning of the gestalt is given in the total configuration and not referred to by the form.[13] References of words or other signs are not meanings of aesthetic objects, but may become elements within a total configuration which carries its own meaning. In Merleau-Ponty's view the problem of sign and signification is quite analogous to that of mind and body:

. . . just as the body and "soul" of a man are only two aspects of its manner of being present to the world, the word and the thought it designates are not to be considered as two terms external to each other; and the word carries its meaning as the body does, in the incarnation of a behavorial pattern.[14]

As the soul is expressed in the behavior of the body, the meaning of the organized gestalt is expressed in its own organization.[15]

In sum then, perceptions are either primary and synthetic or secondary and analytic; the artist deals with perceptions of the first kind, and the scientist with those of the second. The artist is engaged in constructing or reconstructing a universe of unique significance to himself, and the scientist in describing or explaining the manner in which the common universe of human experience is constructed for any rational being. The point being made here is similar, once again, to that made by Croce. What Merleau-Ponty calls a "first, primary and synthetic perception," Croce refers to simply as an "intuition." Finally, the "second, derivative and analytic" perceptions, which according to Merleau-Ponty are the raw materials of scientists, again bear the simple designation, "concepts," in Croce's system. It need only be kept in mind, as Croce had long ago pointed out, that although intuitions are prior to concepts in the order according to which knowledge is gained, concepts may form a part of more complex intuitions. Indeed, if this were not the case, there could be no literary art.

A further and final point of comparison between Merleau-Ponty and Croce becomes apparent when we consider the notion of expression. It may be remembered that Croce had defined art as expression and expression as co-terminous with the field of "spiritual" activity he calls "intuition." The latter is a name he uses for the behavior of artists who give form to the impressions they receive from their environment; as such it is an act of the mind, inexplicable in any terms other than itself. In Croce's own words, "The true artist . . . finds himself big with his theme, he knows not how; he feels the moment of birth drawing near, but he cannot will it or not will it."[16] At this juncture in his aesthetic theory there enters the note of wonder, mystery, and sometimes awesome admiration of aesthetic genius. It is Merleau-Ponty's purpose to reduce the wonder, mystery, and if not the admiration, at least the awesome character of creativity.

In pursuit of his purpose, he first refuses to Croce the distinction of mind and body. As described in *La Structure du comportement,* all human activity is spiritual in the sense of creating a new cultural universe by means of the novel significations projected into the world. This the human animal may do by virtue of his corporeal schema, and the "intentional-arc" by which man, in particular the artist, projects himself into his complex environment to constitute a still more complex human culture. The artist's hand, and his brush or other instrument as an extension of his hand, are as important to creation as his eye and mind.[17] But to understand this non-mystical account of artistic creation it is necessary to re-examine Merleau-Ponty's account of perceptions and the parallel distinctions it implies for a doctrine of aesthetic expression.

It has been a common assumption of critics that an artist can do nothing until his work has been conceived, that consequent upon the conception of the work the artist must execute his design or intent in the symbols of his medium, and that the success or failure of this execution must be judged by referring it to the pre-designed conception. Nothing could be simpler: the conception determines the execution and constitutes a norm by which to judge its excellence. Unfortunately, however, the critics who have maintained this description as a model of artistic communication were unaware of the virtual impossibility of comparing the intention of an artist, a psychic fact, with its physical representation in an art medium, or artifact, a physical fact. Since, in every case of an unsuccessful expression of a pre-ordained conception, the judgment must be based upon what has failed to be expressed in the physical medium—the non-expressed intention—it becomes a total mystery: a thought which can be known by another person only through an act of physical expression of some sort is purportedly judged by reference to what has failed to achieve expression. It is for this reason that the model explained above has come to be called "the intentional fallacy."[18]

A second reason for the fallaciousness of intentionalist criticism is that it confuses, in Merleau-Ponty's terms, a primary with a secondary expression. A primary or successful work of art brings with it a novel significance; it is created, and not copied—even from an artist's vision. The mimetic theory, which holds that the artist does copy nature or a pre-established idea, has not been embarrassed in the least by this inability to explain the novel character of a true work of art; for the most part it has been satisfied to accept as fact the supposition that the purpose of such imitation is the pleasure it may afford to artist or audience. The further contradiction between this purported end of the arts as imitation and the actual physical pain experienced in the work of making the imitative object could, after all, easily be explained by a further assumption, metaphysical this time, that it is the nature of man to make things (*homo faber*) and that anything made for no direct use value must be made for the pleasure of the making. Finally, when a given society has a large number of people capable of so enjoying themselves in artistic pursuits, it has reached a high stage of "culture."

The basic confusion in this series of assumptions is the failure to recognize that almost anything may give pleasure to some kinds of personalities; if this is true, the fact that a given object may give pleasure in the act of contemplation cannot be taken as a distinguishing mark of works of art, good or bad. Merleau-Ponty goes further:

> There is no pleasant art. One can construct objects which give pleasure by relating in a different fashion ideas already received and by presenting forms already seen. Such a picture or secondary expression is what is generally meant by "culture."[19]

In other words, the reinterpretation of a given idea is not art in the creative sense of that word, but already smacks of the secondary discipline of criticism. In order to separate clearly the primary from the secondary Merleau-Ponty denies categorically the imputation that an artist's idea may precede the execution of his work: "Expression cannot . . . be the translation of a thought which is already clear, since clear ideas are those which have already been said either by ourselves or by others. 'Conception' cannot come before 'execution.' "[20] The artist discovers his ideas as he works, and this is what is meant by saying that an artist thinks, if think he must, with the end of his brush. Far from being the initial act of creative expression, conception is rather the final. The artist may stop working when he discovers what he has said; this discovery and aesthetic judgment are one and the same process.

It may be objected at this point that Merleau-Ponty is no less mystical than his idealist adversaries. What, after all, allows an artist to judge that his work is done? The answer to this perplexing question may be found by recalling the first function of aesthetics interpreted as a general theory of linguistics: "The difficulties of Cézanne are those of the first spoken word. He thought he was impotent because he was not onmipotent, because he was not God and he wanted nonetheless to paint the world, to convert it entirely into spectacle, to make *visible* the manner in which it makes its *impression* on us."[21] And one experiences the difficulties of the first act of discourse when one is bereft of a dictionary and the rules of grammar. If these latter are the norms or criteria of rational discourse, then reason must be reinterpreted to include man's first or aesthetic acts: "The meaning of what the artist is going to say *is* nowhere, neither in things nor in his non-formulated life. It calls attention away from a fully constituted reason in which 'cultivated men' enclose themselves, to another which would contain its own origins."[22] As both Croce and Merleau-Ponty have maintained, logic can only grow out of aesthetics; concepts, out of intuitions; secondary, out of primordial expressions. Within aesthetics proper, this can only mean that the significance of works of art must appear on the surface of the work itself, it cannot be reduced to a relation of resemblance.

But, the objection continues, there have been many good realistic paintings, and the techniques for making such works have been known at least since the Renaissance. The objection is well taken, but it over-estimates the value of tradition in the creation of artworks. The problem is no more difficult than a parallel consideration in linguistics. There too, the individual who would speak with originality will find already at his disposal all the constituted meanings of a dictionary and all the established rules of grammar, and these will to an extent define the manner in which the original statement will be made. We need only recall Saussure's distinction between "la langue" and "la parole." The latter, it will be recalled, is the individual and creative use of the former, which may be modified for better or for worse by any neologisms stemming from the individual-social interplay. In linguistics this fact is stated to explain the historical changes in "the living language"; in aesthetics the parallel fact may be cited in explanation of the developments of styles in the history of art.

In commenting upon the individual style of Cézanne, Merleau-Ponty offers an explanation of the new and the old in the paintings of that master. To comprehend the explanation it must be kept in mind that, although Cézanne's paintings may be called "realistic" in that they represent nature, the effect they have produced has been achieved by an intentional violation of naturalistic techniques; their peculiar massive quality has been obtained by juxtaposition of solids without a thought to accurate perspective, and shadows may even be perceived in the "wrong" direction from the source of light. The artist has worked out his paintings stroke upon stroke, and it is the life of the painting, rather than the idea of nature, which guided their application. In this sense nature has provided a motif and the artist has developed the theme according to the necessities of the total construct:

Anatomy and design are present when he makes a stroke, just as the rules of the game are always present in a tennis match. What motivates the painter's gesture, however, is never perspective alone, nor geometry, nor the laws of color analysis or any other bit of knowledge. There is but one motif for all the strokes which form a painting bit by bit, and that is the landscape in its totality and absolute plenitude—what Cézanne appropriately called "a motif."[23]

Susanne Langer refers to such motifs as "commanding forms," which may guide the construction of what she calls the total "presentational symbol."[24]

The emphasis in this terminology is upon the character of the picture itself, and not on any representational elements it may contain. Both Langer and Merleau-Ponty apply the gestaltist principle of *Prägnanz* as source of an artwork's meaning; it reduces to the statement that the meaning of a formal construction of artistic elements is to found in their maximal organization. As Merleau-Ponty puts it, "In the work of art or in theory, as in [the perception of] the sensible thing, the meaning is inseparable from the sign."[25] And he concludes from this statement that "The expression . . . is never completed. The highest form of reason is in the neighborhood of sheer lunacy."[26] A word of explanation for this somewhat arcane inference.

When an artist has embodied his message in the structures of his work, the meaning is there to be perceived by any viewer who commits himself to the discipline of the work. Neither the artist nor the work itself forces the attention of the viewer; the work is there to be perceived. But if it is perceived, some viewer must reorganize its elements in his own experience for the work to appear to him. Creation calls out for appreciation, and the experience of the audience completes the act of creative communication. There is only one restriction to be placed upon this principle, and that is the caution that the viewer's experience be guided by what the artist has put into his work:

In the presence of a novel, poem or film of value, we know that contact has been made with something, that something has been acquired by men and that the work begins to emit an uninterrupted message. . . . But the work is not formulable, either for the artist or for his public, in terms other than the work itself; neither the thought which has made it nor that which has received it is completely self-controlled.[27]

The meaning of a given work of art is not translatable into a set of discursive, or logical, symbols. In practice this means that the work of art must be perceived and that its meaning is clear to anyone who has experienced the structures of the work, for beyond these structures there is nothing to be perceived or understood.

It follows from the above that the critic's job is not to reduce a work of art to a simple logical statement; rather it is to analyze the structures of the work in such a way that a viewer who has failed to perceive the work and understand its significance in the act of perception may be put into a position to have the experience it affords. Creation thus begins and ends in human experience. In the final analysis, the meaning of artworks is judged by human individuals in a direct first-hand experience. The expression is never complete because there is always a further call to interpretation, and each individual interpretation in turn makes its appeal to reflective criticism which, for Merleau-Ponty, is the very essence of philosophy itself.

In moving on to his account of aesthetic criticism—philosophical analysis of primary art expressions—I shall divide the question into two parts. The first will deal with actual criticisms made by Merleau-Ponty on selected extant works of art or art media; the second, with his evaluation of accepted critical procedures. The first will illustrate aesthetics as criticism; the second, as criticism of criticism.

Aesthetics as Criticism.—Merleau Ponty has applied his philosophical method of "critical reflection" to at least three distinct art media: painting, literature, and the film. His aim is not so much the analysis of the particular structures of given works as the development of a critical vocabulary which will allow such analyses. In this first part he will be shown in the guise of an aesthetician looking, in the background of his own art experiences, for a set of general critical categories which may be used in the analysis of further works of art. It should be remembered always that the aesthetician's order of business is secondary; it depends upon the primary activities of artists and their publics, and will in the long run be used to enlighten further contacts with the same area of primitive expressions. Consider first the manner of expression called "painting."

Merleau-Ponty has chosen the life and work of Paul Cézanne to illustrate some of the problems involved in the creation of a visual work of art. Primary among those problems is the nature of the artist's reaction to the motivating stimuli of his environment. Since some painters are predominantly sensuous, and others cerebral, depending upon whether color or design dominates their works, it has been thought that the reflective artist has a choice between chromatic effect or draftsmanship in working out his compositions. A cursory glance at the history of art will bear out the significance of this apparent dichotomy: some artists are known as colorists, others as draftsmen, and many have been the discussions of the relative merits of color and line, forms and space, design and composition in the determination of the value of a particular work.

A common sense solution to this puzzle would indicate that each work is individual, and that each painter develops a personal style. Only an experience of that work or of that style will enable us to judge the validity of the expression. Unfortunately for the student of painting, however, the common sense answer gives no guide for a personal decision in the studio as to which qualities suit his own objectives; that is precisely the position in which Cézanne found himself, giving rise to the serious doubt he entertained concerning the possibility of his ever becoming an artist.[28]

Should the student shift his attention to the area of refined common sense—to that of science or of traditional philosophy—he would be likely to pose the problem in terms of sense impressions and their conceptual analysis; but then the dilemma would become an instance of the old empiricist-rationalist controversy, in which apologists of experience opposed those of reason. Even those cultivated individuals who have little cognizance of the philosophical jargon involved could see the controversy in French painting of the late nineteenth century. The impressionists objected to the rigid, almost mathematical compositions of the academic painters, working under the influence of the Renaissance tradition. The academics were the cerebrals, painters of ideas in clear and distinct portrayal. Their emphasis upon order, thought, and clearness only served to alienate that group of rebels who wanted to return to the world as it is seen. And this they did by their technique of breaking up light into its component parts and placing minute touches of colored pigment in close juxtaposition so that the total impression of the painting was one vibrant plane of iridescent light. For their infinite pains, they were excluded from public exhibition and forced to arrange their own show of the refused paintings. So much for the history; Cézanne found himself in the midst of this controversy. Merleau-Ponty has selected this case, because he felt that Cézanne succeeded in working out an alternative to the academic-impressionistic, or rationalist-empiricist, dichotomy. It will come as no surprise, then, that Cézanne's paintings best illustrate Merleau-Ponty's theory of perception.

In their reaction to the rigidity of the academics, the impressionists succeeded only in their rebellion; in their paintings, they failed to capture the sensuous surface of objective nature. What the appreciator receives from the impressionists' work is light, not the objects which reflect the light. Cézanne insisted that we see things, trees and apples, hills and buildings, and that light is only the medium of transmitting the impression of these things. Evidently then, any painting which makes the light apparent as a value in itself has missed its aim, as naturalistic for the impressionists as for the academics, of presenting nature in the raw. Between paintings of absolute linear perspective and those of color synthesis there could only be a difference of technique.

The reason for this failure of the impressionists, according to Merleau-Ponty, is their inability to understand the nature of painterly expression. To reduce expression to a strict impression of light waves on the eye is to miss the organizing activity of the human organism as it perceives its world, and to attempt to find the organizing principle of perception in the strict concepts and laws of perspectival geometry is to do the same. Neither the rationalist nor the empiricist has a grasp on the world of pure experience. Phenomenologists who would avoid the mistakes of their predecessors could easily have learned their lesson in the work of Cézanne:

Cézanne did not believe he had a choice between sensation and thought, as if between chaos and order. He did not wish to separate the fixed objects of the world which appear to our gaze from their fleeting manner of making an appearance; he wanted, rather, to paint matter in the process of giving itself form, order developing in a spontaneous organization. He did not put the dividing line between "the senses" and "intelligence," but between the spontaneous order of perceived objects and the human order of ideas and of

CÉZANNE, *Village of Gardanne*

science. We perceive things; we have common reactions to them. We are anchored in the world of things, and it is on this pedestal of "nature" that we construct our sciences.[29]

In the light of this interpretation, the relative failure of both academic and impressionistic painters is easily understood. Both used techniques which were derivative from "secondary" perceptions. The laws of color analysis are no more aesthetic, no less scientific, than the laws of perspective.

It matters little whether man's knowledge is derived from the fields of physics, physiology, and psychology or from those of geometry and physics; any technique based upon secondary expression is at least one step removed from the primitive responses of men perceiving the objects of their environment. For this reason, both the academics and the impressionists were thinking instead of painting:

It serves no purpose here to note the distinctions of body and soul, or of vision and thought, since Cézanne returns to the primordial experience from which these notions are taken and which yields them up only as inseparable one from the other. The painter who thinks and looks for his expression before painting misses that mystery, repeated every time we look at someone, according to which the person makes his appearance in nature.[30]

Cézanne's painting gives the "feel" of an object precisely because he painted phenomena; if he continues to be associated with the school of impressionism, the reason may be assigned to his devotion to the phenomenal character of the universe rather than to his use of an abstractly formulable technique. His research into the problems of painting allowed him to differentiate between lived perspective and geometrical perspective according to which men are purported to perceive as if their organism had the structure of a photographic apparatus.[31]

If the painter's eye is not a lens in the same sense as the business end of a camera, the purpose of the painter's art is not to imitate what is seen. Painting, according to Merleau-Ponty, is primordial expression: "In the same way that a word names its object, that is, allows us to grasp it as a recognizable something in a confused situation, the painter . . . 'objectifies,' 'projects,' 'fixes.' "[32] The value of painting, then, is the value of clarification; it presents in image for all the world to see, the visual or perceptual character of the world. It thus becomes a cultural object in its own right and may be placed

in a museum or a home where other kindred spirits may commune in
the celebration of their common humanity:

The painter could only make an image. One must wait for that image to be
animated by others. Then the work of art will have joined those separated
lives; it will no longer exist solely in one of them like a tenacious dream or
persistent delirium, or even in space as a colored canvas; it will inhabit several minds indivisibly, even presumably every possible mind, as a perpetual
[human] acquisition.[33]

The paradox of Cézanne's life and work is expressed in his own
lingering doubt on the quality of his painting. As a glance at the
paintings would suffice to extinguish it, the doubt was baseless, but
it had to be felt for Cézanne to have discovered the visual world enshrined in the paintings themselves. Like Descartes who had to doubt
he was thinking in order to establish that he was, Cézanne redis-
covered painting by doubting he was a painter. As a lived act, moreover, Cézanne's doubt symbolizes the need for continual reflection or
critical appreciation on even the most successful work of art.

The foregoing analysis gives rise to a series of questions, which
will be merely noted here and considered at greater length in the
critical evaluation of Merleau-Ponty's doctrine (below and Chapter
XI). Obviously the case of Cézanne was chosen since his paintings
exhibit the qualities illustrating Merleau-Ponty's distinction between
primordial and secondary expression, as well as his general theory of
perception. Does this mean that Cézanne's paintings become the
touchstones or norms for judging the works of other artists? And
cannot a critic judge a painting, whether pre- or post-impressionistic,
on the grounds of the qualities of the painting itself, abstraction
being made of the manner in which it represents or fails to represent
the perceptual world, and whether or not this perceptual world has
the qualities of "a primordial perception" or of the secondary perceptions of abstract science? Or on the other hand, was Cézanne
chosen merely as representative of the way in which any painter is
led to discover his "idea" of the visual world? That the paintings of
Cézanne are valid artistic expressions will not be doubted by many
art critics; that they should become touchstones of artistic excellence
is quite another matter. And what would become of human freedom
of expression if it could truly be said that Cézanne had discovered
once and for all the formula for producing a successful work of art?

Answers to these queries will be attempted once the two other

media mentioned above have been examined. Since Malraux's aesthetics had been criticized by Merleau-Ponty for the comparison it
draws between painting and literature, we may proceed to Merleau-
Ponty's account of the nature, function, and value of literary expressions.

The guiding thread of Merleau-Ponty's account of the literary
medium is a distinction, reminiscent of that drawn by Sartre between
bourgeois and total literature, of analytic from synthetic writing. Like
painting which has largely been reduced in tradition to a significance
of resemblance and a manner, or style, in which that significance has
been achieved—the idea and its execution, the substance and its
form—literature has been largely dissected into polar elements of its
ideational content and its linguistic form. Content-oriented critics
reduce a novel to a paraphrase of its "idea"; formalists seek out the
techniques used by the author to embody the idea. In painting, where
content may be wholly abstracted from, for example in the presentation of a non-objective design, the distinction under discussion may
be readily comprehended, but few are capable of grasping the intent
of a purely formalistic literary critic who insists that the meaning of
a novel is the manner of an expression abstracted from what has
been expressed in content. Yet the formalists seem to be on the right
track in objecting to the "great commonplace" theory of the inten-
tionalists. If this debate is to be settled, then, it becomes incumbent
upon the aesthetician to reformulate the problem in such a way as
to give each side of the controversy its due.

Not content with this usual bifurcation of the literary product
into the What and the How, Merleau-Ponty is led to look for the
unique structure of a literary expression in the synthetic act by which
the expression takes place. In the unicity of the expressive act, any
distinction between content and form is lost. Consider the case of
irony: the opposite of what is said is intended, and this intention is
understood, in context, by the manner in which it is said. No better
example can be found for the falsity of abstracting a content from its
form, yet it would be false or at least misleading to conclude from
this that irony or paradox is the very definition of poetic language.[34]
There is no paradoxical form which can be understood as paradoxical without reference to a content of pre-established meaning. In
Merleau-Ponty's words, "The correct contrary of formalism is a good
theory of style, or of the spoken word, which puts them above

'technique' or 'means.' "[35] Thus the problem to be solved is how to conceive of the manner in which a new meaning accrues to a language because a writer has put his hand to paper using the old and established meanings of an existent linguistic system. In purely linguistic terms, once again, we must be led to understand how the individual learns to use the social means of communication in such a way that he enriches or impoverishes the established language; in aesthetic terms, how a novel is created.

The best way to miss what is new or creative in a novel is to reduce the story to an analytical account of its events. According to Merleau-Ponty, "The novel considered as a list of events, as the enunciation of ideas, thesis, or conclusions, or as a manifest, prosaic meaning, and the novel considered as an operation of style, or as an oblique and latent meaning, are related simply as homonyms."[36] The word has the same spelling, the same sound, but the meanings differ. Whereas the one would suffice for a scientific or philosophic tract, the second is needed over and above the first if the writer is to create a new value or meaning, and if we are to explain his manner of having done so. It is for this reason that Merleau-Ponty has entitled his study of prose, "Le langage indirect." The paradox of literary prose is that it constitutes a primary expression which uses as elements in the artistic construction words which themselves already constitute a secondary or symbolic manner of expression.

Ostensibly a criticism of Malraux's aesthetics, as explained above, the last mentioned article aims to connect literary expression with Merleau-Ponty's doctrine of bodily expression. If the difficulty of an idealist aesthetic is its distinction of mind and body and their various activities, that difficulty may be obviated by drawing out the parallel between language and meaning on the one hand and body and mind on the other:

Language . . . is not at the service of meaning, nor does it govern meaning. There is no subordination between the two. No one commands, and no one obeys here. What we *want to say* is not before us, out of contact with any spoken word as if it were a pure meaning; it is nothing but the excess of our lived experiences, over and above what has already been said.[37]

Writing, then, is nothing but our manner of living in the symbolic universe of words. Whether or not it is political, as Sartre had maintained, it must be understood as an act. As such it must be understood in the same way as other human acts, as the unique organization of a surrounding environment of special significance to the organizing animal.

An animal sees, says Merleau-Ponty, by organizing spatial and colored configurations of an indefinite number; it moves to a direct attainment of its goal by ignoring its nervous and muscular structures. In much the same way, man writes: "The same function is fulfilled by literary language, when the writer, in a brief and imperious gesture, without transitions and preparations, carries us over from a world already spoken about to something quite distinct."[38] Like the painter who creates a visual universe and calls it his own work, the writer creates his own symbolic universe of words and their meanings, rather than of colors and lines. To compare a Cézanne with the qualities of the "real" or scientific world is to note nothing but a difference; to trace a novel to its pre-established idea is to miss its gesture, its manner of living:

Just as our body can guide us among the things of the world only on the condition that we cease to analyze it in order to make use of it, language is literary, or productive, only on the condition that we cease to demand reasons of it at every turn and follow it where it leads—that we allow the words and all the means of expression incorporated in the book to be enveloped in that halo of signification which is due to their singular arrangement, that we let the writing evolve toward its accessory value, where it seemingly joins the mute radiance of painting.[39]

The fact that an author might not know, at the beginning of his work, exactly what he intends to say does not mean that he has nothing to say; it suffices for him to have discovered that he has said something meaningful at the end of his endeavor. The proof that he has been successful is not in the achievement of an abstract intention, but in the experience of the new meaning: "If the author is a writer, that is to say, capable of finding the elisions and caesuras which are the tokens of a behavioral pattern, the reader responds to his call and joins him at the virtual center of the writing, *even if neither the one nor the other knows it*."[40] To be understood, the writing must be read, its manner of life assumed, and its gesture repeated. The reader may never be able to put into words even the essence of what the novel has communicated.

Nor is conceptual understanding the primary value of the work of literary art. Obviously, when a reader has entered sympathetically into the novel universe of the writer, the two may be said to have communicated. The author has constructed, and the reader reconstructed, a fictional world in which each lives, at least for the time they are engaged in their respective activities. For the author, there is the value of self-expression, in existentialistic terms the commitment to his situation which allows him to surpass the situation:

> Man is capable of surpassing his contingency in what he has created; but every act of expression is, on the same grounds as the highest art, an act of birth for man. The miracle takes place everywhere, and at the level of the ground, not in the privileged skies of the fine arts. The principle of order and of disorder is the same; the contingency of things and our freedom which dominates it are cut from the same cloth.[41]

The only possible gage that the author has been successful is the sympathetic reception of his readers.

But not any sympathetic reader reaction is the mark of an author's success; it is neither an understanding of an abstract idea, nor a moment's release from the reality of the world. The value of a literary masterpiece, for a sympathetic reader, is his acquisition of a new manner of vision:

> What is irreplaceable in a work of art, what makes it more than a simple means of pleasure is that it constitutes an organ of the mind having an analogy with every philosophical and political idea if the latter is productive; the work contains, even better than ideas, *matrices of ideas* furnishing symbols whose meaning we can never exhaust. It is precisely because it is installed and installs us in a world whose significance is foreign to us that it teaches us to see and gives food for thought as no analytical work can, since analysis never finds in its object anything other than what it has already put there.[42]

Like all primary expressions, the literary work calls for continual critical interpretation. When the critical audience is attained, a new kind of society has arisen about the new cultural object. Hence, if writing is not necessarily a political act, it is essentially a social and cultural one.

Merleau-Ponty has chosen the case of a "philosophical" novel to illustrate the manner in which a new meaning may accrue to old words. In this essay on the novel and metaphysics, he has given a review of Beauvoir's *L'Invitée* as an illustration of the relation between the novel as a synthetic or primary expression, and metaphysics as an analytic and secondary one. In gist, the activity of the novelist may be guided by a philosophical vision of the world; but its success will be judged on how well the author has synthesized the meanings of the words in presenting the philosophical abstractions in a concrete context. The philosophical writer does not present a thesis. The *roman à thèse* is not, strictly speaking, a novel at all; it is a philosophical tract. But philosophy may be used to structure the events of the novel's universe:

> The work of a great novelist is always carried by two or three philosophical ideas. Take, for example, the self and freedom in Stendhal; the mystery of history as an appearance of a meaning among adventitious circumstances in Balzac; the occurrence of the past in the present and the presence of what has been lost in time, in Proust. The purpose of the novelist is not to make a thesis of these ideas, but to make them exist before us in the same way as things. It is not the role of Stendhal to hold forth on subjectivity; it suffices for him to render it present.[43]

The novelist of ideas has been successful when he makes his point of view felt, and this he does by presenting the universe as he sees it constructed. If he were properly addressing himself only to the minds of his audience, it would be correct to say that the value of the work is an understanding of its idea; but the novelist is after more important game, the commitment of his reader to the novel's situation. As in painting, it is false to claim that the artist is either a sensualist or a thinker; he is primarily a maker. And to paraphrase the poet, a novel doesn't mean; it is.

An essay in illustration of a novel's making and its appreciation has been presented elsewhere in this treatise;[44] we may now pass on to Merleau-Ponty's analysis of the artistic medium of films. Whereas his account of painting was built upon the paradigm case of Cézanne and that of literature on the case of the existentialist novelists, both analyses end with a description of the aesthetic object as a unique world—call it "frame of reference," if you like—constructed within the synthetic unity of a primordial expression, or humanly significant act, whose significance is pre-rational, demanding continual and indefinite reflective criticism. Since the meaning of works of art is not, according to Merleau-Ponty, formulable in words, or any set of symbols other than the original construction, the only test that the work has communicated is the experience of a new value by the appreciative audience. In considering the final case of Merleau-Ponty's criticism, we shall pay special attention to the manner in which a primary expression is said to be experienced. Without such a description, his

account of aesthetic communication would be open-ended and necessarily incomplete. The problem becomes one of understanding how
an aesthetic object is perceived.

To start with the obvious character of the filmic medium, an audio-
visual stimulus is organized in such a way as to relate a series of
temporally unfolding images, the temporal montage, with a series of
noises or sounds called by Sergei Eisenstein "a vertical montage."
Thus there result two lines of sensorially organized structures: that
of the images themselves, and that of the words or the music, which
interlaces the first. Since the first, or temporal montage, is composed
of images, the analysis of films has been beset by the same problems
as the criticism of painting and writing: the mistaking of the resemblance relation for the meaning of the piece.

Merleau-Ponty's first move is to deny this contention: "The meaning of an image depends upon those which precede it in the film, and
their succession creates a new reality which is not the simple summation of the elements employed."[45] Like any visual object, the film is
constituted by the perceptive apparatus of men which organizes impressions into whole structures. And the primary or temporal montage is supported by the second, so that the total object perceived,
and called a film, is a complex object uniting impressions of various
sense modalities. Here once again, critics have tried to reduce the
role of sound to that of support for the visual message, and Merleau-
Ponty hastens to give still a second denial: "The spoken word does
not have the task, in the cinema, of adding ideas to images; nor
music to associate a feeling with them. The whole tells us something
very precise which is neither a thought, nor the occasion for recalling
the feelings of life."[46] In positive fashion, the double montage is to
be viewed as the means by which the film maker creates a significant
gestalt, a form which bears its significance in the very organization
of the elements united:

... the idea or the prosaic facts are there only in order to give the creator
an occasion to look for sense symbols and to trace out the story in audio-
visual monogram. The meaning of the film is incorporated in its rhythm,
just as the meaning of a gesture is immediately readable in the gesture itself;
and the film "means" nothing other than itself. An idea is here given in its
nascent state, emerging from the temporal structure of the film as does a
painting from the spatial co-existence of its parts.[47]

To grasp the meaning of the filmic work of art it suffices to perceive the totality of its structures; as John Dewey has maintained,[48] criticism is an act of perception. But unlike Dewey, Merleau-Ponty has fortified himself with the assumptions of gestalt psychology: "For the cinema, as for modern psychology, vertigo, pleasure, pain, love, and hate are patterns of conduct."[49]

As a cultural expression of our own, or modern, times, movie making is in a privileged position to make philosophy live as critical reflection on the state of the world. In Merleau-Ponty's view, "If philosophy and the cinema are in accord, if reflection and technical work have taken the same direction, the reason is to be found in that the philosopher and the movie-maker enjoy a common manner of existence and a certain view of the world which is that of our own generation."[50] But it would be a mistake to deduce from this common occupation that philosophic expression and movie making are the same kind of expression. Merleau-Ponty is here remarking only that movie making is an art, and that the job of philosophy consists in reflection on all primary expressions of the human animal:

It is art's good fortune to be able to show how something becomes significant: not by an allusion to ideas already formed and acquired, but by the temporal and spatial alignment of its elements. A film signifies as . . . a thing signifies; neither the one nor the other speaks to a separate understanding, but engages our power of deciphering in tacit fashion both the world and other men, and allows us to co-exist with them.[51]

As with painting and with literature, the aesthetic object of the film is there not to be thought, but to be perceived.[52] Philosophy enters into the picture as criticism, as an attempt to clarify what has been perceived in the primary instance of perception.

As a philosopher, Merleau-Ponty has been working in this sense. He has consciously avoided the traditional critical task of assessing the worth of particular art objects—Dewey calls this "legalistic" criticism—for a generalized description of the manner in which perceived objects begin to take on meaning. The reader who would benefit by this kind of criticism is not presented with the meaning of the work or a statement of its worth: he is put into a position to assume the pose which will allow the work to communicate with him.

Aesthetics as Criticism of Criticism.—As pointed out above, the objection may be made to Merleau-Ponty's doctrine of criticism that it errs in generalizing upon what we have called "paradigm cases." Can even the most correct and perceptive account of Cézanne's work be set up as an ideal for all painters in all times? The answer to the query has already been hinted: if it were being maintained that Cézanne's paintings or even his manner of painting were to be taken as the touchstone by which the excellence of other painters is to be judged, it should readily be admitted that Merleau-Ponty's critical procedure was deficient. The source of the objection is, however, a misapprehension of the role of criticism in aesthetic communication. Critics sometimes act as if it were their job to assess the worth of particular works of art, presumably by comparison with a standard or norm which describes the eminently beautiful. Obviously enough, except for the case of Plato himself and some of his successors, whom we may call "platonic critics" and who profess to have intuited the very idea of beauty, the critic must remain reticent about the manner in which the knowledge of the idea is gained from admittedly imperfect experiences. If Cézanne's case has been chosen, it was merely illustrative of the manner in which a painter solves the problems involved in creating works of visual art that we know, from an actual perception, to be successful expressions. If we give up the overt or covert assumption that a critic's purpose is to evaluate or compare one work of art to another, it will be understood that Merleau-Ponty's position is not only not fallacious, but a useful tool for enhancing aesthetic communication. The critic's task is not primarily a normative one—to compare and to judge; but a descriptive one—to point out the unique structures of expressive works of art. Each and every member of an artist's audience has already criticized or judged the work in question by his act of perceiving it.

Consider the case of legalistic criticism gone wrong: the early condemnation of impressionist works because they "broke the rules," or of contemporary paintings because they "don't look *like* anything." Each painting and each painter must be judged on its or his own merits, and this is precisely what one does when he perceives what is there to be perceived in the work. This does not mean, of course, that everyone will be carried away with a given work of art, or that a viewer may remain passive before a piece of masonite or canvas; but whatever activity he engages in before the work must be dedicated to a discovery of its meaning—a behavioral pattern which must be assumed by creator and appreciator alike if it is to be truly said that artistic communication has taken place.

Before considering the nature of artistic meaning, we may observe some of the kinds of viewer activity which will necessitate that the desired aesthetic perception be missed, in principle. For the sake of simplicity I have divided the various attitudes one might take before a work of art into three distinct types: the formalist, or purist; the intellectualist; and, finally, the existentialist.

Traditionally it is the formalists who have relegated aesthetic perception to the rather rarefied airs of a superior universe above and beyond the one in which a creator and an appreciator must live as men. Appealing to a pleasure which is not physical, to a work of art which is not an object, to an attitude which is the unique property of finer souls, the purists reduce art activity to sheer religious ecstasy. Merleau-Ponty accuses André Gide of puristic formalism for his condemnation of Sartre's "committed literature":

If the religion of art will not admit to being mingled with the subtleties of life, it risks becoming a technique of the pretty. André Gide has said, in a sentence which itself is too pretty, "In art there are no problems to which the work of art is not a satisfactory solution."[53]

No more subtle refutation of the purist's attitude is needed than the bare statement that both creator and appreciator are men, and must perceive aesthetic objects like any other object, with the behavioral patterns of men conditioned by the human environment: physical, biological, and cultural.

The second group of maladjusted critics are those we have called "intellectualist." In the main, they are willing to admit that art activity is engaged in by men limited by the human condition. Their error is in the attempt to describe the work of art or its effects by a series of abstract, or scientific, concepts. More often than not these concepts are derived from a context external to the work of art itself. They may be taken from history, from biography, or even from metaphysics itself. Accordingly, there has been a rash of historical or biographical or metaphysical critics. In America at present there is even a group of individuals calling themselves "Christian critics."

The essence of the intellectualist critic is his drive *to understand* the work. In order to gain this so-called understanding, he must apply his analytical tools; but as Merleau-Ponty says, "Analytical thought breaks the perceptive continuity into separate moments, places, and perspectives, and then attempts to find in the workings of the mind that guarantee of a unity which is already in the object when we perceive it. It is the same with the continuity of culture, which is first broken up into units and then reconstituted from the outside."[54] Merleau-Ponty had learned well the lesson of Bergson's distinction between analysis and intuition. As a method of analysis, intellectualist criticism fails. The misleading emphasis of historical, biographical, or metaphysical critics tends to lead the attention away from the work of art itself. Cultural history and art criticism have nothing in common:

> Criticism may very well confront one manner of literary expression with another and classify a type of narrative as one of a family of many others; but this work is legitimate only when it has been preceded by a perception of the novel, in which the particularities of "technique" are mixed up with those of the total project and its meaning, and when its purpose is to explicate to us what it is we have perceived.[55]

In this quotation Merleau-Ponty is reminding the historical critic that his task is meaningful only when it is based upon a first-hand acquaintance with the expressiveness of the individual work, and when it leads others to have the same kind of experience. Unfortunately however, historical criticism tries to reconstitute history, rather than, as is proper for criticism, to reconstitute the experience of a work of art.

The same effect may be seen in the work of the biographers who assume that the life of the author is particularly significant for determing the meaning of artworks. Like the historians, in some respect they have been seduced by the scientific concept of cause:

> It is certain that the life [of the author] does not *explain* the work, but just as certain that they are related. The truth of the matter is that *the given work demands a certain kind of life*. From its very beginning the life of Cézanne could find equilibrium only by becoming associated with a work to be accomplished in the future, the latter became the project of the former, and the work began to appear premonitorily in the life of the author; but it would be a mistake to take these indications as the cause of the work: they merely make a single venture of both the life and the work.[56]

Paul Valéry had already reversed cause and effect in the biographical critic's venture: the life of an author is not so much the cause of the appearance of the work as it is the effect of its appearance.[57] Biography, like history, must be brought back into a perception of the work if it is to be aesthetically useful: "It remains entirely possible that, by reason of his nervous weaknesses, Cézanne was able to conceive of a form of art valid for all. Left to himself, he knew how to look at nature as only a man can do. The meaning of his work cannot be determined by his life."[58] The critic of Cézanne must lead us to see what Cézanne has seen, and what he has seen is there in his work to be seen by all.

For want of a better term, the final form of intellectualism to be considered has been labeled "metaphysical." Most examples of this kind of criticism will be found in the writings of philosophers who scrutinize art to find problems of philosophy rather than to illuminate the problems of art. In his preface to the Mellon Lectures in the Fine Arts delivered before the National Gallery of Art in Washington, D.C., during 1957, Etienne Gilson goes to great pains to assure painters that he is looking at painting to learn something about philosophy.[59] The very title of his published volume, *Painting and Reality,* will bear out this contention, and illustrates one manner in which a philosopher may approach the subject of art. Rather than a philosophy of art, or an aesthetics properly conceived, Gilson has laid out a field which might be called "philosophy in art." This, too, is a valid intellectual discipline; but it is not especially well placed for calling attention to aesthetic facts. After all, in looking at art to find examples of philosophical problems, it is or should be no surprise that the researchist will find metaphysics at the expense of art.[60]

Thus the question arises whether Merleau-Ponty himself is engaged in the philosophy of art or whether he too is merely looking for philosophy in art. And the question is not any easy one to answer, principally because Merleau-Ponty's attitude toward philosophy is not unambiguous. At times he seems to equate philosophy with metaphysics and the latter with system building:

Metaphysical and moral awareness dies upon contact with the absolute because it is constituted, not within the lifeless limits of habitual or anaesthetized consciousness, but by a living connection of me with myself and of myself with others. Metaphysics is not a construction of concepts by which we try to make our lives less susceptible to paradox; it is, rather, the experience we enjoy in all the situations of our personal and collective history and of those actions which, once assumed as our own, transform history into reason.[61]

It would seem to follow, then, that Merleau-Ponty's quarrel is not so much with philosophy as such, as with a certain manner of "doing" metaphysics. This conclusion is borne out when we consider that he, too, has looked into art to find conclusions for his own personal philosophy:

The sciences of man *in their present orientation* are metaphysical or transnatural in the sense that they bring us to rediscover, by means of the concept of structure and the understanding of various kinds of structures, a dimension of being and a kind of knowledge which is forgotten by man in his natural attitude.[62] [Emphasis added.]

In keeping with the "modern" or existentialist trend, he has defined his approach to philosophy as "critical reflection," a method to be applied to all human experience in an effort to recover what has become lost to man engaged non-reflectively in the push and pull of everyday life. Since Merleau-Ponty was a philosopher and not an artist, his work is necessarily a secondary expression, and is at least one degree removed from the activity of art, which he calls "primary" and whose structures he is trying to elucidate. That his concepts, too, are derivative there can be no doubt, and it is fair play to demand of him that he show, not that concepts may form a part of a complex work of art, but the precise manner in which aesthetic categories are already implicit in the more simple forms of art, containing perhaps no symbols of pre-established meaning, but which, whether they do or not, are of the nature of the forms Croce has called "intuitions." If this were done, we would have gone far in the establishment of "an existentialist aesthetic." But this is precisely what Merleau-Ponty has failed to do. The best we can say is that he has used the concepts of gestalt psychology and those of Saussure's linguistics in such a way as to intimate what an existentialist criticism would be.

Consider the following quotation:

. . . the sciences of man (to say nothing of the others) have shown that every bit of knowledge of man by man is not a pure contemplaton, but inevitably an act by which the knower takes up, insofar as he can, the actions of another person; reactivates, by means of ambiguous signs, an experience which is not peculiarly his own; appropriates as his own a behavioral pattern, which belongs *a priori* to the species of man as a kind of sub-linguistic schema or general climate of opinion. He does not form a definite concept, but reforms an experience like an accomplished pianist who deciphers the score of an unknown musical piece: without intellectually grasping the motives of each gesture or movement and without being able to bring to consciousness all the sedimentary knowledge he is using at the moment.[63]

A person who thinks exhibits behavioral patterns without being completely conscious of them; so does an artist. And this is the basis of the claim to "genius" on the part of gifted and creative people. The task which Merleau-Ponty has left undone is to show how "the sedimentary knowledge" is implicit in the act of perception, preferably in a perception of a particular work of art. Had he succeeded in that task, he would have moved from the field of the philosophy of art to that of aesthetics, and criticism proper. That he did not may be laid, perhaps, to his interest in perception itself, rather than in aesthetics per se. Suffice it to note here that an existentialist criticism would go beyond the limits of "metaphysical background," and go far to constitute a basic organon for humanistic research in the arts. It may be admitted that Merleau-Ponty's writings have brought us to the door, but criticism of criticism must be founded on a solid foundation of viable criticism in the first instance. If we are to go through the door, someone must evaluate the existentialistic foundation of the critical edifice. Thus it is maintained that an existentialist criticism is called for and hinted at in the phenomenology of perception, but it has as yet to be worked out.

XI

Aesthetic Theory in Merleau-Ponty's Phenomenology

The philosophical method used by Merleau-Ponty may cause consternation on the part of those uncritical thinkers who are tempted to seek conclusions without support of critical evidence. His initial reflections are long, in theory unending. Moreover, since he interprets philosophy, everywhere and always, as a reflection on a prior experience whether that experience is itself analytic and secondary or synthetic and primary, he is forced to abandon the scientific method as the criterion of validity. The method of science is merely another kind of experience which must be submitted to the test of critical reflection. This is not to maintain, however, that there is no rational test of the evidence adduced for any theoretical conclusion. In every case that test is whether or not a meaning appears to the inquiring individual, and in every case the test must be applied and re-applied. In this system truth is reduced to an unattainable ideal, and philosophy is properly its pursuit. The job of philosophy, then, is to refine meanings, not by empty logic-chopping, but by continual referral of ideas to the conditions of everyday experience. And when the critical reflective method of philosophy is applied to the area of our experiences of art it is called "aesthetics."

The two preceding chapters have reviewed the significance of aesthetics for the human enterprise as Merleau-Ponty saw it. Concerned as it is with the appearance of artifacts which in some sense communicate a meaning to an appreciative audience, aesthetics has two principal subdivisions. One of these is concerned with a general theory of meaning, or linguistics; the other, with the critical application of the philosophic method to more specific cases of meanings acquired in artistic creations.

Aesthetics as a general theory of linguistics may be considered a branch of philosophy traditionally entitled "epistemology"; its central orientation is towards a rational explanation of expression. And in this connection I have compared Merleau-Ponty's doctrine of "corporeal expressiveness" with the idealistic doctrine of Croce. Following this comparison, I have indicated the nature and functioning of various art media in constituting human expressions, and evaluated some current (art) critical doctrines and practices in the light of Merleau-Ponty's suggestion that perception is already criticism— the evaluation and reconstruction of an individual's basic adjustment to his surrounding world.[1] Thus aesthetics as criticism likewise has two subdivisions. The first of these is criticism proper, containing both a doctrine and suggestions for practice in taking the proper stance before the objects of art. Aesthetics in this sense is a method.

In this area, I have criticized Merleau-Ponty for having limited his investigations to "paradigm cases," although this weakness may be explained by the fact that Merleau-Ponty never did prepare a work dedicated solely to the domain of aesthetics. The value of his examination of paradigm cases is the discovery of the categories he has developed for the evaluation of current critical doctrines. This evaluation, given in the second subdivision of critical aesthetics as the criticism of criticism, indicates the sense in which aesthetics is methodology. But since the criticism of criticism calls for valid criticism in the first instance to serve as a criterion of evaluation, and in the first instance Merleau-Ponty's doctrine possesses the weakness noted above, his theory is incomplete.

When we turn to an evaluation of the whole of Merleau-Ponty's three-fold aesthetics, the first characteristic to strike an academician's eye is the great number of sources used in its construction. To the academician familiar with the development of contemporary aesthetics this will mark the work as eclectic; to a non-academician, such as Simone de Beauvoir, the same work will be called "academic." The property of both of these epithets is a concealed value judgment; both contain an element of pejoration, and both beg the question. An eclectic is one who sifts and winnows, who selects elements from the theories of others to construct his own. There is hidden the implication that the eclectic must do so because of an inherent lack of originality. To the non-academician, an academic is not only one who teaches or communicates a theory, whether his own or someone else's, but also one who is unable to make a successful adjustment to the conditions of life outside of academia. Still more hidden is the implication that the academic refuses to leave the ivory tower because he is unable to make theory work in practice.

In the sense in which both of these epithets are applicable to Merleau-Ponty's doctrine the pejorative implications are decidedly inappropriate. In the first place, although it is true that his theory is eclectic since it has been culled from various sources, he has shown a high degree of originality in developing a thorough-going phenomenology of perception, which maintains the continuity of man with his vital and physical sub-structures. The task of evaluating the theory cannot be limited to the application of a question-begging epithet. What the critic must do is to ascertain the validity of Merleau-Ponty's use of sources. When this is done, when the context of the theory's development is made complete, there may appear still other sources whose influence on the theory is not made entirely manifest, even by the author himself. This is a point to which I shall return—at the risk, it is true, of being considered "academic" myself.

But when one has taken away the spurious pejorative meaning of the word "academic," it will be seen as an appropriate description of Merleau-Ponty's aesthetics. It is quite true that he developed his eclectic theory in the pursuit of his academic role. The critical test here is whether or not he was a good teacher; this can be decided at least in part, on the basis of whether or not what he had to say to students is in some sense true. But to arrive at this decision, we must evaluate at least the central contention of his doctine of expression.

The truth is that Merleau-Ponty is not always as careful as a scholar might be in the use of his source material. There are times when his method of critical reflection becomes less critical than reflective. In a hurry to establish his own interpretation of another author's doctrine he is sometimes guilty of reading into, rather than reading the meaning out of, the original text. Simone de Beauvoir has already called attention to this tendency shown by Merleau-Ponty in his criticism of Sartre's politics.[2] The same tendency may be found in his aesthetic writings. Consider a case in point.

The following quotation is his paraphrase of Saussure:

Saussure was able to show that every expressive act becomes significant only as a kind of modulation of a general system of expression and only in insofar as it is differentiated from other linguistic gestures. The marvel of the fact is that before his time we knew nothing about this; and we still forget it each time we speak, especially when we speak of the idea of Saussure.[3]

From it Merleau-Ponty concludes:

This proves that each partial act of expression, as an act common to the whole of language, is not limited to expending an expressive energy accumulated in the medium of language; the truth of the matter is that the partial act recreates the expressive power of language as it creates language itself by forcing us to varify, within the evidence of a meaning which is lent and received, that speaking subjects can go beyond signs to their meanings.[4]

The first of these citations contains two elements: a rather accurate statement of Saussure's position, and a complex evaluation of it. We are told that Saussure's work is original, that it is little known, and that when it is known it is not known too well.

The irony of this last evaluation is that it may be applied to Merleau-Ponty's own case: his conclusion is not good Saussure. The man who said language is like a piece of paper whose two sides are composed of thought and sound such that if one were to cut the paper it would be impossible to make separations in the one without making them in the other[5]—unless by dint of abstraction one prefers to talk "pure psychology" or "pure phonology"—would never talk of "going beyond" a sign to its meaning. Saussure had defined language as a system of differential signs, each of which constitutes a "value" exchangeable either for another of its own kind or for a "thought," precisely to avoid the artificial abstraction of "sign" and "meaning" from the total sign-function. For Saussure, meaning is given within the internal structures of a sign which is composed of both sonorous material, or sign vehicle, and conceptual idea, or signified meaning. The arbitrary relation of the one to the other is functionally defined in terms of a "form."

Moreover, Saussure's conception of the sign-function, the articulation of ideas in language, is dominated by a rather cloudy idealism inimical to Merleau-Ponty's own metaphysical orientation. Most assuredly Merleau-Ponty cannot be led to agree that there is a realm of thought floating in an amorphous mass above an equally amorphous mass of sounds. The model Saussure sketches re-poses all the old bogeys of the traditional theories of preception, including the relation of mind and body which Merleau-Ponty has defined otherwise in *La Structure du comportement*. The least that should be said for Merleau-Ponty's adaptation of Saussure is that he has tried to replace the lat-

ter's idealism with phenomenology; the most one can say is that both
men are rather rigorous linguistic gestaltists. Merleau-Ponty, at any
rate, has given the impression that the perception of any form, no matter how the elements of that form are constituted, is an original act of
conferring significance. But this is a proposition that must be explained and tested in another place.

Although his reading of Malraux, the second principal source of
his theory of indirect language, seems adequate and his criticisms
cogent, Merleau-Ponty is not quite so profusive in his recognition of
other writers whose works bear favorable comparison with the doctrine we have been considering. One can find at least three such
sources of special interest to the student of recent French philosophy.

In the field of aesthetics, both Alain and Valéry have considered
the central poblem of art theory the explanation of the manner in
which a novel signification is made to inhabit the world; for each
of them aesthetic communication is non-verbal, an aesthetic idea
being the discovery of an artist who manipulates a physical medium
to make a significant form. Each distinguishes between conventional
and primitive signs—a distinction which closely parallels that drawn
by Merleau-Ponty between a secondary and a primary expression;
and Merleau-Ponty's favored expression of an effective perception,
"taken in its nascent state,"[6] may be found in the aesthetic writings
of both.[7] The fact of the matter seems to be that all three of these
men were interested in that marvel of the universe by which a man
becomes conscious of himself, and thus were led to the discovery of
a primary aesthetic fact: that works of art are like a language, yet
are significantly different from any conventional language.

In the field of general philosophy, Bergson readily comes to mind.
Even Merleau-Ponty's interpretation of meaning as a corporeal phenomenon is prefigured in Bergson's doctrine of philosophical intuition. Following a denial that philosophical writing is a superior kind
of system building on the part of one person who uses as building
blocks the ideas already expressed by another, Bergson says,

One might as well say that one speaks by first looking for words which are
then to be sewn together by means of a thought. The truth is that above the
word and above the sentence there is something much simpler than either: a
meaning, which is less like a thing thought than it is a movement of thought,
and less a movement of thought than a sheer direction.[8]

And, finally, it is contended that Bergson's distinction between analysis and intuition[9] could be in part responsible for the shortcomings noted above in Merleau-Ponty's theory of criticism. We shall examine this contention in the concluding chapter.

Whatever Merleau-Ponty has to say about critical aesthetics will stand or fall on the validity of his "phenomenology of perception." I have maintained that Sartre failed to establish his aesthetic doctrine because he begged the question of perception, and Merleau-Ponty will be found to have failed if his doctrine does not survive the test of critical reflection. We may grant his distinction that perception of the things of the world differs when the perceiving subject already possesses the conventional meanings of a pre-existent language; he himself cites ample experimental evidence from the psychological research of others to prove this point. The question is whether or not his own explanation of an "effective or primary perception" is adequately described in his doctrine of expression as bodily movement.

We may divide the question into the following moot points: creative perception is a movement of the human body; the movement of the human body organizes a new object, which is a form; the significance of a form is inseparable from the organization of the elements which enter the complex; "understanding" a form is likewise a bodily reaction: the receiving organism re-creates the form and understands its significance in a way analogous to that in which it was originally created; and the new or created form becomes a cultural object which changes the character of the environment in which both organisms feel newly adjusted.

A word of discussion on each of these points.

It must be remembered in the following discussion that Merleau-Ponty has already poisoned the wells of the opposition. He has made reference to scientific means of refutation impossible by placing the discussion at the level of pre-rational human experience. It is obvious, for example, that the first and second points make the overt assumption of a theory of mind and a theory of objects respectively. According to Merleau-Ponty, referral to the concepts of psychologists and physicists cannot possibly be offered either to substantiate or to refute his contention. Science in its various forms is a secondary expression derivative by means of successive abstraction from the kind of experiences he is treating, and as such must be continually verified by reference to "the structures" of ordinary lived experiences. Does this mean that his theory is irrefutable?

In one sense, yes; in another, no. The sense in which it is irrefutable has been explained in the preceding paragraph. It is not irrefutable in the sense that no counter-instance of his generalizations may be found. The restriction to be observed here is that any counter-instance must come from the same level of experience as the one he is describing. To say that some experiences are pre-rational is not to say that they cannot be known; it is to say, however, that a general principle does not apply to the case in point. Consider the example of Zeno's paradoxes. The mathematical principles of the infinite divisibility of space and time would seem to indicate that Achilles cannot overtake a tortoise if the animal has a head start. To conclude from this that motion is impossible contradicts the rather apparent fact that Achilles does win the race, and he does so merely by running from here to there. Merleau-Ponty would conclude from this that the problem had been falsified for having been conceived on the wrong level of abstraction. An example of misplaced concreteness, Zeno's paradoxes are readily solved in the action of everyday life. Paradoxes are always theoretical, and philosophy will solve more of life's paradoxes if only the researchist be led to reconsider the actual conditions under which they occur.

A further illustration that discussions of mind and matter have been traditionally misformulated is that Merleau-Ponty's account of mind fits no fixed categories of mental activity. One would expect his account to be classified in the category of mind as an intentional act, following his phenomenological orientation; but he differs significantly from the position of Husserl, who, in spite of his own intention to avoid psychologism, remained an idealist. Among the other categories of mind outlined by Professor Morris,[10] the position of Merleau-Ponty could be subsumed under various heads: mind as process, mind as relation, mind as function. The point here is not that Professor Morris' classification of theories is inaccurate, but rather that the problems of mind and body are not properly handled in unique theoretical fashion; they arise in life, and are solved or not solved in action. Although no clearer insight may be gained into Merleau-Ponty's all-pervading anti-intellectualism, "anti-scientistic" is perhaps a better word for describing his position. This property, perhaps more than any other—including its inception in phenomenology—is the mark of an existentialist philosophy.

It remains to be shown, however, that Merleau-Ponty's doctrine is refutable in that the details of primary expression may be known in at least one sense of this term. The most obvious sense to be considered is that knowledge gained by every animal form in its basic experiences: the kind of knowledge Achilles had of motion because he could actually overtake the tortoise. It is for this reason that Merleau-Ponty refers to the facts of aesthetic knowledge to explain perception, and to expressions to explain perception. Moreover, his explanation avoids viciousness in its circularity because each of his five contentions noted above is born out in the common experience of aesthetic objects. Let us consider the propositions, and list the "facts" they would explain:

Creative perception is a movement of the human body. Aesthetically interpreted, this proposition affords the desired correction to Croce, who had distinguished between "intuition" and "externalization" in art. Both Croce and Merleau-Ponty maintain that there is no aesthetic idea which is not expressed; but Merleau-Ponty's claim that expression is a bodily movement allows it to be said that an artist thinks with his materials, not with ideas that he imposes upon them. And this seems to be sound. The concept of "mute, inglorious Miltons" is an absurdity. Stated another way, the artist's genius is his work. After all, no teacher of art will approve his student's claim to creativity if all the student means by this is that he entertains beautiful aesthetic ideas; no idea is aesthetic outside of some kind of physical or symbolic embodiment.

The movement of the human body organizes a new object, which is a form. In terms of aesthetics, this proposition denies as valid what is known in psychology as a specific response. A form is nothing more than an organization of elements. Since the organization of an aesthetic form contains elements of content and structure, aesthetic forms have rightly been described as concrete.[11] Effective irony and successful allusion or indirect discourse are examples of expressiveness through concrete forms.

The significance of a form is inseparable from the organization of its elements. Scientifically this proposition spells out gestaltism; aesthetically, a theory of expressive form.[12] Mrs. Langer, the foremost exponent of this doctrine in America has been severely criticized for her use of such terms as "symbol," "import," and "vital form." But, convinced of the validity of the doctrine of formalism—when this notion is understood in its concrete sense—she has continued to maintain that an art work symbolically transforms human experience into matrices of feelings which are understood when the artwork is correctly perceived. Two serious difficulties arise in the construction of her theory: the first of these is her assumption that the mind is a kind of transformer,[13] and the second, that the feelings which constitute the import of a work of art are not felt, but only conceptualized. If it is true that the brain of man is not a switchboard, it is equally true that it is not a transformer, or anything else describable in terms of a physical model. Merleau-Ponty's dialectic of orders seems to be a corrective to this element of bad science in Mrs. Langer's theory. Her second weakness has proved in at least one teacher's experience the most difficult to make art students accept, their judgments being based upon first-hand experiences of their own. If a gestalt "means" a feeling, if its value is the conceptualization of feeling, all art is representative in this sense, in spite of her reduction of representation in art to the role of a motif.[14] Moreover, artists and appreciators alike continue to insist that aesthetic feelings are felt, and not just as symptoms of an exhilarating contact with successful works of art.[15] In Merleau-Ponty's words, the feeling is perceived, not conceived in any sense at all. This perception is to be discussed further under the following point.

"Understanding" a form is likewise a bodily reaction: the processes of creation and re-creation are analogous. The aesthetic emotion is the emotion of the aesthetic object, and the emotion is controlled by the structures of the object. This proposition rules out, correctly it would seem, the sentimentalism or outrageous responses of over-sensitive audiences which are "sent" by contact with beauty; it is consistent with art educators' ideas of controls used in creation, and in the possibility of teaching creative activity. It has the further advantage of making the artist, and not the audience, the principal agent in aesthetic communication; but it necessitates a criterion of relevance for deciding which of various responses are controlled by the work. This criterion is supplied by the gestaltist principle of *Prägnanz.*

The new or created form becomes a cultural object which changes the character of the environment in which both organisms feel newly adjusted. This final proposition is of extreme importance for both aesthetics and science. The pregnancy of the expression is the source of its effectiveness as a social force. Scientifically, this last proposition crops up as an assumption of contemporary cultural anthropology, which attempts to re-create "lost" societies by an examination of the artifacts produced within them, and which has noted countless examples of reverence for *objets d'art.* Ceremonial and religious uses of artworks are likewise relevant to the application of this proposition to the facts of our aesthetic experience. In this sense, the words "communication" and "communion" become blurred in the common denomination of their etymological root. Finally, from the aesthetic point of view, our fifth proposition would go far to explain the ever present activity of critics to judge the worth of aesthetic creations, as was apparent in the discussion of committed literature in America and France.[16] Merleau-Ponty could likewise have grouped the evidence of the continuity of culture throughout varying epochs and varying societies—an achievement of Malraux's *Les Voix du silence* —among the facts explained in this proposition.

Only one critical notice remains: to become operative, Merleau-Ponty's doctrine of criticism must be strengthened to overcome the weakness we have noted above.[17] There must be developed a theory consistent with these five propositions which would furnish a viable *modus operandi* for two individuals to perceive a unique aesthetic creation. Until this is done, his theory of perception remains incomplete. More on this will occur in the final chapter.

In conclusion, Merleau-Ponty's aesthetics is both epistemological and methodological, but the methodological aspect of it remains incomplete for lack of a working method to be used as a model of aesthetic perception. It is my contention that this limitation is not insurmountable.

*Since . . . art is a social phenomenon, we shall have to
draw upon our knowledge of social psychology to
illumine our analysis of the individual's experience.*

DeWitt H. Parker
The Principles of Aesthetics, *p. 7*

XII

Existentialism and
Aesthetics Proper

We have traced the development of French existentialistic aesthetics
from the appearance of Sartre's *L'Imagination* in 1936 to the publication of Merleau-Ponty's *Les Aventures de la dialectique* in 1955. It
has been my hope to state the doctrines implicit in the various writings of both authors, to show their continuity, along with any comparisons and contrasts they may indicate, to place the existentialistic
aesthetic theory in the general historical context from which it developed, to interpret that context in the light of its divergence from
the dominant trends of British and American thought, and to evaluate the theory in terms of criteria set forth in the Introduction for
the delineation of a field of inquiry I have called "aesthetics proper,"
as distinct from the philosophy of art and discussions of philosophy
in art which pass for aesthetics in our own time.

By "aesthetics proper" is meant "aesthetics properly conceived."
Fully conscious of the movement from the descriptive interpretation of
"proper" in the definiendum to a normative and adverbial use of the
same word in the definiens, I shall now attempt to qualify the conditions which must be achieved before conceding that aesthetics has
been properly conceived, and so defined.[1]

The first of these conditions is that the theory constructed be true to
the facts of everyday aesthetic experiences, and that the facts not be
tailored to fit the requirements of the theory. The surest way of missing
a good many of the facts to be found in an adequate description of
aesthetic experience is to choose one pole of experience, the creative or
the appreciative, at the expense of the other, and to erect that descrip-

tion into a model by which all other aesthetic experiences are to be evaluated. In illustration of this contention may be cited those critics guilty of intentionalistic criticism, who in describing and evaluating the work of art under discussion tend to favor the artist's experience—and only a part of it at that, since the intention or mental act of the artist may be aborted in any act of its physical expression—and those who avoid the intentional fallacy by favoring the appreciator's experience in face of the same work, but who as often as not fall prone to the equally obvious affective fallacy, by which an artwork is described and judged in reference to the psychological effect it may have on an audience. Both of these positions are fallacies in that each taken alone tends to falsify our descriptions of works of art, and both necessitate a principle of relevance which must be taken from our awareness of works of art. Only that intention of the artist is relevant which is actually expressed in the work before the artist and appreciator alike, and if this is the case the intention and the work are the same; only those feelings are relevant to the work which are controlled by the phenomenally objective structures of the work itself, entering into the intersubjective experience of both artistic communicants. It is for this reason that alternatives to the psychological views of art are usually couched in terms of "the work of art" or of "aesthetic judgment." In aesthetic communication, the work serves to mediate the experience of creator and appreciator.

A philosophy of art, then, becomes a reasoned explanation of aesthetic objects. And with this there can be no quarrel, unless one finds grounds for disagreeing with the metaphysics expressed in a particular philosophy of art. For instance, it suffices that a realist perceive the barest hint of idealism or that an idealist perceive the slightest trace of realism in the description of an artwork for the one or the other to reject as false what was not intended to be a metaphysical discussion in the first place. Some philosophers of art, it is true, have felt it necessary to make metaphysical assertions in order to raise our aesthetic experiences to the level of intellectual comprehension, but that these assertions need be interpreted monistically, as applying univocally to all cases of aesthetic objects, is obviously a misleading suggestion. Consider an example. Novels and poems contain ideas and images as well as a sensuous surface; architecture and music usually do not. An idealistic reference would therefore seem perfectly acceptable in the structure of novels and poems, but out of place in the non-representative arts. Metaphysics which makes claims on aesthetic experience going beyond the correct description of the aesthetic object in question can no longer be called a valid part of the philosophy of art, although one could still pursue the metaphysical or epistemological questions involved in the appreciation of a particular work of art. In the latter case art is merely the locus of a strictly metaphysical or epistemological inquiry. A novelist may apparently hold to a given world view, and he may succeed in expressing that world view in one or the other of his novels; but even if this fact should be pointed out, the critic's task would not be completed, since, presumably, there could be good and bad expressions of the same world view.

The temptation of philosophers is to light upon the philosophy expressed either explicitly or implicitly in works of art. And this is perfectly understandable; philosophy is their area of special competence. He who would become a philosopher of art, however, must enlarge his area of competence. Since his job is to reflect critically upon the facts of aesthetic experiences, he must be sure that his reflection is thoroughly founded in his primary aesthetic experiences. A philosopher of art with no artistic ability is conceivable, but one with no taste is not; it would be preferable, however, that the philosopher of art possess an artistic as well as an appreciative talent to bolster his own philosophical competence. He will fail, of course, if he is lacking in either philosophical ability or in taste, and he may do so if he is not creator enough to follow the artist himself in the construction of the work. He must be at least enough of an artist to comprehend the use of certain techniques as the artist has found them useful in the creation of the work. The task of the philosopher of art, then, is to illumine artistic communication; before proceeding to his philosophical criticism, he must have a comprehension of the manner in which an art work is constructed, a perception of the work, and a vigorous appreciation of the work's value.

But there is more. Aesthetics will have been properly conceived only when the vigorous appreciation of an artwork's value includes an awareness of the various uses to which the aesthetic object, qua aesthetic, may be put. I do not intend the rather obvious and fanciful examples such as would afford a piece of sculpture which may be used for a hatrack, or a novel which may entertain or instruct. Neither of the uses mentioned is characteristically aesthetic. What is intended here are the various differences which occur in the life of an individual or the society in which he lives because of the aesthetic experience in question. Thus the primary difference between the philosophy of art and aesthetics proper lies in the scope of inquiry. Usually the philosophy of art limits itself to a description of aesthetic experience: creation, work, appreciation; it is being suggested here that aesthetics proper be conceived of as having a wider range: to include the description of the conditions favorable to creation and appreciation, and of the various consequences creation and appreciation may have upon social and cultural life in general. Should it succeed in this generous, if not too ambitious scheme, aesthetics proper will afford a working theory of art education and a practical guide to criticism, as well as a program of social change. Admittedly this is a large burden to place upon a single person, but it is not too large a task for a group of researchists who are dedicated to the proposition that aesthetic experiences make a difference in one's life. That they do indeed make more of a difference than is accounted for in contemporary British and American philosophy of art is one of the presuppositions of the present study.

If the first condition of an intellectual discipline is to account for as many of the facts within the field of its interest as is possible, the second is to achieve conditions of control. The difference between "accounting for the facts" and "achieving conditions of control" is precisely that between observation and experimentation in the physical sciences, between description of the present facts and prediction of a future event. Can this demand fairly be made of the practitioners of aesthetics proper? At first blush the answer would seem to be no; since the appearance of an aesthetic object depends upon the working of artistic "genius"—imagination or inspiration—there appears to be an uncontrollable individual factor which defies prediction. As the old saw has it, artists are born and not made; it would be absurd to command a Beethoven or a Picasso to step forth from a mob of peasants. But this old saw, like most old wives' tales, is not necessarily true. It is belied by the activity of art educators who do succeed from time to time in producing creative artists, and children who have been observed to create objects, however childish, when given the opportunity and the expressive materials with which to work. It may be true that one is born or not with creative potential, but that creative potential may flourish or not depending upon whether it is put into a favorable environment. No genius and no imagination can work in a vacuum, however fertile they may be in potential. Moreover, since aesthetic communication is communication, the social dynamics of interpersonal reaction is implicit in the field of aesthetics proper. Traditional philosophies of art have put too much emphasis upon individual psychology, however conceived, to the detriment of an understanding of the social nature of art. The psychology of art is social psychology. Art is favored by some social structures and disfavored by others, and everywhere art tends to create a society if none existed before its appearance. Thus the conditions of control are both physical and social, as well as private and personal, as the old saw cited above has led many to believe for so long.

In view of these elements of control, the aesthetician must construct a theory of aesthetic communication which will allow him to describe the appearance of works of art, as well as the conditions favorable to their appearance; the appreciation of works of art, as well as the conditions favorable to their appreciation; and the existence of works of art, as well as the consequences for man and society of the existence of works of art. When this has been achieved, not only will more people be led to realize that aesthetic experiences make a difference to the lives in which they occur, but aesthetics will have proved that it, too, makes a difference, and may even become a privileged area for the education of a cultivated human individual.

The remainder of this conclusion will be divided into three categories: the aesthetic theories of Sartre and Merleau-Ponty, existentialism as a ground for the proper conception of aesthetics, future developments.

The Aesthetics of Sartre and Merleau-Ponty.—The development of Sartre's aesthetics shows at work anything but a simple guileless fool (Luethy), an "intellectual flatfoot" (Kanapa), an idealistic metaphysician (MacDonald), an empirical psychologist (Dufrenne), or even an aesthetician basing his work upon "certain ontological and epistemological presuppositions" (Rau). And although Merleau-Ponty has abused Sartre with the epithet "mandarin," with its connotations of effeteness and lack of existential commitment, he apparently gave the matter a second thought, having included his former associate in the volume he edited, dedicated to *Les Philosophes célèbres.*

The truth of the matter is that Sartre has always been a man of letters. A novelist and a playwright from his youth as well as a trained philosopher, he was interested in the philosophical problems involved in the literary creations he has made (philosophy in art) and has tried to erect a rational explanation of aesthetic experience in general (the philosophy of art). His earliest works on the imagination and the emotions show him a close student of the phenomenology of Husserl, but one who was incapable of accepting the Husserlian interpretation of the intentionality of images. His *Phenomenological Psychology of the Imagination (L'Imaginaire)* was composed to make clear his disagreement with the master, and included, as part of its conclusion, a description of the object of art.

I have interpreted Sartre's description of aesthetic objects to be consistent with the doctrine of the American pragmatist, C. I. Lewis, and have pointed to its efficacy in giving answers to a number of aesthetic problems: the ontological status of artworks; the pleasure of aesthetic experience; aesthetic communication; the paradox of the actor; aesthetic value; and its corollary, the censorship of the arts. His suggested solutions to these problems show him to be a serious philosopher of the arts, and at least three of them contain the seeds for the future development of an aesthetics proper—aesthetic communication, aesthetic value, and art censorship.

Central to his aesthetic doctrine is the notion that man is free because he is possessed of an imagination, the power to "see" what does not exist or what is not present to a perceiving consciousness. Only *after* this conclusion had been reached in his phenomenological study of the imagination did he conceive *L'Etre et le néant*. Given the conclusion that a literary artist does in fact create an object—ideal, to be sure, since a novel is constructed of words and meanings—which did not exist before the novelist's intentional act, Sartre became interested in the "ontological structures" implicit in the act of free creation. Thus, if the historical order of his works is considered, it will be seen that the dialectics of *L'Etre et le néant,* which are more influenced by Heidegger and Hegel than by Husserl, followed upon his aesthetic conclusions rather than supplying the premises upon which his aesthetic conclusions rest. Ontology became one of the directions his thought had taken from its early aesthetic orientation; another was his theory and practice of literature, principally in his novels and plays and in the direction of *Les Temps Modernes,* the journal of committed literature. At present (1960) he is engaged in further developments of both these lines of thought. He has supplied

the book Merleau-Ponty found wanting on the reconciliation of phenomenological ontology with Marxian ideals and practice,[2] and he
continues to direct his journal and otherwise to live by his pen.

After expositing the epistemological assumptions of Sartre's theory, I have criticized his aesthetics on the grounds that it begs the
question of perceptual knowledge. In doing so, I was criticizing
Husserl as well, from whom he borrows the distinction of perception
and imagination. If in an act of perception a person "reads" an essence from the structures of an object present to its consciousness, and
in an act of imagination a person creates an object to fit the requirements of an essence (*savoir imageant*), then, from a strictly empirical point of view, the imagination must have a prior knowledge of
essences in order to be able to create its object. From the same point
of view, the claim that the imagining consciousness creates both the
essence and the object seems to rely too heavily on the power and
authority of a single act. For an empiricist, of course, the imagination becomes capable of constructing new objects by re-aligning the
elements of objects known in a prior experience.

It was to overcome this theoretical shortcoming that Merleau-
Ponty composed his *Phénoménologie de la perception*. It was prepared, essentially, in his first serious philosophical work, *La Structure du comportement,* dedicated to the metaphysical problem of
psycho-physical interaction. Although Merleau-Ponty refuses to accept the empiricist's theory of knowledge, he does practice his method
of philosophy (critical reflection) to criticize the assumptions of
working empirical psychologists. Reflection, for him, is a rational activity which can only grow out of a prior, pre-rational human experience, just as this prior human experience has been observed to grow
out of "lower" forms of behavior. He gives such a wide interpretation to the notion of behavior as to include the sheer physical reaction
of elemental particles, and traces the evolution of human cultural
activity through a dialectic of orders—physical, vital, and human—
in which various kinds of form—syncretic, mutable, and symbolic—
are organized in the behavior of a living organism. Elementary
knowledge he describes in terms of the structuring of forms which
aid the organism to adapt to and to change an environment. An animal knows, in the most primitive sense of this term, when it adjusts:
itself to an environment, or an environment to itself. The superiority
of human behavior is that the subject may transcend its purely phys-

ical and vital nature in the construction of a symbolic and cultural situation. The role of philosophy is conceived of as a continual critical appraisal of man's development in history.

The Hegelian and the Bergsonian influences on Merleau-Ponty's thought are obvious; the Bergsonian, in particular, become apparent in his second work, *Phénoménologie de la perception*. Applying his revised gestaltism to the facts of perception, Merleau-Ponty concludes that an essence is a conventional or arbitrary name tacked on to an already experienced form of behavior. The first and pre-rational experienced form he calls a "primary expression," which he claims may be analyzed and resynthesized in any fashion whatsoever by a human subject in a secondary expression. Science and philosophy are examples of secondary expressions. Their techniques are analytical, proceeding by convention and arbitrary decision. The sum total of primary expressions of men constitutes human history. Human decisions to erect institutions, to react to or to act in accordance with them, form the subject matter of written history, which is likewise a secondary expression, correct or not insofar as the written record corresponds with the facts of the lived experiences. A primary expression, art is a means of introducing new meanings, new directions in the flow of historical events.

As I have pointed out above, Merleau-Ponty's distinction between primary and secondary expressions closely parallels several other famous distinctions in philosophical theory. Aestheticians will note the similarity with Croce's distinction of intuitions and concepts; linguists, with Alain's distinction between relative and absolute languages; philosophers, with Bergson's distinction between intuitive and analytic methods. We may choose the latter to clarify the weakness of all four—including Merleau-Ponty's.

According to Bergson, the method of analysis is incapable of grasping a moving reality or the endurance of anything which comes into being and passes away. The reason for this inability is that the method proceeds by means of immutable concepts, which are at least twice removed from the reality being treated. Concepts are general, and thus abstractions from individual instances; they are symbols, and thus mere pointers to a certain kind of experience. Any movement in thought which does take place in conceptual analysis is from concept to concept, whereas a vital and meaningful movement must be interpreted as proceeding from concept to reality. This our thought cannot perform. Thus, science may be useful but it is not true, in the absolute sense. Bergson maintained, however, that the mind was capable of having an intuition of the movement of actual duration by a process of intellectual sympathy. The objects of such knowledge, although absolute and true, are found to be useless for further intuitions. Each intuition is a closed autonomous act, yielding the totality of its object, but in relation to no other object.[3] Merleau-Ponty's task is to show that primary expressions may be both true and useful; true in at least the pragmatic sense of producing adaptation of organism and environment, and useful in re-directing the forces of history.

To achieve this end he begins with Bergson's claim that it is possible to move in thought from intuitions to analysis. Once the totality of an experience is grasped, it becomes possible to analyze the whole into its constituent elements. Where Bergson appeals to the method of intuition for the starting impetus to thought, Merleau-Ponty begins with his account of a structured behavioral response. Then, by appealing to Saussure's general theory of linguistics, which presupposes a system of communication between organisms, he links primary expressions, intuitions, with the individual *parole,* that is, individual assimilation or modification of the existing *langue vivante.* Thus intuitions and concepts, primary and secondary expressions, interact in such a way as to enrich or impoverish the established language. Art, in this system, assumes its role as a primary expression, and must be accounted for in a general theory of linguistics; the philosophy of art then becomes a thorough-going theory of knowledge. But a theory of knowledge is itself a secondary expression, and must be further scrutinized by the critical reflection of philosophy. This second step in philosophical analysis of the primary expressions of art is criticism. Finally, in its last analysis philosophy becomes the criticism of criticism. Presumably there is no need for further levels or orders of criticism, since philosophical reflection stands to correct itself by referring its symbolic structures to the conditions of the primary experience itself. If all critics of art were as self-critical as they are critical of works of art, moreover, there would be no need for a second order criticism in the first place. It is for this reason that some aestheticians of the British and American tradition limit aesthetics to the journeyman's task of clearing up confusions in art-critical language.[4]

Merleau-Ponty's difficulties are two: he must show how criticism is effective in aesthetic communication—that the analysis of an intuition or primary expression may yield an intuition, a process thought to be impossible by Bergson—and how primary aesthetic expressions become effective to reconstitute the general cultural environment of the artist and his society. It is at this point that the notion of an "aesthetic institution" must be introduced. And to develop it, I move to the second set of conclusions.

Aesthetics Properly Conceived.—The limitations of traditional philosophy of art may be demonstrated by the enshrinement of an object of art in the museums of great cities, where its usual fate is to die for a lack of contact with the lives of people. Once an aesthetic object is looked upon only as an end in itself, as an autonomous object inhabiting a nether realm which one may approach only by adopting the proper attitude, its enclosure in a place outside of contact with the daily lives of a population is thought not only proper, but necessary. This is not to suggest that aesthetic judgments on the uniqueness of art objects and the finality of their value are the only reasons for the existence of museums. Some artworks are patently unique; others are too expensive to be bought by the average person; and in all cases, museums serve a positive function of storing and displaying valuable objects, while educating an audience to the quality of these as true works of art. From time to time a museum may set aside its permanent collection in order to exhibit works of contemporary artists, thereby assuming the function of a gallery in displaying artworks for sale, and in this way it may function to bring an artist and a buying public into contact. What is being deplored is the separation of art experiences from the ordinary kinds of experiences which make up the lives of men. As Dewey has pointed out in *Art as Experience,* this separation is abetted by attitudes of certain aestheticians toward the "fineness" of works of art. It is significant that Merleau-Ponty, like Dewey, may be said to have begun his aesthetics with an account of "the live creature."

The corrective to the misleading and narrowly defined approach to the philosophy of art may be found by refusing to break the art process into its constituent elements: creation, work, and appreciation. Even by starting with the work as central to the communication, aesthetics tends to move into a blind alley. If realism does not do justice to the aesthetic object, then it has been supposed that idealism does; and where both realism and idealism can be shown to fail, pragmatism or phenomenology has stepped into the breach with the refusal to admit distinctions of mind and body in the processes of real life. The question then arises, where do we go from there?

The obvious answer to this query is to consider the process as a whole; the art process is a communication and necessarily implicates a society of men. I propose, then, to consider art activity as a kind of social behavior, and to describe it in terms of an institutional means of intensifying the quality of human existence. Immediately there arise a host of difficulties for the understanding of this concept. First of all, a museum is obviously an institution, possessing the material means of serving its designated social function. Like churches, states, and schools, a museum may be called an "institution." Why must we revert to an older and rarer acceptation of the term?

Precisely because the sociological approach to the study of institutions, which proceeds by classification and abstraction of the necessary and sufficient conditions for the naming of its objects, exemplifies what has come to be known as the "essentialist fallacy." Is a post office an institution? Is a school? a library? a business corporation? Yes, then what do they have in common? Is each a means of social control? If so, does each control social intercourse in the same way? Is each organized in the same fashion? Questions could be proliferated in this way almost *ad infinitum*. The difficulty of this essentialist and absolutistic concept of social institutions is that it tends to set the institution over against the individuals whose conduct is controlled—and, indeed, liberated—by the organized, corporate structures set up in functional relationship by the institution in question. Society is not, after all, merely a means of controlling individual behavior, and is not composed merely of men and institutions; "society" is a functional concept used to refer to the lives of men in the institutions which have been created by them and which may be changed by them as the need arises.

It becomes clearer at this point that my position is based on an older meaning of the term "institution." Elijah Jordan and G. H. Mead have used the same acceptation in their now classical works on social psychology.[5] And for those with a propensity for dictionary authority on the usage of words, it may be pointed out that the essentialistic, "sociological" sense of the term is listed seventh in the Oxford English Dictionary, while the Mead-Jordan concept of social process is listed sixth; in Webster, we fare even better: the sociological concept is listed eighth, although in its broadest sense it is listed as fourth and our alternative is listed as third; it reads as follows: "That which is instituted or established; as . . . (b) A practice, law, custom, *etc.*, which is a material and persistent element in the life or culture of an organized social group. . . ." The point here is not to become engaged in a philological dispute, but to indicate that even a secondary or unusual meaning of a term should be accepted if that meaning is more useful for continued research than the more usual one, even if the more usual *were* the primary meaning.

A second difficulty one might run into when trying to comprehend the notion of an aesthetic institution, is the common assumption on the part of many artists and people knowledgeable in art that it is primarily an individual expression, that an artist must be misunderstood to be effective, that he must separate himself from social controls in order to achieve the ultimate in personal identification with his work. We recognize the picture of the bohemian artist living on the margins of society, alone and inspired, and although starving, too proud to be "caught dead" accepting the benefice of a sponsor or academy. That this picture is still the image of their own personalities held by many contemporary artists, and that it fits the general scheme of the arts in the late nineteenth and early twentieth centuries is too patent to deny. But an admission on both counts does not mean the death of our concept.

Consider the following reasons: many successful artists were well adapted to the social conditions of their own times—Corot is an example of an artist having lived an average bourgeois life in times of artistic rebellion—and although the patron-artist relationship was for the most part destroyed by the French Revolution, artists tend today to be supported by universities and philanthropic foundations.[6] Even the dadaists who quixotically decided to destroy art by creating art to shock the bourgeoisie (*épater le bourgeois*) succeeded in satirizing the falsely aesthetic claims of a basically philistine culture, and in doing so they performed their social function rather well. By acting against society, they succeeded in changing some of the attitudes of the organized social whole. Their mistake, like that of the philistines and of the essentialist sociologists whose concept we have noted above, was to assume that there is no continuity between the organized responses of individuals and the formal customs of the general society.

To show this continuity was, I believe, the intent of Merleau-Ponty's first lecture to the Collège de France, when in describing the function of philosophy in general he proclaimed,

Corresponding to the reciprocal relationship of the will seeking to express itself and the means of expression there is another, between the productive forces and the forms of production or, more generally between the forces of history and [human] institutions. Just as language is a system of signs, which have meaning only relatively to each other and which may be recognized as possessing a certain value that stems from their use in the total language, each institution is a symbolic system that [human] subjects incorporate into their behavior as a certain style of conduct. Institutions function globally, as configurations, and need not be conceived [in order to be effective].[7]

The value of the suggested acception of the term "institution" is that it allows for a continuous development in the organization of human responses. There is no really individual conduct aside from the insignificant release of tensions within individual organisms, just as there are no completely determined examples of socially controlled response. All human activity is more or less individual, which means to say more or less social. The one element of truth cloaked in the bohemian's attitude is that art activity is the one form of social control loosely enough defined to permit a maximum of individual expression. Social customs, habits, and laws often conflict with the individual drive to self expression; and individual self-expressions, be they habitual or merely instinctual, often work to change the customs and laws. What I am arguing for is a reconsideration of the history of art and aesthetic judgment in such a way as to show the social utility of art, without destroying the autonomy of art. And it appears that this can be done only in a society of free institutions.

Examples may elucidate this contention; certain institutions grow so large as to dominate the other forms of behavior in a given society: the Medieval Church, the modern autocratic states, and in our own society, business. As often as not, a religious judgment, a political judgment or an economic evaluation of a work of art may conflict with a purely aesthetic judgment. Each may tend to downgrade or upgrade the value of a work of art. But if so, the judgment is based upon non-aesthetic grounds, and the free institution of creation and appreciation has been interfered with. Paintings have been condemned as sacrilegious and praised as devout without regard to aesthetic excellence. The same non-objective paintings of American action painters have been called "capitalist decadence" by the Soviets and "communist woolly thinking" by American philistines. And probably the most glaring example of interference of one institution with the free workings of another is contained in the "movie industry," whose moguls have succeeded in degrading the noble device of *ars gratia artis* into a greedy pursuit of *ars gratia pecuniae*. The American movie industry has descended from *Intolerance* and *The Birth of a Nation* to *I Was a Teen-age Werewolf* and *The Sexpot Goes to College,* from the aesthetically expressive to the baldly meretricious. Is censorship called for? And if so, by whom must the censoring be perfomed?

The decision as to what legal controls are desirable on truly pornographic works of art is currently being attempted with a modicum of common sense: courts are asking recognized critics for an informed aesthetic judgment differentiating works of art from public obscenities, and so are giving credence to what we have been calling a "free aesthetic institution." The assumption is that a well organized society keeps its institutions in well ordered design, allowing each to function as it is best capable of functioning to permit the maximum development of the human personality. Once the aesthetic institution is put into its rightful place within the corporate structure of society there will be no need for misunderstood geniuses; genius will find its expression in the drive to aesthetic excellence, and society will cease to kill off some of the most valuable of its members. There is no pre-established reason why artists cannot form a profession which may function as other professions in the structure of the global society. When they do, and if they do, they will be remunerated in proportion to the service they render to society. This does not mean that they must become propagandists; indeed it means that they must not, for should they propagandize another institution at the expense of their art they will have ceased to function as artists.

So much for a cursory description of the aesthetic institution. To what extent have the existentialists followed its program? I have already indicated that three of Sartre's conclusions fit well into the program described; they are not conceptually unrelated: aesthetic value, aesthetic communiction, and the censorship of the arts.

If we may assume that Merleau-Ponty has cleared up Sartre's difficulties concerning the theory of perception and that Sartre was patently in error to have generalized upon his description of representational works of art in his treatment of "the aesthetic object," we may consider the value Sartre attributes to literary creations in general society. The literary artist creates, according to Sartre, by imagining what does not already exist; in so doing he posits a value by engaging his own freedom in the present situation. There is nothing mysterious or excessively metaphysical in this description. The author is said to imagine his situation to possess a form other than it has; to do this, he must know the situation and be able to project the value, or desirable state of affairs, on the basis of that knowledge. His creation is the embodiment of that value, which is accepted or rejected by the reader who likewise must engage his freedom in a similar fashion in order to understand the work. The artist proposes an end; the reader disposes of the proposition. The result is free communication.

Aesthetic communication he describes as a community of ends. When the author has formed and the reader has per-formed the work, the two consciousnesses intend the same object; but neither loses any of its autonomy. By joining in the author's "disclosure of being," the reader gains a new manner of seeing. A community of ends shared by autonomous subjects, the literary creation is said to exemplify what Immanuel Kant could place only in a transcendental realm as the locus of interaction of free, self-determining wills. Sartre's merit is to have brought the realm of autonomous subjects back into the arena of social action, where all truly significant communication must take place. Literature is a political act because it may produce this communication, and once produced, the shared value may be further embodied in the social structure each of the participants inhabits with the other.

From this point, the path taken by Sartre's aesthetics may be seen to diverge even as it continues in the same general direction of the program of aesthetic theory I have proposed. First, its continuation in the general direction: since literature may be said to produce a community of ends on earth whenever its success as a communication is manifest, any interference with the communication is an act of tyranny. If the literary arts are censored, the freedom of its participants cannot be engaged; in consequence, the censorship will work for a continuance of the *status quo*. No society which claims to be free, that is, ruled by the very will of the persons entering into its structures, can allow itself the privilege of official censorship. Sartre rendered literary criticism a service when he pointed out the duplicity of the "guardians of society" in the treatment of Jean Genet, and the highmindedness of those recognized authors who interceded in Genet's behalf in order to secure his release from prison. The point was not that a gifted writer should not be placed in prison for a crime: in Genet's case, petty thievery and perversion; but that Genet's works are poignant treatments of thievery, betrayal, and perversion, which may produce the sympathy with the lower depths necessary for a reversal of society's own self-righteous morality. The value of Genet's literature is not that it may institute a society of thieves or perverts, but that it will allow society to understand how criminals are made in, and sometimes by, society itself. The morality involved in making perversion a crime may become an object of discussion following its successful treatment in works of literature. Whether Genet should have been freed or not is a case of legal justice, and any judgment on it must be based upon the legality of the question. It would be romanticism of the worst order to exonerate any person of a crime if the only reason for the exoneration were that the person involved is a talented author. The question is not whether Genet was a succesful *comédien* but the extent to which he was a true *martyr*.[8]

Genet's case exemplifies Sartre's interest in the "bottom-dog." One may agree with Sartre that insofar as Genet's expression is of an imaginary character his books are not a crime, and indeed that their reading may produce the kind of sympathy necessary to re-examine the status of existing law; further, it seems apparent that for a society to honor a perverted author but to abhor his perversion is an anomalous state of affairs. If we put aside the question of legality concerning Genet's release from prison, we may even be forced to admit that a work of art may be good because it has a bad (disapproved) subject matter. We use the word "good" in the last sentence as meaning "possessing desirable social consequences," as tending to the community of ends of free individuals. Lastly, it goes without saying that Genet's works may have had this consequence only if they were, in some aesthetically technical sense, good; otherwise we should have to judge them as outrageous pornography.

Sartre's case for the value of literature begins to diverge from our stated ideal when he departs from the area of fine literature. Although he has written explicitly enough that the social function of literature has nothing in common with propaganda, his interest in the "bottom-dog" has led him to espouse causes which have been formulated in terms of "exploiters" and "the exploited," the bad guys and the good guys. Given the present status of the social sciences, Sartre's position may seem extremely naive. We may grant his point that society, as well as individuals, can and do live in bad faith, without maintaining that class conflicts determine the evolution of societies, but it seems silly in our own time to maintain that bourgeois and proletarian forces control the course of history. And the assumption that society is composed of classes in strife is found not only in his series of articles on "Les communistes et la paix," but is maintained in his recent, *Critique de la raison dialectique,* the first tome of which has appeared, described by its author as a "theory of practical groups."[9]

If we may take American society as an example of a bourgeois dominated one, it will become apparent how members of both so-called classes function within institutions; and many times they do so without regard to economic classification. For instance, the bourgeois and Democratic Wilson created his "New Freedom" in order to continue the work of his predecessor, a bourgeois and Republican Theodore Roosevelt, who had announced in his own "New Nationalism" a "square deal" for the common man against the economic trusts of his time; more recently the high-bourgeois and Democratic F. D. Roosevelt, uniting the best of these two prior administrations, created the New Deal to prove himself a "traitor to his class," as he was called by the people he himself called "economic royalists." The moral of this story is that the history of society is not determined in this hotbed of bourgeois capitalism by a series of class contradictions; not so much, that is, as by institutional structures, which may be altered by the vigorous activity of bourgeoisie and proletariat alike. In the American society, capital and labor have found a means of getting along in a single institution. The battle Marx found going on in capitalist societies has in one sense been won without the destruction of either class, since bourgeois and proletarian now function together in a singly defined institution. And in the sense in which it cannot be said to be won, that classes can be said truly no longer to exist, the structure of the economic system is flexible enough to allow, and to utilize, class differences freely, without even the dictatorship of the proletariat. There are too many men in both the United States and Russia who fall into no clearly defined class relationship. If Hugo of Sartre's *Les Mains sales* could have been talked out of his class consciousness, he might have been found to be recuperable; it was not so much that he was ignorant of psychology, but he and Sartre both were rather poorly acquainted with social psychology.[10]

There is hope that Merleau-Ponty's writings contain the corrective to Sartre's aberration. The clearest indication that Merleau-Ponty has tried to supply an aesthetic theory which would fulfill the deficiencies noted in that of Sartre is his emphasis upon the perceptive quality of aesthetic experiences. It is not sufficient, for example, to point out that Sartre was in error to have generalized upon the function of the imagination found in our experiences of representational works of art. Although it is quite clear that not all works of art are representational, and that therefore the imagination does not always function in the same way in our experiences of artworks, it must be further shown that perception does always function at least in an analogous fashion in the contemplation of works of art whether they be representational or non-objective in character. The point may be made by referring to abstract works in which some subject matter appears, but changed in a manner suitable to the artist's vision of it. In an abstract work, the subject may be changed only by a significant manipulation of the surface materials implicit in the art genre concerned. Paintings become abstract when their surface qualities change the value of the representation as it would be given in the exactness of "naturalism." Any change in the representation considered as a picture of something as it would be in the state of nature must therefore be "understood" in abstract paintings by a perception of the surface qualities by which that change has been enacted; and although anything of a visual nature may be represented in an abstract work, whatever is represented in abstraction has only that significance which the painter's treatment accords to it. Moreover, since it is manifestly impossible to represent nature exactly in that a three-dimensional object must be delineated on a two-dimensional surface even in a *trompe-l'oeil* painting, the same may be said of a naturalistic painting. In this sense, all paintings are abstract; and they are "understood" by a perception of their style.

Malraux, too, describes style as the expressiveness of works of art; but in so doing he tends to abstract the style of a work from its representative content. By criticizing Malraux's notion of style, Merleau-Ponty explains that a truly significant style is describable only in terms of the manner in which a certain subject matter is treated. Thus style is not something placed upon a given content, or a filter through which the content may be said to be poured; it is the formed matter, the content as formed or the form inherent in the content. Merleau-Ponty's notion of aesthetic form is that of a concrete and significant object.

Taking a further note from Ferdinand de Saussure, Merleau-Ponty relates the notion of a concrete form to the evolution of significant discourse. As a speaker always has at his disposal an indefinite set of fixed concepts with which to express himself, the painter has an indefinite set of visual forms supplied by nature itself. Each of these sets of fixed representations supply only the background of an individual expression. In developing a personal style, an individual speaker or an individual painter may effectuate changes in the conventional means of expression; and what he has to say, in every *parole* which is truly *parlante,* may change conventional usage for the better or for the worse. Living languages evolve, just as styles of painting have been observed to evolve; they do so by an intimate kind of interaction between what has already been instituted in the conventional language, on the one hand, and the personal or individual use of pre-existing conventions on the other. It is in this way that painting exemplifies an institutional involvement. Languages grow from an arbitrary decision to formalize one's behavior, with respect to the sounds of vocalization; and painting is an analogous extrapolation of the physiological process of seeing. Quite obviously, when language is applied to what is seen, as in the case of the physical sciences, there will arise the concept of a single universe, which may itself be erected into a regulative principle of further reasoning, as it has been erected into principle by the heuristic assumption that nature is everywhere and always the same.

Merleau-Ponty would correct the traditional theories of knowledge, based upon the uniformity of nature or upon the uniformity of the reasoning process itself, by pointing out the abstract character of these two assumptions. The method of the physical sciences and that of formal logic itself is a conventional extrapolation of man's method of seeing, which is everywhere and always visible on the surface of his artifacts. Our attempts to understand the *voices of silence* may lead us, as it led Malraux, to compare art expressions in such a way as to find a precedent for the one under discussion; but, as Merleau-Ponty has pointed out, we should be in error if we deduced from the phenomenon of historical precedence the existence of a universal genius guiding the work of each individual artist. What the "museum without walls" actually shows is the institutional limitations of an individual's expression. In fine, the individual is limited by his corporeal structure and the use he makes of it (the individual) in reconstructing his physical, vital, and cultural environment (the social). If this interpretation is correct, even the physical environment of an individual is to an extent a social construct, in that the singleness of the universe is a concept deriving from the usage of conventional symbols. As G. H. Mead has expressed it, a symbol becomes significant when two individuals react to its stimulus in the same way.[11] And if this is the case, an understanding of symbols must be found in the patterns of behavior which describe the comportment of the individuals engaged in social intercourse.

It is not clear, however, that Merleau-Ponty wishes to consider individual works of art as a kind of pre-rational symbol; he prefers the term "primary expression." And in our own moment within the development of history, primary expressions are principally reactions against the socially codified "secondary expressions" defining "culture." Philosophy is the conscience of history, continually referring the findings of other secondary expressions to the conditions of the primary and pre-rational experiences they are intended to describe, interpret, or explain. The philosophy of art is in consequence dedicated to a continual criticism of the primary expressions of practicing artists; in the first instance, it is criticism, and in the second, criticism of criticism.

From the foregoing sketch of the development in Merleau-Ponty's aesthetic thought, it may be stated that his primary contribution to the pursuit of aesthetics proper is to place the discussion of art in a context in which its social implications may be made explicit. Sartre's scheme which considers literature as a political act was noted to have done the same thing, but limited as it was to a discussion of the social value of representational works of art it laid itself open, in spite of Sartre's disclaimers, to the criticism of having reduced art to the status of propaganda and the novel to a *roman à thèse*. Since Merleau-Ponty's philosphy of art places the emphasis upon the surface qualities of artworks, his theory is not so easily misinterpreted. What Merleau-Ponty left undone and what he needed to do in order to make clear the social emphasis implicit in his doctrine, was to analyze the aesthetic institution in such a way as to isolate the special social function served by that institution. In a general way this purpose may be stated as the development of novel meanings; for a precedent to this kind of analysis one might recall Mead's interpretation of the religious and economic institutions, dedicated respectively to the expression of universal neighborliness and the exchange of surplus goods.[12]

Dedicated to the creation of novel meanings, artists are quite understandably apt to be misunderstood. Many prospective members of the artist's audience are not prepared either by birth or by education to participate in the artistic communication; and it is the function of critics, who are so prepared, to lead an audience to the fulfillment of the artistic communication. While Merleau-Ponty has expended some effort to give examples of criticism in his consideration of the work of Cézanne and of the media of philosophical literature and cinematography, he failed to provide a method of critical procedure.[13] The demand he puts upon philosophy to criticize first attempts at criticism, moreover, would be easier to justify had he done so. Given the state of the arts as we know them, with practicing artists usually at war with carping critics, it may be suggested that this difference between artist and critic suffices to indicate the need for effective philosophical criticism.

It should not be inferred from the above account that a critic need be a third man intervening between artist and his audience. The artist may himself criticize his own work, as indeed he must in order to be aware of the value of that work; and each member of the audience must criticize the work, perceiving it as a whole, in order to understand its message. Artists are right, however, in insisting that the work is capable of carrying its own message; Merleau-Ponty gives support to this claim by insisting that the work of art must be perceived to be understood. But not all members of a prospective audience are equally perceptive, and those who are may serve to mediate the two experiences, defined as the construction of the work and its correct understanding. Finally, since the critic lays some claim to a "correct understanding," his own work is not exempt from further criticism. In general outline, then, Merleau-Ponty's aesthetics seems sound.

Future Developments.—It was stated above that a theory of knowledge that distinguishes intuitions from conceptual analysis, or primary from secondary expressions, faces a difficulty in explaining how an intuition may be analyzed into concepts for the purpose of resynthesis in the experience of the person who seeks to understand the intuition in a second instance. According to Bergson, the method of analysis is incapable of supplying a knowledge of enduring realities; Merleau-Ponty, whose distinction parallels that of Bergson, seems to face the same difficulty. In terms of our aesthetic institution rather than those of the theory of knowledge, the question then arises as to how a critic must proceed to communicate what some member of the artist's audience may have failed to understand on first contact with a work. Merleau-Ponty has offered examples of criticism, but no method of procedure for critical analysis. Can this method be supplied?

The answer is in nowise apparent, but I think it is affirmative. One may grant Merleau-Ponty that a work of art is a unique act of introducing a novel significance into human culture. The facts that this act produces an object which is perceived at the same time that a subject understands its significance (The significance of a gestalt is the organization of its elements), and that its significance relates to no other object, do not preclude analysis of some sort. What cannot be translated into discursive concepts is the significance, which must be perceived to be understood. The job of the critic, therefore, is not to state what an artwork means; but rather to show how it is constructed, and of what it is constructed, so that a third person may grasp its significance in an act of integral perception. Works of art, like human personalities, have no essence, no nature which determines what they must be; but they are not for this reason subjects[14] or even quasi-subjects.[15] If one were to apply metaphysical language to their description, one would be tempted to call them "individuals." What must be applied to them is not a conceptual or essential analysis, but an existential one. What the critic must possess is not a series of categories, which result from classification of previous artworks, but, if they can be found, the structures which are implicit in the organization of the present artwork.

Merleau-Ponty's examples of criticism illustrate this point. Each of them may be said to emphasize the fact that a critic must be armed with a knowledge of the medium, since the medium itself constitutes one of the limits conditioning aesthetic expression.[16] In more traditional aesthetic theory, discussions of both idealists and realists illustrate this contention. Idealists have emphasized the function of the imagination in creation to such an extent that some aestheticians have described the creative act as entirely mental, as if an artist created his works with ideas rather than with materials; and realists have countered with an overemphasis upon the materials, as if an artist were not possessed of a mind. The truth of the matter seems to be that artists create by thinking with materials; and to be an artist one must learn to think in terms of the symbols of a given art medium.[17]

Expressions of this guide to critical practice are not lacking in the literature of the British and Americans or of the French. Alexander's lecture on "Art and the Material,"[18] like Alain's *Système des beaux-arts,* states that an aesthetic idea is a discovery; and both of these derive in one way or another from Kant's dictum that aesthetic judgment is reflective and not determinant. In the first the "concept" is sought for a given intuition, while in the second intuitions are sought to be subsumed under a given concept. Nor are there lacking manuals in the philosophy of art which exploit the idea that aesthetic perception may be trained by a consideration of the properties of a medium: in American aesthetic literature there are Parker's *Principles of Aesthetics,* Weitz's *Philosophy of the Arts,* and Langer's *Feeling and Form;* and in French, Alain's *Système* and Souriau's *La Correspondance des arts.* One of the best ways to counteract too much "philosophical" discourse on the arts, with its emphasis upon essential and categorial determination, is to introduce the student of aesthetics to the study of a given medium, preferably in a studio with students in the applied arts. As often as not, the philosopher of art will be led to exchange his propensity for essences for a practical concern with the problems involved in manipulating expressive materials for the discovery of individual aesthetic ideas. Merleau-Ponty's criticism of the media of painting, literature, and the movies is in line with this educational program.

But a sound education in the expressiveness of materials is but the first stage in the development of aesthetics proper. As I have defined the term, material or medial education is co-extensive with the philosophy of art, which culminates in the elaboration of criteria for aesthetic judgment. If aesthetics proper is to embrace a wider expanse, the philosopher must be led to consider the consequences of aesthetic judgment. The aesthetic institution may not without some peril to its own existence be isolated from the other institutions of societies.

The multiform questions of value at stake in the conflict of aesthetic judgment with the workings of the other institutions must therefore be met. If I suggest that it be the philosopher of art who must widen his range of interest, I do so on the grounds that the philosopher of art is qualified by his training in philosophy and in art not only to make the bridge between those two disciplines, but to defend the autonomy of the art institution against the claims of other institutions on the behavioral patterns of individuals. As Merleau-Ponty has maintained, philosophy is the constant critique of cultural institutions. This has been its historical role, although at the present time the predominant tendency of British and American philosophy is to limit its scope to the narrower ranges of linguistic institutions, studying either the language of the plain man or of his sophisticated fellow, the scientist. I am arguing merely for an extension of this process to include a study of the "language" of artists when they are speaking in their accustomed "voices of silence."

It is not claimed here that the adjudication of conflicts between aesthetic judgment and other forms of institutional behavior may be decided in a univocal way. There must be a particular judgment on each case of conflict, just as there must be a particular judgment on each case of aesthetic expressiveness. I do maintain, however, that the problem of integrating aesthetic activity into the wider social whole will not be successfully handled until aesthetic activity is conceived of as having an institutional nature affecting the general social life as well as the individuals implicated therein; and when a conflict arises between various institutions, it is the organization of society itself which must resolve the conflict. The spokesmen for the aesthetic institution are none other than artists, critics, and with the kind permission of these, the philosophers of art who have pushed their discipline to the status of an aesthetics proper. In terms of the existentialists, aesthetics must become committed, and to something more than the fineness of an aesthetic product. If this means that more emphasis must be placed upon the social psychology of art, then 'tis a consummation devoutly to be wished. The field is there to be developed by whosoever may wish.[19]

Reference Matter

Appendix A

Mikel Dufrenne on the Phenomenology of Aesthetic Experience

Having concluded the description and evaluation of the phenomenological account of aesthetic experience as found in the writings of Sartre
and Merleau-Ponty, I must now append to my treatise a short review of
the major work of Mikel Dufrenne. A two volume work, it bears the
title, *Phénoménologie de l'expérience esthétique,* and is inspired to a certain extent by the same writings whose merits and limitations I have been
attempting to gauge.

Dufrenne indicates the extent to which the writings of Sartre and
Merleau-Ponty have influenced the development of phenomenology in
France, when, quite early in his text, he explains,

> It will be seen that we are not stringently following Husserl in any literal
> sense. We understand the word "phenomenology" in the sense in which
> Sartre and Merleau-Ponty have acclimated its usage in France: the description
> of an essence, which is defined as a signification immanent to the phenome-
> non and given with it. The essence must be discovered, but by an unveiling
> of the truth and not by a jump from the known to the unknown. Phenome-
> nology is applicable primarily to the human sphere because in it consciousness
> is self-conscious; and that is the very model of our conception of phenome-
> nal existence: the appearance as an appearance to consciousness of a mean-
> ing.[1]

About his inspiration, then, there can be no doubt. One would expect
from this that Dufrenne's phenomenological description of aesthetic
experience would follow rather closely what I have already done, and
that, in consequence, the need for the present work would be seriously
undermined.

A number of reasons militate against this supposed consequence. First
is the fact that Dufrenne has borrowed heavily from other writers, not

359

all of whom have taken the phenomenological point of view: among others, they are Souriau, Lévinas, Alain, Kant, and Heidegger. Secondly, Dufrenne's purpose is the construction of a complete aesthetic theory in phenomenological terms. When he uses the texts of Sartre and Merleau-Ponty, he does so with the aim of assimilating their doctrines in the general framework of his own theory. He is extremely critical of Sartre, and seemingly unaware of the explanatory power of Merleau-Ponty's doctrine of expression. He is not interested, moreover, in the completeness of the theories he assimilates. Thirdly, he insists that although aesthetic experience may be treated from either the producer's or the consumer's point of view, it is more fruitfully considered from the vantage point of the aesthetic contemplator than that of the artist, as maker of the work of art.

In the evaluation of his doctrine I shall consider at greater length each of these critical differences from my own position. For the purposes of the present inquiry, which is devoted only to the gist of Dufrenne's argument, I have divided the subject into five parts: the object of aesthetic inquiry, its method, principal sources, conclusions, and critical evaluation.

The Object of Aesthetic Inquiry.—Noting that recent French aesthetics has taken a turn towards a theory of creation[2] in order to avoid the obvious errors of what he calls "psychologism," and what has come to be known in American aesthetic circles as the intentional and affective fallacies, Dufrenne is skeptical of the results obtained to date by the heavy emphasis placed upon the making of a work of art. His case may be summed up in the following way: although the emphasis upon the artist's activity is designed to avoid intentionalism on the one hand and sentimentalism on the other, it does not guarantee that the aesthetician will succeed in avoiding these pitfalls; indeed, the more one is interested in creative activity itself, the more one is inclined to find an explanation in biography and historical antecedents. That this charge is misleading becomes apparent when one considers the actual writings of both Alain and Valéry,[3] who have been most responsible for producing the change Dufrenne has noted. He misses the point, further, that both of these writers were already working in the tradition established by the third Kantian *Critique,* according to which creation is discovery, and an aesthetic idea, an intuition for which no adequate concept may be found.

Unfortunately for the coherence of his doctrine, Dufrenne is as much influenced by the first *Critique* as by the third. The schemata he develops in the hope of providing a rule for aesthetic analysis may function in a cognitive judgment, but would be denied by Kant as aesthetically effective since they may apply to the work of determinant, but not of reflective judgments. In the former, it will be recalled, a concept is given and is applied to the sensuous manifold of the intuition, while in the latter the sensuous manifold is given, with no rational or empirical concept being adequate to classify its content or to embrace its meaning. Instead of noting the aesthetic influence of Kant, Dufrenne borrows heavily from his epistemology. It is for this reason, perhaps, that he interprets Kant's dictum that genius gives the rule to art as an invitation to consider the character of genius in abstraction from its activity. Consider his reasons for preferring the gallery point of view.

First, a "poetic" genius may seem a very mediocre person. We may recall Sainte-Beuve's astonishment on meeting Henri Beyle, the rather fumbling personality whose genius was published under the name of "Stendhal." Secondly, if a person is a genius, the attribute is freely and correctly accorded only as an inference from works of genius to the quality of mind capable of producing such works. Thus a judgment on the work is a prior condition to the recognition of genius. Merleau-Ponty would make no distinction here: the genius of an artist is his work, nothing more and nothing less. Thirdly, even if aesthetic contemplation is less spectacular than creation, it too has a clearly specifiable character; and taste is as requisite as genius if aesthetic communication is to take place.[4] But the same criticism may be made of the concept of taste as Merleau-Ponty has noted for that of genius. It is an error to abstract one moment of aesthetic communication from the others—if only it were agreed that the phenomenon studied by aesthetics is aesthetic communication, mediated by works of art; the preference for an analytical point of departure may then be justified on the grounds that the work is central to aesthetic communication, and that the total phenomenon is more clearly viewed from the standpoint of the vehicle of communication than from that of the mind sending or receiving the message. It could be argued, further, that the communication takes place between artist and his audience via the aesthetic judgment of works of art, which is the same whether the work is contemplated by the one making the artwork or by the person who merely appreciates what has already been done by someone else. And the condition for the sameness of aesthetic judgment is the objectivity, or at least intersubjectivity, of the work. The point being emphasized here is that Dufrenne might have made his case for the supremacy of aesthetic judgment without laying down the smokescreen against the views of the more operational aestheticians like Alain and Valéry. Both of these men would have freely admitted that an aesthetic judgment completes the act of creation.

Moreover, Dufrenne's own point of view is not without a host of difficulties; but to be fair, it must be stated that he is well aware of them. Distinguishing between the *work of art* which is the physical artifact as it is fashioned by the artist and the *object of art* which appears to a viewer on the occasion of contact with the work, Dufrenne proceeds to enclose himself in a logical circle. He is trying to explain aesthetic experience by reference to a unique object of art, and finds that this latter can be explained only in terms of a unique aesthetic experience: the veridical object of art is one which appears within an adequate aesthetic experience. Dufrenne admits the circle, but denies that it is vicious. And this, primarily because the "work of art" and the "object of art" are different concepts. That the object of art should appear only in an aesthetic experience is not a surprising fact given the phenomenal character of aesthetic perception: consciousness and its object are given simultaneously in every perception, as Sartre and Merleau-Ponty in their fidelity to Husserl have maintained. The real problem is to decide what counts as a work of art, and for the answer to this puzzle he can do no more than to use the plainly empirical decision to accept as a work of art whatever is normally taken to be such. Although some borderline cases may arise, they may be excluded on principle; and it is unthinkable that everything taken to be a work of art should be excluded on this basis.

Dufrenne needlessly complicates his case, however, by appealing to the "opinion of the better."[5] Such an appeal opens the question of norms and preferences and "conditioned liking" which he hopes to avoid. His whole discussion of "beauty" has as its purpose to lay aside the axiology of aesthetic experience.[6] Whereas axiological predicates may name the quality of an aesthetic experience, they do not produce a phenomenological description of aesthetic objects. I am merely pointing out here that the distinction between the work of art and the object of art may afford the third term necessary to destroy the logical circularity involved in the description of the object known only in aesthetic experience; but if it does, the price to be paid for the distinction is that the aesthetician must then pay close attention to the work of art as a sensuous object, made in the creative activity of the artist. And this is precisely the position Dufrenne claimed was of less value when the question arose in connection with the "operational" aestheticians.

For his own reasons, then, he has chosen to study aesthetic experience from the standpoint of the viewer's activity. But instead of characterizing aesthetic experience as a contact with works of art—our knowledge of which has a purely empirical basis—which allows a distinctive aesthetic object to appear, he starts with an eidetic description of aesthetic objects, thereby presupposing that effective contact has already been made with the works.

The Method of Aesthetic Inquiry.—As Sartre and Merleau-Ponty have practiced it, phenomenology is a method of inquiry into human reality and not a metaphysical system. It entails nothing more than a description of the essential properties of the objects isolated in the experience of an observer. In matters aesthetic, one first has an experience, that is, intuits or becomes aware of an object and its essence; then, following an act of reflection, completes the inquiry with an exhaustive description of the object and its essence. Ideally, then, no phenomenological account of the aesthetic object in general is possible, nor desirable in particular. As a uniquely significant creation, each particular art object must be intuited for what it is, and is not to be classified as a mere token of a certain type. Hence any attempt to go beyond the descriptive characterization of a particular experience immediately projects the inquiry into a transcendental sphere; beyond criticism of *an* object, one is supposed to find the eidetic character of *the* aesthetic object. Such an extrapolation of the method of phenomenology had already been outlined by Kant, who gave the name "transcendental deduction" to the study of the conditions making possible an experience of a certain type. Thus, in answering the question, Under what conditions is it possible for men to have experiences of the type x? the aesthetician's method becomes that of transcendental deduction. Finally, in addition to this second step, there may occur the process of metaphysical speculation, which would attempt to ascertain the ontological significance of aesthetic experiences. Dufrenne's method runs the gamut; if his doctrine can be called "phenomenology of aesthetic experience," it is only in the fundamental sense of the term. He gives no analysis of a particular work of art, although he names many. His eidetic description is of the genus of works of art and of objects of art, and his transcendental and metaphysical deductions are based upon the description of the essence he claims to have intuited.

The structure of Dufrenne's work follows this assumed threefold division of the aesthetician's labors. Volume I is dedicated to the phenomenology of the aesthetic object and to an analysis of the work of art. Since the existence of an aesthetic object is understood to be conditioned by the execution of a work of art, the study of the latter may be taken as the first step toward the transcendental deduction, which investigates the conditions of the possibility for a given experience.

Volume II contains a phenomenological description of the kind of experience in which the aesthetic object appears, and thus gives the correlative, in phenomenological terms, to what has been described as proper to aesthetic objects in Volume I. Phenomenology would ordinarily end here; but Dufrenne proceeds once more to the level of transcendental deduction, re-introducing the a priori that phenomenology was originally intended to avoid. The metaphysical deductions are given in the final two chapters of the second volume.

Roughly, then, half of Dufrenne's work is dedicated to phenomenology, and the remaining portion is divided, in a ratio of three to one, between the transcendental deduction of the conditions making possible an aesthetic experience, and his own attempts at metaphysical speculation. Our aim will be the assessment of the phenomenological portions of the work, starting with the sources Dufrenne found in Sartre and Merleau-Ponty.

Principal Sources.—Dufrenne considers Sartre's reduction of aesthetic experience to a phenomenon of the imagination as unsuitable to the richness of the experience. And since his own account of the field of aesthetic inquiry is divided about evenly between a theory of the aesthetic object and a description of the conditions under which it may be said to appear, his criticism may be divided into two corresponding sections. I shall reverse the order, and treat the conditions of aesthetic experience first.

Sartre erred, according to Dufrenne, in drawing a hard and fast line of distinction between the perceptive and the imaginative attitudes. It will be remembered that for Sartre the perceptive consciousness intends a real object of the spatio-temporal continuum we normally call the real world, while in imaginative experience, consciousness intends an unreal or absent object which may appear only on the margins of the real world. Dufrenne notes two theoretical difficulties arising from this distinction: first, the explanation of perceptions, which always intend more than what is actually given in the several profiles of the object perceived; second, why the imaginary object need be conceived as "unreal," in precisely the sense Sartre has attributed to this term. A few words on both of these difficulties, which are not unrelated to Dufrenne's metaphysical orientation.

Admittedly we perceive more than we see. What is the phenomenological interpretation of this experience? According to Sartre, who follows Husserl on this point, some conscious acts are composed of empty intentions which correspond to states of anticipation having or lacking a future fulfillment. Thus what one sees may be taken as a hyletic content which comes to be formed by an intention, demanding further experimental content if the original "perception" is to be verified in further experience. Strictly speaking, of course, the concept of an "empty intention," is itself empty of significance, since it entails the existence of a form without a content. Husserl was saved this inconvenience by his doctrine of the independence of essential knowledge from our knowledge of empirical fact. He tried to show this independence by appealing to the functioning of the imagination (*Phantasie*).[7] Unfortunately, however, and on this point Sartre follows Husserl, the imagination cannot function without intending some *kind of object*. If a tree is not given in experience, then at least the form of a tree is given to the imagination. And this form might be clear and distinct, or fuzzy and blending into its background. As we have objected to Sartre we shall object to Husserl, that the imagination must be preconditioned to some knowledge of a given essence before it may serve to organize a manifold of impressions to fit its character. Husserl uses the term *Ideation,* and Sartre, *savoir imageant* to admit this point. Both should have remembered Descartes' speculation in the dream hypothesis of the first *Meditation,* that should man be possessed of an imagination so powerful that it could form objects having no resemblance to the objects of the real world, then for its objects to be of an imaginal character, visual in this case, and appear to a given subject, color must be given in the experience; and if color, then space. Hume was working in a similar vein when he visualized the co-existent points of external space to be purple: they had to be of some color, if they were to be perceived. The point to be registered here is that no intention is entirely empty.

Dufrenne merely states that Husserl and Sartre play with the meanings of "empty" and "full."[8] What I don't see in a given perception I fill in with imaginary objects. But if this is the case, then Sartre is faced with another difficulty: to explain how an unreal object—or an absent one, albeit present in its absence—can be conceived to fill in the vague outline of the essence which is fully present and fully real. The question is a metaphysical one, and Dufrenne refuses to follow Sartre into the relations of figure and ground, the "nihilation" of the present by the absent, and at rock bottom, the dialectics of being and nothingness. He would seem to be correct, however, in his implication that Sartre's theory of the imagination is groundless without the support of his phenomenological ontology. And one might suppose that it is for this reason that *L'Etre et le néant* was composed after *L'Imaginaire:* to supply the lacking ground.

Dufrenne's second criticism reflects this refusal to follow Sartre into the paradoxical ways of being and nothingness; he questions the conception of an imaginary object as unreal. He would suggest "pre-real" to indicate the anticipatory activity of the imagination as it functions to fulfill the broad outlines of unclear perceptions. If our perceptions are false, then, as Alain indicated,[9] we have imagined that we saw what in fact we did not. The distinction Dufrenne wishes to bring out is that between *Einbildung* and *Phantasie* in German, "imagination" and "fancy" in English. Sartre, according to Dufrenne, has made a single function of the imagination, creation, to encompass the whole, anticipation-creation. And, as I have pointed out in Chapter II, the imagination cannot be separated radically from our perceptions. When we imagine that we see, we are anticipating what is possible to be perceived clearly and distinctly. If this were not the case, it would be impossible to conceive how our empty intentions become fulfilled, and how literature as imaginary creation may be said to reveal, or uncover some aspect of the real world. Dufrenne concludes from this that the imagination is always involved in aesthetic perception; we shall see how in a further section of this appendix.

Correlative to this criticism of Sartre's account of the experience of imaginary objects, Dufrenne has given an evaluation of Sartre's description of the ontological status of aesthetic objects. The difficulty arises, once again, from Sartre's radical distinction between the imagination and perception. According to Sartre, the aesthetic object is neither a representation, a psychic entity, nor a thing, a real object. As an imaginary object, it is intended by an attitude of consciousness which denies the relevance of the real world without for that matter assimilating it as an object immanent to itself. Always in situation, human consciousness may accept or reject its impressions of external reality; standing before a portrait painting, one may become aware of the physical properties of the canvas and pigments, or one may become aware of the person whose portrait is presented in the painting. A carpenter and an art critic do not exhibit the same attitude before the physical thing. Yet, there is always the physical thing to be perceived. Sartre calls it the "analogue"; what can be made of the analogue doctrine in terms of aesthetic perception?

Dufrenne finds two difficulties, both of which have been pointed out in our discussion of Sartre's phenomenology. In the first place, Sartre has used as his model of explanation the phenomenal characteristics of a portrait-image. The question immediately arises as to whether this model may be extended to non-representative forms of art. And, in the second place, if it cannot be applied to non-representative forms of art, can we give any credence to its specious applicability to representative arts? There is, for example, another attitude besides that of the carpenter and the art critic before a portrait painting. If one were to consider the attitudes of the subject or of the person interested in the likeness given in portrait, we shall discover that such persons are interested primarily in the exactness of representation, and if not that, at least in the degree to which the likeness flatters or "fails to do justice" to the subject. And these attitudes are as non-aesthetic as that of the carpenter, who is inter-

ested, qua carpenter, only in measuring the painting's physical dimensions for crating and shipping it to another location.[10]

The physical painting taken only as an analogue for the imaginary
presence of its subject is, then, merely the occasion or "motivation" of
the aesthetic experience. Referring to an external thing, or situation, its
"meaning" is external to itself. But if it is possible for an aesthetic perception to have meaning when there is no representative content in the
work of art, on what grounds can it be said that the meaning of a representative piece is limited to its external signification? The answer to this
query may be found, it is suggested, only by reconsidering the phenomenology of perception in such a way as to make a place for a meaning
which is intrinsic to the work. Thus, contrary to Sartre's attempt to find
a *tertium quid* between the existence of things on the one hand and
mental or psychological contents on the other, Dufrenne is led to accept
the existence of the work of art as a thing in its own right, not a mere
analogue of another, and bearing a meaning which is not based upon the
relation of resemblance. He is, however, unwilling to go the whole way
with Merleau-Ponty and describe the object entirely in terms of perception,[11] but conceives the problem as one of explaining how the aesthetic
object can be at one and the same time a thing and a meaning existing
outside of my control—the work is already made—but which makes its
appearance by virtue of my aesthetic attitude—the phenomenal character
of contemplative experience. We shall examine this possibility in a following section.

It may be of some note here, however, to indicate the cavalier manner
in which Sartre's theory is linked with that of Husserl. True, Sartre
makes allusion to empty and fulfilled intentions, and retains Husserl's
distinction of matter and form within an intentional act. But to see
nothing but this similarity is to have missed what Sartre was aiming to
do in his work on the imagination. In *L'Imagination* Sartre had indicated
that he could not go along with Husserl's statement that an image and
a perception have the same matter, and that the difference between the
two was one of form. And it is for this reason that he undertook the
writing of *L'Imaginaire,* to show that images and perceptions differ in
the degree to which matter is taken from the perceived world, from the
inner world of bodily movements and feeling, or from both of these
worlds. And it is from a description of the function of the imagination
in its various forms that Sartre has derived his own theory of the imagination. To say, as Dufrenne does,[12] that Sartre's analyses hardly leave
the realm of the empirical is to say that he is not phenomenological—
that is, Husserlian—enough;[13] and this is to go back on his own stated

intention of giving an analysis of aesthetic experience more in keeping with the phenomenology of Sartre and Merleau-Ponty than with the original doctrine of Husserl himself.

The tone of Dufrenne's last criticism may recall one of the earlier American attempts to evaluate Sartre's contribution to aesthetic theory. Catherine Rau begins her article by stating that Sartre had given "a clearly conceived and emphatically stated contextualist view of art,"[14] and then moves on to say that he could achieve no more than he did because of his ignorance of psychology. According to her, Sartre was not empirical enough. She concludes her account of Sartre's theory with a pathetic plea of ignorance on her own part: "His aesthetics, in so far as he has a single settled view, is formulated to accord with certain ontological and epistemological presuppositions which it is not in the scope of the present study to examine."[15] As long as his critics persist in their refusal to follow the lines of his argument taken as a whole, there is need of the kind of study we have undertaken.

Dufrenne's debt to Merleau-Ponty is deeper, perhaps, than is made explicit in the documentation of his text. His motive for consulting Merleau-Ponty's phenomenology was, as pointed out above, the theoretical impossibility of separating radically the function of the imagination from that of perception in describing the appearance of objects to conscious subjects. Since Sartre's theory of the imagination is haunted by the specter of idealism by which consciousness is said to be constitutive of its objects,[16] and since Merleau-Ponty proposed a phenomenological theory in which he claimed that subject and object are reconciled at the level of experience an organism is capable of having of its "body proper," the transition from Sartre to Merleau-Ponty is quite natural. Moreover, since Sartre's weakness is due in part to his uncritical acceptance of Husserl's doctrine of the fulfillment of empty intentions, Merleau-Ponty's contribution to phenomenology will be measured to some extent by the way in which he departs from Husserl's accepted terminology and method of inquiry.

That Merleau-Ponty has established a new direction to phenomenological inquiry is readily perceived in Dufrenne's threefold analysis of Merleau-Ponty's position: First the transcendental reduction—the last, which places consciousness in relationship to itself following the earlier "phenomenological" and "eidetic" reductions—is a patent impossibility; as Sartre had already pointed out, consciousness is always pre-reflectively self-conscious, and any attempt to bracket off the world and the realm of essences on the level of reflection will always find consciousness already intending some kind of object. Secondly, the non-reflective relation between consciousness and its object is always lived, and given to the whole organism, not just to intellect or to feeling. Finally, intentionality, therefore, is not a mere psychic act; it is, by experience that one has of it, a project in which man's drive to knowledge of himself in abstraction from his situation as history is self-defeating. What one attains in this project is a subject and an object which are already correlated in a still more primitive experience than the one in question. I have indicated this last point in explaining Merleau-Ponty's "anti-intellectualism," which is nothing more than his attempt to face up to the "given" of intellectual or philosophical inquiry. And de Waelhens has shown how Sartre's phenomenological ontology has failed to give an adequate explanation of this given pre-reflective, and thus pre-rational, experience.[17]

In order to make good his claim that subject and object are given already related in a prior experience, Merleau-Ponty has gone through the analysis of the structure of behavioral patterns. Central to his explanation is the re-interpretation of gestalt psychology. A form, or gestalt, is not merely a configuration of physical stimuli, but rather of the subject-object, which is the object of philosophical reflection. As indicated above, any separation of subject from object or object from subject is the result of an arbitrary distinction or an abstraction from lived reality. Merleau-Ponty's analysis of the methods and presuppositions of the behavioral sciences was undertaken to establish this conclusion.

When the first or phenomenological reduction is practiced, the person who brackets off the rest of the world finds himself intending an object which is always "already there." He does not constitute the object in his act of perception; the perceived object is *en-soi–pour-nous*. It exists in itself, but for a perceiver. That the object should exist in itself means, for Merleau-Ponty, that it is present to consciousness, and not a construct of consciousness; but since the object is never exhausted in a single perspectival perception, its status as object is ambiguous. It is present, but not entirely so, and for this reason no perception is entirely clear and distinct. Each and every perception demands unlimited criticism, or philosophical reflection. Finally, philosophical reflection is based ultimately upon the lived experience of a "body proper." Consciousness is of an object because a consciousness is not distinct from the corporeal nature of man which already enjoys physical commerce with the objects of the real world.

For a more concise statement of Merleau-Ponty's position one would have to look a long time; not even his own inaugural lecture to the Collège de France is so explicit or so precise. Interested only in constructing his own phenomenology of aesthetic experience, Dufrenne cites Merleau-Ponty's results without following the intricacies of their development. Thus his own work calls for, rather than supplants, a treatise of the kind I have been constructing. It remains to show how Dufrenne has used Merleau-Ponty's theoretical framework.

In short, he takes the description of objects of perception as an *en-soi–pour-nous* as definitive of what Pepper has called "the object of criticism."[18] Aesthetic perceptions are controlled by what is objectively present to an observer, and relatively invariant from observer to observer. The variance is explained by the structures of the work as it has been made by the artist (*l'oeuvre d'art*); the purely subjective differences in the psychological make-up of various perceivers is underplayed in Pepper's scheme because of the "considerable degree of uniformity in the perceptive capacities of different spectators."[19] Merleau-Ponty has been more explicit in the statement of the causes of this uniformity. A necessary condition for the perception of an object of art is the physical existence of the artifact; the structures of the work of art guide the perceiver's attention before which the phenomenal object appears. It need only be added that the physical presence of the work of art is "known" pre-reflectively, in Merleau-Ponty's view, by an attitude of the body proper.

Dufrenne accepts this account of the work of art, but rejects the pre-reflective relation between body and object as constitutive of the affective content of the object of art, the phenomenal appearance of the work. But in so doing, he likewise rejects Merleau-Ponty's solution of the feeling-form paradox.[20] Merleau-Ponty could say that the feeling is in the form, because the form is a configuration of the subject-object complex, and bodily attitudes and movements, feelings physiologically considered, are properly conceived as parts of the subject as it lives its body-proper. The reason for Dufrenne's disagreement may be made clearer by a quotation:

Meaning is truly comprehended only when the body is in accord with the sign, when it is present, from its innermost depths, to the aesthetic object. But that lived presence is not the feeling; it is rather the condition of the feeling. And not the only condition at that; for it is not sufficient that the object be present to a perceiver, it must likewise be represented. The corporeal grasp of the object is at first only a condition of conscious perception, and by virtue of the feeling it arouses. Thus the feeling loses its factual immediacy, even if it retains its formal immediacy: it is immediate when the object is given to us and we are available to its charm, but there still must be an object given along with it.[21]

Dufrenne has introduced the distinction between the object and its feeling in order to account for a "thickening of the surface"; starting with the physical presence, he moves to an aroused feeling, to a represented object, to an expressed "world." Thus, although he admits that Merleau-Ponty's account of the physical presence of the work oi the art is accurate, he rejects the doctrine promulgated by Merleau-Ponty that each corporeal perception is a complete expression. The question therefore arises as to whether he can accept what he has, while rejecting the rest. I shall postpone the answer to this query until the sketch of Dufrenne's entire theory has been completed.

In moving to the second manner in which Dufrenne has made use of Merleau-Ponty's phenomenology, I am forced to state that on neither of the following points has Merleau-Ponty been given full credit. With respect to Merleau-Ponty's aesthetics, Dufrenne's index and notes are mysteriously incomplete. I have found at least four such lapses, the explanation of which may be either the fact that Merleau-Ponty's doctrine was not considered as a complete aesthetic or that Merleau-Ponty himself was heavily indebted to other writers for these features of his thought.

The first lapse concerns the description of an aesthetic form as a concrete structure, as opposed to a bare outline or manner of presentation. In stating that the meaning of a work of art is not a simple organization of sensuous elements, Dufrenne maintains that "The aesthetic object is one whose matter continues to endure only if the form is not lost."[22] As for Merleau-Ponty, meaning is equated with perception of a gestalt, when the notion of the gestalt is enriched by the inclusion of a preordained relationship between the structures of the perceiving organism and its environment. The sign-signification unity is all of the expression for Merleau-Ponty; but in Dufrenne's scheme this same form gives rise to a second configuration, that of object-representation.

Secondly, in commenting upon Schloezer's treatise on the music of Bach, Dufrenne states, following Goldstein, that the unity of the meaningful perception constitutes the unity of the aesthetic object.[23] Judging the work as a presentation, as Merleau-Ponty does, and not as a representation as Dufrenne insists we must, the meaning can only be measured in terms of a bodily reaction, and our knowledge of works of art is limited by its presence to our perceptive apparatus. The following quotation is pure Merleau-Ponty:

. . . if meaning can unify and constitute the object, the reason is that it develops from the object's innermost depths and that it does not reside uniquely in any representations the object may propose. The work can be said to be one only on the condition of receiving a unity more profound than that of logical coherence found in a rational meaning, a unity which comprehends both the sign and its significance and gives the work its true personality. It is that unity which constitutes the ultimate peripateia of the aesthetic object's meaning, and without which the object exists only as a mediocre sign, deprived of both its rigor and its fullness.[24]

Once again the question arises whether there is anything above and beyond this meaning to be perceived; to state, as Dufrenne does, that "the aesthetic object doesn't have a form, it is a form"[25] would lead one to suspect that the theorist would accept Merleau-Ponty's consequences. That Dufrenne accepts the statement of fact but denies its consequences will be made clear in the sequel. The doubt in connection with Dufrenne's account is the meaning one may attribute to a representation which represents only itself. In traditional epistemology the reflexive relation between representative vehicle and represented object is exactly the substance of a presentation.

The third and fourth instances of Merleau-Ponty's influence on Dufrenne's treatise occur in the final metaphysical speculations on the philosophical value of aesthetic perception. Dufrenne accepts Merleau-Ponty's doctrine of an indirect language, which had already been clearly outlined by Alain: ". . . the literary work is true, like the fable, by its secondary meaning and not by the immediate meaning which the words represent. The function of representation is not so much to imitate the real as to permit an expression which allows us to grasp reality."[26] This is to say, as Merleau-Ponty has maintained, that literature constructs its objects of language, and becomes a means of non-verbal communication in that its own language is indirect.

Finally, sense and nonsense, meaning and its opposite, are accepted as the limits within which aesthetic perceptions take place. Where Merleau-Ponty has exemplified this thesis in his *Sens et non-sens,* whose title is to be taken as symbolic of the incompleteness of all expressions, Dufrenne has gone beyond the empirical description of actual behavioral patterns to a concept of reality and being, in keeping with Hegel's dialectical metaphysics. While Merleau-Ponty was drawing a distinction between what is "living" and what is "dead" in the philosophy of Hegel, Dufrenne accepts both indiscriminately. He states, "Being bears meaning, which is expressed in reality and understood by man";[27] and, as if one violation of the principle of economy were not enough, offers the following explanation:

This does not imply that the real is identical to meaning: it is, as in Hegel's dialectic, other than meaning and thus that which overflows meaning's bounds; it is inexhaustible, and nonsense. But what is nonsense to man still has meaning for being; it is meaning become nature.[28]

At this stage of the game it is clear that Dufrenne has left the area of the phenomenology of aesthetic experience, of aesthetics properly so-called, and has joined many of his confreres in the practice of philosophy in the arts. I am glad to leave him there. Like Merleau-Ponty, I am content to accept the limits of sense and nonsense as they define man's historical and anthropological project.

Dufrenne's criticism of Merleau-Ponty derives precisely from this limitation. The relation of organism and environment, he claims, is nothing more than an analogy in terms of which Merleau-Ponty has been able to reformulate the gestalt hypothesis; but a new deception arises in that the analogy fails to interpret the existence of things (objects of representation), the objects of intentions, even if the intentions are corporeal rather than intellectual in nature. Without an object which calls out the proper responses of the living organism, it would have to be said that the body-proper constitutes its objects in pursuit of its biological and vital functions; and this would be an inverted form of idealism.[29] Merleau-Ponty's difficulty, according to Dufrenne, is to have moved from Heidegger's descriptions of *Dasein,* an existence which reveals being because it is in-the-world, to Sartre's latent idealism, and in an attempt to correct the latter, to the biologism of Goldstein.[30] But this is to say no more than what he has already said, that Merleau-Ponty fails or refuses to make the transcendental leap.

Dufrenne's Phenomenological Conclusions.—Having criticized Sartre for too limited a view of the imagination and Merleau-Ponty for too broad a view of perception, Dufrenne has undertaken the task of re-formulating the relation of the functions of both these faculties as they operate in aesthetic awareness. In aesthetic rather than epistemological terms, Sartre has given a thick doctrine, and Merleau-Ponty a thin. But to account for representative depth in the aesthetic object, Sartre has made appeal to objects, unreal or absent, which constitute the meanings of the physical analogue perceived, and thereby has destroyed the notion of an autonomous art object; Merleau-Ponty has tried to retain the autonomous object by reducing all depth content to a perception of an artwork's surface. According to Dufrenne, a faithful phenomenological theory will account for both surface and depth expression only by considering the manner in which our surface perceptions are thickened by an awareness of the depth dimensions of an aesthetic object. The depth elements are supplied, according to Dufrenne, by the aesthetic contemplator's mind. This process is not unakin to that described by Ingarden, who has isolated various strata within the literary art object.[31]

Since aesthetic perception is said to begin with the physical presence of the work of art as constructed by an artist, it would not be a falsification of Dufrenne's theory to start with a statement of the limits of criticism. The object of art appears in an adequate perception of the work, and the first step to insure an adequate perception is to avoid the obvious pitfalls of unenlightened criticism. Speaking on the manner in which works of genius are recognized, he states,

The genius is that one person one will be able to pick out of a thousand, who, even if by no will of his own, has no equal. But let's understand this matter correctly; in listening to Mozart, I have to hear Mozart. If in recognizing the work as Mozart's I say that the work belongs to a certain classical style, I am criticizing, and losing contact with the work; and I may even cease to perceive aesthetically in order to know objectively [classify]. This passage from the individual to the type is quite assuredly the result of an abstraction, if I proceed from an external point of view, making my appeal to varying techniques and influences and the whole history of similar works of art.[32]

He begins, then, from the proper standpoint; the work must be known for what it is and does rather than for any comparisons it may suggest with other works. Aesthetic perception is object-centered.

Although I should insist that classification of art works is not even criticism—no criticism worthy of the name will allow itself to lose contact with the work—it seems apparent that no aesthetic object will appear if the work itself is viewed only in relation to something else. The difficulty arises when Dufrenne states that, all things considered, whatever is expressed by the work is inexpressible in any terms other than itself, other than an actual perception. This difficulty is, however, one of critical practice, and not of formal aesthetic theory. If whatever is expressed in a unique work of art were expressible in terms not of itself, there would be no need for the artist to go through the trouble of making the artifact. Since there are no established dictionaries for the elements of art language and no grammatical rules for composing messages, there is no manner of translating or transliterating the message. Either the work is experienced or remains forever unknown. The difficulty then becomes one of finding a procedure for producing a complete and adequate perception of the work if for any reason a person remains insensitive to the work's significance.

It is here that Dufrenne outlines a series of schemata, the comprehension and application of which will allow the intuition of the work's unique universe. He divides the arts into those of time and space, and shows that whether the particular art be of time or of space, both space and time are generated by the structuring of the work. He follows Kant both in his description of the abstract and formal character of space and time, and of the maner in which objects are said to be apprehended within their formal schematization: "The relation of subject to object is prefigured at the very heart of the subject by the relation obtaining between time and space; and movement, which is movement in the subject before being movement of the object, expresses the same relation in the object."[33] The life of an aesthetic object is comprehended, then, either on the basis of an analogy with our self-knowledge—transcendental for Kant and for Dufrenne—or, if argument by analogy is to be eschewed, the direct metaphysical attribution of subjective qualities to objective entities. Artists often speak of the "movement" or "activity" or "feeling" of the piece, and Dufrenne gratifies their propensity by referring to an aesthetic object as a "quasi-subject."[34]

In Dufrenne's view, it is easier to know a quasi-subject than a full-blown and authentic subject exemplified in every human being. The critic proceeds from the objective structures of the object as constructed, to an intuition of the intimate structures of the quasi-subject. The object, of course, is here the work of art; the quasi-subject, the object of art. Further, the movement from objective perception to aesthetic intuition is guided by the application of structural schemata, which allow the subject to perceive the "temporalization of space" and the "spatialization of time" characteristic of the object of art. The schemata he proposes are the traditional aesthetic categories: harmony, rhythm, and melody.

Harmony he defines as a relationship between the work and the environment in which it is realized, an ideal space with assignable intervals; as such, it delimits a universe in which the work may move. The movement within the ideal space of harmony he calls rhythm. It is number and measure, the latter of which allows the subject to recognize equal intervals and to perceive repeated emphases. Numbered, rhythm is quantitative; accented, it is qualitative. Where harmony provides the space for the appearance of an aesthetic object, rhythm supplies its time; and melody fills in its indefinable essence. Following Bergson, Dufrenne refers to melody as the object's duration (*durée*).

The intellectual tour de force is to apply these schemata to the primarily spatial arts. But Dufrenne has already prepared his reader by the metaphysical analysis of space and time. He begins with an account of the temporalization of space.[35] Our awareness of the simultaneity of the work is mediated by the perception of various elements as co-existent, the points of a line, the places of solid figures, the progression and regression of colors; the only danger here is to be carried away by the representational qualities of a painting. If we are not so carried away, we may perceive harmony and rhythm, and, indeed, even the melody of a spatial creation.

Spatial harmony is established by color intervals, and once again sets up the ideal space in which the painting may "move." The palette or spectrum is to the painter what the harmonic scale is to the musician. The movement is controlled by design, and so rhythm is describable in terms of architectonic, delineation of lines of force, distribution of masses within the harmonic space, which establishes the number, and repetition, which is here the whole design as it is prefigured in each part. In a painting, he says, ". . . the movement is nothing more than the development of an essence, the adventure of a being always constant with itself throughout its metamorphoses, like a theme throughout its variations."[36] Thus pictorial rhythm is conceived as mediating harmony on the one hand and melody on the other; as in music, the melody is the unique significance of the unification of the perceivable elements. Accentual rhythm is possible in painting by the variations in the qualities of line—intensity, value, direction, attitude—as well as by those of color —brightness, hue, saturation. It must be emphasized, however, that these aesthetic categories are only schemata and do not determine what a given work of art will contain; the actual content of a work is supplied by the manner in which the artist organizes his creation.

It is for this reason that our aesthetic perception must start with the work of art as constructed. When the structural schemes become apparent, the perceiver may move from his knowledge of the work to an intuition of the object because he has had aroused in him the spatial and temporal characteristics of the object itself. To explain this intuition Dufrenne must make appeal to the transcendental relationship of subject and object; I can perceive the work of art as a quasi-subject because I am directly aware of my own space and my own time as feeling in general. According to Dufrenne, feeling in this sense is a form of knowing; phenomenologically, it is a feeling of the piece. Kant had explained this knowledge in the *Critique of Judgment* in terms of a felt harmony of all our cognitive faculties, the perception of which is aesthetic pleasure. But since our cognitive faculties are not themselves cognized empirically —being the supersensible substrate of the transcendental subject—aesthetic analysis at this point must yield to transcendental deduction. Dufrenne admits the case, and offers a chapter on the a priori character of human affectivity.[37] In sum, analysis of the work of art in terms of its structural schemata permits the appearance of the object of art primarily because it engages man's a priori affective nature.

I shall continue the sketch of Dufrenne's phenomenology by correlating the strata of the object which appears with a phenomenological description of the conditions which permit its appearance. In contradistinction to the four strata isolated in Souriau's comparative aesthetics,[38] Dufrenne finds only three: the sensuous basis, the represented object, and the "world" expressed. We may save some motion by considering the properties of the object as they follow from the phases of a complete act of perception: physical presence, imaginative representation, and affective expression; or more briefly: presence, representation, and reflection. Each of these levels is composed of a reflexive relation: between sign and significance, between representative vehicle and represented object, and between the world expressed and its feeling. The theoretical trick, then, is to show how each reflexive duality spills over into the next until there is reached the final dyad which unifies the entire construct.

For a description of the physical presence of the aesthetic object Dufrenne is satisfied to accept Merleau-Ponty's account of corporeal communication with the world:

. . . meaning is not primarily something that I think with detachment; it produces concern, and determines my conduct; resonates within, and moves me. The signification in its pure state, which I contemplate without adhering to it, will be deduced from this prior meaning that evokes my conviction because it moves me, giving, as it does, a summary appeal to which I respond with my whole body.[39]

A second condition for the appearance of a meaning at this corporeal level of response is that the sign and its referent be given simultaneously in a single configuration.[40] This too is Merleau-Ponty. But that is as far as Merleau-Ponty goes: expression is perception, and perception is bodily comprehension.

Dufrenne insists there is more to the experience; if there were not, he argues, the most beautiful work would be the most moving. That this consequence is a *reductio ad absurdum,* however, only Dufrenne would seem to comprehend. He supports his claim by adding that too violent a bodily reaction often inhibits the engagement of *mind.* As I have shown, Merleau-Ponty makes no distinction between mind and body; mind is merely a way in which the body behaves under certain circumstances. Dufrenne will have none of this psycho-physical monism, and makes appeal to a doctrine of the imagination as the mediating ground of a transition from sheer physical presence to contemplative representation. It would seem incumbent upon him, therefore, to give a purely phenomenological account of mind. He must, like Husserl, practice the transcendental *époché* (reduction), which Merleau-Ponty deems impossible because self-defeating. He proceeds by attempting to correct Sartre on the function of the imagination.

According to Dufrenne, it will be remembered, Sartre had mistaken one of the functions of the imagination (fantasy) for an adequate description of the entire role played in aesthetic contemplation by our image-making faculty. What Sartre has failed to take into account is that the perception of the physical analogue itself, the artifact, already involves a kind of contemplation. But since Dufrenne maintains that all aesthetic objects, representational or abstract, must be represented in their totality in the imagination, it is clear that his notion is epistemological, and not aesthetic. The possible confusion of "representational" for "imaginative representation" is difficult to avoid here. As in most of his cases of theoretical conflict, Dufrenne seeks clarity in a distinction of metaphysical terms:

I perceive only in the past, and from the future; in the present I can only act. To contemplate is to go back to the past in order to take hold of the future by surprise; I can cease to be one with the object, as I am by its physical presence to me, only by detaching myself from the present in which I am lost in the world of things. The "re" of "representation" expresses that internalization, just as the "con" of "contemplate" expresses the possibility of passage and simultaneity which suggests a concept of space; for space is contemporaneous with time.[41]

As for Kant, space and time are given transcendentally, if only in their formal abstract character, in every intuition of an object of representation.

The task then becomes one of showing how the transcendental imagination relates to an empirical act of the perceiver. And according to Dufrenne, the transcendental prefigures and makes possible the empirical: ". . . it expresses the possibility of a representation, while the empirical [imagination] renders account of the significance of a represented object by integrating it with the representation of a world."[42] In an ordinary perception of the objects in the real world, the representation of an object is interpreted as a sign of other objects; in aesthetic perception, on the other hand, the significance of the representation must be read on the surface of the represented object itself. Instead of perceiving real space and real time, the aesthetic perceiver must become aware of the space and time of the object perceived; the perception of a real object produces action, and the perception of an imagined object produces contemplation.

Given Kant's transcendental categories, Dufrenne's account of the imagination would seem to make sense, provided that his epistemological orientation did not falsify the facts of aesthetic perception; and one of the ways of testing whether such falsification has taken place is to judge whether he has slipped from one meaning of "representation" to another without being aware of the shift. He must, for instance, give examples of both objective and non-objective artworks to substantiate his claim that he is using the word in a univocal sense in different contexts. He cites painting and architecture.

In a realistic painting, he says, the subject must appear.[43] If it does not, the perceiver is aware of colors and lines or free forms, but cannot be said to have grasped the represented object. Here, one will observe, is the slip that indicates theoretical ambiguity. If it is true that a subject appears only to structure the space and to animate the time of a realistic painting, it becomes difficult to understand why painters have chosen this subject as opposed to any other in any given representational universe. Abstract painters, of course, agree; it is for this reason that they present no recognizable subject-matter in their works. For them, a subject is irrelevant to the formal values of painting; and painting is, like architecture, a representation only in the epistemological sense. Dufrenne makes the case for abstract art in the following description of a "non-objective representation":

> . . . in order for us to grasp the aesthetic object as such, it must appear to us . . . as figuring a represented object; in this case that represented object is the idea of the cathedral which is had through the appearance of the cathedral: the sign and its representation are objectively indistinguishable, since the cathedral has no subject other than itself. But subjectively there is a distinction to be drawn between them in that the sign requires an indefinite exploration, which the imagination supplies in its own way, while the representation is seized as immediately given in each perception.[44]

But this non-objective representation is nothing more than the presented object already fully comprehended as a physical presence.

Moreover, if the idea of a cathedral can be given to perception, then it would seem that the idea of a painting can be given in the same fashion; and the representation of the one is similar to the representation of the other. This epistemological sense of "representation" then goes nowhere to explain the special aesthetic meaning of a representational painting in which both a presentational object and a subject-theme appear. Dufrenne himself seems to admit this point in his several statements that artistic truth has nothing in common with logical or empirical truth and that one gives evidence of aesthetic sensitivity to the extent that one refrains from commenting upon the subject of a representational piece.[45]

This may be the case; but if so, one must still give an answer to the prior question: what function is served by the depiction of a given subject? In answer one might say that no function is served at all, or that the subject serves to model the space and to generate the time of the piece, or that art is at the service of education or moral edification. It would seem obvious that the first and last alternatives are mistaken, and that the second more closely corresponds to what happens in aesthetic perception. And if this is the case, it cannot be said that the representation of reality in works of art gains for being of one kind rather than of another; a religious painting is not aesthetically distinguishable from a sacrilegious one, a politically conformist novel from a radical one.

In the face of such a conclusion, the critic will be forced to admit that the aesthetic value of an object derives from something other than its represented reality, and will assume the task of showing how the representational content of an objective piece helps *to give form to* the object perceived. In this sense, representation is a motif guiding the development of an artwork's unique world. At times Dufrenne is aware of this, but at others his attention slips. Where he states that both objective and nonobjective art engage the imagination, he is interested in the perception of aesthetic form, which eventually constitutes the expressive vehicle; where he claims that the subject must be "understood" he goes beyond the given of the experience, for that understanding is not the representation which is involved in *all* aesthetic perceptions. He is not in consequence describing *the* aesthetic object, but only one kind of aesthetic object.

Having distinguished surface and depth expression in the structure of works or art, he ends with an overlay of strata as if the represented stratum were placed upon the physical presence with no essential relation obtaining between the layers, except that both underlayers act as support for a third, the stratum of expression or sentiment, which is thought to produce the unity of a single aesthetic experience.

For this level of the experience Dufrenne again follows Kant. Feeling is supplied by the perceiving subject, and not by the subject perceived (representation in an objective work), although the subject matter of represented objects is said to control the expressiveness of the piece. The mode of access to the feeling of an artwork is reflection, which may begin after the analysis of the structures of the piece, but which in the end refers the total construct to the significance inherent in those structures: the inexpressible and inexhaustible depth of aesthetic expressions. Reflection calls out the feeling which in turn guides further reflection. Since the complete aesthetic object does not appear until the level of reflection has been achieved, and an aesthetic feeling is the sign that it has been achieved, criticism proceeds from feeling to analysis to reinforced feeling. The total experience is thus reflexive, and may be conceived on the model of the existence of psychological subjects.

Following this line of reasoning, Dufrenne maintains that an aesthetic object is a quasi-subject; it is known by sympathetic reflection. Kant had achieved the same result, the description of a pre-existent harmony of the subjective and the objective in his notion of purposiveness without purpose, the aesthetic object being completed in the feeling of the relationship of subjective faculties. And Dufrenne admits his debt:

That affinity which is manifested between nature and myself is not only understood by an act of reflection; it is also experienced, particularly in aesthetic experience, as a sort of communion between the object and myself. And that communion is a way of access to the feeling.[46]

Thus Dufrenne goes beyond the phenomenology of Merleau-Ponty, who describes the immanent structures of physical presence, as he eventually goes beyond Kant, who described the a priori structures of imaginative representation; his own contribution is to have attempted the description of the a priori structures of human affectivity, which lead him to a level of speculation yielding a "pure aesthetic."

The point of relevance to our thesis is the case he makes for finding the unity of the experience in the third, or expressive stratum. Why, in particular, must the feeling of a work of art be attributed analogically to a phenomenal object? Why cannot the attribution be made to the form of an experience which is properly conceived as partly objective (the work) and partly subjective (the attitudes of the body proper as it assimilates the work)? Why, in short, does Dufrenne add stratum to stratum in order to explain the thickening of aesthetic experience?

At first blush the answer seems apparent: the problem is epistemological, and Dufrenne is tracing the appearance of a special kind of object before an attentive consciousness. Thus he finds physical presence buttressed by the special mental function of the imagination, which provides a representation for further assimilation by reason, the faculty of judgment. Agreeing with Kant that the judgment involved at this stage of the experience is reflective, rather than determinant (the object is given; the concept sought), the only proof that the given object is assimilated by reason is the felt harmony of the faculties engaged by the experience. And this felt harmony is an immediate quality of the aesthetic experience. Once it is experienced, analysis of the work of art, which caused it in the first place, may begin. The difference between Dufrenne and Kant is that in the latter's aesthetics there is no differentiation in kinds of aesthetic feeling. The feeling is one of the harmony of the faculties, a pleasure before beautiful objects and transmuted pain in the case of sublime objects. Dufrenne's concept of a general a priori human affective consciousness is an attempt to allow variations and determinations within the pleasure-pain continuum. He fortifies himself to some extent by Heidegger's notion of Befindlichkeit, the given affective character of a conscious being as it is present to a world.[47]

But the question then becomes one of clarification. Why cannot the immediate feeling of physical presence account for the immediacy of aesthetic response? And how can there be two "immediate" feelings engaged in the same experience? Dufrenne offers three reasons for distinguishing the feeling of the object from that of our subjective faculties involved in aesthetic judgment: because the two feelings reveal distinct objects, because they appear only on the occasion of distinct attitudes of the subject, and because the one precedes and the other follows the completion of the aesthetic object as a representation.[48]

A word of explanation on each of these reasons. First, the distinction between objects of feeling. The feeling of physical presence is nothing more than the attitude of the body which assimilates the object, and is thus external to the object itself, while the feeling of the total artwork is internal to or inherent in the structures of the work, a function of the space and time generated by the representation. Second, the distinction in attitude on the part of the perceiver. The feeling of physical presence is provoked by the object as that object indicates a meaning for the vital and physical substructures of the subject, and as such the meaning is of a surface nature; while the feeling of the entire object reveals a depth which can be comprehended only by the full depth of the perceiving consciousness. And it is for this reason that Dufrenne calls aesthetic communication a communion between beings, depth in the object responded to by depth in the subject. Third, the temporal distinction between the two. Physical presence is the first step in the comprehension of an object; reflection, the measure of its full assimilation. Following his original existentialistic inspiration, Dufrenne refers to the feeling of the entire piece (*sentiment*) as the authentic feeling of the work of art. The authenticity of the feeling is guaranteed by the authenticity of the aesthetic attitude of the perceiving subject.[49]

In a word, the aesthetic attitude is authentic when it allows the perceiver to have the immediate feeling of the entire work of art as that work was structured in the first place; and in a case of ideal perception the distinction previously drawn between the work of art and the object of art is factitious, having been made at the start merely for a point of departure. But if this is the case, Dufrenne is faced again with the logical circularity the original distinction between the two was intended to avoid.[50]

In sum, the analysis of an aesthetic object will cover three distinct strata of meaning: the materials, which are given in their sheer physical presence; the subject, which may be either an objective representation or a non-objective structuring of a unique frame of reference; and the expression, the inexhaustible depth of feeling derived from the world as structured within that framework.[51] Since Merleau-Ponty's analysis had stopped with the first stratum, it behooves us to evaluate Dufrenne's attempt to complete Merleau-Ponty's insight into the non-reflective character of aesthetic expression.

Critical Evaluation.—The first difficulty is to be found at the level of representation. As discussed above, the error is to have interpreted a distinctly aesthetic term "representation" or "subject" in a more general epistemological sense. Dufrenne has done this, it will be recalled, to avoid the difficulty facing Sartre in conceiving the object of representation to be external to the work itself. But in moving from the aesthetic to the logical[52] intension of the term, as Dufrenne does in stating that a cathedral or an absolute musical piece represents itself even if it does not in the strictest sense represent another object, there is a double confusion: first, the self-representing and the other-representing objects become indistinguishable in theory, even though they are clearly distinguishable in fact; and secondly, the peculiar quality of the other-representing object becomes a mystery solvable only by reference to the artist's taste or preference, if not to his "genius." In this respect, Dufrenne states,

The artist chooses a given subject because it is consubstantial with him, because the subject evokes in him a certain emotion, provokes a certain questioning. It is not a matter of copying the subject, but of giving by its means the sensuous equivalent of the affective or intellectual meaning it has for him: Roualt does not paint a Christ, but the pictorial equivalent of what Christ signifies to him.[53]

If, however, Roualt's Christ is not a representation of Christ, but a particular feeling congenial to Roualt's felt universe in general, then in principle an explanation of the second level of the experience depends upon our having already reached the third. And if this is the case, the same feeling may be represented without Christ's appearance at all, that is, it would have been possible for Roualt to have portrayed the same feeling non-objectively, passing from the manipulation of color and line directly to the stratum of expression without giving us the picture of Christ he quite obviously did. And this, too, is to destroy the uniqueness of Roualt's expression. To reduce the representation of Christ to a means of expression is not to do away with Christ altogether. To understand Roualt's Christ we must see the Christ, otherwise we violate the stated principle of taking aesthetic representations as representative of self before they may become expressive of a universe. Only those objects which fully represent the total subject pictured are capable of bearing the function Dufrenne places upon them.

Moreover, there is a second violation of stated principle in appealing to an artist's preference since an appeal is made to the psychology of creation, which had been excluded from the area of investigation in the earlier parts of the treatise under discussion. This is all the more serious since the creative act is not explicated in terms of the object created, but rather in terms of the artist's feeling, and this is to have sunk to the level of psychologism Dufrenne's aesthetics was to have avoided.

The only honest conclusion that an aesthetician can draw from the facts of representational and non-representational art is that the two

objects differ in kind, and necessitate a consequent difference of explanation. To subsume both objective and non-objective art under the concept
of (even) epistemological representation is an intellectual tour de force
which fails to accomplish what it was designed to do. If we do make this
identification, we cannot fail to do an injustice to the one or the other:
objective works intend another object and non-objective works do not.
The relation between surface and depth in a work of art may be harmonious or contrasting, and of any degree of differentiation in between;
and aesthetic analysis may begin with surface or with depth as long as
surface and depth are perceived in relation, for it is this relationship
which constitutes the expressiveness of an objective representation.

Having explained the difficulties with the second stratum of an aesthetic object, I may be briefer with those attending the third. A world is
said to be expressed by virtue of the subject. But if a subject is incon-
ceivable in aesthetic terms for a non-objective work, the passage from
materials to expressiveness is blocked, and we must fall back upon the
feeling of the physical presence of the work. All the pains Dufrenne has
taken to differentiate intellectual depth from the depths of emotive
expression derive from the fact, expressed in Kantian terms, that the
aesthetic judgment is reflective and not determinant. This same explanation may be given for the conclusion that the expressiveness of artworks
is not amenable to analysis. If an object is given to perception for which
a suitable concept cannot be found, the concepts of philosophy, if they
enter into an artwork at all, must perform the same function as any
other subject matter or content, contributing to the structure of the object,[54] which structure controls the feeling of the piece.

The objective evaluation of Dufrenne's treatise may be concluded
with an examination of his description of the total structure of the triple
leveled object. What does it mean to say that it is a quasi-subject? First,
that it is an object. It is something which exists for our perception, and
is not constituted by that perception. The latter alternative would be
idealism. But what about the former? Is it any less idealistic to suppose
that the aesthetic object is only a quasi-subject? Dufrenne's idealism is
transcendental and rational, like Kant's, rather than subjective and
empirical, like Berkeley's; but it is nonetheless idealistic. What evidence
does he have that the imagination must function to supply an object to
reflection, if not that "a transcendental imagination" prefigures and
makes possible the empirical act? It would seem, then, that in his
attempt to be something more rigorously intellectual than an empirical
investigator Dufrenne has not become phenomenological, but, like
Sartre, has retreated to Kant's critical method.[55] Instead of insisting, as
phenomenologists always do, that consciousness and its object are given

in a conscious act, Dufrenne states that consciousness of a radically non-empirical sort is presupposed in each consciously empirical act. In so doing, he has put the presuppositions back into a nominally presuppositionless philosophy. The question therefore remains whether anything can be known, phenomenologically or empirically, of "the" aesthetic object.

In telling us that the aesthetic object is a quasi-subject, Dufrenne is expressing in quasi-metaphysical terms what every good critic has known for a long time: that the object expresses whatever is expressed in a work of art, and that the author's intention and a perceiver's reaction may be falsified, as criteria of judgment, by a reconsideration of the object's internal structures, in a word, that aesthetic perception is at its best always object-centered. It comes as no surprise, then, that Dufrenne's transcendentalism, which re-introduces a quasi-subjectivity into aesthetic perception, falsifies this common-sense, but sound, critical maxim.

Appendix B

Toward a Concept of
Existentialist Literature: An
Essay in Philosophy and the Novel

As the subtitle of this appendix indicates, the purpose is to consider the relations obtaining between two disparate, yet mutually complementary, humanistic disciplines. They are disparate, since the primary function of philosophy is to amass evidence for the acceptability of knowledge claims, whether of a very particular and restricted scope—as in the stipulation of the conditions for the truth of a given proposition—or of the widest, most general applicability—as in the construction of metaphysical hypotheses which purport to explain the truth of the universe at large. Literature, on the other hand, has no necessary connection with fact. The writer as often as not utilizes his imagination to the prejudice of his observational and explanatory faculties. A philosopher must be judged, then, on the logic of the manner in which he founds his claims; and a writer, on the degree to which his imaginative construction holds the attention of a critical reader. In common, the two disciplines have the medium of words, arbitrary signs or symbols to which have been assigned conventional meanings; and, at least on the surface, an interest in man and his purposes in face of an often hostile environment.

It would be too easy, however, to look into the common medium and the common interest to pursue our present purpose. Anyone the least bit familiar with contemporary philosophy knows the degree to which philosophers are enamored of words and their meanings; it would be foolhardy indeed to deny that the business of writing starts, not with having something to say, but with having the words for saying anything at all. Thus, the superficial comparison of the linguistic media of philosophers and writers leads nowhere beyond the surface, which is already quite apparent. And without further insight into the differences with which philosophers and writers handle their primary interest in the human condition, the second common element of the two disciplines is no more fruitful than the first. Either, then, we pursue the differences, or we remain on the surface.

The prima facie difficulty of pursuing the differences between philosophy and literature is to become so puristic in the one or the other that an eventual comparison between the two becomes all but impossible. What of the philosopher whose purpose cannot be turned away from the attainment of truth? In his attempt to talk nothing but the clearest of sense he often fails to recognize that if truth is not always stranger than fiction, fiction quite often seems as true as the most apparent of facts. And any philosopher incapable of distinguishing between what merely seems to be and what actually is the case has no authority for his pronouncements on the superiority of the truth. In answer to the sophomoric question, *What is the truth?*, Friedrich Nietzsche once remarked with a great deal of penetration that truth is a necessary lie.

But Nietzsche, aside from founding the atheistic brand of existentialism, was a poet-philosopher whose literary reputation has suffered much in contemporary evaluation. The reason for this maltreatment is neither his atheism nor the possessiveness of a sister too closely associated with officialdom of the Nazi party; rather, it lies in his desire to be more a writer than a philosopher. What he did gain in the purity of his poetry he lost in the clearness of his expression, and consequently in the conviction of his audience. Realizing that any bastardization of the philosophic medium will almost universally result in a like consequence, philosophers generally eschew the literary enterprise althogether. This attitude is nowhere clearer than in a famous essay by the American, C. S. Peirce, generally considered the founder of pragmatism.

Both John Dewey and William James credit Peirce with the institution of pragmatism as a philosophy; in the opinion of others, he thus contributed the first and only original American push to the development of philosophy as an intellectual discipline. Although "pragmatism" was already used in its adjectival form by Immanuel Kant, Peirce claimed credit for having established the word in its substantival sense. Pragmatism, as a philosophy, centered upon the so-called pragmatic test for meanings, and Peirce was pleased when James and others took up the word as a suitable rubric for the growing development in humanistic philosophy. Nevertheless, when the word became current in the writings of humanists of another stripe, he pulled up short: "But at present, the word begins to be met with occasionally in the literary journals, where it gets abused in the merciless way that words have to expect when they fall into literary clutches."[1] In an effort to avoid misunderstanding and to keep his meaning clearly philosophical he suggested the alternate, "pragmaticism," a word he deemed "ugly enough to be safe from kidnappers."[2]

If philosophers have not been too sympathetic to the proposed marriage between their discipline and that of writers, the latter have, on the other hand, been a bit too eager to join hands, if not bodies, with philosophers to produce a philosophic literature. Numerous are the novels of ideas in which a character or an author is given to spouting a philosophic line. Dostoievsky, Mann, and Pasternak found convenience in this sort of marriage; but the difficulty with each has been the quality of its off-spring. The novels themselves have suffered for an inadequate embodiment of the philosophical idea; the "philosophy" of a Dostoievsky or of a Mann remains an ornament, of Pasternak, a digression; and in spite of the semblance of profundity that such an ornament or digression will produce, the essential quality of the novel, its form or structure, is either hidden or obscured by what can only be labeled a philosophical intrusion on the novelist's basic task—forming an imaginary universe in which to depict some aspect of man's fate.[3] Too much discourse on fate either on the part of the author or one of his characters is quite apt to produce a work in which philosophy is used in this superficial and ornamental sense.

To be successful, it seems to me that the appropriate merger must conform to the following conditions: first, philosophical literature is to be philosophical in a rigorous manner, that is, the idea must have import for the pursuit of philosophy as such, and secondly, it must be literary in the best sense of that word, which is to say that the work produced must possess artistic merit and be judged on aesthetic grounds, just as any other non-philosophical literary work is to be judged, on the basis of its goodness or badness as art. The first of these conditions is stipulated to avoid philosophical dilettantism of the kind which had so upset Peirce; the second is to avoid dilettantism in literature, exhibited by those critics who find anything with a philosophical idea, no matter how poorly embodied, great and its author, ever so elegant, ever so intelligent.

The question as to who is best qualified to meet these conditions is purely academic. Until philosophers become writers or writers philosophers there is little chance of success, even though it may appear that a writer has a better chance of becoming a philosopher than a philosopher of becoming a writer. The reason for this, again, is the philosopher's preoccupation with the truth. It may well be true that writers are born and not made, but it seems to me that philosophers are always made in long years of training, which, once acquired, may be applied to a great many experiences of individual life. The question remains aca-

demic, however, since all a critic must do is to comb the literary products of his culture or of any other in order to find the qualities described
in the conditions laid down above. In its best moments this is what we
find in the contemporary existentialist movement. But before proceeding
to the demonstration, I shall pause to elaborate on the conditions mentioned above.

Philosophical Rigor.—Since their purposes vary, the philosopher and
the writer are not judged on the same grounds. The one produces an
argument to be judged by virtue of its soundness; the other, a work of
art to be judged by virtue of its expressiveness. Yet it would seem that,
should the writer choose a philosophical idea, it becomes incumbent
upon him to be aware of, and to utilize, both the idea itself and any of
its important consequences or implications which have a bearing upon
his story.

His story concerns people, and those people are placed in some kind
of environment. We have in those elements two distinct yet related
dimensions: character and plot. The very word "character" suggests a
philosophical consideration: morals. But the morality of a given character cannot be shown in isolation from the events in his environment or
his relationships with the various other characters. The events, on the
other hand, suggest a second philosophical consideration: metaphysics,
the philosopher's concern with the nature of reality. Thus, by analyzing
two elements of the product of literary art we are brought face to face
with two important areas in which philosophy and literature overlap.
It may be stated in passing that any concern with either metaphysics or
morals which is both consistent and empirically applicable will meet the
condition of philosophical rigor set down above. Without consistency,
moreover, the story embodying the philosophical idea will be lacking
in coherence, and so, in aesthetic unity. In this respect, the two disciplines are found to overlap in ideals, in the quality each of them seeks
in its products. Finally, as to adequacy, it may be suggested that a reader's impression that life or the universe "could be like that" is sufficient
to satisfy this second aspect of philosophical rigor.

Strictly speaking, of course, the requirement of empirical adequacy
demands the existence of an objective criterion for the establishment of
"truth." As granted above, the writer need not be limited to the statement of empirical truths. It would seem, then, that a further bit of
rationalization is necessary to establish the fact that we have here another
area of overlap between philosophy and literature, but this rationalization
is not difficult to supply.

First of all, philosophers are not themselves agreed upon what constitutes reality; they differ as much as the position of common sense,
which states that things are as they are—the brute character of facts—

and that our knowledge of them diverges according to our ability to perceive them adequately, differs from that of objective idealism, which states that things must exist according to the designs of an all-encompassing and objectifying reason. According to the first, whenever a further observation contradicts an idea we have of the character of the universe we are bound to change our idea, or to submit our observation to further test; according to the latter, when an observation contradicts our idea of the structure of the universe which is given by the abstract character of reason itself, we are led to doubt the validity of our observation no matter how many times it has been verified. And there are a number of philosophical positions to be maintained in between.

From these observations it is clear that philosophers themselves are not in a position to stipulate what constitutes empirical adequacy as long as their researches are of a metaphysical character. And this is necessarily. so, since metaphysics puts the very question of reality at stake; for a philosopher to take one stand at the expense of another is quite clearly to beg the question. All that any writer can do in such a situation is to take as true whatever appears to him to be true, and develop its consequences. In philosophy this position has come to be called "the ego-centric predicament," and in literature one hears of "a willing suspension of disbelief."

But no matter how egocentric the writer's predicament, nor how willing the reader to suspend his natural disbelief of anything contradicting common sense, the writer is not freed from some kind of concern with empirical adequacy. It is suggested here, in second place, that the very possibility of suspending disbelief constitutes a kind of empirical adequacy, freely and largely interpreted. If the reader cannot suspend his skeptical judgment, he cannot accept the plot or characters of a story as true; if he can and does, then the story contains verisimilitude and meets the demand of empirical adequacy at least in this psychological sense. If the story cannot be taken as literally true, it may be true—given the writer's egocentric predicament, or his philosophical orientation. Thus the writer is freed from the strict requirement of empirical adequacy, even though he must meet it in some sense if he is to have an interested reader. Didactic readers find the point of a story, its message or moral, in this larger sense of empirical adequacy. The writer is assumed to "have something to say," and we as readers must allow him leeway to assume any position it may fit his design to adopt.

Freed from the strict requirement of non-metaphysical philosophical enquiry, the writer gains in the variety of possibilities for expressing his point of view. He can pick and choose from among those philosophical ideas which seem to him the most valid expression of the values of human life. Not concerned primarily with the way life really is—except in the case of realism or naturalism—he is freed to explain a value—the way life could conceivably be, if only one made the correct assumptions.

Existentialism, like philosophical naturalism or Platonic idealism, is merely one way in which a writer may structure the events of his story. But of that, more later. It suffices here to state that the conditions of coherence and empirical adequacy philosophers demand of each others' work serve likewise to promote the cause of aesthetic unity and reader interest, respectively, when philosophy in this rigorous sense is embodied in a literary work.

Literary Excellence.—It is not my purpose to lay down a set of conditions sufficient to define a universal beauty, whatever that might be. In contemporary aesthetics, the word "beauty" is almost completely passé, limited in use to describe the effect of women and horses, or other natural objects, on the physiological economy of a beholder. No one, to my knowledge, has successfully defined "beauty," and for the purposes of aesthetics its definition is not requisite. Nor is it apropos, in its stead, to seek a list of qualities which a successful work of literature might possess, such as the coherence and interest noted above. From this point of view, it might be argued that philosophy, either in its metaphysical or ethical phases, has already yielded a number of such qualities; in addition to those stated above, one might claim as primary universality, due the supposed generality of philosophical knowledge, and poignancy, due the intellectual sympathy the depiction of human character is capable of producing, whether in its heroic or its pathetic dimension. Both of these approaches seem to be in error.

Consider the following reasons. The philosophical critic who approaches the individual work from the standpoint of an abstract ideal of beauty must defend his claim of possessing knowledge of the ideal. If he claims such knowledge is based upon an intimate acquaintance with prior works of art, then he must establish the assumption that his samples, or touchstones, were in fact beautiful to start with. In other words, there must be an appeal to another sample, or to some kind of non-empirical knowledge of the beautiful. In this approach, then, aesthetics must face the dilemma of a choice between an infinite regress and mysticism; and neither of these is capable of convincing a truly skeptical critic. One can always ask with meaning the following question: How do you know that X defines beauty?

If definition, by its abstractness, leads to a blind alley, it might be thought that a simple listing of concrete properties of various works may be substituted in its place. But just as there could be *an infinite regress* of touchstones by the way of abstract definition, there must be *an open list* of properties which any given successful work might possess; and one could never wish to exhaust all the properties a truly expressive work will have. Once again we are faced with a difficulty of principle.

A common-sense approach to this difficulty is one which seeks its categories or structures from a knowledge of the general properties of a given medium. The task is to consider the medium with which the literary artist must work in an effort to describe the kind of object he will produce as a writer, and then to judge a particular work in terms of the author's achievement of that kind of object. We are here concerned primarily with the novel, a particular literary genre having its history and evolution as a form of literary expression. But neither its history nor its evolution need be relevant to our judgment of a given novel written, for example, in the twentieth century. We may avoid this fruitless appeal to history by considering the medium of the novel.

A novel is made of words and their meanings, that is to say, not of ideas or meanings alone, so that a judgment on the excellence of a particular novel will entail the direct experience of the qualities of the physical expression of the novel, the words as sounded or heard, as well as of those qualities which derive from the intellectual depth of the piece, the system of meanings constituted by the conventional definitions of the words. As a temporary conclusion, then, it might be stated that every novel must contain the two kinds of expressiveness noted: surface and depth. A novel without depth, or meanings, would be a series of nonsense syllables, and consequently not a novel; a novel without surface would be a system of ideas unexpressed, and so likewise not a novel. It need only be added that a judgment on the concrete fact of a novel's existence is made on the fitness of the one to express the other. A novel is to be judged not on depth alone, nor on surface alone; in terms perhaps more familiar to literary critics, neither on conception in the abstract, nor on execution abstracted from the conception. Thus to say that a novel is good or great because it contains a philosophical idea is a fallacy of judgment: abstraction will have been made of the quality of that idea's surface expression. And, correspondingly, it is equally fallacious to say that a novel is good merely because it contains poetic language; for, in this case, abstraction will have been made of the novel's depth. The critical task is to perceive the relatedness of surface and depth; for in so doing we will have perceived the novel, or, more properly said, have had its experience.

The second condition for a successful merger of philosophy and literature may be viewed in light of the foregoing aesthetic characteristics of the novel. It becomes apparent that metaphysics and morals may supply the plots and characters; but if they do, they have furnished nothing but the depth of the experience. The critic's task in evaluating a novel of ideas is to judge the manner in which the story is achieved or constructed. If it be assumed that a given novel is constructed according to a certain philosophical idea, that idea may be taken as an hypothesis —from among any others—which makes a maximal interpretation of the details found in a novel's depth. The next step becomes the task of determining the extent to which the depth in question reflects upon the surface in the communication of the novel's experience.

The question may arise here whether a novelist must start his creation with the conception of the plot and characters, or whether he may not start by playing with the techniques of his writing craft in an effort to discover the conception of his story. Again, the question is purely academic, since quite obviously he may start and end either way. For the reader, on the other hand, first contact is made with the surface, or textural, qualities of the story. But since his judgment is held in abeyance until he has realized the artist's conception, he may start with the conception and relate in retrospect his eventual knowledge of the story's depth with his first acquaintance of the story's surface. Where the depth meaning of a story is not apparent, a hypothesis must be entertained and checked against the details which are understandable; often the texture itself will supply a clue for such hypotheses. Only in those rare cases when a novelist is using a clearly defined philosophical system of ideas are the depth elements of the story readily understandable as a whole. In the case of existentialism the philosophical ideas were, for the most part, worked out in the abstract before they became concretized in the form of an existentialist novel.[4]

We may turn now to an analysis of two early novels of the French existentialist movement.[5] In each case the analysis is my own. I shall consider in brief the structure and texture of Sartre's *La Nausée* and of Camus' *L'Etranger*.

Philosophically, existentialism is perhaps best understood in terms of its reaction to the Hegelianism rife on the continent. According to the Hegelians, objective idealists of the most extreme sort, the absolute idea unfolds itself in time to create contemporary history. Everything which has happened or which will happen is already implicit in this all-inclusive process, beginning with logic and ending, religiously, in Christianity; politically, in the German State; and philosophically, in Hegel's own thought. If this seems a closed circle, it was certainly intended to be one. It constitutes the absolute idealism Marx tried to turn right side up by making its universal determinism depend upon the material and economic conditions of life, which are working their way, as we all know, through a series of contradictions to a state of the classless society. Man's conduct, determined in part by the current of the historical flow and in part by his essence as man, could be free only through the recognition of, and acquiescence in, the direction of history. Quite naturally, then, the romantic or democratic belief that the human individual was of supreme worth was thought to be baseless in the very nature of things. The romantic sentiments of some and the religious or political convictions of others brought about the reaction. If the individual was lost sight of in the Hegelian-Marxistic systems of thought, it would become necessary to construct a metaphysics more suitable to man's "subjectivity," which is perhaps best interpreted as man's intuitive self-awareness. Kierkegaard founded the theistic, and Nietzsche the atheistic developments in existentialist thought. Both Sartre and Camus are closer to Nietzsche than to Kierkegaard.

Prediction of a human event is thought by both Hegelian and Marxist to depend upon essential determination: because a given object is a such and such, it must act in a way proper to things of that kind. *Aqua regia* will always reduce gold because of the essential relations of the properties of the two substances. Likewise, a man whose essence is given in his "human nature" is such that he will always react in like manner to like circumstance. Existentialists are willing to admit that physical nature runs according to the pattern thus described, but deny that man possesses an essence or nature which will determine his actions. For all natural and cultural objects, the very being of the object depends upon having an essence; whereas, for man, existence precedes or determines his essence. And this is to say no more than that natural or cultural objects are made, while man is capable of making himself. All things become, or come into existence in time; but man becomes what he intends that he should be. This is not to be interpreted too literally, for there is always a "coefficient of adversity," or implication within a natural and cultural situation which sets limits upon the effectiveness of human choice.

The result of these assumptions is the statement that there are two kinds of existents: a being-in-itself, which has already become what it will always be, and being-for-itself, which is always in the process of becoming something else. The first describes the existence of things; the second, of human consciousness. Moreover, whenever there is consciousness there already exists a world of some sort which is the object of that consciousness. One merely finds oneself in a situation, and from the point of view of that consciousness there is no rational explanation of the character of that world. Hence, a basic contingency, or absurdity, conditions the life of man. This does not mean, of course, that man's life need continue to run in an absurd fashion, since man is capable of interjecting his own plans or intentions into the situation in which he happens to find himself. It does mean, however, that his existence is superfluous and contingent, not essential and necessary.

In sum, then, existentialism may be described as a metaphysical interpretation of the events of the world, which maintains that the human scene depends upon an absolute contingency—as opposed to the absolute rationality of the Hegelians—and that the human individual is free to determine himself by injecting his own values into his environing situation—as opposed to the more rigid determinism of both Hegel's and Marx's thought. With this freedom, of course, comes the dreadful awareness that man is responsible for whatever happens to him.

The principal theme of both *La Nausée* and *L'Etranger* is the developing awareness on the part of a protagonist of his own "metaphysical," or existentialistic, condition. But Sartre and Camus treat the subject in different manners, and it is primarily in the treatment of the theme that they differ in their early work.

The overall structure of *La Nausée* follows a simple pattern. An intellectual finds himself in Bouville finishing research for a biography of a late eighteenth century nobleman who had combined his talents as a spy with his natural propensities as a rake. While pursuing his task, the intellectual hero, Roquentin, is the witness of strange events beginning to occur in his own life. Natural objects lose their familiar phenomenal character; a piece of paper resists being touched, a glass of beer being drunk. People become something less than people: the protagonist's only friend is known to him merely as the "self-taught man," reading books in the library classified by author from A through Z, and giving in from time to time to his homosexual tendency; his former girl friend is an incomprehensible female in search of "privileged situations" and "perfect moments" to ply her trade, which is acting; his present mistress is a sexual automaton, who when in a hurry to climax asks to keep her stockings on. The whole town is presided over by the dead, enshrined in portrait form in the local art gallery. On a Sunday morning one can see the equally dead descendants marching ceremoniously to adoration in a church built over a former fish market—the bourgeoisie must live on the produce of the proletariat, even if it is already dead and stinking! Only one experience gives him any relief from his queasiness, listening to that oldtime jazz piece, "Some of These Days."

All these events are recounted in the author's, Roquentin's, diary, which quite conveniently affords a moment of reflection on the events of the day. When, finally, the root of a chestnut tree loses its character

as root to become *that*—being-in-itself, which consciousness cannot reduce to a rational explanation of any sort—the awareness of the absurdity dawns; and although the condition returns periodically when the
hero's attention shifts from the phenomenal characteristics of objects to
being in itself, he now knows the cause and is capable of changing the
mood by consciously shifting attention. He decides to quit living
vicariously the life of his subject, seeks to renew the relationship with
his actress friend, finds that impossible because of a new lover in her
life, and returns to Bouville from Paris only to clean up his affairs and
then to take up life in the capital. He finally realizes that his only salvation is like that of the negress and the Jew, the singer and songwriter—
characteristically and ironically known only by their essence—to live by
creating works of his own. But here the story must end, since an awareness can go no further.

When we turn to the execution of the story, we meet the first criticism
leveled at Sartre's technique. The diary form, it has been said, is too
artificial to be convincing. Critics who have made this charge seem to
forget that everything in a novel is artificial; any work of art can be
nothing more than human artifice, and that is precisely why it is cherished. In Sartre's case, the diary form is a useful means to achieve the
metaphysical structure of the story. It may be defended on three grounds.
First of all, it permits the reflection necessary for final awareness to
develop, and it permits the author, Sartre, to present the development
of that awareness in slow moving tempo. Secondly, the diary form is not
out of character, and succeeds in revealing just what sort of person is
capable of having the metaphysical "anguish." And lastly, it permits
the author, Sartre-Roquentin, to change writing styles and points of view
as the exigencies of the story demand. A few paragraphs in explanation
of this last virtue.

There are at least three distinct writing styles employed in *La Nausée*.
I use "style" here to refer to a manner of representing reality. The first
and predominant may be called *reportage*, an objective account of the
events of the story as they would happen, for example, in a naturalistic
novel. As stated before, existentialists accept the determinism of natural
events. The story begins and ends in this style, and one will find it in
all those moments when the diarist is most lucid in perceiving history
as it is occurring. *Reportage* is demanded of the author when the content of the diary is given in straightforward report. It changes when
"the crud," his metaphysical awareness, or nausea, appears.

This change is likewise dictated by the philosophical content. Since
the change in the diarist's attitude is from the objectivity of events to
the impression of objects upon his own inner state, the style develops

into complete *impressionism*. The people, the town, the events are, in this style, depicted as they touch the author's consciousness, and reflect a first level of heightening subjectivity. In this mood, given in the impressionistic style, the author is concerned primarily with the phenomenal attributes of things and people; from his point of view they all seem to be just a little bit odd—with a hint that still odder things are yet to come.

Impressionism, of course, is an apt literary tool to express subjective idealism, the philosophical doctrine which states that objects exist as they are perceived. This metaphysical system was propounded in England by Berkeley—and confounded by Dr. Johnson; it, too, has its empirical adequacy as I have interpreted it. The "taint" of subjective idealism in Sartre's later metaphysics finds its expression in these stages of Roquentin's developing consciousness.

If the point of the story had been that things are not what they seem, there would have been no more than these two styles: for things as they are, reportage suffices; for things as they seem, impressionism suffices. But existentialism as Sartre understands it demands that consciousness become aware of being itself; and when Roquentin achieves this awareness, he is hit with that awful urge. As a matter of fact, nausea is that awareness; it is a privileged way of being aware of being-in-itself. How, for a writer, to move from a knowledge of things as they seem, to one of being-in-itself?

Sartre chose a third style to permit the transition from impressionism to his mystical state of metaphysical nausea, and back again. It is called *surrealism*.[6] When in the heightened state of impressionistic awareness objects make their effect felt upon Roquentin's consciousness, he realizes that he may make objects appear in any way whatever, that he is free to join what nature has left asunder, and so amuses himself in imagining the most horrible of objects. He no longer has to feel his face with his hand to make sure he has a body, he can change his own tongue into a crawling thing merely by imagining it to be such. In this awareness man is finally freed from the tyranny of objectivity. But this freedom is only a function of his imagination, and to be made meaningful must be expended in the creation of something new and significant to the creator himself. This is the realization which floats into Roquentin's consciousness behind the strains of "Some of These Days."

The last mentioned device of depicting a double consciousness is possible only in the manner of stream of consciousness, where the significance of the events themselves may be lost, at least to the character himself, or of reflective reportage, where their significance is retained and may be dilated upon by the character in question. According to the demands of his plot, Sartre uses the latter. In the diary entry which records the luncheon of Roquentin with the self-taught man, there is a simultaneous recounting of the philosophical discussion between the two men and the intermittent impression upon Roquentin's awareness of the conversation between two lovers at a neighboring table; both of these sequences of events are objectively reported in the diary. But since the one is objective and the other subjective, the two needed, and found, unification in a single consciousness as it is recorded.

This portion of the diary, however, is written in the historical present tense, which gives an illusion of immediacy to the recorded action. It is for this reason that the technique may be termed "reflective stream of consciousness." And if it should be objected that the stream of consciousness technique as it has been used by Joyce differs radically from Sartre's prose, it would be apropos to state that consciousness may differ according to what passes in the stream and to the character of the person whose consciousness it is. Roquentin is depicted as a reflective individual. This distinction is important philosophically as well as literarily. In a later philosophical work Sartre distinguishes between two kinds of self-awareness, that of a pre-reflective as differentiated from a reflective *cogito*. The *cogito* is an experience of thinking, unique as the source of our self-knowledge. The knowledge one has of his own being which is not an act of reflection is only implicit—and this is what has made Joyce's literary technique an effective device for making character explicitly known to a perceptive reader. But the character of the personality whose consciousness is deployed in a stream, or interior monologue, does not usually include reflection; if it did, the stream would be stopped, only to start again after a moment's reflection. The effect of Sartre's prose was to have saved the impression of immediate action, while at the same time introducing a reflective act of self-awareness. The diary form, then, becomes a necessary device following upon the literary conception; it is to be viewed as a literary technique for unifying diverse writing styles, which are demanded by the character of the events being recounted.

From the foregoing it is to be concluded that the artificial devices used by Sartre to fulfill the conception of his novel were rather skillfully employed; the structure of the depth and the texture of the surface yield a lasting impression of a well-made novel, and careful attention paid to the philosophical depth in relationship to the literary surface of the story will most probably confirm this judgment. The story is not good because it has philosophical content; nor is it good because it "preaches" a new philosophy, that of existentialism; if it is good, it is because the philosophical content has dictated its overall form, which is cohesive and meaningful. Like naturalistic novels, or those of any other describable form, there are good and bad existentialistic novels. We may proceed to apply the same test to Camus' *The Stranger*.

The title of Camus' story has an unfortunate English translation. The sense would be more adequate, so it seems to me, if *L'Etranger* were rendered by the more closely cognate, "estranged one"; for estrangement implies a separation more pronounced or violent than simple strangeness, although that sense, too, is contained in the development of the story. Moreover, estrangement implies a moral connotation which is lacking in the usual English translation. Meursault, the protagonist, is estranged from his world at first without being aware of his condition; when at last he realizes the conditions of his estrangement, it is ironically too late for him to do anything about his state.

Two lines of development are suggested in the preceding remarks. The first is that Camus adds a moral dimension, which becomes an existentialist dilemma, to the notion of the sheer metaphysical absurdity of Sartre—a fact which will appear in the depth of Camus' novel; the second, which will make its appearance on the surface, in the ironic tone of the author, is that man's condition is marked by a deep paradox. The following analysis will be devoted to an explanation of these characteristics of the work.

Just as *La Nausée* was an exposé of the superfluity of man and the contingency of the universe which must remain a surd to his reasoning ability, Camus accepts the basic irrationality of the world and adds a moral dimension in defining the absurd as a violent contradiction felt by man to exist between his desires and his knowledge of what the world is and has to offer by way of satisfying desire. This addition is permitted him in French, since the word *conscience* harbors an ambiguity; it means consciousness, or awareness in the multiple sense already exploited by Sartre, and it means conscience, or moral awareness of what one ought to do. The consciousness which develops through the vagaries of Meursault's life will therefore have to be understood in this richer sense in which metaphysics is buttressed by morals.

As a guide to the thread of the story one might suggest that it presents an answer to the question, What ought one do after one has been led to realize what one is? That no definitive answer to this question will be given in the novel will not come as a surprise since no man, by the existentialist code, will ever be able to tell what he is—except in aspiration; and only when he dies will others be able to make the summing up. Meursault dies: his name may be considered a composite of "meurs" and "saut" (*Je meurs si je fais le saut!*);[7] but he dies in spite of his refusal to make the leap into the absolute of religion or into the regular and determined life of the stably functioning society; and we, as readers of his life's story, should be qualified to determine his essence.

The structure of *L'Etranger* is guided, as suggested above, by the estrangement Meursault progressively feels towards the world, towards others, and towards himself. The story opens with his receipt of a telegram announcing the death of his mother, but he can't remember on which day. The formalistic, legalistic language of the telegram insinuates into his awareness the impersonality of her later life, as well as the impersonality of his own. The event leaves him indifferent; he cannot play the dutiful son. He is estranged. Even though he makes all the required gestures, he is incapable of perceiving in them any innate significance.

Neither the death nor the funeral keeps him from meeting a girl he makes his mistress. They go swimming and enjoy a comic film, starring Fernandel, before he takes her home. Although he confides to her that he does not love her, he offers to continue the relationship if only she would care to. He had gone to pay his respects to his mother, and after refusing to have the screws removed from the coffin lid so that he could view her last remains, he had felt the need of a cigarette and made the social blunder of enjoying one, along with coffee. He attended the funeral, and now tries his best to go on living. This he does as if absolutely nothing had happened.

In the days immediately following, he befriends a pimp, and defends him by lying to the police who have come to arrest the character for having beaten one of his charges, an Arabian girl. He accepts an invitation to a week-end party at the beach, which he spends with his mistress, the pimp, and a few others. At the party he meets the brother of the victimized Arabian girl in two different encounters. In the first nothing happens, but in the second Meursault has a gun and the Arab has a knife. He fires once, and in his trial, later, he might have pleaded self-defense if only he hadn't pulled the trigger four more times. When asked why, his explanation is that the sun was hot.

The rest of the story draws out the implications of this series of events as they are reviewed by the various members of the social organism who must see them from a fixed point of view inevitably at variance with the narrator's own. Meursault is visited by the magistrate, the chaplain, and Marie, his mistress. At trial, the prosecutor pictures him as an antisocial ogre; to do so he has only to recount the series of events outlined above. The defense can make no case. Meursault is found guilty and sentenced to death by the guillotine. His last wish, that at least the audience enjoy his death, is his final irony to be flaunted in the face of society: by their enjoyment, to be expressed by "howls of execration," they will have become implicated in the responsibility for his death.

The sheer listing of the events in the story tends to take away its poignancy. It merely states what has happened and what has been reviewed. The manner of review, however, serves to reinforce the reader's knowledge of Meursault's basic estrangement. He has lived what Simone de Beauvoir calls "a passionate life," giving away to the impulse of the moment, and never reflecting enough to know that is what he was doing; nor did he understand that there is a reason why he should have, until he finds himself in prison. Conscience, after all, is an act of reflection; it is for this reason that the ambiguity noted above is permitted in the French. But if Meursault had reflected there would have been no estrangement and no novel by the name, *L'Etranger*.

Meursault's self-awareness takes place gradually, and once again irony has its part in the development. Listening to the prosecutor and to the defense attorney, Meursault knows they must be talking about him, but fails to recognize himself in their speeches. He begins to note the disparity between his character as it is described in concepts by others, and the inner felt necessity to be other than described and known by others. What he feels and what he hears do not jibe; the world as it is described and the world as he feels it should be are not the same. They cannot be the same, since the one contradicts the essence of the other. It is as if he finally became a part of society by being its victim: absurd, but that is it, the metaphysical awareness. One is free to feel other, and is free only as one does so. But this awareness comes to Meursault when he is behind bars, fated to die by decapitation in the name of the French people. And therein lies still another irony.

The moral dilemma, which can be solved only by quick action, can no longer be solved, unless it be by adding the last fateful wish to incriminate others in his own death. By capturing their consciousnesses in the fascination of his last agony, he will have expressed himself freely and fully consciously for the only time of his life. His fate is ironic, but superior to theirs: he knows what is happening to them and they are mistaken about him.

In all this complicated depth, there is one outstanding symbol: the Algerian sun. It has been thought that Meursault's explanation of the murder was entirely fanciful, a cynical denial of responsibility for his act. And so it was interpreted at the trial. At the time it was given, the explanation was correct and fraught with significance of which even Meursault was ignorant. Why did he pull the trigger the second and succeeding times? Because the sun was hot.

Some critics have interpreted this answer as a statement of the absurd, due to the *non sequitur* contained therein. A statement of the absurd it is, but not because of the alleged *non sequitur*. The clue to the symbol is given in Meursault's musing following the trial, when, in jail, he tries to reconstruct for himself the significance of the events he has just lived through.

The awareness of the sun's significance is given simultaneously with that of his freedom. It signifies the contingent universe which is the real world of the naturalists, and as such constitutes that reactive field which a man's freedom must possess if his actions are to be effective. It need not be adverse, but is always there, indifferent. Meursault did not pull the trigger, as a naturalist would have it, because he was forced to it by the adversity of events; there is no freedom, no life to be found in that gambit. He pulled the trigger for no reason at all; in doing so, he was living his freedom. Finally, he was not guilty of murder by premeditation because he had no intention of killing his adversary; rather, he was guilty because in the exercise of his freedom he took away the freedom of another; in living, he caused death. And all this he could now read from the effect of that sun, when he was no longer affected by its brilliance or its heat because of the prison walls which shielded him from the blinding glare. Again, there is irony: the sun may blind only if one is free and exposed to its rays; perceived indirectly, by reflection from an object, the sun yields light even if that light is reflected off prison bars.

The hell of his incarceration is experienced as a set of deprivations, and Meursault dies in spite of his refusal to take the leap; but he dies at the hands of an ignorant society which is in no position to feel either the glare and the heat or to perceive the light of the sun. And for their crime, which is to have needlessly taken Meursault's life, he becomes the judge and condemns them to enjoy the sight of his decapitated body.

The expressiveness of Camus' story is extremely acute, since the irony of the depth is constantly mirrored in the ironic tone of the first person narrator. To show the disparity between fact and human desire Camus needs only show the growing gulf between Meursault and his accusers— as well as his defenders. The significance of this disparity is continually insinuated, never insisted upon. Even Meursault's own thoughts are never clearly stated; they run together and are blurred by the hint of an emotion, which is felt sometimes toward the thoughts of others, sometimes toward one of his own thoughts. But just as Sartre had used a variegated style, Camus switches from impressionism to reportage, and from reportage back to impressionism, depending upon the function of objectivity in the telling of the story. When the position of the world and its metaphysical absurdity or the views of another on Meursault's character dominates the narration, reportage is used; impressionism allows the consciousness to appear; and when it becomes fully self-conscious, as it does just before his last wish, the novel ends on its final note of moral absurdity.

Still more important for our case is the order in which the styles appear. Part I is written almost wholly impressionistically; it depicts Meursault's life of listless passion as it is interrupted by his mother's death. In Part II reportage dominates, since the events of Part I are reviewed by others; as such, they are seen by the reader and the narrator in the same instant but at the distance of one remove from actuality, the point of view taken by the other, whether friendly and "helpful" or official and opposing. This remove, given in the objectivity of reportage, permits the narrator's reflection, which must, in its conclusion, revert to impressionism. The universe is then seen as completely indifferent to man's wishes, but even this felt realization cannot prevent the last wish.

The sun riddle, the solving of which is one of the major developments in the story, is put forth in both styles: its presence on the day of the murder is registered impressionistically, and later is assigned as the reason of the murder. When the reason is to be given in court, the sun's effect cannot be effectively registered in an objective report. It is given in a negative fashion: the prisoner can state only that he had no intention of killing the victim; when put into a positive statement, the reason seems absurd and the audience titters. Once the riddle is solved, however, and the prisoner realizes that the universe is benignly indifferent to his every wish, his consciousness achieves full self-awareness only to be ironically extinguished. A final paradox expressed in a final irony, Meursault's enlightenment is not rendered directly into prose; it is the ultimate and unexpressed conclusion which the author has left to the reader's cooperative imagination.

In conclusion it may be stated that the story is efficiently conceived and masterfully executed. It was conceived on the basis of its metaphysical and moral significance, and executed as that paradoxically significant episode could best be executed, in the impressive ironies of a first person narrator. *The Stranger* therefore meets both conditions we have laid down for a successful novel of ideas: it presents an abstract idea in the full integument of a concrete, imaginative context. No one could look for more, either from a philosopher or from a man of letters.

That existentialist philosophy has been successful in interpreting life in post-war Europe there can be no doubt. A group of writers have been successful in embodying the basic existentialistic hypotheses in a series of novels and have thereby produced what has come to be called "existentialist literature." The movement at present bids fair to outgrow its original context, but it is to be hoped that this further growth will never lose contact with its philosophical roots. Existentialist literature need not be European but it must remain philosophical in the sense I have tried to explain. How far the existentialist literatures of other cultures are imitative, and how far original, is, however, a matter of future historical judgment. But if my test for the literary judgment of a philosophical novel is correct, the critic's task is to consider the manner in which the metaphysical or moral idea has been embodied in the writer's medium. Nothing less than this formal judgment will substantiate the claims made for an existentialist literature.[8]

Notes

The titles of works frequently mentioned in the notes are abbreviated. Full titles and bibliographical information for all articles and books are included in the bibliography.

CHAPTER I

1 See Croce's *Aesthetic as Science of Expression;* the book is divided into two parts, theory and the history of aesthetics. For commentaries by American authors, see Hospers, *Philosophy,* XXXI (1956), 291–308, and Zink, *Journal of Philosophy,* XLVII (1950), 210–16.
2 See Bosanquet's *Three Lectures on Aesthetic.*
3 See Collingwood's *Principles of Art.*
4 See Alexander's essay in *Philosophical and Literary Pieces,* ed. Laird, pp. 211–32, and his *Beauty and Other Forms of Value.*
5 In his *Principles of Literary Criticism* and his *Science and Poetry.*
6 Elton, ed., *Essays.*
7 Santayana, *Sense of Beauty,* p. 9.
8 *Ibid.,* p. 10.
9 For his treatment of the sensuous character of an aesthetic surface, see his *Aesthetic Judgment,* Chaps. III–V; for his definition of the field of ·aesthetic inquiry see his *Aesthetic Analysis,* p. 5.
10 For a commentary on Dewey's formalist doctrine, see Ames's article in *Journal of Aesthetics and Art Criticism,* XV (1956), 85–93.
11 Besides the critical edifice of his own two earlier *Critiques,* Kant has used the sources he found in Hume, Burke, and Gérard. In discussing judgments of taste as a function of the reflective faculties of the human mind, Kant freed aesthetics of the notion that an artist, or genius, creates with respect to a preconceived notion or concept; it followed immediately therefrom that "genius" alone gives the rule to art, and that the product it thus produces is not translatable into terms other than itself. Thus was depicted the notion of an autonomous art object which is the cornerstone of "modern" aesthetics. Creation as discovery is a central thesis in the aesthetics of Alexander and of the Frenchman, Alain.
    The recent French aesthetician, Alain (Emile Chartier), sums up Kant's contribution to contemporary aesthetics in the following way: "Je dois avertir qu'après une étude suffisante de cette oeuvre vénérable, je n'y ai rien trouvé qui ne m'ait semblé capital et à jamais acquis en ce difficile sujet." *Système,* p. 7. This judgment seems to be borne out by the consistent attempts to describe aesthetic judgments in terms, other than those

necessitated by Kant's own transcendental method, of a unique qualitative experience.

12   Mrs. Langer's philosophy of art has been undergoing continual revision in the following series of her aesthetic works: *Philosophy in a New Key* (1942), *Feeling and Form* (1953), and *Problems of Art* (1957).

13   See his essay in *Collected Papers,* eds. Hartshorne and Weiss, V, 388–402.

14   *Sense of Beauty,* p. 166. Santayana thus has had the honor of presaging the linguistic theory of the *Tractatus.* When Wittgenstein later became interested in the sources of various languages, he dropped this model as an ideal and referred to various possible languages which are governed by different sets of rules like so many arbitrary games. See his *Philosophical Investigations,* pp. 5 ff.

15   *Feeling and Form,* p. ix.

16   See his *Philosophy of Art.*

17   Morris has developed his aesthetic views in a series of articles: "Esthetics and the Theory of Signs," *Journal of Unified Science, VIII* (June, 1939), 131–50; "Science, Art and Technology," *Kenyon Review,* I (1939), 409–23; "Significance, Signification, and Painting," in *Language of Value,* ed. Lepley, pp. 58–76, 274–80.

18   *Art as Experience.*

19   See his article in *International Journal of Ethics,* XXXVI (1926), 382–93; See also *Mind, Self and Society,* ed. Professor Morris, which contains a quasi-complete bibliographical account of Mead's semiotic writings.

20   *Philosophy of the Arts.*

21   See his article in *Journal of Aesthetics and Art Criticism,* XV (1956), 27–35. In editing his later *Problems in Aesthetics,* Weitz asked for a criticism of his later position from Erich Kahler; it appeared in that volume, pp. 157–71.

22   Arnheim's earlier works appeared in German. Since his transplantation, two editions have appeared in English: *Art and Visual Perception,* and *Film as Art.* The latter work is a revision of an earlier German work on the film.

23   *Work of Art.* This work grew out of the earlier *Basis of Criticism in the Arts,* which is an application of the four metaphysical doctrines—mechanism, contextualism, organicism, and formism—to criticism. The final essay in this earlier volume was entitled "Supplementary Essay: The Aesthetic Work of Art." For an explanation of his metaphysical categories, see his *World Hypotheses.*

24   In *The Journal of Philosophy,* LIV (1957), 429–42.

25   In *Essays,* ed. Elton, pp. 170–86.

26   The treatment of the relations between philosophy and literature varies greatly: from the outright confusion of the two disciplines in Kaufman's *Existentialism,* via some attempts to clarify the philosophical value of literature in Berger's *Existentialism and Literature in Action,* U. of

Buffalo Studies, and Knight's excellent study, *Literature Considered as Philosophy*, to the application of philosophy to explain the very structure of literary forms, as in Harper's *Sleeping Beauty* and Barnes's *Literature of Possibility*.

I have included my own analysis of the philosophical structure of two French novels to illustrate the contention that traditional philosophy may serve as a source of hypotheses to interpret the surface and depth qualities of a novel; see Appendix B.

27 Pp. 7–10.

28 *Aesthetic Analysis*, p. 5.

29 Santayana, *Sense of Beauty*, pp. 20–21; Parker, *Principles of Aesthetics*, pp. 2 ff.

30 Given its connection with the Aesthetics Society of America, the *JAAC* is one of the best sources of our knowledge concerning the direction the study of aesthetics has taken in our own day. Originally published by The Philosophical Library under the editorship of D. D. Runes, the journal was presented to the ASA in 1945, when Thomas Munro assumed the editorship. Runes was the titular editor of the journal from its foundation in 1941 until its transfer to Munro in 1945.

31 See his article in *Essays*, ed. Elton, pp. 169 ff.

32 For a rather dogmatic statement of the causes of aesthetics' low status, see Passmore's article in *Essays*, ed. Elton, pp. 36–55.

33 The conception of aesthetics as a discipline dealing with creative activity within the structures of social institutions is today being soft-pedalled in favor of philosophers' greater concern with logic and linguistics—a point which may be made by examining the contents of a standard book of readings in aesthetics: Rader, *Modern Book of Esthetics*, which has undergone two revisions since 1935, in 1952 and 1960.

In the first edition of this text, the topic was listed under the rubric "Instrumentalist Theories" and contained articles by Morris, Dewey, and Whitehead; in the second, the rubric became "Art and Society," and the Dewey article was replaced by Mumford's "The Esthetic Assimilation of the Machine." In the last edition the topic of art and society was dropped, Mumford's article relegated to a discussion of "form and function," and those of Dewey and Whitehead classified as theories concerned with art as "vivid experience."

34 Merleau-Ponty has given an account of his early relationship with Sartre in *Sens et non-sens*, pp. 83–96.

CHAPTER II

1 Besides his unorthodox ideas in philosophy and in politics, Sartre's love of expressive language has caused him to be classified as a "scandalous" writer. See Merleau-Ponty's "Un auteur scandaleux", *Sens et non-sens*, pp. 83–96.

2 Beigbeder recounts that Sartre's first literary attempts were to put the

Fables of La Fontaine into classical alexandrines at the age of six; at eighteen he published his first play in the *Revue Sans Titre,* founded by himself in collaboration with some school friends, among whom was Paul Nizan. His first novel, like his first collection of essays, was refused publication. See Beigbeder's *L'Homme Sartre, passim.*

3   A fairer evaluation of the works of Mme. de Beauvoir would be, perhaps, to say she has collaborated with Sartre in the development of their ideas. She has contributed an ethics to the movement, and is perhaps best known for her study of woman's condition in an existentialist world. See her *Deuxième sexe.* A brilliant novelist in her own right, she is a constant contributor to *Temps Modernes.*

4   Mathematician and professor of applied science, Campbell has been a close student of the development of existentialism in France. His study of the philosophy in Sartre's literature is clear and fair-minded: *Jean-Paul Sartre, ou une littérature philosophique.* The basis of Campbell's acceptance of Sartre is given in the introduction to this book as Sartre's belief in freedom.

5   See his *Structure,* and *Phénoménologie.*

6   This thesis, expounded in *L'Etre,* is repeated by the hero of *L'Age de raison,* and has led some critics to claim that the tetralogy is in fact an autobiography.

7   See Beigbeder, *L'Homme Sartre,* p. 17; I have given a literary analysis of the book in Appendix B.

8   French teacher, philosopher, and essayist whose theory of the imagination was developed into a philosophy of art in *Système* and expanded to include a naturalistic philosophy of religion in *Les Dieux.*

9   See the pre-reflective *cogito, L'Etre,* pp. 16–23.

10   Sartre examines Berkeley's dictum, *esse est percipi,* in the Introduction to *L'Etre,* pp. 23–27.

11   See de Waelhen's "Une philosophie de l'ambiguïté," published as an introduction to Merleau-Ponty's *Structure,* pp. v–xv.

12   See this study, pp. 32–33.

13   See Sartre's article in *Recherches Philosophiques* VI (1936–37), 85–123, especially 107 ff.

14   This technique is borrowed from Merleau-Ponty who indicates the relevance of the so-called mind-body problem for the phenomenology of perception in his *Structure.*

15   Stated in *L'Etre,* p. 34.

16   *L'Imagination,* p. 19.

17   *Ibid.,* p. 14. The "phosphorescence" of Hume's impression is not easily established. If one consults the texts, only the purple color of the points of extension by which the idea of space is built up would seem to afford some evidence; see Hume, *Treatise of Human Nature* I, II, 3. Sartre seems to assume that anything seen (and Hume's impressions are supposedly seen) must be capable of reflecting light; whence the phosphorescence of the impressions.

18   *Ibid.,* p. 13.
19   *Ibid.*
20   See *L'Imaginaire,* p. 11; and Sartre's article in *Recherches Philoso-phiques,* VI (1936–37), 85–123, *passim.*
21   See his article in *Recherches Philosophiques,* VI (1936–37), pp. 116–23.
22   "On appelle spontanée une existence qui se détermine par elle-même à exister. En d'autres termes, exister spontanément, c'est exister pour soi et par soi. Une seule réalité mérite donc le nom de spontanée; c'est la con-science. Pour elle, en effet, exister et avoir conscience d'exister ne font qu'un."—*L'Imagination,* p. 125.
23   In *Recherches Philosophiques,* VI (1936–37), p. 114.
24   For Sartre's refutation of Alain's theory of the imagination, see his *L'Imagination,* pp. 135–38.
25   "Nous avons tous lu Brunschvicg, Lalande et Meyerson, nous avons tous cru que l'Esprit-Araignée attirait les choses dans sa toile, les couvrait d'une bave blanche et lentement les déglutissait, les réduisait à sa propre substance."—Sartre, in *Nouvelle Revue Française,* LII (1939), 129.
26   Cf. the explanation of these terms in pre-Sartrean existentialism by Wahl, *Existence Humaine et Transcendance;* and "Experience and Tran-scendence," *Philosophic Thought in France and the United States,* ed. Farber, pp. 87–102.
27   Cf. *Husserliana,* Band I. A refutation of Sartre's position is given by Natanson in the *Festschrift, For Roman Ingarden,* pp. 42–53.
28   *Husserliana,* Band III, pp. 269–70.
29   Cf. Dufrenne's *Phénoménologie,* and his article in *Revue Philosophique,* CXLIV (1954), 75–84.
30   See below, pp. 43 ff.
31   *L'Imagination,* p. 158.
32   *L'Imaginaire,* p. 14.
33   See Lanteri-Laura's article in *Etudes Philosophiques,* IX (1954), 57–72.
34   Sartre quotes the following passage in support of his contention: "Now, as it is impossible to form an idea of an object that is possessed of quan-tity and quality, and yet is possessed of no precise degree of either, it follows, that there is an equal impossibility of forming an idea that is not limited and confined in both these particulars. . . ."—Hume, *Treatise* (I, I, 7); cf. *L'Imaginaire,* p. 15.
35   *L'Imaginaire,* p. 17.
36   *Ibid.,* p. 18.
37   *Ibid.,* pp. 19–22.
38   *Ibid.,* p. 25.
39   "La condition pour qu'une conscience puisse imaginer est donc double: il faut à la fois qu'elle puisse poser le monde dans sa totalité synthétique et, à la fois, qu'elle puisse poser l'objet imaginé comme hors d'atteinte par rapport à cet ensemble synthétique, c'est-à-dire poser le monde comme un néant par rapport à l'image."—*Ibid.,* p. 233.

40 "L'objet intentionnel de la conscience imageante a ceci de particulier qu'il n'est pas là et qu'il est posé comme tel, ou encore qu'il n'existe pas et qu'il est posé comme inexistant, ou qu'il n'est pas posé du tout."— *Ibid.*, p. 25.

41 *Ibid.*, p. 170.

42 *Ibid.*, pp. 161–75.

43 See *L'Etre*, pp. 508–61.

44 ". . . un acte qui vise dans sa corporéité un objet absent ou inexistant à travers un continu physique ou psychique qui ne se donne pas en propre, mais à titre de 'représentant analogique' de l'objet visé."—*L'Imaginaire*, p. 75.

45 *Ibid.*, pp. 30–34.

46 *Ibid.*, p. 70.

47 *Ibid.*, p. 76.

48 *Ibid.*

49 See *L'Etre*, pp. 11–14.

50 *L'Imaginaire*, p. 155.

51 *Ibid.*, p. 156.

52 Merleau-Ponty's treatise appears in the same collection as Sartre's two major works: Gallimard's *Bibliothèque des Idées*.

53 See his *Phénoménologie*.

54 In his article published as Introduction to Merleau-Ponty's *Structure*, pp. v–xv.

55 *L'Imaginaire*, pp. 79–92.

56 The psychological case history used as a basis for the description of this metaphysical state first occurred in "La transcendance de l'Ego"; it re-occurs, with a change in example, in *L'Etre*, pp. 67–79.

57 In his *Les Idées et les âges*, Vol. I, pp. 25 ff.

58 See his *L'Imaginaire*, pp. 79–92.

59 Essences are sometimes said to be "projected" upon the profiles of objects, and in this way consciousness is said to create its objects. But in order to be able to "project" essences upon the appearances of an object the consciousness in question must be possessed of them, if not innately, then by an intuition or abstraction. The consequences of these assumptions are considered below.

60 Pp. 11–14. I am rendering *raison* as "ratio."

61 See his *L'Existentialisme est un humanisme*, pp. 17–18.

62 Pp. 508–61.

63 See Welch's *Edmund Husserl*, pp. 229–37.

64 *L'Imaginaire* is subtitled *Psychologie phénoménologique de l'imagination; L'Etre, Essai d'ontologie phénoménologique.* In the former work Sartre blandly assumes that the two methods will give substitutable results. His stated reason for so doing is that the philosophical world is not yet used to the method of "pure phenomenology." See his *L'Imaginaire*, p. 228. This substitution is consistently made in *L'Etre*.

65 See this study, pp. 35–36.

66 See this study, pp. 46–48; for Sartre's admission of his debt to Husserl, see also his *L'Imagination,* p. 157.

CHAPTER III

1 See MacDonald's essay in *Essays,* ed. Elton, pp. 114–30. Miss Mac-Donald states that the distinction between the physical object and the "work of art" is usually made, and that it is the philosopher's business to solve the linguistic problems arising from the distinction. For some arts (the plastic ones) the physical object and the work of art are the same, whereas in others they are not. She does not think it possible to give a complete elucidation of the term 'work of art.'

2 *Ibid.,* pp. 123–24.

3 See his *Treatise* I, I, 3.

4 See above, pp. 35–42.

5 "Poser une image c'est constituer un objet en marge de la totalité du réel, c'est donc tenir le réel à distance, s'en affranchir, en un mot le nier."—*L'Imaginaire,* p. 233.

6 Cf. *ibid.,* pp. 234 ff.

7 *Ibid.,* p. 233.

8 See his *Literary Criticism,* and *Science and Poetry, passim.*

9 See this study, pp. 66–67.

10 *L'Imaginaire,* pp. 239–40.

11 For an elucidation of this point, see Zink's article in *Journal of Philosophy,* XLVII (1950), 210–16.

12 *Feeling and Form,* p. ix.

13 See MacDonald's article in *Essays,* ed. Elton, p. 123.

14 See Sartre's refutation of Alain's theory of the imagination in *L'Imagination,* pp. 135–38.

15 See MacDonald's article in *Essays,* ed. Elton, p. 123.

16 The dependence upon Descartes' theory of knowledge is clearly evident here. I have traced the sources of Alain's aesthetic theory in my unpublished doctoral dissertation, *Alain, Aesthetician: An Essay in the Philosophy of Art,* submitted to the faculty of the University of Illinois in June, 1954.

17 In his "Fixer l'imaginaire, c'est peut-être le but de tous les beaux-arts." *Vingt leçons,* p. 33.

18 Buffon has been so often misquoted, and the misquotations corrected, that a reference to the source of the quotation is perhaps somewhat overbearing. In his *Discours sur le style,* delivered to the Académie Française on August 25, 1753, he elaborated the connection between style and the form writing; "Le style n'est que l'ordre et le mouvement qu'on met dans ses pensées." And he concludes, ". . . le style est de l'homme même." Extracts of the speech are included in a standard student anthology by Schinz, *Eighteenth Century French Readings,* pp. 253–57.

19 *Système,* p. 388.

20   This remark was made more precisely against Renan's *Jesus* and *Marcus Aurelius*. Alain had the habit of bracketing Renan, Sainte-Beuve, and Taine as the gods presiding over the Ecole Normale, and did his best to destroy their literary reputations. More specifically he calls Taine's *Intelligence* and *Napoléon* unworthy of consideration. These episodes of his school days are recounted in *Histoire de mes pensées*, pp. 38–39.

21   Interspersed throughout the ten volumes of Comte, six of the *Cours de philosophie positive* and four of *Système de politique positive*. For specific references to the genesis of a society through the use of signs, see *Système de politique positive*, II, 87, 101, and 220–59. Most important for contemporary aesthetics is Comte's description of the social significance of ambiguity.

22   See Church's *Essay on Critical Appreciation*, Chap. V.

23   As Langer considered them in her *Philosophy in a New Key*, pp. 75–83; her terminology is revised in *Feeling and Form*, p. 26.

24   ". . . le langage absolu se retrouve dans tous les arts, qui, en ce sens, sont comme des énigmes, signifiant impérieusement et beaucoup, sans qu'on puisse dire quoi."—*Vingt leçons*, p. 66.

25   "Toujours, autant que l'oeuvre est d'artisan, le modèle de l'oeuvre est hors de l'oeuvre; mais autant que l'oeuvre est d'artiste, c'est l'oeuvre même qui est le modèle. Enfin ce qui renvoie à un autre objet est plat, ce qui renvoie à la sagesse de l'auteur est pédant; mais quand l'oeuvre répond à elle-même et instruit l'artiste aussi bien, elle est de style alors. Et ce n'est pas par hasard que ce beau mot désigne aussi l'outil pointu qui sculptait autrefois l'écriture."—*Système*, pp. 387–88.

26   The influence of Alain, the teacher, on one of France's most prolific writers is described by Maurois in *Alain*.

27   *Préliminaires à l'esthétique*, pp. 37–38.

28   "On reconnaît donc ici comme dans la musique un accord entre les démarches intellectuelles et la nature corporelle, ce qui faisait dire à Kant que le beau enferme une finalité sans fin extérieure. Le beau, autrement dit, nous fait sentir en nous-mêmes l'accord entre le haut et le bas, si vainement cherché par la sagesse."—*Vingt leçons*, p. 40.

29   Richards, *Principles of Literary Criticism* and *Science and Poetry;* Ducasse, *Philosophy of Art*.

30   *L'Imagination*, pp. 135–38.

31   See Chap. II above, where Sartre's refutation of Alain is outlined at some length.

32   See Chaps. II–IV.

33   This assertion is one of the reasons I have taken exception to the treatment of Sartre by MacDonald.

34   See Croce, *Aesthetic*, p. 111: "We cannot will or not will our aesthetic vision. . . ." and p. 51: "The true artist . . . finds himself big with his theme, he knows not how he feels the moment of birth drawing near, but he cannot will it or not will it."

35   *Analysis of Knowledge*, p. 478.

36 *L'Imaginaire,* p. 239.
37 *Analysis of Knowledge,* p. 478.
38 Expressed in an essay in *Selected Essays, 1917–1932,* pp. 121–26.
39 *Feeling and Form,* p. xi, pp. 45–46.
40 Explained in Chap. II, above.
41 *L'Imaginaire,* p. 245.
42 See his *Sense of Beauty.*
43 See her chapter by the same name in *Feeling and Form,* pp. 12–23.
44 *Ibid.,* Chap. I.
45 Hospers has isolated the various senses of the term "expression" as used in aesthetics in his article in *Proceedings of the Aristotelian Society,* 1954–5, pp. 313–44.
46 *Tractatus Logico-Philosophicus,* 4.021, 4.0311.
    Santayana uses the same notion to explain the form of literary expression in *Sense of Beauty,* Sec. 42. Langer's first development of this idea is in *Philosophy in a New Key,* pp. 63–68.
47 The theory here developed is merely sketched in outline as a partial conclusion to the work under discussion.
48 See his article in *Nouvelle Revue Française,* Jan., 1939, pp. 129–32.
49 Sartre thought phenomenological theory would serve to "liberate" the reading public from Proust; he had in mind, of course, Proust's stylistic habit of associating a physical event with a complex state of mind. See *Situations I,* p. 34.
50 "C'est une *propriété* de ce masque japonais que d'être terrible, une inépuisable, irréductible propriété qui constitue sa nature même—et non la somme de nos réactions subjectives à un morceau de bois sculpté. Husserl a réinstallé l'horreur et le charme dans les choses. Il nous a restitué le monde des artistes et des prophètes: effrayant, hostile, dangereux, avec des havres de grâce et d'amour."—*Ibid.*
51 *Esquisse d'une théorie des émotions,* p. 5.
52 *Ibid.,* p. 7.
53 *Ibid.,* p. 49.
54 *Ibid.,* p. 41.
55 *Ibid.;* Dufrenne develops this notion of "affective schemata" in his *Phénoménologie,* Vol. II, Part. 4.
56 *Esquisse d'une théorie des émotions,* p. 41.
57 "La conscience ne se borne pas à projeter des significations affectives sur le monde qui l'entoure: elle *vit* le monde nouveau qu'elle vient de constituer. Elle le vit directement, elle s'y intéresse, elle souffre les qualités que les conduites ont ébauchées. Cela signifie que, lorsque, toutes voies étant barrées, la conscience se précipite dans le monde magique de l'émotion, elle s'y précipite tout entière en se dégradant; elle est nouvelle conscience en face du monde nouveau et c'est avec ce qu'elle a de plus intime en elle qu'elle le constitue, avec cette présence à elle-même, sans distance, de son point de vue sur le monde."—*Ibid.,* pp. 41–42.

58 ". . . une manière d'appréhender l'object irréel et, loin de se diriger sur le tableau réel, elle sert à constituer à travers la toile réelle l'objet imaginaire."—*L'Imaginaire*, p. 242.

59 Ziff has tried to elucidate the senses of the pertinent aesthetic terms in his article in *Essays*, ed. Elton, pp. 170–86. When he legitimizes the sense of "object of art" in common usage to refer to the physical object which might have to be crated for shipment, he seems to give too much weight to the distinction abhorred by Miss MacDonald; his distinctively aesthetic interpretation of the same object, it may be noted, lacks the psychological or metaphysical background Sartre attempted to give the distinction. It is part of my thesis that the aesthetician can, however, by-pass the metaphysics of realism or idealism; in this, I am in agreement with Professor Ziff.

60 See Blackmur's article in *Lectures in Criticism*, Bollingen Series, XVI (1949), pp. 187–209.

61 For an edition of this classic with opinions of various actors concerning the validity of Diderot's "paradox," see *Paradoxe sur le comédien*.

62 In *Eighteenth Century French Readings*, ed. Schinz, pp. 477–78.

63 Schinz gives a brief discussion of this controversy, citing A. Morize, *Problems and Methods of Literary History* (New York: Ginn & Co., 1923), pp. 158–69.—*Eighteenth Century French Readings*, pp. 477 ff.

64 "C'est vous qui remportez toutes ces impressions. L'acteur est las, et vous tristes; c'est qu'il s'est démené sans rien sentir, et que vous avez senti sans vous démener. S'il en était autrement, la condition du comédien serait la plus malheureuse des conditions; mais il n'est pas le personnage, il le joue et le joue si bien que vous le prenez pour tel: l'illusion n'est que pour vous, il sait bien, lui, qu'il ne l'est pas."—Diderot, *Paradoxe*, p. 22.

65 *My Life in Art*, pp. 163–64.

66 *L'Imaginaire*, p. 242.

67 *Ibid.*, p. 243.

68 *Ibid.*

69 In her article in *Essays*, ed. Elton.

70 See above, pp. 64–66.

71 *Philosophy in a New Key*, pp. 63–83; *Feeling and Form*, pp. 24–41. For the use of the same device in literary criticism, see Burke, *Philosophy of Literary Form*, pp. 1–137.

72 See Flew's article in *Mind* n.s. LXV (1956), 392–99, in review of Shorter, also in *Mind* n.s. LXI (1952), 528–42, which in turn was written in criticism of Ryle's *Concept of Mind*, Chap. VIII.

73 See this study, Chap. IV, for a discussion of Sartre's treatment of the novel.

74 "A présent, voici la matière: un rocher, simple grumeau d'espace. Avec de l'espace, il faut donc que Giacometti fasse un homme; il faut qu'il inscrive le mouvement dans la totale immobilité, l'unité dans la multiplicité infinie, l'absolu dans la relativité pure, l'avenir dans le présent éternel, le bavardage des signes dans le silence obstiné des choses."—*Situations III*, p. 290.

75 "Voici Ganymède sur son socle. Si vous me demandez à quelle distance il est de moi, je vous répondrai que je ne sais pas de quoi vous parlez. Entendez-vous par 'Ganymède' le jouvenceau qui fut enlevé par l'aigle de Jupiter? En ce cas, je dirai qu'il n'y a de lui à moi aucune relation *réelle* de distance, pour la raison qu'il n'existe pas. Faites-vous allusion, au contraire, au bloc de marbre que le sculpteur a façonné à l'image du mignon? En ce cas, il s'agit d'une chose vraie, d'un minéral existant et nous pouvons mesurer."—*Ibid.*, p. 296.

76 "Calder ne suggère rien: il attrape de vrais mouvements vivants et les façonne. Ses mobiles ne signifient ríen, ne renvoient à ríen qu'à eux-mêmes: ils sont, voilà tout; ce sont des absolus. En eux, la "part du Diable" est plus forte peut-être qu'en tout autre création de l'homme. Ils ont trop de ressorts, et trop compliqués, pour qu'une tête humaine puisse prévoir toutes leurs combinaisons, même celle de leur créateur."—*Ibid.*, p. 308.

77 See Merleau-Ponty's evaluation of "metaphysical" criticism, Chapter X, below; and Munro's *Scientific Method.*

CHAPTER IV

1 The inclusion of the study of creativity, and its relation to social function, is the distinctive characteristic of Sartre's theory of literature. Traditionally it follows a pattern set by Alain and Valéry; Dufrenne, in *Phénoménologie,* Vol. I, pp. 1–7, argues for a reversal, with the emphasis placed on the activity of the aesthetic consumer.

2 For Beauvoir's contribution, see *Temps Modernes* II (1946), 1153–63.

3 *Sens et non-sens,* pp. 51–81.

4 After Beauvoir's novel, *Les Mandarins,* in which the inner movements of the group were rendered in fiction. Following his defection, Merleau-Ponty criticized Sartre's later emphasis on the political functions of literature as based upon the "myth" of the mandarin. See this study, Chap. VI.

5 See his article on Dos Passos in *Nouvelle Revue Française,* August, 1938.

6 In *Nouvelle Revue Française,* L (1938), 323–28; and LII (1939), 1057–61.

7 For an analysis of Wright's style, see below, pp. 111 ff. The French translation of Algren's *Man With the Golden Arm* appeared serially, as *L'Homme au bras d'or,* in *Temps Modernes,* Vol. X (1954–55).

8 For a description of Sartre's notion of freedom as it applies to a subjugated people, see *Situations III,* pp. 11–14.

9 See his *Great Tradition.*

10 *Ibid.,* p. 19.

11 *Ibid.*

12 For Farrell's recognition of his debt, see his *Note on Literary Criticism,* p. 12.

13 *Ibid.* pp. 12–13.

14 See his *Creative Criticism,* pp. 3–44.

15 *Note on Literary Criticism,* pp. 134–79; see also his "The Categories of 'Bourgeois' and 'Proletarian,' " pp. 77–94.

16 For a description of the concrete relation between "subject matter" and "form," see below, pp. 109 ff.

17 His theory of meaning is the source of this claim; see this study, pp. 29–30 and 57–62.

18 Farrell, *Note on Literary Criticism,* pp. 148 ff.

19 For Farrell's case, see *Literature and Morality,* pp. 35–78; for Blackmur's, *Language as Gesture,* pp. 400–420, and "A Critic's Job of Work," pp. 372–99.

20 These articles are reprinted in his *Philosophy of Literary Form,* pp. 314–22.

21 This confusion of the individual and the social aspects of literature is even more surprising since Burke was a student of Mead's philosophy and social psychology; see "George Herbert Mead," in his *Philosophy of Literary Form,* pp. 379–82.

22 Cf. Sartre's *L'Etre,* Part II, Chap. I; for a readable, sympathetic commentary, see Desan's *Tragic Finale,* Chaps. II, IV, and V.

23 *Situations I,* pp. 70–81.

24 This thesis was explained and defended in an article by Shorer, in *Hudson Review,* I (1948), 67–87.

25 See Farrell's defense of Proust against the criticism of Hicks, in his *Note on Literary Criticism,* pp. 77-94.

26 Farrell is concerned with applying economic categories to the aesthetic product; Sartre, with the morality of authors: see *Situations II,* pp. 9–30.

27 *Ibid.,* p. 19.

28 *Ibid.,* p. 17.

29 Pédéraste, Proust a cru pouvoir s'aider de son expérience homosexuelle lorsqu'il a voulu dépeindre l'amour de Swann pour Odette; bourgeois, il présente ce sentiment d'un bourgeois riche et oisif pour une femme entretenue comme le prototype de l'amour: c'est donc qu'il croit à l'existence de passions universelles dont le mécanisme ne varie pas sensiblement quand on modifie les caractères sexuels, la condition sociale, la nation ou l'époque des individus qui les ressentent. Après avoir ainsi 'isolé' ces affections immuables, il pourra entreprendre de les réduire, à leur tour, à des particules élémentaires. Fidèle aux postulats de l'esprit d'analyse, il n'imagine même pas qu'il puisse y avoir une dialectique des sentiments, mais seulement un mécanisme."—*Ibid.,* p. 20.

30 *Ibid.,* p. 21.

31 *Ibid.,* pp. 21–22.

32 *Ibid.,* p. 22.

33 *Ibid.*

34 Two rather unsympathetic commentaries in English are those of Grene, *Dreadful Freedom,* and Stern, *Sartre: His Philosophy and Psychoanalysis.* Of a different stamp is that of Desan, cited above.

35 See the discussion of these contradictions, later in this chapter. Following this writing Sartre has published his first attempt to clear up the

confusions we have noted in detail; see his *Critique de la raison dialectique*.

36 After a novel by Edward Dahlberg, *Bottom Dog*, cited by Farrell, *Literature and Morality*, p. 21.

37 *Situations II*, pp. 261–77.

38 *Ibid.*, p. 16.

39 "Je rappelle, en effet, que dans la 'littérature engagée,' *l'engagement* ne doit, en aucun cas, faire oublier la *littérature* et que notre préoccupation doit être de servir la littérature en lui infusant un sang nouveau, tout autant que de servir la collectivité en essayant de lui donner la littérature qui lui convient."—*Ibid.*, p. 30.

40 The word "existentialist" has already entered the American dictionary as descriptive of a literary movement; see *Webster's New Collegiate Dictionary* (Springfield, Mass: Merriam, 1953), p. 289: "2. Lit. The theory or practice which aims to give readers a sense of an individual's passionate awareness of personal contingency and freedom." More metaphysical than literary, this definition misses the reference to literary techniques necessary to clarify the relationship between metaphysics and and fine literature. See Appendix B.

41 *Situations II*, p. 16.

42 For Alain's classification of the arts, see his *Système des beaux-arts*.

43 *What is Literature?* (translation by Frechtman of Sartre's *Qu'est-ce que la littérature?*), p. 20.

44 See his *L'Etre*, Part III, Chap. II; the literary interpretation of this principle follows below.

45 Frechtman, *What Is Literature?*, pp. 12–13.

46 *Ibid.*, pp. 19–20.

47 *Ibid.*, p. 13.

48 See below, Chap. VIII.

49 The coincidence of the aesthetic theories of Alain and Valéry reached its climax in Alain's commentaries on Valéry's poetry; See *Charmes* and *La Jeune Parque*.

50 Frechtman, *What Is Literature?*, p. 44.

51 See his *Situations II*, pp. 89–115.

52 See *L'Etre*, Part IV, Chap. I.

53 Cf. MacDonald, "Some Distinctive Features of Arguments used in Criticism of the Arts," in *Essays*, ed. Elton, pp. 114–30.

54 *L'Existentialisme*, pp. 17 ff.

55 Frechtman, *What Is Literature?*, p. 24.

56 Kant, *Fundamental Principles of the Metaphysics of Morals*.

57 Frechtman, *What Is Literature?*, p. 50.

58 *Ibid.*, p. 59.

59 The inadequacy of the so-called aesthetic categories has been shown by Weitz, *Philosophy of the Arts*, pp. 35–41, and by Burke, in his discussion of the form-content distinction in "The Philosophy of Literary Form," title essay of the longer work, pp. 89–102.

60 Frechtman, *What Is Literature?*, p. 239.

61 *Ibid.*, p. 284.
62 *Ibid.*, p. 224.
63 *Ibid.*, pp. 224 ff.
64 *Ibid.*, pp. 224–225.
65 *Ibid.*, p. 229.
66 *Sens et non-sens*, pp. 51–52.
67 Frechtman, *What Is Literature?*, pp. 77 ff.
68 This discrimination is part of the subject of the third in a series of articles entitled "Les communistes et la paix," in *Temps Modernes*, IX (1954), 1731–1819.
69 Frechtman, p. 240. The concept of "total literature" is intended to unite two functions served by the novelist as maker and consumer of society's products. The following scheme illustrates the two approaches to the literary profession and their intended synthesis in a total literature:

TOTAL LITERATURE

	Bourgeois	*Proletarian*
Dominant metaphysical categories	être	faire
Historical emphases	exis	praxis
Purpose of literary work	enjoyment	dévoilement
Literary techniques	analysis	synthesis

Sartre's theory of literature can therefore be called neither bourgeois nor proletarian, although it is more the latter than the former. See *Situations II*, pp. 261–66.
70 Frechtman, *What Is Literature?*, p. 156.
71 Through Brentano and his influence on Husserl. See Chap. II, this study.
72 See Vendôme's article in *Etudes*, CCLIX (1948), 39–54.
73 Sartre's earlier disagreement with the French Communist Party is expounded in *Situations II*, pp. 277 ff. See also his *Situations III*, pp. 135–225.
74 Frechtman, *What Is Literature?*, pp. 222-23.

CHAPTER V

1 See his *L'Esprit libre.*
2 *Situations II*, pp. 9–30.
3 See his article in *Etudes*, CCLIX (1948), 43–44.
4 Sartre condemns "collaborationist" writers on precisely this point; see his *Situations II*, p. 46.
5 "En vain tenterions-nous de devenir notre propre historien: l'historien lui-même est créature historique. Nous devons nous contenter de *faire* notre histoire à l'aveuglette, au jour le jour, en choisissant de tous les partis celui qui nous semble présentement le meilleur; mais nous ne pourrons jamais prendre sur elle ces vues cavalières qui ont fait la fortune de Taine et de Michelet; nous sommes dedans."—*Ibid.*, p. 42.

6 "Lire, pour un contemporain de l'auteur, roulé dans la même subjectivité historique, c'est participer aux risques de l'entreprise. Le livre est neuf, inconnu, sans importance: il faut y entrer sans guide; peut-être laisserons-nous passer sans les voir les qualités les plus rares, peut-être, au contraire, un éclat superficiel nous induira-t-il en erreur."—*Ibid.*, p. 43.

7 *Ibid.*, p. 44.

8 Cf. Hyman's *Armed Vision*, p. 407.

9 ". . . une invention technique, une oeuvre d'art ont un contenu positif qui demeure irréductible; quand vous aurez expliqué Racine par son époque, par son milieu, par son enfance, il restera *Phèdre*, l'inexplicable."—*Saint Genet comédien et martyr*, p. 222.

10 Frechtman, *What is Literature?*, p. 264.

11 See *Situations III*, pp. 11–14.

12 *L'Etre*, pp. 139–47, and 561–638.

13 Frechtman, *What Is Literature?*, p. 47.

14 See above, Chaps. II and III.

15 *Genet*, p. 321.

16 Frechtman, *What Is Literature?*, p. 57.

17 *Ibid.*, p. 58.

18 *Ibid.*

19 *Ibid.*

20 "En effet nous ne pouvons à la fois nous placer sur le plan esthétique où paraît cet 'elle-même' irréel que nous admirons et sur le plan réalisant de la possession physique."—*L'Imaginaire*, p. 246.

21 See his article in *Law and Contemporary Problems*, XX (1955), 544–59.

22 In *Temps Modernes*, VII (1951–52), 1002–33 and 1197–1230.

23 *Ibid.*, pp. 1005–6.

24 *Ibid.*, p. 1004.

25 *Ibid.*, p. 1003.

26 Part I, Chap. II.

27 "En choisissant l'érotisme, Sade a choisi l'imaginaire; dans l'imaginaire seulement il réussira à s'installer avec certitude sans risquer de déception; il l'a répété tout au long de son oeuvre: 'La jouissance des sens est toujours réglée sur l'imagination.' 'L'homme ne peut prétendre à la félicité qu'en servant tous les caprices de son imagination.' "—*Temps Modernes*, VII (1951), 1033.

28 *Marquis de Sade*, ed. Dinnage, p. 82.

29 *Ibid.*

30 *Genet*, p. 424.

31 See his *Baudelaire;* for the theoretical construction of the method, see *L'Etre*, pp. 643–63.

32 In *Anchor Review*, No. 2, pp. 241–54.

33 "Montrer les limites de l'interprétation psychanalytique et de l'explication marxiste et que seule la liberté peut rendre compte d'une personne

en sa totalité, faire voir cette liberté aux prises avec le destin, d'abord écrasée par ses fatalités puis se retournant sur elles pour les digérer peu à peu, prouver que le génie n'est pas un don mais l'issue qu'on invente dans les cas désespérés, retrouver le choix qu'un écrivain fait de lui-même, de sa vie et du sens de l'univers jusque dans les caractères formels de son style et de sa composition, jusque dans la structure de ses images, et dans la particularité de ses goûts, retracer en détail l'histoire d'une libération: voilà ce que j'ai voulu; le lecteur dira si j'ai réussi."— *Genet*, p. 536.

34 *Ibid.*, pp. 447–500. The title recalls a statement of Breton to the effect that the epitome of surrealism would be reached by descending upon an anonymous crowd with a loaded pistol and beginning to fire at random. See Breton, *Manifestes du surréalisme*, p. 94.

35 "Puisque la synthèse du Non-Etre de l'Etre et de l'Etre du Non-Etre c'est l'apparence, et puisque l'apparence manifeste au méchant son horrible liberté, si Genet, par un effort extraordinaire, transformait les actes en gestes, l'être en imaginaire, le monde en fantasmagorie et soi-même en apparence? S'il remplaçait la destruction impossible de l'univers par son *irréalisation?* Si ce garçon se transformait—comme Divine —en femme imaginaire? Et si, par cette comédie, il entraînait tout, arbres, plantes, ustensiles, animaux, femmes et hommes dans un tourbillon irréalisant? Nous apprendrons plus loin que cette folle tentative pour remplacer le monde entier par une apparence de monde se nomme l'esthétique et que l'esthète est un méchant. Dix ans de sa vie Genet a été esthète et la beauté ne fut d'abord pour lui qu'un rêve haineux de conflagration universelle."—*Genet* p. 155.

36 *Ibid.*, p. 428.

37 *Ibid.*, p. 449.

38 *Ibid.*, p. 390. Sartre is reminded of this point in the final evaluation of the so-called new phase of his attitude toward the French Communist Party; see this study. Chap. VI.

39 "Autrement dit, la *réalité* d'une société comporte la socialisation de certaines *irréalités*. Imaginaires en tant qu'elles se rapportent à des événements qui n'ont jamais eu lieu ou à des personnages qui n'ont jamais existé, parfois même à des lois qui ne sont pas celles de notre univers, les oeuvres 'reçues' sont *réelles* en ceci qu'elles provoquent des actions réelles, des sentiments réels et qu'elles définissent le développement historique d'une société. A vrai dire, les collectivités se défendent aussi longtemps qu'elles peuvent contre les images: on charge des spécialistes nommés 'critiques' de retarder leur admission. Genet le sait: mais il sait aussi que, s'il gagne, il rentrera avec les honneurs de la guerre dans la communauté des Justes qui l'a exilé."—*Ibid.*

40 "Ils s'arrêtaient au vocabulaire de Genet pour se garder d'entrer dans son délire; ils admiraient la forme pour se défendre de *réaliser* le contenu. Mais forme et contenu ne font qu'un: c'est *ce* contenu qui exige *cette* forme; tant que vous jouerez l'amoralisme, vous resterez au seuil de l'oeuvre."—*Ibid.*, p. 537.

41 "A propos de 'Le Bruit et la fureur'; la temporalité chez Faulkner."
42 *Genet,* pp. 395–414.
43 *Ibid.,* pp. 429–46.
44 *Ibid.,* pp. 472–79.
45 As to Luethy, in his article in *Anchor Review,* No. 2.
46 *History of Aesthetic,* Chap. III.

CHAPTER VI

1 In *Anchor Review,* No. 2, p. 245.
2 Merleau-Ponty, *Les Aventures,* pp. 131–271.
3 *Situations II,* pp. 207 ff.
4 "L'engagement a été d'abord la résolution de se montrer au dehors tel
   qu'on est au dedans, de confronter les conduites avec leur principe,
   chaque conduite avec toutes les autres, de tout dire, donc, et de tout
   peser à nouveau, d'inventer une conduite totale en réponse au tout du
   monde."—*Les Aventures,* p. 255.
5 *Ibid.,* pp. 255–57.
6 "Il est vrai: le but de cet article est de déclarer mon accord avec les
   communistes sur des sujets précis et limités, en raisonnant à partir de
   mes principes et non des *leurs;* on verra pourquoi."—*Temps Modernes,*
   VIII (1952), 706.
7 In *Temps Modernes* VIII (1952), 727–28.
8 *Ibid.,* p. 726.
9 "La classe, unité *réelle* de foules et de masses historiques, se manifeste
   par une opération datée et qui renvoie à une intention; elle n'est jamais
   séparable de la volonté concrète qui l'anime ni des fins qu'elle poursuit.
   Le prolétariat se fait lui-même par son action quotidienne; il n'est qu'en
   acte, il est acte; s'il cesse d'agir, il se décompose."—*Ibid.,* p. 732.
10 *Ibid.,* p. 760.
11 *Ibid.,* p. 761.
12 *Ibid.*
13 "Pour moi, je tiens que le développement du capital, pris dans sa gé-
   néralité, rend compte des aspects communs à tous les mouvements ou-
   vriers. Mais ces considérations de principe n'expliqueront jamais par
   elles seules les traits particuliers de la lutte des classes en France ou en
   Angleterre entre telle date et telle autre. Un fait concret est, à sa manière, l'expression singulière de relations universelles; mais il ne peut
   être expliqué dans sa singularité que par des raisons singulières: à vou-
   loir le déduire d'un savoir absolu mais vide ou d'un principe formel de
   développement, on perd son temps et sa peine. En vérité, il y a des
   dialectiques et elles sont dans les faits, à nous de les y découvrir et non
   de les y mettre."—*Temps Modernes,* IX (1954), 1732–33.
14 *Ibid.,* pp. 1755 ff.
15 See *Temps Modernes,* IX (1954), 1723–28.
16 See his *Les Aventures,* Sec. III. Merleau-Ponty is interpreting Sartre,
   rather than quoting him when he says, "Le même terme de praxis que

les *Thèses sur Feuerbach* employaient pour désigner une activité immanente à l'objet de l'histoire, Sartre le reprend pour désigner l'activité
'pure' qui fait être dans l'histoire le prolétariat. Le 'je ne sais quoi'
sartrien—la liberté radicale—prend possession de la praxis."—p. 178.
       Beauvoir criticizes this interpretation of Sartre's new position in
Temps Modernes, X (1955), 2072–2122.

17   *Les Aventures*, pp. 210–11.
18   "Il y a un centre de l'histoire qui est l'action politique, et une périphérie,
       qui est la culture. Il y a les infrastructures et les superstructures. Les
       choses ne vont pas ici et là du même pas. Un écrivain remplit son rôle
       quand il fait voir des situations et des conduites typiques, même si le
       commentaire politique reste à faire, même si l'ouvrage, disait Engels,
       est en thèse."—*Ibid.*, p. 212.
19   In *Sens et non-sens*, pp. 83–96.
20   "Pour Sartre . . . comme il n'y a pas une seule histoire derrière nous à
       laquelle notre littérature et notre politique appartiennent ensemble,
       comme leur unité est à faire par nous, comme il les prend à leur source
       unique, la conscience, si elles doivent toucher les choses, il faut que la
       littérature traite de politique, et d'ailleurs que l'action, comme un roman,
       colle à l'événement sans distance."—*Les Aventures*, p. 212.
21   *Ibid.*, p. 213.
22   *L'Etre*, p. 708.
23   *Les Aventures*, p. 240.
24   "L'action de dévoilement a ses facilités et ses tourments qui sont ceux
       de la contemplation. Ce sont problèmes et solutions de mandarins. Le
       mythe du mandarin réunit le phantasme du savoir total et de l'action
       pure. Le mandarin est supposé présent par sa science partout où se pose
       un problème, et capable d'agir immédiatement, en tout lieu, à distance,
       par efficience pure, comme si *ce qu'il fait* tombait en milieu inerte, et
       n'était pas, en même temps théâtre, manifestation, object de scandale ou
       d'enthousiasme. La conscience spectatrice est trop occupée de voir pour
       se voir elle-même comme conscience 'spéciale,' et elle rêve d'une action
       qui serait une autre ubiquité. Telle est la naïveté et la ruse du nar-
       cissisme."—*Ibid.*, pp. 238–39.
25   *Ibid.*, p. 221.
26   "Reconnaître la littérature et la politique comme des activités distinctes,
       c'est peut-être enfin la seule façon d'être fidèle à l'action comme à la
       littérature, et, au contraire, proposer l'unité d'action, quand on est
       écrivain, à un parti, c'est peut-être attester qu'on reste dans l'univers de
       l'écrivain . . ."—*Ibid.*, p. 271.
27   "Pour en juger autrement, il faut vivre dans un univers où tout est signi-
       fication, la politique comme la littérature, il faut être écrivain. La lit-
       térature et la politique sont liées entre elles et avec l'événement, mais
       d'une autre façon, comme deux couches d'une seule vie symbolique ou
       histoire."—*Ibid.*
28   *Ibid.*, pp. 270–71.
29   See her *Les Mandarins.*

30 The work alluded to has appeared as *Critique de la raison dialectique*.
31 *Les Aventures,* p. 270.
32 *Ibid.,* p. 262.
33 See Abel's "Operation Called 'Verstehen,' " in *Readings in the Philosophy of Science,* eds. Feigl and Brodbeck, pp. 677–87.
34 Frechtman, *What is Literature?,* p. 229.
35 This thesis is Alain's; see Chap. III, this study. For a similar treatment of the meaning of literature, see Blackmur's *Literature as Gesture.*
36 *Great Tradition.*
37 *Literature and Reality.*
38 Utilitarianism is condemned by Sartre as bourgeois, in *Situations II,* p. 274. Simone de Beauvoir has been struck with the problem of the conflict between two absolute freedoms which have entered into competition, in *Ethics of Ambiguity,* pp. 111–15; her *L'Invitée* is a fictional treatment of the same theme. Merleau-Ponty's interpretation of the latter work appears in his *Sens et non-sens,* pp. 51–81.
39 Aristotle, *Poetics,* 9.1451[b]5.
40 From the same point of view, anthropologists have often attempted to reconstruct a given social pattern from an examination of the literal truth of an artistic construct: see Métraux and Mead, *Themes in French Culture,* especially the supporting paper entitled "Plot and Character in Selected French Films: An Analysis of Fantasy," pp. 89–108.
41 At this writing it is not clear whether Sartre is aware of the "naturalistic fallacy" as G. E. Moore has developed this concept in value theory; his analysis of value as an object of desire is found in *L'Etre,* pp. 720–22. In Sartre's phenomenology a value is experienced as a felt lack, the fulfillment of which becomes the aim of the human consciousness which felt the lack. One of the modes of experiencing anguish, the phenomenological access to "nothingness," is described as "anguish before values"; see *ibid.,* pp. 75–76. Finally, Sartre discusses God as symbolic of the ultimate in human values in that God is a being (a self-contradictory *en-soi–pour-soi*) which, as perfect, could experience no lack; see *ibid.,* pp. 652–55.

CHAPTER VII

1 See the commemorative issue of *Etudes Philosophiques,* VI, Nos. 2 and 3, 1951.
2 *Eloge de la philosophie,* pp. 77–78.
3 Subtitled "Essai sur le problème communiste."
4 The book containing the essay which Lefebvre has called a "settling of accounts" between Sartre and Merleau-Ponty.
5 Sartre, "Les communistes et la paix."
6 *Les Aventures,* pp. 131–271.
7 See his "Questions de méthode," in *Temps Modernes,* XIII (1957), 338–417 and 658–98.
8 In *Pensée,* LXVIII (1956), 44–58, and LXXIII (1957), 37–52.

9   This supposed superiority constitutes the theme of de Waelhens' article, "Une philosophie de l'ambiguïté," published as Introduction to Merleau-Ponty's *Structure*.
10 See this study, Chap. II.
11 *L'Etre*, p. 120.
12 *Ibid.*, p. 225.
13 *Problems of Philosophy*, Chap. V.
14 For Sartre's existentialistic account, see his *L'Etre*, pp. 365 ff.; Beauvoir's defense of Sartre's doctrine against the "pseudo-Sartre" of Merleau-Ponty occurs in *Temps Modernes*, X (1955), 2072–2122. For her statement of Merleau-Ponty's foreknowledge of Sartre's intention to attack the problems raised by ontology for the phenomenological method, see pp. 2121–22. At this writing the projected work has not appeared.
15 Sartre, *L'Etre*, pp. 236–37.
16 De Waelhens, Introd. to Merleau-Ponty's *Structure*, p. viii.
17 See this study, Chap. II.
18 In his Introd. to Merleau-Ponty's *Structure*, pp. ix–xi.
19 *L'Etre*, pp. 643–63.
20 *Structure*, pp. 5–48.
21 *Ibid.*, pp. 48–49.
22 *Ibid.*, p. 53.
23 *Ibid.*, p. 54.
24 *Ibid.*
25 *Ibid.*
26 *Ibid.*, pp. 56–59.
27 *Ibid.*, p. 59.
28 *Ibid.*, pp. 59–60.
29 *Ibid.*, p. 62.
30 *Ibid.*, p. 69.
31 "La conduite du malade ne se déduit pas de la conduite du normal par simple soustraction de parties, elle représente une altération *qualitative,* et c'est dans la mesure où elles exigent une attitude dont le sujet n'est plus capable que certaines actions sont électivement troublées. Ici apparaît donc un nouveau genre d'analyse, qui ne consiste plus à isoler des éléments, mais à comprendre l'allure d'un ensemble et sa loi immanente."—*Ibid.*, p. 70.
32 *Ibid.*
33 " 'Les modes de pensée, les processus associatifs peuvent s'effectuer autour d'un noyau sensoriel prédominant avec des différences suivant les individus, et chez un individu donné, suivant les circonstances.' "—*Ibid.*, p. 79.
34 "Les excitations locales réparties à la surface des récepteurs subissent, dès leur entrée dans les centres spécialisés de l'écorce, une série de structurations qui les dissocient du contexte d'événements spatio-temporels où elles étaient réellement engagées pour les ordonner selon les dimensions originales de l'activité organique et humaine."—*Ibid.*, p. 81.

35   *Ibid.*, pp. 83–4.

36   "Ici les éléments coordonnés ne sont pas seulement accolés les uns aux autres. Ils constituent ensemble, par leur réunion même, un tout qui a sa loi propre et la manifeste dès que les premiers éléments de l'excitation sont donnés, comme les premières notes d'une mélodie assignent à l'ensemble un certain mode de résolution."—*Ibid.*, p. 96.

37   *Ibid.*, p. 97.

38   "A mesure qu'on avance vers le centre de l'écorce, les conditions des comportements, au lieu de se trouver dans la substance nerveuse en tant que telle, comme il arrive à la périphérie, se trouvent de plus en plus dans les modes qualitativement variables de son fonctionnement global."—*Ibid.*, p. 102.

39   *Ibid.*, p. 106.

40   *Ibid.*, p. 108.

41   "Le stimulus conditionnel n'agit que comme le représentant de toute une catégorie de stimuli devenus réflexogènes en même temps que lui; le mouvement de réponse primitif n'est fixé que comme un cas particulier d'une aptitude générale qui peut varier autour d'un même thème fondamental."—*Ibid.*

42   *Ibid.*, p. 109.

43   *Ibid.*, p. 112.

44   *Ibid.*, p. 113.

45   The "ambiguity" in this expression is not a linguistic reference; the term refers rather to the character of the human being whose essence is to be inserted within a given situation, and at the same time capable of "transcending" the physical limits of expression set up by that situation. Sartre, Beauvoir, and Merleau-Ponty use the same definition, which was initiated, so it would appear, by Heidegger. See his *Existence and Being*, pp. 353–92.

46   *Ibid.*

47   This expression has been inspired by the title of one of his later works, *Les Aventures de la dialectique.*

48   Miller's article, entitled "A Reply to Sign-Gestalt or Conditioned Reflex," appears in *Psychological Review*, XLII (1935), 280–92.

49   Merleau-Ponty, *Structure*, p. 117.

50   Mead's analysis, given from the standpoint of social behaviorism (*Mind, Self and Society*), is supported by Merleau-Ponty's theory of the manner in which the objects are created in an environment by a living organism. Rather than establishing any kind of influence of Mead on Merleau-Ponty, this coincidence would seem to follow consequentially from their common interest in biology. It appears that Merleau-Ponty would have profited by relating his own conclusions on behaviorism to the newer direction Mead gave behavioristic psychology.

51   Merleau-Ponty, *Structure*, p. 133; again, comparison with Mead's doctrine of the significant symbol would help clear up the difficulties posed by the almost discrete distinction Merleau-Ponty draws between the vital and

the human orders. Cf. Mead, *Mind, Self and Society*, Part II, secs. 9, 10, 11, 16, and Part IV, sec. 30.

52 *Structure*, p. 131, footnote 2.

53 *Ibid.*

54 See Alain's *Système*, and Valéry's *Introduction à la poétique*.

55 *Structure*, p. 133.

56 *Ibid.*, pp. 133–35. Merleau-Ponty's debt to Valéry is the topic of a later chapter of this treatise.

57 *Ibid.*, pp. 135–38; cf. Mead's *Mind, Self and Society*, *passim*, but especially "meaning," pp. 75 ff.

58 *Ibid.*, p. 140.

59 See his *Accent on Form.*

60 Merleau-Ponty, *Structure*, p. 148.

61 *Ibid.*, p. 149.

62 *Ibid.*, p. 155.

63 *Ibid.*, p. 157.

64 *Ibid.*, p. 174; the appeal to "occasions" has its source in Descartes, rather than his continental followers bearing the "occasionalist" label. Cf. Merleau-Ponty's discussion of Descartes' *Dioptrique*, *ibid.*, pp. 206 ff. Merleau-Ponty's appeal to this concept is reminiscent of Sartre's "motivation" of a given consciousness. See this study, Chap. II.

65 "En reconnaissant que les comportements ont un sens et dépendent de la signification vitale des situations, la science biologique s'interdit de les concevoir comme des choses en soi qui existeraient, *partes extra partes, dans* le système nerveux ou *dans* le corps, elle voit en eux des dialectiques incarnées qui s'irradient sur un milieu qui leur est immanent."—*Ibid.*, p. 174.

66 *Ibid.*, p. 175.

67 *Ibid.*

68 *Ibid.*

69 *Structure*, p. 179.

70 *Ibid.*, p. 182.

71 "Ce qui définit l'homme n'est pas la capacité de créer une seconde nature—économique, sociale, culturelle—au delà de la nature biologique, c'est plutôt celle de dépasser les structures créées pour en créer d'autres." —*Ibid.*, p. 189.

72 *Ibid.*, pp. 210–11.

73 *Ibid.*

74 "De ce point de vue la perception ne pouvait plus apparaître comme l'effet en nous de l'action d'une chose extérieure, ni le corps comme l'intermédiaire de cette action causale; la chose extérieure et le corps, définis par la 'pensée du' corps—par la signification chose et la signification corps—devenaient indubitables tels qu'ils se présentent à nous dans une expérience lucide, en même temps qu'ils perdaient les pouvoirs occultes que le réalisme philosophique leur donne."—*Ibid.*, p. 211.

75 *Ibid.*, p. 212.

76 *Ibid.*, p. 215.

77 "Pour marquer à la fois l'intimité des objets au sujet et la présence
en eux de structures solides qui les distinguent des apparences, on les
appellera des 'phénomènes' et la philosophie, dans la mesure où elle
s'en tient à ce thème, devient une phénoménologie, c'est-à-dire un inventaire de la conscience comme milieu d'univers."—*Ibid.*

78 *Ibid.*, p. 217.

79 *Ibid.*

80 *Ibid.*

81 *Ibid.*, p. 218.

82 *Ibid.*

83 *Ibid.*, pp. 219–20; cf. the definition of "ambiquity," above, note 45.

84 ". . . il y a le corps comme masse de composés chimiques en interaction,
le corps comme dialectique du vivant et de son milieu biologique, le
corps comme dialectique du sujet social et de son groupe, et même
toutes nos habitudes sont un corps impalpable pour le moi de chaque
instant. Chacun de ces degrés est âme à l'égard du précédent, corps à
l'égard du suivant."—*Ibid.*, p. 227.

85 *Ibid*; in the same place, Merleau-Ponty recognizes his debt to Hegel, if
only one makes the substitution of "*Gestalt*" for the Hegelian "*Begriff*":
"La notion de *Gestalt* nous ramenait, par un développement naturel, à
son sens hégélien, c'est-à-dire au concept avant qu'il soit devenu conscience de soi." For a clearer admission of Merleau-Ponty's debt to
Hegel, see his *Sens et non-sens*, pp. 125–39.

86 This preference of Merleau-Ponty has been stated by de Waelhens in his
Introduction to Merleau-Ponty's *Structure*, p. xiv; the second treatise is
examined in the next chapter of this study.

87 This work begins with a chapter on "The Live Creature," pp. 3–19.

88 "*La Structure du comportement* se place donc au niveau de l'expérience
non pas naturelle mais scientifique et s'efforce de prouver que cette expérience elle-même—c'est-à-dire l'ensemble des faits qui, mis en lumière
par *l'investigation scientifique*, constitue le comportement—n'est pas
compréhensible dans les perspectives ontologiques que la science adopte
spontanément."—De Waelhen's Introduction to Merleau-Ponty's *Structure*, p. xiii.

89 *Ibid.*, note.

90 "La réduction eidétique c'est . . . la résolution de faire apparaître le
monde tel qu'il est avant tout retour sur nous-mêmes, c'est l'ambition
d'égaler la réflexion à la vie irréfléchie de la conscience."—*Phénoménologie*, pp. x–xi.

91 In *Nouvelle Revue Française*, LII (1939), 129–32.

92 *Ibid.*, p. 131.

93 In *Temps Modernes*, I (1945), 1–21.

94 In this second long portrayal of jealousy, the man is primarily jealous

of a feminine rival for the possession of the beloved. Although the fact has no relevance to the quality of the novel, critics have pointed out, thereby giving some credence to Sartre's account, that the real life model situation which is being transformed in the novel has been inverted: Proust had a homosexual attachment for, among others, his secretary-chauffeur and kept him a prisoner as Marcel did Albertine; if there is no record of jealousy in Proust over his chauffeur's promiscuity or over his marriage, the imprisonment of the beloved would seem to indicate Proust was motivated by the kind of possessiveness felt, in the story's context, by both Swann and Marcel.

95   Dufrenne, *Phénoménologie,* I, 4, note.

CHAPTER VIII

1   In his Introduction to Merleau-Ponty's *Structure.*

2   See her review of the book in *Temps Modernes,* I (1945), 363–67.

3   See his article in *Pensée,* LXVIII (1956), 44–58.

4   Merleau-Ponty's account of the philosophical errors of traditional attempts to codify human behavior; see Chap. VII, this study, for the explanation of Merleau-Ponty's method and the list of the traditional "errors."

5   See Bayer's *Merleau-Ponty's Existentialism,* University of Buffalo Studies. For an expression of Merleau-Ponty's anti-rationalism in aesthetic theory, see Bayer's essay in *Philosophic Thought,* ed. Farber.

6   *Phénoménologie,* pp. 494–95, and Part II, Chap. III, *passim.*

7   *Ibid.,* p. 335.

8   *Structure,* pp. 116 ff., and pp. 139 ff.

9   Cf. his *L'Imagination,* pp. 12 ff; the term is used explicitly in his *L'Imaginaire,* p. 15.

10   See his "Qualitative Thought," *Philosophy and Civilization,* pp. 93–116.

11   "Il nous faut reconnaître l'indéterminé comme un phénomène positif. C'est dans cette atmosphère que se présente la qualité. Le sens qu'elle renferme est un sens équivoque, il s'agit d'une valeur expressive plutôt que d'une signification logique. La qualité déterminée, par laquelle l'empirisme voulait définir la sensation, est un objet, non un élément, de la conscience, et c'est l'objet tardif d'une conscience scientifique."— *Phénoménologie,* p. 12.

12   *Structure,* pp. 157–73.

13   Sartre's objection to the "naive ontology" of Hume's position has been shown in Chap. II of this study; Merleau-Ponty is here objecting to the psychological doctrine. The latter's account is similar again to Dewey's analysis of "resemblance" and "contiguity" found in the essay cited above, note 10.

14   Dewey, *Creative Intelligence,* p. 108–16.

15   ". . . il n'agit qu'en rendant probable ou tentante une intention de repro-

duction, il n'opère qu'en vertu du sens qu'il a pris dans le contexte de l'expérience ancienne. . . ."—*Phénoménologie*, p. 26.

16 "Les atomes du physicien paraîtront toujours plus réels que la figure historique et qualitative de ce monde, les processus psycho-chimiques plus réels que les formes organiques, les atomes psychiques de l'empirisme plus réels que les phénomènes perçus, les atomes intellectuels que sont les 'significations' de l'Ecole de Vienne plus réels que la conscience, tant que l'on cherchera à construire la figure de ce monde, la perception, l'esprit, au lieu de reconnaître, comme source toute proche et comme dernière instance de nos connaissances à leur sujet, *l'expérience* que nous en avons."—*Ibid.*, p. 31.

17 Primarily in his *Meditations*, I and II.

18 In his *Recherche de la vérité*, I, Chap. I.

19 In his *Célèbres leçons*, the essay entitled "Cours sur la perception," pp. 129–82.

20 In his *Eléments de philosophie*.

21 Alain, *Système*, Book I, Chap. III, and notes to same, pp. 390–92.

22 "Faire attention, ce n'est pas seulement éclairer davantage des données préexistantes, c'est réaliser en elles une articulation nouvelle en les prenant pour *figures*. Elles ne sont préformées que comme des *horizons*, elles constituent vraiment de nouvelles régions dans le monde total. C'est précisément la structure originale qu'elles apportent qui fait apparaître l'identité de l'objet avant et après l'acte d'attention."—*Phénoménologie*, p. 38.

23 For Merleau-Ponty's explanation of this concept, see his *Phénoménologie*, p. 61, and his *Structure*, pp. 234–35.

24 "La perception est une interprétation de l'intuition primitive, interprétation en apparence immédiate, mais en réalité acquise par l'habitude, corrigée par le raisonnement . . ."—Lagneau, *Célèbres leçons*, p. 179.

25 Merleau-Ponty, *Phénoménologie*, p. 43.

26 *Ibid.*, pp. 58–60.

27 *Ibid.*, pp. 60–61.

28 *Ibid.*, p. 61.

29 ". . . il y a une raison d'être qui oriente le flux des phénomènes sans être explicitement posée en aucun d'eux, une sorte de raison opérante."—*Ibid.*

30 The reference here is to the position taken in American pragmatism against the "spectator theory of knowledge." See James' *Essays in Radical Empiricism*, in particular "Does Consciousness Exist?" and "A World of Pure Experience"; and John Dewey's concise statement of the problem in *Creative Intelligence*, pp. 3–69.

31 See Chap. VII of this study. Merleau-Ponty's *Structure* seems to be an attempt at making explicit the "anti-psychologism" of Husserl (*Logische Untersuchungen*). As explained in Chap. VII, the inadequacies of the psychological viewpoint are criticized in favor of a "philosophical anthropology." In the light of Merleau-Ponty's second treatise, however,

the anti-psychological analyses of the first seem to lead to a phenomenological explanation of perception centering about a concept of *bodily
schema* which transcends the traditional subject-object distinction.

32 Cited by Merleau-Ponty, *Phénoménologie*, p. 68.

33 *Ibid.*, p. 69.

34 Sartre is responsible for the term "existential psychoanalysis"; for the
principles of the method, see *L'Etre*, IV, II, 1, pp. 643–63. American
clinical psychologists have already been introduced to "existential analysis" by May, *Existence;* and a new journal of "existential psychoanalysis" has recently made its appearance.

35 The same charge was made against pragmatism, and for similar reasons,
as noted above; see notes 5 and 30.

36 *Sense of Beauty* p. 76.

37 See his description of the "facticity" of the body, *L'Etre*, pp. 368–404.

38 Merleau-Ponty's account of the body proper was foreshadowed in his
Structure, pp. 230 ff., and given in detail in *Phénoménologie*, Part I,
pp. 81–232. Without a prior reading of the first treatise it would appear
that Merleau-Ponty's conclusions were strongly influenced by Sartre's
account of the body as "facticity." See note 37.

39 "S'il doit parvenir à une parfaite densité, en d'autres termes s'il doit
y avoir un object absolu, il faut qu'il soit une infinité de perspectives
différentes contractées dans une co-existence rigoureuse, et qu'il soit
donné comme par une seule vision à mille regards."—*Phénoménologie*,
p. 84.

40 Such a consciousness would be unconscious, and self-contradictory.
Sartre uses this absurdity to establish his "ontological proof" of the
"transphenomenality" of being, *L'Etre*, pp. 27–29. The pre-reflective
cogito argued for on the basis of the same absurdity is given *ibid.*, p.
18.

41 *Structure*, pp. 139 ff.

42 See above pp. 217 ff.

43 Sartre gives the ontological description of this phenomenon in his
discussion of *mauvaise foi*, *L'Etre*, pp. 85–111.

44 "Le malade sait donc sa déchéance justement en tant qu'il l'ignore et
l'ignore justement en tant qu'il la sait."—*Phénoménologie*, p. 97.

45 Sartre, "Mauvaise Foi," *L'Etre*, pp. 85–111, and Heidegger, *Sein und
Zeit*, pp. 73 ff.

46 This loss of spontaneity by the consciousness for its being committed
to a personal history in the universal course of historical events is precisely the difference between the Sartrean and Merleau-Pontyan metaphysics of existence. See de Waelhens' Introduction to Merleau-Ponty's
Structure.

47 Merleau-Ponty, *Phénoménologie*, p. 123, and Part I, Chap. III, *passim*.

48 *Ibid.*, p. 115–16.

49 Merleau-Ponty treats the body as a "sexed being" in a separate chapter,
ibid., pp. 180–202. For his interpretation of Konrad's revision of
Schilder, see *ibid.*, pp. 116–17.

50 *Psychologische Analysen Hirnpathologischer Faelle*, pp. 157–250; see also Goldstein's article in *Monatsschrift fuer Psychiatrie und Neurologie*, LIV (1923), 141–94, and *Der Nervenarzt*, IV (1931), 53–66. For an account in English of Goldstein's distinction between "abstract" and "concrete" patterns of behavior, see his *Abstract and Concrete Behavior*. The emphasis in this English monograph is on the experimental tests designed to measure efficiency in the two types of conduct.

51 In criticizing the rationalistic (*l'analyse intellectualiste*) approach to mental disturbance, Merleau-Ponty seems to be aiming, whether intentionally or not, at the metaphysical explanation of Sartre. See his "Après tout, le trouble de Schn. n'est pas métaphysique d'abord, c'est un éclat d'obus qui l'a blessé dans la région occipitale. . . . C'est par la vision qu'en lui l'Esprit a été atteint." *Phénoménologie*, p. 146. De Waelhens, in his Introduction to Merleau-Ponty's *Structure*, makes much of this basic difference between Sartre and Merleau-Ponty.

52 Cf. the following description of mental aberration taken from the point of view of a pure spontaneity, existing for itself:
"Si la conscience est placée hors de l'être, elle ne saurait se laisser entamer par lui, la variété empirique des consciences—la conscience morbide, la conscience primitive, la conscience enfantine, la conscience d'autrui—ne peut pas être prise au sérieux, il n'y a rien là qui soit à connaître ou à comprendre, une seule chose est compréhensible, c'est la pure essence de la conscience. Aucune de ces consciences ne saurait manquer d'effectuer le *Cogito*. Le fou, *en arrière de* ses délires, de ses obsessions et de ses mensonges, *sait qu'il* délire, qu'il s'obsède lui-même, qu'il ment, et, pour finir il n'*est* pas fou, *il pense l'être*. Tout est donc pour le mieux et la folie n'est que mauvaise volonté."—*Phénoménolgie*, pp. 145–46.

53 See his article in *Pensée*, LXVII (1956), 44–58; LXXIII (1957), 37–52.

54 ". . . la vie de la conscience—vie connaissante, vie du désir, ou vie perceptive—est sous-tendue par un 'arc intentionnel' qui projette autour de nous notre passé, notre avenir, notre milieu humain, notre situation physique, notre situation idéologique, notre situation morale, ou plutôt qui fait que nous soyons situés sous tous ces rapports. C'est cet arc intentionnel qui fait l'unité des sens, celle des sens et de l'intelligence, celle de la sensibilité et de la motricité. C'est lui qui se 'détend' dans la maladie." *Phénoménologie*, p. 158.

55 *Ibid.*, p. 160.

56 This theme is embroidered in his *Mind, Self and Society*.

57 "Le romancier n'a pas pour rôle d'exposer des idées ou même d'analyser des caractères, mais de présenter un événement interhumain, de le faire mûrir et éclater sans commentaire idéologique, à tel point que tout changement dans l'ordre du récit ou dans le choix des perspectives modifierait le sens *romanesque* de l'événement."—*Phénoménologie*, p. 177.

58 "Un roman, un poème, un tableau, un morceau de musique sont des individus, c'est-à-dire des êtres où l'on ne peut distinguer l'expression

de l'exprimé, dont le sens n'est accessible que par un contact direct et qui rayonnent leur signification sans quitter leur place temporelle et spatiale."—*Ibid*.

59   "En deçà des moyens d'expression conventionnels, qui ne manifestent à autrui ma pensée que parce que déjà chez moi comme chez lui sont données, pour chaque signe, des significations, et qui en ce sens ne réalisent pas une communication véritable, il faut bien, verrons-nous, reconnaître une opération primordiale de signification où l'exprimé n'existe pas à part l'expression et où les signes eux-mêmes induisent au dehors leurs sens."—*Ibid.*, p. 193.

60   "Ce sens incarné est le phénomène central dont corps et esprit, signe et signification sont des moments abstraits."—*Ibid*.

61   See Chap. II, this study.

62   Strictly speaking, this characterization is inexact. I have given an account of Sartre's phenomenology of the imagination; his metaphysical principles are outlined in the later, *L'Etre et le néant*. Moreover, when Merleau-Ponty directly assaulted Sartre's metaphysical explanations in "Sartre et l'ultra-bolchévisme," (*Les Aventures*), Beauvoir came to Sartre's defense by stating that he was aware of the difficulties Merleau-Ponty mentioned, and was planning to publish his solution in the near future. See note 14, Chap. VII, this study.

63   See his *Meditations*, I and II.

64   See his *Aesthetic*.

65   "Phenomenology," *Encyclopedia Britannica*, XVII (1957), 700–702. Prof. Findlay's criticisms of Husserl's system are almost prophetic of Merleau-Ponty's later interpretations. See his statement: "His program is, in fact, not very different from that of modern British and U.S. analytic philosophy. We may note further that his analyses of mental states do little more than bring out what is involved in their 'intentionality' or *direction* to objects. But since this property is as much a characteristic of outward actions as of inward experience—for our actions can be shown to be oriented to things and to situations—there is much in his analyses that could be given a behavioristic interpretation." [Emphasis added.]

The purpose of Merleau-Ponty's *Structure* is to examine the validity of behaviorism's claim to explain "intentionality"; and although Merleau-Ponty rejects psychologism, his reference to the "intentional-arc" established pre-cognitively by the body-proper of the organism in its environment seems to carry out the program suggested in Findlay's criticism.

66   Further historical comment on this point may be of some value. Merleau-Ponty is following the phenomenological line laid down by Husserl in the *Logische Untersuchungen* by destroying the "psychologistic" view of philosophy. But Husserl had no adequate notion of the bodily organism; see his exegete, Welch, *Edmund Husserl,* p. 254: "What, then, was Husserl's attitude toward the bodily organism? He never dealt with this specific problem, but it can be inferred from his general out-

look that he viewed it as a means whereby the realm of essences announces its presence through concrete manifestations, commonly referred to as sense qualities."

If this is correct, Merleau-Ponty's use of the triple reduction in such a way as to bring the consciousness in relation to the living organism in a primitive "intentional arc" can be interpreted as bringing Husserl's transcendental and idealistic metaphysics back down to the real essence of the lived situation. More than Sartre, then, Merleau-Ponty is seen as a direct descendant of Husserl, contributing to the future development of phenomenology. This is the historical significance of his philosophy.

67 "S'il y a pour moi un cube à six faces égales et si je peux rejoindre l'objet, ce n'est pas que je le constitue de l'intérieur: c'est que je m'enfonce dans l'épaisseur du monde par l'expérience perceptive. Le cube à six faces égales est l'idée-limite par laquelle j'exprime la présence charnelle du cube qui est là, sous mes yeux, sous mes mains, dans son évidence perceptive."—*Phénoménologie*, pp. 236–37.

68 "Toute perception extérieure est immédiatement synonyme d'une certaine perception de mon corps comme toute perception de mon corps s'explicite dans le langage de la perception extérieure."—*Ibid.*, p. 239.

69 Sartre, *L'Etre*, p. 371.

70 See his "World of Pure Experience," *Essays in Radical Empiricism.*

71 *Philosophy and Civilization*, pp. 96 ff.

72 *Ibid.*, p. 100.

73 *Ibid.*, p. 103.

74 Heidegger, *Existence and Being*, pp. 360–61.

75 See Lanteri-Laura's article in *Etudes Philosophiques*, IX (1954), 57–72.

76 In connection with Sartre's use of the concept; See Chap. II, this study.

CHAPTER IX

1 See his *Aesthetic as Science of Expression and General Linguistic.*

2 *Ibid.*, Chap. XV.

3 Hyman, *Armed Vision.*

4 The term "new criticism," owes its coinage to Spingarn, whose *Creative Criticism* is dedicated to Croce. Perhaps the most comprehensive work of the new critics is *Theory of Literature* by Welleck and Warren. The authors are interested primarily in establishing a method of literary criticism based upon Croce's doctrine of the autonomy of a work of art.

5 Cf. the parallel discussion of this matter in Dewey, *Experience and Nature*, p. 398.

6 *Phénoménologie*, Part I, Chaps. IV and VI; pp. 333 ff., 372–73, and 445 ff.

7 In his *Cours de linguistique générale.*

8 In his *Voix du silence.*

9 In an advertisement to the edition cited above, R. L. Wagner gives a

short summary of the work's importance. The advertisement is drawn from an account of Saussure's influence which had appeared in *Temps Modernes*, III (1948), 1583–1611. This fact is cited as further evidence of the connection between the earlier careers of Sartre, the director of *Temps Modernes*, and Merleau-Ponty, who once served as an editor on its staff. The journal has consistently served its principal purpose as an "intellectual clearing house" for the problems of contemporary society. That they should tackle Saussure is *prima facie* evidence that its editors have not always eschewed "academic" topics.

10   *Cours de linguistique générale*, p. 33.
11   *Collected Papers of C. S. S. Peirce*, Vol. II.
12   The system of Saussure bears closer comparison with the earlier work of Professor Morris. Cf. the latter's *Foundations of a Theory of Signs*, Vol. I, No. 2, in the *Encyclopedia of Unified Science* (Chicago: The University Press, 1938).
13   *Mind, Self and Society.*
14   *Cours de linguistique générale*, p. 140.
15   "Le rôle caractéristique de la langue vis-à-vis de la pensée n'est pas de créer un moyen phonique matériel pour l'expression des idées, mais de servir d'intermédiaire entre la pensée et le son, dans des conditions telles que leur union aboutit nécessairement à des délimitations réciproques d'unités. La pensée, chaotique de sa nature, est forcée de se préciser en se décomposant. Il n'y a donc ni matérialisation des pensées, ni spiritualisation des sons, mais il s'agit de ce fait en quelque sorte mystérieux, que la 'pensée-son' implique des divisions et que la langue élabore ses unités en se constituant entre deux masses amorphes."—*Ibid.*, p. 156.
16   *Ibid.*
17   *Ibid.*, p. 157.
18   "Tout ce qui précède revient à dire que *dans la langue il n'y a que des différences*. Bien plus: une différence suppose en général des termes positifs entre lesquels elle s'établit; mais dans la langue il n'y a que des différences *sans termes positifs*. Qu'on prenne le signifié ou le signifiant, la langue ne comporte ni des idées ni des sons qui préexisteraient au système linguistique, mais seulement des différences conceptuelles et des différences phoniques issues de ce système."—*Ibid.*, p. 166.
19   Merleau-Ponty, "Le langage indirect et les voix du silence," *Temps Modernes*, VII (1952), 2113.
20   *Ibid.*, pp. 2118 ff.
21   *Ibid.*, p. 2117.
22   *Ibid.*, p. 2119.
23   "Il y a, pour les expressions déjà acquises, un sens direct, qui correspond point par point à des tournures, des formes, des mots institués. En apparence, point de lacunes ici, aucun silence parlant. Mais le sens des expressions en train de s'accomplir ne peut être de cette sorte: c'est un sens latéral ou oblique, qui fuse entre les mots—c'est une autre manière de secouer l'appareil du langage ou du récit pour lui arracher un son neuf."—*Ibid.*, p. 2122.

24 "Ce sens naissant au bord des signes, cette immanence du tout dans les parties se retrouvent dans toute l'histoire de la culture."—*Ibid.*, p. 2115.

25 The development of Merleau-Ponty's philosophy from *Structure du comportement* to *Aventures de la dialectique* is a series of variations on this single theme. He attempted a systematic account of the relations between "history" and "philosophy" in his inaugural lecture at the Collège de France, published as *Eloge de la philosophie.*

26 *Voix du silence.* Merleau-Ponty's notion of an indirect language is intended as a corrective to Malraux' conception of the function of prose literature which is compared, as an artistic medium, with that of painting in the text cited.

27 *Romans,* pp. 163–78.

28 *Voix du silence,* p. 341.

29 "Mais le faussaire traditionnel ne tente pas de rivaliser avec le génie, il tente d'en imiter la manière, ou, s'il vise les époques d'anonymat, le style. Ce dernier agit si puissamment sur nous, que tout ce qu'il marqua devient art."—*Ibid.*, p. 369.

30 "Tout style crée son univers propre en conjuguant les éléments du monde qui permettent d'orienter celui-ci vers une part essentielle de l'homme." —*Ibid.*, p. 322.

31 "La peinture moderne pose un tout autre problème que celui du retour à l'individu: le problème de savoir comment on peut communiquer sans le secours d'une Nature préétablie et sur laquelle nos sens à tous ouvriraient, comment nous sommes entés sur l'universel par ce que nous avons de plus propre."—In *Temps Modernes,* VII (1952), 2129.

32 "C'est ce qui fait que les oeuvres des classiques ont un autre sens et plus de sens peut-être qu'ils ne croyaient, qu'ils anticipent souvent une peinture délivrée de leurs canons ct restent les intercesseurs désignés de toute initiation à la peinture. Au moment même où, les yeux fixés sur le monde, ils croyaient lui demander le secret d'une représentation suffisante, ils opéraient à leur insu cette *métamorphose* dont la peinture est plus tard devenue consciente."—*Ibid.*, p. 2124.

33 "La perspective est beaucoup plus qu'un secret technique pour imiter une réalité qui se donnerait telle quelle à tous les hommes: elle est l'invention d'un monde dominé, possédé de part en part dans une synthèse instantanée dont le regard spontané nous donne tout au plus l'ébauche quand il essaie vainement de tenir ensemble toutes les choses dont chacune le veut en entier."—*Ibid.*, p. 2127.

34 "La peinture moderne, comme en général la pensée moderne, nous oblige à admettre une vérité qui ne ressemble pas aux choses, qui soit sans modèle extérieur, sans instruments d'expression prédestinés, et qui soit cependant vérité."—*Ibid.*, p. 2135.

35 "On ne peut pas plus faire l'inventaire d'une peinture—dire ce qui y est et ce qui n'y est pas—que, selon les linguistes, on ne peut recenser un vocabulaire, et pour la même raison: ici et là, il ne s'agit pas d'une somme finie de signes, mais d'un champ ouvert ou d'un nouvel organe de la culture humaine."—*Ibid.*, p. 2138.

36 "Toute perception, toute action qui la suppose, bref tout usage humain du corps est déja *expression primordiale*—non pas ce travail dérivé qui substitue à l'exprimé des signes donnés par ailleurs avec leur sens et leur règle d'emploi, mais l'opération première qui d'abord constitue les signes en signes, fait habiter en eux l'exprimé par la seule éloquence de leur arrangement et de leur configuration, implante un sens dans ce qui n'en avait pas, et qui donc, loin de s'épuiser dans l'instant où elle a lieu, inaugure un ordre, fonde une institution ou une tradition. . . ."—Merleau-Ponty, *Temps Modernes,* VIII (1952), 73.

37 "Les mots, même dans l'art de la prose, transportent celui qui parle et celui qui les entend dans un univers commun en les entraînant vers une signification nouvelle par une puissance de désignation qui excède leur définition reçue. . . ."—*Ibid.,* p. 83.

38 "Cette spontanéité du langage qui nous unit n'est pas une consigne, l'histoire qu'elle fonde n'est pas une idole extérieure: elle est nous-mêmes avec nos racines, notre poussée et, comme on dit, les fruits de notre travail."—*Ibid.*

39 "Toute la merveille d'un style déjà présent dans les éléments invisibles d'une oeuvre revient donc à ceci que, travaillant dans le monde humain des choses perçues, l'artiste se trouve mettre sa marque jusque dans le monde inhumain que révèlent les appareils d'optique, comme le nageur survole à son insu tout un univers enseveli qu'il s'effraie de découvrir à la lunette sous-marine. . . ."—*Ibid.,* p. 71.

40 "Et comme l'opération du corps, celle des mots ou des peintures me reste obscure: les mots, les traits, les couleurs qui m'expriment sortent de moi comme mes gestes, ils me sont arrachés par ce que je veux dire comme mes gestes par ce que je veux faire."—*Ibid.,* p. 83.

41 "Le mouvement de l'artiste traçant son arabesque dans la matière infinie amplifie, mais aussi continue, la simple merveille de la locomotion dirigée ou des gestes de prise."—*Ibid.,* p. 73.

42 See above, Chap. VII.

43 "Le fait central auquel la dialectique de Hegel revient de cent façons, c'est que nous n'avons pas à choisir entre le *pour soi* et le *pour autrui,* entre la pensée selon nous-mêmes et la pensée selon autrui, mais que dans le moment de l'expression, l'autre à qui je m'adresse et moi qui m'exprime sommes liés sans concession."—Merleau-Ponty, *Temps Modernes,* VIII (1952), 81.

44 "Et il ne s'agit pas, entre ces deux problèmes, d'une simple *analogie:* c'est l'opération expressive du corps, commencée par la moindre perception, qui s'amplifie en peinture et en art. Le champ des significations picturales est ouvert depuis qu'un homme a paru dans le monde. Et le premier dessin aux murs des cavernes ne fondait une tradition que parce qu'il en recueillait une autre: celle de la perception."—*Ibid.,* p. 76.

45 "Le langage indirect," Parts I and II, is the last of Merleau-Ponty's pieces to appear in *Temps Modernes,* in June and July of 1952. He was appointed to the chair of philosophy in the Collège de France in the following year.

46 See this study, Chap. II. This conclusion is shared by another of Sartre's interpreters, Professor Dufrenne, who places the debate on aesthetic grounds rather than the purely epistemological ground I have established in the chapter noted.—See his *Phénoménologie de l'expérience esthétique*, 259–66.

47 Merleau-Ponty, *Phénoménologie*, p. 206.

48 *Mind, Self and Society*, ed., Morris.

49 ". . . . je commence à comprendre une philosophie en me glissant dans la manière d'exister de cette pensée, en reproduisant le ton, l'accent du philosophe."—*Phénoménologie*, p. 209.

50 In the title essay of his *Language as Gesture*.

51 "Mais, à vrai dire, le sens d'un ouvrage littéraire est moins fait par le sens commun des mots qu'il ne contribue à le modifier. Il y a donc, soit chez celui qui écoute ou lit, soit chez celui qui parle ou écrit, une *pensée dans la parole* que l'intellectualisme ne soupçonne pas."—Merleau-Ponty, *Phénoménologie*, p. 209.

52 See her *Philosophy in a New Key*, Chapter IV.

53 See this study, Chapter II.

54 Merleau-Ponty, *Phénoménologie*, pp. 210–11.

55 *Ibid.*, p. 211.

56 "Il faut que, d'une manière ou de l'autre, le mot et la parole cessent d'être une manière de désigner l'objet ou la pensée, pour devenir la présence de cette pensée dans le monde. . . ."—*Ibid.*, p. 212.

57 "Ce qui nous trompe là-dessus, ce qui nous fait croire à une pensée qui existerait pour soi avant l'expression, ce sont les pensées déjà constituées et déjà exprimées que nous pouvons rappeler à nous silencieusement et par lesquelles nous nous donnons l'illusion d'une vie intérieure. Mais en réalité ce silence prétendu est bruissant de paroles, cette vie intérieure est un langage intérieur."—*Ibid.*, p. 213.

58 "L'intention significative nouvelle ne se connaît elle-même qu'en se recouvrant de significations déjà disponibles, résultat d'actes d'expression antérieurs. Les significations disponibles s'entrelacent soudain selon une loi inconnue, et une fois pour toutes un nouvel être culturel a commencé d'exister."—*Ibid.*

59 "La parole est un véritable geste et elle contient son sens comme le geste contient le sien. C'est ce qui rend possible la communication."—*Ibid.*, p. 214.

60 Merleau-Ponty published a long essay on the phenomenology of language in which he relates his doctrine of corporeal expressivity to the beginnings of a phenomenological study of language left by Husserl.— See "Sur la phénoménologie du langage," in his *Signes*, pp. 105–22.

CHAPTER X

1 "L'histoire n'a pas de sens si son sens est compris comme celui d'une rivière qui coule sous l'action de causes toutes-puissantes vers un océan où elle disparaît."—*Eloge de la philosophie*, p. 71.

2   "La théorie du signe, telle que la linguistique l'élabore, implique peut-être une théorie du sens historique qui passe outre à l'alternative des *choses* et des *consciences*. Le langage vivant est cette concrétion de l'esprit et de la chose qui fait difficulté. Dans l'acte de parler, dans son ton et dans son style, le sujet atteste son autonomie, puisque rien ne lui est plus propre, et cependant il est au même moment et sans contradiction tourné vers la communauté linguistique et tributaire de la langue. La volonté de parler est une même chose avec la volonté d'être compris. La présence de l'individu à l'institution et de l'institution à l'individu est claire dans le cas du changement linguistique."—*Ibid.,* p. 74.

3   See her article in *Temps Modernes,* X (1955), 2072–2122.

4   "Comme la langue est un système de signes qui n'ont de sens que relativement les uns aux autres et dont chacun se reconnaît à une certaine valeur d'emploi qui lui revient dans le tout de la langue, chaque institution est un système symbolique que le sujet s'incorpore comme style de fonctionnement, comme configuration globale, sans qu'il ait besoin de la concevoir."—*Eloge,* pp. 75–76.

5   "C'est à ce titre, et comme autant de logiques de conduites, qu 'existent les formes et les processus historiques, les classes, les époques dont nous nous demandions où elles étaient: elles sont dans un espace social, culturel ou symbolique qui n'est pas moins réel que l'espace physique et qui, d'ailleurs, prend appui sur lui."—*Ibid.,* p. 76.

6   "La philosophie se retourne vers l'activité symbolique anonyme d'où nous émergeons et vers le discours personnel qui se construit en nous-mêmes, qui est nous, elle scrute ce pouvoir d'expression que les autres symbolismes se bornent à exercer. . . . elle récupère et aussi elle pousse au delà de toute limite le devenir de vérité qui suppose et qui fait qu'il y a une seule histoire et un seul monde."—*Ibid.,* p. 78.

7   "Philosophy recovers itself when it ceases to be a device for dealing with the problems of philosophers, and becomes a method, cultivated by philosophers, for dealing with the problems of men."—Dewey, "The Need for a Recovery of Philosophy" in *Creative Intelligence,* p. 65.

8   See his *Eléments de philosophie,* formerly published as *81 Chapitres sur l'esprit et les passions,* and cited by Merleau-Ponty, *Phénoménologie,* p. 68.

9   "La perception n'est pas une sorte de science commençante, et un premier exercice de l'intelligence, il nous faut retrouver un commerce avec le monde et une présence au monde plus vieux que l'intelligence."—Merleau-Ponty, *Sens et non-sens,* p. 106.

10 "Ma perception n'est donc pas une somme de données visuelles, tactiles, auditives, je perçois d'une manière indivise avec mon être total, je saisis une structure unique de la chose, une unique manière d'exister qui parle à la fois à tous mes sens."—*Ibid.,* p. 101.

11 "La permanence des couleurs et des objets n'est donc pas construite par l'intelligence, mais saisie par le regard en tant qu'il épouse ou adopte l'organisation du champ visuel. . . . Les objets et l'éclairage forment un

système qui tend vers une certaine constance et vers un certain niveau stable, non par l'opération de l'intelligence, mais par la configuration même du champ."—*Ibid.,* pp. 104–5.

12 *Ibid.,* pp. 107 ff.

13 In recent American aesthetics this thesis has been maintained by Langer; see her *Feeling and Form,* Chap. III, and *Problems of Art,* Chaps. II, III, and IV.

14 ". . . de même que le corps et 'l'âme' d'un homme ne sont que deux aspects de sa manière d'être au monde, de même le mot et la pensée qu'il désigne ne doivent pas être considérés comme deux termes extérieurs et le mot porte sa signification comme le corps est l'incarnation d'un comportement."—*Sens et non-sens,* pp. 109–10.

15 For Merleau-Ponty's account of the body's functioning in the organization of its objects, see Chapter VII, this study.

16 *Aesthetic,* p. 51.

17 This thesis is one of the principal elements of the aesthetic theory promulgated by Alain and Valéry. See Alain's *Entretiens chez le sculpteur,* p. 15; and Valéry's *Introduction à la poétique,* p. 40.

18 One of the principal exponents of this doctrine is Beardsley; see his *Aesthetics,* pp. 17–29.

19 "Il n'y a donc pas d'art d'agrément. On peut fabriquer des objets qui font plaisir en liant autrement des idées déjà prêtes et en présentant des formes déjà vues. Cette peinture ou cette parole seconde est ce qu'on entend généralement par culture."—*Sens et non-sens,* pp. 34–35.

20 "L'expression ne peut alors pas être la traduction d'une pensée déjà claire, puisque les pensées claires sont celles qui ont déjà été dites en nous-mêmes ou par les autres. La 'conception' ne peut pas précéder 'l'exécution.' "—*Ibid.,* p. 35.

21 "Les difficultés de Cézanne sont celles de la première parole. Il s'est cru impuissant parce qu'il n'était pas omnipotent, parce qu'il n'était pas Dieu et qu'il voulait pourtant peindre le monde, le convertir entièrement en spectacle, faire *voir* comment il nous *touche.*"—*Ibid.,* p. 36.

22 "Le sens de ce que va dire l'artiste *n'est* nulle part, ni dans les choses, qui ne sont pas encore sens, ni en lui-même, dans sa vie informulée. Il appelle de la raison déjà constituée, et dans laquelle s'enferment les 'hommes cultivés,' à une raison qui embrasserait ses propres origines."—*Ibid.,* pp. 35–36.

23 "L'anatomie et le dessin sont présents, quand il pose une touche, comme les règles du jeu dans une partie de tennis. Ce qui motive un geste du peintre, ce ne peut jamais être la perspective seule ou la géométrie seule ou les lois de la décomposition des couleurs ou quelque connaissance que ce soit. Pour tous les gestes qui peu à peu font un tableau, il n'y a qu'un seul motif, c'est le paysage dans sa totalité et dans sa plénitude absolue—que justement Cézanne appelait un 'motif.' "—*Ibid.,* p. 31.

24 *Feeling and Form,* Chap. V, *passim.*

25 "Dans l'oeuvre d'art ou dans la théorie comme dans la chose sensible, le

sens est inséparable du signe."—*Sens et non-sens,* p. 9.

26 "L'expression, donc, n'est jamais achevée. La plus haute raison voisine avec la déraison."—*Ibid.*

27 "En présence d'un roman, d'un poème, d'une peinture, d'un film valables, nous savons qu'il y a eu contact avec quelque chose, quelque chose est acquis pour les hommes et l'oeuvre commence d'émettre un message ininterrompu. . . . Mais ni pour l'artiste, ni pour le public le sens de l'oeuvre n'est formulable autrement que par l'oeuvre elle-même; ni la pensée qui l'a faite, ni celle qui la reçoit n'est tout à fait maîtresse de soi."—*Ibid.,* p. 8.

28 See Merleau-Ponty's interpretation of Cézanne's dilemma, "Le doute de Cézanne," *ibid.,* pp. 15–49.

29 "Cézanne n'a pas cru devoir choisir entre la sensation et la pensée, comme entre le chaos et l'ordre. Il ne veut pas séparer les choses fixes qui apparaissent sous notre regard et leur manière fuyante d'apparaître, il veut peindre la matière en train de se donner forme, l'ordre naissant par une organisation spontanée. Il ne met pas la coupure entre 'les sens' et 'l'intelligence,' mais entre l'ordre spontané des choses perçues et l'ordre humain des idées et des sciences. Nous percevons des choses, nous nous entendons sur elles, nous sommes ancrés en elles et c'est sur ce socle de 'nature' que nous construisons des sciences."—*Ibid.,* p. 24.

30 "Il ne sert à rien d'opposer ici les distinctions de l'âme et du corps, de la pensée et de la vision, puisque Cézanne revient justement à l'expérience primordiale d'où ces notions sont tirées et qui nous les donne inséparables. Le peintre qui pense et qui cherche l'expression d'abord manque le mystère, renouvelé chaque fois que nous regardons quelqu'un, de son apparition dans la nature."—*Ibid.,* p. 29.

31 *Ibid.,* p. 25; for Merleau-Ponty's criticism of physical models used to explain psychic activity, see Chap. VII, this study.

32 "Comme la parole nomme, c'est-à-dire saisit dans sa nature et place devant nous à titre d'objet reconnaissable ce qui apparaissait confusément, le peintre, dit Gasquet, 'objective,' 'projette,' 'fixe.' "—*Ibid.,* p. 32.

33 "Le peintre n'a pu que construire une image. Il faut attendre que cette image s'anime pour les autres. Alors l'oeuvre d'art aura joint ces vies séparées, elle n'existera plus seulement en l'une d'elles comme un rêve tenace ou un délire persistant, ou dans l'espace comme une toile coloriée, elle habitera indivise dans plusieurs esprits, présomptivement dans tout esprit possible, comme une acquisition pour toujours."—*Ibid.,* p. 37.

34 As it is maintained by Brooks; see "Language of Paradox," in his *Well Wrought Urn,* pp. 3–20.

35 "Le vrai contraire du formalisme est une bonne théorie du style, ou de la parole, qui les mette au-dessus de la 'technique' ou de 'l'instrument.' "—Stated in an article in *Temps Modernes,* VIII (July, 1952), 85.

36 "Le roman comme compte rendu d'événements, comme énoncé d'idées, thèse ou conclusions, comme signification manifeste ou prosaïque, et le

roman comme opération d'un style, signification oblique ou latente sont dans un simple rapport d'homonymie."—*Ibid.*

37 "Le langage . . . n'est pas au service du sens et ne gouverne pourtant pas le sens. Il n'y a pas de subordination entre eux. Ici personne ne commande et personne n'obéit. Ce que nous *voulons dire* est devant nous, hors de toute parole, comme une pure signification. Ce n'est que l'excès de ce que nous vivons sur ce qui a été déjà dit."—*Ibid.*, p. 93.

38 C'est un office du même genre que remplit le langage littéraire, c'est de la même manière impérieuse et brève que l'écrivain, sans transitions ni préparations, nous transporte du monde déjà dit à autre chose."—*Ibid.*, p. 86.

39 "Et comme notre corps ne nous guide parmi les choses qu'à condition que nous cessions de l'analyser pour user de lui, le langage n'est littéraire, c'est-à-dire productif, qu'à condition que nous cessions de lui demander à chaque instant des justifications pour le suivre où il va, que nous laissons les mots et tous les moyens d'expression du livre s'envelopper de cette auréole de signification qu'ils doivent à leur arrangement singulier, et tout l'écrit virer vers une valeur seconde où il rejoint presque le rayonnement muet de la peinture."—*Ibid.*, pp. 86–87.

40 "Si l'auteur est écrivain, c'est-à-dire capable de trouver les élisions et les césures qui signent la conduite, le lecteur répond à son appel et le rejoint au centre virtuel de l'écrit, *même si l'un ni l'autre ne le connaissent.*"—*Ibid.*, p. 85.

41 "L'homme peut dépasser sa contingence dans ce qu'il crée, mais toute expression, au même titre que le Grand Art, est un acte de naissance de l'homme. Le miracle se passe partout et à ras de terre, non dans le ciel privilégié des beaux-arts. Le principe de l'ordre et celui du désordre sont un seul principe, la contingence des choses et notre liberté qui la domine sont faites d'une même étoffe."—Merleau-Ponty, *Sens et non-sens,* p. 91.

42 "Ce qui n'est pas remplaçable dans l'oeuvre d'art, ce qui fait d'elle beaucoup plus qu'un moyen de plaisir: un organe de l'esprit, dont l'analogue se retrouve en toute pensée philosophique ou politique si elle est productive, c'est qu'elle contient, mieux que des idées, des *matrices d'idées,* qu'elle nous fournit d'emblèmes dont nous n'avons jamais fini de développer le sens, que, justement parce qu'elle s'installe et nous installe dans un monde dont nous n'avons pas la clef, elle nous apprend à voir et finalement nous donne à penser comme aucun ouvrage analytique ne peut le faire, parce que l'analyse ne trouve dans l'objet que ce que nous y avons mis."—In *Temps Modernes,* VII (July, 1952), 86.

43 "L'oeuvre d'un grand romancier est toujours portée par deux ou trois idées philosophiques. Soit par exemple le Moi et la Liberté chez Stendhal, chez Balzac le mystère de l'histoire comme apparition d'un sens dans le hasard des événements, chez Proust l'enveloppement du passé dans le présent et la présence du temps perdu. La fonction du romancier n'est pas de thématiser ces idées, elle est de les faire exister devant nous

à la manière des choses. Ce n'est pas le rôle de Stendhal de discourir sur la subjectivité, il lui suffit de la rendre présente."—*Sens et non-sens,* pp. 51–52

44   See this study, Appendix B.

45   "Le sens d'une image dépend donc de celles qui la précèdent dans le film, et leur succession crée une réalité nouvelle qui n'est pas la simple somme des éléments employés."—*Sens et non-sens,* p. 111.

46   "La parole, au cinéma, n'est pas chargée d'ajouter des idées aux images, ni la musique des sentiments. L'ensemble nous dit quelque chose de très précis qui n'est ni une pensée, ni un rappel des sentiments de la vie."—*Ibid.,* p. 116.

47   ". . . l'idée ou les faits prosaïques ne sont là que pour donner au créateur l'occasion de leur chercher des emblèmes sensibles et d'en tracer le monogramme visible et sonore. Le sens du film est incorporé à son rythme comme le sens d'un geste est immédiatement lisible dans le geste, et le film ne veut rien dire que lui-même. L'idée est ici rendue à l'état naissant, elle émerge de la structure temporelle du film, comme dans un tableau de la coexistence de ses parties."—*Ibid.,* p. 118.

48   *Art as Experience,* Chap. XVIII.

49   "Pour le cinéma comme pour la psychologie moderne, le vertige, le plaisir, la douleur, l'amour, la haine sont des conduites."—*Sens et non-sens,* p. 120.

50   "Si donc la philosophie et le cinéma sont d'accord, si la réflexion et le travail technique vont dans le même sens, c'est parce que le philosophe et le cinéaste ont en commun une certaine manière d'être, une certaine vue du monde qui est celle d'une génération."—*Ibid.,* pp. 121–22.

51   "C'est le bonheur de l'art de montrer comment quelque chose se met à signifier, non par allusion à des idées déjà formées et acquises, mais par l'arrangement temporel ou spatial des éléments. Un film signifie comme . . . une chose signifie: l'un et l'autre ne parlent pas à un entendement séparé, mais s'adressent à notre pouvoir de déchiffrer tacitement le monde et les hommes et de coexister avec eux."—*Ibid.,* pp. 118–19.

52   *Ibid.,* p. 119.

53   "Si la religion de l'art n'admet pas d'être mêlée à l'à-peu-près de la vie, elle risque de devenir une technique de joli. 'En art, il n'est pas de problèmes, dit Gide dans une phrase elle-même trop jolie, dont l'oeuvre d'art ne soit une suffisante solution.' "—*Ibid.,* p. 88.

54   "La pensée analytique brise la transition perceptive d'un moment à un autre, d'un lieu à un autre, d'une perspective à une autre, et cherche ensuite du côté de l'esprit la garantie d'une unité qui est déjà là quand nous percevons. Elle brise aussi l'unité de la culture et cherche ensuite à la reconstituer du dehors."—*Temps Modernes,* VIII (1952), 75.

55   "La critique pourra bien confronter le mode d'expression d'un romancier avec celui d'un autre, faire rentrer tel type de récit dans une famille d'autres possibles. Ce travail n'est légitime que s'il est précédé par une perception du roman, ou les particularités de la 'technique' se confon-

dent avec celles du projet d'ensemble et du sens, et s'il est destiné
seulement à nous expliquer à nous-mêmes ce que nous avons perçu."—
Ibid., p. 87.

56   "Il est certain que la vie n'*explique* pas l'oeuvre, mais certain aussi
qu'elles communiquent. La vérité est que *cette oeuvre à faire exigeait
cette vie.* Dès son début, la vie de Cézanne ne trouvait d'équilibre qu'en
s'appuyant à l'oeuvre encore future, elle en était le projet, et l'oeuvre
s'y annonçait par des signes prémonitoires que nous aurions tort de
prendre pour des causes, mais qui font de l'oeuvre et de la vie une seule
aventure."—Merleau-Ponty, *Sens et non-sens,* p. 38.

57   *Introduction à la méthode de Léonard de Vinci,* p. 38.

58   "Il reste possible que, à l'occasion de ses faiblesses nerveuses, Cézanne
ait conçu une forme d'art valable pour tous. Laissé à lui-même, il a pu
regarder la nature comme seul un homme sait le faire. Le sens de son
oeuvre ne peut être déterminé par sa vie."—Merleau-Ponty, *Sens et non-
sens,* p. 19.

59   *Painting and Reality,* pp. 7–10.

60   Sartre has been criticized by MacDonald for his "metaphysical" idealism.
Although the title of her article is promising, she neglects to show how
metaphysical idealism fails to enlighten an audience on the problems of
art criticism: "Some Distinctive Features of Arguments Used in Criticism of the Arts," in *Essays,* ed. Elton, pp. 114–30. I have tried to show
that the epithets "idealism" and "realism" are strictly metaphysical
terms, and are applicable to aesthetic objects only in a derived sense.
The aesthetic question is whether or not the metaphysical positions of
idealism and realism solve the problems of aesthetic analysis. See this
study, Chap. III.

61   "La conscience métaphysique et morale meurt au contact de l'absolu
parce qu'elle est elle-même, par delà le monde plat de la conscience
habituée ou endormie, la connexion vivante de moi avec moi et de moi
avec autrui. La métaphysique n'est pas une construction de concepts par
lesquels nous essaierions de rendre moins sensibles nos paradoxes; c'est
l'expérience que nous faisons dans toutes les situations de l'histoire per-
sonnelle et collective—et des actions qui, les assumant, les transforment
en raison."—*Sens et non-sens,* p. 191.

62   "Les sciences de l'homme, dans leur orientation présente, sont métaphysique ou transnaturelles en ce sens qu'elles nous font redécouvrir,
avec la structure et la compréhension des structures, une dimension d'être
et un type de connaissance que l'homme oublie dans l'attitude qui lui
est naturelle."—*Ibid.,* p. 185.

63   ". . . les sciences de l'homme (pour ne rien dire des autres) ont fait
voir que toute connaissance de l'homme par l'homme est inévitablement,
non pas contemplation pure, mais reprise par chacun, selon ce qu'il
peut, des actes d'autrui, réactivation à partir de signes ambigus d'une
expérience qui n'est pas la sienne, appropriation par lui d'une structure
—*a priori* de l'espèce, schème sublinguistique ou esprit d'une civilisa-

tion—dont il ne forme pas un concept distinct et qu'il restitue comme
le pianiste exercé déchiffre une musique inconnue: sans saisir lui-même
les motifs de chaque geste ou de chaque opération, sans pouvoir réveil-
ler tout le savoir sédimenté dont il fait usage à ce moment."—*Ibid.*,
pp. 185–86.

CHAPTER XI

1 For an American reader this proposition may bring to mind the pragmatic position of John Dewey; the French source is, however, probably
   to be found in Bergson, *Matière et mémoire,* Chap. I.
2 See her "Merleau-Ponty et le pseudo-Sartrisme," in *Temps Modernes,*
   X (1955), pp. 2072–2122.
3 "Saussure peut bien montrer que chaque acte d'expression ne devient
   signifiant que comme modulation d'un système général d'expression et
   en tant qu'il se différencie des autres gestes linguistiques—la merveille
   est qu'avant lui nous n'en savions rien et que nous l'oublions encore
   chaque fois que nous parlons, et pour commencer quand nous parlons
   des idées de Saussure."—*Temps Modernes,* VIII (1952), 90.
4 "Cela prouve que chaque acte partiel d'expression, comme acte commun
   du tout de la langue, ne se borne pas à dépenser un pouvoir expressif
   accumulé en elle, mais le recrée et la recrée, en nous faisant vérifier,
   dans l'évidence du sens donné et reçu, le pouvoir qu'ont les sujets
   parlants de dépasser les signes vers le sens."—*Ibid.*, pp. 90–91.
5 Cf. Saussure, *Cours de linguistique générale,* p. 157.
6 *Phénoménologie,* p. 48.
7 Cf. Valéry:
   "La formation de figures est indivisible de celle du langage lui-même,
   dont tous les mots 'abstraits' sont obtenus par quelque abus ou quelque
   transport de signification, suivi d'un oubli du sens primitif. Le poète
   qui multiplie les figures ne fait donc que retrouver en lui-même le
   langage à l'état naissant."—*Introduction à la poétique,* p. 12.
      Alain, who had written commentaries on two of Valéry's longer poems,
   uses a comparable expression in his distinction between "primitive" and
   "conventional" signs. Moreover, like Valéry and Merleau-Ponty, he
   insists that meanings are not, in their nascent state, intellectual, but
   actions of the human body: "Le corps humain, par sa structure, nous offre
   deux formes du langage naturel, le geste et la voix. On aperçoit aussitôt
   que la danse correspond au premier, et la musique au second. Toutefois
   si l'on veut comprendre en quel sens l'art est langage, *il faut prendre
   le langage aux racines.* Et il est clair que le premier et le plus puissant
   langage, c'est l'action. Agir, c'est signifier."—*Vingt leçons,* p. 60.
   [Emphasis added.]
8 "Autant vaudrait croire que, pour parler, nous allons chercher des mots
   que nous cousons ensuite ensemble au moyen d'une pensée. La vérité
   est qu'au-dessus du mot et au-dessus de la phrase il y a quelque chose
   de beaucoup plus simple qu'une phrase et même qu'un mot: le sens,

qui est moins une chose pensée qu'un mouvement de pensée, moins un mouvement qu'une direction."—*Pensée et le mouvant,* p. 133; see also *Matière et mémoire,* Chap. I.

9   See this study, Chap. XII.
10 *Six Theories of Mind.*
11 See Nahm's *Artist as Creator,* Book II, Chap. 8.
12 The vagaries of this aesthetic notion have been many since its beginning in Bell's *Art;* Langer has taken up the same notion for a third time in her *Problems of Art,* Chap. 2.
13 *Philosophy in a New Key,* Chap. 2.
14 *Feeling and Form,* Chap. V.
15 *Ibid.,* pp. 395–97.
16 See this study, Chap. IV.
17 See this study, Chap. X.

CHAPTER XII

1   I am mindful also of the fact that the word "proper" usually indicates a restriction in the scope of the term to which it is applied, as "Greece proper" refers to the Greek homeland, which was only a smaller part of the total ancient Greek civilization and empire. The word "aesthetics," then, could be conceived as applied to the narrower interest of philosophers in a "science of the beautiful," and the term "philosophy of art" saved for the wider interest I am attempting to delineate.

I offer the following reasons for not accepting the conventional acceptation of the term: (a) The distinction between objects of natural beauty and successful artistic expressions is not specious, but has little consequence for the development of an aesthetics or a philosophy of art, no matter how conceived. See Alexander's essay "Art and the Material," in his *Philosophical and Literary Pieces,* pp. 231–32. (b) Should the term "philosophy of art" be applied to our wider concept, we would be forced to extend the notion of "art," and it seems better that this term be restricted (if for no other reason than to protect the autonomy of the artist's expression). (c) The term "philosophy of art" as I am using it is consistent with the contemporary practice of philosophers, who are engaged in a secondary intellectual discipline dedicated to the understanding of the workings of a primary discipline. It is in this sense that it may be said that *the philosophy of* various other first order disciplines has replaced the more traditional interest in "first philosophy," or metaphysics.

2   *Critique de la raison dialectique.*
3   See his *Pensée et le mouvant,* pp. 177–227.
4   This point of view has been developed in *Essays,* ed. Elton.
5   Jordan, *Forms of Individuality,* and Mead, *Mind, Self and Society.*
6   The case for a contemporary reintegration of the artist with society has been made by the sociologist, Griff, in *Arts in Society,* No. 3, pp. 43–54 (Fall), 1959.

7 "Aux rapports réciproques de la volonté expressive et des moyens d'expression correspondent ceux des forces productives et des formes de production, plus généralement des forces historiques et des institutions. Comme la langue est un système de signes qui n'ont de sens que relativement les uns aux autres et dont chacun se reconnaît à une certaine valeur d'emploi qui lui revient dans le tout de la langue, chaque institution est un système symbolique que le sujet s'incorpore comme style de fonctionnement, comme configuration globale, sans qu'il ait besoin de le concevoir."—*Eloge de la philosophie,* pp. 75–76.

8 See Sartre's *Saint Genet comédien et martyr.*

9 Although Sartre's discussion of social groupings has some relevance to an understanding of his differences with Merleau-Ponty, it seems to go beyond the scope of the present treatise. It should be noted, however, that any discussion of Sartre's social philosophy would be incomplete without an analysis of this work.

10 Sartre has objected to the autobiographical interpretation of *Les Mains sales,* claiming that the protagonist of the story is Hoederer, whose conscience is controlled by the directives of the party line and a policy of political expediency. French Communists have condemned the play as anti-Communistic, while Sartre interprets it as showing his sympathy for Communist activity. If the character of Hugo was not built upon Sartre's own ambivalent attitude toward Communism, the similarity with the facts of Sartre's life are striking: the conflict of an intellectual before the dual demand of authenticity of existence and practicality of action. This conflict, it seems to me, is at the basis of the quarrel between Sartre and Merleau-Ponty.

11 *Mind, Self and Society,* pp. 71–72.

12 *Ibid.,* Part IV, *passim.*

13 The recent controversy between advocates of the New Criticism and the more traditional exponents of "historical criticism" was gone through to some extent for the purpose of improving education of the liberal arts, with particular reference to literature; see Wellek and Warren, *Theory of Literature,* Chap. XX.

14 Accepting Croce's denial of the validity of "aesthetic types," Spingarn reduced literary criticism to a two-fold practice: to determine what the author wanted to say, and to show how the author accomplished what he wanted to say. See his "The New Criticism," in *Creative Criticism,* pp. 3–44. In an effort to avoid Spingarn's intentionalism, some critics refer to the "intent" of the piece, which would allow the critic to consider the work as if it contained, in its own right, the subjective qualities usually associated only with human beings.

15 See Dufrenne's *Phénoménologie de l'expérience esthétique, passim.* Dufrenne refers to the work of art as a quasi-subject much on the same grounds as those of the earlier New Critics; he further supplies the metaphysical categories of contemporary existentialism to substantiate his claims. See also Appendix A, this study.

16 Weitz has included a discussion of the value of the medium to artistic expression in his *Problems in Aesthetics,* pp. 246–59.

17 Hospers has indicated this interpretation for Croce's theory of intuition; see his article in *Philosophy,* XXXI (1956), 291–308.

18 In his *Philosophical and Literary Pieces,* ed. Laird.

19 There has already appeared a book entitled *Social Psychology of Music,* in which the author, Farnsworth, applies the techniques of his specialty to the field of music. Although he describes the psychological approach to music as comprised of a triple function (descriptive, explanatory, and predictive), his descriptions are all given in terms of correlations between noted preferences and the social classification of his subjects; his explanations are all *post hoc,* and he gives no predictions.

What the book lacks in order to achieve the conception of an aesthetics proper is a serious consideration of the aesthetic value of music (which may be relative, and not absolute as Farnsworth seems to think it must be in a philosophical context), and the influence of relative value judgments on the structures of society itself. Mr. Farnsworth also seems to think that although "culture" determines our value judgments the aesthetic values of music have no influence on society other than as a means of psychological therapy or of increasing the industrial efficiency of workers. The greatest weakness of the book is Farnsworth's naive notion of social "causality." In two places where the aesthetic knowledgeability of his subjects influence his results, Farnsworth tends to ignore this factor. See Chap. VI, "The Nature of Musical Taste."

The book does contain an excellent bibliography of the literature on the psychology of music.

APPENDIX A

1 "On verra que nous ne nous astreignons pas à suivre la lettre de Husserl. Nous entendons 'phénoménologie' au sens où MM. Sartre et Merleau-Ponty ont acclimaté ce terme en France: description qui vise une essence, elle-même définie comme signification immanente au phénomène et donnée avec lui. L'essence est à découvrir, mais par un dévoilement et non par un saut du connu à l'inconnu. La phénoménologie s'applique en premier à l'humain parce que la conscience est conscience de soi: c'est là qu'est le modèle du phénomène, l'apparaître comme apparaître du sens à lui-même."—*Phénoménologie,* pp. 4–5, note.

2 *Ibid.,* pp. 1–4.

3 For the principal aesthetic works of Alain, see his *Système* and *Vingt leçons;* of Valéry, his *Introduction à la méthode de Leonard de Vinci* and *Variété IV* and the two dialogues on architecture and the dance published together in a volume entitled *Eupalinos.*

4 Dufrenne, *Phénoménologie,* pp. 3–4.

5 *Ibid.,* p. 16.

6   *Ibid.*, pp. 22 ff.
7   Edmund Husserl, *Ideen zu einer reinen Phaenomenoiogie und phaenome-nologischen Philosophie*, Bk. I, Part I, Chap. I, sec. 4.
8   *Phénoménologie*, p. 443.
9   *Système*, Book I.
10 This distinction is taken from Ziff's article in *Essays*, ed. Elton, pp. 170–86. Ziff refuses to distinguish between two kinds of object, the work of art and the object of art, because all differences between the two concepts reduce to varying descriptions of the same object.
11 *Phénoménologie*, p. 265.
12 *Ibid.*, p. 442.
13 The rather wide variation on the application of the term "phenomenology" is explained adequately in Lalande's *Vocabulaire technique et critique de la philosophie*, pp. 749–51.
14 In *Journal of Aesthetics and Art Criticism*, IX (1950), 139.
15 *Ibid.*, p. 147.
16 Sartre's theory of creation as a function of the imagination, which in its free activity "nihilates" the perceived or real world, and his doctrine of representative meaning smack more of idealistic metaphysics than of phenomenology. MacDonald has selected this feature of Sartre's aesthetics as dominating; see her article in *Essays*, ed. Elton, pp. 114–30.
17 See his Introduction to Merleau-Ponty's *Structure*, pp. v–xv.
18 *Basis of Criticism in the Arts*, pp. 168–69.
19 *Ibid.*, p. 71.
20 See this study, Chap. XI.
21 "La signification n'est vraiment saisie que lorsque le corps s'accorde avec le signe, lorsqu'il est présent du fond de lui-même à l'objet esthétique; cette présence vécue n'est pas le sentiment, elle en est la condition. Et pas la seule condition, car il ne suffit pas que l'objet nous soit présent, il faut qu'il soit représenté; la prise corporelle sur l'objet n'est d'abord qu'une condition de la perception consciente, et par ce détour du sentiment. Ainsi le sentiment perd son immédiateté de fait, s'il garde une immédiateté de droit: il est immédiat quand l'objet nous est donné et que nous sommes disponibles, mais encore faut-il que l'objet nous soit donné."—*Phénoménologie*, pp. 516–17.
22 "L'objet esthétique est celui où la matière ne demeure que si la forme ne se perd pas."—*Ibid.*, p. 132.
23 *Ibid.*, p. 276.
24 "Mais si le sens peut ainsi unifier et constituer l'objet, c'est qu'il procède du plus profond de lui et qu'il ne réside pas seulement dans les représentations que l'objet peut proposer: l'oeuvre n'est vraiment une qu'à condition de receler une unité plus profonde que la cohérence logique d'un sens rationnel, une unité qui rassemble toute, signifié et signifiant, et qui lui donne vraiment sa personnalité; c'est cette unité qui constitue la péripétie ultime du sens de l'objet esthétique, faute de quoi cet objet n'a plus que l'être d'un signe quelconque et perd à la fois sa rigueur et sa plénitude."—*Ibid.*

25 "L'objet esthétique n'a pas une forme, il est forme."—*Ibid.*, p. 293.

26 ". . . l'oeuvre littéraire est vraie, comme la fable, par son sens second et non par le sens immédiat de ce qu'elle représente; la fonction de la représentation n'est pas tant d'imiter le réel que de servir l'expression qui permettra de le saisir."—*Ibid.*, p. 643. See also pp. 620–31.

27 *Ibid.*, p. 657.

28 "Cela n'implique pas que le réel soit identique au sens: il est, comme dans la dialectique hégélienne, l'autre du sens; et c'est ainsi qu'il est le débordant, l'inépuisable, le non-sens. Mais ce qui est non-sens par rapport à l'homme est encore sens par rapport à l'être: c'est le sens devenu nature."—*Ibid.*, note.

29 *Ibid.*, p. 283.

30 *Ibid.*, note 1.

31 In *Das literarische Kunstwerk*, Part II. Cf. Dufrenne, pp. 266–73.

32 "Le génie est celui que je reconnais entre mille, celui qui, même s'il ne l'a pas voulu, n'a pas son pareil. Mais comprenons bien: en entendant du Mozart, je dois reconnaître Mozart; et si, l'ayant reconnu, je dis que Mozart appartient à un certain style classique, alors je fais oeuvre de critique, je décolle de l'oeuvre, je cesse de percevoir esthétiquement pour connaître objectivement: le passage de l'individu au genre est bien ici le résultat d'une abstraction, si c'est du dehors que je l'opère, en confrontant les techniques, les influences, et toute l'histoire des oeuvres."—*Phénoménologie*, p. 157.

33 "La relation du sujet à l'objet est préfigurée au sein même du sujet par la relation du temps à l'espace; et le mouvement, qui est mouvement dans le sujet avant d'être mouvement dans l'objet, exprime dans l'objet même cette relation."—*Ibid.*, p. 313.

34 *Ibid.* The quasi-subjectivity of an object of art is a recurring idea in Dufrenne's work; see especially p. 255.

35 *Ibid.*, pp. 346–355.

36 ". . . le mouvement n'est rien d'autre que ce développement d'une essence, l'aventure d'un être égal à lui-même à travers ses métamorphoses, comme du thème à travers les variations."—*Ibid.*, p. 371.

37 *Ibid.*, Part IV, Chap. I.

38 See his *Correspondance des arts*, Part III.

39 ". . . le sens n'est pas d'abord quelque chose que je pense avec détachement, mais quelque chose qui me concerne et me détermine, qui résonne en moi et m'émeut; la signification pure que je contemple sans y adhérer sera prélevée sur cette signification primitive, qui me convainc parce qu'elle m'ébranle, où le sens est une sommation à laquelle je réponds avec mon corps."—*Phénoménologie*, p. 422.

40 *Ibid.*

41 "Je ne perçois qu'au passé, et du futur; au présent, je fais seulement. Contempler c'est revenir au passé pour surprendre le futur; je ne cesse d'être un avec l'objet par la présence qu'en me détachant du présent où je suis perdu dans les choses. Le 're' de représentation exprime cette intériorisation, de même que le 'com' de contempler exprime la possi-

bilité d'un survol et d'une simultanéité qui en appellent à l'espace. Car l'espace est contemporain du temps."—*Ibid.*, p. 434.

42 . . . il exprime la possibilité de la représentation, l'empirique rend compte de la possibilité qu'a telle représentation d'être signifiante et de s'intégrer à la représentation d'un monde."—*Ibid.*, p. 435.

43 *Ibid.*, p. 451.

44 ". . . pour que nous saisissions l'objet esthétique comme tel, il faut encore, nous l'avons dit, qu'il nous apparaisse comme figurant un objet représenté; cet objet représenté est ici l'idée de la cathédrale: représentant et représenté objectivement se confondent, puisque la cathédrale n'a d'autre sujet qu'elle-même; mais ils se distinguent tout de même subjectivement en ceci que le premier requiert une exploration infinie que l'imagination comble à sa façon, tandis que le second est saisi comme immédiatement donné dans chaque perception."—*Ibid.*, p. 454.

45 *Ibid.*, Part IV, Chap. III, *passim.*

46 "Cette affinité qui se manifeste entre la nature et moi n'est pas seulement comprise par la réflexion, elle est éprouvée, particulièrement dans l'expérience esthétique, dans une sorte de communion entre l'objet et moi. Et cette communion est une voie d'accès au sentiment."—*Ibid.*, p. 468.

47 *Ibid.*, pp. 253–56; see especially p. 254, note 2.

48 *Ibid.*, pp. 469 ff.

49 *Ibid.*, Part III, Chap. 5.

50 See this appendix, p. 362.

51 *Phénoménologie*, Part II, Ch. 4.

52 Dufrenne uses the term "logical" in order to encompass the sense of "representation" I have referred to as "epistemological."—See *ibid.*, p. 389.

53 "L'artiste choisit tel sujet parce qu'il lui est consubstantiel, parce que ce sujet éveille en lui une certaine émotion, entretient une certaine interrogation; il ne s'agit pas pour lui de copier ce sujet, mais de donner à travers lui un équivalent sensible de la signification affective autant qu'intellectuelle que ce sujet a pour lui: Roualt ne peint pas un Christ, mais à travers le Christ un équivalent pictural de ce que le Christ signifie pour lui." *Ibid.*, pp. 393–94.

54 For a demonstration of the manner in which the contribution is made, see Appendix B, this study.

55 See his *Phénoménologie*, Part IV, "Critique de l'expérience esthétique," pp. 543–94.

APPENDIX B

1 Peirce, *Collected Papers*, V, 276.

2 *Ibid.*, p. 277.

3 Dostoievsky's inclusion in this trio of novelists may be thought unjust. Of his novels familiar to me only *The Idiot* seems to be a successful

embodiment of a philosophical idea, the Christian ideal of universal charity.

4 Sartre had published no major philosophical work before the appearance of *La Nausée* in 1938. His *L'Imagination*, however, appeared in 1936; and he had published an article in *Recherches Philosophiques*, VI (1936-37), 85–123. *L'Etre et le néant* did not come out until 1943; it contains Sartre's major contribution to metaphysics.

5 It must be remembered that Camus denied he was an existentialist, whether from the modest motive of wishing to deny any claim to the status of philosopher or from the more confused motive of not wishing to be associated with a growing clique of writers. If not existentialist, the philosophy embodied in his early work is clearly existentialistic. Later, when the problem of conscience becomes ramified in his thinking to include the doctrine of revolt, his work appears less so. Beauvoir draws the picture of "the passionate man" in her *Ethics of Ambiguity*, which takes its inspiration from Camus' position in *Myth of Sisyphus*. A non-existentialistic reading of Camus' novel is given by Champigny in his *Sur un héros païen*.

6 The author is indebted for certain revisions in this text to Miss Germaine Brée, whose interpretation of Camus' work is based upon her intimate knowledge of all his original manuscripts. See her *Camus*.

Miss Brée has indicated that Sartre is not, strictly speaking, using the surrealistic writing technique of automatic "psychical" expression. Cf. Breton, *Manifestes du surréalisme*, p. 45. She correctly points out that Sartre is in full control of his literary expression. The point remains, however, that Roquentin has undergone what Breton calls "the surrealist experience" (pp. 91–93), and is depicted by Sartre as having passed on the experience in the pages of the "discovered" diary. Roquentin has undergone the surrealist's act of freely metamorphosizing reality as it is intercut with images of dream-like quality into a new experience of the "surreal." And Sartre depicts this experience in what I have called "reflective stream of consciousness," to show the third and final step in the liberation of Roquentin's consciousness.

Surrealist painters are called "surrealist" in an analogous fashion. The style referred to is a manner of depicting reality.

7 This suggestion has already been made by Viggiani, in *Publications of the Modern Language Association*, LXXI (1956), 865–87, and is reported as having been rejected by Camus as not intended. In spite of the author's own rejection of the hypothesis, the name is here asserted as symbolic in view of the two denials of Meursault to accept essential determination in religion (the repentent sinner) and in society (the criminal). Meursault refuses to take either of these leaps and adheres to his own inner conviction of innocence. He refuses to lie, and prefers an actual death to the symbolic end of his existence which religion and society both represent in their own way.

Moreover, the concern with death is undeniable in the structure of the story: Meursault finds himself standing over the dead body of the Arab (following his vigil over his mother's coffin), and this scene is repeated in anticipation with the image of the audience who are to witness Meursault's execution. For those who are given to an external critical criterion, it might be further indicated that the subject of *Mythe de Sisyphe,* published the same year as *L'Etranger,* is precisely concerned with the inauthenticity of religious and social determinations of human nature; and, finally, the good which may be experienced by men is exposited there in terms of what Simone de Beauvoir has called "the passionate life." Any association of Meursault's name with that of the wine seems completely adventitious within the fictional context of the story considered in itself.

The author of this essay is grateful to Miss Brée for calling his attention to the Viggiani article.

8 For an example of the intellectual confusion which results from the separation of the philosophical and the literary questions in considerations of a "philosophical" literature, see *Wisconsin Studies in Contemporary Literature,* I, No. 3 (1960).

Bibliography

BOOKS

Alain [*pseud.* of Emile Chartier]. *Système des beaux-arts.* Paris. Gallimard, 1920.

———. *Les Idées et les âges,* 8th ed., Paris: Gallimard, 1927. 2 vols.

———. *Histoire de mes pensées.* Paris: Gallimard, 1936.

———. *Préliminaires à l'esthétique.* Paris: Gallimard, 1939.

———. *Vingt leçons sur les beaux-arts,* new ed. Paris: Gallimard, 1939.

———. *Les Dieux,* 9th ed. Paris: Gallimard, 1947.

———. *Entretiens chez le sculpteur,* new ed. Paris: Hartmann, 1949.

———. *Eléments de philosophie,* 20th ed. Paris: Gallimard, 1953.

Alexander, Samuel. *Beauty and Other Forms of Value.* London: Macmillan, 1933.

———. *Philosophical and Literary Pieces.* John Laird, ed. London: Macmillan, 1939.

Algren, Nelson. *The Man with the Golden Arm.* Published serially in the French translation of Boris Vian as *L'Homme au bras d'or* in *Les Temps Modernes,* X (1954), 769–820; X (1955), 1013–52, 1253–69, 1409–32.

Aristotle. *De Poetica.* In *Introduction to Aristotle.* Richard McKeon, ed. New York: The Modern Library, 1947.

Arnheim, Rudolph. *Art and Visual Perception.* Berkeley: University of California Press, 1954.

———. *Film as Art.* Berkeley: University of California Press, 1957.

Barnes, Hazel Estella. *The Literature of Possibility.* Lincoln: University of Nebraska Press, 1959.

Beardsley, Monroe C. *Aesthetics: Problems in the Philosophy of Criticism.* New York: Harcourt, Brace and Co., 1958.

Beauvoir, Simone de. *Pour une morale de l'ambiguïté.* Published serially in *Les Temps Modernes,* II (1946–47), 193–211, 385–408, 638–664, 846–874.

———. *The Ethics of Ambiguity.* Bernard Frechtman, trans. New York: The Philosophical Library, 1948.

———. *Le Deuxième sexe.* Paris: Gallimard, 1949. 2 vols.

———. *L'Invitée.* Translated as *She Came to Stay.* Cleveland: World Publishing Co., 1954.

———. *Les Mandarins.* Paris: Gallimard, 1954.

Beigbeder, Marc. *L'Homme Sartre.* Paris: Bordas, 1947.

Bell, Clive. *Art,* reprint ed. New York: Capricorn Books (Putnam's Sons), 1958.

Bergson, Henri. *Matière et mémoire,* 50th ed. Paris: Presses Universitaires de France, 1949.

————. *La Pensée et le mouvant,* 27th ed. Paris: Presses Universitaires de France, 1950.

Blackmur, R. P. *Language as Gesture.* New York: Harcourt, Brace and Co., 1952.

Bosanquet, Bernard. *A History of Aesthetic.* New York: Macmillan, 1904.

————. *Three Lectures on Aesthetic.* London: Macmillan, 1931.

Brée, Germaine. *Camus.* New Brunswick: Rutgers University Press, 1959.

Breton, André. *Les Manifestes du surréalisme.* Paris: éditions du Sagittaire, 1946.

Brooks, Cleanth. *The Well Wrought Urn.* New York: Reynal and Hitchcock, 1947.

Burke, Kenneth. *The Philosophy of Literary Form.* Baton Rouge: Louisiana State University Press, 1938.

Campbell, Robert. *Jean-Paul Sartre ou une littérature philosophique,* 3d ed. Paris: Ardent, 1947.

Camus, Albert. *Le Mythe de Sisyphe.* Paris: Gallimard, 1942.

Champigny, Robert. *Stages on Sartre's Way.* Bloomington: Indiana University Press, 1959.

————. *Sur un héros païen.* Paris: Gallimard, 1959.

Church, Ralph W. *An Essay on Critical Appreciation.* Ithaca: Cornell University Press, 1938.

Collingwood, R. G. *The Principles of Art,* paperback reprint. New York: Oxford University Press, 1958.

Comte, Auguste. *Cours de philosophie positive,* 5th ed. Paris: au siège de la société positiviste, 1892–94. 6 vols.

————. *Système de politique positive.* Paris: à la librairie scientifique de L. Mathias, 1951–54. 4 vols.

Croce, Benedetto. *Aesthetic as Science of Expression and General Linguistic.* Douglas Ainslie, trans. London: Macmillan, 1909.

Desan, Wilfrid. *The Tragic Finale.* Cambridge, Mass: Harvard University Press, 1954.

Dewey, John. *Experience and Nature.* Chicago and London: Open Court Publishing Co., 1925.

————. *Philosophy and Civilization.* New York and London: Putnam's Sons, 1931.

————. *Art as Experience.* New York: Minton, Balch and Co., 1934.

————, *et al. Creative Intelligence.* New York: Holt and Co., 1917.

Diderot, Denis. *Le Paradoxe sur le comédien.* Paris: éditions Nord-Sud, 1949.

Dinnage, Paul, ed. *The Marquis de Sade.* New York: The Grove Press, 1953.

Ducasse, Curt J. *Philosophy of Art.* New York: The Dial Press, 1929.

Dufrenne, Mikel. *Phénoménologie de l'expérience esthétique.* Paris: Presses Universitaires de France, 1953. 2 vols.

Eliot, T. S. *Selected Essays, 1917–32.* New York: Harcourt, Brace and Co., 1932.

Elton, William, ed. *Essays in Aesthetics and Language.* Oxford: Blackwell, 1954.

Farber, Marvin, ed. *Philosophic Thought in France and the United States.* Buffalo: University of Buffalo, 1950.

Farnsworth, Paul R. *The Social Psychology of Music.* New York: Dryden Press, 1958.

Farrell, James T. *A Note on Literary Criticism.* New York: Vanguard Press, 1936.

———. *Literature and Morality.* New York: Vanguard Press, 1947.

Fast, Howard. *Literature and Reality.* New York: International Publishers, 1950.

Gelb, Adhemar, and Kurt Goldstein. *Psychologische Analysen Hirnpathologischer Faelle.* Leipzig: Bath, 1920.

Genet, Jean. *Querelle de Brest.* n.p.: no publisher, 1947.

———. *Notre-Dame des fleurs.* Lyon: L'Arbalète, 1948.

———. *Pompes funèbres.* n.p.: no publisher, 1948.

Gilson, Etienne. *Painting and Reality,* reprint edition. New York: Meridian Books, Inc., 1959.

Goldstein, Kurt. *The Organism.* Translation of his *Der Aufbau des Organismus,* 1934. New York, Cincinnati: American Book Co., 1939.

———, and Martin Scheerer. *Abstract and Concrete Behavior.* Psychological Monographs, J. F. Dashiell, ed., Vol. 53, No. 2. Evanston, Ill.: American Psychological Association, Inc., 1941.

Gotshalk, D. W. *Art and the Social Order.* Chicago: University of Chicago Press, 1947.

Grene, Marjorie. *Dreadful Freedom.* Chicago: University of Chicago Press, 1948.

Harper, Ralph. *The Sleeping Beauty.* London: The Harvill Press, 1955.

Hartshorne, Charles. *The Philosophy and Psychology of Sensation.* Chicago: University of Chicago Press, 1934.

Heidegger, Martin. *Sein und Zeit.* Halle a.d.S.: Max Neimeyer, 1927.

———. *Existence and Being.* Chicago: Regnery and Co., 1949.

———. *Kant und das Problem der Metaphysik,* 2d ed. Frankfurt am Main: Vittorio Klostermann, 1951. 1st ed., 1929.

———. *Was ist Metaphysik?* 7th ed. Frankfurt am Main: Vittorio Klostermann, 1955.

———. *Hölderlin und das Wesen der Dichtung.* Munich: Albert Langen-Georg Mueller Verlag, 1937.

Hicks, Granville. *The Great Tradition.* New York: Macmillan, 1933.

Hospers, John. *Meaning and Truth in the Arts.* Chapel Hill: University of North Carolina Press, 1946.

Hume, David. *A Treatise of Human Nature.* Everyman's Library. New York: Dutton and Co., 1949. 2 vols.

Husserl, Edmund. *Husserliana. Gesammelte Werke,* ed. directed by H. L. Van Breda. The Hague: Martinus Nijhoff, 1950–56. 7 vols.

Huxley, Aldous. *Point Counter Point.* Harper's Modern Classics. New York: Harper and Bros., 1947.

Hyman, Stanley E. *The Armed Vision.* New York: Knopf, 1948.

Ingarden, Roman. *Das literarische Kunstwerk.* Halle: Max Niemeyer Verlag, 1931.

James, William. *Essays in Radical Empiricism.* London and New York: Longmans, Green and Co., 1912.

Jeanson, Francis, ed. *Sartre par lui-même.* Paris: aux éditions du Seuil, 1955.

Jordan, Elijah. *Forms of Individuality.* Bloomington, Ind.: Principia Press, 1927.

Kant, Immanuel. *Kritik der reinen Vernunft,* 1st and 2d eds. collated by Raymund Schmidt. Hamburg: Verlag von Felix Mainer, 1952.

———. *Kritik der Urtheilskraft,* 2d ed. Berlin: F. T. Lagarde, 1793.

———. *Critique of Judgment.* J. H. Bernard, trans. New York: Hafner, 1951.

———. *Fundamental Principles of the Metaphysics of Morals.* T. K. Abbot, trans. New York: Liberal Arts Press, 1949.

Kaufmann, Walter. *Existentialism from Dostoevsky to Sartre.* New York: Meridian Books, 1957.

Knight, Everett W. *Literature Considered as Philosophy.* New York: Macmillan, 1958.

Lagneau, Jules. *Célèbres leçons et fragments.* Paris: Presses Universitaires de France, 1950.

Lalande, André. *Vocabulaire technique et critique de la philosophie.* Paris: Presses Universitaires de France, 1947.

Langer, Susanne K. *Philosophy in a New Key,* paperback reprint. New York: Penguin Books, Inc., 1948.

———. *Feeling and Form.* New York: Scribner's Sons, 1953.

———. *Problems of Art.* New York: Scribner's Sons, 1957.

Lévinas, Emmanuel. *De l'existence à l'existant.* Paris: éditions de la Revue Fontaine, 1947.

Lewis, C. I. *An Analysis of Knowledge and Valuation.* LaSalle, Ill.: Open Court Publishing Co., 1946.

Malebranche, Nicolas. *De la recherche de la vérité.* Paris: Flammarion, 2 vols. [1935]. 1st ed., 1674; 6th ed., 1712.

Malraux, André. *Romans* [*Les Conquérants, La Condition humaine, L'Espoir*]. Paris: NRF, éditions de la Pléiade, 1947.

———. *Les Voix du silence.* Paris: NRF, La Galérie de la Pléiade, 1951.

Maurois, André. *Alain.* Paris: Domat, 1950.

May, Rollo, *et. al. Existence.* New York: Basic Books, Inc., 1958.

Mead, George H. *Mind, Self and Society.* Charles Morris, ed. Chicago: University of Chicago Press, 1934.

Merleau-Ponty, Maurice. *La Structure du comportement,* new ed. Paris: Presses Universitaires de France, 1949. Original, 1942.

———. *Phénoménologie de la perception.* Paris: Gallimard, 1945.

———. *Humanisme et terreur,* in the collection *Les Essais.* Paris: Gallimard, 1947.

———. *Sens et non-sens.* Paris: Editions Nagel, 1948.

———. *Eloge de la philosophie.* Paris: Gallimard, 1953.

———. *Les Aventures de la dialectique.* Paris: Gallimard, 1955.

———, ed. *Les Philosophes célèbres.* Paris: Mazenod, 1956.

———. *Signes.* Paris: Gallimard, 1960.

Métraux, Rhoda, and Margaret Mead. *Themes in French Culture.* The Hoover Institute Studies, Series D, No. 1. Stanford: Stanford University Press, 1954.

Morris, Chas. W. *Six Theories of Mind.* Chicago: University of Chicago Press, 1932.

Munro, Thomas. *Scientific Method in Aesthetics.* New York: W. W. Norton and Co., 1928.

Nahm, Milton C. *The Artist as Creator.* Baltimore: Johns Hopkins Press, 1956.

Parker, DeWitt H. *The Principles of Aesthetics,* 2d ed. New York: F. S. Crofts and Co., 1947.

Peirce, Charles S. *Collected Papers.* Charles Hartshorne and Paul Weiss, eds. Cambridge: Harvard University Press, 1934. Vols. 2 and 5.

Pepper, Stephen C. *Aesthetic Quality.* New York: Scribner's Sons, 1938.

———. *World Hypotheses.* Berkeley and Los Angeles: University of California Press, 1942.

———. *The Basis of Criticism in the Arts.* Cambridge: Harvard University Press, 1949.

———. *The Work of Art.* Bloomington: Indiana University Press, 1955.

Prall, David W. *Aesthetic Judgment.* New York: Thomas Y. Crowell Co., 1929.

———. *Aesthetic Analysis.* New York: Crowell, 1936.

Rader, Melvin M., ed. *A Modern Book of Esthetics.* New York: Henry Holt and Co., 1935. Re-edited, 1952, 1960.

Richards, I. A. *Principles of Literary Criticism,* new ed. New York: Harcourt, Brace and Co., 1947. Original, 1924.

———. *Science and Poetry,* 2d ed. London: Kegan, Paul, Trench, Trubner and Co., Ltd., 1935. Original, 1926.

Rolland, Romain. *L'Esprit Libre.* Paris: Editions Albin Michel, 1953.

Ross, Julian. *Philosophy in Literature.* Syracuse: University Press, 1949.

Russell, Bertrand. *Problems of Philosophy.* Home University Library. New York: H. Holt and Co., n.d.

Ryle, Gilbert. *The Concept of Mind.* London, New York: Hutchinson's University Library, 1949.

Santayana, George. *The Sense of Beauty.* New York: Modern Library, 1955. Original, 1896.

Sartre, Jean-Paul. *L'Imagination,* 3d ed. Paris: Presses Universitaires de France, 1950. Original, 1936.

———. *L'Imaginaire,* 18th ed. Paris: Gallimard, 1948. Original, 1939.

————. *L'Etre et le néant.* Bibliothèque des Idées. Paris: Gallimard, 1943.

————. *Being and Nothingness.* Hazel Barnes, trans. New York: Philosophical Library, 1956.

————. *L'Existentialisme est un humanisme.* Paris: Nagel, 1946.

————. *Baudelaire.* Paris: Gallimard, 1947.

————. *Situations I–III.* Paris: Gallimard, 1947-49. 3 vols.

————. *What Is Literature?* Bernard Frechtman, trans. New York: Philosophical Library, 1949. Contains the greater part of *Situations II.*

————. *Esquisse d'une théorie des émotions,* 2d ed. Paris: Hermann et Cie., 1948.

————. *Les Mains sales.* Paris: Gallimard, 1948.

————. *Saint Genet comédien et martyr,* 3d ed. Paris: Gallimard, 1952.

————. *Critique de la raison dialectique.* Bibliotheque des Idées. Paris: Gallimard, 1960.

Saussure, Ferdinand de. *Cours de linguistique générale.* Ch. Bally, Albert Sechehaye, Albert Riedlinger, eds. Paris: Payot, 1949.

Schinz, Albert, ed. *Eighteenth Century French Readings.* New York: Henry Holt and Co., 1923.

Souriau, Etienne. *L'Avenir de l'esthétique.* Paris: Felix Alcan, 1929.

————. *La Correspondance des arts.* Paris: Flammarion, 1947.

Spingarn, Joel E. *Creative Criticism.* New York: Holt and Co., 1917.

Stern, Alfred. *Sartre: His Philosophy and Psychoanalysis.* New York: Liberal Arts Press, 1953.

Stanislavski, Constantin. *My Life in Art,* new ed. n.p.: Theatre Arts Books, 1948.

Valéry, Paul. *Introduction à la méthode de Leonard de Vinci.* Paris: éditions de la NRF, 1919.

————. *Eupalinos.* Preceded by *L'Ame et la danse.* Paris: Gallimard, 1924.

————. *Littérature.* Paris: Gallimard, 1930.

————. *Variété, IV,* 29th ed. Paris: Gallimard, 1938.

————. *Introduction à la poétique.* Paris: Gallimard, 1938.

Wahl, Jean. *Existence humaine et transcendance.* Neuchâtel: éditions de la Baconnière, 1944.

Weitz, Morris. *Philosophy of the Arts.* Cambridge: Harvard University Press, 1950.

————, ed. *Problems in Aesthetics.* New York: Macmillan, 1959.

Welch, E. Parl. *The Philosophy of Edmund Husserl.* New York: Columbia University Press, 1941.

Wellck, René, and Austin Warren. *Theory of Literature.* London: J. Cape, 1949.

Whyte, L. L., ed. *Aspects of Form.* London and Bradford: Lund Humphries and Co., Ltd., 1951.

————. *Accent on Form.* Vol. 2 in *World Perspectives, An Anticipation of the Science of Tomorrow.* New York: Harper and Bros., 1954.

Wittgenstein, Ludwig. *Tractatus Logico-Philosophicus.* Intro. by Bertrand Russell, F.R.S. New York: Harcourt, Brace and Co., Inc., 1922.

————. *Philosophical Investigations.* G. E. M. Anscombe, trans. New York: Macmillan, 1953. German and English on facing pages.

ARTICLES AND ESSAYS

Abel, Theodore. "The Operation called 'Verstehen,' " in Feigl and Brodbeck, *Readings in the Philosophy of Science.* New York: Appleton-Century-Crofts, Inc., 1953. Pp. 677–87.

Ames, Van Meter. "What is Form?" *Journal of Aesthetics and Art Criticism,* XV (1956), 85–93.

Baensch, Otto. "Kunst und Gefuehl," *Logos,* XII (1923–24), 1–28.

Bayer, Raymond. "Recent Esthetic Thought in France," in Marvin Farber, ed. *Philosophic Thought in France and the United States.* Buffalo: University of Buffalo, 1950. Pp. 267–79.

————. *Merleau-Ponty's Existentialism,* University of Buffalo Studies, Vol. 19, No. 3. Buffalo, 1951.

Beauvoir, Simone de. "*La Phénoménologie de la perception* de Merleau-Ponty," *Les Temps Modernes,* I (1945), 363–67.

————. "Littérature et métaphysique," *Les Temps Modernes,* I (1946), 1153–63.

————. "Faut-il brûler Sade?" *Les Temps Modernes,* VII (1951), 1002–33; VII (1952), 1197–1230.

————. "Must We Burn Sade?" Trans. of above in *The Marquis de Sade.* Paul Dinnage, ed. New York: The Grove Press, 1953. Pp. 9–82.

————. "Merleau-Ponty et le pseudo-Sartrisme," *Les Temps Modernes,* X (1955), 2072–2122.

Berger, Gaston. *Existentialism and Literature in Action,* University of Buffalo Studies, Vol. 18, No. 4. Buffalo, 1948.

————. "Experience and Transcendence," in Marvin Farber, ed. *Philosophic Thought in France and the United States.* Buffalo: University of Buffalo, 1950. Pp. 87–102.

Blackmur, R. P. "A Burden for Critics," in *Lectures in Criticism,* XVI, Bollingen Series. New York: Pantheon Books, 1949. Pp. 187–209.

Campbell, Robert. "Existentialism in France since the Liberation," in Marvin Farber, ed. *Philosophic Thought in France and the United States.* Buffalo: University of Buffalo, 1950. Pp. 137–50.

Dufrenne, Mikel. "Intentionnalité et esthétique," *Revue Philosophique,* CXLIV (1954), 75–84.

Eliot, T. S. "Hamlet and his Problems," in *Sacred Wood.* London: Methuen and Co., Ltd., 1920. Pp. 87–94.

Findlay, John Niemeyer. "Phenomenology," *Encyclopedia Britannica.* Chicago, London, Toronto: Encyclopedia Britannica Inc., 1957. XVII, pp. 700–702.

Flew, Anthony. "Facts and Imagination," *Mind* (NS), LXV (1956), 392–99.

Goldstein, Kurt. "Ueber die Abhaengigkeit der Bewegungen von optischen Vorgaengen," *Monatsschrift für Psychiatrie und Neurologie,* LIV (1923), 141–94.

———. "Ueber Zeigen und Greifen," *Der Nervenarzt*, IV (1931), 453–66.

Griff, Mason. "Alientation and the Artist," *Arts in Society*, No. 3 (Fall, 1959), pp. 43–54.

Heidegger, Martin. "What is Metaphysics?" in his *Existence and Being*. Chicago: Regnery and Co., 1949. Pp. 353–92.

Henze, Donald F. "The Work of Art," *The Journal of Philosophy*, LIV (1957), 429–42.

Hering, Jean. "Phenomenology in France," in Marvin Farber, ed. *Philosophic Thought in France and the United States*. Buffalo: University of Buffalo, 1950. Pp. 67–85.

Hospers, John. "The Concept of Artistic Expression," *Proceedings of the Aristotelian Society*, 1954–55. Pp. 313–44.

———. "The Croce-Collingwood Theory of Art," *Philosophy*, XXXI (1956), 291–308.

Julia, Didier. "Analyse de *Phénoménologie de l'expérience esthétique*," *Revue d'Esthétique*, VI (1953), 332–35.

Kanapa, Jean. "Un 'nouveau' révisionnisme à l'usage des intellectuels," in *L'Humanité* (Paris), February 22, 1954, p. 2.

Kaplan, Abraham. "Obscenity as an Esthetic Category," *Law and Contemporary Problems*, XX (1955), 544-59.

Lalande, André. "Phénoménologie," lexicographical entry in *Vocabulaire technique et critique de la philosophie*, 5th ed. Paris: Presses Universitaires de France, 1947. Pp. 749–51.

Lanteri-Laura, G. "L'usage de l'exemple dans la phénoménologie," *Les Etudes Philosophiques*, IX (1954), 57–72.

Lefebvre, Henri. "Merleau-Ponty et la philosophie de l'ambiquïte," *Pensée*, LXVIII (1956), 44–58; LXXIII (1957), 37–52.

Leuthy, Herbert. "The Void of Jean-Paul Sartre," in *The Anchor Review*, No. 2. Garden City: Doubleday Anchor Books, 1957. Pp. 251–54.

MacDonald, Margaret. "Some Distinctive Features of Arguments used in Criticism of the Arts," in William Elton, ed. *Essays in Aesthetics and Language*. Oxford: Blackwell, 1954. Pp. 114–30.

Mead, George H. "The Nature of Aesthetic Experience," *International Journal of Ethics*, XXXVI (1926), 382–93.

Merleau-Ponty, Maurice. "Un auteur scandaleux," in *Sens et non-sens*, pp. 83–96.

———. "Le roman et la métaphysique," in *Sens et non-sens*, pp. 51–81.

———. "Le langage indirect et les voix du silence," in *Les Temps Modernes*, VII (June, 1952), 2113–44; VII (July, 1952), 70–94.

Miller, Neal E. "A Reply to Sign-Gestalt or Conditioned Reflex," *Psychological Review*, XLII (1935), 280–92.

Morris, Charles W. "Esthetics and the Theory of Signs," *The Journal of Unified Science*, VIII (1939), 131–50.

———. "Science, Art and Technology," *Kenyon Review*, I (1939), 409–23.

———. "Significance, Signification, and Painting," in *The Language of Value*. R. Lepley, ed. New York: Columbia University Press, 1957, Pp. 58–76, 274–80.

Natanson, Maurice. "The Empirical and Transcendental Ego," in *For Roman Ingarden: Nine Essays in Phenomenology.* A. T. Tymieniecka, ed. The Hague: Martinus Nijhoff, 1959. Pp. 42–53.

Rau, Catherine. "The Aestheitc Views of Jean-Paul Sartre," *Journal of Aesthetics and Art Criticism,* IX (1950), 139–47.

Sartre, Jean-Paul. "La transcendance de l'Ego," *Recherches Philosophiques,* VI (1936–37), 85–123.

——. "Sartoris," *Nouvelle Revue Française,* L (1938), 323–28; collected in *Situations* I, pp. 7–13.

——. "A propos de Dos Passos et de '1919,'" *Nouvelle Revue Française,* LI (1938); collected in *Situations* I, pp. 292–301.

——. "A propos de 'Le Bruit et la fureur': la temporalité chez Faulkner," *Nouvelle Revue Française* LII (1939), 1057–61; LIII (1939) 147–51; collected in *Situations* I, pp. 70–81.

——. "Une idée fondamentale de la 'Phénoménologie' de Husserl, l'intentionnalité" *Nouvelle Revue Française,* LII (1939), 129–32.

——. "Présentation des *Temps Modernes,*" *Les Temps Modernes,* I (1945), 1–21.

——. "Les communistes et la paix," *Les Temps Modernes,* VIII (1952), 1–50, 695–763; IX (1954), 1731–1819.

——. "Réponse à Lefort," *Les Temps Modernes,* VIII (1953), 1571–1629.

——. "Opération Kanapa," *Les Temps Modernes,* IX (1954), 1723–28.

——. "Les peintures de Giacometti," *Les Temps Modernes,* IX (1954), 2221–32.

——. "Questions de méthode," *Les Temps Modernes,* XIII (1957), 338–417, 658–98.

Shorer, Mark. "Technique as Discovery," *Hudson Review,* I (1948), 67–87.

Shorter, J. M. "Imagination," *Mind* (NS), LXI (1952), 528–42.

Tolman, E. C. "Sign-Gestalt or Conditioned Reflex," *Psychological Review,* XL (1933), 246–55.

Vendôme, André. "Jean-Paul Sartre et la littérature," *Etudes,* CCLIX (1948), 39–54.

Viggiani, Carl A. "Camus' *L'Etranger,*" *PMLA,* LXXI (1956), 865–87.

Waelhens, Alphonse de. "Une philosophie de l'ambiguïté," Introduction to Merleau-Ponty, *La Structure du comportement,* pp. x–xv.

Wagner, R. L. "Le langage et l'homme," *Les Temps Modernes,* III (1948), 1583–1611.

Wahl, Jean. "Present Situation and the Present Future of French Philosophy," in Marvin Farber, ed. *Philosophic Thought in France and the United States.* Buffalo: University of Buffalo, 1950. Pp. 27–35.

Weitz, Morris. "The Role of Theory in Aesthetics," *Journal of Aesthetics and Art Criticism,* XV (1956), 27–35.

Ziff, Paul. "Art and the 'Object of Art,'" in William Elton, ed. *Essays in Aesthetics and Language.* Oxford: Blackwell, 1954. Pp. 170–86.

Zink, Sidney. "Intuition and Externalization in Croce's *Aesthetic,*" *Journal of Philosophy,* XLVII (1950), 210–16.

Index